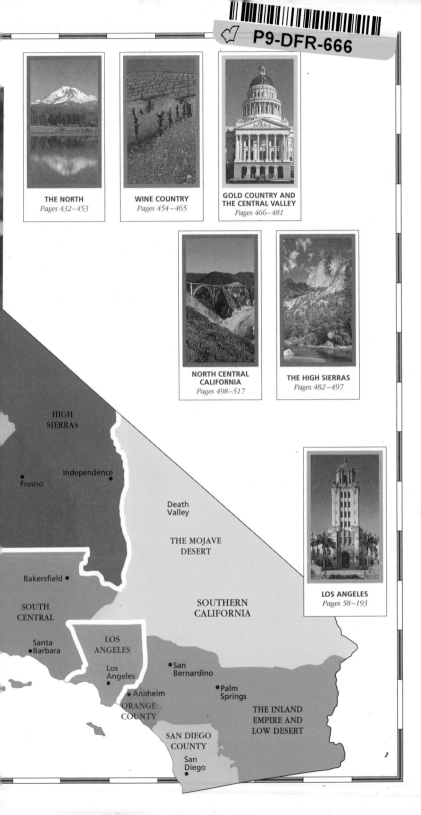

**THE NORTH**
*Pages 432–453*

**WINE COUNTRY**
*Pages 454–465*

**GOLD COUNTRY AND THE CENTRAL VALLEY**
*Pages 466–481*

**NORTH CENTRAL CALIFORNIA**
*Pages 498–517*

**THE HIGH SIERRAS**
*Pages 482–497*

HIGH
SIERRAS

Independence
Fresno

Death
Valley

THE MOJAVE
DESERT

**LOS ANGELES**
*Pages 58–193*

Bakersfield

SOUTH
CENTRAL

SOUTHERN
CALIFORNIA

Santa
Barbara

LOS
ANGELES

Los
Angeles

San
Bernardino

Anaheim

Palm
Springs

ORANGE
COUNTY

THE INLAND
EMPIRE AND
LOW DESERT

SAN DIEGO
COUNTY

San
Diego

# EYEWITNESS TRAVEL
# CALIFORNIA

# EYEWITNESS TRAVEL
# CALIFORNIA

DK

LONDON, NEW YORK,
MELBOURNE, MUNICH AND DELHI
www.dk.com

Produced by Duncan Baird Publishers, London, England

MANAGING ART EDITOR Clare Sullivan
EDITORS Slaney Begley, Joanne Levêque, Zoë Ross
EDITORIAL ASSISTANT Leo Hollis
DESIGNERS Christine Keilty, Susan Knight, Jill Mumford, Alison Verity

MAIN CONTRIBUTORS Jamie Jensen, Barry Parr,
Ellen Payne, J Kingston Pierce, Rebecca Poole Forée,
Nigel Tisdall, John Wilcock, Stanley Young

PHOTOGRAPHERS
Max Alexander, Peter Anderson, John Heseltine, Dave King,
Neil Lukas, Andrew McKinney, Neil Setchfield

PICTURE RESEARCH Lindsay Hunt

ILLUSTRATORS
Arcana Studios, Joanna Cameron, Stephen Conlin,
Dean Entwhistle, Nick Lipscombe, Lee Peters, Robbie Polley,
Kevin Robinson, John Woodcock

REPRODUCED BY Colourscan (Singapore)
PRINTED AND BOUND BY South China Printing Co., Ltd., China

First American Edition, 1997
12 13 14 15 10 9 8 7 6 5 4 3 2 1

Published in the United States by
DK Publishing, 375 Hudson Street,
New York, New York 10014

Reprinted with revisions 1999, 2000, 2001, 2002,
2003, 2004, 2005, 2006, 2007, 2008, 2009, 2010, 2012

Published in Great Britain by Dorling Kindersley Limited.

A CATALOG RECORD FOR THIS BOOK IS AVAILABLE FROM THE
LIBRARY OF CONGRESS.

ISSN 1542-1554
ISBN 978-0-75668-560-7

Front cover main image: California redwoods

MIX
Paper from
responsible sources
FSC
www.fsc.org   FSC™ C018179

---

**The information in this
DK Eyewitness Travel Guide is checked regularly.**
Every effort has been made to ensure that this book is as up-to-date
as possible at the time of going to press. Some details, however, such
as telephone numbers, opening hours, prices, gallery hanging
arrangements and travel information are liable to change. The
publishers cannot accept responsibility for any consequences arising
from the use of this book, nor for any material on third party
websites, and cannot guarantee that any website address in this book
will be a suitable source of travel information. We value the views
and suggestions of our readers very highly. Please write to: Publisher,
DK Eyewitness Travel Guides, Dorling Kindersley, 80 Strand, London
...s@dk.com.

**32530607923065**

◁ Heisler Park in Laguna Beach showing panoramic view of coastline

# CONTENTS

Volleyball on Pismo Beach

## LOS ANGELES

Half Dome in Yosemite National Park

State Capitol
building in
Sacramento

# HOW TO USE THIS GUIDE

This guide helps you to get the most from your stay in California. *Introducing California* maps the whole state and sets it in its historical and cultural context. The ten regional chapters, plus *Los Angeles* and *San Francisco and the Bay Area*, describe important sights with maps, pictures,

and illustrations, as well as introductory features on subjects of regional interest.

Suggestions on restaurants, accommodations, shopping, and entertainment are in *Travelers' Needs*. The *Survival Guide* has tips on getting around the state. LA, San Francisco, and San Diego have their own *Practical Information* sections.

## LOS ANGELES AND SAN FRANCISCO AND THE BAY AREA

The centers of the two major cities have been divided into a number of sightseeing areas. Each area has its own chapter that opens with a list of the sights described. All the sights are numbered and plotted on an *Area Map*. Information on each sight is easy to locate within the chapter as it follows the numerical order on the map.

**Sights at a Glance** lists the chapter's sights by category: Historic Streets and Buildings, Shops, Modern Architecture, etc.

**A locator map** shows where you are in relation to other areas of the city center.

**All pages** relating to Los Angeles have lilac thumb tabs. San Francisco pages have grass-green thumb tabs.

**1 Area Map**
*For easy reference, the sights are numbered and located on a map. The sights are also shown on the* Los Angeles Street Finder *(see pp182–93) or the* San Francisco Street Finder *(see pp400–9).*

**2 Street-by-Street Map**
*This gives a bird's-eye view of the heart of each sightseeing area.*

**A suggested route** for a walk covers the more interesting streets in the area.

**Stars** indicate sights that no visitor should miss.

**3 Detailed Information on Each Sight**
*All the sights in Los Angeles and in San Francisco and the Bay Area are described individually. Addresses and practical information are provided. The key to the symbols used in the information block is shown on the back flap.*

**Story boxes** explore specific subjects in more detail.

### 1 Introduction
*The landscape, history, and character of each region is described here, showing how the area has developed over the centuries and what it offers to the visitor today.*

## NORTHERN CALIFORNIA AND SOUTHERN CALIFORNIA
Apart from San Francisco and the Bay Area and Los Angeles, California has been divided into two regions (Northern and Southern California), each of which has five separate area chapters. The most interesting towns and places to visit are numbered on a *Regional Map* at the beginning of each chapter.

**Each area** of California can be identified quickly by its own color coding, which is shown on the inside front cover.

### 2 Regional Map
*This shows the main road network and gives an illustrated overview of the whole area. All entries are numbered, and there are also useful tips on getting around the region.*

### 3 Detailed Information
*All the important towns and other places to visit are described individually. They are listed in order, following the numbering on the Regional Map. Within each entry, information is given on the most important sights. A map reference refers the reader to the road map inside the back cover.*

**For all the top sights**, a visitors' checklist provides the practical information you need to plan your visit.

### 4 California's Top Sights
*These are given two or more full pages. Historic buildings are dissected to reveal their interiors; museums and galleries have color-coded floor plans to help you locate the most interesting exhibits; national parks and forests have maps showing facilities and trails.*

# INTRODUCING
# CALIFORNIA

# DISCOVERING CALIFORNIA

California is a land of breath-taking extremes. Its rugged, redwood-covered bluffs, idyllic sun-drenched sands, soaring granite cliffs, and snow-capped peaks have inspired generations of artists, athletes, and explorers. Since the 1840s Gold Rush, the state

MARILYN MONROE

Hollywood's Walk of fame

has exerted great cultural and political influence. A lifetime could be spent discovering every unique town and temperament, so the following pages give a taste of the 12 distinct regions to help you determine which aspects are of most interest.

**Mann's Chinese Theatre, one of Hollywood's most famous landmarks**

## LOS ANGELES

- **Hollywood landmarks**
- **Fantastic art collections**
- **Vibrant Downtown**

Los Angeles is a city of paradoxes. The same place that spawned the commercial Hollywood **Walk of Fame** *(see p111)* and **Sunset Strip** *(see pp102–104)* also accommodates **Griffith Park** *(see pp150–51)*, one of the largest urban wildernesses in the US. An identity rooted in the film industry belies one of the greatest concentrations of museums in the world, including the **J Paul Getty Museum at the Getty Center** *(see pp82–5)*, the **Los Angeles County Museum of Art** *(see pp114–7)*, and the **Huntington Library, Art Collections, and Botanical Gardens** *(see pp158–61)*. Visitors can experience the glamour of the movie industry by taking a tour of one of the major studios in **Burbank** *(see pp144–5)*, or

of **Universal Studios®** *(see pp146–7)*. Downtown LA's resurgence is evident in the undulating forms of Frank Gehry's Disney Theatre at the **Music Center** *(see p125)* as much as in the bustling stands of the **Grand Central Market** *(see p124)*. Beach communities such as those in **Venice** *(see p80)*, **Santa Monica** *(see pp76–9)*, and **Malibu** *(see pp86–7)* delight with their distinctiveness.

**Marine life abounds on the coast of South Central California**

## SOUTH CENTRAL CALIFORNIA

- **Palatial Hearst Castle**
- **Whale watching**
- **Santa Ynez wineries**

Massive hills define this rugged region, forming an imposing backdrop to the affluent, handsome city of **Santa Barbara** *(see pp220–23)* to the south, and enhancing the jaw-dropping grandeur of fairytale **Hearst Castle** *(see pp212–15)* to the north. **Ojai** *(see p225)* is a favored getaway among the Hollywood elite for spa treatments and spiritual-wellness retreats. Marine biology buffs flock to **Channel Islands National Park** *(see p224)* for their remoteness and favorable odds for seeing gray whale pods, while at **Los Padres National Forest** *(see p225)* visitors may spot a condor patrolling the park's almost perennially cloudless skies.

Toward the coast, take a tour of one of the many wineries of the **Santa Ynez Valley** *(see p218)*. Winemakers in this region take advantage of the more temperate climate to produce famed and distinctive wines.

## ORANGE COUNTY

- **Wealthy seaside villages**
- **Legendary Disneyland®**
- **Catalina Island**

The profile of Los Angeles' sprawling southern neighbor has risen dramatically since Walt Disney's vision of a

◁ *Yosemite Valley* (1868) by Albert Bierstadt

magic kingdom blossomed in 1955, and Orange County now counts some of the world's richest individuals among its handsome beach communities and rustic mountainside ranches. The world-famous, original **Disneyland® Resort** *(see pp232–5)* enchants children of all ages, and neighboring **Knott's Berry Farm® and Soak City** *(see pp236–7)* pick up where Disney's more forgiving thrill rides leave off. Along the **Orange County Coastline** *(see pp230–31)*, places such as Laguna, Newport, and Huntington State Beach bear the distinctive Orange County hallmarks of surf, beach volleyball, stellar seafood, and stunning beachfront homes. Offshore, charming **Catalina Island** *(see pp242–3)* beckons weekenders from the bustle of Los Angeles with promises of fair breezes, quaint harbors, and a herd of bison.

The enchanting façade of Mission San Luis Rey, San Diego County

Surfers riding waves along the Orange County coastline

## SAN DIEGO COUNTY

- Mission architecture
- San Diego Zoo and the Gaslamp Quarter
- La Jolla

Located close to the busiest border crossing in the world at **Tijuana** *(see p265)*, **San Diego** *(see pp250–59)* offers an irresistible study in contrasts. In 1769, the first Franciscan mission of 21 in California, **Mission San Diego de Alacalà** *(see pp260–61)*, was founded here, marking

the city as a historic colonial center. **Mission San Luis Rey** *(see pp262–3)* is a striking example of Mission Archi-tecture. In 1915, the Panama-Pacific Expo, held at **Balboa Park** *(see pp256–9)*, ushered in impressive public works such as the world-renowned **San Diego Zoo** *(see pp256–9)*, and Spanish-Colonial style pavilions. Next to the city's gleaming, modern Financial District, the **Gaslamp Quarter** *(see pp252–3)* preserves many Victorian-era buildings, housing excellent bars, cafés, and restaurants. On the city's outskirts, seaside hamlet **La Jolla** *(see p261)* ranks among the wealthiest, most exclusive communities in the US. Also, given the region's ideal climate, San Diego County is a sports enthusiast's paradise, with fantastic hiking trails in **Cuyamaca Rancho State Park** *(see p264)*, while **Mission Bay** *(see pp260–61)* offers every water sport conceivable.

## INLAND EMPIRE & LOW DESERT

- San Bernardino mountains
- Palm Springs and Riverside
- Joshua Tree National Park

The Inland Empire and Low Desert offer city-weary Angelenos and San Diegans readily accessible outdoor recreation. With some of the most varied climates and topography in the state, one can remove tire chains from

a ski trip in the stunning **San Bernardino Mountains** *(see p272)* just one hour before tee time on the golf courses outside historic **Riverside** *(see p273)*. To the south in Coachella Valley, **Palm Springs** *(see pp274–6)* has a reputation as the state's de facto retirement community. It is far from dull, however, with first-rate luxury shopping in Palm Desert, renowned health spas, and, in neighboring Indio, an annual date festival with camel and ostrich races. Legendary **Joshua Tree National Park** *(see pp278–9)* presents a distinctive landscape, with undulating rock formations, palm-ringed oases, tumbleweed, and groves of the contorted, ancient joshua trees that give the park its name.

Rugged desert dunes near Palm Springs

The unique and isolated beauty of Death Valley National Park

## MOJAVE DESERT

- **Death Valley**
- **London Bridge and Las Vegas**
- **Edwards Air Force Base and Aeronautics Center**

Over 90 years have passed since the all-time highest temperature in US history was recorded in the Mojave Desert, yet today, in tourism terms, the expanse of arid land west of **Las Vegas** *(see p289)* is hotter than ever. **Death Valley National Park** *(see pp290–93)* earns its name with the hottest mean temperature on earth. Visitors can take in Stovepipe Wells' mesmerizing sand dunes, the sub-sea-level altitudes of Badwater, sweeping desert panoramas from Dante's View, or opt for the climate-controlled confines of the mirage-like Scotty's Castle. Other incongruous delights include the original London Bridge spanning manmade **Lake Havasu** *(see p288)*, and the unrepentant glitz of nearby Las Vegas, rising from the desert floor. **Edwards Air Force Base** *(see p284)* completes this otherworldly landscape, allowing visitors to learn about the country's space program.

## SAN FRANCISCO & THE BAY AREA

- **Legendary Golden Gate Bridge**
- **Gay and Lesbian scene**
- **Marin Headlands**

The Bay Area is a dynamic, unpredictable environment where chilling fog yields to brilliant sunshine in a matter of minutes, architecture responds to landscape in creative, sometimes stubborn ways, and where an active seismic fault line is never far. Yet despite its occasionally volatile character, this region nurtures one of the world's great cities, San Francisco. Landmarks such as the **Golden Gate Bridge** *(see pp380–81)*, the junction of **Haight Ashbury** *(see p358)*, and the **Transamerica Pyramid** *(see p315)* are emblems of the city's myriad lifestyles. Vibrant enclaves include Italian North Beach, Chinatown, and the Castro, center of the thriving gay community. Off the peninsula, visit **Oakland** *(see pp422–5)*, windswept **Point Reyes National Seashore** *(see p414)*, and the **Marin Headlands** *(see pp416–17)*.

Steaming, sulfurous pools, Lassen Volcanic National Park

## THE NORTH

- **Rugged Lost Coast**
- **Redwood National Park**
- **Towering Mount Shasta and Mount Lassen**

A realm of heavily wooded, desolate coastline, and primordial, volcanic mountain ranges, the North offers some of California's most varied, yet least visited, terrain. North of Cape Mendocino are the isolated rocky beaches and excellent hiking trails of the **Lost Coast** *(see p449)*. Further north, **Redwood National Park** *(see pp448–9)* protects one of the world's largest remaining old-growth redwood stands. The logging legacy of the North can be experienced in rural, personable towns such as **Weaverville** *(see p449)* and **Eureka** *(see p446)*. The imposing snow-covered peak of **Mount Shasta** *(see p452)*, and dramatic **Lassen Volcanic National Park** *(see p453)* are magnets for avid hikers. Glimpses of Lassen's fiery origins can be seen in the vast network of lava tubes and crystal-filled caves at **Lava Beds National Monument** *(see p453)*.

Dazzling views across San Francisco Bay

## WINE COUNTRY

- **Napa Valley wine tastings**
- **Hot springs at Calistoga**
- **Delightful Mendocino**

The soil, climate, and groundwater conditions of this rolling landscape provide for North America's premium winemaking region, founded in **Sonoma Valley** *(see pp464–5)*. The heart of the industry lies in the scenic and internationally renowned **Napa Valley** *(see pp462–3)*, home to more than 350 wineries; tastings and tours here are readily available. Stop nearby at the hot springs in **Calistoga** *(see p461)* for a relaxing volcanic mud bath or spa treatment.

The legacy of New England shipbuilders and fishermen who settled in California in the 19th century can be seen in the charming and quaint residences, galleries, and bed and breakfasts in **Mendocino** *(see p442)*. The coastline here is fantastic for bird- and whale-watching.

Vineyards in the Napa Valley, famous for wineries

## GOLD COUNTRY & THE CENTRAL VALLEY

- **Gold Rush-era towns**
- **Native American village re-creations**
- **Historic Sacramento**

In 1848, amid the heavily wooded Sierra foothills, James Marshall discovered gold flakes on his employer's land. The ensuing **Gold Rush** *(see pp48–9)* forever transformed California. Boom towns that survived after the Mother Lode had been completely depleted, include impeccably preserved and picturesque **Columbia State Historic Park** *(see pp480–81)*, and **Jackson** *(see p477)*, a thriving gateway town to the Sierras.

Northeast of Jackson, the fascinating **Chaw'se Indian Grinding Rock State Historic Park** *(see p477)* recreates a pre-European-encounter Miwok village. To the west,

**Sutter Creek** *(see pp476–7)* is a delightful Gold Country town to stop at on the way to **Sacramento** *(see pp472–5)*, California's capital city. Highlights here include the grand State Capitol building with its striking rotunda, as well as a network of historic structures that line the waterfront of the well preserved old district.

Soaring granite peaks, Yosemite National Park

## THE HIGH SIERRAS

- **Staggering natural wonders**
- **Yosemite and Lake Tahoe**
- **Lively Stateline casinos**

The High Sierras boast some of the country's most super-lative natural wonders from **Mount Whitney** *(see p495)*, the highest peak in the 48 contiguous United States, to the breathtaking **Sequoia and Kings Canyon National Parks** *(see pp496–7)*, whose giant sequoia trees are the world's largest living organisms

above sea level. The high camps of **Yosemite National Park** *(see pp488–91)* remain pristine, little-known gems. To the north, **Lake Tahoe** *(see pp486–7)*, the country's second deepest lake, sparkles year round, as do Stateline's gaudy casinos on its southern shore. Winter-sports enthusiasts flock here to ski and snowboard on the surrounding peaks, and watersports on the lake itself include fishing, kite surfing, canoeing, and scuba diving.

## NORTH CENTRAL CALIFORNIA

- **Bohemian Santa Cruz**
- **Enchanting Monterey**
- **Magnificent Carmel Mission**

Rocky beachside bluffs, serene harbors, and Spanish missions define this un-spoiled region. Visit inspiring seaside cliffs and secret waterfalls in **Big Sur** *(see pp514–15)*. Enjoy the bohemian café-bookstore culture in downtown **Santa Cruz** *(see pp506–7)*. The original capital of California, **Monterey** *(see pp508–11)*, has one of the country's largest aquariums, and a fish-packing district made infamous by John Steinbeck's 1945 novel *Cannery Row*. Just south, in the hills surrounding Carmel, Father Junípero Serra founded the delightful **Carmel Mission** *(see pp512–13)*, one of California's most beautiful churches.

# Putting California on the Map

California is the third largest state in the US (after Texas and Alaska) and, with over 36 million people, the most populous. Situated on the Pacific Coast, it is 800 miles (1,300 km) long and 250 miles (400 km) wide, covering an area of 158,710 sq miles (411,060 sq km). The state has two major cities: San Francisco and Los Angeles. Most visitors arrive via the airports in one of these cities; the main cities and towns are linked with each other and with other states by an extensive rail (Amtrak) and road system.

**Downtown Los Angeles at dawn**

Satellite view of the San Francisco Bay Area

# A PORTRAIT OF CALIFORNIA

*I*mpressive for both its size and its sway over modern culture, *California symbolizes the United States' diversity and sense of prosperity. Here can be found towering forests, deserts within half a day's drive of ocean beaches, and two of the world's foremost cities, San Francisco and Los Angeles.*

Perceptions of California vary so greatly that some now joke that there are two states. The first is geographic: California is the third-largest state in the Union (after Alaska and Texas), containing its largest county, San Bernardino, which covers 20,155 sq miles (52,200 sq km) – larger than Vermont and New Hampshire combined. This California has 840 miles (1,350 km) of coastline and measures 365 miles (587 km) at its widest point. It claims the second highest peak in the country (Mount Whitney) and its lowest expanse of dry land (Death Valley). More than 1,500 plant species grow here that cannot be found anywhere else on earth.

State seal

Roughly one in every eight Americans is a Californian, making this the most populous of the 50 states, represented by the largest congressional delegation.

And that other California? It is a realm of romance, formed by flickering celluloid images. Think "California" and pictures are immediately conjured up of bikini-clad beachcombers, middle-class suburban families in ranch houses, and film stars emerging from limousines into hordes of autograph-seekers. These stereotypes are perpetuated by the entertainment and tourism media.

Hollywood is only partly to blame for this blurring of fact and fiction. It goes back to Spanish legends of an exotic outpost called California, flung

Sun-worshipers on Manhattan Beach, Los Angeles

◁ Roller coaster at Knott's Berry Farm, Orange County

**Joshua Tree National Park**

out at the edge of the sea. Most of the world, though, knew nothing of this spot until the Gold Rush of 1849. Tales of the riches to be found encouraged thousands of would-be Croesuses to invade the region. Whether they found their fortunes or not, prospectors spread the same message: California was not as colorful or seductive as they had been told. It was even more so.

### SOCIETY AND POLITICS

If the US as a whole is a melting pot of people, California is an ethnic microcosm. It receives the highest number of immigrants (more than 200,000 annually), and the racial make-up is the most diverse in the nation. The percentage of whites and African-Americans is lower than the national average, but the Asian residency is more than triple the national level. Hispanics account for more than a quarter of all Californians – three times the US average. Walk through any of the four most-populated cities

**Golden Gate Bridge, San Francisco**

(LA, San Diego, San Jose, and San Francisco), and you receive an immediate taste of this ethnic cocktail. It is still more potent during *Mexican Cinco de Mayo* (May 5) festivities, Chinese New Year bashes, and other multicultural events held around the state.

Racial prejudice has plagued the state since its early days. Abolitionists prevented California's 1849 constitutional convention from barring the entry of blacks into this land, but in the 1870s nativist orators such as Denis Kearney endorsed violence against Chinese immigrants, said to be "stealing" white jobs. Sadly, overcrowding is reigniting racial tensions today, with overpopulation having a negative effect on law enforcement and education. It is raising the already high student–teacher ratios in California's schools, which have been short of funding since property taxes, a source of revenue for state and local governments, were cut and capped in 1978.

But the most inevitable result of population growth has been an altered balance between rural and urban sectors. More people means that more land is needed for housing. The value of California's

**Surfer**

**Red Rock Canyon in the Mojave Desert**

agricultural goods still outranks that of all other states, but its farmland has declined steadily since the 1950s. Lumber workers have also had a hard time, because of conservation measures and a continuing shrinkage

**California oranges**

of the state's forests. The fastest-expanding job markets now are in service industries and high technology, which suggest a more metropolitan than pastoral future. Visitors usually come to California to see one of two cities: San Francisco or Los Angeles. In the north and south of the state respectively, these cities define the opposing sides of its character: San Francisco is older and more compact. Although California in general is recognized for its eccentricities and is still the birthplace of new trends, San Francisco is particularly proud of its nonconformity and open-mindedness. It was here that the "Big Four" railroad barons built their millionaire's mansions, but the city has since evolved into a pro-labor hotbed, with a history of activism (the Bay Area was a hub of the anti-Vietnam War movement). It also

has one of the world's largest concentrations of gays and lesbians, with a substantial gay vote.

In contrast to San Francisco, LA is a sprawling city without a real focal point. The car rules, demanding a network of freeways that have hemmed in some of the city's historical buildings and which grind to smoggy standstills during rush hours. The façades of wealth, fame, and glamour leave LA as a dimensionless creation of bright lights and fairly conservative politics.

**Wild poppies in Antelope Valley**

This is not to say that the north is entirely Democrat (left wing) and the south, Republican (right wing). Hollywood is a chief sponsor of liberal causes, and there are pockets of antigovernment rebels in the northeast. But the conflicting power that the two cities exert on state government in Sacramento

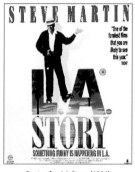

**Poster for *LA Story* (1991)**

and the state's representatives in Washington, DC explains why California may appear a little schizophrenic.

### CULTURE AND LEISURE

High- and low-brow art enjoy comparable support here. For most people, the state's contributions to culture are the many blockbusters made by Hollywood movie studios or televised sitcoms shot on LA sound stages. This is art in unashamed pursuit of the almighty dollar, complete with tabloid scandals and giant movie billboards blotting out the Los Angeles sun. But another creativity reveals itself through the state's history of landscape painting, portraiture, and 20th-century avant-garde art. Modern artists John

McLaughlin and Elmer Bischoff, and ceramists Peter Voulkos and Robert Arneson have all made international reputations. So have a few pioneers of photographic art, such as Imogen Cunningham and Ansel Adams. British artist David Hockney lived here for many years, capturing the state's sun-soaked image on canvas. California is also home to some of the world's finest art museums, including LACMA, the Oakland Museum, the San Francisco MOMA, and the two J Paul Getty Museums. Victorian architecture in the Bay Area has always been a major tourist attraction, as have the many historic buildings across the state designed by Californians such as Willis Polk and Bernard Maybeck. Visiting designers Frank Lloyd Wright

**Al Pacino receiving an Academy Award in 1993**

and Daniel Burnham have left their

**Napa Valley Train in Wine Country**

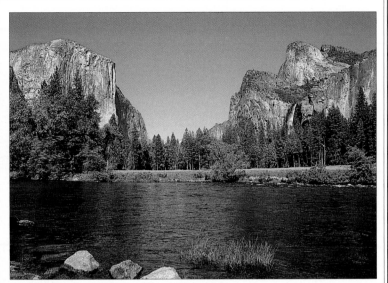

El Capitán (left) and the Three Brothers at Yosemite National Park

mark here, too. Recent influential architects include residents Frank Gehry and Joe Esherick.

The state has seen many writers over the years, including Nobel prize-winner John Steinbeck and Beat authors Jack Kerouac and Allen Ginsburg. The tradition continues with Armistead Maupin *(Tales of the City)*, detective novelist Sue Grafton, and Amy Tan *(The Joy Luck Club)*, among others. Music also plays a major role, whether the work of the cities' orchestras or rock musicians. This is where the Beach Boys, Janis Joplin, the Grateful Dead, and Red Hot Chili Peppers launched their careers.

Californians love to eat out, and chefs Wolfgang Puck and Alice Waters have made their name promoting "California cuisine" – a blend of local ingredients and Asian techniques. This, combined with a selection of local world-class wines, is proof that Californians take care of their palates. Yet residents

are also body-conscious, aware that they live among the "beautiful people" who come here with dreams of film stardom. So they become slaves to the gym or take up a sport. On any weekend, in various parts of the state, you will see cyclists, surfers, in-line skaters, even white-water rafters. Californians are eager supporters of professional baseball and football, but they like to be active themselves. Luckily, surrounded by some of the nation's most beautiful countryside and the gentlest climate, they don't have to go far to enjoy a satisfying outdoor experience.

Padres baseball stadium in San Diego

# California's Landscape and Geology

California's dramatic landscape includes the highest and lowest points in the lower 48 states of the US, Mount Whitney in the High Sierras, and Death Valley in the southern deserts. Millions of years ago, subduction of the Pacific Ocean floor beneath the North American Plate created the Coastal Range, the Central Valley, and the granitic rocks of the Sierra Nevada Mountains. Later, the granites were uplifted and tilted westward. The movement of tectonic plates along the San Andreas Fault is still changing the shape of California.

**The Coastal Range** *along the Pacific Coast was created around 25 million years ago, when fragments of the ocean floor and oceanic islands were pushed up by plate movements.*

## HOW THE WEST WAS MADE

Over a period of 150 million years, ending about 15 million years ago, the movement of the Pacific Plate and North American Plate formed the western margin of California.

Off-shore Pacific islands

Shallow water sediment

Pacific Plate

North American Plate

**100 million years BC**

Subduction zone where the two plates meet

**1** The North American Plate, moving westward, sweeps up any off-shore islands.

**25 million years BC**

Coastal Range

**2** As the ocean floor moves north, the fragments of off-shore islands are scattered along the coast. They are then pushed up to form the Coastal Range.

San Andreas Fault

Sierra Nevada

**Present Day**

Central Valley basin filled by sediment

**3** The boundary between the North American Plate and the Pacific Plate is marked by the San Andreas Fault *(see pp24–5).*

*MOUNT SHASTA* 14,162 ft (4,317 m)

**Mount Lassen** (see p453) *and Mount Shasta (see p452) are part of the Cascades, a range of extinct and active volcanoes (including Mount St. Helen created by a subduction zone beneath the north-western corner of the North American Plate. Both Mount Lassen and Mount Shasta are still considere active. When young, the Sierra Nevada range m have resembled the Cascades.*

**Lemon trees** *flourish in central California. The highly fertile surface sediments of the flat Central Valley come from erosion of the surrounding mountains. The sediments have accumulated over the last few hundred thousand years.*

**Mount Whitney** *(see p495) in the High Sierras is the highest point in the continental United States, rising to 14,494 ft (4,418 m). The process that raised the Sierra Nevada Mountains began more than 50 million years ago, but peaked a few million years ago.*

NORTH PALISADE
**14,242 ft (4,341 m)**

MOUNT
DANA
**13,053 ft
3,979 m)**

MOUNT WHITNEY
**14,494 ft (4,418 m)**

DEATH
VALLEY

BIG PINE MOUNTAIN
**6,826 ft (2,081 m)**

0 kilometers 100

0 miles 100

**il wells** *sprang up at a frantic pace when oil was iscovered in California. The drilling was so intense at the extraction of oil and gas deflated the land. art of Los Angeles County subsided 28 ft (8.5 m) efore oil companies were required to pump sea water own the wells to replace the extracted fuels.*

**Death Valley** *(see pp290–3) in the Mojave Desert has extreme height variations. Surrounded by some of the highest mountains on the continent, the valley floor lies 280 ft (85 m) below sea level. Death Valley was formed less than 15 million years ago when the North American Plate began to stretch due to the northwest drag created by the Pacific Plate.*

# California's Earthquakes

The San Andreas Fault extends almost the full length of California, some 600 miles (965 km) from the Gulf of California northwest to Cape Mendocino. It is not the only fault in California but is the line of most activity. Each year, on average, the Pacific Plate moves 1–1.6 inches (2.5–4 cm) to the northwest. Earthquakes occur when this movement is resisted. Stresses build up and eventually they are released, causing an earthquake. Many of California's major earthquakes have occurred in the northern section of the fault. The terrible fire of 1906 that destroyed San Francisco was caused by an earthquake estimated at 7.8 on the Richter Scale. More recently, the earthquake of October 1989, south of San Francisco, killed 62 people and caused at least $6 billion worth of damage *(see p505)*. In 1994, the Northridge quake, magnitude R6.7, rocked Los Angeles and was felt in Las Vegas, Nevada. Scientists now predict that the next major earthquake, the "Big One," will hit Southern California.

**The San Andreas Fault** *is one of the few sites on earth where an active plate boundary occurs on land.*

Hayward Fault

1989 earthquake epicenter

**1989 earthquake hypocenter**

**The 1906 earthquake** *confounded contemporary geologists and led to the "elastic rebound" theory of earthquake formation, which is still in use today.*

**The 1989 earthquake** *struck the Santa Cruz Mountains in central California.*

## TIMELINE

| | 1750 | 1800 | 1850 | 1900 | 1950 |
|---|---|---|---|---|---|
| | | **1769** Members of Portolá's expedition are first Europeans to experience an earthquake in California | **1865** San Francisco hit by its first major earthquake on October 9 and another on October 23 | **1872** Town of Lone Pine is destroyed and Sierra Nevada Mountains rise 13 ft (4m) | **1952** Kern County (R7.7) <br> **1940** Imperial Valley (R7.1) | **1992** Yucca Valley outside LA (R7.4) <br> **1989** Loma Prieta (R7.1) strikes San Francisco area |
| | | *Don Gaspar de Portolá* | **1857** Fort Tejon (R8) is followed by smaller earth tremors in Bay Area | **1906** San Francisco earthquake (R7.8) causes a devastating three-day fire that leaves 3,000 dead and 250,000 homeless | **1994** Northridge (R6.7). At least 56 people killed, more than 7,000 injured, and 20,000 made homeless. Anaheim Stadium and several Los Angeles freeways are badly damaged | |

**The 1994 earthquake** *caused havoc in the Los Angeles area. Collapsed overpasses closed the Santa Monica Freeway and Interstate 5 near Valencia. Fires caused damage in the San Fernando Valley and in Malibu and Venice.*

**Seismically safe housing** *is designed to withstand the stresses caused by the ground shaking during an earthquake. Every time a strong earthquake occurs, scientists carefully measure how various structural designs respond to earthquake motion.*

**The movement of plates** is most pronounced along the San Andreas Fault Zone. Friction sometimes causes the fault to "stick."

Garlock Fault

Elsinore Fault

Los Angeles

Santa Barbara

San Diego

San Andreas Fault

S (secondary) waves travel, through solid parts of the crust.

North American Plate

## PACIFIC PLATE MEETS NORTH AMERICAN PLATE

The San Andreas Fault is a major fracture in the earth's crust. It is the result of friction where two plates meet – the Pacific Plate (consisting of most of the Pacific Ocean and the California coastline) and the North American Plate.

Pacific Plate

Hypocenter

P (primary) waves travel through the earth's core.

P waves    S waves    L waves

**It is possible** *to calculate the magnitude of an earthquake from a seismograph recording. Printouts show the intensity of earthquake vibrations graphically. The magnitude of the earthquake is registered on the Richter Scale (R).*

**Earthquake energy vibrations** *move through the earth's crust in waves. There are three types of wave: P or primary waves, S or secondary waves, and L or surface waves. The waves change as energy moves from the hypocenter to the earth's surface. Surface waves cause most of the damage associated with earthquakes.*

# Literary California

As journalist Carey McWilliams remarked in 1946, "What America is, California is, with accents, in italics." The chance to study the nation in microcosm has been especially appealing to authors. Many, such as Robert Louis Stevenson (1850–94), have simply passed through. He arrived in Monterey in 1879 and later based scenes in *Treasure Island* on the surrounding coastline. But California has not lacked for resident wordsmiths. This, after all, is where Henry Miller (1891–1980) blended erotic and verbal inventiveness and William Saroyan (1908–81) found his eccentric rural characters. Nobel prize-winning playwright Eugene O'Neill (1888–1953) produced some of his best work at Tao House in the Ramon Valley *(see p426)*. California is also where several successful contemporary writers, such as Amy Tan (born in 1952), now chase their muse.

**Mask used in plays at Tao House**

**Robert Louis Stevenson, author of *Treasure Island***

## THE PIONEERS

Much of the very early writing about California was unsophisticated, satisfying readers who simply wanted a taste of the frontier environment. But the Gold Rush *(see pp48–9)* created a market for prose that captured the poignancy, romance, and raw humor of life in the West. Bay Area literary journals such as *The Golden Era* and *The Overland Monthly* nurtured many local fiction writers. These included Bret Harte (1836–1902), the author of *The Luck of Roaring Camp*, essayist Henry George (1839–97), and bards ranging from Joaquin Miller (1837–1913) to Ina Coolbrith (the nation's first poet laureate in 1915).

The literary journals also provided an apprenticeship for San Franciscan writer Samuel Clemens (1835–1910). His 1865 publication of the Gold Country yarn, "The Celebrated Jumping Frog of Calaveras County," introduced him to a national readership as Mark Twain.

**Writer Samuel Clemens, alias Mark Twain**

## THE SOCIAL CRITICS

Ambrose Bierce (1842–1914) ranked among the first of many California writers who used their art to advocate wide-ranging political and social reforms. During the late 19th century, Bierce filled his *San Francisco Examiner* column with tirades against hypocrites and bureaucrats. His poisonous articles helped to trim the overweening influence of the vast Southern Pacific Railroad Company *(see pp50–51)*.

Frank Norris (1870–1902) attacked America's greed in his novel, *McTeague* (1899). In *The Octopus*, Norris also lashed out at the Southern Pacific, this time for its monopolistic mistreatment of ranchers in the San Joaquin Valley.

Back from the Klondike Gold Rush (setting for *The Call of the Wild*), working-class author Jack London alternated between writing adventure novels and stories – such as *The Iron Heel* – that showed his faith in Marxism.

Upton Sinclair (1878–1968) had already published *The Jungle*, his exposé of the Chicago stockyards, when he moved to California after World War I. But it was in Pasadena that he wrote most of his novels, campaigning against poverty and inequality.

Social injustice was a frequent theme for Salinas-born novelist John Steinbeck (1902–68). *Tortilla Flat* (1935), about a band of Mexican-American outcasts, was his first success. It was *The Grapes of Wrath* (1939), however, that brought him the prestigious Pulitzer Prize for

**Jack London at his Sonoma Valley ranch**

**Steinbeck on the Californian coast**

Literature. Steinbeck's book so powerfully portrayed the miseries endured by migratory laborers that it was banned from public libraries in some parts of the state.

## THE CRIME WRITERS

Three California writers established the American school of private-eye fiction. The first of these was Dashiell Hammett (1884–1961), a tubercular former Pinkerton Agency detective and San Francisco resident. He began writing for *Black Mask* and other "pulp" crime-fiction magazines in the 1920s. He then went on to produce five novels, including *The Maltese Falcon* (1930). Hammett's work boasted a grim realism not found in either British whodunits or more venal tales by pulp writers lacking his investigative credentials.

Raymond Chandler (1888–1959) was less intimate with urban "mean streets," but was a more lyrical storyteller.

**Poster for the film adaptation of Hammett's *The Maltese Falcon***

Chandler was an oil company executive in Los Angeles until he was sacked for drunkenness. He went on to create the quintessential American detective–Philip Marlowe, star of seven novels, the best being *Farewell, My Lovely* and *The Long Goodbye*. But it was Ross Macdonald (né Kenneth Millar) who finally rounded off his genre's rough edges and confirmed LA as its ideal setting. Macdonald was also the most prolific of this trio. He wrote 19 novels about sleuth Lew Archer, including *The Underground Man.*

**Beat writers and friends, Jack Kerouac and Neal Cassady**

## THE BEATS

Protest against the political conservatism of President Eisenhower's America and against the conventions of society and art combined to produce San Francisco's "Beat Movement" of the 1950s. The Beats (or "Beatniks," as *San Francisco Chronicle* columnist Herb Caen labeled them) were led by the writers Allen Ginsberg (1926–97), Jack Kerouac (1922–69), and William Burroughs (1914–97). They extolled poetry made up of random word usages, produced stream-of-consciousness, drug-assisted narratives, and shunned social, literary, and sexual restraints.

The Beatniks' rebellion officially began in December, 1955, when Ginsberg gave a public reading of his poem

"Howl," which was more like a shouting. Despite protests that "Howl" was obscene, it was subsequently published by San Franciscan Lawrence Ferlinghetti, poet and owner of City Lights *(see p340)*, the first paperbacks-only bookshop in the United States.

Two years later, Kerouac's novel *On the Road* spread the Beats' bohemian ethic nationwide. The most influential of the Beat writers, Kerouac also wrote *Desolation Angels* and *The Dharma Bums,* both novels set in California. By 1960 the Beat movement was waning, but not before it had paved the way for that decade's hippie movement.

## THE MODERNS

Today, most best-seller lists feature at least one novel by a California author. The state has many distinctive young voices, such as Ethan Canin (*The Palace Thief,* 1988), Michael Chabon (*The Wonder Boys,* 1995), and Ron Hansen (*Mariette in Ecstasy,* 1991). More established authors, such as Joan Didion (*A Book of Common Prayer,* 1977), Amy Tan (*The Joy Luck Club,* 1989, *The Bonesetter's Daughter,* 2001), and Alice Walker (*The Color Purple,* 1985), are still shining as brightly as ever. There are also many genre writers in California, including James Ellroy (*LA Confidential,* 1990), Dean Koontz (*Sole Survivor,* 2000), and Sue Grafton (*U is for Undertow,* 2009), all adding new depth to detective fiction.

**Novelist Amy Tan**

# Art in California

In the wake of the Gold Rush *(see pp48–9)*, California became both a magnet and a breeding ground for artists. They generally eschewed native folk traditions, however, in favor of European aesthetics that, while making the most of this new land and its people, were not dramatically changed by it. Only after World War II did Californians – including painter Richard Diebenkorn and photographer Imogen Cunningham – shed subservience to Old World art movements in order to develop distinctive visual trends, which then spread internationally. Since the 1950s, Los Angeles has challenged San Francisco's cultural primacy, and California art has become a highly valued investment.

*Figure on a Porch* (1959) by Richard Diebenkorn

environment. In the south, Guy Rose (1867–1925) led an Impressionist school that used the region's vibrant colors and brighter light to produce Monet-like effects.

Prohibition-era Los Angeles flirted with the Synchromist style of Stanton Macdonald-Wright (1890–1973). San Francisco was enchanted by Cubist Realists such as Otis Oldfield (1890–1969). Another popular artist there was the great Mexican muralist Diego Rivera, who in 1940 composed *Panamerican Mind*, an enormous fresco that can be seen at the City College.

Modernism flowered fully in California after World War II. It was at that time that David Park (1911–60), Richard Diebenkorn (born in 1922), and other members of the Bay Area Figurative School began to blend Expressionism with realistic imagery. In Southern California, Hard-Edge Abstractionists such as Helen Lundeberg and John McLaughlin (1898–1976) drew critical acclaim with their large-scale geometric shapes.

What is remarkable about contemporary California painters is not simply the worldwide recognition that they have earned, but their stylistic breadth. They range from Pop Artist Ed Ruscha (born in 1937) and urban landscapist Wayne Thiebaud (born in 1920), to cutting-edge British émigré David Hockney (born in 1937) and Arthur Carraway (born in 1927), whose work celebrates his African-American heritage.

## PAINTERS

California's mountain and desert landscapes and dramatic ocean shores dominated painters' attention here during the late 19th century. Thomas Hill (1829–1908) was born in England and trained in Paris. He moved to California in 1861 and began to produce epic natural panoramas, especially of the stunning Yosemite Valley *(see pp488–91)*. His work not only attracted new visitors to the West Coast but also helped win Yosemite its national park status in 1890. Even more popular was William Keith (1838–1911), a Scotsman who spent 50 years portraying the state's virgin wilderness. At that time, cities and people may have seemed comparatively pale inspirations. Yet Gilded Age California *(see pp50–51)* could not now be fully understood without such talents as William Hahn (1829–87), a German immigrant who captured life in nascent San Francisco; Grace Carpenter Hudson (1865–1937), renowned for her portraits of coastal natives; and William A Coulter (1849–1936), who recorded maritime scenes.

As early as 1900, the state's two halves displayed stylistically disparate growth. In the north, Xavier Martinez (1869–1943) and his fellow Tonalists filled canvases with the familiar hazy light and gray-brown hues of their

*Afternoon in Piedmont (Elsie at the Window)* by Xavier Martinez

*Two Callas* by Imogen Cunningham

## PHOTOGRAPHERS

Many early California photographs were either portraits or straightforward documentary scenes done by surveyors. Some photographers, however, such as Eadweard James Muybridge (1830–1904), found photography no less powerful than painting in depicting nature. Others preferred to focus on human subjects. Allegorical nudes and other images by Anne Brigman (1869–1950) found fans even in New York City. Arnold Genthe (1869–1942) studied the Bay Area's Asian community, producing (with writer Will Irwin) a 1913 volume called *Pictures of Old Chinatown*.

In 1932 an Oakland group called "f/64" mounted a major exhibition at the MH de Young Memorial Museum in San Francisco *(see pp372–3)*. Members of f/64, among them Ansel Adams (1902–84), Imogen Cunningham (1883–1976), and Edward Weston (1886–1958), believed photography should emphasize realism. This approach was riveting when used in close-ups of plants, or as Dorothea Lange (1895–1965) applied it in her portraits of Californians during the Great Depression.

The range of approaches now includes the snapshot aesthetics of Judy Dater (born in 1941) and photographs of Weimaraner dogs by William Wegman (born in 1942).

## SCULPTORS

German-born Rupert Schmid (1864–1932) arrived in San Francisco in the 1880s. He soon became famous for figurative works employing western themes, such as *California Venus* (1895), his life-size female nude adorned with California poppies. More important still was Douglas Tilden (1860–1935), a sculptor from Chico who created impressive civic monuments. Arthur Putnam (1873–1930) also won notoriety with his sensual representations of wild animals.

Schmid's *California Venus*

Californians have been expanding the parallel fields of sculpture and ceramics since the early part of this century. Peter Voulkos (born in 1924) experimented in large-scale fired clay sculptures. Robert Arneson (1930–1992) abandoned more traditional vessel aesthetics to pursue startling and amusing Pop Art ceramics, while Bruce Beasley (born in 1939) and Michael Heizer (born in 1944) have created pieces that take on different dimensions depending on the weather.

---

### ART PATRONAGE IN CALIFORNIA

Private and public patronage have been essential to the vitality of California culture since the late 19th century. Had it not been for railroad baron Henry Huntington's money and interest in art treasures, there would be no Huntington Library, Art Galleries, and Botanical Gardens in Pasadena *(see pp158–9)*. The public would not have access to that institution's collection of 18th-century British art, including Thomas Gainsborough's *The Blue Boy* (c.1770) and many other masterpieces. Multimillionaire J Paul Getty brought together the world-famous collection of Greek and Roman antiquities housed in the J Paul Getty Villa in Malibu *(see p88)* and the painting, sculpture, and decorative arts collection occupying the new J Paul Getty Center in Brentwood *(see pp82–3)*. Another multimillionaire, Norton Simon, amassed the renowned selection of Goyas, Picassos, Rembrandts, and Van Goghs now on public display in the Norton Simon Museum *(see pp156–7)*.

Public financing, too, has enriched the state's art offerings. In the 1930s, the New Deal paid artists to paint the frescoes in San Francisco's Coit Tower *(see p331)* and embellish public structures throughout the state. More recently, city funds have been used to make Los Angeles one of the most important centers of mural art in the world.

**Henry Huntington**

# Architecture in California

California's architectural history began with the
arrival of the Europeans in the 18th century *(see
pp46–7)*. Many of the Spanish missions of the late 18th
and early 19th centuries were adaptations of Mexican
baroque architecture, and the Spanish-Mexican influence continued to dominate California buildings until
the middle of the 19th century. Later, the population
influx caused by the Gold Rush led to this Hispanic
vernacular merging with styles imported by settlers
from the eastern United States and Europe. Architects
such as Henry Cleaveland, S & J Newsom, and
Bernard Maybeck were all influential in creating the
state's unique Victorian style.

**Hale House in Heritage Square,
Los Angeles**

## MISSION

Franciscan missionaries,
arriving in California from
Mexico, established a chain
of 21 missions from San
Diego to Sonoma as centers
from which to colonize the
state. They were all designed
to be within a day's journey
of their nearest neighbors.
These provincial versions of
Mexican churches and their
communal buildings were
designed by friars and built
of adobe bricks and wood
by unskilled Native American laborers. Over the years
their crude constructions
decayed and were shaken by
earthquakes, but many have
been carefully restored in
the 20th century. Distinctive
features include massive
walls covered with white
lime cement, small window
openings, rounded gables,
and tiered bell towers.

**Distinctive rounded bell tower
at Carmel Mission**

**Small
round
window**

**Rounded gable**

**Lime
cement
wall**

**Mission San Luis Rey** *(1811–51) was the 18th mission
to be established and was so architecturally impressive
that it was often referred to as a "palace."*

## MONTEREY

In the 1850s and 1860s, East
Coast settlers flooded into
the newly declared 31st state,
bringing with them styles
that were already going out
of fashion on the East Coast,
such as Greek Revival. Monterey, the state capital under
Mexican rule, gave its name
to an architecture that is, in
essence, a wooden Greek
temple wrapped around a
Mexican adobe. Features
include two-story wooden
porticoes supported by slim
square posts, wood shingle
roofs, and a chaste symmetry
of plan and elevation.

**Monterey-style Rancho
Los Cerritos, Long Beach**

**Square post**

**Wood shingle
roof**

**Wooden
portico**

**Adobe wall**

**Larkin House** *(1837), built by Thomas Larkin, was the first
Monterey-style house, with its two stories of adobe brick.*

## VICTORIAN

Three major styles emerged in California during the Victorian era: Italianate, most popular in San Francisco (see pp300–301), Queen Anne, and Eastlake. The two latter styles achieved a pinnacle of exuberance in California during the 19th century when they were brought to the state by migrants from the East Coast. The restrained Eastlake style, with its geometrically patterned façades and ornamentation, was often combined with the more extravagant Queen Anne style, notable for its gables, turrets, wraparound porches, and splendidly confused anthology of classical details.

Turret

Decorative gable

Decorative window on a Victorian house in Napa

Wraparound porch

**Carson Mansion** *in Eureka (1886) was built by S & J Newsom, who were masters of the Queen Anne style. Now a private club, the house may be California's ultimate Victorian folly.*

## ARTS AND CRAFTS

Pioneered by William Morris and Charles Voysey in England, the Arts and Crafts movement flourished briefly in California in the early 20th century. Also known as Craftsman style, its leading proponents included Bernard Maybeck and Charles and Henry Greene. Its emphasis is on simplicity and refinement on the outside and in the handcrafted interiors.

Characteristic beamed roof at Gamble House, Pasadena

Clapboard wall

Shady porch

**The First Church of Christ Science** *in Berkeley (1907) is the finest example of Bernard Maybeck's Arts and Crafts designs.*

## MISSION REVIVAL

The Spanish-Mexican style was dormant during the second half of the 19th century. Decorative or pared-down versions were then enthusiastically revived in the early 20th century. The style is distinguishable by its rounded arches, harmonious proportions, and absence of ornamentation.

Red-tiled roof at the Beverly Hills Hotel

White stucco wall

Red-tiled roof

Rounded arch

**The Women's Club** *(1913) in La Jolla was designed by Irving Gill, a pioneer of modernism who used poured concrete and stucco to create elegant versions of the Mission style.*

# Twentieth-Century California Architecture

In the early 20th century an architecture distinctive to California emerged, after a brief return to the state's Hispanic roots and an Art Deco style imported from Europe. This California style borrowed post-and-beam construction and wide porches from traditional Japanese buildings. Later, during the postwar building boom of the 1950s, the whole country was influenced by Cliff May's California ranch house, with its fusion of indoor and outdoor living. In more recent years, many architects, such as Craig Ellwood and Frank Gehry, have helped to make LA a center of modern architectural innovation *(see pp72–3)*.

**San Francisco Museum of Modern Art (1995)**

## SPANISH COLONIAL

Ornate versions of traditional Spanish architecture were first given wide currency by the Panama-California Exposition in San Diego in 1915 *(see pp256–7)*, where many buildings were decorated in this style. Simplified versions became the popular style for houses and public buildings throughout the 1920s. Distinguishing features included ornamental wood, stone, and ironwork, used to set off expanses of white stucco, red pantiled roofs, and lush gardens.

George Washington Smith, the Montecito-based architect, was a master of the style, creating abstracted Andalusian-style villages, such as **Ostoff House** (1924) in San Marino and Casa del Herrero (1925), a private house in Montecito. Another striking example of this style is William Mooser's **Santa Barbara County Courthouse** (1929), with its hand-painted ceilings, murals, and sunken gardens.

## STREAMLINE MODERNE

Art Deco made a brief appearance in California at the end of the 1920s, with jazzy reliefs and tile façades. It was superseded by Streamline Moderne, where sleek, rounded forms are animated by ribs, canopies, and reliefs. Its inspirations were machine-age imagery. The style is best seen in movie theaters, such as the **Academy Cathedral** (1939) in Inglewood and Oakland's **Paramount Theater** (Miller & Pflueger, 1931).

## PWA MODERNE

This movement was named after the Public Works Administration, established in the 1930s to fund public buildings. It is a marriage of Beaux-Arts formality and the simplicity of Modernism. It is notable for its stone façades, pilasters, and carved ornamentation. A good example is the **Monterey County Courthouse** (1937) in Salinas.

## LATE 20TH CENTURY

A diversity of approaches by leading architects has resulted in some striking contemporary buildings. Among the notable achievements of recent years are the ground-hugging, barnlike structures of **Sea Ranch**. This ecologically friendly vacation-home community on the Northern California coast began as a cluster of condominiums by Moore Lyndon Turnbull Whittaker in 1965. In sharp contrast is the **Salk Institute**, in La Jolla (Louis Kahn, 1959–65). State-of-the-art laboratories of poured concrete flank a bare travertine-paved plaza; a symbolic meeting place that links the continent and the ocean.

The **San Francisco Museum of Modern Art** (1995) by Swiss architect Mario Botta is both a civic symbol and an indoor plaza. A cylindrical skylight reaches up from stacked, top-lit galleries clad in precast panels of plain and angled bricks, to light an expansive foyer.

## POST-MODERNISM

Reacting to the impersonality of corporate towers, architects such as Michael Graves, Venturi Scott-Brown,

**George Washington Smith's Casa del Herrero in Montecito (1925)**

and Robert Stern popularized a more decorative approach to Modernism in the 1970s. Buildings such as **The Library** (1984) by Robert Stern in San Juan Capistrano make playful use of historical elements (columns, pediments, and pergolas) while employing colorful palettes.

Jon Jerde scrambles colors and architectural references with even greater abandon in his popular shopping centers, most notably **Westfield Horton Plaza** (1989) in San Diego. This multilevel outdoor shopping mall with domes and tilework echoes local Spanish-style buildings.

**Post-Modern Horton Plaza**

**Programmatic Donut Hole in La Puente, east of Los Angeles**

## PROGRAMMATIC BUILDINGS

The automobile began to reshape California as early as the 1920s, and there was fierce competition to attract the attention of passing motorists on the commercial strips that linked scattered communities. An exuberant roadside architecture developed, in which travelers were invited to sleep in wigwam motels or have their shoes repaired inside a building in the shape of a huge shoe (Doschander's Shoe Repair Shop, Bakersfield, 1947). Most of these fantasies have been demolished, but a few remain in outlying areas, such as the drive-thru **Donut Hole** (1958) in La Puente.

## WHERE TO FIND THE BUILDINGS

### FRANK LLOYD WRIGHT

Born in Wisconsin, Frank Lloyd Wright (1867–1959) lived in California in the 1920s and designed buildings in the state throughout his career. He began with **Hollyhock House** (1917–20) in Hollywood, and ended with the **Marin County Civic Center** in San Rafael, north of San Francisco, completed in 1972. Other notable buildings are the old VC Morris store (1949), now the **Union Square Frank Lloyd Wright Building** in San Francisco, and several LA "textile block" houses, inspired by Mayan temples.

**Frank Lloyd Wright's Hollyhock House in Hollywood**

# Multicultural California

California is the most ethnically diverse state in the Union. In the 19th century, the discovery of gold, silver, and oil each brought an influx of migrants of many nationalities to California; the landscape and climate still attract farmers, fishermen, and vintners from all over the world. By the mid-21st century, many believe California will be a hybrid of cultures, with no clear ethnic majority. The concentration of races varies statewide: a greater number of Hispanics reside in the south, while the Silicon Valley and northern farmlands have attracted Asians and Europeans. Most ethnic communities still celebrate their cultures with festivals *(see pp36–9)*.

Japanese sign

San Francisco's Chinatown

entire areas of cities. Although many of the younger Chinese have now moved to middle-class areas, the Chinatowns of LA and San Francisco still attract tourists to their traditional shops and restaurants.

Mexican street musicians in Los Angeles

## THE NATIVE AMERICANS

California has more resident Native Americans than any other state. The indigenous population grew in the 1960s when they gained more political rights. A few Native Americans still live on reservations, but the majority have opted for integration throughout the state.

## THE HISPANIC-AMERICANS

You cannot go far in California without becoming aware of the state's Hispanic heritage. Spanish explorers who arrived in the 17th and 18th centuries *(see pp46–7)* established many of today's cities. As early as the 1940s the state was home to the largest population of Mexicans outside their own country. Political and economic troubles in Central and South America have continued to fuel Hispanic immigration. Today, almost every city has Mexican influences in its architecture, cuisine, and art. The Hispanics are also responsible for some of the brightest fiestas, including the extravagant *Cinco de Mayo* (May 5) *(see p36)*.

## THE CHINESE

Chinese immigrants first arrived in California during the Gold Rush *(see pp48–9)*. A further influx escaped the economic problems of their homeland in the 1860s to work as cheap labor building the transcontinental railroad *(see pp50–51)*. Following its completion, they remained in California, setting up laundries and other businesses, but were met with racial violence by activists claiming they were stealing "white jobs." In the 1880s Congress severely limited Chinese immigration, a law that was not repealed until 1943.

Such antipathy resulted in ghettolike Chinese communities, which dominated

Girl in Native American dress

## THE AFRICAN-AMERICANS

African-Americans have been present in California since the days of Mexican rule. It was the increase in heavy industry during World War II, however, that led to the largest influx from the poorer southern states.

**Rotchev House at Fort Ross**

In the years that followed, low social standing and racism resulted in the growth of urban ghettos. Racial problems still persist in the US, but many African-Americans are making their mark in government, entertainment, and business. Cities like Oakland (see pp422–5) continue to celebrate traditional festivals.

## THE JAPANESE

The Japanese arrived in California in the early 20th century. The majority of them were farmers who literally sowed the seeds of the state's agricultural industry. During World War II, however, Japanese-Americans were considered a risk to national security and were interned for the duration of the war. The succeeding generation has overridden these events, and Japanese businesses have continued to grow since the 1980s property boom.

## THE ITALIANS

Italians, predominantly fishermen, arrived in California in the late 19th century, and settled in North Beach, San Francisco (see pp340–43). The climate and soil also tempted Italian vintners, who founded what is now a highly respected wine industry.

## THE RUSSIANS

Fur trappers from Russia and Alaska were among the first European settlers in California, arriving in the early 1800s. For a short time, they established a successful settlement at Fort Ross (see p460), and today there is a Russian population of some 25,000 in and around San Francisco.

## THE IRISH

Fewer people of Irish descent reside on the West Coast than on the East Coast, and there are no distinct Irish districts in California. The Irish have largely integrated into a multicultural way of life, but their presence is still felt in the many Irish city bars, and particularly during the statewide parades on St. Patrick's Day (see p36).

**Santa Monica English pub sign**

## THE MELTING POT

Over the last few decades there has been a steady rise in immigrants from Asia. Long Beach has the largest population of Cambodians outside Cambodia, and the district is known as "Little Phnom Penh." Wars in Korea and Vietnam brought natives of these countries to the liberal atmosphere of California in the 1950s and 1970s. Made to settle in the poorer areas of inner cities, they have now turned many of these into thriving communities. Fresno (see p516) has the second largest Hmong population outside Laos in the world.

The technological opportunities of Silicon Valley (see p428) have continued to attract Indians and Pakistanis to the region since the 1970s. Santa Monica is home to a large British contingent, complete with "authentic" pubs (see pp76–7). The town of Solvang (see p219) was founded by immigrants from Denmark in 1911 and retains its Danish heritage. California also has the second largest Jewish community in the US, two-thirds of whom live in LA.

**Danish windmill in Solvang**

# CALIFORNIA THROUGH THE YEAR

California generally enjoys a moderate climate (see pp40–41), which explains how residents can schedule annual events without concern for the weather. The size of the state, however, means that a range of activities can be pursued in different locations: winter can be spent skiing in the north or soaking up the sun in the warmer south. Californians love to celebrate, and the calendar is full of parades and festivals. Many are related to the state's agricultural heritage; others have been inspired by its social history, such as the Gold Rush, or its ethnic diversity. There are also cultural events, including jazz and film festivals, and national sports fixtures.

**Runners in the Los Angeles Marathon**

## SPRING

There's a clear sense of re-emergence in spring, when wildflowers carpet California's coastal headlands, gray whales swim north with their newborn offspring, and people start searching frantically for the sunglasses they tucked away the previous October. *Cinco de Mayo* (May 5) celebrations in Los Angeles and San Francisco, Hollywood's glamorous Academy Awards® ceremony, baseball games, and San Francisco's Bay-to-Breakers run are all familiar elements of the season.

## MARCH

**Los Angeles Marathon** *(first Sun)*. Takes place in the heart of the city and offers more live entertainment than any other marathon.
**Snowfest** *(first ten days)*, Tahoe City. The winter carnival features ski competitions, a "polar bear" (cold water) swim, parades, races, theater, and live music.
**St. Patrick's Day Parade** *(weekend nearest Mar 17)*, San Francisco. A parade down Market Street is usually followed by Irish coffee in the city's Irish bars.
**Return of the Swallows** *(Mar 19)*, Mission San Juan Capistrano *(see pp240–41)*.

**Swallows returning to Mission San Juan Capistrano**

**St. Patrick's Day shamrock**

Crowds gather to see the birds fly back to the mission gardens from their winter homes in Argentina. Live music, food, and children's activities feature.
**Redwood Coast Dixieland Jazz Festival** *(end Mar)*, Eureka. Some of the world's finest Dixieland bands gather for this annual event.

## APRIL

**Major League Baseball** *(Apr–Sep)*. The San Francisco Giants, LA Dodgers, Anaheim Angels, Oakland Athletics, and San Diego Padres compete.
**Grand National Rodeo** *(early Apr)*. Daly City. The largest two-day rodeo in the US. Lassoing mustangs and a livestock exposition.
**Toyota Grand Prix** *(mid-Apr)*, Long Beach. The biggest street race in the US.
**Agua Cahuilla Indian Heritage Festival** *(mid-Apr)*, Palm Springs. Festivities honor the Native Americans who discovered the local hot springs.
**Cherry Blossom Festival** *(mid-Apr)*, San Francisco. Japanese dancing and martial arts displays are all part of this traditional annual event *(see p352)*.
**San Francisco International Film Festival** *(mid-Apr – early May)*. Independent films from around the world are shown in venues throughout the city.

## MAY

**Raisin Festival** *(early May)*, Selma. A parade, art competitions and the Raisin Queen.

**Cinco de Mayo** *(May 5)*, LA and San Francisco. The state's largest Mexican celebrations feature folk dancing and mariachi music.

**Calaveras County Fair** *(mid-May)*, Angels Camp. The famous frog jumping contest *(see p479)* and a rodeo.

**California Strawberry Festival** *(mid-May)*, Oxnard. Food booths, arts and crafts, and contests.

**Bay-to-Breakers** *(third Sun)*, San Francisco. The world's largest fun run is 7.5-miles (12.5-km) from the Embarcadero to Ocean Beach.

**Carnaval** *(last weekend)*, San Francisco. The Mission District turns Latin American, with salsa and reggae bands.

**Sacramento Jazz Jubilee** *(last weekend)*.

Mexican dancer at the *Cinco de Mayo* festival in Los Angeles

## SUMMER

At no other time of year are the clichés of California so evident. Beaches are crowded with tanned, muscled bodies and daredevil surfers, and colorfully dressed gays and lesbians parade through San Francisco streets in June. Tourists flood into the state, attending its many outdoor music events, Wild West celebrations (such as Old Miners' Days in Big Bear Lake), and the renowned annual Gilroy Garlic Festival.

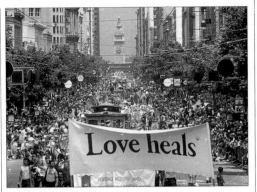

Lesbian and Gay Pride parade in San Francisco

## JUNE

**Mainly Mozart Festival** *mid-Jun)*, San Diego. Leading orchestras perform Mozart.

**Lesbian and Gay Pride Day** *(Sun in late Jun)*, San Francisco. The largest gay parade.

**Lumber Jubilee** *(end Jun)*, Tuolumne. The history of California's lumber industry.

**Monterey Blues Festival** *(end Jun)*. Star blues.

**Juneteenth** *(end Jun)*, Oakland. African-American celebration, featuring jazz and gospel.

## JULY

**Fourth of July Fireworks** Particularly good displays are at Disneyland and on Santa Monica Pier.

**Mammoth Lakes Jazz Jubilee** *(first weekend after Jul 4)*. Some dozen world-class jazz bands perform.

**Obon Festival** *(mid-Jul)*, San Jose. Taiko drummers and dancers join in this Japanese-American party.

**Carmel Bach Festival** *(mid-Jul–early Aug)*. Bach concerts and classes.

**California Indian Center Pow-wow** *(end Jul)*, Los Angeles. A celebration of Native American food and culture.

**Gilroy Garlic Festival** *(end Jul)*. Garlic in all kinds of dishes.

**Old Miners' Days** *(end Jul–mid-Aug)*, Big Bear Lake. The Gold Rush is recalled with a chili cook-off.

**Festival of the Arts** *(Jul–Aug)*, Laguna Beach.

**International Surf Festival** *(late Jul/Aug)*. Body boarding and surfing events take place at various LA beaches.

## AUGUST

**San Francisco Marathon** *(late Jul or early Aug)*.

**Old Spanish Days Fiesta** *(early Aug)*, Santa Barbara. Spanish markets, a carnival.

**San Mateo County Fair** *(early–mid-Aug)*, Thousands of attractions. Horse racing.

**Nisei Week** *(mid-Aug)*, Japanese festival in LA's Little Tokyo.

**Pebble Beach Concours d'Elegance** *(mid-Aug)*. Classic automobile show.

**California State Fair** *(mid-Aug–early Sep)*, Sacramento. Everything from star-studded entertainment to pig races.

**Bigfoot Days** *(end Aug/early Sep)*, Willow Creek. A parade and ice-cream social at this homage to California's legendary hermit.

Native American dancers at a powwow

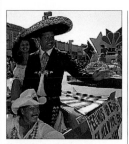

Mexican Independence Day
parade in Santa Monica

## AUTUMN

In the High Sierras, leaves
of deciduous trees turn
stunning shades of red and
yellow. The Napa Valley
wineries (see pp462–3) invite
visitors to help celebrate
their grape harvests with wine
tastings and live music. All
over the state, Oktoberfests
serve up foamy mugs of
beer and the "oom-pah-pah"
of German bands, while
rodeos dramatize California's
frontier past.

## SEPTEMBER

**Pro Football** (Sep–Dec). The
San Francisco '49ers,
Oakland Raiders,
and San Diego
Chargers take
to the field.
**Los Angeles
County Fair** (whole
month), Pomona.
This vast county fair
includes horse races, an
operational farm, outdoor
miniature railroad, and
entertainment acts.
**California State Gold
Panning Championship**
(early Sep), Foresthill. The
1849 Gold Rush is remem-
bered with a gold panning
competition.
**Oktoberfest** (mid-Sep–
mid-Oct), Torrance. The
largest German beer festival
in Southern California. Entry
to the festival is for those
aged 21 years and over only,
except family day on Sunday.
The event features German
dancers, contests, and food.
**Mexican Independence Day**
(Sep 16). Mexican dancing,

**Football**

music and food in Los Angeles, Calexico, and Santa Maria.
**Monterey Jazz Festival**
(third weekend). Running
since 1958, this is the
world's oldest continuously
held annual jazz festival,
attracting over 500 top artists.
All the greats have played
here at one time.
**Danish Days** (mid–Sep),
Solvang. Danish food stands
and parades (see p219).
**Sonoma County Harvest
Fair** (late Sep/early Oct),
Santa Rosa. A grape stomp
and a 6-mile (10-km) run are
highlights of this annual fair.
**Tarfest** (late Sep). Three-day
festival of film, music, and
art in Los Angeles.

## OCTOBER

**Black Cowboy Parade**
(early Oct), Oakland.
Commemorating the part
African-Americans played in
settling the American West.
**Columbus Day Parade**
(Sun nearest Oct 12), San
Francisco. Bands and floats
proceed down Columbus
Avenue to Fisherman's Wharf.
**San Francisco Jazz Festival**
(end Oct–early Nov).
All-star jazz perform-
ances throughout
the city.
**Pumpkin Festi-
val** (mid-Oct),
Half Moon Bay.
The World Heavy-
weight Pumpkin
Championship, pump-
kin carving, and pumpkin
dishes are served in every
edible variety.

**Craftsman Weekend** (mid-
Oct), San Gabriel Valley.
Largest celebration of the
Arts and Crafts movement in
western US, including tours.
**Halloween** (Oct 31), San
Francisco. Costumed
residents parade through
the city streets.
**Butterflies** (end Oct–mid-
Mar), Pacific Grove.
Thousands of monarch
butterflies migrate here
annually (see p510).

Costumed participants in
Pasadena's Doo Dah Parade

## NOVEMBER

*Dia de los Muertos*/Day of the
Dead (Nov 1). Festivities in
LA's El Pueblo and San Francisco's Mission District highlight this Mexican religious
festival, when the souls of the
dead are said to visit their
surviving relatives. Scholars
trace the origins to indigenous
observances dating back
thousands of years.
**Death Valley '49ers
Encampment** (early Nov).
Fiddle, banjo, mandolin, and
guitar competitions, pioneer
costume and horseshoe
contests, cowboy poetry, and
gold panning.

Mexican musicians at the *Dia de los Muertos* festival

Gray whale approaching a boat off Baja California

## WINTER

Californians love bright lights, and this is most apparent at Christmas, when every building and public square seems to be draped in twinkling bulbs. Churches resound with Christmas carols, and film stars take part in seasonal parades. As Lake Tahoe's ski season gets under way, highways jam up with avid skiers traveling north.

## DECEMBER

**Hollywood Christmas Parade** (*first Thu after Thanksgiving*), Los Angeles. Hollywood and Sunset Boulevards are crowded with this celebrity-heavy extravaganza, held since 1931.
**Newport Beach Christmas Boat Parade** (*mid-Dec*). Five nights of carol singing and almost a hundred glittering vessels that light up the Newport waterfront.

Christmas decorations in Carmel Plaza

**International Tamale Festival** (*early Dec*), Indio. Mexican dancing accompanies the *tamale* (spicy corn husk rolls) gluttony.
**Whale-watching** (*end Dec–Apr*). California gray whales, migrating south annually from the Bering Strait to Baja, can be sighted along the coast or from whale-watching boats out of many coastal cities (*see p614*).

Float at the Tournament of Roses Parade in Pasadena

## JANUARY

**Bald Eagles** (*Jan–Feb*), Mount Shasta. See bald eagles that nest here.
**Tournament of Roses Parade** (*Jan 1*), Pasadena. A pageant, followed by the Rose Bowl intercollegiate football game (*see p154*).
**Doo Dah Parade** (*mid-Jan*), Pasadena. Costumed parody of the Rose Parade.
**Palm Springs International Film Festival** (*early–mid-Jan*). Screenings and awards.
**Gold Discovery Day** (*Jan 24*), Coloma. Anniversary of the first gold discovery (*see p475*).

**Napa Valley International Mustard Festival** (*Jan–Mar*), Valley-wide. Mustards and wines available for tasting.

## FEBRUARY

**Academy Awards Ceremony** (*Feb*), Los Angeles. Hollywood's finest gather to honor the year's top films and actors.
**AT&T Pebble Beach Pro-Am Golf Tournament** (*end Jan–early Feb*). Pros and celebrities play golf together.
**Dickens Festival** (*early Feb*), Riverside. Writer Charles Dickens' life is celebrated in a re-creation of a mid-19th-century London marketplace.
**Riverside County Fair and National Date Festival** (*mid–late Feb*), Indio. Date dishes and camel and ostrich races.
**Chinese New Year Festival** (*mid-Feb–early Mar*), San Francisco. The nation's largest Chinese New Year festival.

Chinese New Year celebrations in San Francisco

# The Climate of California

Apart from the extremes of the mountains and the deserts, the state's climate is neither oppressive in summer nor too cold in winter. The Northern Coastal Range is temperate, although wet in the winter. To the east, rain turns to snow on the Sierra Nevada Mountains. Central California and the Central Valley have a Mediterranean climate. The weather becomes drier and warmer toward the south with soaring temperatures in the desert during the summer.

## THE NORTH

| °F | | | |
|---|---|---|---|
| 61 | 63 | 61 | 54 |
| 48 | 52 | 48 | 41 |
| 55 % | 52 % | 49 % | 42 % |
| 2.9 in | 0.1 in | 1.9 in | 5.6 in |
| month Apr | Jul | Oct | Jan |

Average monthly maximum temperature
Average monthly minimum temperature
Average monthly sunshine during daylight hours (%)
Average monthly rainfall

## WINE COUNTRY

| °F | | | |
|---|---|---|---|
| 70 | 82 | 77 | 57 |
| 43 | 54 | 48 | 37 |
| 75 % | 85 % | 80 % | 52 % |
| 1.6 in | 0 in | 1.7 in | 5.4 in |
| month Apr | Jul | Oct | Jan |

## SAN FRANCISCO AND THE BAY AREA

| °F | | | |
|---|---|---|---|
| 63 | 68 | 72 | 57 |
| 50 | 54 | 55 | 46 |
| 73 % | 66 % | 70 % | 56 % |
| 1.3 in | 0 in | 1.3 in | 4 in |
| month Apr | Jul | Oct | Jan |

## GOLD COUNTRY

| °F | | | |
|---|---|---|---|
| 66 | 91 | 73 | 54 |
| 39 | 55 | 45 | 32 |
| 70 % | 89 % | 78 % | 54 % |
| 3 in | 0.2 in | 2.3 in | 6.7 in |
| month Apr | Jul | Oct | Jan |

## NORTH CENTRAL CALIFORNIA

| °F | | | |
|---|---|---|---|
| 75 | 99 | 81 | 54 |
| 48 | 64 | 50 | 37 |
| 85 % | 96 % | 88 % | 51 % |
| 0.9 in | 0 in | 0.5 in | 1.9 in |
| month Apr | Jul | Oct | Jan |

## SOUTH CENTRAL CALIFORNIA

| °F | | | |
|---|---|---|---|
| 70 | 82 | 77 | 61 |
| 45 | 54 | 48 | 36 |
| 83 % | 97 % | 87 % | 46 % |
| 1.1 in | 0.7 in | 0.3 in | 2.9 in |
| month Apr | Jul | Oct | Jan |

Eureka
Redding
Chico
Tahoe City
Santa Rosa
Sacramento
Stockton
San Francisco
Modesto
San Jose
Monterey
San Obi

**HIGH SIERRAS**

| °F | | | | |
|---|---|---|---|---|
| | 50 | 77 | 59 | 41 |
| | 27 | 45 | 32 | 19 |
| ☀ | 65 % | 82 % | 70 % | 50 % |
| ☂ | 2 in | 0.3 in | 2.1 in | 5.6 in |
| month | Apr | Jul | Oct | Jan |

**MOJAVE DESERT**

| °F | | | | |
|---|---|---|---|---|
| | 79 | 100 | 82 | 61 |
| | 48 | 66 | 52 | 32 |
| ☀ | 91 % | 93 % | 91 % | 81 % |
| ☂ | 0.2 in | 0.3 in | 0.2 in | 0.5 in |
| month | Apr | Jul | Oct | Jan |

**LOS ANGELES**

| °F | | | | |
|---|---|---|---|---|
| | 72 | 84 | 72 | 68 |
| | 55 | 64 | 61 | 50 |
| ☀ | 70 % | 67 % | 80 % | 76 % |
| ☂ | 1.2 in | 0.2 in | 0.4 in | 2.7 in |
| month | Apr | Jul | Oct | Jan |

**ORANGE COUNTY**

| °F | | | | |
|---|---|---|---|---|
| | 70 | 82 | 77 | 66 |
| | 54 | 63 | 59 | 48 |
| ☀ | 70 % | 67 % | 80 % | 76 % |
| ☂ | 0.8 in | 0 in | 0.2 in | 2.5 in |
| month | Apr | Jul | Oct | Jan |

**PALM SPRINGS**

| °F | | | | |
|---|---|---|---|---|
| | 88 | 109 | 91 | 70 |
| | 54 | 75 | 59 | 43 |
| ☀ | 94 % | 91 % | 92 % | 84 % |
| ☂ | 0.1 in | 0.2 in | 0.2 in | 1 in |
| month | Apr | Jul | Oct | Jan |

**SAN DIEGO**

| °F | | | | |
|---|---|---|---|---|
| | 70 | 77 | 75 | 66 |
| | 57 | 66 | 61 | 50 |
| ☀ | 66 % | 67 % | 70 % | 72 % |
| ☂ | 0.8 in | 0 in | 0.4 in | 1.8 in |
| month | Apr | Jul | Oct | Jan |

Independence

Death Valley

field

a
ara

Los Angeles

San Bernardino

Anaheim

Palm Springs

San Diego

# THE HISTORY OF CALIFORNIA

An early 16th-century chivalric Spanish novel, *Las Sergas de Esplanadían (The Exploits of Esplanadían)*, first gave the name *California* to a mythical island, plump with natural wealth and ruled by Calafía, a pagan queen. By 1542, when the Portuguese navigator Juan Rodríguez Cabrillo (João Rodrigues Cabrilho) sailed north from Mexico on Spain's behalf and discovered what he believed to be an island, the name California was already familiar enough for him to use it in his journal. Two centuries would pass, however, before Spain made a real claim on the land, sending Father Junípero Serra in 1769 to establish Franciscan missions along the length of California.

**State seal**

### THE GOLD RUSH

Still, the territory remained remote until 1848; the same year that Mexico ceded California to the US, gold was found in the Sierra Nevada foothills. By 1849, hordes of fortune seekers had arrived in Northern California. The Gold Rush, followed by silver finds in the western Sierras and the completion of the transcontinental railroad in 1869, brought prosperity to the whole state. But the changes caused social rifts: whites charged Chinese immigrants with "stealing" their jobs, and by the beginning of the 20th century, economic divisions left over from the time of plenty had helped to create powerful labor unions.

### 20TH-CENTURY CALIFORNIA

San Francisco's earthquake in 1906 convinced many that California's heyday was over. However, during the next 90 years, Hollywood drew international attention with its moviemaking. Oil wells serviced the needs of increasingly car-dependent residents, and by 1937 orange groves had become a symbol of the state's fertile future. When the UN charter was signed in San Francisco in 1945, it was clear that California, once considered at the edge of civilization, was finally a player at center stage.

Early map of the United States, showing California as an island

◁ Mural at the Santa Barbara County Courthouse showing Cabrillo's landing in California

# Early California

It is estimated that, at the time of European discovery, between 100,000 and 275,000 natives lived in California. They were not warlike, nor did they have much in the way of government. Only on the Colorado River did they practice agriculture; most relied on hunting, fishing, or the gathering of staples such as acorns for food. Their religion and medical beliefs were bound together in the person of a shaman, said to be in direct communication with the spirit world. They congregated in villages of 100 to 150 inhabitants generally living in conical or dome-shaped dwellings. Social classes were almost nonexistent, but there were great language divisions between different tribes.

**Early basketry**

**Tcholovoni People**
*Various tribes, including these Tcholovoni people, settled in small villages on the shores of San Francisco Bay.*

**Money Box**
*Natives of Northern California used dentalium shells for money, held in ornately carved boxes.*

**Jewelry**
*This necklace, made of abalone and clamshells, is thought to be one of the earliest artifacts of Native California life.*

**Gift baskets**, such as this Miwok example, were often decorated with beads.

**Quail feathers** and geometric dancers decorate this basket of the Yokut people.

**Eel trapper**

## BASKETRY
Basket-weaving was the primary native activity. They used a wide range of materials, which were twined or coiled into imaginative or symbolic designs. Baskets were used in all walks of life, including hunting, storage, cooking, and eating.

**Headdresses**
*This headpiece, made out of black and white magpie feathers, derives from the native Miwok people.*

## TIMELINE

**3,400,000 BC** Volcanic ash from Mount St. Helens creates the Petrified Forest at Calistoga (*see p461*)

**200,000 BC** Early inhabitants, possibly predecessors of *Homo sapiens*, live near what is now Calico (*see p285*)

*Early flint stone tool*

| 3,400,000 BC | 2,000,000 BC | 200,000 BC |
|---|---|---|

**3,000,000 BC** Plate movements form Redrock Canyon in Death Valley (*see pp290–93*)

*Sabre-toothed tiger skeleton from La Brea Tar Pits*

**40,000 BC** Mammoths, tigers, and other Pleistocene epoch creatures are trapped in Los Angeles' La Brea Tar Pits

**Kule Loklo People**
*These early Bay Area inhabitants were depicted by Anton Refregier in his mural in the foyer of the Rincon Center (see p317).*

## WHERE TO SEE EARLY CALIFORNIA
The George C Page Museum of La Brea Discoveries *(see p118)* includes fossil reconstructions of creatures recovered from the nearby tar pits. The Chumash Painted Cave State Historic Park *(p219)* has rare pictographs executed by the Chumash people. LA's Southwest Museum *(p153)* and the California Academy of Sciences in San Francisco *(pp370–71)* both feature Native American artifacts.

**Painted caves** *dating back thousands of years have been carefully preserved in the Chumash Painted Cave State Historic Park in Southern California.*

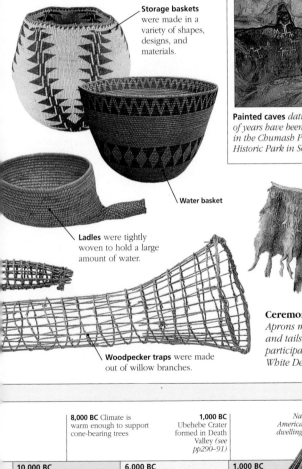

**Storage baskets** were made in a variety of shapes, designs, and materials.

**Water basket**

**Ladles** were tightly woven to hold a large amount of water.

**Woodpecker traps** were made out of willow branches.

**Ceremonial Costumes**
*Aprons made of animal skins and tails were worn by participants in the traditional White Deerskin Dance.*

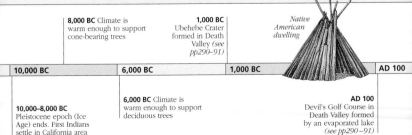

**8,000 BC** Climate is warm enough to support cone-bearing trees

**1,000 BC** Ubehebe Crater formed in Death Valley *(see pp290–91)*

*Native American dwelling*

| 10,000 BC | 6,000 BC | 1,000 BC | AD 100 |
| --- | --- | --- | --- |

**10,000–8,000 BC** Pleistocene epoch (Ice Age) ends. First Indians settle in California area

**6,000 BC** Climate is warm enough to support deciduous trees

**AD 100** Devil's Golf Course in Death Valley formed by an evaporated lake *(see pp290–91)*

# The Colonial Period

Although the Spanish "discovered" California in 1542, they did not colonize the area until the 18th century. Their rule was enforced through a trio of institutions – the mission (church), the *presidio* (fort), and the *pueblo* (town). Of these, the mission was the most influential. Beginning at San Diego in 1769, Franciscan friars founded 21 missions at approximately 30-mile (48-km) intervals along *El Camino Real* ("the Royal Road"). Missionaries wanted to bring religion to the "benighted Indian," but they also used natives as cheap labor. European colonists committed a more serious crime by spreading diseases that would reduce the native population to about 16,000 by 1900.

**Mission statue**

• San Francisco de Solano *(1823)*
• San Rafael Arcangel *(1817)*
• San Francisco de Asis *(1776)*
• San Jose *(1797)*
• Santa Clara de Asis *(1777)*
Santa Cruz *(1791)*
• San Juan Bautista *(1797)*
• Nuestra Señora de la Soledad *(17*
San Carlos Borromeo de Carmelo *(1770)*
• San Antonio de Padua *(1771)*

*El Camino Real*

San Miguel Arcangel *(1797)*

San Luis Obispo de To *(1772)*

La Purisma Concepcic *(1787)*

• Santa Ines *(1804*

Santa Barbara *(17*

San Buenaventura *(1782)* •

**Sir Francis Drake**
*The English navigator landed in California in 1579 to make repairs to his ship, the* Golden Hind. *He named the land "Nova Albion" and claimed it for Queen Elizabeth I.*

**Father Junípero Serra**
*Originally from the Spanish island of Majorca, Father Junípero Serra led the Franciscan expedition to establish a chain of missions in California.*

**Jedediah Smith**
*In 1828, a fur-trapper, Jedediah "Strong" Smith, was the first white man to reach California overland across the Sierra Nevada Mountains, from the eastern United States.*

## TIMELINE

**1524** Hernán Cortés, Spanish conqueror of Mexico, encourages King Charles V to seize control of the "California Islands"

**1579** English privateer Francis Drake anchors his *Golden Hind* near Point Reyes *(see pp412–13)*

| 1500 | 1600 | 1650 |
|---|---|---|

**1542** Juan Rodríguez Cabrillo (João Rodrigues Cabrilho) sails north from Mexico to San Diego harbor, making him the official discoverer of California

**1595** Portuguese navigator Sebastián Rodríguez Cermeño discovers Monterey Bay

*Juan Rodríguez Cabrillo*

**1602** Spanish merchant-adventurer Sebastián Vizcaíno sails up the California coast, naming landmarks as he goes – including San Diego, Santa Barbara, Point Concepcíon, and Carmel

**Mission San Gabriel Arcángel**
*Ferdinand Deppe's 1832 work is thought to be the
first painting of a mission. It depicts the central
role of the mission in the community, surrounded
by Native American dwellings.*

### WHERE TO SEE COLONIAL CALIFORNIA

**Restored living quarters** *are displayed at
the Santa Barbara Mission Museum.*

Mission-era artifacts can be found at
San Francisco's Mission Dolores *(see
p361)*, the Oakland Museum of California *(pp424–5)*, the Mission
San Carlos Borromeo in Carmel
*(pp512–13)*, and the Mission Santa
Barbara *(pp222–3)*. Most of the 21
missions offer public tours.

■ Fernando Rey de España *(1797)*

● San Gabriel Arcangel *(1771)*

  ● San Juan Capistranol *(1776)*

    ● San Luis rey de Francia *(1798)*

    ● San Diego de Alcalá *(1769)*

**US Victory**
*On July 9, 1846, 70
US sailors and marines
marched ashore at
San Francisco (then
Yerba Buena) and
claimed it for the US.*

**Mission Artifacts**
*The Franciscan friars brought
many items from Spain and
Mexico to California. As well as
decorative objects, some, such as
these prayer bells, had
practical purposes.*

### EL CAMINO REAL

The 21 missions along El Camino Real, from San
Diego to Sonoma, were planned so that each was
one day's journey on horseback from the next.

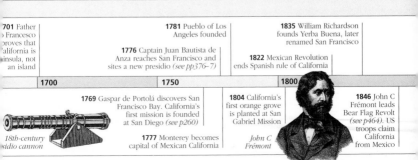

**1701** Father
Francesco
proves that
California is
peninsula, not
an island

**1781** Pueblo of Los
Angeles founded

**1776** Captain Juan Bautista de
Anza reaches San Francisco and
sites a new presidio *(see pp376–7)*

**1835** William Richardson
founds Yerba Buena, later
renamed San Francisco

**1822** Mexican Revolution
ends Spanish rule of California

| 1700 | 1750 | 1800 |
|------|------|------|

**1769** Gaspar de Portolá discovers San
Francisco Bay. California's
first mission is founded
at San Diego *(see p260)*

**1804** California's
first orange grove
is planted at San
Gabriel Mission

**1846** John C
Frémont leads
Bear Flag Revolt
*(see p464)*. US
troops claim
California
from Mexico

*18th-century
sidio cannon*

**1777** Monterey becomes
capital of Mexican California

*John C
Frémont*

# The Rush For Riches

In 1848 newspaperman Sam Brannan brandished nuggets that had been found in the Sacramento Valley, shouting "Gold! Gold! Gold from the American River!" Most of the prospectors who thereafter stampeded California's Mother Lode did not find fortune. But the gold-seeking hordes changed the area forever – especially San Francisco. Between 1848 and 1850, the town's population shot from 812 to 25,000. Food and property prices skyrocketed and crime thrived. In 1859, after the Gold Rush had ended, silver ore (the Comstock Lode) was exposed on the eastern Sierras, and Northern California boomed again.

**Nugget of Californian gold**

**Forty-Niners**
*Gold prospectors from all over the US traveled to California in 1849, hence their name. They carried tools, weapons, and food provisions on their journey.*

**Barbary Coast Saloon**
*Gambling and prostitution were rife in San Francisco's Barbary Coast region, and men were often pressed into naval service.*

**Pickaxes** were used to loosen hard rock ready for the sluice.

**State Capital**
*Once little more than farmland, Sacramento grew into a bustling city within two years of the Gold Rush. It became the state capital in 1854.*

**The sluice** was a long trough with wooden bars. As water was flushed along, gold particles were trapped behind the bars.

## TIMELINE

**1848** California is annexed by the US. Gold discovered at Sutter's Mill *(see p475)*

**1849** Almost 800 ships leave New York, full of men bound for the gold fields

*Sign from the Flying Cloud clipper ship*

**1854** Sacramento becomes California state capital

| 1848 | 1850 | 1852 | 18 |

**1850** California becomes 31st state in the Union

**1851** San Francisco vigilante movement hangs several lawbreakers. Clipper ship *Flying Cloud* sails from New York to San Francisco in a record 89 days

**1853** Levi Strauss lands in the Bay Area and begins selling his canvas trousers *(see p343)*

*John Sutter (1802– 1880)*

**Count Agoston Haraszthy**
*The Hungarian was the first vintner to plant European grape-vine cuttings in California.*

**Hydraulic mining** blasted away rock with water to uncover gold underneath.

### WHERE TO SEE THE ERA OF RICHES

Many of the settlements that were once thronged with gold miners have since disintegrated into ghost towns, such as Bodie (p494) and Calico (p285). But you can still get a feel for the times at Columbia State Historic Park (pp480–81), a restored Mother Lode town. The Wells Fargo History Museum in San Francisco (p314) has mementos of the Gold Rush. The Jackson Square Historical District (p314) was once part of the Barbary Coast.

**Old schoolhouse at Calico ghost town**

**Comstock Lode Silver**
*Between 1859 and the mid-1880s, 400 million dollars worth of silver was extracted from mines in the High Sierras.*

**Gold panning** involved swirling dirt and water around a flat-bottomed pan until only gold residue remained.

**Emperor Norton**
*Self-proclaimed Emperor of the United States and Protector of Mexico, the eccentric Joshua Norton printed his own currency and gave advice to Sacramento legislators.*

### OLD MINING TECHNIQUES

the rush for gold increased, ways of racting the ore became more sophisti-ed. What began as an adventure came a highly developed industry.

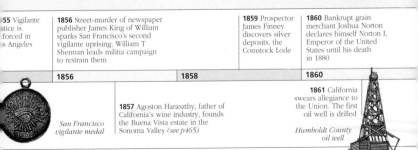

| **55** Vigilante stice is forced in s Angeles | **1856** Street-murder of newspaper publisher James King of William sparks San Francisco's second vigilante uprising; William T Sherman leads militia campaign to restrain them | | **1859** Prospector James Finney discovers silver deposits, the Comstock Lode | **1860** Bankrupt grain merchant Joshua Norton declares himself Norton I, Emperor of the United States until his death in 1880 |
|---|---|---|---|---|
| | **1856** | **1858** | **1860** | **1861** California swears allegiance to the Union. The first oil well is drilled |
| *San Francisco vigilante medal* | | **1857** Agoston Haraszthy, father of California's wine industry, founds the Buena Vista estate in the Sonoma Valley (see p465) | | *Humboldt County oil well* |

# The Gilded Age

For California's *nouveaux riches*, the smartest address during the late 19th century was on Nob Hill in San Francisco *(see p330)*, where grand mansions were built. This was a time of ostentation but also of expansion, thanks to train connections with the East and South. California oranges could now be exported easily to New York markets; taking the return trip were European immigrants and others hoping for a better life on the West Coast. Land prices increased in LA County, and by 1900 San Francisco's population exceeded 300,000.

**Gold pocket watch**

**Victorian Décor**
*Windows in the Winchester Mystery House (see pp430–31) are typically ornate.*

**Transcontinental Railroad**
*On May 12, 1869, the final spike was driven for the new railroad, linking the East and West Coasts.*

Bathroom, with original bath tub and tiles

Front parlor

Dining room

**The "Big Four"**
*Charles Crocker, Leland Stanford, Collis Huntington, and Mark Hopkins made millions investing in the transcontinental railroad.*

## TIMELINE

**1863** Construction begins on the Central Pacific Railroad

**1869** Transcontinental railroad is completed

**1870**

**1871** Racial violence in LA leaves about 20 Chinese dead

**1873** Andrew Hallidie tests San Francisco's first cable car

*San Francisco's first cable car*

**1873–5** Orange planting begins in Riverside

**1875**

**1876** Southern Pacific Railroad reaches Los Angeles

*California oranges*

**1877** San Franciscans torch Chinese stores and laundries to protest against cheap labor

**1880**

**1882** US Congress passes the Chinese Exclusion Act, limiting Chinese immigration

**1884** Sarah chester emb on her 38 house-bui project in San *(see pp430*

**Sutro Baths**
*The largest swimming pool in San Francisco stood from 1896 until the 1960s.*

**Yosemite National Park**
*Made a national park in 1890, Yosemite also became California's first tourist attraction and a popular image for advertisers.*

## WHERE TO SEE GILDED AGE CALIFORNIA

Public tours are held at the Haas-Lilienthal House *(see p348)* and the first cable car is on display at the Cable Car Barn *(p331)*, both in San Francisco. The "golden spike" from the transcontinental railroad is displayed, along with Big Four mementos, at the Stanford University Art Museum *(p427)*. Train buffs will also enjoy the California State Railroad Museum in Sacramento *(p473)*.

**The California State Railroad Museum** *is a celebration of rail travel on the West Coast.*

**The living room** was originally the master bedroom.

**Porch**

**Hall, with Victorian corner sofa**

**Chinese Immigrants**
*The "coolies" who helped build the transcontinental railroad stayed and set up businesses, such as laundries and restaurants, but were met with racism.*

## HAAS-LILIENTHAL HOUSE

Grocer William Haas built this elaborate Queen Anne-style house in 1886, one of many in San Francisco. Today it is a museum, and shows how a wealthy family would have lived at the end of the 19th century *(see p348)*.

**1890** Yosemite wins national park status *(see pp488–91)*

*Stanford University seal*

**1893** San Andreas Fault discovered by University of California geologist Andrew Lawson

**1896** Comstock tunnel builder Adolph Sutro opens the world's largest indoor saltwater swimming center in San Francisco

1885

1890

1895

**1888** Hotel del Coronado opens in San Diego *(see p255)*

**1891** Stanford University opens *(see p427)*; future president Herbert Hoover is in the first graduating class

**1894** West Coast's first world's fair is held in San Francisco's Golden Gate Park

**1897** San Francisco merchants prosper by outfitting gold miners traveling to Canada's Klondike River

# The Rise of Hollywood

In 1887, Kansas prohibitionist Harvey Henderson Wilcox wanted to call his farm and the LA suburb surrounding it "Figwood," after his chief crop. His wife chose instead a name she had overheard on a train: "Hollywood." By the 1920s, the film industry was making the town famous and offering Americans entertainment to help them escape the reality of World War I, Prohibition, and later, the Great Depression. Silent film stars such as Mary Pickford and Charlie Chaplin were succeeded by icons of a more glamorous Hollywood, such as Mae West and Errol Flynn. Wall Street bankers were quick to realize their potential and invested heavily in the film industry.

**Oscar® statuette**

**Panama Canal**
*Two world fairs celebrated the completion of the canal in 1915.*

**Clara Bow**, dubbed the "It" girl, was one of Hollywood's first sex symbols.

**Actors** were chosen for their looks and often had little stage experience.

**San Francisco Earthquake and Fire**
*After the 1906 disaster, many buildings had to be demolished.*

**Los Angeles Aqueduct**
*The vast aqueduct was built at a cost of $24.5 million to irrigate the arid south with melted snow from the High Sierras.*

## HOLLYWOOD'S SILENT ERA
The movie industry grew rapidly and soon large corporate studios emerged. *Mantrap* (1927) was one of hundreds of silent movies made each month.

---

## TIMELINE

**1905** Tobacco magnate Abbot Kinney opens his many-canaled resort of Venice *(see p76)*, west of LA. Excavations begin on La Brea Tar Pits *(see p115)*

**1907** San Francisco political "boss" Abraham Ruef pleads guilty to extortion and brings down Mayor Eugene Schmitz

**1913** Opening of Owens Valley–Los Angeles aqueduct improves LA access to water

**1900**          **1905**          **1910**

**1901** A three-month waterfront labor strike affects San Francisco business; four men die and 300 are injured in hostilities

**1906** San Francisco is struck on April 18 by the worst ever US earthquake, at an estimated 8.3 on the Richter scale: 3,000 die and 25,000 are left homeless

*Early Hollywood film camera*

**1911** *The Law of the Range*, shot by William and David Horsley, is the first film made in Hollywood

**Prohibition** *(1920–33)*
*Los Angeles became a popular port of entry for smugglers bringing illegal alcohol into the United States from Mexico during the nationwide ban.*

**Studios** operated like factories, filming different movies on adjacent sets.

**Cameramen** used 35 mm cameras, operating at 24 frames per second.

**Directors** also found fame and fortune in the new industry.

**Orchestras** were often hired to play in the background of a scene during filming to create the right mood for the actors.

## WHERE TO SEE CLASSIC HOLLYWOOD

The likenesses of numerous movie stars are displayed at the Hollywood Wax Museum *(p105)*. The Hollywood Studio Museum *(p108)*, once Cecil B De Mille's offices, now exhibits movie mementos. Some 200 stars have cemented their fame in front of Grauman's Chinese Theatre *(p106)*.

**Grauman's Chinese Theatre** *has hand-prints, footprints, and autographs of film stars cemented in its forecourt.*

**Paramount Studios** *are the only studios now located in Hollywood and still attract would-be stars* (p109).

**Aimee Semple McPherson**
*In 1923 the controversial evangelist and spiritualist opened her Angelus Temple in LA where she held regular spiritual revivalist meetings.*

**1916** The Lockheed brothers start building airplanes in Santa Barbara

*WR Hearst*

**1924** LA eclipses San Francisco as the most important port on the West Coast

**1929** Stock exchange crash causes national Depression. Actor Douglas Fairbanks, Sr. hosts the first Academy Awards® presentation

**1915**

**1920**

**1925**

**1915** San Francisco and San Diego both hold Panama-Pacific Expositions

**1917** The US enters World War I

**1919** WR Hearst begins construction of his magnificent castle at San Simeon *(see pp202–205)*

*Norma Talmadge*

**1927** Actress Norma Talmadge is the first star to cement her foot-prints at Mann's Chinese Theatre *(see p106)*

**1928** Cartoonist Walt Disney creates character of Mickey Mouse

# The California Dream

Movies and the new medium of television made California *the* symbol of America's postwar resurgence – suddenly everybody wanted the prosperous middle-class existence they believed was common here. The airplane industry, shipyards, and agriculture had burgeoned during the war, and a sense of prosperity lasted through the 1950s. Suburbs sprang up to meet the needs of returning soldiers, while new highways were laid to make them accessible. Yet at the same time, state schools lacked funds, African- and Mexican-Americans faced discrimination and violence, and Hollywood found itself attacked by politicians as a hotbed of Marxist Communism.

**Olympic Games 1932**
*Los Angeles won the bid to hold the 1932 games and built Exposition Park for the event (see pp164–5).*

**Longshoreman's Strike**
*On July 5, 1934, police opened fire on dockers striking for better conditions, killing two.*

**Kitchen units** became more practical, with Formica counters.

**Household appliances** became more widely available, easing domestic duties.

**Hoover Dam**
*In 1936 Hoover Dam was built on the Colorado River to supply electricity.*

## TIMELINE

| | | | | | |
|---|---|---|---|---|---|
| **1932** LA hosts its first Olympic Games | **1934** Alcatraz Island becomes a maximum security penitentiary *(see pp32–3)* | **1936** Hoover Dam begins supplying Southern California with much-needed electricity | **1940** Los Angeles opens its first freeway – Arroyo Seco Parkway | | **1942** Japanese Americans se to relocation camps for "w security reaso *(see p495)* |
| **1930** | | **1935** | | **1940** | |
| **1933** Prohibition ends. "Sunny Jim" Rolph, a popular San Francisco mayor turned California governor, shocks supporters by praising a lynch mob in San Jose | | **1937** The Golden Gate Bridge opens | **1939** San Francisco's third world's fair, the Golden Gate Exposition, is held on Treasure Island | **1941** Japan attacks US fleet at Pearl Harbor | **1943** California becomes nation's leading agricultural state |

*"Sunny Jim" Rolph*

**Golden Gate Bridge**
*On May 28, 1937, an official convoy of black limousines were the first vehicles to cross the bridge, which links San Francisco with Marin County.*

## WHERE TO SEE THE CALIFORNIA DREAM

LA's Petersen Automotive Museum celebrates California's love affair with the car *(see p118)*. At the Treasure Island Museum in San Francisco, memorabilia from the Golden Gate International Exposition is displayed *(p412)*. A trip to the Sleeping Beauty Castle in Disneyland® is the ultimate California Dream experience *(p233)*.

**The Petersen Automotive Museum**
*displays many classic models. This 1959 Cadillac epitomizes California cars.*

**Land of Plenty**
*California's agricultural industry boomed in the 1940s, and its farmland was the most productive in the US.*

**Large refrigerators**, stocked with food, were a symbol of the California "good life."

**San Francisco Giant**
*Willie Mays was part of the first team to bring professional baseball to California in 1958.*

## THE CALIFORNIA HOME

Eduardo Paolozzi's image is a pastiche of California's white, middle-class lifestyle in the 1950s. Nuclear families, ranch houses, and outdoor living were all part of the "dream."

**1945** End of World War II. International delegates meet at San Francisco April 25–June 25 to found the United Nations

**1945**

**1950**

**1955** Disneyland® opens in Anaheim. Actor James Dean, 24, dies in a car accident near Paso Robles

*James Dean*

**1955**

*United Nations flag*

**1953** Beginning of Cold War is a boost to California defense industry

**1958** New York Giants baseball team moves to San Francisco, finally bringing Major League baseball to the West Coast

# California Today

Since 1962, when California surpassed New York as the most populous state in the Union, it has become the focus of many of the country's most significant issues. UC Berkeley was home to America's Free Speech Movement during the 1960s, and Haight Ashbury in San Francisco was the mecca for the "hippie" movement. Silicon Valley leads high-tech development in the US, and California benefits commercially from its proximity to the Far East. However, the state is still at risk from earthquakes; San Francisco has a high proportion of the country's AIDS cases; and racial tension, especially in LA, has led to riots.

**1984** LA hosts its second Olympic Games

**1968** Democratic presidential candidate Robert Kennedy is assassinated at LA's Ambassador Hotel on June 5 after announcing his victory in the California primary

**1967** Haight Ashbury is swamped by half a million young people celebrating the "Summer of Love" *(see p359)*

**1962** Actress Marilyn Monroe dies in Hollywood, at age 36, from an overdose of sleeping pills

**1978** Apple Computer produces its first personal computer

**1970s** Huey Newton, a founder of Oakland's Black Panther Party, is arrested in 1967 and becomes a symbol of resistance during the 1970s

**1987** Film director Steven Spielberg starts his own studio, Dreamworks

| 1960 | 1970 | 1980 |
| --- | --- | --- |

| 1960 | 1970 | 1980 |
| --- | --- | --- |

**1960** Winter Olympic Games are held at Squaw Valley near Lake Tahoe

**1966** LA becomes the most populous county in the nation, with more than 7 million inhabitants

**1969** American Indian Movement occupies Alcatraz Island *(see pp338–9)* to publicize its differences with the Bureau of Indian Affairs

**1978** San Francisco Mayor George Moscone and his deputy Harvey Milk are assassinated at City Hall on November 27 by former policeman Dan White

**1968** Richard Nixon becomes the first native-born Californian to be elected President of the United States. Discredited, Nixon retired to San Clemente in 1974 *(see p238)*

**1976** French judges award California the top two prizes for wine at a blind tasting

**1963** Surfing becomes a popular sport in California

**1989** The Bay Area endures its second worst earthquake, measuring 7.1 on the Richter Scale. 67 people die, another 1,800 are left homeless

**1992** Riots in LA follow the acquittal of four white police officers who were videotaped beating a black motorist, Rodney King

**1994** An earthquake measuring 6.8 on the Richter scale strikes LA, killing more than 60 people, injuring 9,000, and destroying freeways

**2004** Iconic, Austrian movie star and former bodybuilder Arnold Schwarzenegger, married to news journalist Maria Shriver, is elected as the 38th governor of California

**2006** San Francisco congresswoman Nancy Pelosi is the first woman to become elected speaker of the United States House of Representatives

**2008** The contemporary Jewish Museum, designed by Daniel Libeskind, opens in San Francisco

| | 2000 | 2010 | 2020 |

**2001** An energy crisis grips the state, with rolling blackouts affecting all major cities

**1996** After 15 years as the speaker of the California Assembly, Democrat Willie Brown is sworn in as San Francisco's first black mayor

**1995** The world-famous America's Cup yacht race, in which five countries compete, is held in San Diego from January to May

**1991** AIDS becomes San Fransisco's number one killer of men

# LOS ANGELES

# Los Angeles at a Glance

Greater Los Angeles is made up of 88 different towns, with a total population of more than 9.8 million and covering more than 460 sq miles (1,200 sq km). In this book, LA has been divided into six areas. Downtown is a cultural melting pot, juxtaposing Hispanic El Pueblo, Chinatown, Little Tokyo, and the Business District. The glamour of the movies is just one aspect of Hollywood and West Hollywood, which today is a vibrant area of museums and galleries. Beverly Hills, Bel Air, and Westwood are still the playgrounds of the stars. Beaches and ports in the coastal regions of Santa Monica Bay, Palos Verdes, and Long Beach show the importance of the sea to Angelenos. Around Downtown covers some of the outlying towns and areas of the city, including Pasadena.

**AROUND DOWNTOWN**
*(See pp140–65)*

**BEVERLY HILLS, BEL AIR, AND WESTWOOD**
*(See pp88–99)*

**SANTA MONICA BAY**
*(See pp74–87)*

**Sunset Boulevard** (see pp102–7) *is one of the most famous roads in the world. Lined with clubs and hotels, the section known as Sunset Strip is the center of LA's nightlife.*

0 kilometers 5

0 miles 5

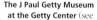

**The J Paul Getty Museum at the Getty Center** (see pp82–5) *is situated on a hill and has stunning views across Los Angeles and the Santa Monica Mountains. Included in its world-class collection is Joseph Nollekens' marble statue of Venus (1773).*

**LACMA** (see pp114–17) *has been located in Hancock Park since 1965, and has expanded west along Wilshire Boulevard. LACMA is currently undergoing a major renovation.*

◁ City of Los Angeles

**At Universal Studios®** (see pp146–9), *just north of Hollywood, visitors can see working film sets on the Studio Tour. A series of thrilling rides, based on the studios' movies, includes Jurassic Park–The Ride.*

**The Huntington Library, Art Collections, and Botanical Gardens** (see pp158–61) *in Pasadena have a wealth of treasures. The North Vista is one of the gardens' loveliest views.*

**HOLLYWOOD
AND WEST
HOLLYWOOD**
*(See pp100–19)*

**DOWNTOWN
LOS ANGELES**
*(See pp120–29)*

**AROUND DOWNTOWN**
*(See pp140–65)*

**El Pueblo** (see pp124–5), *in the heart of Downtown Los Angeles, is the site of the city's first settlement. The area's Mexican population throngs its churches, plaza, and colorful markets, especially at festival time.*

**The Queen Mary** (see pp134–5), *one of the most famous liners in the world, is now permanently docked in Long Beach. The ship is still in use as a tourist attraction and luxury hotel. Many of its Art Deco features remain intact.*

**LONG BEACH AND
PALOS VERDES**
*(See pp130–39)*

# The Shape of Los Angeles

The city of Los Angeles sits in a broad, flat basin, facing the Pacific Ocean and enclosed by mountains. The San Gabriel Mountains and the Traverse Range come from the north, meeting the Santa Ana Mountains east of the city. The Santa Monica Mountains and the Hollywood Hills in the northwest split the basin, dividing the city center from the San Fernando Valley in the north. The shoreline varies from the rocky cliffs of Palos Verdes to the sands of Santa Monica Bay. Downtown, with the impressive skyscrapers of the Business District, sits in the center of the basin. Hollywood, Beverly Hills, and Santa Monica lie to the west.

**Hollywood** (see pp100–19) *is the birthplace of the modern film industry. Its famous sign* (see p145) *stands out like a beacon above Tinseltown.*

**The San Fernando Valley** *(see p144)*, the city's great suburban sprawl, is home to the Mission San Fernando Rey de España.

SAN GABRIEL MOUNTAINS

⑤

BURBANK

SANTA SUSANA MOUNTAINS

101   HOLLYW

SAN FERNANDO VALLEY

Mulholland Drive

101   405   Sunset Boulevard

SANTA MONICA MOUNTAINS

10

①

**Malibu** *(see pp86–7)* is an area of fine surfing beaches, wildlife havens, and private beach colonies nestled below rugged mountains.

**Santa Monica** (see pp76–9), *perched on palm-lined bluffs overlooking the Pacific Ocean, is a small independent city with LA's most accessible beaches. It has all the traditional seaside attractions, such as a pier and amusement park. Santa Monica is also known for its excellent restaurants, boutiques, exciting nightlife, and vibrant arts scene.*

**Beverly Hills** (see pp88–97) *is home to the rich and famous of Los Angeles. Their lifestyle is epitomized by the exclusive shops that line Rodeo Drive.*

**Pasadena** (see pp154–61) *is an affluent community, with an ornate city hall. It grew up as a winter retreat for wealthy Easterners in the 19th century. Site of the Rose Bowl stadium, it has fine museums as well as excellent shopping and dining.*

**Watts** has the Watts Towers (*see p163*).

**Downtown Los Angeles** *is a diverse area* (see pp120–29). *Attractions range from the skyscrapers of the Business District to the ethnic delights of Little Tokyo and Chinatown.*

**The City of Long Beach** has a strong nautical tradition (*see pp132–5*).

ERDUGO
OUNTAINS

SAN RAFAEL
HILLS

MONTEREY
HILLS

PUENTE HILLS

5

DOWNEY

605

LDWIN
IILLS

42

INGLEWOOD

105

COMPTON

710

DOMINGUEZ
HILLS

405

SIGNAL
HILL

110

TORRANCE

1

SANTA
MONICA
BAY

PALOS VERDES
HILLS

SAN PEDRO

SAN
PEDRO
BAY

**Los Angeles International Airport**, *known simply as LAX, lies along the coast. It is well placed for easy access to most areas of the city and near major freeways leading out of town.*

**Point Fermin lighthouse** *is a Victorian landmark among the rocky cliffs of Palos Verdes* (see pp138–9).

# North Los Angeles Coastline

Each year more than 30 million people visit the
beaches around Los Angeles, making them the most
popular destination on the West Coast. The Malibu
headland, from Point Dume to Malibu Lagoon,
alternates between rocky shorelines and beaches.
Farther south, the shoreline becomes a long sandy
strand leading to the renowned beaches at Santa
Monica and Venice. Inland, the terrain of the Santa
Monica Mountains is rugged and largely unspoiled,
with plenty of hiking trails leading to panoramic
views of the Pacific Ocean. The waters off the Malibu
Pier, Leo Carillo, and Topanga state beaches are
considered to be the best for surfing.

*Castro Crest is characterized by
large areas of exposed reddish
purple sandstone and oak
woodland. The park's hiking trails
offer magnificent views inland of
the Santa Susana mountains and,
offshore, the Channel Islands.*

**Cold Creek Canyon Preserve** *was set up in 1970 to
protect the rich diversity of fauna and flora found in
the Santa Monica Mountains, including the bobcat, the
Pacific tree frog, and the stream orchid.*

**★ Leo Carillo State Beach ①**
At low tide it is possible to explore
the wide variety of life in the rock
pools around Sequit Point.

**★ Surfrider County Beach ⑤**
One of California's finest surfing
beaches, Surfrider has featured in many
surfing films. Malibu Pier is a good
place from which to watch the action.

### Zuma County Beach ②
🚶 ⛱ 🏊 🚻 ♿ 🚹
The white sands of Malibu's largest beach are very popular during the summer. There is good surfing and swimming, but be careful of the hazardous rip tides.

### Point Dume County Beach ③
🚶 ⛱ 🏊 🚻 ♿ 🚹
Surf fishing, diving, sunbathing, and exploring the rock pools beneath Point Dume are all popular activities on this sandy sheltered beach.

### Paradise Cove ④
⛱ 🏊 🚻 ♿ 🚹 🚗
This privately owned cove was featured in the TV series *The Rockford Files*. The pier is a good place for surf fishing, and the beach is ideal for sunbathing and swimming.

### Topanga State Beach ⑥
🚶 ⛱ 🏊 🚻 ♿ 🚹 🅿 🚗
This narrow sandy beach is popular with windsurfers. It is divided in two by the mouth of Topanga Creek.

### Marina del Rey Harbor ⑩
⛱ 🏊 ♿ 🚹
This is one of the world's largest artificial harbors *(see p80)*. The quaint Fisherman's Village, next to Basin H, has shops, cafés, and restaurants.

**LOCATOR MAP**

**KEY**

| | |
|---|---|
| ▬▬ | Freeway |
| ▬▬ | Major road |
| ▬▬ | Minor road |
| ⌒ | River |
| ☀ | Viewpoint |

★ **Venice Beach ⑨**
🚶 ⛱ 🏊 🚻 ♿ 🚹
Backed by picturesque Venice *(see p80)*, Venice Beach offers an eclectic mix of street performers, skaters, and body builders, working out on Muscle Beach.

HOLLYWOOD

COLD CREEK
CANYON PRESERVE

PACIFIC
PALISADES

Topanga Canyon Road 27

Sunset Blvd

SANTA
MONICA

Wilshire Blvd

BEVERLY
HILLS

DOWNTOWN
LOS ANGELES

10

187

405

VENICE

LONG
BEACH

PALOS
VERDES

★ **Will Rogers State Beach ⑦**
🚶 ⛱ 🏊 🚻 ♿ 🚹 🚗
Named after the Hollywood actor *(see p81)*, this is a good beach for body surfing.

★ **Santa Monica State Beach ⑧**
🚶 ⛱ 🏊 🚻 ♿ 🚹
This is one of Santa Monica's *(see pp76–9)* most popular beaches. The group of houses at the western end of the beach are known collectively as "the Gold Coast."

# South Los Angeles Coastline

The coast between Dockweiler State Beach and Torrance County Beach boasts shallow waters and wide stretches of sand, which are ideal for families. The two main communities, Manhattan Beach and Redondo Beach, have some of the cleanest waters in the area. Farther down the coast, the rocky bluffs of the Palos Verdes Peninsula shelter coves with rock pools teeming with marine life. Beyond the commercial and cruise port at San Pedro, the coastline turns into a vista of white sand and rolling waves bordering Long Beach. Belmont Shores is popular with anglers. Windsurfers, sea kayakers, and jet-skiers frequent Alamitos Bay, home to the man-made canals and islands of Naples.

*HOLLYWOOD BEVERLY HILLS*

*SANTA MONICA*

*Vista del Mar Boulevard*

*Sepulveda Boulevard*

*42*

*405*

*1*

*105*

*Manhattan Blv*

*Artesia Blvd*

*107*

**TORRAN**

*Torrance*

*1*

*N7*

*Palos Verde Penins*

*Palos Verdes*

*Drive*

★ **Manhattan State Beach** ②
🚶 ⛱ 🏊 🚻 ♿ 🚻
Backed by the coastal cycle path, this long wide beach is good for swimming, surfing, and fishing.

★ **Hermosa City Beach** ③
🚶 ⛱ 🏊 🚻 ♿ 🚻
This family beach is ideal for all types of beach sports, as well as being popular with anglers who fish the surf for perch.

**Worldport LA**, *with its 28 miles (45 km) of waterfront, includes an oil terminal, cruise ship, and cargo port. It is also home to the country's second largest fishing fleet.*

★ **Torrance County Beach** ⑤
🚶 ⛱ 🏊 🚻 ♿ 🚻
Popular with surfers, swimmers, anglers, and divers alike, this beach marks the end of the Santa Monica Bay coastal cycle path *(see p178).*

★ **Redondo State Beach** ④
🚶 ⛱ 🏊 🚻 ♿ 🚻
A bronze bust commemorates George Freeth, who introduced surfing to California in 1907 at Redondo Beach.

### Dockweiler State Beach ①
🏃 ⛱ 🏊 ⚓ ♿ 🚻
The north end of Dockweiler, beyond the harbor entrance, includes a nesting area for the rare California least tern.

### Cabrillo Beach ⑥
🏃 ⛱ 🏊 ⚓ ♿ 🚻
Split in two by the breakwater, Cabrillo has a fishing pier on the ocean side and a protected stretch of sand within San Pedro Bay.

### Long Beach City Beach ⑦
🏃 ⛱ 🏊 ⚓ ♿ 🚻
At the western end of Long Beach Strand, as it is also known, stands the old clapboard lifeguard headquarters, now a lifeguard museum.

### Belmont Shores ⑧
🏃 ⛱ 🏊 ⚓ ♿ 🚻
Belmont Pier, situated at the northern end of the beach, is used by anglers fishing for halibut, bonito, and perch. It is also a roosting site for the endangered California brown pelican. The beach stretches south as far as the mouth of the San Gabriel River.

**LOCATOR MAP**

### Alamitos Bay ⑨
⛱ 🏊 ♿ 🚻
Windsurfing, waterskiing, and swimming are all popular activities in the protected waters of the bay.

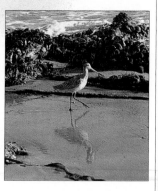

**Palos Verdes Peninsula** *rises 1,300 ft (400 m) above the rocky shoreline, which is home to many wading birds. Steep trails connect the shore to the clifftop with its panoramic views.*

### KEY

| | |
|---|---|
| ▒▒ | Freeway |
| ▬ | Major road |
| ▬ | Minor road |
| ⌒ | River |
| ☀ | Viewpoint |

# The Movies in Los Angeles

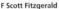

**Hollywood street sign**

When people refer to Los Angeles as an "industry town," they invariably mean the movie industry. Its great fantasy factories employ more than 60,000 people and pump about $4 billion into the LA economy every year. Hollywood Boulevard has sadly lost much of its glamour over the years; some film companies have decamped to cheaper movie-making places. But the air of Hollywood as a dream-maker, a place where a secretary named Ava Gardner or college football player John Wayne could be "discovered" and go on to earn million-dollar salaries, still persists.

**Film crews** *shooting location scenes for various Hollywood movies are a regular sight on Los Angeles' streets.*

**The Griffith Observatory** (see p150) *was the setting for the teenage school trip and dramatic car race at the climax of the legendary film* Rebel Without A Cause *(1955). The film catapulted James Dean to stardom, but he was to die in a car crash later the same year.*

## WRITERS IN HOLLYWOOD

Hollywood novels have been a literary feature since the 1930s. Some writers, such as Nathaneal West and F Scott Fitzgerald, worked in Hollywood, only to turn against the town and publish novels that exposed its shallow and often cruel sides. West's *The Day of the Locust* (1939) is still considered the classic literary put-down of the film industry. Fitzgerald's posthumous *The Last Tycoon* (1941) sentimentalizes the career of Irving Thalberg, one of the most influential producers during Hollywood's "Golden Age." More recent is James Ellroy's *LA Confidential* (1997), a retro, atmospheric story of corruption and redemption in 1950s Los Angeles.

**The Last Action Hero**, *Arnold Schwarzenegger's 1993 blockbuster, filled this LA street with the excitement of controlled explosions, car chases, and stuntmen flying through the air.*

## LA LOCATIONS

As well as utilizing the man-made sets erected on the backlots of the major studios in the 1940s and 1950s, film directors now regularly turn to the local landmarks of Los Angeles as locations for their films, often disguising them as other towns and cities. As a consequence, many of these places have become familiar to moviegoers all over the world.

**F Scott Fitzgerald**

**Million-dollar contracts** *have been a feature of Hollywood since Charlie Chaplin's eight-picture deal in 1917. Leonardo DiCaprio is currently Hollywood's highest-paid actor, earning $77 million in 2010–2011. Johnny Depp and Adam Sandler earn at least $40 million a year, while Julia Roberts and Harrison Ford are also in the eight-figure category. Studio executives justify the salaries by saying that big stars attract a large enough audience to recoup the high production costs.*

Julia Roberts          Harrison Ford

**The Venice district** (see p80) *saw actress Sarah Jessica Parker dancing around Steve Martin, in his 1991 hit film* LA Story. *The colorful buildings and characters of the area make it a popular film location.*

### TOP GROSSING FILMS

Critics gush over *Citizen Kane* (1941), and *Casablanca* (1943) is the most popular Hollywood love story ever made. Yet neither of these films is on trade paper *Variety*'s list of the U.S. film industry's highest-grossing films of all time:

1. *Avatar* (2009)
2. *Titanic* (1997)
3. *The Dark Knight* (2008)
4. *Star Wars* (1977)
5. *Shrek 2* (2004)
6. *E.T.: the Extra Terrestrial* (1982)
7. *Star Wars: Episode I – The Phantom Menace* (1999)
8. *Pirates of the Caribbean: Dead Man's Chest* (2006)
9. *Toy Story 3* (2010)
10. *Spider-Man* (2002)

The only films made before 1980 on the top 100 list are *Star Wars* (1977), at No. 4, and *Jaws* (1975), at No. 56.

**Santa Monica Pier** (see p78) *should be familiar to fans of the gangster film* The Sting *(1973), starring actors Robert Redford and Paul Newman.*

**Stargazing** *is enjoyed by both visitors and locals in LA's many glamorous venues. Good opportunities to spot actors, directors, and film executives can be found at Wolfgang Puck's trendy Spago* (see p569) *and the Polo Lounge at the Beverly Hills Hotel* (see p525).

**Film poster for *E.T.: the Extra Terrestrial***

# Los Angeles's Best: Museums and Galleries

The museums of LA reflect the great diversity of the city. Collections ranging from natural history to Native American artifacts and from cowboy heritage to the history of the Holocaust educate and inspire the visitor. The city also contains many museums of art. Some of these display the private collections of the wealthy, such as Norton Simon, J Paul Getty, Eli Broad, and Henry and Arabella Huntington, and feature internationally acclaimed Old Masters, Impressionist paintings, and European and Asian works of art. "Museum Row" on Wilshire Boulevard has five museums, including the renowned LACMA.

**LACMA** *is one of the top US art museums. Its collection includes* La Trahison des Images (Ceci n'est pas une pipe), *painted by René Magritte in around 1929. (See pp114–17.)*

*Around Downtown*

*Santa Monica Bay*

**J Paul Getty Museum** *has relocated most of its antiquities to the Getty Villa.* La Promenade *(1870) by Pierre-Auguste Renoir is just one of the extraordinary paintings in the Impressionist collection. (See pp82–5.)*

0 kilometers    5

0 miles    5

**The Museum of Tolerance** *aims to promote understanding between peoples. This sculpture of President Sadat of Egypt, with President Carter of the United States and Prime Minister Begin of Israel, illustrates that aim. (See p93.)*

**The Southwest Museum of the American Indian** *exhibits thousands of artifacts of the native cultures of the Americas, including this ceramic jar, which was produced around 1900.* (See p153.) *Closed through 2013.*

**The Autry National Center** *is dedicated to preserving the history of the American West by exploring the connections among the area's varied Native American and Western cultures. Wax models, such as this one of outlaw Billy the Kid, are on display.* (See p151.)

**Norton Simon Museum of Art** *was built in 1969. It houses a superb collection of European, Indian, and Southeast Asian art that spans more than 2,000 years.* (See pp156–7.)

*ywood*
*1 West*
*ywood*

*Downtown Los Angeles*

**The Huntington Library, Art Collections, and Botanical Gardens** *are in Pasadena. Roger van der Weyden's 15th-century Madonna and Child is one of the many works of art on display.* (See pp158–61.)

**Natural History Museum of Los Angeles County** *is one of three museums in Exposition Park. The exhibits include this eight-million-year-old skeleton of a short-legged rhinoceros.* (See p164.)

# Twentieth-Century Architecture in Los Angeles

For more than a century after it was founded in 1781, LA remained a small town of modest adobe buildings. It was not until the late 19th century that settlers from the East and Midwest introduced the Victorian styles of building they had grown up with. When the transcontinental railroad reached LA in 1887 there was a building boom, and the city has been expanding ever since. In the 20th century, LA's finest contributions to architecture were the inventive reworkings of past styles. In recent years, architects have remodeled dilapidated commercial buildings to create lively, fashionable structures.

**Kate Mantilini's** *(198* *This building-within-a-buildi restaurant is typical of LA's avan garde deconstructivism (see p568*

*Around Downtown*

**2 Rodeo**
*(1990)*
*This pastiche of European architecture, including a replica of Rome's Spanish Steps, is part of the famous shopping district (see p94). This area has Victorian-style streetlamps and a cobblestone street.*

*Beverly Hills, Bel Air, and Westwood*

*Santa Monica Bay*

**Eames House** *(1949)*
*This steel-framed house and studio were designed by Charles and Ray Eames as one of 36 projects commissioned by* Arts & Architecture *magazine.*

**TBWA Chiat/Day Advertising Agency** *(1991)*
*Frank Gehry, the leading LA architect, designed this striking building (see p78).*

**Disney® Studio Office Building** *(1991)*
*Michael Graves' Post-Modern Disney® building in Burbank includes a classically inspired pediment supported by 19-ft (5.7-m) statues of the Seven Dwarfs. Inside, chairs incorporate Mickey Mouse in their design (see pp144–5).*

**Ennis House** *(1923)*
*The base, plan, and textured interiors of this house are typical of Frank Lloyd Wright's "textile block" houses.*

**Gamble House**
*(1908)*
*This is the finest example of Charles and Henry Greene's turn-of-the-century Arts and Crafts bungalows. Its expansive eaves, outdoor sleeping porches, and elegant interior are characteristic of the brothers' style (see p154).*

*Hollywood and West Hollywood*

*Downtown Los Angeles*

**Union Station** *(1939)*
*The last of the great American railroad terminals, the vaulted concourse, arches, waiting room, and patios combine Mission Revival and Streamline Moderne styles (see p128).*

**Eastern Columbia Building** *(1930)*
*This Art Deco building, designed by Claude Beelman, is one of the most impressive of its kind in LA.*

EASTERN

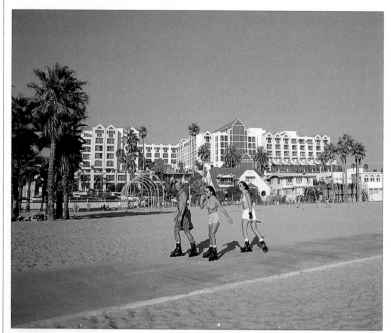

In-line skaters on Venice Beach bike path

PACIFIC
OCEAN

## SIGHTS AT A GLANCE

**Districts**
Malibu Colony **11**
Marina del Rey **3**
*Santa Monica pp76–9* **1**
Venice **2**

**Museums**
Adamson House and Malibu
  Lagoon Museum **9**
*J Paul Getty Museum at the
  Getty Center pp82–5* **5**

The Getty Villa **8**
Museum of Flying **4**

**Parks and Beaches**
Malibu Creek State
  Park **12**
Malibu Lagoon State
  Beach **10**
Topanga State Park **7**
Will Rogers State
  Historic Park **6**

**KEY**

Street-by-Street map
*See pp76–7*

0 kilometers          2

0 miles               2

# SANTA MONICA BAY

With its warm sun, cool sea breezes, miles of sandy beaches, excellent surf, and world-class museums, Santa Monica Bay epitomizes the best of California. The area was inhabited by the Chumash and Tongva/Gabrielino peoples for 2,500 years before the arrival in 1542 of the Spanish explorer Juan Cabrillo *(see p46)*. In the early 19th century, Santa Monica Bay was divided into several land grants, including Rancho San Vicente y Santa Monica and Rancho Topanga Malibu Sequit. In 1875, Nevada senator John Percival Jones bought control of the former, hoping the port of Los Angeles would be built there. Thankfully, that honor went to

**Swimmer in Venice Beach**

San Pedro *(see pp138–9)* and the beach resort sections of Santa Monica and Venice were developed in its place. These areas have remained two of the most attractive and lively parts of Los Angeles.

Farther along the coast, the Rancho Topanga Malibu Sequit was bought in 1887 by Frederick and May Rindge. The Rindge family fought with the state for many years to keep their property secluded. Eventually failing, they sold much of Malibu to the rich and famous. Large mountain areas backing Santa Monica Bay have remained undeveloped, however. The vast Topanga and Malibu Creek state parks help to improve Los Angeles's air quality and offer miles of hiking trails.

**GETTING THERE**

Santa Monica lies at the end of the Santa Monica Freeway (I-10) and is linked to Malibu by the Pacific Coast Highway. Santa Monica and Venice are well served by the Santa Monica Blue Bus Company. Possibly the best way to see the area is by renting a bicycle and taking the coastal bike path *(see p178)*.

# Street-by-Street: Santa Monica ●

**View from Palisades Park**
*The cliff top park offers pano-ramic views of Santa Monica Bay. Looking northward, you can see all the way to Malibu.*

**Street entertainer**

Santa Monica's fresh sea breezes, mild climate (on average, the sun shines here 328 days a year), and pedestrian-friendly streets make it one of the best places in LA to go for a stroll. The city is perched on a high cliff over-looking Santa Monica Bay and miles of broad, sandy beach. Running along the cliff edge is palm-shaded Palisades Park, a narrow, 26-acre (10-ha) garden offering spectacular views, especially at sunset. A stairway leads down to Santa Monica's famous beach and pier. A few blocks inland from the hotel-lined seafront is Third Street Promenade – a great place to sit outside a café or restaurant and people-watch.

**★ Third Street Promenade**
*Metal and topiary animals decorate these three lively blocks. This is one of the best outdoor shopping areas in LA.*

SANTA MONICA BLVD

ARIZONA AVENUE

WILSHIRE BOULEVARD

**Hotels** line the beach.

**★ Palisades Park**
*This narrow strip of park-land, planted with mature palm trees, is a good place to walk, jog, or sit on a bench and admire the view. In the evening, many people come here to watch the sun go down.*

## STAR SIGHTS

★ Palisades Park

★ Santa Monica Pier

★ Third Street Promenade

## KEY

– – – Suggested route

0 meters                200
0 yards                 200

For hotels and restaurants in this region see pp524–31 and pp568–76

**Santa Monica Place**

*This lively shopping mall, designed by architect Frank Gehry in 1979, has since undergone a major renovation. The modern, open-air complex features upscale stores and rooftop dining.*

**LOCATOR MAP**

**★ Santa Monica Pier**
*Since 1908, Angelenos and visitors alike have flocked to this landmark pier. With its long boardwalk, arcades, and fishing areas, it still has plenty to offer. A small amusement area, Pacific Park, has a Ferris wheel, roller coaster, and bumper cars.*

Tourist information

**Beach**
*Following the success of the television series* Baywatch, *Santa Monica's beaches are famous throughout the world.*

# Exploring Santa Monica

Santa Monica has been the star of LA's coast-line since the 1890s, when trolleys linked it to the city, and beach parties became the rage. In the early days, it lived a dual life as a sleepy coast town and the headquarters for offshore gambling ships. In the 1920s and 1930s, movie stars such as Cary Grant and Mary Pickford bought land here, creating "the Gold Coast." The beach and pier are still major attractions, but the city is now also famous for its restaurants (*see p573*). With the cleanest air in LA, Santa Monica offers many outdoor shopping areas and an active arts scene. Bergamot Station and the Edgemar complex on Main Street have a range of galleries.

**Statue in Bergamot Station gallery**

**Frank Gehry's innovative design for the TBWA Chiat/Day Advertising Agency**

## Around Santa Monica

Grassy parks dot the city's landscape, with none quite as beautiful or revered as **Palisades Park** on the bluff overlooking the ocean. Stretching 1.5 miles (2.5 km) along the cliff's edge, this narrow, well-manicured park is one of the best spots to watch the sun go down. For the quintessential California experience, take a walk or jog along the paths, with the ocean as a backdrop and the towering palms overhead. The landscaping is beautiful, with semitropical trees and plants. At the northern end, the aptly named Inspiration Point has great views of the bay, stretching from Malibu to Palos Verdes.

Inland, between Wilshire Boulevard and Broadway, is **Third Street Promenade**. Once a decaying shopping street, this boulevard has undergone a major face-lift and is now one of the liveliest places in Los Angeles. Its three pedestrian blocks are lined with shops, coffee houses, restaurants, bookstores,

and cinemas. At night the mood is especially festive. Street performers entertain passers-by with music, dance, puppet shows, and magic tricks. Nearby, on Arizona Avenue, a farmers' market on Saturdays and Wednesdays is one of the best in the city.

Santa Monica's other important shopping area is **Main Street**, which runs south toward Venice (*see p80*). At the turn of the 20th century, Main Street was the commercial district for Pacific Ocean Park, an amusement park, baths, and pier. By the early 1970s, however, the majority of the neighborhood's attractions had been demolished, and Main Street itself had become a slum.

Today, this revitalized street abounds with a wide range of

**Chain Reaction by Paul Conrad**

shops, superb restaurants, and first-rate art galleries.

There are many examples of public art displayed along Main Street. Sculptor Paul Conrad's *Chain Reaction* (1991) is a stainless-steel and copper-link chain statement against nuclear war. It stands next to the Civic Auditorium. *Ocean Park Pier* (1976), a mural by Jane Golden and Barbara Stoll, is situated at the junction with Ocean Park Boulevard and depicts the Pacific Ocean Park in the early 1900s.

A lovely example of Spanish Colonial architecture remains at the northwest corner of Main Street and Pier Avenue. Nearby, the TWBA Chiat/Day Advertising Agency building, designed in 1991 by Frank Gehry and shaped like a giant pair of binoculars, dominates the street (*see p72*).

### 🎠 Santa Monica Pier

Colorado & Ocean Aves. *Tel (310) 458-8900.* **Looff Carousel** ◯ *11am–4pm daily.* **Arcade** ◯ *10am–mid-night Sun–Thu (to 2am Fri–Sat).* **Pacific Park** ◯ *call for hours (310 260-8774).* 🖳 www.santamonicapier.org

This popular 1909 landmark is the West Coast's oldest amusement pier, with popcorn, cotton candy, bumper cars, and an amusement arcade. At the western end, Pacific Park has a Ferris wheel rising 11 stories high. Nearby, the 1922 Looff Carousel, similar to that in Santa Cruz (*see p506*), with 44 handcrafted horses, was featured in George Roy Hill's

**Beach apartments along the front of Palisades Park**

1973 film *The Sting (see p69)*. You can fish without a permit from the balconies on the pier's lower deck. On Thursday evenings during the summer, there is free dancing and live music *(see p173)*.

### 🏛 Bergamot Station
2525 Michigan Ave. *Tel (310) 829-5854.* ⬜ *10am–6pm Tue–Fri, 11am–5:30pm Sat.* ⬤ *Sun.* ♿

Bergamot Station is a 5.5-acre (2-ha) arts complex that stands on the site of an abandoned Red Line trolley station. The crude buildings are constructed from aluminum siding, with an added touch of high-tech styling. More than 25 galleries and a small museum showcase the latest works in contemporary and radical art, including painting, sculpture, photography, and glass, plus collectibles and African art. Bergamot Station also houses some artists' studios.

**A typical poster on display in Bergamot Station**

### 🏛 California Heritage Museum
2612 Main St. *Tel (310) 392-8537.* ⬜ *11am–4pm Wed–Sun.* ⬤ *Jan 1, Jul 4, Thanksgiving, Dec 25.* 📷 ♿ www.californiaheritagemuseum.org

The Queen Anne museum building was built in 1894 by architect Sumner P Hunt as the home of Roy Jones, son of the founder of Santa Monica *(see p75)*. On the first floor, the rooms depict the lifestyle of various periods in Southern California history: a Victorian dining room, an Arts and Crafts living room, and a 1930s kitchen. Upstairs,

**Victorian façade of the California Heritage Museum**

there are changing exhibitions on topics such as surfing *(see pp198–9)*, the Hollywood Western, quilts, and Monterey Rancho-style furniture.

### 🏛 Santa Monica Museum of Art
Building G-1, Bergamot Station. *Tel (310) 586-6488.* ⬜ *11am–6pm Tue–Sat.* ⬤ *Jan 1, Jul 4, Thanksgiving, Dec 25.* ♿ www.smmoa.org

The Santa Monica Museum of Art is dedicated to both contemporary and modern

art. Its main aim is to publicize the work of living artists, particularly those involved in performance and multimedia art. In May 1998 the museum re-opened after moving to its exciting new, 930 sq m (10,000 sq ft) home. It is located in the large arts complex, Bergamot Station, along with over 20 other galleries. Although the museum does not have any permanent collections, a wide range of artists' work is represented in the individual exhibitions. The museum has an excellent art book shop.

## RAYMOND CHANDLER

Novelist and screenwriter Raymond Chandler (1888–1959) set several of his works wholly or partly in Santa Monica, a city that he loathed and that he thinly disguised as sleazy Bay City in *Farewell, My Lovely*. There was some truth in Chandler's portrayal of Santa Monica. Corruption and vice in the 1920s and 1930s are well documented. Illegal gambling ships were anchored offshore, including the *Rex*, 5 miles (8 km) out in Santa Monica Bay, called the *Royal Crown* in *Farewell, My Lovely*.

Chandler's novels *Farewell, My Lovely*, *The Big Sleep*, *The High Window*, *The Little Sister*, and *The Long Goodbye* were made into films that portrayed the shadowy side of LA. With an elegant, dark style, he wrote vivid dialogue in the voice of the common man. His character Philip Marlowe was the definitive detective. A loner with a hard-boiled veneer often hiding a soft heart, Marlowe uttered tough one-liners, played by the rules, and usually didn't get the girl.

**Film poster for *The Big Sleep* (1946)**

## Venice ②

**Road map** inset A.
**Tel** *(310) 822-5425.*
*www.*venicechamber.net

Since its inception, Venice has attracted a bohemian society, from the rowdy crowd who frequented its dance hall and bathhouse in the 1910s to beatniks in the 1950s. Today, the town has a large population of artists, whose studios line the streets.

The community was founded in 1905 by tobacco magnate Abbot Kinney as a US version of Venice, Italy. Hoping to spark a cultural renaissance in southern California, he built a system of canals and imported gondolas and gondoliers to punt along the waterways. Unfortunately, Kinney did not take the tides into consideration when designing Venice, and the area was constantly dogged by sewage problems.

Today, only a few of the original 7 miles (11 km) of canals remain, the rest having been filled in during 1927. The traffic circle at Windward Avenue was the main lagoon, and Grand Boulevard, which runs southeast from there, was the Grand Canal. The best place to see the remaining canals is on Dell Avenue, where old bridges, boats, and ducks grace the waterways.

Over the years, the circus atmosphere of Venice Beach has never faltered. On the boardwalk during weekends, semiclad men and women whiz past on bicycles and skates, while a zany array of street performers, like chainsaw jugglers and one-man bands, captivates the crowds. Muscle Beach, where Arnold Schwarzenegger used to work out, still attracts body builders.

While Venice Beach is safe to explore on foot by day, caution is advised at night.

**Yachts moored in the harbor at Marina del Rey**

## Marina del Rey ③

**Road map** inset A. ▮ *4701 Admiralty Ave, Marina del Rey (310) 305-9545.*
*www.*visitmarinadelrey.com

Covering an area of just 1.3 sq miles (3.4 sq km), approximately half of which is water, Marina del Rey has the world's largest artificial small-craft harbor. Those attracted to this town tend to be young and single or with families, and enjoy outdoor activities such as skating, cycling, and water sports. Everything from paddle boats to yachts can be rented, or you can charter boats for deep-sea fishing or a luxury cruise.

Fisherman's Village, on Fiji Way, resembles a New England fishing town. It has a variety of shops, restaurants, and cafés, many of which offer views of the harbor.

## Museum of Flying ④

▢ *check website for details and address.* **www.**museumofflying.com

The Museum of Flying places heavy emphasis on the history of the Santa Monica Airport, where it is located, as well as the prominent role that the Douglas Aircraft Company played in the early development of commercial and military aviation. The museum is remodeling a building to exhibit an impressive collection of aircraft, artifacts, and aviation art, plus expanded educational offerings with hands-on, interactive exhibits. When complete, nearly two

**Man-made canal in Venice**

dozen aircraft will chronicle the history of flight, from a Wright Flyer replica to aircraft from the jet age.

Yellow Peril Boeing Stearman at the Museum of Flying

## THE WILDLIFE OF SANTA MONICA BAY

Among the marine mammals that inhabit the waters of Santa Monica Bay are harbor seals, California sea lions, and bottlenosed dolphins. From December to February gray whales can be seen migrating from Alaska to Baja California to calve. One of the best places in Los Angeles for whale-spotting is Point Dume. In the mountains, the range of wildlife is exceptional. The rare mountain lion can reach a size of 7 ft (2 m) in length and tends to live in the rockier, more remote areas. Its cousin the bobcat is smaller, with tufts of hair on the ends of its ears. Coyotes come out at dusk, often preying on the pets of people living in the hills. The bold, intelligent raccoon raids camp sites even when people are present. Mule deer, desert cottontail, and striped skunk also abound. Birds seen here include golden eagles and red-tailed hawks.

Raccoon (Procyon lotor)

## J Paul Getty Center ❺

*See pp82–5.*

## Will Rogers State Historic Park ❻

1501 Will Rogers State Park Road, Pacific Palisades. **Road map** inset A. **Tel** *(310) 454-8212.* ⬤ *8am–sunset daily.* ⬤ *Jan 1, Thanksgiving, Dec 25.* 🖾 🚻 *lawn area.* 🅿 www.parks.ca.gov

Will Rogers (1879–1935) started life as a cowboy and went on to become a film star, radio commentator, and newspaper columnist. Called the "Cowboy Philosopher," he was famous for his homespun humor and shrewd comments on current events, usually made while performing rope tricks. His show business career lasted from 1905 until his death. When his widow, Betty, died in 1944, she deeded the house and the surrounding land to the state, stipulating that nothing in the house be changed and that polo matches be held on weekends (Rogers was an avid polo player).

Hiking trails lead up from the ranch, many of them originally cut by Rogers. The lawn just east of the house is an ideal setting for a picnic. Tours of the house include the living room where Rogers used to practice his roping skills.

## Topanga State Park ❼

20825 Entrada Rd, Topanga. **Road map** inset A. **Tel** *(310) 455-2465 & (805) 488-8147 for fire conditions in summer & autumn.* ⬤ *8am–sunset daily.* 🖾 🚻 www.parks.ca.gov

Topanga State Park stretches from the Pacific Palisades to the San Fernando Valley (see p144). Topanga is thought to be an Indian term meaning "the place where the mountains meet the sea." The area was inhabited by the Tongva/Gabrielino and Chumash Indians 5,000 years ago. Today, its groves of sycamore and oak trees attract residents seeking an alternative way of life.

The marked entrance to the 13,000-acre (5,300-ha) park lies just north of Topanga village, off Hwy 27 on Entrada Road. Most of the land falls within the LA city boundary, making it the largest city park in the US. As such, it vastly improves the region's air quality and provides ample space for hiking and riding.

As you ascend the Santa Monica Mountains, canyons, cliffs, and meadows give way to vistas of the ocean and the San Fernando Valley. Four trails begin from the park's headquarters at Trippet Ranch: a 1-mile (1.6-km) self-guided nature trail; the Dead Horse Trail; Musch Ranch Trail (which leads to a camp site); and East Topanga Fire Road, which connects with Eagle Junction. The 2.5-mile (4-km) Eagle Rock/Eagle Spring Trail from Eagle Junction is one of the most popular.

Bicycles are allowed on the park's dirt fire roads, and horses on all but one of the trails.

Hiking trails crossing the Santa Monica Mountains in Topanga State Park

# J Paul Getty Museum at the Getty Center ❺

The Getty Center, which opened in December 1997, holds a commanding physical and cultural position in the city. It is situated amid the wild beauty of the Santa Monica Mountains, in the Sepulveda Pass, next to the San Diego Freeway (I-405). The complex houses not only the museum but also the Getty's research, conservation, and grant programs (the Getty Foundation). Getty made his fortune in the oil business and became an ardent collector of art. He wanted his collection, which focuses on European art from the Renaissance to Post-Impressionism, to be open to the public without charge. Greek, Etruscan, and Roman antiquities are displayed at the Getty Villa in Malibu *(see p86)*.

**LOCATOR MAP**

Illustrated area

Research, conservation, education, administration, restaurant, café, and auditorium buildings

Tram station

**East Pavilion**

**★ Irises** *(1889)*
*This work was painted by Vincent Van Gogh while he was in the asylum at St-Rémy. Its graphic style reveals the influence of artists such as Paul Gauguin (1848–1903) and the Japanese print-maker Hokusai (1760–1849).*

**Hispano-Moresque Deep Dish**
*This elaborately decorated earthenware dish was made in Valencia, Spain, in the mid-15th century. The use of lustrous colors was a specialty of Moorish potters at that time.*

**North Pavilion**

**Courtyard**

## STAR PAINTINGS

★ Wheatstacks, Snow Effect, Morning by Claude Monet

★ The Abduction of Europa by Rembrandt

★ Irises by Vincent Van Gogh

**Entrance**

### Cabinet on Stand

*Attributed to the French master craftsman André-Charles Boulle, this 17th-century cabinet was made to celebrate the victories of Louis XIV.*

**South Pavilion**

**West Pavilion**

**South Promontory**

### Korean Man

*(c.1617)*
*This drawing in black and red chalk is by the Flemish artist Peter Paul Rubens. It is one of many drawings displayed on rotation.*

### ★ Wheatstacks, Snow Effect, Morning *(1891)*

*This is one in a series of works by Monet that shows the same landscape at different times of the day and year.*

**Temporary exhibitions**
and the garden café are housed in this building.

### GUIDE TO THE GETTY CENTER

*From below, the Getty Center (designed by architect Richard Meier) may look like a fortress, but once on top, the scale is intimate, with fountains, walkways, courtyards, and niches. An electric tram brings visitors from the parking area to the complex. The museum has a tall, airy foyer that opens onto a central courtyard. From here radiate five two-story pavilions. The Conceptualist artist Robert Irwin has created a garden to the west of the museum. Across the main plaza from the tram station there is a café and restaurant. Another café and a bookstore are located within the museum.*

**★ The Abduction of Europa** *(1632)*
*One of Rembrandt's few landscapes, this depicts the Roman god Jupiter, disguised as a bull, kidnapping Europa, princess of Tyre.*

# Exploring the Getty Museum

J Paul Getty (1892–1976) amassed a remarkable collection of antiquities, European painting, sculpture, and decorative arts, focusing on pre-20th-century artistic movements. Getty was a bold collector who enjoyed the pursuit of an object almost more than the possession of it. Since his death, the Getty Trust has strengthened the museum's holdings by purchasing works of the highest quality. New departments in related areas such as photographs (which includes 19th and 20th-century American and European photographs), drawings, and manuscripts have also been added.

**Man with a Hoe, painted between 1860 and 1862 by Jean-François Millet**

## EUROPEAN PAINTINGS AND SCULPTURE

The museum boasts a superb collection of European paintings, dating from the 13th century to the late 19th century. Italian works from the Renaissance and Baroque periods include *The Adoration of the Magi* (c.1495–1505) by Andrea Mantegna and *View of the Arch of Constantine with Colosseum* (1742–5) by Canaletto. Rembrandt's *The Abduction of Europa* (1632) is a highlight from the Flemish and Dutch collections, which also include an oil sketch by Peter Paul Rubens (1577–1640) and a portrait by Anthony Van Dyck (1599–1641).

Of the French artworks on display, *The Race of the Riderless Horses* (1817) is an important painting by the Romantic painter Théodore Géricault. In *Still Life with Apples* (1894) by Paul Cézanne, the artist's preoccupation with gradations of light and color reveals the progression in the late 19th century from the old, realistic style of painting, to a more modern, abstract approach.

This painting, along with Claude Monet's *Wheatstacks, Snow Effect, Morning (see p83)*, Vincent Van Gogh's *Irises (see p82)*, and Paul Gauguin's *The Royal End*, has helped elevate the museum's collection of Impressionists and Post-Impressionists.

European sculptures in the Getty date from the 16th century to the end of the 19th century. Pier Jacopo Antico's *Bust of a Young Man* (1520) was created at the end of the High Renaissance in Italy. The elongated body favored by the Mannerists can be seen in Benvenuto Cellini's *Satyr* (c.1542). Fine examples of Baroque sculpture are *Pluto Abducting Proserpine* (c.1693–1710) by François Girardon and Bernini's *Boy with a Dragon* (c.1614). Neo-Classical works include three statues by Joseph Nollekens.

## DRAWINGS

The purchase in 1981 of Rembrandt's red chalk study of *Nude Woman with a Snake* (c.1637) marked the beginning of the museum's drawings collection. Today, the collection contains more than 400 works in a wide range of media, spanning the 15th to the late 19th century. *The Stag Beetle* (1505) by Albrecht Dürer is an exquisitely detailed illustration in watercolor and gouache. By contrast, Leonardo da Vinci's *Studies for the Christ Child with a Lamb* (c.1503–6) is a looser pen-and-ink study.

Peter Paul Rubens' *Korean Man (see p83)* is one of several portrait drawings. The *Self-Portrait* (c.1857–8) by Edgar Degas, executed in oil on paper and showing the young artist on the threshold of his extraordinary career, is another.

## PHOTOGRAPHS

The museum launched its photographic department in 1984 with the purchase of several major private collections, including those of Bruno Bischofberger, Arnold Crane, and Samuel Wagstaff. The holdings focus on European and American photography up to the 1950s. Exceptionally rich in works from the early 1840s, the collection features

**Cape Horn, Oregon (1881–3) by Carleton E Watkins**

many of the pioneers of photography. In daguerreotypes, the identity of the sitter was often more important than that of the maker. The museum has one portrait of Louis-Jacques-Mande Daguerre himself, taken in 1848 by Charles R Meade.

Englishman William Henry Fox Talbot (1800–1877) was the first to make prints from negatives. A lovely example of his work is *Oak Tree in Winter* (1841). Other early practitioners on display include Hyppolyte Bayard (1801–87), portraitist Julia Margaret Cameron (1815–79), war photographer Roger Fenton (1819–69), Gustave Le Gray (1820–82), and Nadar (1820–1910).

Among the important early 20th-century artists represented are Edward Weston (1886–1958), who created beautiful still lifes, and Walker Evans (1903–75), who was a pivotal influence in American documentary photography.

Renaissance chalcedony, or agate, glass bowl, made in Venice, Italy, in around 1500

## APPLIED ARTS

Applied arts in the museum encompass pre-1650 European pieces and works from southern Europe from 1650 to 1900. They have been chosen to complement the Getty's extensive holdings of French decorative arts.

Highlights include glass and earthenware from Italy and Spain; metalwork from France, Germany, and Italy; and highly decorated furniture. An extravagantly inlaid display cabinet from Augsburg in Germany (c.1620–30) falls into this last category. All four of the piece's sides open to reveal numerous drawers and compartments for collectibles.

Sèvres porcelain basket, dating from the mid-18th century

## DECORATIVE ARTS

Decorative arts were Getty's first love as a collector, after he rented a New York penthouse furnished with 18th-century French and English antiques. Originally, his collection focused on furnishings from the reign of Louis XIV to the Napoleonic era (1643–1815), encompassing the Regency, Rococo, and Empire periods.

The age of Louis XIV saw the development of French furniture reach great artistic heights, where appearances mattered more than function. The premier craftsman during that time was André-Charles Boulle (1642–1732), who was noted for his complex veneers and marquetry. The museum has several pieces attributed to Boulle from the French royal household. Two coffers on stands (c.1680– 85), made for the Grand Dauphin, son of Louis XIV, probably held jewelry and valuable objects.

Several of the tapestries in the collection have remained in excellent condition, with their colors still vibrant. They include one woven by Jean de la Croix (active 1662–1712) for Louis XIV. The holdings also include ceramics, silver and gilded objects such as chandeliers and wall lights.

Pieces from Germany, Italy, and northern Europe have also been added. A Neo-Classical rolltop desk (c.1785), made by the German David Roentgen, has a weight-operated, concealed writing stand. This type of elaborate mechanical feature was Roentgen's trademark.

## MANUSCRIPTS

The museum began collecting illuminated manuscripts in 1983 with the purchase of the Ludwig Collection of 144 works, which emphasized German and Central European texts. Tracing the development of illumination from the 6th to the 16th century, the collection today has masterpieces from the Byzantine, Ottoman, Romanesque, Gothic, and Renaissance periods.

Illuminated manuscripts were written and decorated entirely by hand. Initially, most were produced in monasteries, which were then the center of European intellectual life. Later, in the 12th century, they were also produced in the growing number of universities. Most books contained religious material, but some also preserved the philosophy, history, literature, law, and science of Western civilization. Kings, nobles, and church leaders commissioned these richly painted books, some of which were decorated with jewels and precious metals.

The manuscripts, as well as drawings and photos, are all rotated. Highlights include an Ottoman Gospel lectionary from either Reichenau or St. Gall (950–75); an English Gothic Apocalypse (1255–60); two Byzantine Gospel books; *The Visions of Tondal* (1475), in the Flemish holdings; and the *Hours of Simon de Varie*, illuminated by French artist Jean Fouquet in 1455.

Saint John the Evangelist (c.1120– 40) from the German Abbey of Helmarshausen's Gospel book

# The Getty Villa

17985 Pacific Coast Hwy. *Tel (310) 440-7300.* ☐ *10am–5pm Wed–Mon (visits scheduled by phone).* ● *major holidays.* ⓴ *www.getty.edu*

The Getty Villa is the home of the Antiquities collection of the J Paul Getty Museum (*see pp82–5*). Getty's vision – of a museum where his collection of antiquities could be displayed in a place where such art might originally have been seen – has finally come to fruition. The museum displays ancient art from Greece, Rome, and Etruria on both floors of the building.

The Villa is based on the Villa dei Papiri, the country estate of a Roman consul. The Outer Peristyle garden is spectacular, with its large pool bordered by bronze statuary replicas. The buildings combine authentic Roman detailing with modern technology.

Getty's original home on this property, and the site of the first Getty Museum, holds a research library, seminar room, classroom, reading room, conservation labs, and offices for scholars and staff. The outdoor amphitheater presents Greek drama and dance performances, and there is an upscale café.

**Intricate tile detail in Adamson House**

Decorative façade and grounds of Adamson House

## Adamson House and Malibu Lagoon Museum ⑨

23200 Pacific Coast Hwy. **Road map** inset A. *Tel (310) 456-8432.* ☐ *11am–3pm Wed–Sat.* ● *Jan 1, Jul 4, Thanksgiving, Dec 25.* 🎫 ⓴ 📷 📷 *last tour 2pm.* www.adamsonhouse.org

Adamson House was built in 1930 for husband and wife Merritt and Rhoda Adamson. Rhoda was the daughter of Frederick and May Rindge, the last owners of the Rancho Malibu Spanish land grant. Until 1928, the family owned 24 miles (39 km) of Malibu coastline.

Situated on the beach, the idyllic house, designed by Stiles Clements, and its 6 acres (2.5 ha) of gardens overlook Malibu Pier and Malibu Lagoon. The Spanish Colonial style building is covered with vivid tiles from the Malibu Potteries – a ceramics firm that was started by May Rindge and owned by the family. Hundreds of these individually designed tiles are featured throughout the house and grounds. The floors, walls, doorways, and fountains are all intricately decorated. The house's original 1920s furnishings are also on display.

Located in the converted garage of Adamson House is the Malibu Lagoon Museum, which is devoted to the history of Malibu. Artifacts, documents, and photographs tell the story not only of the Rindge family but also of the early Chumash population and José Tapia, who in 1802 became Malibu's first Spanish landowner.

## Malibu Lagoon State Beach ⑩

**Road map** inset A. *Tel (818) 880-0367.* ☐ *8am–sunset daily.* 🎫 ⓴ www.parks.ca.gov

The Chumash people built Humaliwo, their largest village, on the shores of this lagoon. By the 16th century, about 1,000 people had their home here, making it one of the most populated Native American villages north of what is now Mexico.

The estuary supports a wide range of marine life and is an important feeding ground for up to 200 species of

**The Getty Villa's Outer Peristyle garden**

Exclusive beach houses in Malibu Colony

migratory and native birds. To the east of the lagoon, the 35-acre (14-ha) Surfrider County Beach is devoted to surfers. With its rare point break, Malibu is one of the finest surfing spots in southern California. The area closest to the pier is thought to have the best waves for longboarding.

View across Malibu Lagoon to the Santa Monica Mountains

## Malibu Colony ⑪

**Road map** inset A. 🚌 🛈 23554 *Malibu Colony Rd.*

In 1928, to raise money for an ongoing battle to keep Malibu in the family, May Rindge sold this section of shoreline to film stars such as Bing Crosby, Gary Cooper, and Barbara Stanwyck. Today, the colony is a private, gated compound, still favored by

people working within the entertainment industry. Public access to the beach is difficult, but stars can often be spotted in the Malibu Colony Plaza, which is located near the entrance.

## Malibu Creek State Park ⑫

**Road map** inset A. **Tel** *(818) 880-0367 or (800) 444-7275 for camp site reservations.* ◯ *dawn–dusk daily.* 🐾 🔥 🅿 **www**.parks.ca.gov

This 10,000-acre (4,000-ha) park was inhabited by the Chumash Indians until the mid-19th century. A varied landscape of forests, meadows, and rocky outcrops create the illusion of a vast wilderness, miles away from civilization.

Some 2,000 acres (800 ha) of the park were once owned by 20th Century Fox, which made it a favorite location for movie-making *(see pp68–9).*

*M\*A\*S\*H* (1970), *Butch Cassidy and the Sundance Kid* (1969), and *Planet of the Apes* (1968) were all filmed here. The state bought the land back from the film company in 1974.

The information center is close to the parking lot and has exhibits on the area's history, flora, and fauna. The stunning Gorge Trail starts from the center of the park and leads to a rock pool, which was used as a pseudo-tropical location to film the movies *South Pacific* (1958) and *Tarzan* (1959).

Off Crags Road, the marshy Century Lake harbors catfish, bass, bluefish, red-winged blackbirds, buffleheads, coots, and mallards. In spring the meadows are a riot of colorful wildflowers. Groves of live and valley oaks, redwood, and dogwood trees are scattered throughout the park.

Within the park there are 20 trails for hiking, cycling, or horseback riding; a nature center; and many picnic areas.

Malibu Creek State Park, near Castro Crest *(see p64)*

# BEVERLY HILLS, BEL AIR, AND WESTWOOD

everly Hills is a city, independent of Los Angeles and with its own laws and regulations. Since the early 1920s it has been the entertainment industry's favorite residential address. Beverly Hills' Golden Triangle is the West Coast's answer to New York's

**City limits sign**

Madison Avenue, with its array of restaurants, shops, and coffee bars. South of Bel Air's shady canyons, youthful Westwood Village brims with UCLA students. In the business-minded Century City, high-rises crowd the skyline. Together, these areas are known as the Westside.

## SIGHTS AT A GLANCE

**Historic Buildings**
Beverly Hills Civic Center ❶
Beverly Hills Hotel ❽
Hotel Bel-Air ⓫

**Parks and Gardens**
Greystone Park and Mansion ❼
Virginia Robinson Gardens ❾

**Shopping Areas**
Century City ❻
*Rodeo Drive p94* ❸
2 Rodeo ❹

**Tours**
Tour of the Stars' Homes
*pp96–7* ❿

**Museums**
The Paley Center for Media ❷
Museum of Tolerance ❺

**Universities**
UCLA and Westwood
Village ⓬

## GETTING THERE

A car is essential when visiting this area, which has many parking lots. From the San Diego Freeway (I-405) take Wilshire or Sunset Boulevards east to Westwood, Bel Air, and Beverly Hills.

0 kilometers 1
0 miles 0.5

### KEY

Street-by-Street map
See pp90–91

Illustrated tour
See pp96–7

◁ **Distinctive tower of Beverly Hills City Hall, part of the Civic Center**

# Street-by-Street  The Golden Triangle

The area bordered by Santa Monica Boulevard, Wilshire Boulevard, and North Crescent Drive, known as the "Golden Triangle," is the business district of Beverly Hills. The shops, restaurants, and art galleries lining the streets are some of the most luxurious in the world. Cutting through the middle is Rodeo Drive, where many international designer boutiques are to be found. On Wilshire Boulevard, the cream of American department stores offer a heady mix of style and opulence. To the north are the beautifully mani-cured Beverly Gardens, the elegant Civic Center with its landmark City Hall, and the Paley Center for Media, formerly the Museum of Television and Radio.

★ **The Paley Center for Media**
*A valuable addition to the Golden Triangle, this museum gives a comprehensive history of broadcasting* ❷

**The Electric Fountain** was built in 1930. The statue on the top is of a Native American praying for rain. Scenes from California history are depicted on the base frieze.

SANTA MONICA BOULEVARD

LITTLE SANTA MONICA BOULEVARD

NORTH CAMDEN DRIVE

NORTH BEDFORD DRIVE

BRIGHTON WAY

NORTH ROXBURY DRIVE

**Saks Fifth Avenue** is one of the four major department stores along Wilshire Boulevard.

**The Creative Artists Agency** building, with curving, mirrored glass and marble walls, was built in 1989 by architect IM Pei. (CAA has moved its offices.)

★ **Beverly Hills Civic Center**
*The 1932 Spanish Renaissance
City Hall has been restored and
a series of new administration
and public buildings
added* ❶

**LOCATOR MAP**
*See Street Finder, map 5*

**Anderson Court**
was designed by
Frank Lloyd Wright
in 1953.

**2 Rodeo**
*When built in 1990,
this center included
the first new street in
Beverly Hills since
the city established
independence
from LA in
1914* ❹

**The MGM Building** was
built in the 1920s by Louis
B Mayer. The white and
gold Art Deco structure
was the headquarters of
the newly formed
Metro-Goldwyn-
Mayer film studios.

**Rodeo Drive**
*These three blocks of
Rodeo Drive are among
the most famous shopping
areas in the world* ❸

**0 meters** 100
**0 yards** 100

**KEY**

– – – Suggested route

**The Beverly Wilshire** Hotel
first opened in 1928. In 1970 a
second wing was added to the
original Beaux-Arts building. A
private, cobblestone street links
the two wings *(see p525)*.

**STAR SIGHTS**

★ Beverly Hills
Civic Center

★ The Paley Center for
Media

**Beverly Hills Civic Center with City Hall in the background**

screenings on specialized subjects and selected actors or directors.

The collection of more than 75,000 television and radio programs includes such timeless classics as *I Love Lucy (see p199)* and *The Honeymooners*. Favorite television and radio commercials, encompassing the industry's advertising history, are also available.

The museum's holdings duplicate those of New York's highly successful Museum of Television and Radio, which was created in 1975 by the late William S Paley, when he was the head of CBS Television.

## Rodeo Drive ❸

*See p94.*

## 2 Rodeo ❹

**Map** 5 F3. 268 N. Rodeo Drive (310-247-7040). **www**.2rodeo.com

Developed in 1990 on the corner of Rodeo Drive *(see p94)* and Wilshire Boulevard, 2 Rodeo is one of the most expensive retail centers ever made. It looks like a film set of a European street, complete with a public square and Victorian-style streetlamps. Exclusive shops such as Versace and Jimmy Choo line Via Rodeo, the cobbled lane

## Beverly Hills Civic Center ❶

455 N Rexford Drive. **Map** 5 F3. **Tel** (310) 285-1000. 7:30am–5:30pm Mon–Thu, 8am–5pm Fri. public hols. **www**.beverlyhills.org

The Spanish Colonial City Hall, with its majestic tower capped by a tiled cupola, was designed in 1932 by local firm Koerner and Gage. Over the years it has become a symbol of the elegant, European-inspired city of Beverly Hills.

In 1990, architect Charles Moore linked the building to a new Civic Center by a series of diagonal landscaped and pedestrianized courtyards. On the upper levels, balconies and arcaded corridors continue the Spanish Colonial theme. The harmonious modern addition houses a beautiful public library as well as the local fire and police stations.

Billboards are banned in the area, and a height restriction of three stories or 45 ft (14 m) is imposed on any new buildings, leaving City Hall to dominate the skyline.

## The Paley Center for Media ❷

465 N Beverly Drive. **Map** 5 F3. **Tel** (310) 786-1091. noon–5pm Wed–Sun. public hols. **www**.paleycenter.org

Visitors to the Paley Center, formerly the Museum of Television and Radio, may watch and listen to news and a collection of entertainment and sports programs from the earliest days of radio and television to the present.

Pop music fans can see footage of the early Beatles or a young Elvis Presley making his television debut. Sports fans can relive classic Olympic competitions.

Visitors can select up to four extracts from the library's computerized catalogue at any one time. These are then played on small private consoles. The museum also has a 150-seat theater, which hosts major exhibitions, seminars, and

**Lucille Ball, the most popular television star during the 1950s**

**Spanish Steps leading to 2 Rodeo**

that bisects the center. Via Rodeo meanders to the Spanish Steps, which descend to Wilshire Boulevard.

## Museum of Tolerance **❺**

9786 W Pico Blvd. **Map** 5 F5.
**Tel** (310) 553-8403. ◯ 10am–5pm Mon–Fri, 11am–5pm Sun. ◉ Jan 1, Thanksgiving, Dec 25, and all major Jewish holidays. 🖼 🔊 ♿ 🎥 📷
**www**.museumoftolerance.com

This museum is dedicated to the promotion of respect and understanding among all people. Its two primary areas of focus are the history of racism and prejudice in the United States and the European Holocaust experience, examined in both historical and contemporary contexts.

The museum tour begins in the Tolerancenter, where visitors are challenged to confront racism and bigotry through interactive exhibits. A recreation of a 1950s diner has a menu of controversial topics focusing on personal responsibility, and a film on Bosnia and Rwanda and contemporary hate groups brings human rights violations up-to-date.

A 16-screen video wall depicts the 1960s civil rights struggle in America. Interactive video monitors ask visitors for their personal

profiles and then challenge them on questions of responsible citizenship and social justice. They also offer footage of the LA riots of 1992 (see p57), with follow-up interviews.

At the beginning of the Holocaust section, each visitor is given the details and photograph of a child whose life was in some way altered by that period. Throughout the tour, the child's history is updated and, at the end, his or her fate is revealed. During the tour, visitors become a witness to events in Nazi Germany. Wax models in an outdoor café scene, set in prewar Berlin, seem to discuss the impending Nazi takeover of Germany. In a re-creation of the Wannsee Conference, the Third Reich leaders decide on the "The Final Solution of the Jewish Question." Videotaped interviews with concentration camp survivors shown in the "Hall of Testimony" tell of their harrowing experiences. Artifacts on display include Anne Frank's original letters and memorabilia from the camps.

Visitors must call ahead for reservations, as tickets are issued for allocated slots and specific exhibitions. There is a short orientation before a self-guided tour. Some of the exhibits, including the Holocaust portion, are not recommended for children under the age of 12.

**History of racial prejudice at the Museum of Tolerance**

## Century City **❻**

**Map** 5 D5. 🛈 2029 Century Park East, 90067 (310-553-2222).
**www**.centurycitycc.com

This site used to be part of 20th Century Fox's backlot. It was sold in 1961 to the developers of Century City, who designed a high-rise complex of offices, stores, and homes on the 180 acres (73 ha).

Today lawyers, agents, and production companies fill the office blocks. Despite this, the area has never developed a community feel.

The Westfield Century City Shopping Center, however, is a notable success and has been remodeled into an outdoor complex with some 150 stores and restaurants, and a 15-screen cinema.

**Westfield Century City**

## Greystone Park and Mansion **❼**

905 Loma Vista Drive. **Map** 5 F1.
**Tel** (310) 550-4796. **Park** ◯ 10am–5pm (to 6pm summer) daily. ◉ Jan 1, Dec 25. ♿ terrace & lower grounds.

In 1928 Edward L Doheny, an oil millionaire, built this 55-room mock-Tudor manor house for his son. Just three weeks after moving in with his family, Doheny's son was found dead in his bedroom with a male secretary, an apparent murder-suicide. His wife and children soon moved out, and since then the mansion has often been vacant.

Now owned by the city of Beverly Hills, Greystone is used in films, music videos, and commercials. The house is closed to the public, but visitors can walk or picnic in the beautiful 18-acre (7-ha) terraced gardens, which offer views across Los Angeles.

# Rodeo Drive ❸

The name Rodeo Drive is derived from *El Rancho Rodeo de las Aguas* ("the ranch of the gathering of waters"), the name of an early Spanish land grant that included Beverly Hills. Today, Rodeo Drive is one of the most celebrated and exclusive shopping streets in the world, with Italian designer boutiques, the best of French fashion, world-class jewelers, and some of the leading LA retailers. For those who enjoy celebrity-spotting, Rodeo Drive is a prime area.

**Cartier**, *at No.370, is well-known for its classic-style watches and diamond rings.*

**Barakat** *sells fine jewelry and also has an impressive collection of pre-Columbian and ancient Greek artifacts, at No. 405.*

411 •

• 421

GUESS U.S.A.

bijan

BRIGHTON WAY

**Gucci,** *at No. 347, is a leading Italian boutique. Best known for its leather accessories and colorful scarves, it also produces furnishings, such as this cushion.*

• 370

• 434

HERMES

• 317

Hammacher Schlemmer & Co

VAN CLEEF & ARPELS

DAYTON WAY

RODEO DRIVE

**Lalique**, *at No. 238, is famous for its Art Deco and Art Nouveau glassware. The shop's frosted lamps are typical of Lalique's style.*

Christian Dior

**Christian Dior**, *at No. 309, is one of the leading names in French* haute couture. *The founder of the house was responsible for the 1950s "New Look."*

**Rodeo Drive's** *wide sidewalks, bordered by trees, help create a pleasant shopping environment.*

• 273

• 230

TIFFANY & CO

| 0 meters | 50 |
| 0 yards | 50 |

The landmark Beverly Hills Hotel

## Beverly Hills Hotel ❽

9641 Sunset Blvd. **Map** 5 D2. **Tel** *(310) 276-2251, (800) 283-8885.* ⬭ *daily.* 🖳 www.beverlyhillshotel.com
See *Where to Stay p525.*

Dubbed "the Pink Palace," this extravagant Mission Revival-style hotel was built in 1912 by developer Burton E Green. The hotel's 21 secluded bungalows, set in 12 acres (5 ha) of landscaped gardens, have been romantic hideaways for film stars such as Marilyn Monroe, Clark Gable, Richard Burton, and Elizabeth Taylor.

The Beverly Hills Hotel has undergone a $100 million program of renovations, reviving the style of Hollywood's heyday. Its legendary pool and cabanas have remained one of the places to be seen and heard in Los Angeles, and its famous restaurants, The Polo Lounge and Polo Grill, are once more at the center of the movie industry's deal-making.

## Virginia Robinson Gardens ❾

1008 Elden Way. **Map** 5 D1. **Tel** *(310) 276-5367.* ⬭ *Tue–Fri.* 🌑 *public hols.* 📷 🖳 🗗 *obligatory 10am & 1pm Tue–Fri. Advance reservations required.* www.robinsongardens.org

In 1908, department-store heir Harry Robinson and his wife, Virginia, bought a plot of land in Beverly Hills. Three years later they completed the city's first house here and planted 6 acres (2.5 ha) of landscaped gardens set amid terraces, ponds, and fountains.

Bequeathed to LA County, the gardens were opened to the public in 1982. One of the most impressive sights is the 2.5-acre (1-ha) palm forest, where you can see the largest king palms outside Australia.

The organized tour includes part of the house, which still has its original furnishings.

## Tour of the Stars' Homes ❿

*See pp96–7.*

## Hotel Bel-Air ⓫

701 Stone Canyon Rd. **Map** 4 A1. **Tel** *(310) 472-1211, (800) 648-4097.* ⬭ *daily.* 🖳 www.hotelbelair.com
See *Where to Stay p524.*

Considered one of the best hotels in the US, Hotel Bel-Air is located in a heavily wooded canyon, giving it an air of privacy and tranquillity. The 1920s Mission Revival-style buildings are set in 11 acres (4.5 ha) of beautiful gardens, interspersed with fountains and intimate courtyards.

Among the trees and shrubs rarely seen in Southern California are coastal redwoods, white-flowering bird of paradise trees, and a floss silk tree – the largest of its kind outside its native South America. The gardens are fragrant with roses, gardenias, jasmine, and orange blossoms. In fact, the Bel-Air is so perfect that one guest stayed for 40 years.

Pool at Hotel Bel-Air, surrounded by attractive gardens

*For hotels and restaurants in this region see pp524–31 and pp568–76*

# Tour of the Stars' Homes ❿

Beverly Hills has long been the symbol of success for those in the entertainment industry. When, in 1920, Mary Pickford and Douglas Fairbanks built their mansion, Pickfair, at the top of Summit Drive, everyone else followed – and stayed. Sunset Boulevard divides the haves from the have-nots: people who live south of it may be rich, but it is those who live to the north of the road who are considered to be the super-rich. A bus tour will take you around if you don't wish to drive yourself *(see p179)*. Be aware that most of the addresses are the former homes of celebrities, who no longer live there.

**Security guard sign**

**Jimmy Stewart's former home at No. 918 Roxbury Drive ⑬**

### South of Sunset

Start at No. 714 Palm Drive, the elegant home of Faye Dunaway ①, who starred with Warren Beatty in *Bonnie and Clyde* (1967). Continue south and turn right on Elevado Avenue. The former home of Rita Hayworth ② is situated on the corner at No. 512 Palm Drive.

At Maple Drive, turn right. No. 720 is the white and green New England-style home of the late George Burns and Gracie Allen ③. Continue north and just before Sunset Boulevard make a sharp left onto Lomitas Avenue. Go two blocks and turn left onto Foothill Road. On the corner, at No. 701, is the unassuming house of Carroll Baker ④. This blonde-haired beauty made her debut in *Giant* (1956) with James Dean. At one time she was being groomed to be the next Marilyn Monroe.

Turn right onto Elevado Avenue, take the next right onto Alpine Drive, left onto Lomitas Avenue, and left at Crescent Drive. Doris Day's modest house ⑤ is barely

visible at No. 713, hidden behind a tall hedge and gate.

Turn right on Carmelita Avenue and right again at Cañon Drive. The pretty house ⑥ where Robert Wagner and Natalie Wood once lived can be seen through the low wall at No. 603. Continue north to the junction with Elevado Avenue. Just across the road, at No. 707 Cañon Drive, lush palm trees in the front mark the beginning of Kirk Douglas's walled and gated property ⑦.

Turn left onto Elevado Avenue. As you cross Rodeo Drive, look to your right. The lovely home of the late Gene Kelly ⑧ is at No. 725 Rodeo Drive. This renowned Hollywood icon performed in such classics as *An American in Paris* (1951) and *Singing in the Rain* (1952).

Continue along Elevado Avenue, then turn right on Bedford Drive. The comedian and actor Steve Martin ⑨ has a home at No. 721. A modern block structure, it has no front windows and can be only partially glimpsed behind a bougainvillea hedge. Lana Turner's scandal-ridden house ⑩ at No. 730, on the

**Faye Dunaway's house at No. 714 Palm Drive ①**

### KEY

– – –  Tour route

**Gene Hackman's house at No. 9906 Sunset Boulevard** ⑭

**LOCATOR MAP**
*See Street Finder, map 5*

His former neighbors at No. 1000 Roxbury Drive were Lucille Ball and Desi Arnaz ⑫. Their successful show *I Love Lucy (see pp92 and 149)* reruns daily on television. Nearby, at No. 918, is the mock-Tudor former home of the much-respected Jimmy Stewart ⑬.

At Sunset Boulevard, turn right. Gene Hackman's house is at No. 9906 ⑭, on the southwest corner of Sunset Boulevard, just past Greenway Drive. The actor became famous in the 1970s after his Academy-award winning role in *The French Connection*.

Turn right onto North Carolwood Drive. Just to the right, at No. 144 Monovale Drive ⑮, is one of rock-and-roll king Elvis Presley's former homes. Only the tennis courts can be seen from the street.

Continue along Carolwood Drive. Barbra Streisand ⑯ has lived at No. 301 on a heavily guarded estate. The actress won an academy award in 1969 for her role as Fanny Brice in the musical *Funny Girl*. The late Walt Disney, who captured the imagination of the world with his cartoon characters, used to live just north of here at No. 355 Carolwood Drive ⑰. His house is on a bend, behind a gate.

**Walt Disney's mailbox** ⑰

### North of Sunset

Cross Sunset Boulevard, taking the street farthest to the left, which is now Benedict Canyon Drive. On the corner is the Beverly Hills Hotel, *(see p95),* long a celebrity rumor mill. The private bungalows behind its pink façade saw many a romantic tryst, including, it is said, those between Marilyn Monroe and John and Robert Kennedy.

At Roxbury Drive, turn left and curve south with the road. At No. 1002 is the late Jack Benny's traditional-looking brick house ⑪, which he occasionally used in his shows.

corner of Bedford Drive and Lomitas Avenue, was where her gangster-lover Johnny Stompanato was stabbed to death with a kitchen knife by her daughter, Cheryl Crane.

Turn right onto Lomitas Avenue, then make a sharp left on Cañon Drive.

### TIPS FOR DRIVERS

*Tour length:* 5 miles (8 km).
*Warning:* Film stars' homes or former homes are private residences. Do not attempt to trespass or you may be arrested.

# University of California Los Angeles, Westwood Village  ⓑ

A large university with a first-rate reputation, UCLA has a wide range of academic departments and professional schools, including the respected UCLA Hospital. Sited on 419 acres (170 ha), with more than 35,000 students, it is a city within a city. The original campus was designed in 1925 to resemble the Romanesque towns of southern Europe. The first four buildings followed this theme, but as the university expanded more modern architecture was favored. The disappointing mix of bland structures that resulted is redeemed by the beautiful landscaped grounds.

Romanesque-style façade of UCLA's Royce Hall

## Exploring UCLA and Westwood Village

Since it was first developed in 1928, Westwood Village, at the foot of the UCLA campus, has been a meet and greet place for college students and anyone looking for a break from the city. This always lively enclave is chockablock with shops catering mostly to students and

**Detail of ceiling in Royce Hall**

restaurants of all kinds, plus the biggest lineup of movie theaters in LA. In fact, on any evening there is the possibility to see stars walking the red carpet at the Fox or the Bruin, since Hollywood favors these venerable theaters for its gala premieres.

### 🏛 Royce Quadrangle

Dickson Plaza. *Tel (310) 825-2101.* ◯ *daily.*
The four buildings that make up the Royce Quadrangle are the oldest on UCLA's campus in Westwood. Built of red brick in the Italian Romanesque style, Royce, Kinsey, and Haines halls, and Powell

Library far surpass the other buildings at UCLA in beauty. The best of them all is Royce Hall, which is based on the basilica of San Ambrogio in Milan, Italy. Its auditorium hosts professional music, dance, and theater shows throughout the year. Across the quad, Powell Library's grand rotunda was modeled on San Sepolcro in Bologna, Italy.

### 🏛 Armand Hammer Museum of Art and Cultural Center

10899 Wilshire Blvd. *Tel (310) 443-7000.* ◯ *11am–7pm Tue, Wed, Fri, Sat; 11am–9pm Thu; 11am–5pm Sun.* ● *Jan 1, Jul 4, Thanksgiving, Dec 25.* 🎟 *free 11am–9pm Thu.* 🚻 🎫 🛍 www.hammer.ucla.edu
The museum presents selections from the collection of businessman Armand Hammer (1899–1990). Works are largely Impressionist or Post-Impressionist by artists such as Mary Cassatt (1845–1926), Claude Monet (1840–1926), Camille Pissarro (1830–1903), John Singer Sargent (1856–1925), and

Vincent Van Gogh (1853–90). Exhibits from the Armand Hammer Daumier and Contemporaries Collection are also shown on a rotating basis and include paintings, sculptures, and lithographs by Daumier and his contemporaries. Displays are also drawn from the UCLA Grunwald Center for the Graphic Arts, which holds more than 35,000 works on paper dating from the Renaissance to the present day.

### 🍃 Franklin D Murphy Sculpture Garden

*Tel (310) 443-7041.* ◯ *daily.*
This is the largest sculpture garden on the West Coast with more than 70 20th-century sculptures. The highlights

## UCLA AND WESTWOOD VILLAGE

Entrance to UCLA's Armand Hammer Museum of Art

*Automne (Autumn, 1948) by Henri Laurens*

*Key to map:*
1. Franklin D Murphy Sculpture Garden
2. Fowler Museum
3. Royce angle
4. Mildred E Mathias Botanical Garden
5. Westwood Village
6. Armand Hammer Museum
7. Westwood Memorial Park

0 meters 500
0 yards 500

## VISITORS' CHECKLIST

**Map** 4 A3. 20, 21, 22. **UCLA Campus** 310 825-4321. **www**.ucla.edu **Westwood Village** 2990 S Sepulveda Blvd (310 481-0600). **www**. westwoodvillageonline.com

include Henry Moore's *Two-Piece Reclining Figure, No. 3* (1961) and Jacques Lipchitz's *Baigneuse* (*Bather*, 1923–5).

### ♣ Mildred E Mathias Botanical Garden

*Tel* (310) 825-1260. ☐ 8am–5pm Mon–Fri, 8am–4pm Sat & Sun. ● *public hols.* &

Tucked away in a small shady canyon, this serene garden contains almost 4,000 rare and native species. Divided into 13 thematic sections, the gardens feature both subtropical and tropical plants. The trees are spectacular and include some outstanding Australian eucalyptus and some large specimens of dawn redwoods.

### �m Fowler Museum of Cultural History

*Tel* (310) 825-4361. ☐ noon–5pm Wed–Sun (until 8pm Thu). ● *public hols.*

This university museum is committed to enriching the community's understanding of other cultures. Its exhibitions focus on the prehistoric, historic, and contemporary societies of Africa, Asia, the Americas, and Oceania. The collection of 750,000 artifacts makes it one of the nation's leading university museums.

### ⊞ Westwood Memorial Park

1218 Glendon Ave. *Tel* (310) 474-1579. ☐ 8am–dusk daily. &

Off the beaten track, this small cemetery is located behind the Avco Center theaters and parking lot. The tranquil grounds are now the final resting place for celebrities such as Dean Martin, Peter Lorre, Buddy Rich, Natalie Wood, and Marilyn Monroe. For several decades after her death, Monroe's second husband, Joe DiMaggio, used to have six red roses placed on her tomb every week.

Tranquil Westwood Memorial Park, shaded by trees

### MARILYN MONROE

Born Norma Jean Baker in the charity ward of Los Angeles General Hospital, Marilyn Monroe (1926–62) was placed in foster care by her mother when she was two weeks old. Her first marriage, at the age of 16, lasted four years, before she gave it up to pursue her dream of being an actress. In 1950, her career took off with *The Asphalt Jungle* and *All About Eve*. With films such as *The Seven-Year Itch* (1955) and *Some Like It Hot* (1959), she became the biggest sex symbol Hollywood has ever seen. In the latter part of her life, she struggled to escape the narrow confines of her on-screen persona.

**Marilyn Monroe's memorial plaque**

**Key to Symbols** *see back flap*

# HOLLYWOOD AND WEST HOLLYWOOD

In 1887, Harvey Henderson Wilcox and his wife, Daeida, set up a Christian community, free of saloons and gambling, in a Los Angeles suburb and called it Hollywood. It is ironic that the movie business, with all its decadence, came to replace their Utopia. In 1913, Cecil B De Mille filmed *The Squaw Man* in a barn at the corner of Vine and Selma, and for several decades the studios

**Hollywood's Walk of Fame**

were based here, generating wealth and glamor. During the 1980s and 90s the area fell into decline, but has since revived. Together with Sunset Boulevard, Hollywood is now the hub for Los Angeles nightlife. West Hollywood, with its large gay community, is also a lively area, Wilshire Boulevard between La Brea and Fairfax Avenues is known as the Miracle Mile, or Museum Row.

## SIGHTS AT A GLANCE

**Museums**
Craft and Folk Art Museum ⑲
Hollywood Heritage Museum ⑨
Hollywood Museum ⑦
*Los Angeles County Museum of Art pp114–17* ⑭
Madame Tussaud's Hollywood ②
Page Museum at the La Brea Tar Pits ⑱
Petersen Automotive Museum ⑯

**Historic Streets and Buildings**
Hollywood Bowl ⑧

Hollywood Roosevelt Hotel ①
Miracle Mile ⑮
Paramount Studios ⑫
Walk of Fame ⑥

**Cemeteries**
Hollywood Forever Cemetery ⑪

**Cinemas and Theaters**
El Capitan Theater ⑤

Grauman's Chinese Theatre ③
Hollywood and Highland ④
Pantages Theater ⑩
The Improv ⑰
Wiltern Theater ⑳

**Shops and Markets**
Farmers Market ⑬

See pp108–9
See pp102–4
See pp105–7

**0 kilometers** 2
**0 miles** 1

## GETTING THERE

The Metro runs from Union Station to Wilshire Boulevard, Hollywood Boulevard, and to North Hollywood. Bus services from Downtown include: No. 1 (along Hollywood Boulevard), No. 2 (Sunset Boulevard), No. 4 (Santa Monica Boulevard), No. 10 (Melrose Avenue), and Nos. 20, 21, and 22 (Wilshire Boulevard). Freeway 101 runs through Hollywood from Downtown and on to Ventura.

**KEY**

Illustrated areas

M Metro station

◁ **Grauman's Chinese Theatre, a lavish remnant of Hollywood's Golden Age**

# A View of Sunset Boulevard: Sunset Strip

Sunset Boulevard curves west for 26 miles (42 km) from downtown LA to the Pacific Coast Highway. Sunset has been associated with the movies since the 1920s, when it was a dirt track linking the burgeoning film studios in Hollywood with the hillside homes of the screen stars. Today, much of the boulevard is still lined with the mansions of the rich and famous *(see pp96–7)*. Sunset Strip is the liveliest and most historically rich stretch, filled with restaurants, luxury hotels, and nightclubs. The 1.5-mile (2.4-km) section was first paved in the mid-1930s. Its lack of local government made it a magnet for gambling and bootlegging. Famous nightclubs included the Trocadero, Ciro's, and the Mocambo – where young Margarita Cansino met studio boss Harry Cohen, who renamed her Rita Hayworth. Sunset Strip is still the center of LA's nightlife today.

**Sunset Strip and the Santa Monica Mountains from Crescent Heights**

### Rainbow Bar & Grill
*The walls of this restaurant, at No. 9015, are lined with wine casks and gold records. Formerly the Villa Nova, Vincente Minnelli proposed to Judy Garland here and, eight years later in 1953, Marilyn Monroe met Joe DiMaggio here on a blind date.*

### The Original Spago
*Wolfgang Puck, who is regarded by many as the founder of Californian cuisine, had his first LA restaurant at No. 8795 until 1997. During the 1970s and 1980s Oscar® night parties were held here, hosted by the legendary Hollywood agent Irving "Swifty" Lazar.*

### The Roxy on Sunset
*This trendy nightclub, at No. 9009, occupies the site of the old Club Largo.*

**The Viper Room**, at No. 8852, is a popular live music club *(see p174)*, co-founded and once owned by the actor Johnny Depp. In October 1993 young film star River Phoenix, having taken a lethal cocktail of drugs, collapsed and died on the sidewalk outside.

CLARK ST

LARRABEE ST

HORN AVE

HAMMOND ST

HILLDALE AVE

SAN VICENTE BLVD

HOLLOWAY

### Andaz West Hollywood Hotel

*Formerly known as the "Riot Hyatt", visiting rock stars often stay at this hotel, at No. 8401 (see p530). Jim Morrison was a guest here when he performed nearby.*

### Sunset Tower Hotel

*This hotel is an Art Deco high-rise. In Hollywood's heyday it was an apartment complex and home to Jean Harlow, Clark Gable, and other luminaries. (See p531.)*

**Cabo Cantina (The Source)** at No. 8301 is where Woody Allen rants about LA in his film *Annie Hall* (1977).

### The Comedy Store

*This is a world-famous spot for stand-up comedy, often enjoying television coverage. It stands on the site of the 1940s nightclub, Ciro's.*

```
0 meters     100
0 yards      100
```

N LA CIENEGA BLVD

OLIVE DRIVE

**The Mondrian Hotel**, at No. 8440 *(see p531)*, was decorated with stripes as a tribute to artist Piet Mondrian when it was built, but has since been repainted.

### The House of Blues

*This tin-roofed blues bar, at No. 8430, has been transported from Clarksdale, Mississippi. It was co-founded by the actor Dan Ackroyd, who starred with John Belushi in the 1980 cult movie* The Blues Brothers *(see p174).*

### Sunset Plaza

*This area is lined with chic stores and cafés. It is a good section to explore on foot.*

# Sunset Strip continued

**Miyagi's**, behind the big billboard to the west of the Chateau Marmont hotel, is currently popular with college crowds. It stands on the site of the Players Club, which was owned in the 1940s by movie director Preston Sturges.

**Chateau Marmont**
*The hotel at No. 8221 (see p531) was modeled on a Loire Valley château. When it opened in 1929, it attracted actors such as Errol Flynn and Greta Garbo. Today's regulars have included Winona Ryder and Christopher Walken.*

N LAUREL AVE

N FAIRFAX AVE

TO OI
STUI
DISTI
(2KM

**The Trocadero** nightclub, at No. 8610, had Nat "King" Cole as its pianist in its heyday. Only three steps remain of the old building.

**Directors' Guild of America**
*This is one of the many offices on Sunset Boulevard connected with the entertainment industry.*

**Schwab's**
*The former drugstore was a popular meeting place for film stars and columnists. Across Crescent Heights was the legendary Garden of Allah apartment complex whose residents included Scott Fitzgerald and Dorothy Parker, and which was torn down in 1959.*

## BILLBOARDS

The most visible pieces of art along Sunset Strip are the huge, hand-painted billboards, produced by some of Hollywood's finest artists to advertise new films, records, and personalities. They are often three-dimensional, a technique introduced in 1953 when Las Vegas's Sahara Hotel rented a billboard, erected a real swimming pool, and filled it with swimsuited models. During the 1960s the billboards were dominated by the music industry, with advertising space along Sunset Strip even being written into some rock stars' contracts. LA's well-known antipathy toward smoking now shows up in anti-smoking ads, which mimic the Marlboro cowboy style, on the massive boards outside the Chateau Marmont. The city is now trying to ban billboards.

**Famous Marlboro billboard, now gone from Sunset Strip**

# A View of Sunset Boulevard: Old Studio District

During the first half of the 20th century, this 2-mile (3-km) stretch of Sunset Boulevard, was the center of Hollywood's film industry. This historic district is located 1.2 miles (2 km) to the east of the fashionable nightlife and boutiques of Sunset Strip *(see pp102–4)*. Major studios, including 20th Century Fox, RKO, Warner Bros., Paramount, and United Artists, were all in the vicinity, and the streets were filled with directors, actors, and would-be film stars. In the area known as Gower Gulch, low-budget outfits churned out Westerns by the score.

**Sunset Boulevard during its heyday in the 1940s**

**Jim Henson Company**
*These buildings, stretching from the southeast corner of Sunset Boulevard down La Brea Avenue, were constructed by Charlie Chaplin as homes for workers at his studio.*

**Crossroads of the World**
*Hollywood's first shopping mall, built in 1936, is located at No. 6621. Designed to resemble an ocean liner, with a globe-topped tower on its prow, it has now been converted into offices.*

**Hollywood High School**
*A long list of famous alumni have attended Hollywood High School, at No. 6800, including Lana Turner. The actress was first discovered in 1936 by director Mervyn LeRoy, sipping a soda in the now-defunct Top Hat Malt Shop. Its site, opposite the school, is now occupied by a garage.*

*For hotels and restaurants in this region see pp524–31 and pp568–76*

# Old Studio District continued

**Hollywood Athletic Club**
*Stars of the 1930s and 1940s exercised here.* Flash
Gordon *star Buster Crabbe trained here before
winning a gold medal at the 1932 Olympics.*

**ArcLight Cinerama Dome**
*The distinctive dome of
No. 6360 was the first
wide-screen movie theater
on the West Coast.*

CASSIL PLACE · N HUDSON AVE · N CAHUENGA BLVD · IVAR AVE · MORNINGSIDE CT

SEWARD ST · WILCOX AVE · COLE PLACE · VINE ST

**The Cat and Fiddle**
*This British-style pub,
at No. 6530, is built
around an attractive
Mediterranean-style
patio. British beers are
served along with pub
food, such as bangers
and mash. There is a
dartboard inside.*

## TIME CAPSULE

In 1954 the Los Angeles Chamber of Commerce decided to preserve the history of
Hollywood with a time capsule. A copy of
Bing Crosby's hit record "White Christmas,"
released that year, a script of the most
successful film made to date, *Gone
With the Wind*, and various contemporary radio and television tapes were
deposited under the sidewalk at the
famous intersection between Sunset

**Singer Bing Crosby**

Boulevard and Vine Street. The time capsule was retrieved
50 years after it was planted, in 2004.

A sidewalk plaque marking
the site notes that the legend
of Hollywood was born here in
1913 with the making of the first
feature-length film, *The Squaw
Man*, by Cecil B De Mille and
Jesse Lasky. The actual location
of their barn studio, now
preserved on North Highland
Avenue *(see p112)*, was farther
up the block at No. 1521 Vine
Street. Hollywood had also
been incorporated as a town
ten years earlier and numerous
short films had been made here
during that decade.

**Poster of Gone With the Wind (1939)**

### Hollywood Palladium
*Norman Chandler, of the* Los Angeles Times *dynasty, built this theater and dance hall at No. 6215. It was opened by Lana Turner in 1940, when Frank Sinatra gave a concert here.*

### Warner Bros. Studio
*The first talkie, Al Jolson's* The Jazz Singer *(1927), was made here at No. 5858. The following year the studio moved to Burbank (see p145). The building now houses local radio stations.*

0 meters 100
0 yards 100

N GORDON ST

N BRONSON AVE

HOLLYWOOD FREEWAY

GOWER GULCH

TAMARIND AVE

### Gower Gulch
*In the 1930s, Gower Street earned the name "Gower Gulch" because of all the extras in cowboy costumes. Today, the Gower Gulch strip mall sits on the southwest corner of Sunset and Gower. An actual chuck wagon (see left) remains as a reminder of that era.*

**Sunset Boulevard Theater**
*Showman Earl Carroll's Vanities Theater originally occupied this site at No. 6220 in the 1940s. It had the world's largest revolving stage, which held 60 dancers.*

**VISITORS' TIP**

*This section of Sunset Boulevard, east of Vine St, was run down and frequented by drug dealers and prostitutes for many years. The gentrification of Hollywood has made a positive impact, however, and visitors need only observe the rules for safety as in any large city. Lock your car, keep your wallet in an inconspicuous place, and don't wear valuable jewelry.*

# A View of Hollywood Boulevard

Hollywood Boulevard is one of the most famous streets in the world, and its name is still redolent with glamor. Visitors wishing to recapture a Golden Age of film should visit the Grauman's Chinese Theatre and its autograph patio, and stroll down the Walk of Fame to spot the stars of icons such as Marilyn Monroe. World premieres of Disney films at the El Capitan Theater often feature a live revue by the Magic Kingdom®'s favorite characters. Other attractions include Madame Tussaud's, the Hollywood Guinness World of Records Museum, Ripley's Believe It or Not!®, and the Kodak Theatre, home of the Academy Awards®.

**First National Bank detail**

**LOCATOR MAP**
*See Street Finder, map 2*

★ **Grauman's Chinese Theatre**
*Famous for stars' autographs* ❸

**The Kodak Theatre**, home to the Academy Awards®, has hosted a range of stars including Celine Dion and Princ

**HOLLYWOOD BOULEVARD NORTH SIDE** ▶▶▶▶▶▶▶▶▶▶▶▶▶▶▶▶▶▶▶▶▶▶▶▶▶▶▶▶▶▶▶▶▶▶▶

★ **Walk of Fame**
*Marilyn Monroe's star is embedded in the sidewalk at No. 6776 Hollywood Boulevard. The camera symbol below her name indicates her career as a film actress* ❻

MARILYN MONROE

**Hollywood Guinness World of Records Museum** uses models, videos, and special effects to bring record-breaking achievements alive. It is housed in the area's first movie theater.

**Ripley's Believe It or Not!®** is a museum devoted to the bizarre. The building, topped by a model *Tyrannosaurus rex*, contains more than 300 exhibits, such as shrunken heads and two-headed calves.

**HOLLYWOOD BOULEVARD SOUTH SIDE** ▶▶▶▶▶▶▶▶▶▶▶▶▶▶▶▶▶▶▶▶▶▶▶▶▶▶▶▶▶▶▶▶▶▶▶

For hotels and restaurants in this region see pp524–31 and pp568–76

**KEY**

▶▶▶▶▶▶ North Side walking east

◀◀◀◀◀◀ South Side walking west

**STAR SIGHTS**

★ Grauman's Chinese Theatre

★ Walk of Fame

**First National Bank** marks the junction with Highland Avenue. Its tiered façade is decorated with stone reliefs of historical figures such as Christopher Columbus and Nicolaus Copernicus.

**Hollywood and Highland** *is great for retail shops and entertainment* ❹

**Madame Tussaud's** has branches all over the world, and this site focuses on Hollywood stars. To create many of the figures, Tussaud's brought the celebrities in and measured them using computers, to make life-size, meticulously crafted wax figures, which are set up to make close-up viewing and photos easy.

meters 200

yards 200

**Hollywood Roosevelt Hotel**
*An image of the actor Charlie Chaplin (1889–1977) decorates the wall of this 1920s hotel* ❶

**El Capitan Theater**
*Neon lights welcome filmgoers to this beautifully restored Art Deco theater. Movies can be seen in old-fashioned comfort, but with state-of-the art sound* ❺

**The old Masonic Hall** is now a TV studio owned by Disney.

Sid Grauman's famous Chinese Theatre (now Grauman's)

# Hollywood Roosevelt Hotel ❶

7000 Hollywood Blvd. **Map** 2 B4.
**Tel** (323) 466-7000, (800) 950-7667.
🚫 see **Where to Stay** p527.
**www**.hollywoodroosevelt.com

Named after US president Theodore Roosevelt, this hotel was opened in 1927 by joint owners Louis B Mayer, Mary Pickford, Marcus Loewe, Douglas Fairbanks, Sr., and Joseph Schenk. Marilyn Monroe, Ernest Hemingway, and Clark Gable were all visitors and, on May 16, 1929, the first Academy Awards® banquet was held in the Roosevelt's Blossom Room.

Renovations in 1986 revealed a Spanish Colonial design. The following year the pool was decorated by David Hockney *(see p28)*. The Hollywood Historical Review exhibition, documents the area's history.

**Hollywood Roosevelt Hotel, locale for the first Academy Awards®**

# Madame Tussaud's Hollywood ❷

6933 Hollywood Blvd. **Map** 2 B4. **Tel** (213) 595-5505. 🕐 10am–8pm daily (last admission 7pm); May 25–Sep 7: 10am–10pm (last admission 9pm). 🚫 **www**.madametussauds.com

Madame Tussaud's Hollywood is the first of the nine Tussaud's to be built from the ground up. The three-story structure features wax figures of hot Hollywood icons and stars including Johnny Depp, Nicole Kidman, Denzel Washington, Clarke Gable, James Dean, and Audrey Hepburn. Sports figures, pop stars, and movie characters are also represented. Over 80 figures are displayed in 11 themed areas, including The Red Carpet, and visitors can touch the figures and take photos with them.

# Grauman's Chinese Theatre ❸

6925 Hollywood Blvd. **Map** 2 B4. **Tel** (323) 461-3331. 📧 (323) 464-8111. 🕐 daily. 🎬 🚫 **www**.chinesetheatres.com

One of the most famous sights in Hollywood has not changed much since it opened in 1927 with the gala premiere of Cecil B De Mille's *King of Kings*. The exterior is an ornate medley of Chinese temples, pagodas, lions, and dragons, reflecting the keen sense of showmanship of the theater's creator, Sid Grauman.

Grauman also thought up one of the longest-running publicity stunts in Hollywood history: inviting movie stars to impress their handprints, footprints, and autographs in the cement courtyard of his theater. There are many versions of how this custom began. One tells of silent screen star Norma Talmadge accidentally stepping in the wet cement at the gala opening *(see p53)*. Another is that the French stonemason, Jean Klossner, put his hand in the wet cement for posterity. Whatever the precedent, Sid Grauman liked the idea and invited Norma Talmadge, Mary Pickford, and Douglas Fairbanks, Sr. to legitimately leave their mark in the cement on May 17, 1927.

Anyone can visit the courtyard, but only filmgoers can see the extravagant interior.

# Hollywood and Highland ❹

6801 Hollywood Boulevard. **Map** 2 B4. **Tel** (323) 467 6412. 🕐 10am–10pm Mon–Sat, 10am–7pm Sun. 🅿 🚫 **www**.hollywoodandhighland.com

Opened after a major refurbishment of this once-neglected area, this shopping and entertainment complex features restaurants, clubs, retail shops, a hotel, and a cinema. Visitors can also see a play or concert and take a tour of the **Kodak Theatre**, the home of the Academy Awards® ceremonies.

## El Capitan Theater ❺

6838 Hollywood Blvd. **Map** 2 B4.
**Tel** (818) 845-3110. ◯ daily. 📷
www.elcapitan.go.com

Built in 1926 as a legitimate theater, El Capitan was later converted to a movie house. It was the venue for many premieres, such as Orson Welles's *Citizen Kane* (1941). In 1942 El Capitan was renamed the Hollywood Paramount and in 1991 it was bought by Disney and Pacific Theaters who restored the Art Deco interior. Today, Disney feature animations open here.

## Walk of Fame ❻

**Map** 2 B4. 🏛 *7018 Hollywood Blvd*
🎬 (323) 469-8311.
www.hollywoodchamber.net

The Walk of Fame is set with more than 2,000 polished marble stars. Since February 1960, celebrities from the worlds of film, radio, TV, theater, and music have been immortalized on Hollywood Boulevard and Vine Street. Each has to be sponsored and approved by the Chamber of Commerce, and pay a $25,000 installation fee. Among the most famous are Charlie Chaplin (No. 6751) and Alfred Hitchcock (No. 6506).

**Some of the marble stars on The Walk of Fame**

## Hollywood Museum ❼

1660 N Highland Ave. **Map** 2 B4.
**Tel** (323) 464-7776.
◯ 10am–5pm Wed–Sun. ♿
www.thehollywoodmuseum.com

This museum is housed in a restored 1930s Art Deco building, which was once make-up artist Max Factor's studios. Three floors display fabulous costumes worn in films by stars such as Marilyn Monroe, Judy Garland, Elizabeth Taylor, Humphrey Bogart, and Jodie Foster. The collectibles exhibition displays Sylvester Stallone's boxing gloves and W.C. Field's top hat among other oddities. The basement contains Hannibal Lecter's entire prison cell.

The museum offers two hour tours of The Magic Castle, a members-only magicians' club nearby (reservations required).

## Hollywood Bowl ❽

2301 N Highland Ave. **Map** 2 B3.
**Tel** (323) 850-2000. ◯ late Jun–late Sep. 📷 ♿ **Box office** ◯ 10am–6pm Tue–Sun. **Edmund D Edelman Hollywood Bowl Museum**
**Tel** (323) 850-2058. ◯ noon–6pm Tue–Sun. www.hollywoodbowl.com

Situated in a natural amphitheater, once revered by the Cahuenga Pass Gabrielino Indians, the Bowl is now sacred to Angelenos. Since 1922 it has been the summer home of the LA Philharmonic (*see p125*).

Thousands gather on warm evenings to picnic – often in high style – under the stars and listen to the orchestra. Jazz, country, folk, and pop concerts are also performed here while popular events include the Fourth of July concert with fireworks, the Easter Sunrise Service, and a Tchaikovsky Spectacular with cannons, fireworks, and a military band.

The shell-shaped stage was originally designed in 1929 by Lloyd Wright, son of architect Frank Lloyd Wright, and the Bowl and its privately-owned front-row boxes seat 18,000 people.

The Edmund D Edelman Hollywood Bowl Museum explores the rich history of the Bowl, through videos, old programs and posters, and memorabilia of the artists who have come here, from violinist Jascha Heifetz to The Beatles.

**Hollywood Bowl, nestling in the Hollywood Hills**

**Mausoleum of William A Clark, Jr. in Hollywood Forever Cemetery**

## Hollywood Heritage Museum ❾

2100 N Highland Ave. **Map** 2 B3.
***Tel*** *(323) 874-2276.* ◯ *noon–4pm Wed–Sun.* 🖼 ⬥ 🖾
**www**.hollywoodheritage.org

In 1913, Cecil B De Mille and the Jesse L Lasky Feature Play Company rented this barn, then located on Vine Street, just north of Sunset Boulevard. That year De Mille used the building to make *The Squaw Man*, the first feature-length movie produced in Hollywood. In 1935 the company was renamed Paramount Pictures.

The barn was moved to its present site, in the Hollywood Bowl parking lot *(see p111)*, in 1983. Thirteen years later a fire prompted a major renovation. Today the barn is a museum, displaying props, costumes, photographs, and other memorabilia from the early days of filmmaking.

## Pantages Theater ❿

6233 Hollywood Blvd. **Map** 2 C4.
***Tel*** *(323) 468-1770.* ◯ *daily.* 🖼 ⬥

To attend a show at the Pantages is to experience the glory days of the 1930s movie palaces. Built in 1929, the marble and bronze Art Deco

theater catered to the comfort of its audience, with a spacious foyer and luxurious lounges. It opened in 1930 with *The Floradora Girl*, starring Marion Davies, the mistress of WR Hearst *(see p214)*. Between 1949 and 1959 the Academy Awards Ceremony was also held here.

Splendidly renovated in the 1980s, today Pantages is used to stage Broadway musicals. Only show ticket holders are allowed into the breathtaking interior, with its magnificent chandeliers, vaulted ceilings, and columns decorated with geometric patterns.

**Elegant Art Deco façade of the Pantages Theater**

## Hollywood Forever Cemetery ⓫

6000 Santa Monica Blvd. **Map** 8 C1.
***Tel*** *(323) 469-1181.* ◯ *8am–5pm Mon–Fri; 8:30am–4:30pm Sat–Sun.* ⬤ *public hols.* ⬥
**www**.hollywoodforever.com

The map of this cemetery (available at the front office) reads like a history of film. Tyrone Power has a white memorial overlooking a pond on the eastern side. Next to him, the mausoleum of Marion Davies bears her family name of Douras. Cecil B De Mille, Nelson Eddy, and many others from Hollywood's heyday are buried here. Douglas Fairbanks Sr.'s grave has a reflecting pool and monument, reputed to have been paid for by his ex-wife, the silent film star Mary Pickford. Inside the gloomy Cathedral Mausoleum is the tomb of Rudolph Valentino, still the cemetery's biggest attraction. Every year, on August 23, a "Lady in Black" pays her respects to the actor on the anniversary of his death.

The back of Paramount Studios forms the southern wall of the cemetery, and Columbia used to be to the north. Columbia boss Harry Cohn is said to have picked his plot so that he could keep an eye on his studio.

*For hotels and restaurants in this region see pp524–31 and pp568–76*

# Paramount Studios ⑫

5555 Melrose Ave. **Map** 8 C1. *Tel (323) 956-5000.* **Visitors' Center and Ticket Window** 860 N Gower St. *Tel (323) 956-1777.* ☐ *for tours: 9am–6pm Mon–Fri (reservations only).* 🌐 *Jan 1, Easter Sun, Thanksgiving, Dec 25.* www.paramount.com

The last major studio still located in Hollywood, Paramount was also the first in operation. Cecil B. De Mille, Jesse Lasky, and Samuel Goldwyn joined forces with Adolph Zukor in 1914 to form what became known as the directors' studio. The roster of stars was equally impressive: Gloria Swanson, Rudolph Valentino, Mae West, Marlene Dietrich, Gary Cooper, and Bing Crosby all signed with Paramount.

Aspiring actors still hug the wrought-iron gates at Bronson Avenue and Marathon Street. Seeking luck, they quote Norma Desmond's final line in *Sunset Boulevard*: "I'm ready for my close-up, Mr. De Mille."

Classics such as *The Ten Commandments, The War of the Worlds, The Greatest Show on Earth,* and the *Godfather Parts I, II,* and *III* were all made in Paramount's 63 acres (25 ha) of backlot and sound stages. The studio closed to the public after September 11, 2001 but has now re-opened. A two-hour tour details its history and gives visitors a behind-the-scenes view of films and television shows currently in production *(see p175).*

## MELROSE AVENUE

Once a bland avenue, Melrose burst onto the Los Angeles street scene in the mid-1980s with quirky shops and good restaurants. The prime area stretches for 16 blocks between La Brea and Fairfax avenues, providing a rare opportunity to walk and shop outdoors in the city. From Fifties to punk to classic, the clothing, shoe, and accessory boutiques offer a wide range of styles and goods and stay open until late *(see pp176–7).* The same can also be said of the avenue's many restaurants, which represent the diverse ethnic flavors of Los Angeles. Mexican and Thai are two of the favorite cuisines, but pasta and pizza dominate the street, as they do the rest of the city.

At the western end of Melrose, at San Vincente Boulevard, is the huge 600-ft (183-m) high blue-glass Pacific Design Center, known to the locals as the Blue Whale. Designed by César Pelli in 1975, this showcase for interior designers and architects is the largest on the West Coast. Although it caters mainly to trade, the center also welcomes the general public. Admission charges and purchasing policies may vary between individual showrooms.

**Colorful shop window on Melrose Avenue**

# Farmers Market ⑬

6333 W 3rd St. **Map** 7 D3. *Tel (323) 933-9211.* ☐ *9am–9pm Mon–Fri, 9am–8pm Sat, 10am–7pm Sun.* 🌐 *Jan 1, Easter Sun, Memorial Day, Jul 4, Labor Day, Thanksgiving, Dec 25.* ♿ www.farmersmarketla.com

In 1934, during the Great Depression *(see p53),* a group of farmers began selling their produce directly to the public in a field then at the edge of town. Since then, Farmers Market has become a favorite meeting place for Angelenos and tourists. There are stalls

**Clock tower at entrance to Farmers Market**

selling fresh flowers, meats, cheeses, fruit, vegetables, breads and gourmet foods. There are also more than 100 shops that sell everything from antiques to T-shirts and garden supplies. Among the best of the numerous cafés and restaurants are Bob's Donuts, Magee's Kitchen for roast or corned beef, turkey, and ham platters; and The Gumbo Pot, with sweet *beignets* (dough fritters) and traditional Cajun food *(see p570).* Next to the market is The Grove, a deluxe retail complex with shops, restaurants and cinema.

**Poster for Paramount's** *The War of the Worlds* **(1953)**

# Los Angeles County Museum of Art ⓮

The largest art museum west of Chicago, the Los Angeles County Museum of Art (LACMA) has one of the finest collections of art in the country and boasts the stunning Broad Contemporary Art Museum, built to exhibit the comprehensive private collection of contemporary art donated by its billionaire founder and art connoisseur Eli Broad. The world-renowned architect Renzo Piano designed the building and has been supervising the overhaul of the entire museum campus, which consists of nine museum venues along Wilshire Boulevard from the La Brea Tar Pits in Hancock Park to Fairfax Avenue. Due to ongoing updating, specific works of art may change location.

★ **In the Woods at Giverny**
*This work of 1887, subtitled "Blanche Hoschedé at her easel with Suzanne Hoschedé reading," depicts the daughters of Monet's mistress.*

★ **Soap Bubbles** *(after 1739)*
*Parisian artist Jean-Baptiste-Siméon Chardin's work predominantly depicts small scenes of domestic life such as this.*

**The Hope Athena**
*This marble statue is a 2nd century AD Roman copy of the 5th century BC Greek original.*

### KEY

▢ Exhibition space

▢ Non-exhibition space

### STAR PAINTINGS

★ In the Woods at Giverny by Claude Monet

★ Soap Bubbles by Jean-Baptiste-Siméon Chardin

★ Mulholland Drive by David Hockney

Third level

Second level

Entranc

Plaza level

Lynda and Stewart Resnick Exhibition Pavilion

American Art

ENTRANCE PAVILION

Lower level

LACMA West

BROAD CONTEMPORARY ART MUSEUM BUILDING

## VISITORS' CHECKLIST

5905 Wilshire Blvd. **Map** 7 E4.
**Tel** (323) 857-6000. 20.
noon–8pm Mon, Tue, Thu
(until 9pm Fri), 11am–8pm Sat &
Sun. Wed, Thnksg., Dec 25.
(free 2nd Tue of month).
www.lacma.org

★ **Mulholland Drive: The Road
to the Studio** (1980)
*British artist David Hockney has made
his home in LA. This painting of one
of the city's most famous roads (see
p144) follows the route to his studio.*

**Japanese Plate**
*This 17th-century
glazed porcelain
plate forms part of
the museum's excep-
tional collection of
Japanese art.*

Second
level

Plaza
level

Entrance

**HAMMER
BUILDING**

Third
level

Second
level

Entrance

Plaza
level

**PAVILION FOR
JAPANESE ART**

Second
level

Plaza
level

Entrance

**BING
CENTER**

Plaza
level

Main entrance

**MODERN AND
CONTEMPORARY
ART BUILDING**

**AHMANSON
BUILDING**

## MUSEUM GUIDE

*European and modern works
of art are displayed in the
Ahmanson and Broad
buildings. The Art of the
Americas Building holds the
American and Latin American
collection. The Sculpture
Garden has bronzes by
Auguste Rodin. The Plaza
Café is located in the Bing
Center. LACMA West is
at the corner of Fairfax Ave.*

**MUSEUM PLAN**

- [ ] Ahmanson Building
- [ ] Art of the Americas
  Building
- [ ] Hammer Building
- [ ] Bing Center
- [ ] Pavilion for Japanese Art
- [ ] Broad Contemporary Art
  Museum Building
- [ ] Lynda and Stewart Resnick
  Exhibition Pavilion
- [ ] LACMA West

# Exploring LACMA

A tour of LACMA offers a comprehensive survey of the history of art throughout the world. The museum has more than 100,000 objects that represent many cultures, dating from prehistoric to modern and contemporary periods. Ancient art treasures encompass pre-Columbian finds as well as the largest Islamic art collection in the western United States. Decorative arts, which include European and American pieces from medieval times to the

**Standing Warrior**

present, are exhibited alongside paintings and sculpture from the same period. The museum also has a superb collection of costumes and textiles. A program of world-class traveling exhibitions complements the permanent collection.

**Magdalen with the Smoking Flame (c.1640) by Georges de la Tour**

## AMERICAN ART

The collection of paintings traces the history of American art from the 1700s to the 1940s. Dating from the Colonial period are John Singleton Copley's *Portrait of a Lady* (1771) and Benjamin West's *Cymon and Iphigenia* (1773).

In the mid-1800s American artists such as Edwin Church (1826–1900), Winslow Homer (1836–1910), and Thomas Moran (1837–1926) turned from portrait painting and Classical subjects to landscapes of the New World. Notable Impressionist works include Childe Hassam's *Avenue of the Allies* (1918), while among the European art is Jean-Baptiste-Siméon Chardin's *Soap Bubbles (see p114)*.

Decorative arts range from Chippendale and Federal-style furniture to lamps by Louis Comfort Tiffany (1848–1933).

**Monument to Balzac, sculpted in the 1890s by Auguste Rodin**

## EUROPEAN PAINTING, SCULPTURE, AND DECORATIVE ARTS

The collection of European works of art spans the 12th to early 20th centuries, beginning with medieval religious objects. Fine portraits by Lucas Cranach (1472–1553) and Hans Holbein (1497–1543) represent the Northern Renaissance.

Religious paintings by Fra Bartolommeo (1472–1517) and Titian (c.1490–1576) date from the Italian Renaissance.

One of the European collection's strengths is its 17th-century Dutch and Flemish canvases. Rembrandt's *The Raising of Lazarus* (c.1630) and Anthony Van Dyck's *Andromeda Chained to the Rock* (1637–8) are among the highlights. Works displayed from the French and Italian schools include Georges de la Tour's *Magdalen with the Smoking Flame,* painted around 1640, and Guido Reni's *Portrait of Cardinal Roberto Ubaldino,* which dates from before 1625. The French collections from the 18th and 19th centuries are also impressive, with works by Eugène Delacroix (1798–1863) and Camille Corot (1796–1875). The sculpture collection concentrates mostly on 19th-century French artists, with more than 40 works by Auguste Rodin (1840–1917).

Two highlights of the Impressionist and Post-Impressionist collection are *In the Woods at Giverny* by Claude Monet *(see p114)* and Edgar Degas' *The Bellelli Sisters* (1862–4). Others include paintings by Pierre Auguste Renoir (1841–1919), Vincent Van Gogh (1853–90), and Paul Cézanne (1839–1906).

Among the finest decorative arts pieces are a Venetian enameled and gilded blue glass ewer, dating from about 1500, and a mid-16th-century Limoges plaque that depicts Psyche and Cupid.

**The Cotton Pickers (1876) by Winslow Homer**

## MODERN AND CONTEMPORARY ART

The Broad Contemporary Art Museum on the LACMA campus is a bright, airy home for contemporary art displayed for its fullest impact, no matter what its size or shape. The building itself is a piece of art, funded by the Los Angeles philanthropist Eli Broad. It houses some 200 pieces from his own cutting-edge collection, plus LACMA's own growing assemblage of modern holdings, and visiting collections. Its span covers painting, sculpture, and constructions ranging from 1945 to the present. Works include Richard Serra's *Band* (2006), John Baldessari's *Wrong* (1966-68), and Roy Lichtenstein's *Cold Shoulder* (1963).

## PHOTOGRAPHY, PRINTS, AND DRAWINGS

The museum's outstanding photography holdings give a rare overview of the medium. Exhibits range from early 19th-century daguerreotypes and albumen prints to abstract mixed media images. A large group of works by Edward Weston (1886–1958) is filled with texture and sensuality.

LACMA's holdings of prints and drawings includes the Robert Gore Rifkind Collection of German Expressionist works. Erich Heckel's woodcut, *Standing Child* (1910), is just one of its outstanding prints.

## ANCIENT AND ISLAMIC ART

The ancient art of Egypt, western Asia, Iran, Greece, and Rome make up an impressive collection of artifacts. Items include massive carved stone panels from a 9th-century BC Assyrian palace; a rare Egyptian bronze from the 25th Dynasty; and delicate Iranian figures, some dating from 3,000 BC. The Islamic art collection spans almost 1,400 years. Its Iranian and Turkish holdings are particularly strong.

Carved stone objects and ceramic vessels and statues from Central America and Peru comprise the pre-Columbian holdings. *Standing Warrior* (100 BC–AD 300), a Mexican effigy, is the largest known work of its kind.

## INDIAN AND SOUTHEAST ASIAN ART

With more than 5,000 works dating from the 3rd century BC, the museum has one of the most comprehensive collections outside Asia. It is especially strong in Indian arts, from splendid sculpture to intricate watercolors on cloth and paper. There are manuscripts and *thankas* (paintings on cloth) from Tibet and Nepal, and stone and bronze sculptures from Indonesia, Thailand, Sri Lanka, Cambodia, and Myanmar (Burma).

**Pair of Officials (618–907),
from the Tang dynasty, China**

## FAR EASTERN ART

This section includes ceramics, sculpture, screens, and scrolls from China, Japan, and Korea. The highlight, however, is the Shin'enkan Collection which features 200 screens and scroll paintings from the Edo period (1615–1868). These examples are considered to be the most outstanding in the Western world. Masterpieces include Ito Jakuchu's 18th-century hanging scroll, *Rooster, Hen and Hydrangea*, and Suzuki Kiitsu's 19th-century *Seashells and Plums*. The Bushell Collection of *netsukes* (carved toggles used to secure a small container), ceramics, sculpture, and woodblock prints is also impressive.

## COSTUMES AND TEXTILES

An encyclopedia of clothing and textiles, the collection boasts some 55,000 artifacts that represent more than 300 of the world's cultures. The oldest pieces are embroidered Peruvian burial shrouds that date from 100 BC and an Egyptian Coptic tunic from the 5th century AD. One of the most important pieces is the early 16th-century Iranian "Ardebil" carpet, named after a shrine in northwest Iran for which it was commissioned. A French noblewoman's gown, made from silk, gold, and silver, is one of only two complete 17th-century dresses in the US.

*Dunes, Oceano* **(1936) by Edward Weston**

## Miracle Mile ⓯

Wilshire Blvd between La Brea &
Fairfax Aves. **Map** 7 D4. ℹ️ 685
*S Figueroa St (213) 689-8822; 6801
Hollywood Blvd (323) 467-6412.*
**www**.seemyla.com

In 1920, the developer A W
Ross bought 18 acres (7.2 ha)
of land along Wilshire Boulevard and built a shopping
district aimed at the wealthy
families living in nearby
Hancock Park. With its
Art Deco and Streamline
Moderne buildings, wide
sidewalks and streets built
for cars rather than carriages,
it earned the nickname
"Miracle Mile." The suburban
department stores were
designed with parking lots,
a convenience that attracted
hordes of shoppers from the
city. It was the start of LA's
decentralization.

Today, this stretch of
boulevard is a shadow of
its former self, dotted with
grocery stores catering to
various ethnic communities,
although it is still vibrant.

The western end of the
Miracle Mile has fared better,
however. Anchoring the
corner of Fairfax Avenue,
is the old May Company
department store building,
now LACMA West. With
several other major museums
besides LACMA *(see pp114–
17)* within a one mile radius,
the area has now become
known as Museum Row.

**Gold façade of the old May Company
building on Wilshire Boulevard**

**Round door Rolls Royce at the Petersen Automotive Museum**

## Petersen Automotive Museum ⓰

6060 Wilshire Blvd. **Map** 7 D4. *Tel
(323) 930-2277.* ⭕ 10am–6pm Tue–
Sun. ◑ Jan 1, Thanksgiving, Dec 25.
🖼️ 🅱️ 🈂️ 🖫 **www**.petersen.org

Dioramas and temporary
exhibitions illustrate the
evolution of the United States'
car culture *(see pp200–201)*.
On the first floor there are
highly detailed displays featuring cars such as the 1911
American Underslung "Stuck
in the Mud" and Earl Cooper's
1915 "White Squadron" Stutz
Racer. A 1922 Ford Model-T
is shown in a scene from a
Laurel and Hardy film, and a
trio of beautiful vintage cars
appear in a 1920s street setting.

Other displays include a
1920s garage; a 1930s car
showroom, whose opulence
defied the Depression; and a
1950s drive-in restaurant.
A 1930s billboard shows how
advertising was used to boost
the popularity of the car.

Upstairs, five galleries showcase everything from hot rods
and motorcycles to vintage
classics and cars of the stars.
Vehicles that fall into the last
category are Rita Hayworth's
1953 Cadillac and Clark Gable's
1941 Cadillac Coupe.

## The Improv ⓱

8162 Melrose Ave. **Map** 8 B2.
*Tel (323) 651-2583.* ⭕ 8pm
Mon–Thu, 8:30pm & 10:30pm Sat &
Sun. 🖼️ 🅱️ **www**.improv.com

When it opened in 1975, the
Improv immediately became
one of the finest comedy
clubs in town, and today it is
known throughout the world.
Famous names such as Jay
Leno, Richard Lewis, and
Damon Wayans appear
regularly, and Drew Carey

performs most Thursdays
with co-stars from the Drew
Carey Show. The club is also
a great place to see talented
newcomers, many of whom
have glittering careers ahead.

Food can be bought in the
showroom itself or in the
restaurant, Hell's Kitchen,
which specializes in Italian
food, and a minimum of two
drinks per head can be
ordered at the bar.

Given the club's popularity,
it is best to book a table a day
or two in advance.

**Popular comedian Drew Carey
performing at the Improv club**

## Page Museum at the La Brea Tar Pits ⓲

5801 Wilshire Blvd. **Map** 7 E4.
*Tel (323) 934-7243.*
⭕ 9:30am–5pm daily. ◑ Jan 1,
Jul 4, Thanksgiving, Dec 25.
🖼️ (free first Tue of month.) 🅱️ 🈂️
🖫 **www**.tarpits.org

Opened in 1976, the Page
Museum has a collection of
more than one million fossils
that were discovered at the
La Brea Tar Pits. These
include more than 500 types

## LA BREA TAR PITS

The tar in the La Brea Pits was formed some 42,000 years ago by oil rising to the earth's surface and gelling. Animals entering the pits to drink the water became stuck in the tar and died. Their bones were then fossilized.

For centuries the tar was used by Gabrielino Indians to waterproof baskets and boats. Later, Mexican and Spanish settlers tarred their roofs with it. In 1906 geologists discovered the largest collection of fossils from the Pleistocene Epoch ever found in one place, and the pits began to attract greater attention. The land was deeded to the county in 1916.

Models at the La Brea Tar Pits depicting how animals were trapped

of mammals, birds, reptiles, plants, and insects. Some of the pieces date back around 40,000 years. Among the highlights are mastodons, saber-toothed cats, American lions, and an imperial mammoth. The display of more than 400 wolf skulls shows just how much variation can occur within a single species.

The only human skeleton to have been found in the pits is that of "La Brea Woman." A hologram changes her from a skeleton to a fully fleshed person and back again.

Pit 91 has produced most of the fossils. During the summer, visitors on the viewing station can watch paleontologists at work. Inside the museum, a glass-walled laboratory allows observation of the cleaning and identification of the fossils.

Mammoth skeleton at the George C Page Museum

## Craft and Folk Art Museum ⓳

5814 Wilshire Blvd. **Map** 7 E4. *Tel* (323) 937-4230. ◯ 11am–5pm Tue–Fri, noon–4pm Sat & Sun. ◯ Jan 1, Thanksgiving, Dec 25. ▨ ▨ (Wed). ◻ www.cafam.org

The museum's collection has more than 3,000 folk art and craft objects from around the world, ranging from 19th-century American quilts to contemporary furniture, to African masks. There are also regular exhibitions on subjects such as toys, glassware, and textiles.

Mexican artworks here include papier-mâché pieces from the Linares family.

A series of exhibitions is held throughout the year, and every October the museum runs the International Festival of Masks in nearby Hancock Park.

African mask at the Craft Museum

## Wiltern Theater ⓴

3790 Wilshire Blvd. **Map** 9 D4. *Tel* (213) 380-5005. ◯ performances only. ▨ ▨ ▨

Built as a movie theater in 1931, the Wiltern Theater was restored in 1985 and is a center for the performing arts. Its Art Deco tower and wings are faced with turquoise-glazed terra-cotta, and its main entrance is marked by a sun-burst canopy. The sun motif continues in the auditorium, where rays of low-relief skyscrapers decorate the interior ceiling.

To see inside the Wiltern Theater visitors must buy a ticket to a show.

# DOWNTOWN LOS ANGELES

Considered a backwater a little over a hundred years ago, Los Angeles has confounded its critics by becoming a powerful worldwide influence. The city's Spanish roots are here, at El Pueblo, where the Avila Adobe and Old Plaza Church stand as reminders of Mexican frontier days, when *rancheros* and their *señoras* strolled through the streets. To the north of El Pueblo is Chinatown, with its numerous Asian shops and restaurants. To the south, Little

**Detail from the Fine Arts Building on West 7th Street**

Tokyo is the heart of the largest Japanese-American community in North America. Downtown's business district is centered around Bunker Hill, once a wealthy neighborhood where the city's Victorian elite lived. Today, office towers such as the First Interstate World Center and the Wells Fargo Center dominate the Downtown landscape. The district is also home to the Museum of Contemporary Art (MOCA) and the Music Center for the performing arts.

## SIGHTS AT A GLANCE

**Historic Districts and Buildings**
Angels Flight ❷
Bradbury Building ❹
Chinatown ❽
El Pueblo pp126–7 ❼
Grand Central Market ❸
Little Tokyo ⓬
Los Angeles Central Library ❶
Los Angeles City Hall ⓫
Union Station ❾

**Museums and Galleries**
Geffen Contemporary at MOCA ❿
Japanese American National Museum ⓭
Fashion Institute of Design and Merchandising ⓮
Museum of Contemporary Art ❺

**Arts Complex**
Music Center ❻

**Churches**
Cathedral of Our Lady of the Angels ⓯

**GETTING THERE**
The Metro stops at 7th Street/Metro Center, Pershing Square, Civic Center, and Union Station. The Metro Blue Line runs between Long Beach and 7th Street/Metro Center. DASH buses also serve the district.

0 meters 500
0 yards 500

**KEY**
Street-by-Street map See pp122–3
Street-by-Street map See pp126–7
Amtrak station
Metro station

◁ **Wells Fargo Center, slicing the Downtown skyline**

# Street-by-Street: Business District

The 20th century saw LA expand west toward the ocean, temporarily relegating Downtown to a minor role in the city. All that has changed. Today a revitalized business district has developed around Flower Street, and the sidewalks are once more filled with tourists and Angelenos alike. California's banking industry has its headquarters here, housed in striking skyscrapers such as the Wells Fargo Center. The revival has continued eastward across Downtown, where the jewelry, toy, food, and garment wholesale industries are flourishing. A commitment to the arts has also borne fruit. The Museum of Contemporary Art (MOCA), Music Center, and Los Angeles Central Library have together encouraged a thriving cultural environment that has drawn people back to the city's center.

**The Westin Bonaventure Hotel** has external elevators with views of the business district.

**The First Interstate World Center**, a 73-story office block designed by I M Pei, opened in 1989. At 1,017 ft (310 m) it is the tallest building in LA.

**Fine Arts Building**

**7th Street/ Metro Center**

0 meters 500
0 yards 500

★ **Los Angeles Central Library**
*The beautiful Beaux-Arts library is decorated with carvings and inscriptions based on the theme "the Light of Learning"* ❶

**The Oviatt Building** (1925) is a marvelous example of Art Deco styling. René Lalique made some of the glass.

**The Millennium Biltmore Hotel** was one of LA's most luxurious hotels when it opened in 1923 (see p526).

**★ Museum of Contemporary Art**
*Located off California Plaza, MOCA's sandstone building was greeted with acclaim when it opened in 1986. The collection gives an exciting overview of post-1940 art* ❺

**LOCATOR MAP**
*See Street Finder, map 11*

**The Wells Fargo Center**, the LA branch of this California company *(see p314)*, has a museum and sculpture court, with works by artists such as Jean Dubuffet.

**Angels Flight**
*The funicular runs from South Hill Street to California Plaza* ❷

**Pershing Square Metro station**

**★ Bradbury Building**
*The atrium of this unassuming Victorian office block is one of the finest of its kind in the US* ❹

**Grand Central Market**
*This indoor market lies at the heart of the old theater district* ❸

**Pershing Square** was designated the city's first public park in 1866. The now-concreted square is still a popular meeting place and has been landscaped with trees, benches, and statuary.

**KEY**

- - - Suggested route

**STAR SIGHTS**

★ Bradbury Building

★ Los Angeles
   Central Library

★ Museum of
   Contemporary Art

Façade of the Los Angeles Central Library

# Los Angeles Central Library **❶**

630 W 5th St. **Map** 11 D4.
**Tel** (213) 228-7000. ◯ 10am–8pm
Tue & Thu, 10am–5:30pm Wed,
Fri & Sat. ◉ public hols. ♿
www.lapl.org

Built in 1926, this civic
treasure was struck by an
arson attack in 1986. It was
closed for seven years while
a $213.9 million renovation
program was carried out.
Sympathetic to the
original architecture, the
improvements have
doubled the library's
capacity to more than
2.1 million books.
The original building
combines Beaux-Arts
grandeur with Byzan-
tine, Egyptian, and
Roman architectural
elements, inscriptions,
and sculpture on the
theme "the Light of
Learning." The murals
in the rotunda, painted
by Dean Cornwell
(1892–1960), depict the
history of California and
are well worth seeing.
The attention given to detail
in the Tom Bradley wing is
impressive. One example is
the three atrium chandeliers,
created by Therman Statom to
represent the natural, ethereal,
and technological worlds.
The Central Library's garden
is situated by the Flower Street
entrance. Weary sightseers
will appreciate its fountains,
sculptures, shaded benches,
and restaurant.

**Statue on the library wall**

A varied program of arts
events takes place within the
library, including prose and
poetry readings, lectures,
concerts, and plays.

# Angels Flight **❷**

Between Grand, Hill, 3rd & 4th Sts.
**Map** 11 D4. **Tel** (213) 626-1901.

Billed as the "shortest railway
in the world," Angels Flight
transported riders the 315 ft
(96 m) between Hill Street
and Bunker Hill for almost
70 years. Built in 1901, the
funicular quickly became
a familiar and much-loved
method of travel. But, by
1969, Bunker Hill had
sadly degenerated and
was considered an eye-
sore. The city dismantled
Angels Flight, but
promised to reinstall the
funicular once the area
had been redeveloped.
It reopened in 1996 but
was closed again after
an accident. A volunteer
group is now working
to repair and re-open
the funicular.

# Grand Central Market **❸**

317 S Broadway. **Map** 11 E4.
**Tel** (213) 624-2378. ◯ 9am–6pm
daily. ◉ Jan 1, Thanksgiving, Dec 25.
♿ www.grandcentralsquare.com

Angelenos have been coming
to this vibrant indoor bazaar
since 1917. Today, more than
40 stallholders operate inside
the marketplace. Neatly
arranged mounds of bargain-
priced fresh fruits and
vegetables line the many
produce stands, and friendly
stallholders frequently offer
free samples of fruit.
Almost all the signs are in
English and Spanish. The
market's predominantly Latin-
American clientele come here
to buy exotic products from
their home countries, such as
fresh Nogales cacti and beans
from El Salvador. The seafood
stands are filled with an array
of fish caught in the waters
off Southern California. Goat
heads and tripe are offered
alongside the more familiar
cuts of meat at the butcher
stalls. Herb stands offer a range
of homeopathic alternatives for
minor ills. Amid all this bustle,
fragrant aromas of powdered
chilies, herbs, and spicy foods
waft through the air.
Among the many cafés and
food stands in the market is
China Café, which has been
serving its popular chow mein
since the 1930s. Visitors can
enjoy watching a rickety
assembly-line machine turn
*masa* (corn flour dough)
into tortillas and then partake
of the free samples on the
counter. Mexican stalls, such
as Ana Maria, sell tacos and
burritos, which are filled with
all kinds of meat and seafood.
Venturing from the market
onto Broadway, you will find
yourself on the main
shopping street of Los
Angeles' Hispanic community.
Before World War II, this was
the movie district, with
extravagant theaters and
fashionable shops. Today,
most of the theaters have
either closed down or are
being used for religious
meetings conducted in
Spanish. The street has a
great deal of energy – the feel
is that of Mexico City or Lima,
Peru – but tourists should be
wary of pickpockets.

China Café in the market

**Atrium of the Bradbury Building**

## Bradbury Building ❹

304 S Broadway. **Map** 11 E4. **Tel** (213) 626-1893. ☐ 9am–6pm Mon–Fri, 9am–5pm Sat & Sun. ♿ from 3rd St.

The Bradbury Building was designed by architectural draftsman George Herbert Wyman in 1893. It is one of the few surviving Victorian structures in LA. Although the red façade is simple, the atrium is outstanding, with its lace-work of wrought-iron railings, oak paneling, glazed brick walls, two open-cage elevators, and a glass roof. It is the only office building in LA to be designated a National Historic Landmark. Visitors may get a feeling of *déjà vu* – the building is a popular film location, with Ridley Scott's *Blade Runner* (1982) just one of the movies shot here.

## Museum of Contemporary Art ❺

250 S Grand Ave. **Map** 11 D4. **Tel** (213) 621-2766. ☐ 11am–5pm Mon & Fri (to 8pm Thu), 11am–6pm Sat & Sun. ☐ Jan 1, Jul 4, Thanksgiving, Dec 25. ☒ (free 5–8pm Thu.) ♿ www.moca.org

Rated by the American Institute of Architects as one of the best works of architecture in the US, this museum's building is as

interesting as its collection. It is an intriguing combination of pyramids, cylinders, and cubes, designed in 1986 by Japanese architect Arata Isozaki. Its warm native sandstone walls, which sit on a red granite foundation, are in pleasing contrast to the cool tones of the district's surrounding skyscrapers.

The gallery area lies off the sunken entrance courtyard and is reached via a sweeping staircase. Four of the seven galleries are naturally lit from pyramid-shaped skylights that punctuate the roofline.

Founded in 1979, the Museum of Contemporary Art has quickly amassed a respected selection of post-1940 work from artists such as Piet Mondrian, Jackson Pollock, Louise Nevelson, and Julian Schnabel. Added weight is given by the Panza Collection of 80 works of Pop Art and Abstract Expressionism by artists such as Robert Rauschen-berg, Mark Rothko, and Claes Oldenburg.

In 1995, MOCA acquired the 2,100-print Freidus Collection of photographs, which traces the development of documentary photography in the United States from the 1940s through the 1980s. The collection includes works by Diane Arbus and Robert Frank.

MOCA stands at the northern end of the 11-acre (4.5-ha)

*Coca-Cola Plan (1958) by Robert Rauschenberg*

California Plaza. This vast development funded the creation of MOCA, donating 1.5 percent of its budget, as stipulated by LA law, to public art. The spectacular fountain at the center of the plaza repeats its synchronized program every 20 minutes. The finale drops a 10,000-gal (45,500-litre) wave that washes over the fountain edge.

## Music Center ❻

135 N Grand Ave. **Map** 11 E3. **Tel** (213) 972-7211. ☒ ♿ **Dorothy Chandler Pavilion box office** ☐ 10am–6pm Thu–Sat. **Mark Taper Forum & Ahmanson Theater box offices** ☐ noon–8pm Tue–Sat, 11am–7pm Sun. **Walt Disney Concert Hall box office** ☐ noon–5pm Tue–Sun. www.musiccenter.org

This complex is one of the three largest performing arts venues in the US. The Walt Disney Concert Hall, designed by architect Frank Gehry, opened in 2003. This striking 2,265-seat venue is the home of the Los Angeles Philharmonic Master Chorale. The Dorothy Chandler Pavilion is the venue for the LA Music Center Opera, LA Master Chorale, and LA Philharmonic. The Ahmanson Theater stages Broadway plays, while the intimate Mark Taper Forum presents first-class plays.

**The Walt Disney Concert Hall designed by architect Frank Gehry**

# Street-by-Street: El Pueblo **⑦**

Statue of LA's founder, Felipe de Neve

El Pueblo de la Reina de Los Angeles, the oldest part of the city, was founded in 1781 by Felipe de Neve, the Spanish governor of California. Today, El Pueblo is a State Historic Monument. The shops along Olvera Street sell colorful Mexican dresses, leather *huaraches* (sandals), *piñatas* (clay or paper-mâché animals), and snacks like *churros*, a Spanish-Mexican fried bread. During its festivals El Pueblo is ablaze with color and sound. The Blessing of the Animals, *Cinco de Mayo* (May 5), the Mexican Independence Day fiesta (September 13–15), and the candlelight procession of *Las Posadas* (December 16–24) are celebrated with passion *(see pp36–9)*.

★ **Our Lady Queen of the Angels Church**
The Annunciation *(1981)*, a mosaic by Isabel Piczek, is on the city's oldest church's façade

**Pico House**
*California's last Mexican governor, Pío Pico, constructed the three-story Pico House in 1870. The colonial-style building was for many years the area's finest hotel.*

**Site of the** first cemetery in Los Angeles.

NORTH MAL

**Plaza**
*A wrought-iron bandstand is set in the middle of the plaza. Nearby is a list of the first 44 settlers and a statue of Felipe de Neve.*

ARCADIA STREET

NORTH LOS ANGELES

**Firehouse**

---

**STAR SIGHTS**

★ Avila Adobe

★ Our Lady Church

**KEY**

– – – Suggested route

LOCATOR MAP
See Street Finder, map 11

**David Alfaro Siqueiros'** mural, *Tropical America*, was created in 1932.

**Sepulveda House**

◄ **Avila Adobe**
*The Avila Adobe is the oldest existing house in Los Angeles. It is furnished as it would have been in the late 1840s.*

**Plaza Methodist Church**

| 0 meters | 50 |
| 0 yards | 50 |

**Olvera Street**
*This pedestrian street was preserved in the 1930s as a Mexican market-place following a campaign by local civic leader Christine Sterling.*

# Chinatown ❽

**Map** 11 F2. ⓘ 727 N Broadway, Suite 208 (213 680-0243).
**www**.chinatownla.com

The Chinese first came to California during the Gold Rush *(see pp48–9)* to work in the mines and build the railroads. Confronted by prejudice, they developed tightknit communities. LA's first Chinatown was established in 1870 on the present-day site of Union Station *(see p128)*. It was relocated about 900 yds (820 m) northward in 1938. Today it is the home of over 12,000 people, who live and work in this colorful district.

The ornate East Gate on North Broadway leads into Gin Ling Way and the New Chinatown Central Plaza. This pedestrian precinct is lined with brightly painted buildings that have exaggerated pagoda-style roofs. Here, import shops sell everything from exquisite jade jewelry and antiques to inexpensive trinkets.

In the surrounding streets, the buildings are more bland, but tantalizing restaurants offer all manner of Chinese food, from dim sum (filled, steamed, or grilled dumplings, *see p564*) to spicy Szechuan dishes.

Although on a smaller scale than the celebrations in San Francisco *(see p39)*, LA has its own Chinese New Year Parade in early February. The festivities include dragon and lion dancers, who are accompanied by drums, cymbals, floats, and firecrackers.

**Restaurant in Chinatown, topped by a pagoda**

Unique blending of architectural styles on Union Station's façade

## Union Station ❾

800 N Alameda St. **Map** 11 F3.
**Tel** (800) 872-7245. ⬭ 24 hours
daily. ♿ **www**.amtrak.com

Dating from 1939, this grand
railroad passenger terminal was
the last of its kind to be built in
the United States. The exterior
is a successful merging of
Spanish Mission, Moorish,
and Streamline Moderne styles
(see pp30–33). The tiles edging
the interior walls, the inlaid
marble designs of the floors,
and the filigree work over the
windows and doorways all
use Spanish motifs.

The vast concourse, with its
52-ft (15.8-m) high roof, will
be familiar to any fan of 1940s
films – stars were frequently
photographed here arriving in
Los Angeles. In recent years it

has been the location for several movies, including Sydney
Pollack's *The Way We Were*
(1973) and Barry Levinson's
*Bugsy* (1991). Today the station
is quieter, but there are still
daily departures to Chicago,
Seattle, and San Diego.

## Geffen Contemporary at MOCA ❿

152 N Central Ave. **Map** 11 F4.
**Tel** (213) 426-6222. ⬭ 11am–5pm
Mon & Fri, 11am–8pm Thu, 11am–
6pm Sat & Sun. ⬤ Tue–Wed, Jan 1,
Jul 4, Thanksgiving, Dec 25. 🎟 (free
5–8pm Thu). ♿ 🏛 **www**.moca.org

In 1983, this old police garage
was used as a temporary
exhibition space until MOCA's
California Plaza facilities were

completed (see p125). Frank
Gehry's renovations were so
successful that the warehouse
became a permanent fixture.
Exhibitions often include highlights from MOCA's collection.

## Los Angeles City Hall ⓫

200 N Spring St. **Map** 11 E4. **Tel** (213)
485-2121. ⬭ 8am–5pm Mon–Fri.
⬤ public hols. ♿ from Main St. 🏛
advance booking; call (213) 978-1995.

Until 1957, this 28-story
structure was the tallest in
Downtown – all others were
limited to 12 floors. When it
was built in 1928, sand from
every California county and
water from each of the state's
21 missions was added to the
City Hall's mortar.

Today City Hall is dwarfed
by surrounding skyscrapers,
but its distinctive tower is still
one of Los Angeles's most
familiar landmarks. Among
its many film and television
roles it has been the location
for the *Daily Planet*, Clark
Kent's place of work in the
television series *Superman*.

Inside, the rotunda has a
beautiful inlaid-tile dome
and excellent acoustics.
The dome is decorated with
eight figures showing the
building's major concerns:
education, health, law, art,
service, government,
protection, and trust.

Onizuka Street in Little Tokyo, looking toward Los Angeles City Hall

*For hotels and restaurants in this region see pp524–31 and pp568–76*

Organized groups who take the 45-minute tour of the City Hall can ascend to an observation area in the tower, which has been restored after damage by the 1994 Northridge earthquake *(see p57)*. From here there are panoramic views across the city.

**Rotunda of LA City Hall**

## Little Tokyo ⓬

**Map** 11 E4. 🛈 *244 S San Pedro St. (213 628-2725).* **www**.visitlittletokyo.com

Lying between First, Third, Los Angeles, and Alameda streets, the bustling area of Little Tokyo has more than 200,000 visitors who throng its Japanese markets, shops, restaurants, and temples.

The first Japanese settled here in 1884. Today, the heart of the area is the Japanese American Cultural and Community Center at No. 244 South San Pedro Street, from which cultural activities and festivals such as Nisei Week *(see p37)* are organized. The center's fan-shaped Japan America Theater is often a venue for performers from Japan, such as the Grand Kabuki.

The Japanese Village Plaza at No. 335 East Second Street has been built in the style of a rural Japanese village, with blue roof tiles, exposed wood frames, and paths landscaped with pools and rocks. A traditional fire watchtower marks the plaza's First Street entrance. Stores include Enbun Market, one of Little Tokyo's oldest businesses, and the Mikawaya Candy Store. Off San Pedro Street, Onizuka Street offers more upscale shops.

## Japanese American National Museum ⓭

369 E 1st St. **Map** 11 F4. **Tel** *(213) 625-0414.* 🕐 *11am–5pm Tue, Wed & Fri–Sun, noon–8pm Thu.* 🔴 *Jan 1, Thanksgiving, Dec 25.* 📷 ♿ 📷 **www**.janm.org

The former Nishi Hongwanji Buddhist Temple is now a museum. In 1925, architect Edgar Cline designed a building with a dual personality. The First Street entrance has an unremarkable brick façade, but the ceremonial entrance, on Central Avenue, mixes oriental and Egyptian motifs.

The museum is committed to preserving the history of Japanese-Americans in the US and has the largest collection of Japanese-American memorabilia in the world. Past exhibitions have covered the "Issei Pioneers," "America's Concentration Camps," and "Japanese-American Soldiers." Workshops are also offered.

## Fashion Institute of Design and Merchandising ⓮

919 South Grand Avenue. **Map** 10 C5. **Tel** *(800) 424-1200, (213) 624-2001.* 🕐 *10am–4pm Mon–Sat.* ♿ 📷 *12:15pm Mon–Fri.* **www**.fidm.edu

The Fashion Institute of Design and Merchandising pays homage to the fashion, graphics, interior design, and entertainment industries. Ranging from the late 18th century to the present day, there are some 12,000 pieces

**Central Avenue entrance to the Japanese American Museum**

in the collection, from ready-to-wear garments to couture, film and theater costumes, bold textiles, ethnic fabrics, and accessories. World-renowned designers such as Commes des Garçons, Christian Dior, Issey Miyake, and Yves Saint Laurent are represented here. Many garments were worn by famous people, including Marlene Dietrich, Fred Astaire, and Carole Lombard.

## Cathedral of Our Lady of the Angels ⓯

555 W Temple St. **Map** 11 E3. **Tel** *(213) 680-5200.* 🕐 *early morning–6pm daily.*

LA's Catholic cathedral, dedicated in 2002, has drawn kudos and criticism ever since it opened. Designed by Spanish architect José Rafael Moneo, its contemporary design is loved by some, yet scorned by others for its lack of stained glass and a steeple.

**Costume display at the Fashion Institute of Design and Merchandising**

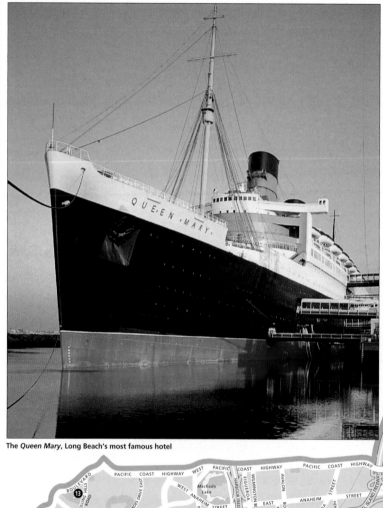

The *Queen Mary*, Long Beach's most famous hotel

# LONG BEACH AND PALOS VERDES

**Statue in Ports O'Call Marketplace**

The ocean is the unifying force of this disparate region, where waves crash against the cliffs of the Palos Verdes Peninsula and tankers head for the busy ports of Los Angeles and Long Beach. The peninsula, a magnificent stretch of coastline, is an affluent area, with mansions and stables set amid the rolling hills. On its southeastern side, working-class San Pedro is home to the Port of Los Angeles as well as generations of fishermen. The big city in the area – the fifth-largest in the state – is Long Beach. Aptly named for its 5.5-mile (9-km) expanse of white sand, this community has long attracted those who love the ocean. Its most famous landmark is the ocean liner *Queen Mary*.

## SIGHTS AT A GLANCE

**Historic Ships**
*Queen Mary pp134–5* ❻

**Districts**
Long Beach ❶
Naples ❹
Ports O'Call Marketplace ❽
San Pedro ⓫

**Historic Buildings**
Rancho Los Alamitos ❸
Rancho Los Cerritos ❷

**Modern Architecture**
Wayfarers Chapel ⓬

**Parks and Gardens**
Point Fermin Park ❿
South Coast Botanic Garden ⓭

**Museums**
Aquarium of the Pacific ❺
Cabrillo Marine Aquarium ❾
Los Angeles Maritime Museum ❼

**GETTING THERE**
The Metro Blue Line connects Long Beach to downtown Los Angeles. The busy port is well served by freeways that link it to the rest of the city. A free shuttle bus, the Runabout, makes frequent trips between downtown Long Beach, Shoreline Village, the *Queen Mary*, and the Catalina Island terminal *(see pp242–3)*. Cyclists can take the Oceanside Bike Path *(see p178)* from Long Beach to Naples.

### KEY

Street-by-Street map
*See pp132–3*

Ⓜ Metro station

0 kilometers    2

0 miles    2

# Street-by-Street: Long Beach ●

**Shoreline Village sign**

With palm trees and the ocean as a backdrop, downtown Long Beach is a mixture of carefully restored buildings and modern glass high-rises. At its heart, Pine Avenue still retains the early mid-western charm that gave the city its nickname of "Iowa by the Sea." The trendy atmosphere attracts locals, who come to relax, enjoy a cup of espresso, and sample some of the best food in the area. Nearby, Long Beach Convention and Entertainment Center was once the site of the Pike Amusement Park, famous for its roller coaster. Now the Terrace Theater's respected music and dance programs draw the crowds. Along the ocean, the shops and restaurants in Shoreline Village offer views of the *Queen Mary*.

**Farmers and Merchants Bank Tower**
*When erected in 1922, this terra-cotta building was Long Beach's first skyscraper. Its hall is a fine example of period styling.*

**Transit Mall Metro station**

**Long Beach Municipal Auditorium Mural**
*This 1938 mural of a day at the beach was originally housed in the Municipal Auditorium. It was moved in 1979 when that building was demolished to make way for the Terrace Theater.*

**The Promenade** is the site of Long Beach's farmer's market. Every Friday the street is filled with stands selling fruit, vegetables, and crafts.

**The 1929 Mediterranean-style** Ocean Center Building was the start of the Pike Amusement Park's Walk of a Thousand Lights.

**KEY**

– – – Suggested route

**STAR SIGHTS**

★ Pine Avenue

★ Shoreline Village

**★ Pine Avenue**
*The center of down-town Long Beach, Pine Avenue is lined with stores, cafés, and restaurants. Some of these businesses are housed in historic buildings, such as the 1903 Masonic Temple at No. 230.*

AROUND DOWNTOWN

LONG BEACH AND
PALOS VERDES

**LOCATOR MAP**

**1st Street Metro station**

**Convention and Entertainment Center**
*This newly expanded complex includes the Terrace Theater, the home of Long Beach's symphony orchestra and opera company.*

**The Breakers** (1925), an elegant former hotel, now houses senior citizens.

**Planet Ocean** (1992)
*Recognized as the world's largest mural, artist Wyland's Planet Ocean covers the 116,000-sq-ft (11,000-sq-m) surface of Long Beach Arena with life-size sea creatures.*

**The Hyatt Regency Hotel** adjoins the Convention Center (see p528).

**★ Shoreline Village**
*This waterfront complex of restaurants and shops boasts a 1906 Looff merry-go-round. Shoreline Village is a good place to view the Queen Mary (see pp134–5).*

**The tall ship Californian** is docked at Shoreline Village. Both short and long cruises are available.

| 0 meters | | 200 |
|---|---|---|
| 0 yards | | 200 |

# Rancho Los Cerritos ❷

4600 Virginia Rd. **Tel** (562) 570-1755.
⬜ 1–5pm Wed–Sun. ⬤ Jan 1,
Easter Sun, Thanksgiving, Dec 25. ♿
📷 1pm, 2pm, 3pm, 4pm Sat & Sun
only. **www.**rancholoscerritos.org

Rancho Los Cerritos was once part of a 300,000-acre (121,400-ha) land grant, given between 1784 and 1790 to Spanish soldier Manuel Nieto. Mission San Gabriel reclaimed nearly half of the property, and the rest was left to Nieto's children on his death in 1804.

In 1844 John Temple bought the ranch, built the adobe house, and later sold up to the firm Flint, Bixby & Co. The ranch was gradually sold off, but in 1955 the City of Long Beach bought the house and its 5 acres (2 ha). Today, it is a museum, focusing on those who lived here from 1840 to 1940. The Monterey-style house (see p30) is furnished to reflect the late 1870s.

# Rancho Los Alamitos ❸

6400 Bixby Hill Rd. **Tel** (562) 431-3541. ⬜ 1–5pm Wed–Sun.
⬤ Jan 1, Easter Sun, Thanksgiving, Dec 25. **Donation**. ♿ 📷
**www.**ranchoslosalamitos.com

Rancho Los Alamitos stands on a mesa inhabited since AD 500. In 1790 it formed part of the Manuel Nieto land grant. The house was built in 1806 and changed hands frequently until it was bought by the Bixby family in 1881. In 1968 the ranch was given to the

**Cactus Garden on the grounds of Rancho Los Alamitos**

City of Long Beach, and today the house is furnished as it was in the 1920s and 1930s. The grounds are a rare example of a pioneer garden.

# Queen Mary ❻

Pier J, 1126 Queens Hwy. **Road map** inset A. **Tel** (800) 437-2934, (562) 435-3511. ⬜ 10am–5pm daily. 📷 ♿ 📷 see **Where to Stay** p528 and **Where to Eat** p571. **www.**queenmary.com

Named after the wife of British King George V, this liner set new standards in ocean travel with its maiden voyage of May 27, 1936. The jewel in the crown of the Cunard White Star Line, the Queen Mary sailed weekly from Southampton, England to New York City. Although the second- and third-class quarters may look small next

**Royal Jubilee Week, 1935 by AR Thomson, above the bar in the Observation Lounge**

to the grandeur of the first-class rooms, they were considered chic and spacious for their time. On its five-day trips, the liner carried an average of 3,000 passengers and crew. There were two swimming pools, two chapels, a synagogue, gym, ballroom, and children's playrooms. Anyone who was anyone sailed on the Queen Mary, from royalty to Hollywood stars.

From 1939 to 1946, the liner was converted into a troopship

Sir Winston's Restaurant

Wedding Chapel

Sir Winston's Piano Bar

Royal Salon

Queen's Salon

Chelsea Restaurant

Britannia Salon

Verandah Grill

Grand Salon

## Naples ❹

**Road map** inset A. Long Beach.
One World Trade Center, Suite 300
(562 436-3645). **Gondola Getaway**
5437 E Ocean Blvd (562 433-9595).
www.visitlongbeach.com

In 1903, developer Arthur
Parson began creating his own
version of the city of Naples
in Italy, complete with winding
streets and waterways (even
though the real Naples does
not have canals and gondolas).

Taking heed of the mistakes
made by Abbot Kinney in
Venice (see p80), Parson
designed his canals so that
the Pacific Ocean's tidal flows
would keep them clean.

Finished in the late 1920s,
this charming Long Beach
neighborhood is actually
three islands in the middle
of Alamitos Bay. An eclectic
architectural mix
of shingled
Mission Revival,
Victorian, and Arts
and Crafts houses
(see pp30–33) line
the Italian-named
streets. The Rivo
Alto Canal is the
largest in the
network and you
can book a cruise
on an authentic
Venetian gondola.

Canal in residential Naples, with boats moored
alongside the private jetties

## Aquarium of the Pacific ❺

100 Aquarium Way, Long Beach.
**Road map** inset A. **Tel** (562) 590-
3100. 9am–6pm daily. Grand
Prix weekend at Long Beach, Dec 25.
combined ticket packages available
(see website for details).
www.aquariumofpacific.org

Learn about the inhabitants
and ecosystems of the Pacific
Ocean in this, one of the
largest aquariums in the US.
Over 500 species fill 19 major
habitats and 32 exhibits which
guide visitors on a journey
through the Pacific's three
regions: Southern California,
the Tropical Pacific, and the
Northern Pacific.

called the *Grey Ghost*, carrying
more than 800,000 soldiers
during its wartime career. At
the end of the war, it
transported more
than 22,000 war
brides and children
to the US during
"Operation
Diaper."

In 1967, after
1,001 transatlantic
crossings, the liner
was bought by the
City of Long Beach. It was
permanently docked for use as
a hotel and tourist attraction.

Detail inside the ship's
**Grand Salon**

Today, visitors can view part of
the original Engine
Room, examples of
the different travel
accommodations,
and an exhibition
on the war years.
Many of the original
Art Deco features,
created by more
than 30 artists,
still decorate the
interior. Open to
the public for
dining, the Grand Salon and
Observation Lounge are fine
examples of period styling.

Dual set of brass steering wheels in
the *Queen Mary*'s wheelhouse

Crow's Nest
**W6R0 Amateur Radio Station**
**Bridge Wheelhouse**
Officers' Quarters
QUEEN MARY
**Promenade Café and Bar**
**Piccadilly Circus**
Observation Lounge

**Relaxing on Redondo Beach, LA** (see p66) ▷

# Los Angeles Maritime Museum ❼

Berth 84, 6th St, San Pedro. **Road map** inset A. **Tel** (310) 548-7618. ◯ 10am–5pm Tue–Sun. ⬤ Easter Sun, Thanksgiving, Dec 25. **Donation.** ♿ www.lamaritimemuseum.org

Housed in a restored ferry terminal building, the Los Angeles Maritime Museum contains an array of nautical paintings and memorabilia, including a wooden figurehead of British Queen Victoria. Highlights of the exhibition include its extensive model ship collection. Also on display is the bow and bridge of US Navy cruiser USS *Los Angeles*, and there are ever-changing temporary exhibitions. Early 20th-century Monterey fishing boats *(see p509)* can be seen in the dock.

**Figurehead of Queen Victoria**

# Ports O'Call Marketplace ❽

Berths 75–79, San Pedro. **Road map** inset A. **Tel** (310) 548-8076. ◯ 11am–7pm Sun–Thu, 11am–8pm Fri & Sat. www.sanpedro.com

Ports O'Call Marketplace is a pastiche of many different seaports from all around the world. Building styles range from a 19th-century New England fishing village, to a Mediterranean harbor, to a Mexican town.

The village's quaint shops and restaurants are linked by charming cobblestone walkways. Seafood is a specialty here, and the restaurants all serve locally caught, delicious fresh fish. From the dockside boardwalk visitors can watch the huge cargo ships and cruise liners sail by. Daily harbor cruises tour the inner harbor, coastguard station, marina, freighter operations, and scrap yards. Helicopter rides offer a birds' eye view of the harbor, and in winter, whale-watching cruises leave from this area.

# Cabrillo Marine Aquarium ❾

3720 Stephen White Dr, San Pedro. **Road map** inset A. **Tel** (310) 548-7562. ◯ noon–5pm Tue–Fri, 10am–5pm Sat & Sun. ⬤ Thanksgiving, Dec 25. 💲 for parking only. ♿ 📷 www.cabrillomarineaquarium.org

Designed by architect Frank Gehry and surrounded by a geometric chain-link fence, the Cabrillo Marine Aquarium houses one of the largest collections of Southern California marine life. Sharks, moray eels, and rays thrill thousands of visitors each year. The exhibition hall includes interpretive displays that explain the typical plants and animals of the region. It is divided into three environments – rocky shores, beaches and mudflats, and open ocean.

An outdoor rock pool tank contains sea cucumbers, sea anemones, starfish, and sea urchins that visitors are permitted to touch. This small museum also boasts 14,150 gallons (64,400 liters) of circulating sea water, as well as a tidal tank that allows viewers to see below a wave. Another exhibit shows how human activities have altered Los Angeles Harbor.

The beautifully maintained clapboard Point Fermin Lighthouse

# Point Fermin Park ❿

807 Paseo del Mar, San Pedro. **Road map** inset A. **Tel** (310) 548-7705. ◯ daily. www.sanpedro.com

This tranquil 37-acre (15-ha) park sits on a bluff overlooking the Pacific Ocean. Between January and March, migrating gray whales can be spotted offshore and, on a clear day, there are views of Catalina Island. The charming Eastlake-style lighthouse dates from 1874. Its bricks and lumber were shipped around Cape Horn. The lighthouse originally used oil lamps that emitted approximately 2,100 candlepower. They were replaced by an electric lamp in 1925.

# San Pedro ⓫

**Road map** inset A. ✈ LAX, 15 miles (24 km) NW of San Pedro. 🚌 MTA. ℹ San Pedro Chamber of Commerce, 390 W 7th St (310) 832-7272. www.sanpedro.com

Famous for the Worldport LA, blue-collar pride, and a tradition of family fishermen, San Pedro ("San Peedro" to the locals) has a strong Eastern European and Mediterranean flavor. The harbor is the nation's busiest import-export site. The houses are tiny compared to those in Palos Verdes, but this is a very important center of industry.

**Street scene in the picturesque Ports O'Call Marketplace**

**Korean Friendship Bell in Angels Gate Park, San Pedro**

In Angels Park, at the end of Gaffey Street, there is a Korean Friendship Bell, given to the United States in 1976 by South Korea.

**Steps leading to the hilltop Wayfarers Chapel**

## Wayfarers Chapel ⑫

5755 Palos Verdes Drive S, Rancho Palos Verdes. **Road map** inset A. **Tel** (310) 377-1650. ◯ call ahead (frequently booked for weddings). **Gardens** ◯ 8am–5pm daily. ♿ www.wayfarerschapel.org

This glass and redwood-framed chapel sits on a hilltop above the ocean. From the street below, all that can be seen is a thin stone and concrete tower rising from the greenery.

When the architect Lloyd Wright (son of Frank Lloyd Wright) designed the chapel in 1949, he tried to create a natural place of worship, surrounding it by trees. Today, its charm makes it a popular site for weddings.

The chapel is sponsored by the Swedenborgian church, which follows the teaching of Emanuel Swedenborg, the 18th-century Swedish theologian and mystic.

## South Coast Botanic Garden ⑬

26300 S Crenshaw Blvd, Palos Verdes. **Road map** inset A. **Tel** (310) 544-1948. ◯ 9am–5pm daily. ◉ Dec 25. ♿ www.southcoastbotanicgarden.org

This 87-acre (35-ha) garden was created on top of some 3,175,000 tons of waste that were dumped here from 1956 to 1960. Prior to that, the area was the location of a mine for algae-rich diatomaceous earth. Today, gas formed underground as a result of the waste decomposing is collected and used to generate electricity.

The garden is a study in land reclamation, with an emphasis on drought-resistant landscaping. Specimens from all the continents except Antarctica are planted within the grounds.

In the Herb Garden plants are divided into three main categories: fragrant, medicinal, and culinary. The Rose Garden has more than 1,600 roses, including old-fashioned and miniature roses, floribundas, hybrid teas, and grandifloras.

One of the most innovative areas is the Garden for the Senses. Here, plants are chosen for their extraordinary qualities of color, smell, or touch.

**Children's Garden in the South Coast Botanic Garden**

# AROUND DOWNTOWN

*F*rom the freeways, it is hard to appreciate the many treasures that lie within Los Angeles's sprawl. But a short drive beyond the central sights to nearby areas can be surprisingly rewarding. Up-scale Pasadena, with its delightful Old Town, also has the excellent Norton Simon Museum as well as the Huntington Library, Art Collections, and Botanical Gardens.

Northeast of Downtown are the Heritage Square Museum with its historic buildings, and Lummis House. Just north of Hollywood, hilly Griffith Park offers precious open spaces for picnicking, hiking, and horseback riding as well as the Los Angeles Zoo, Griffith Observatory, the outdoor Greek Theater, and Autry Museum of Western Heritage.

Nearby, Universal Studios offers tours of its backlots as well as theme park rides. Universal is one of four major studios based in Burbank, which has replaced Hollywood as the head-quarters for

the film and television industries. Farther north n the broad, flat San Fernando Valley, Mission San Fernando Rey de España provides a historical insight into California's origins.

South of Downtown, the Natural History Museum of Los Angeles County and the California Museum of Science and Industry are among the top attractions at Exposition Park, along with the stately buildings of the University of Southern California.

For sheer scenic delight and outstanding views over the city and San Fernando Valley, twisting mountainous Mulholland Drive is hard to beat.

**Tranquil Japanese Garden at the Huntington Botanical Gardens**

◁ **Monument to astronomers outside the Griffith Observatory**

# Exploring Around Downtown

The outlying areas of Los Angeles contain a vast range of museums, galleries, historic buildings, and parks. A little forward planning is necessary, however, to make the best use of time. The Heritage Square and Southwest museums are easily visited on the way to Pasadena. While Universal Studios needs a day to itself, other studio tours in Burbank can be combined with a trip to Griffith Park or to Mission San Fernando Rey de España. Get an early morning start at the Flower Market before tackling the three museums at Exposition Park, or take a trip east to see the Watts Towers in between museum visits.

## SIGHTS AT A GLANCE

0 kilometers    5

0 miles    5

**Los Angeles Memorial Coliseum and Downtown skyline viewed from Exposition Park**

View of San Fernando Valley from Mulholland Drive

# San Fernando Valley ❶

**Road map** inset A. ✈ Burbank-Glendale-Pasadena, 20 miles (32 km) SE of San Fernando. 🚌 MTA. 🛈 200 Magnolia Blvd, (818) 377-6388. **www**.thevalley.net

The city of Los Angeles is split into two distinct halves by the Santa Monica Mountains (see pp62–3). To the north, the San Fernando Valley spreads out in a seemingly endless vista of neat houses, freeways, and shopping malls, such as the Sherman Oaks Galleria (see p166). Residents south of the mountains tend to dismiss "the Valley," as they call it, as it is more smoggy and noticeably hotter in the summer.

In the 19th century, the San Fernando Valley was made up of ranches, orange groves, and nonirrigated farms. With the completion of the LA Aqueduct in 1913 (see pp202–3), the city was insured a plentiful water supply. As a result, the Valley quickly developed into a mass of suburbs. Today, more than a million people live in this area of Los Angeles, which encompasses only 177 sq miles (460 sq km).

On January 17, 1994, San Fernando Valley was at the epicenter of a devastating earthquake, which measured 6.8 on the Richter Scale (see pp24–5). The area had also been badly damaged by the February 1971 earthquake.

# Mission San Fernando Rey de España ❷

15151 San Fernando Mission Blvd, Mission Hills. **Road map** inset A. **Tel** (818) 361-0186. ⏰ 9am–5pm daily. ⬤ Thanksgiving, Dec 25. 🎦 ♿ grounds only. 🎫 **www**.missiontour.org

One of 21 Franciscan missions in California (see pp46–7), San Fernando Rey de España was founded in 1797 and named after King Ferdinand III of Spain. The present church is an exact replica of the original, which was destroyed in the 1971 earthquake. The convento (living quarters) has a 21-arch portico and is the largest mission building still standing in California.

**Mission altar detail**

A tour of the complex explores the early days of Spanish rule, when the monks and Native Americans worked together to make the mission self-sufficient.

# Mulholland Drive ❸

Off Hwys 1 & 27, from Hollywood Fwy to Leo Carrillo State Beach. **Map** 1 C2. 🛈 Malibu Chamber of Commerce, 23805 Stuart Ranch Rd, Ste 100 (310) 456-9025.

Mulholland Drive, one of the most famous roads in Los Angeles, runs for nearly 50 miles (80 km) from north Hollywood to the Malibu coast (see pp64–5). As it winds along the ridge of the Santa Monica mountains, the route has spectacular views across the city, San Fernando Valley, and some of LA's most exclusive houses. Its spirit was captured in David Hockney's painting of the area, which hangs in LACMA (see p115).

The road was named after William Mulholland (see p202). Although better known for his work on the LA Aqueduct, he oversaw the completion of Mulholland Drive in 1924.

# Children's Museum of Los Angeles ❹

Hansen Dam Recreation Park, 11800 Foothill Blvd, Lakeview Terrace, San Fernando Valley. **Road map** Inset A. **Tel** (818) 686-9280. ⬤ for renovation; see website for details. **www**.childrensmuseumla.org

Set within the beautiful Hansen Dam Recreation Park, the Children's Museum is housed within an ecologically progressive building. The hands-on museum aims to stimulate the imagination of children by encouraging them to explore their self-expression, from painting to putting on plays.

Mission San Fernando Rey de España in the Mission Hills

**Warner Bros Studios in Burbank**

## Burbank **5**

**Road map** inset A. ⬛ *Burbank-Glendale-Pasadena*. ⬛ *MTA*.
🅸 *200 W Magnolia Burbank (818 846-3111). See **Entertainment in Los Angeles** pp174–5.*
**www**.*burbankchamber.org*

Since 1915, when Universal Studios moved near here *(see pp146–9)*, Burbank has been competing with Hollywood as the true center of the Los Angeles film industry. Today there are four major studios: Universal, Disney, NBC, and Warner Bros. Disney's studios are closed to the public, but the fanciful building, designed by Michael Graves, can be seen from Alameda Avenue.

At NBC, visitors are offered a tour of the production studios and *The Tonight Show* set. Warner Bros offers an extensive tour, and a studio tour is included at the Universal Studios Hollywood℠ theme park.

## Universal Studios Hollywood℠ **6**

*See pp146–9.*

## Hollywood Sign **7**

*Mt Cahuenga, above Hollywood.*
🅸 *Hollywood Visitors Information Center, 6801 Hollywood Blvd (323) 467-6412.* **www**.*hollywoodsign.org*

The Hollywood Sign is an internationally recognized symbol of the movie business. Set high up in the Hollywood Hills, it is now a protected historic site. It is visible for miles from many parts of Los Angeles, but it is not possible for the public to reach the sign itself as there is no legitimate trail leading up to the 45-ft (13-m) tall letters.

Erected in 1923, it originally advertised the Hollywoodland housing development of the former *LA Times* publisher

Harry Chandler *(see p125)*. The "land" was removed in 1949. Nearly 30 years later, donors pledged $27,000 per letter for a new sign.

It has been the scene of one suicide – that of disappointed would-be actress Peg Entwistle, who jumped off the "H" in 1932.

## Hollyhock House **8**

*4800 Hollywood Blvd.* **Tel** *(323) 644-6269.* ⬜ *park open 5am–10:30pm daily.* 📷 *Wed–Sun (tours of the house).* **www**.*hollyhockhouse.net*

American architect Frank Lloyd Wright *(see p33)* designed a number of houses in LA. Hollyhock House was the first and remains one of the best known. An excellent example of Wright's infatuation with pre-Columbian styles, the hilltop house resembles a Mayan temple. The house is undergoing renovation, but there are tours of the exterior.

It was completed in 1921 for oil heiress Aline Barnsdall, who asked that her favorite flower, the hollyhock, be used as a decorative motif throughout the building. A band of stylized hollyhocks, fashioned in concrete, therefore adorns the exterior of the house. The flowers also feature as ornamentation inside, such as on the dining room chairs and other Wright-designed furnishings. The 11-acre Barnsdall Park, once the grounds of the estate, is now a public art park with galleries.

**Hollywood Sign, high above Los Angeles in the Hollywood Hills**

# Universal Studios Hollywood<sup>SM</sup> ❺

**Universal Studios Logo**

Carl Laemmle bought a chicken ranch on this site in 1915 and moved his film studio here from Hollywood. He charged visitors 25 cents to see films being made, and guests could also buy fresh eggs. With the advent of the "talkies" in 1927, the sets needed quiet and the visits stopped. In 1964, Universal Studios Hollywood<sup>SM</sup> was launched as a behind-the-scenes tram ride. The Studio Tour through Universal's 415 acres brings visitors face-to-face with soundstages and movie sets. Here, everything is, or looks like, a film set. The attractions, from Shrek to the latest virtual-reality thrill ride, create a world of magic and Hollywood glamor.

**LOCATOR MAP**

- ▨ Universal City
- ☐ Universal Studios

The Studio Tour takes in over 500 sets and façades on the backlot

## TACKLING THE PARK

Spread over 415 acres (168 ha) Universal Studios Hollywood<sup>SM</sup> is the world's largest working movie and television studio and theme park. The complex is divided into three areas: the Entertainment Center, Studio Center, and the studio lots.

As soon as you walk through the gate, visitors stroll through the Streets of the World, which are actual working sets depicting anything from a 1950s America to a European village. The Studio Tour, boarded from the Entertainment Center, is the only way of seeing Universal's main television and movie stages, sets, and movie stars. The Entertainment Center is also the place to catch such spectacular shows as the Blues Brothers Show

and Animal Actors. A futuristic escalator, the Starway, links the upper and lower portions of the studio lot. The lower level is where the major thrill rides, such as Revenge of the Mummy – The Ride can be found. Universal CityWalk® connects the working studios, the theme park, the Gibson indoor amphitheater, and 18-theater cinemas. There are also more than 65 different retail and entertainment venues.

## STUDIO TOUR

The original Universal Studios attraction, this classic Studio Tour gives visitors an up-close and personal view of the past, present, and future of Hollywood movie-making. Guests sit in mobile movie

theaters that are fitted with state-of-the-art, high-definition monitors and digital playback systems. Comedian Jimmy Fallon is the video host of the tour. The star of *Late Night with Jimmy Fallon* introduces hundreds of clips of well-known films and hit TV shows. Guests also experience an earthquake, see King Kong and Jaws, and survive a collapsing bridge, flash flood, and avalanche. The tour passes the Bates Motel, from *Psycho* (1960), and Who-ville from Dr Seuss' *How the Grinch Stole Christmas*.

A favorite part of the tour is the "Before They Were Stars" montage and the special weather-effects demonstrations. The 35 different soundstages, various movie and TV sets, props, cameras, lights, and lots of action give guests a first-hand look into filmland's realities and illusions. Special installations of "The Mummy," "Earthquake – The Big One," "King Kong,"

---

### SET LOCATIONS ON THE BACKLOT

Guests on the Studio Tour will see these working sets for hundreds of movies and TV productions, many of which are instantly recognizable. Each tram has an LCD flat screen, audio system, and DVD player to put a frame of reference to every set visited.

1. **Courthouse Square:** most frequently used set (***Back to the Future*** film series, ***To Kill a Mockingbird***, ***Batman & Robin***, ***Bruce Almighty***, ***Dr Seuss' The Cat In The Hat***).
2. **Psycho House/Bates Motel:** most famous set (***Psycho*** original and the remake of the same movie).
3. **Who-ville:** main town scenes from ***Dr Seuss' How the Grinch Stole Christmas***.
4. **Denver Street:** 7/8 scale to make actors in Westerns look larger than life (***Winchester '73, Babe***).
5. **Falls Lake with Backdrop:** most flexible set (***Apollo 13***, ***Charlie's Angels***, ***O Brother, Where Art Thou?***, ***Van Helsing***).

---

*For hotels and restaurants in this region see pp524–31 and pp568–76*

## VISITORS' CHECKLIST

100 Universal City Plaza, Universal City. **Road map** inset A. **Tel** *(800) 864-8377.* ▣ *424.* ☐ *Jun–Aug: 9am–8pm daily; Sep–May: 10am–6pm daily.* ● *Thanksgiving, Dec 25.* ▣ ▣ ▣ ▣ ▣ ▣ **www.** universalstudioshollywood.com

and "Jaws Lake" let visitors experience the live action of each working set. *The Tonight Show with Jay Leno* is filmed at the Universal Studios Lot. The show's state-of-the-art studio is now a featured showpiece on the tour.

In spite of all the virtual-reality, thrill rides, and modern attractions, the Studio Tour is really what a visit to Universal Studios Hollywood℠ is all about.

## UNIVERSAL CITYWALK®

In 1993, American architect Jon Jerde designed a festive assortment of façades for the shops and restaurants that make up CityWalk®'s promenade. Now, with the addition of more than 30 new attractions, including bars, nightclubs, and theaters Universal's CityWalk® is being hailed as the entertainment mecca of Southern California.

## UNIVERSAL STUDIOS HOLLYWOOD℠ TICKETS AND PASSES

General Admission: Tickets are either Adult or Child (3–9). Parking is extra.
1. Southern California Pass: Admission to Universal Studios and four Southern California attractions. Valid for 30 days.
2. Front of Line Pass: All day admission with priority entry to all attractions and reserved seating at all shows.
3. Annual Pass: Unlimited park access for one year (contains 30 blackout days) and free guest pass Sep–Dec.
4. VIP: Admission, guided tour of studio backlot, front-of-line privileges, and escorted priority access to rides and shows.
5. Southern California Value Pass: Admission to Universal Studios and SeaWorld San Diego. Valid for 14 days.
For more information, call 1-800-UNIVERSAL (1-800-864-8377) or visit the website.

Designed to appeal to guests' sense of whimsy, a giant neon-lit baseball player swings his bat above a sports store. To enter an ice-cream store, visitors must walk under an upside-down pink convertible that has crashed through a Hollywood Freeway sign. Jillian's Hi-Life Lanes, a multimedia rock 'n' roll bowling alley gives guests a chance to work off some extra energy; Howl at the Moon, a duelling piano bar, encourages audience participation; and the festive Cafe TuTu Tango offers tapas and a decor that mimics an artist's loft, complete with paintbrushes on the tables, artworks in progress,

**An upside-down car hangs above the entrance to a CityWalk® store**

and sometimes spontaneous performances by dancers and musicians.

The three-story IMAX® 3-D theater shows the latest venture into knock-your-socks-off film, and the NASCAR virtual racecar experience can be an antidote to the newest retail shops, name-brand outlets, and restaurants. This spectacular venture into California fantasy and entertainment is still one of the prime areas where you can buy Hollywood souvenirs and memorabilia.

## TOP 5 ATTRACTIONS

★ Animal Actors

★ Studio Tour

★ Universal CityWalk®

★ Terminator 2: 3-D®

★ Jurassic Park®

**Bright lights, big buildings, and prime entertainment in CityWalk®**

# Rides and Special Effects

Thrill rides are what theme parks do best. Not only does Universal offer some of the most spectacular rides but, coupled with the special effects at this working studio, some of the best in the business. The newest is Revenge of the Mummy – The Ride, which is a mix of high-speed roller coaster and space-age robotics, while an updated ride, complete with more horrifying monsters, is the Terminator 2: 3-D®. Visitors can also see King Kong on the world's largest soundstage and may get the rare chance to get a sneak peek at one of dozens of the films currently in production. Each attraction here is a thrill ride in itself, where the excitement of movies literally comes alive.

**Filming at the Studios**

A star of Animal Actors shows a talented paw

## ENTERTAINMENT CENTER

The entertainment center has dozens of themed souvenir shops and restaurants. The spectacular shows in this area of the park give visitors an insight into the stunts and special effects used to make a film.

### Animal Actors
Animal stars, multi-media effects, human co-stars, and unique sketches from TV's Animal Planet Network offer warm, family entertainment.

### Terminator 2: 3-D®
This show has been hailed as the world's most advanced film-based attraction. Arnold Schwarzenegger and the rest of the original cast from *Terminator 2: Judgment Day* (1991) star in this sequel, which continues the science-fiction epic in startling 3-D. Interactive virtual adventures and spectacular stunts are projected onto the world's largest 3-D screen.

### WaterWorld – A Live Sea War Spectacular
The audience is part of the action, and right in the middle of this thrilling, high-tech show, which packs dazzling pyrotechnics – a giant fireball that rises 50 feet (15 m) in the air – battle scenes, extraordinary stunts, and some wild jet-skiing into 16 minutes of daredevil action.

### Shrek 4-D
This superb "multi-sensory" attraction continues Shrek's adventures in the "greatest fairytale never told." Picking up where the DreamWorks movie left off, the second comic installment features ground-breaking "Ogre Vision" animation.

### The Simpsons Ride
Homer, Marge, Bart, Lisa, and Maggie Simpson – stars of TV's longest running series – ride along with guests in this mega-attraction at Universal Orlando Resort and Universal Studios Hollywood℠. Guests are rocketed along with the Simpson family on a hysterical, almost unimaginable adventure. On the way they experience a side of Springfield previously unexplored, as they enjoy the ride's interpretation of the thrill rides, dark rides, and "live" shows that make up a fantasy amusement park dreamed up by the show's cantankerous Krusty the Clown.

### King Kong 360 3-D
The King Kong 360 3-D is the first theme park attraction created by Peter Jackson, director of the Oscar-winning 2005 film upon which it is based. Guests on the Universal tram are given 3-D glasses and enter into a world where the film and tram are tied into a motion simulator that creates a titanic struggle between the 30-ft- (9-m-) tall gorilla and a 35-ft- (11-m-) tall Tyrannosaurus Rex. Surrounded by two curved screens, Studio Tour guests are completely swept up in the action. It is the first theme park attraction to win an award for "outstanding visual effect in a special venue project," from the Visual Effects Society.

Terrifying the audience at the Terminator 2: 3D® show

## Blues Brothers Show

This 20-minute live music stage show celebrates the antics and blues songs of the Blues Brothers. There's plenty of audience participation, with dancing, sing-alongs, and some outrageous humor.

## Fear Factor Live!

Based on the long-running *Fear Factor* – which showed on US TV until 2006 – Fear Factor Live! marks the first time a reality television show has been transformed into a theme park experience. Members of the audience are chosen to participate in the thrill of the blockbuster series.

In each show, a number of park guests compete against each other in a progression of extreme stunts which have been developed in conjunction with the original *Fear Factor* creators, and are designed to test the physical and emotional limits of each contestant.

## STUDIO CENTER

The Starway, which links the upper and lower portions of Universal's working lots, offers some spectacular views. The Studio Center on the lower lot has three super-thrilling rides and several other attractions that reveal the secrets of some of the studio's most successful films and television series. There are, of course, lots of photo opportunities around each corner, from the giant 24-ft (7-m) hanging shark to Universal's mascot Woody

**Jurassic Park® – The Ride roars to life**

Woodpecker. Or you might bump into a host of characters, including Charlie Chaplin, Frankenstein, the Mummy, Dracula, or Marilyn Monroe.

## Backdraft

In a re-creation of the final scene from the firefighting film *Backdraft* (1992), the audience can literally feel the heat of the film's blazing warehouse inferno. Beforehand, a technician explains how the scenes were created and controlled. The temperature rises when the firestorm explodes, causing red-hot ashes to rain down and overhead pipes to burst, leaving the audience scared and thrilled. The experience may be too frightening for young children.

## Revenge of the Mummy℠ – The Ride

This is California's fastest indoor roller coaster, and uses some of the most advanced animatronics ever engineered, together with spaceage robotics and technology to create a thrilling, scream-worthy ride. Light levels change from daylight to total darkness and don't forget to watch out for the skeleton warriors.

## Jurassic Park® – The Ride

Based on one of the most successful films of all time, *Jurassic Park* – The Ride takes visitors on a 5.5-minute trip through 6 acres (2.5 ha) of exotic prehistsoric wilderness. Steven Spielberg's epic movie leaps and roars to life with the most sophisticated state-of-the-art computer and robotic technology ever designed. Guests are hurled into the steamy world of Jurassic Park, where huge

**Jurassic Park® sign**

five-story dinosaurs swoop to within inches of riders' faces, and a terrifying *Tyrannosaurus rex* with a mouthful of razorsharp teeth considers each rider part of his dinner. The ride ends with an 84-ft (25-m) drop into complete darkness.

## Behind the Scenes of Universal Pictures

This attraction gives an extraordinary, close-up view of never-before-seen props, costumes, artifacts, and special effects items pulled from many of Universal's most celebrated productions, including hits and major motion pictures that have yet to be released.

Highlights include the Oscar® statuette for *The Sting*, props and costumes from Guillermo del Toro's *Hellboy II: The Golden Army*, the Speak 'N Spell transmitter from *E.T.: The Extra-Terrestrial*, Gregory Peck's briefcase and glasses from *To Kill a Mockingbird*, and military props from *All Quiet on the Western Front*. Material from new movies and artifacts from the studio's archives update the displays on a regular basis.

**King Kong, beloved of filmgoers, on Universal's Studio Tour**

# Griffith Park ❾

**Merry-go-round horse**

Griffith Park is a 4,000-acre (1,600-ha) wilderness of rugged hills, forested valleys, and green meadows in the center of LA. The land was donated to the city in 1896 by Colonel Griffith J Griffith, a Welshman who emigrated to the United States in 1865 and made his money speculating in mining and property. Today, people come to Griffith Park to escape from the city crowds, visit the sights, picnic, hike, or go horseback riding. The park is safe during the day, but it should be avoided at night.

**Griffith Observatory on Mount Hollywood**

## Exploring Griffith Park

The ranger station, located on Crystal Springs Drive, has maps of the park showing its numerous picnic areas and miles of hiking trails and bridle paths. There are two public 18-hole golf courses on the eastern side of the park and tennis courts on Riverside Drive and in Vermont Canyon.

In the hills just off Griffith Park Drive is a 1926 merry-go-round. Adults and children can still ride on its 66 carved horses and listen to its giant band organ. Across the street, an informal Sunday gathering of drummers has been meeting since the 1960s.

Fern Dell, at the Western Avenue entrance, is a beautiful shady glen with a flowing stream and small waterfalls.

### 🏛 Griffith Observatory

2800 Observatory Rd. **Tel** (213) 473-0800. ⬚ noon–10pm Wed–Fri,10am–10pm Sat & Sun. 🎦 Planetarium. **www**.griffithobservatory.org

Situated on Mount Hollywood, Griffith Observatory commands stunning views of the Los Angeles basin below. The Art Deco observatory is divided into three main areas: the Hall of Science museum, the Planetarium theater, and the telescopes.

The planetarium has a seamless dome and the world's most advanced projector. In the Main Rotunda of the Hall of Science, the Foucault Pendulum demonstrates the speed of the earth's rotation. Above the pendulum are murals on

a scientific theme, painted by Hugo Ballin in 1934. Characters from Classical mythology are depicted on the domed ceiling.

Visitors are taken on a journey through space and time, as stars, moons, and planets are projected onto the ceiling. On the roof, the Zeiss Telescope is open to the public on clear nights.

### 🏛 Travel Town

5200 W Zoo Drive. **Tel** (323) 662-5874. ⬚ 10am–4pm Mon–Fri, 10am–6pm Sat & Sun. 🚫 Dec 25. **www**.lacity.org

The spirit of the rails comes alive at this outdoor collection of vintage trains and cars. Children and adults can climb aboard freight cars and railroad carriages, or ride on a small train.

East of Travel Town, on Zoo Drive, miniature steam trains take people on rides during weekends.

**Steam locomotive from 1922, one of 16 steam trains in Travel Town**

### 🎭 Greek Theatre

2700 N Vermont Ave. **Tel** (323) 665-5857. ⬚ open for engagements only. 🎦 for concerts. **www**.greektheatrela.com

Styled after an ancient Greek amphitheater, this open-air music venue has excellent acoustics. On summer nights, over 6,000 people can sit under the stars and enjoy performances by leading popular and classical musicians. Bring a sweater as evenings can be chilly.

**Flamingos at Los Angeles Zoo**

### 🐾 Los Angeles Zoo

5333 Zoo Drive. *Tel (323) 644-4200.*
⬜ 10am–5pm daily. ⬛ Dec 25. 🌐
www.lazoo.org

This 113-acre (46-ha) hilly compound has more than 1,200 mammals, reptiles, and birds living in simulations of their natural habitats.

Many newborn creatures can be seen in the Animal Nursery, including some from the zoo's breeding program for rare and endangered species. The Koala House is dimly lit to encourage the nocturnal creatures to be active. Adventure Island focuses on Southwestern animals and habitats. Visitors can also enjoy the Pachyderm Exhibit, the Rainforest of the Americas, and the Insect Interpretation Center. There are several animal shows that are aimed toward a young audience. Be prepared to walk long distances, or use the Safari Shuttle bus.

### 🏛 Autry National Center

4700 Western Heritage Way (opposite the zoo). *Tel (323) 667-2000.*
⬜ 10am–5pm Tue–Sun (to 8pm Thu in summer). ⬛ Thanksgiving, Dec 25. 🌐 (free second Tue of month).
www.autrynationalcenter.org

The Autry Museum of Western Heritage explores the many cultures that have shaped the American West. Artworks by such artists as Albert Bierstadt and Frederic Remington *(see pp28–9)* depict a romantic view of life in the region. Tools, firearms, tribal clothing, and religious figurines are some of the artifacts that show the diversity of the people who have lived here. Founded by the film star Gene Autry, "the singing cowboy," the museum also houses movie and television memorabilia. The museum is planning a major new facility in Burbank for 2020, and so some galleries and exhibits may be closed or not on show.

**Deerskin Sioux dress**

### 🐾 Bird Sanctuary

Vermont Canyon Rd (just N of Greek Theater). *Tel (323) 913-4688.*
⬜ 10am–5pm daily.

Many trees and bushes have been planted in this secluded canyon to encourage local birds to nest here. Although you may not see too many birds, you will definitely hear their song. Depending on the season, water may be running in the stream, adding to the serenity of the area.

## GRIFFITH PARK

0 kilometers          1

0 miles          0.5

**KEY**

🛈 Tourist information

SAN FERNANDO VALLEY
VENTURA
DRIVE
ZOO DRIVE
PASADENA
GRIFFITH
PARK
CRYSTAL SPRINGS DRIVE
DRIVE
GOLDEN STATE FREEWAY
VAL DRIVE
MINERAL WELLS TRAIL
VISTA DEL VALLE DRIVE
FERN CANYON TRAIL
VERMONT CANYON ROAD
COOLIDGE TRAIL
CRYSTAL SPRINGS DRIVE
GRIFFITH PARK DRIVE
DOWNTOWN LOS ANGELES

# Dodger Stadium ❿

1000 Elysian Park Ave (at Stadium
Way). **Map** 11 F1. **Tel** (323) 224-
1500. **Tickets Tel** (323) 224-1471.
◻ for special events only. 🎟 ♿
**www**.dodgers.com

This baseball stadium seats
56,000 spectators. Built in
1962 for the Brooklyn team
which had moved to LA in
1958, the stadium has a canti-
levered design that guarantees
every seat an unobstructed
view of the field.

From the stadium there are
equally impressive panoramas
of the city. To the south is
Downtown LA, to the north
and east are the San Gabriel
Mountains. The stadium has
undergone a multi-million-
dollar renovation, resulting in
a sleek, contemporary, and
luxurious venue.

**Queen Anne-style Hale House at
Heritage Square Museum**

# Heritage Square
Museum ⓫

3800 Homer St, Los Angeles.
**Tel** (323) 225-2700. ◻ late Mar–
Oct: noon–5pm Fri–Sun; Nov–mid-
Mar: 11:30–4:30pm Fri–Sun. 🎟 ♿
🎬 **www**.heritagesquare.org

Most Victorian buildings in
Los Angeles were demolished
during redevelopments, but
some were saved by the
Cultural Heritage Board and
moved here. Dating from 1865
to 1914, they include a carriage
barn, train depot, and church.
Hale House, a Queen Anne-
style building (see p31), has
been authentically restored.

**Restored interior of the 19th-
century Lummis House**

# Lummis House ⓬

200 East Ave 43, Los Angeles.
**Tel** (323) 222-0546. ◻ 8:30am–
5pm Mon–Fri. **Donation**. ♿ 🎬

Also known as "El Alisal,"
Spanish for "Place of the
Sycamore," this house was
the home of Charles Fletcher
Lummis (1859–1928), who
built it out of concrete and
rocks from the local riverbed.
The structure's various design
elements – Native American,
Mission Revival, and Arts and
Crafts – reveal the dominant

influences of Lummis's life.
Constructed between 1898
and 1910, mostly by his own
hands, the design reveals a
creative, independent thinker.

Lummis was a newspaper
editor, writer, photographer,
artist, and historian. In 1885
he walked across the United
States, from Ohio to LA,
where he settled. He played
a central role in the city's
cultural life, editing the *LA
Times*. As a co-founder of the
California Land-mark Club,
he campaigned successfully
for the preservation of the
state's missions (see pp46–7).
His collection of Native
American artifacts was the
basis of the holdings at the
Southwest Museum.

Today, Lummis House is the
headquarters of the Historical
Society of Southern California.
Although few of Lummis's
be-longings remain in the
house, there are some Native
American artifacts. The built-in
furnishings include a splendid
Art Nouveau fireplace.

The garden was originally
planted with vegetables and
fruit trees. It was redesigned
in 1985 and now grows a
number of drought-tolerant
and native Southern California
plant species.

## THE DODGERS

The Dodgers originated in 1890 in Brooklyn, New York.
They used to train by dodging the trolleys that traveled
down that borough's streets, thus earning their name. Since
moving to Los Angeles in 1958, they have become one of
the most successful baseball teams in the United States.
In 1955, they won the first of five world championships.

Over the years the team
has had a number of
outstanding players, notable
examples were Sandy
Koufax and Roy Campanella.
In 1947, the Dodgers made
headlines when they signed
Pasadena-born Jackie
Robinson, the first African-
American to play in the
major leagues.

Japanese star pitcher Hideo
Nomo joined the Dodgers
team in 1995, and created a
sensation in his first season.
During the playoffs, crowds
brought Tokyo to a standstill
as Nomo prepared to pitch
on the other side of the
Pacific Ocean.

**Part of the victorious 1959 world
championship team**

## GALLERY GUIDE

*The galleries are closed while restoration of the building and conservation of the museum's rare collection of Native American artifacts is in progress. Because of its small size, only two percent of the museum's 250,000 items are displayed at any one time, and during renovations artifacts will be stored and curated. The museum is closed until 2013, but the museum store is open at weekends, and programs and events are still on offer to the public.*

**Southwest Museum of the American Indian**

# Southwest Museum of the American Indian ⓭

234 Museum Drive, Los Angeles.
***Tel** (323) 221-2165.* 🔵 *for repairs until 2012.* 🖼️ 🎫 🚪 *noon–5pm Sat & Sun.* **www**.autrynationalcenter.org

A part of the Autry National Center of the American West, this museum is one of the oldest in Los Angeles. It was founded by Charles Fletcher Lummis, a photographer, amateur anthropologist, and prolific historian of the south-western United States who helped popularize the idea of Los Angeles as a multicultural city. In 1884, Lummis walked from Ohio to California in a pair of knicerbockers and street shoes to take a job as a reporter for the Los Angeles Times. In the process he gained a national following as well as a deep appreciation for both the natural beauty and cultural diversity of the Southwest, where he remained for the rest of his life. In 1903, Lummis set out to create "a great, characteristic Southern California museum". When it opened in 1914, the museum included halls of conchology and Asian and European art,

**Sequoyah Indian relief**

along with displays of Southwestern and California archaeological materials, the Munk Library of Arizoniana, and the Lummis Library. In the 1920s the museum narrowed its focus to anthropology and its subject matter to the cultural history and prehistory of the indigenous peoples of the Americas.

Upper level

Entrance

Lower level

### KEY

- ☐ The Northwest Coast
- ☐ Preservation wing
- ☐ The Plains
- ☐ People of California
- ☐ Contemporary Art
- ☐ People of the Southwest
- ☐ Non-exhibition space

# Pasadena ⑭

With the completion of the Santa Fe Railroad in 1887, wealthy people from the East Coast began to spend the winter in the warmth and sunshine of Southern California. Many settled in Pasadena and were soon joined by artists and bohemians, who were also seeking the sun. This mix of creativity and wealth has resulted in a city with a splendid cultural legacy. The highlights of the area include the Huntington Library, Art Collections, and Botanical

**Rose Bowl statue**

Gardens *(see pp158–61)*, and the outstanding collection of Old Masters and Impressionist paintings at the Norton Simon Museum *(see pp156–7)*.

### Exploring Pasadena

Just east of the Norton Simon Museum is **Old Pasadena**, once a decaying section of town. A dozen blocks of commercial buildings dating from the 1880s and 1890s have been restored and are now filled with stores, restaurants, and movie theaters. The mixture of Victorian, Spanish Colonial, and Art Deco architecture adds to the area's pleasant environment. The stately Beaux-Arts **Civic Center**, on Union Street at Garfield Avenue, was designed by Edward Bennett in the early 1920s. It includes the city hall, police station, post office, library, and civic auditorium. The neighborhood northeast of Gamble House has many examples of Arts and Crafts architecture *(see p31)*, most notably along tree-lined **Prospect Boulevard**.

### 🏟 Rose Bowl

1001 Rose Bowl Drive.
**Tel** (626) 577-3101. 🈂
**www**.rosebowlstadium.com
Sited in a wealthy neighborhood, the stadium seats more than 100,000 people. It was built in 1922 for the annual Rose Bowl football game, which matches college teams from the Midwest and the West Coast.

The first collegiate game played here was delayed for more than an hour when the visiting team was stuck in traffic, a fate that befalls many visitors today. This is the home of UCLA's football team, the Bruins. Numerous Super Bowl games have also been played here as well as the World Cup Championships in 1994 and the 1984 Summer Olympics soccer competitions. There is also a flea market here every month.

**Tiffany lamp in the Gamble House**

Pasadena's city hall in the Beaux-Arts Civic Center

### 🏟 Gamble House

4 Westmoreland Place. **Tel** (626) 793-3334. ◯ noon–3pm Thu–Sun. ◖ public hols. 🈂 📷 obligatory.
**www**.gamblehouse.org
A masterpiece of the era, this wooden house epitomizes the Arts and Crafts movement, which stressed simplicity of design with superior craftsmanship. The dwelling was built in 1908 for David Gamble, of the Procter and Gamble Company. It is considered the crowning achievement of brothers Charles and Henry Greene, Boston-trained architects who visited Pasadena in 1893 and never left *(see p31)*.

Gamble House was tailor-made for LA's climate. Its terraces and open porches facilitate indoor-outdoor living, and broad overhanging eaves shade the house. At certain times of day, the sun illuminates the stained-glass front door, a dazzling sight.

### 🏛 Pacific-Asia Museum

46 N Los Robles Ave. **Tel** (626) 449-2742. ◯ 10am–6pm Wed–Sun. ◖ public hols. 🈂 📷
**www**.pacificasiamuseum.org
Built in 1924 to a traditional northern Chinese design, the Pacific-Asia Museum houses a collection of Far Eastern art founded by Grace Nicholson. Changing exhibitions on the arts of Asia and the Pacific Basin supplement the permanent collection. The museum's lovely courtyard garden is one of only a few authentic Chinese gardens in the United States.

A packed Rose Bowl during a football game

*For hotels and restaurants in this region see pp524–31 and pp568–76*

### ❧ LA State and County Arboretum

301 N Baldwin Ave, Arcadia. *Tel (626) 821-3222.* ☐ *9am–4:30pm daily.* ⬤ *Dec 25.* 🖾 ♿ ☑ *(free third Tue every month).* **www**.arboretum.org
Situated on 127 acres (51 ha) east of Pasadena, the arboretum has more than 30,000 plant species displayed according to their geographical origin. The park includes a herb garden, a waterfall, lily ponds, and a tropical jungle. It was used as the backdrop for all of Johnny Weissmuller's

**Tropical landscaping in the LA State and County Arboretum**

*Tarzan* films (1932–48) and for some parts of Humphrey Bogart's *African Queen* (1951). Among the historical buildings in the grounds are Gabrielino Native American *wickiups* (huts) and the reconstructed 1839 Hugo Reid adobe.

### 🏛 Kidspace Children's Museum

480 North Arroyo Blvd, Pasadena. *Tel (626) 449-9144.* ☐ *10am–5pm daily (closed Mon in winter).* ⬤ *public hols.* 🖾 ♿ **www**.kidspacemuseum.org
This museum engages children and families by sparking creativity and imagination

**VISITORS' CHECKLIST**

**Road map** inset A. 🏘 *145,000.*
🚌 *79 from Downtown LA.*
ℹ️ *300 E. Green St (626) 795-9311, (800) 307-7977.*
🎏 *Tournament of Roses Parade (Jan 1).* **www**.pasadenacal.com

through the 17 different indoor exhibits and 10 outdoor learning environments in the museum's Brookside Park location. There are also continually changing educational programs, as well as a café and a learning store.

### THE ROSE PARADE

In 1890 the Pasadena Valley Hunt Club decided to hold the first Tournament of Roses to celebrate – and advertise – the region's balmy winters. Little did they know that their horse-drawn carriages would be the start of this world-famous New Year's day extravaganza, with the world watching its marching bands and riders and gigantic electronically animated floats covered in flowers, grasses or seeds.

**Rose Parade float**

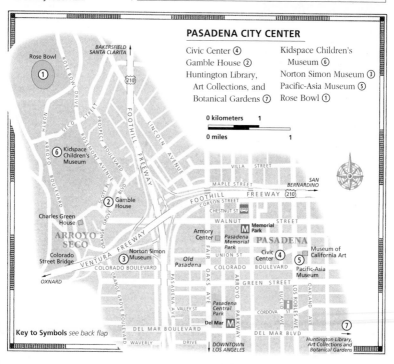

**PASADENA CITY CENTER**

Civic Center ④
Gamble House ②
Huntington Library, Art Collections, and Botanical Gardens ⑦
Kidspace Children's Museum ⑥
Norton Simon Museum ③
Pacific-Asia Museum ⑤
Rose Bowl ①

0 kilometers 1

0 miles 1

# Norton Simon Museum

Norton Simon (1907–93) was a businessman who combined running his multinational corporation with forming an internationally acclaimed collection of works of art. From the 1950s to the 1980s, he amassed, with the genius of a connoisseur, masterpieces spanning more than 2,000 years of Western and Asian art. Within the European holdings, the Old Masters and Impressionist paintings are especially strong. Renaissance, Post-Impressionism, German Expressionism, and the modern period are also well represented. Sculptures from India and Southeast Asia are among the finest outside the region and offer an insight into the complex roles art and religion play in these cultures.

**Main level**

**Sculpture Garden**

**Lower level**

★ **Woman with a Book** *(1932)*
*Pablo Picasso, one of the great artistic forces of the 20th century, was a major influence on both the Cubist and Surrealist movements. His mistress Marie-Thérèse Walter, was the subject of a number of his paintings in the 1930s.*

**Self-Portrait** *(c.1636–8)*
*Rembrandt painted nearly 100 self-portraits during his lifetime. This one shows the artist in his early thirties.*

★ **Still Life with Lemons, Oranges and a Rose** *(1633)*
*The Spanish painter Francisco Zurbarán excelled at contemplative still lifes. Many of his works were exported to the Spanish Americas, where they influenced colonial painters.*

## STAR PAINTINGS

★ Still Life with Lemons, Oranges and a Rose by Francisco Zurbarán

★ Woman with a Book by Pablo Picasso

## GALLERY GUIDE

*The museum's galleries are on two floors. European paintings, prints, sculpture, and tapestries, dating from the Renaissance to the 20th century, as well as special exhibitions, are on the main level. The lower galleries showcase the Norton Simon's impressive collection of Indian and Southeast Asian works. Visitors can also enjoy the gallery's outdoor space, which takes the form of a huge sculpture garden with a natural pond in the center, inspired by the artworks of Claude Monet.*

### VISITORS' CHECKLIST

411 W Colorado Blvd. **Tel** (626) 449-6840. 181, 182.
noon–6pm (9pm Fri) Wed–Mon. Jan 1, Thanksgiving, Dec 25.
www.nortonsimon.org

**Saints Paul and Frediano** (c.1483)
*This is one of a pair of religious panels executed by Florentine artist Filippino Lippi. It shows the influence of Lippi's more famous father, Fra Filippo Lippi, and his other mentor, Botticelli.*

Theatre

Spiral staircase

Main entrance

Spiral staircase

### KEY

- 14th–17th centuries
- 17th–18th centuries
- 19th century
- 20th century
- South Asian
- Special exhibitions
- Non-exhibition space

**Little Dancer Aged Fourteen** (1878–81)
*This bronze is one of more than 100 works by Edgar Degas in the museum. It features one of the artist's favorite subjects, the ballet.*

**Buddha**
*This bronze was made in Kashmir in India in the 8th century. It is inlaid with silver and copper.*

# Huntington Library, Art Collections, and Botanical Gardens

Detail from garden urn

Visitors and scholars alike are united in their love of the Huntington. The Beaux-Arts mansion was built between 1909 and 1911 for Henry Huntington (1850–1927), who made his fortune building a network of interurban trams in Los Angeles. In 1913 he married his uncle's widow, Arabella. Together they amassed one of the most important libraries and collections of 18th-century British art in the world. An expansion has more than doubled the exhibit space for its growing American art collection.

**Mausoleum**
*Designed by the architect John Russell Pope, this building in the form of a Greek temple is made of Colorado yule marble.*

**Main entrance**

**Orange Grove**

**Rose Hills Foundation Conservatory for Botanical Science**

**Children's Gar**

**Camellia Garden**

**Chinese Garden**

**Virginia Steele Scott Galleries**

**Boone Gallery**

**North Vista**
*Backed by the San Gabriel Mountains, the vista re-creates the feel of a 17th-century European garden, complete with an Italian Baroque fountain at one end.*

**Herb Garden**

**Japanese House**

**Zen Garden**

**★ Japanese Garden**
*Designed as a place for quiet contemplation, this typical Japanese garden includes a small lake, crossed by a curved moon bridge, and a traditional Japanese house.*

**STAR EXHIBITS**

* ★ The Blue Boy by Thomas Gainsborough
* ★ Gutenberg Bible
* ★ Japanese Garden

### ★ Gutenberg Bible
*This Bible was printed on vellum around 1450–55 by Johannes Gutenberg in Mainz, Germany. It is the oldest printed book in the Huntington Library.*

**VISITORS' CHECKLIST**

1151 Oxford Rd. **Tel** (626) 405-2100. ⬤ Jun–Aug: 10:30am–4:30pm Wed–Mon; Sep–May: noon–4:30pm Mon, Wed–Fri; 10:30am–4:30pm Sat & Sun. ⬤ pub hols. 🎫 📷 ♿ 🏪 ⬤ 📖 ⬤

### Jungle Garden
*The palms, ferns, gingers, and other plants in this garden are all typical of a tropical rainforest. The waterfalls add to the lush beauty of the garden.*

**Dibner Hall of the History of Science**

**e Munger esearch Center**

**Shakespeare Garden**

**Huntington Library**

**Palm Garden**

**Desert Garden**

**Lily Ponds**

**Huntington Art Gallery**

**Subtropical Garden**

**Australian Garden**

### Rose Garden
*Nearly 1,200 rose varieties trace the development of the flower from the early blooms of classic antiquity to modern hybrids.*

### ★ The Blue Boy (c.1770)
*Thomas Gainsborough's portrait of Jonathan Buttall, a merchant's son, is one of the collection's most famous paintings.*

# Exploring the Huntington

In 1919 Henry and Arabella Huntington put their home and gardens into a trust, creating a nonprofit research institution. Today, the Huntington has undergone a $20 million renovation, adding an educational facility and cultural center, serving scholars and the public. The institution comprises one of the world's great research libraries, an outstanding art collection, and over 130 acres (50 ha) of botanical gardens. The Huntington is only open to the public for a few hours each day.

*Diana Huntress* **(1782) by Jean-Antoine Houdon**

## HUNTINGTON LIBRARY

Built in 1920, the library specializes in British and American history and literature. It attracts nearly 2,000 scholars every year. The public can view key items and exhibits in the Library Exhibition Hall.

Among the 600,000 books and six million manuscripts are Benjamin Franklin's autobiography and the Ellesmere manuscript of Chaucer's *Canterbury Tales* (c.1410). The collection includes a Gutenberg Bible (c.1455) – one of only 12 surviving copies printed on vellum in the world.

There are first editions and manuscripts by noted authors, including Mark Twain, Charles Dickens, and Lord Tennyson, and early editions of Shakespeare's plays. Letters written by George Washington, Benjamin Franklin, and Abraham Lincoln are also part of the collection.

**Pilgrim from *The Canterbury Tales***

## HUNTINGTON ART GALLERY

The Huntingtons' mansion houses the majority of the art collection, including British and French art from the 18th and early 19th centuries. The most famous works are the portraits in the Thornton Portrait Gallery, which provide an unrivaled opportunity to study British art. On display are Thomas Gainsborough's *The Blue Boy* (c.1770) and Lawrence's *Pinkie* (1794), as well as paintings by Constable, Romney, Reynolds, Van Dyck, and Turner.

The Large Library Room contains some outstanding 18th-century furnishings, which include two Savonnerie carpets made for Louis XIV, and five Beauvais tapestries. On the second floor of this palatial home, formerly occupied by the Huntingtons, are Renaissance paintings and bronzes and more choice pieces of French and British art.

## DIBNER HALL OF THE HISTORY OF SCIENCE

How beautiful ideas in science have changed the world is the theme of this exhibit. The Burndy Library, formerly at MIT, plus the Huntingdon's own history of science collection, are combined here in four galleries to present the findings of world-renowned scientists from Ptolemy to Einstein.

Visitors will be able to make use of a reading room to study translations and modern editions of work in the collection.

## BOONE GALLERY

The Boone Gallery displays temporary exhibitions of American and English art, rare books, and manuscripts, as well as items from the Huntington's permanent collection.

Built in 1911 as a garage for Mr Huntington's fleet of automobiles, the Neoclassical building later fell into disrepair. Its restoration in 2000, funded by MaryLou and George Boone, provides 4,000 sq ft of additional exhibition space.

## VIRGINIA STEELE SCOTT GALLERIES OF AMERICAN ART

A major expansion added 16,379 sq ft (1,522 sq m) of gallery space that combines the old Virginia Steele Scott

**French furniture in the Large Library Room**

Gallery and the Lois and Robert F. Erburu Gallery. The space is one of the largest presentations in Southern California of American art from the colonial period through the mid-20th century. Some of the most well-known works in the collection are *The Meeting of Lear and Cordelia* (1784), by Benjamin West (1738–1820); *Chimborazo* (1864), by Frederic Edwin Church (1826–1900); and *Breakfast in Bed* (1897), by Mary Cassatt (1844–1926). The gallery also features the marble sculpture *Zenobia in Chains* (1859), by Harriet Hosmer (1830–1908), which was discovered in a private collection afer years of being presumed lost or destroyed. Other notable artists include Edward Hopper (1882–1967); and a group of seminal photographs by Edward Henry Weston (1886–1958).

**Desert Garden**

## BOTANICAL GARDENS

In 1904, Henry Huntington hired landscape gardener William Hertrich to develop the grounds, which now contain 15 principal gardens.

The 12-acre (5-ha) Desert Garden has more than 4,000 drought-tolerant species from around the world. In the Rose Garden, a walkway traces the history of the species over 1,000 years, with 2,000 varieties. The oldest are found in the Shakespeare Garden.

One of the most popular areas is the Japanese Garden, with a moon bridge, Zen Garden, and Japanese plants.

## HUNTINGTON ART GALLERY

**First floor**

**Second floor**

1 Large Library Room
2 Large Drawing Room
3 Small Drawing Room
4 Dining Room
5 Anteroom
6 Thornton Portrait Gallery
7 Hall
8 Small Library
9 European and Renaissance art
10 Ceramics
11 British art
12 Wedgwood vases
13 Silver
14 Miniatures and early 19th-century oil sketches
15 Morris and Co. stained glass window

## DIBNER HALL OF THE HISTORY OF SCIENCE

1 Astronomy
2 Natural History
3 Medicine
4 Light
5 Reading Room

## HUNTINGTON LIBRARY

1 Medieval Manuscripts and Early Printing
2 English and American Literature
3 American History
4 Temporary Exhibitions

**First floor**

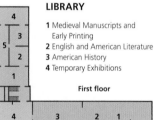

## VIRGINIA STEELE SCOTT GALLERIES OF AMERICAN ART

1 20th century
2 19th century
3 Sculpture
4 18th century
5 17th century
6 Dorothy Collins Brown Wing
7 Susan and Stephen Chandler Wing: temporary exhibitions

**First floor**

**Cowboy boot stand at El Mercado**

# El Mercado ⑮

3425 E 1st St. *Tel (323) 268-3451.*
⬚ *10am–8pm daily.* ♿
www.elmercadodelosangeles.com

East Los Angeles is the heart
of the Mexican-American
community *(see p34)*, and this
marketplace caters to the
locals. Its three levels bustle
with taco vendors, *mariachis*
(Mexican street musicians),
and families out for a good
meal. Unlike Olvera Street
*(see p127)*, El Mercado is not
designed as a tourist spot.
The greatest attraction here is
the authentic Mexican food
and regional music.

On the main floor, stands
offer everything from chilies
to snack food. A *tortillaria*
sells fresh, hot tortillas;
bakeries display traditional
Mexican breads and pastries;
and delicatessens have meats
you may never have seen
before. To hear the *mariachis*,
go to the mezzanine level,
which is also where the
cafeteria-style restaurants are.

---

**THE LAKERS AND BASKETBALL**

Basketball originated in Springfield, Massachusetts in 1891 as
a team sport that could be played indoors during the harsh
winters. LA's winter may be warm, but people still love the
fast-paced, high-scoring game. The city's team, the Lakers,
has a huge following. Such
illustrious players as Magic
Johnson, Wilt Chamberlain,
Kareem Abdul-Jabbar,
Shaquile O'Neal, and Kobe
Bryant have helped make
the team one of the most
successful in the National
Basketball Association (NBA).
The Lakers started out in
Minnesota; in 1960 they came
to LA; they won the NBA
Championship four times in
the 1980s, and now play in
the state-of-the-art Staples
Center (pictured below).

**Magic Johnson**

---

Brightly colored Mexican
clothing, furniture, and crafts
fill the shops in the basement,
along with the sounds of
Latin American salsa music.
It gets crowded on Sundays.

# Flower Market ⑯

754 Wall St. *Tel (213) 627-2482.*
⬚ *8am–noon Mon, Wed, Fri,*
*6am–noon Tue, Thu, Sat.* ♿
www.laflowerdistrict.com

In the early hours before
sunrise the city's florists
flock to this two-block long
area to buy wholesale flowers
and plants. Warehouses lined
with tables and stands are
laden with brightly colored

blossoms that contrast sharply
with the gray surrounding
buildings. An enormous
range of flowers is offered,
so that California varieties
compete with plants from
Columbia, New Zealand,
France, and Holland.

Anyone can take advantage
of the low prices (bargains
are available after 8am).
However, it is advisable to
arrive early because supplies
sell out quickly.

# Exposition Park and University of Southern California ⑰

*See pp164–5.*

# LA Live ⑱

Downtown. **Map** 10 C5. *Tel (213)*
*689-8822, (323) 467-4270.*
www.lalive.com

Downtown LA has long been
overlooked as a residential
and shopping district but is
rapidly changing with its abundance of trendy apartments,
theaters, hotels, restaurants,
and clubs surrounding the
Los Angeles Convention Center
and the Staples Center *(see
p163)*. All are part of the
massive $1.7 billion LA Live
development project.

**The Staples Center, home to the LA Lakers and LA Clippers**

## Staples Center ⓳

1111 S Figueroa St. **Map** 10 C5.
*Tel (213) 742-7340 (Box office).*
◯ *for events.* 🅿 *for events.*
**www**.staplescenter.com

Home to three professional
ball clubs, the LA Lakers, the
LA Clippers (basketball), and
the LA Kings (ice hockey),
this stadium has revitalized
downtown LA for sports
fans. It also hosts the US
Figure Skating Champion-
ships, major rock and pop
concerts, WWF wrestling,
and Hollywood awards
events, as well as grad-
uation ceremonies.

## Hollywood Park Racetrack ⓴

1050 S Prairie Ave, Inglewood.
**Road map** inset A.
*Tel (310) 419-1500.*
◯ *call for post times.* 🅿 ♿
**www**.hollywoodpark.com

From April to July and
November to December
racing enthusiasts, Hollywood
stars, and tourists come to
Hollywood Park to bet on
the thoroughbreds. This is
an elegant and beautifully
landscaped racetrack,
designed by noted racetrack
architect Arthur Froehlich,
and is conveniently located
near LAX. A large computer-
operated screen relays the
action from the obscured
back straight, and shows
instant replays, photo finishes,
and race statistics.

**Landscaped racetrack at
Hollywood Park in Inglewood**

**Watts Towers, covered in shells, china, and glass**

## Watts Towers ㉑

1727 E 107th St, Watts. **Road
map** inset A. *Tel (213) 847-4646.*
📅 *10am–4pm Wed–Sat, noon–4pm
Sun.* 🅿 *Towers only.* ♿ *Arts
Center only.*

Watts Towers is a masterpiece
of folk art that embodies the
perseverance and vision of
Simon Rodia, an immigrant
from Naples, Italy. Between
1921 and 1954, the tile-worker
sculpted steel rods, pipes,
and whatever else he could
find into a huge skeletal
framework. The highest tower
reaches 100 ft (30 m). Rodia
adorned the cemented surface
with fragments of seashell,
tile, china, and glass. He never
gave a reason for building the
towers and, upon finishing, he
deeded the land to a neighbor
and left Los Angeles.

Despite several attempts to
have Watts Towers razed, it is
now a State Historic Site and
is undergoing extensive
renovation. It stands as a
symbol of hope in this area
that, in 1965, was the site of
the worst riots in Los Angeles.

Adjacent to the monument is
the Watts Towers Arts Center.
This complex displays temporary exhibitions of work by
African-American artists in the
community and hosts work-
shops for artists of all ages.

South Central LA, which
includes Watts, is an
impoverished and somewhat
high-crime neighborhood.
Visitors should not stay
in the area after dark. Take
common-sense precautions.

# Exposition Park and University of Southern California ⓱

**Bovard Administration Building**

Exposition Park began life in the 1880s as an area of open-air markets, carnivals, and horse-racing. By the end of the century, the district was rife with drinking, gambling, and prostitution. When Judge William Miller Bowen's nearby Sunday school pupils began skipping church to enjoy local temptations, he pushed for the transformation of the area into a cultural landmark that today includes three museums. The Exposition Park Rose Garden in their midst contains more than 19,000 rose bushes.

*Tommy Trojan statue*

Across the street, the University of Southern California (USC) covers 152 acres (62 ha) and is attended by almost 28,000 students. Founded in 1880, it is the oldest and largest private university in the western United States.

### 🏛 Doheny Memorial Library

Corner of Hoover Blvd and Childs Way, USC. **Tel** *(213) 740-4039.* ◯ *daily.*

A majestic building with Italian Romanesque, Egyptian, and Moorish design influences, USC's main reference library was built in 1932 in memory of Edward L Doheny, Jr., a trustee of the university. There is a monumental marble staircase at the entrance, and ornate stone and woodwork throughout.

### 🏛 Natural History Museum of Los Angeles County

900 Exposition Blvd. **Tel** *(213) 763-3466.* ◯ *9:30am–5pm daily.* ● *Jan 1, Jul 4, Thanksgiving, Dec 25.* 🖼 www.nhm.org

This museum is one of the country's most important natural and cultural history museums. A $135 million, seven-year renovation that began in 2006 has restored the Beaux-Arts 1913 building at its core, as well as a wing added to the museum in the

1920s. Both buildings house the Age of Mammals exhibit and the Dinosaur Hall. In 2012 a permanent exhibition, and The Nature Lab, and indoor-outdoor science hub, will open. The collection aims to highlight southern California's natural and cultural treasures.

### 🏛 Bovard Administration Building

Hahn Plaza, USC. ◯ *daily.*

This Italian Romanesque structure was named after USC's fourth president, George Bovard. The former bell tower has sculpted figures of John Wesley, Abraham Lincoln, Theodore Roosevelt, Cicero, and Plato. The Gothic Norris Auditorium seats 1,600 people. *Tommy Trojan*, a statue of a Trojan warrior by the main entrance, was sculpted in 1930 by Roger Nobel Burnham.

### SIGHTS AT A GLANCE

0 meters 200
0 yards 200

SANTA BEVER

Tr Sta

CHILDS

McCLINTOCK AVENUE

DOWNEY WAY

WEST 37TH STREET

WAY

↑ HOLLYWOOD

Lindhurst Galleries

Sculpture Garden

EXPOSITION

⑥ Natural History Museum of Los Angeles County

VERMONT

MENLO

COLISEUM DRIVE N

AVENUE

Los Ar Mem Colis

LEIGHTON AVE

SOUTH PARK DR

MARTIN LUTHER

**Key to Symbols** *see back flap*

**Natural History Museum in Exposition Park**

**Los Angeles Memorial Coliseum**

## 🏟 Los Angeles Memorial Coliseum

3911 S Figueroa St. **Tel** (213) 747-7111. ⬜ for events. 🏷 🎥 by request. **www**.lacoliseumlive.com
Built in 1928, this is the only facility in the world to host two Olympiads, two Super Bowls, and a World Series.

Home court for the USC football team, it has also hosted rock concerts, Nelson Mandela's triumphant return to the US, Pope John Paul II's Mass in 1987, and John F. Kennedy's 1960 acceptance speech as the Democratic party's candidate for president. The venue also benefits from a sound system, videoboards, and seating.

## 🏛 California Science Center

700 Exposition Park Drive. **Tel** (323) 724-3623. ⬜ 10am–5pm daily. ● Jan 1, Thanksgiving, Dec 25. 🎥 **www**.californiasciencecenter.org
One of the largest of its kind in the US, the California Science Center aims to make science accessible to people of all ages. The World of Life exhibit in the Kinsey Hall of Health explores how living things function, with Body Works, a 50-ft- (15-m-) long transparent human figure with illuminated organs, as its centerpiece. The Creative World area shows how people create what they need, following an idea from inception to production. Ecosystems invites visitors to explore eight different environments. The IMAX® Theater at the museum has a seven-story-high screen presenting nature-related movies. The Aerospace Museum, designed by Frank Gehry, has an F-104 Starfighter jet bolted to its façade. It features all kinds of winged craft, from a Wright Brothers' glider to a Gemini 11 space capsule. Once decommissioned, the spaceshuttle *Endeavour* will be held here.

## 🏛 USC Fisher Museum of Art

Harris Hall, USC. **Tel** (213) 740-4561. ⬜ noon–5pm Tue–Sat. ● public hols & summer. **www**.uscfishermuseumofart.org
Named after the gallery's benefactor, Mrs. Walter Harrison Fisher, the collection includes 19th-century French and American landscapes and works by Peter Paul Rubens.

DOWNTOWN LOS ANGELES

## 🏛 California African American Museum

600 State Drive. **Tel** (213) 744-7432. ⬜ 10am–5pm Tue–Sat, 11am–5pm Sun. ● Jan 1, Thanksgiving, Dec 25. **www**.caamuseum.org
This museum is a record of African American achievements in the arts, sciences, politics, religion, and sports. The permanent art collection includes works by artists such as Martin Pierré, Betye Saar, Noah Purifoy, and the 19th-century landscape painter Robert Duncanson. Frequent temporary exhibitions are held in the sculpture court.

## 🏟 Mudd Memorial Hall

Corner of Trousdale Parkway and Exposition Blvd, USC. ⬜ daily.
The philosophy department's hall is predominantly pre-Renaissance Tuscan in style. Its bell tower is 146 ft (44 m) high and was used in the 1939 film *The Hunchback of Notre Dame*. Statues of great philosophers are detailed on the exterior, with the Cynic Diogenes placed over the entrance. The Hoose Library of Philosophy has more than 60,000 volumes and is considered to be one of the best in the country.

**Italianate façade of the Mudd Memorial Hall**

### Map labels

JEFFERSON
4TH STREET
BOULEVARD
SOUTH
USC School of Cinema-Television
TROUSDALE PARKWAY
HOOVER ST
① Bovard Administration Building
② Tommy Trojan
WEST 35TH ST
③ Doheny Memorial Library
FIGUEROA
STREET
UNIVERSITY OF SOUTHERN CALIFORNIA
Mudd Memorial Hall
BOULEVARD
Aerospace Museum
KINSEY DRIVE
⑦
STATE DRIVE
⑨
⑧ California Afro-American Museum
California Science Center
Exposition Park
FIGUEROA STREET
MENLO DRIVE
LA Sports Arena
DRIVE
BOULEVARD
LONG BEACH ↓

# SHOPPING IN LOS ANGELES

Whatever money can buy can be found in Los Angeles, from Cartier necklaces to organic farm produce. LA's temperate climate also allows for many pleasant outdoor alternatives to the ubiquitous malls. Melrose Avenue *(see p113)* and Santa Monica's Third Street Promenade *(see p78)* are both vibrant areas. Upscale Rodeo Drive *(see p94)* and Golden Triangle *(see p90)* are

**LA shopper**

famous for high couture houses and jewelers. Santa Monica's chic Montana Avenue is favored by both Hollywood wives and movie stars. The best areas for the latest in fashion and home decor are Robertson Boulevard near Burton Way, and Beverly Boulevard at Martel Avenue. Shopping is a pleasure in Old Pasadena *(see p154)*, which has many unique shops in restored, late 19th-century buildings.

**Interior of the Westside Pavilion, just south of Westwood Village**

## SHOPPING CENTERS AND MALLS

Shopping centers in LA tend to outclass most other American malls. One of the newest outdoor malls in the city, **The Grove** offers a blend of shopping and entertainment venues. The street is popular with families and teens who, between all the stores, cinemas, and restaurants, find plenty to keep themselves busy. Also check out the adjacent Farmers Market *(see p113)*, where you will find many quaint souvenir shops, and inexpensive, yet excellent outdoor food stands.

For a smooth indoor mall experience, try the trendy **Beverly Center**, which boasts a selection of more than 160 stores. Surrounded by Century City's office towers and in an open-air setting, **Westfield Century City** shopping center has more than 120 shops. The newly built stadium-style cinemas and posh outdoor

dining terrace make this mall a popular weekend hangout. Nearby, **Westside Pavilion** has an excellent array of clothing stores for children. A new cineplex adds to its appeal. **Santa Monica Place** *(see p77)* is a short walk from the beach, and is next door to the delightful Third Street Promenade. In the suburban San Fernando Valley, **Westfield Fashion Square** offers an eclectic shopping mix, with special appeal to families. One of the smaller malls, **Sherman Oaks Galleria** also boasts a fitness center and spa, in addition to its cineplex, shops, and restaurants.

## DEPARTMENT STORES

Every shopping mall has at least one department store, all of which stock a wide variety of goods, from cosmetics and clothes to cutlery and crockery. The old favorites are **Bloomingdale's**, best known for its shop-within-a-shop boutiques, and **Macy's**, with its in-house clothing lines that offer reasonably-priced designer fashion. The Beverly Hills section of Wilshire Boulevard *(see pp90–91)* has come to be known as Department Store Row. Among

**Shop logo on Melrose Avenue**

its big-name retailers are **Barneys New York** and **Saks Fifth Avenue**. Barneys rooftop deli is packed at lunchtime with shoppers and crowds from the film industry.

The shoe department at the high-end **Nordstrom** is legendary, as are its January and June half-price sales.

## DISCOUNT STORES

Many of LA's discount stores are part of national chains. A dollar goes a long way at such outlets, but it's strictly no-frills shopping. **Target** is popular for household items, toys, camping gear, and casual clothes, while **Costco** vends everything from bulk food items to computers. Wine and liquor are especially well priced here. Some even sell gas, though an annual membership fee is required.

**Upscale shops on Rodeo Drive *(see p94)***

Bargain hunters will delight in **99 Cents Only** stores. It is hard to predict what will be in stock, but items range from food to flower pots. **Nordstrom Rack**, the outlet for the chain, has top quality clothes, cosmetics, and lingerie. Again, the products in stock here vary by day and season. **Ross** and **Marshall's** stores carry the latest fashion with big discounts.

## FOOD AND WINE

Food markets in LA reflect the region's ethnic diversity and obsession with a healthy lifestyle. Downtown, Grand Central Market *(see p124)* sells produce and also has plenty of inexpensive food stalls. Farmers Market *(see p113)* offers fresh fruit, vegetables, and specialties such as freshly ground peanut butter. Dining alfresco here at vintage tables is a popular pastime. The market is also home to **Monsieur Marcel**, a gourmet French mini-market and deli, which specializes in cheeses, wines, and several other delicacies.

LA's homegrown food emporium, **Trader Joe's** sells an array of healthy foods, ready-to-eat meals, and wines. You can find everything from vitamins to fresh seafood here. **Whole Foods Market** also services the

health-conscious, discerning customers. Prepared delights, from soups and salads to sushi, can be consumed on the spot at tables here, making it a great choice for a quick bite. **Bristol Farms** is the city's most upscale grocer and wine merchant. All of the branches are spectacular, with in-store sushi bars and cafés.

A paradise for cheese lovers, **The Cheese Store of Beverly Hills** has the widest selection of domestic and imported cheeses in LA. It also stocks luxuries such as truffles and truffle oils.

In Beverly Hills, **The Wine Merchant** keeps one of the most superb cellars in town. Specializing in California-grown estate wines, **Silverlake Wine** offers weekly tastings and friendly service.

There is no dearth of ethnic food and spices in LA, and you will find Mexican, Chinese, and Thai markets dotted around. A must-try among ethnic stores is **India Sweets and Spices**, which stocks all things Indian, and also serves vegetarian delicacies in its small cafeteria.

## CLOTHES

Casual, of-the-moment styles dominate LA's fashion scene. The influence of Hollywood and its legion of slim actresses means that most trendy outlets stock breathtakingly small sizes. Unsurprisingly, custom-made haute couture is best in Beverly Hills, where you will find glitzy, red-carpet outfits throughout the shopping district. Rodeo Drive's tenants are among the who's who of the fashion world, from **Armani** to **Chanel** and **Versace**, all the most important fashion labels are within walking distance. These stores also offer sophisticated leather goods and signature fragrances. Prepare to be put on a waiting list for in-demand items. Also on Rodeo Drive is the architecturally magnificent **Prada**, which looks more like a museum than a retail store, with clothes, shoes, and purses that are must-haves for the upwardly mobile.

For unusual and trendsetting women's fashions at relatively affordable rates, **Anthropologie** is a fashionista's dream come true. **Eduardo Lucero** and

*A Gucci cushion*

Colorful stalls of produce in Grand Central Market *(see p124)*

**Trina Turk** are two of the city's most popular designers, and both sell distinctive designs in their eponymous boutiques. **American Rag** features both new and second-hand clothes and shoes for men, women, and children.

In West Hollywood, **Fred Segal** is more a collection of boutiques than a single store, and is frequented by many celebrities and movie stars. **Maxfield** also attracts fashionable and well-heeled clients, who love the exciting and stylish range of labels available. A companion to Fred Segal and Maxfield on Melrose Avenue, **Betsey Johnson** is known for her fun, colorful, and sometimes outrageous fashions for women.

For men, **Ermenegildo Zegna** and **John Varvatos** have some of the finest fashions in stock, while for the ultimate hip LA look, visit **Urban Outfitters**, the favorite of the college-aged crowd. If you've left home without your bikini, try the trendy **Everything But Water**.

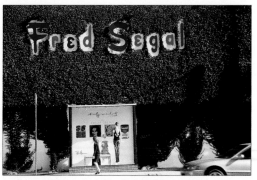

A Hollywood classic, Fred Segal boutique on Melrose Avenue

## CHILDREN'S CLOTHES

Seasonal styles sell quickly at big box retailer Target (see p166), which offers good value for children's clothing. **Old Navy** has low-priced, trendy styles, and popular end-of-season sales, while **GapKids** can be found at most malls, selling the popular casual jeans and T-shirt look. Kids with a high-end brand sensibility can visit Bloomingdale's (see p166) for labels such as Guess and Juicy Couture.

For designer kids' clothes, be prepared to spend at speciality boutiques such as **Flicka** on Larchmont Avenue. **Rightstart** offers quality gear, toys, books, accessories, and safety items. For the baby who has everything, **James Perse** is the store for sophisticated all-cotton clothing that has won over many Hollywood moms.

## VINTAGE CLOTHES

Vintage clothes in LA can be anything from hardly worn designer styles, clothes from decades past, or yesterday's cast-offs. Sifting through the racks takes time at charity-run thrift stores such as **Out of the Closet** and **Goodwill**. You may well find treasures among the donated goods, but it's all hit-and-miss.

Hipsters and teens favor shops trading in funky recycled fashions. **Squaresville** on Vermont Avenue and **Wasteland** on Melrose Avenue have some of the most popular retro looks in stock. Don't be surprised by some of the high prices, as some vintage clothes are quite valuable.

**reVamp** produces new vintage-inspired clothing, focusing on fashions from between 1910 and 1950. For slightly more contemporary styles, try **Buffalo Exchange**.

Clothes that come straight from film and TV show wardrobe departments can be found in the Valley at **It's A Wrap**.

## SPECIALTY SHOPS

Hollywood memorabilia is on sale throughout LA. **Fantasies Come True** sells only Disney-related items. Located in the heart of Hollywood, **Larry Edmund's Cinema Bookshop** is a cinephile's dream. It has new and used books, plus vintage posters. **Dark Delicacies** has everything for the horror fan, with some truly creepy items on sale. **Every Picture Tells A Story** sells original art from children's books and has a comfortable reading room for youngsters. For unique, handmade items, **The Folk**

**Tree** in Pasadena has a superb selection of Latin American arts and crafts, while **New Stone Age** sells unusual artisan ceramics and jewelry.

## ART & ANTIQUES

Fine antiques shops are found everywhere in the city. Those in Beverly Hills and West Hollywood cater to buyers with deep pockets. **Richard Shapiro** is filled with wonderful museum-quality pieces. His vine-covered building is close to more than 25 other dealers such as **Rose Tarlow**, also known for fabrics and candles, and **Off the Wall**, which offers mid-century furniture and decor items. Window shopping in this neighborhood is a rarefied pleasure. On Sunset Boulevard, **Wells Antiques** has the city's best collection of vintage tiles and California pottery.

In addition to LA's diverse antiques shops, its art galleries also span the gamut from the edgy grad-student work of Chung King Road, to the renowned contemporary artists at **Gagosian Gallery**. Bergamot Station (see p79) is home to several galleries, including top photograph dealer **Peter Fetterman**. Check newspaper listings for weekend gallery openings that bring out LA's art crowd.

# DIRECTORY

| SHOPPING CENTERS AND MALLS | DEPARTMENT STORES | DISCOUNT STORES |
|---|---|---|

**SHOPPING CENTERS AND MALLS**

**Beverly Center**
8500 Beverly Blvd.
**Map** 6 C2.
**Tel** (310) 854-0070.

**The Grove**
189 The Grove Drive.
**Map** 7 D3.
**Tel** (323) 900-8080.

**Santa Monica Place**
395 Santa Monica Place,
Santa Monica.
**Tel** (310) 394-5451.

**Sherman Oaks Galleria**
15301 Ventura Blvd,
Sherman Oaks.
**Tel** (818) 382-4100.

**Westfield Century City**
10250 Santa Monica Blvd,
Century City.
**Tel** (310) 277-3898.

**Westfield Fashion Square**
14006 Riverside Drive,
Sherman Oaks.
**Tel** (818) 783-0550.

**Westside Pavilion**
10800 W Pico Blvd.
**Tel** (310) 470-8752.

**DEPARTMENT STORES**

**Barneys New York**
9570 Wilshire Blvd. **Map** 5 F4. **Tel** (310) 276-4400.

**Bloomingdale's**
Beverly Center, 8500 Beverly Blvd. **Map** 6 C2.
**Tel** (310) 360-2700.

**Macy's**
Beverly Center, 8500 Beverly Blvd. **Map** 6 C2.
**Tel** (310) 854-6655.

**Nordstrom**
Westside Pavilion,
10830 W Pico Blvd.
**Tel** (310) 470-6155.

**Saks Fifth Avenue**
9600 Wilshire Blvd.
**Map** 5 E4.
**Tel** (310) 275-4211.

**DISCOUNT STORES**

**99 Cents Only**
601 S Fairfax Ave.
**Map** 7 D4.
**Tel** (323) 936-3972.

**Costco**
2901 Los Feliz Blvd.
**Tel** (323) 644-5201.

**Nordstrom Rack**
227 N Glendale Ave,
Glendale.
**Tel** (818) 240-2404.

**Target**
7100 Santa Monica Blvd,
W Hollywood. **Map** 7 F1.
**Tel** (323) 603-0004.

# DIRECTORY

## FOOD AND WINE

**Bristol Farms**
9039 Beverly Blvd. **Map** 6
A2. **Tel** (310) 248-2804.
www.bristolfarms.com

**The Cheese Store
of Beverly Hills**
419 N Beverly Drive,
Beverly Hills. **Map** 5 F3.
**Tel** (310) 278-2855.
www.cheesestorebh.com

**India Sweets
and Spices**
3126 Los Feliz Blvd.
**Tel** (323) 345-0360.

**Monsieur Marcel**
Farmers Market, 6333
W 3rd St. **Map** 7 D3.
**Tel** (323) 939-7792.
www.mrmarcel.com

**Silverlake Wine**
2395 Glendale Blvd.
**Tel** (323) 662-9024.
www.silverlakewine.com

**Trader Joe's**
7304 Santa Monica Blvd.
**Map** 7 F1.
**Tel** (323) 851-9772.
www.traderjoes.com

**Whole Foods Market**
6350 W 3rd St. **Map** 7 D3.
**Tel** (323) 964-6800.
www.wholefoods.com

**The Wine Merchant**
228 N Canon Drive. **Map**
5 F3. **Tel** (310) 278-7322.
www.beverlyhillswine
merchant.com

## CLOTHES

**American Rag**
150 S La Brea Ave. **Map** 7
F2. **Tel** (323) 935-3154.
www.amrag.com

**Anthropologie**
320 N Beverly Drive,
Beverly Hills. **Map** 5 F3.
**Tel** (310) 385-7390.
www.anthropologie.com

**Betsey Johnson**
8050 Melrose Ave.
**Map** 7 D2.
**Tel** (323) 852-1534.
www.betseyjohnson.com

**Chanel**
400 N Rodeo Drive,
Beverly Hills. **Map** 5 F3.
**Tel** (310) 278-5500.
www.chanel.com

**Eduardo Lucero**
7378 Beverly Blvd. **Map** 7
E2. **Tel** (323) 933-2778.

**Ermenegildo Zegna**
301 N Rodeo Drive,
Beverly Hills. **Map** 5 F3.
**Tel** (310) 247-8827.
www.zegna.com

**Everything But
Water**
Beverly Center, 8500
Beverly Blvd. **Map** 6 C2.
**Tel** (310) 289-1550.

**Fred Segal**
8118 Melrose Ave. **Map** 7
D1. **Tel** (323) 651-1935.

**Giorgio Armani
Boutique**
436 N Rodeo Drive,
Beverly Hills. **Map** 5 F3.
**Tel** (310) 271-5555.
www.armani.com

**John Varvatos**
8800 Melrose Ave. **Map** 6
B2. **Tel** (310) 859-2970.

**Marshall's**
2206 Sawtelle Blvd.
**Tel** (310) 312-1266.

**Maxfield**
8825 Melrose Ave. **Map** 6
B2. **Tel** (310) 274-8800.

**Prada**
343 N Rodeo Drive,
Beverly Hills. **Map** 5 F3.
**Tel** (310) 278-8661.
www.prada.com

**Ross**
6298 W 3rd St.
**Tel** (323) 936-2864.

**Trina Turk**
8008 W 3rd St. **Map** 6 C3.
**Tel** (323) 651-1382.
www.trinaturk.com

**Urban Outfitters**
1440 Third St Promenade,
Santa Monica.
**Tel** (310) 394-1404.

**Versace**
248 N Rodeo Drive,
Beverly Hills. **Map** 5 F3.
**Tel** (310) 205-3921.
www.versace.com

## CHILDREN'S
CLOTHES

**Flicka**
204 N Larchmont Blvd.
**Map** 8 B3.
**Tel** (323) 466-5822.

**GapKids**
6801 Hollywood Blvd.
**Map** 2 B4. **Tel** (323) 462-
6124. www.gap.com

**James Perse**
8914 Melrose Ave. **Map** 6
A2. **Tel** (310) 276-7277.
www.jamesperse.com

**Old Navy**
8487 W 3rd St. **Map** 6 C3.
**Tel** (323) 658-5292.
www.oldnavy.com

**Rightstart**
2212 Wilshire Place,
Santa Monica. **Map** 10 B3.
**Tel** (310) 829-5135.
www.rightstart.com

## VINTAGE CLOTHES

**Buffalo Exchange**
131 N La Brea Ave.
**Map** 7 F3.
**Tel** (323) 938-8604.

**Goodwill**
4575 Hollywood Blvd,
Hollywood.
**Tel** (323) 644-1517.
www.goodwill.com

**It's A Wrap**
3315 N Magnolia Ave,
Burbank.
**Tel** (818) 567-7366.

**Out of the Closet**
360 N Fairfax Ave.
**Map** 7 D2.
**Tel** (323) 934-1956.

**reVamp**
834 S Broadway.
**Map** 10 D5.
**Tel** (213) 488-3387.
www.revampvintage.com

**Wasteland**
7428 Melrose Ave.
**Map** 7 E2.
**Tel** (323) 653-3028.

## SPECIALTY SHOPS

**Dark Delicacies**
4213 Burbank Blvd,
Burbank.
**Tel** (818) 556-6660.
www.darkdel.com

**Every Picture Tells
A Story**
1311-C Montana Ave,
Santa Monica.
**Tel** (310) 451-2700.
www.everypicture.com

**Fantasies Come True**
4383 Tujunga Ave, Studio
City. **Map** 2 A1.
**Tel** (818) 985-2636. www.
fantasiescometrue.com

**The Folk Tree**
217 S Fair Oaks Ave,
Pasadena. **Tel** (626) 795-
8733. www.folktree.com

**Larry Edmund's
Cinema Bookshop**
6644 Hollywood Blvd. **Map**
2 B4. **Tel** (323) 463-3273.
www.larryedmunds.com

**New Stone Age**
8407 W 3rd St. **Map** 6 C3.
**Tel** (323) 658-5969.
www.newstoneagela.com

## ART AND
ANTIQUES

**Gagosian Gallery**
456 N Camden Drive,
Beverly Hills. **Map** 6 A2.
**Tel** (310) 271-9400.
www.gagosian.com

**Off the Wall**
7325 Melrose Ave,
W Hollywood.
**Map** 6 B2. **Tel** (323)
930-1185. www.
offthewallantiques.com

**Peter Fetterman
Gallery**
Bergamot Station
2525 Michigan Ave,
Gallery A7, Santa Monica.
**Tel** (310) 453-6463.
www.peterfetterman.com

**Richard Shapiro**
8905 Melrose Ave,
W Hollywood. **Map** 6 A2.
**Tel** (310) 275-6700. www.
rshapiroantiques.com

**Rose Tarlow**
8540 Melrose Place,
W Hollywood. **Map** 6 C1.
**Tel** (323) 651-2202.
www.rosetarlow.com

**Wells Antiques**
2162 Sunset Blvd.
**Tel** (213) 413-0558.
www.wellstile.com

*Many of the listings have
multiple branches. Shops
will be happy to provide
information of their
nearest branch.*

## BOOKS & MUSIC

Residents of LA buy more books than in any other city in the country. Some of the most popular independent book-shops are **Book Soup** and **Skylight Books**. Each of these old favorites regularly host readings by major writers. Also, the staff at these shops tend to be more knowledgeable about their merchandise than chain outlets. Book Soup has a great selection of art books and guidebooks devoted to California and LA, while **Hennessey & Ingalls** has one of the largest collections of art and architecture books on the west coast.

Many large bookstore chains, such as **Barnes & Noble**, have coffee bars and stock music CDs as well. **Amoeba Music**, located in Hollywood, is the city's largest independent music store with two floors of new and used records and CDs. The weekly in-store perfor-mances are free and fun.

**Origami** is a vinyl record store that carries a curated selection of new, reissued, and used vinyls. They often host in-store performances by new indie bands.

## FARMERS' MARKETS

With 80 certified Farmers' Markets held in the city each week, there is no shortage of opportunities to see and taste Southern California's seasonal, newly harvested bounty. Each outdoor farmers' market has vendors selling a range of fresh produce, including organically grown fruits and vegetables straight from the fields. Many markets also feature stalls, which offer prepared food as well as arts and crafts. Check out the **Farmernet** website for exact times and locations of the various markets.

The popular **Santa Monica's Wednesday and Saturday Farmers' Market** at Arizona and Second Streets is the largest. The high quality of the produce on sale is attested to by the well-known chefs who frequent the stalls. Savvy buyers prefer to start their shopping early. On Sunday mornings, visit Ivar Avenue's **Hollywood Farmers' Market**, which attracts a very hip crowd. Famous faces can often be spotted browsing amidst the crowd. **Santa Monica Sunday Farmers' Market** on Main Street is a favorite with families who line up for delicious, freshly made crêpes and omelets to picnic on in the busy street-side green.

## FLEA MARKETS

Most of LA's best-known flea markets take place on Sundays at varying locations. All are in the open, with hundreds, and sometimes thousands of vendors spreading out their wares over massive parking lots. Be prepared to spend more than a couple of hours browsing, bargaining, and walking. Comfortable shoes and a discriminating eye are a must. It is possible to find outstanding bargains for antiques, jewelry, vintage clothes, and assorted knick-knacks.

On the first Sunday of the month, the **Pasadena City College Flea Market** adds huge numbers of used records to the mix, while on second Sundays, the **Rose Bowl Flea Market**, one of the largest and best-loved markets in LA, sells hard-to-find collectibles. However, those who arrive early have to pay an extra entry fee. The **Long Beach Outdoor Antique & Collectible Market** runs on the third Sunday of every month and offers bargains galore.

## HOME ACCESSORIES

There's an entire universe of stores dedicated to outfitting LA's sprawl of homes and apartments. **IKEA** does basic home furnishings stylishly, and at extremely affordable prices. These items are generally home assembly and emphasis is more on looks than longlasting quality. **Pottery Barn** and **Crate & Barrel** serve those who do not mind spending more for durability and good design. Both have several outlets, as does the home accessory superstore, **Bed, Bath &** **Beyond**. Look here for items such as kitchen gadgets, picture frames, towels, and clever decorative accessories.

Anthropologie *(see p169)* offers endearingly whimsical, flea market-style goods for the home. Glassware and crockery change palettes and styles with each season. **Shabby Chic** on Montana Avenue helped popularize the casual Southern California look, as is evident from its oversized, comfortable, and slip-covered sofas and chairs.

For both vintage as well as modern reproduction furnish-ings, survey the stores along Beverly Boulevard from La Brea west, to Crescent Heights. Shops such as **Modern One**, **Twentieth Design**, and **Modernica** feature the best of sleek, mid-20th-century design. **Thai Teak** specializes in modern Asian-style furnishings, while **Grace Home Furnishings** is known for its eclectic new and retro furniture. Chic and tasteful, **Bountiful** sells period furniture along with luxurious bath and home products on Venice's charming Abbot Kinney Boulevard.

## GIFTS AND TOYS

Some of the best luxury gift products, ranging from picture frames to fine jewelry, can be found in Beverly Hills' **Gearys**, a shop also known for its opulent bridal and gift registry. At the other end of the price spectrum, **Wing Hop Fung** in Chinatown stocks all sorts of imported goods, from cheap toys to tea sets. Other smaller gift shops in the area are also within easy walking distance and are good for inexpensive shopping.

**Sumi's** in Silver Lake features local designers, as well as lines from around the world. Jewelry is the star here. **Compantes Chocolatier** sells handmade chocolates packaged in beautifully wrapped boxes.

For toys, Target *(see p166)* and **Toys 'R' Us** have several branches selling many brands, games, and smaller sporting goods. **PuzzleZoo** has puzzles, games, and the most in-demand action figures.

**Wound and Wound** is one of the many toy shops at Universal CityWalk® that sell items for both children and adults.

## HAIR AND BEAUTY

LA is no less than the world's beauty capital. Credit goes to the youth-obsessed film and television business for the proliferation of high-quality soap-and-salve emporiums.

Glossy skin care and make-up superstore **Sephora** displays dozens of product lines. Sales clerks here are helpful and offer many samples. **Aveda** adheres to organic principles in its fragrant, natural skin- and hair-care lines. Shoppers can ask for a brief, relaxing chair massage and tea. **Wilshire Beauty** was a laboratory for Rita Hayworth's colorist and Bette Davis's make-up artist, and stocks premier beauty products. **The Salon** at Fred Segal's Santa Monica branch specializes in what can be termed beauty couture. Fragrances can be made to order and make-up artists stand by for quick make-overs, using boutique brands such as Stilla. **Cost Plus World Market** has bath products and candles at reasonable prices. Trader Joe's *(see p167)* has its own line of organic hair- and skin-care products, such as salt scrubs and lavender-scented shampoo. Many spas such as **Equinox Spa** sell higher-end skin-care lines and anti-aging regimes. Notable hair salons, including **Privé Salon**, also a spa, sells its own line of elegant hair care products. **MAC** is known for its seasonally changing color palette and alliances with top Hollywood make-up artists and stars.

# DIRECTORY

## BOOKS & MUSIC

**Amoeba Music**
6400 Sunset Blvd. **Map 2**
C5. **Tel** *(323) 245-6400.*

**Barnes & Noble**
1201 3rd St Promenade,
Santa Monica.
**Tel** *(310) 260-9110.*

**Book Soup**
8818 W Sunset Blvd. **Map**
1 A5. **Tel** *(310) 659-3110.*

**Hennessey & Ingalls**
214 Wilshire Blvd,
Santa Monica.
**Tel** *(310) 458-9074.*

**Origami Vinyl**
1816 W Sunset Blvd.
**Map 10** C1.
**Tel** *(213) 413-3030.*

**Skylight Books**
1818 N Vermont Ave.
**Tel** *(323) 660-1175.*

## FARMERS' MARKETS

**Farmernet**
For markets in your area
see: **www**.farmernet.com

**Hollywood Sunday Farmers' Market**
Ivar and Selma Aves. **Map**
2 C4. **Tel** *(323) 463-3171.*

**Santa Monica Sunday Farmers' Market**
Ocean Park & Main Sts,
Santa Monica.
**Tel** *(310) 458-8712.*

**Santa Monica Wednesday and Saturday Farmers' Market**
Arizona & 2nd Sts, Santa
Monica. **Tel** *(310) 458-8712.*

## FLEA MARKETS

**Long Beach Outdoor Antique & Collectible Market**
Veterans Stadium, Faculty
Ave & Conant St, Long
Beach. **Tel** *(323) 655-5703.*

**Pasadena City College Flea Market**
1570 E Colorado Blvd,
Pasadena.
**Tel** *(626) 585-7906.*

**Rose Bowl Flea Market**
1001 Rosebowl Drive,
Pasadena.
**Tel** *(323) 560-7469.*

## HOME ACCESSORIES

**Bed, Bath & Beyond**
1557 Vine St. **Map 2** C5.
**Tel** *(323) 460-4500.*

**Bountiful**
1335 Abbot Kinney Blvd,
Venice. **Tel** *(310) 450-3620.*

**Crate & Barrel**
189 The Grove Drive. **Map**
7 D3. **Tel** *(323) 297-0370.*

**Grace Home Furnishings**
11632 Barrington Ct.
**Tel** *(310) 476-7176.*

## IKEA
600 N San Fernando Blvd,
Burbank.
**Tel** *(818) 842-4532.*

**Modern One**
7956 Beverly Blvd. **Map**
7 D2. **Tel** *(323) 651-5082.*

**Modernica**
7366 Beverly Blvd. **Map**
7 E2. **Tel** *(323) 933-0383.*

**Pottery Barn**
300 N Beverly Drive. **Map**
6 B3. **Tel** *(310) 860-9506.*

**Shabby Chic**
1013 Montana Ave,
Santa Monica.
**Tel** *(310) 394-1975.*

**Thai Teak**
2400 Main St, Santa
Monica. **Tel** *(310) 581-4255.*

**Twentieth Design**
8057 Beverly Blvd. **Map 7**
D2. **Tel** *(323) 904-1200.*

## GIFTS AND TOYS

**Compartes Chocolatier**
912 S Barrington Ave.
**Tel** *(310) 826-3380.*

**Gearys**
351 N Beverly Drive,
Beverly Hills. **Map 5** F3.
**Tel** *(310) 273-4741.*

**PuzzleZoo**
1411 3rd St Promenade,
Santa Monica.
**Tel** *(310) 393-9201.*

**Sumi's**
3204 Sunset Blvd.
**Tel** *(323) 284-4712.*

## Toys 'R' Us
11136 Jefferson Blvd,
Culver City.
**Tel** *(310) 398-5775.*

**Wing Hop Fung**
725 W Garvey Ave,
Monterey Park.
**Tel** *(323) 940-8000.*

**Wound and Wound**
100 Universal City Plaza.
**Tel** *(818) 509-8129.*

## HAIR AND BEAUTY

**Aveda**
6801 Hollywood Blvd.
**Map 2** B4. **Tel** *(323)
962-1596.*

**Cost Plus World Market**
6333 W 3rd St. **Map 7** D3.
**Tel** *(323) 935-5530.*

**Equinox Spa**
2025 Ave of the Stars. **Map**
5 D5. **Tel** *(310) 556-2256.*

**MAC**
133 N Robertson Blvd.
**Map 6** B2.
**Tel** *(310) 854-0860.*

**Privé Salon**
7373 Beverly Blvd. **Map**
7 E2. **Tel** *(323) 931-5559.*

**The Salon**
500 Broadway, Santa
Monica.
**Tel** *(310) 394-8509.*

**Sephora**
6801 Hollywood Blvd.
**Map 2** B4.
**Tel** *(323) 462-6898.*

**Wilshire Beauty**
5401 Wilshire Blvd.
**Map 7** F4.
**Tel** *(323) 937-2000.*

# ENTERTAINMENT IN LOS ANGELES

As the center of the film industry, Los Angeles has dominated the world stage during much of the 20th century. It is therefore not surprising that the city sees itself as the Entertainment Capital of the World. LA's large and successful artistic community ensures that there is always plenty to do in the city, although only small areas tend to be lively after dark.

Hollywood movie sign

LA also has a huge number of theaters, which range from 1930s movie palaces to state-of-the-art multiplexes. Stage productions are also plentiful and diverse. The city has a well-respected symphony orchestra and opera company, which in the summer give outdoor concerts in places such as the Hollywood Bowl (see p111). Jazz and blues bars and clubs are centered on Sunset Boulevard.

**LA listings publications**

## INFORMATION

Various publications can help sift through the city's embarrassment of entertainment riches. The *LA Weekly* – a free paper available at bars, clubs, and corner stands across the city – has the most comprehensive entertainment and arts listings. It is aimed at the younger generation and outshines the *Los Angeles Times* in that respect, although the *Los Angeles Times* is also a reliable source for information.

The monthly publications include the popular *Los Angeles Magazine*, which lists all the main events in the city and also has good restaurant reviews. More up-to-date and reliable information, aimed at tourists, is provided in the monthly *Where Magazine*, which is available in most hotels.

Listings for gay and lesbian readers include *Odyssey Magazine*, *Edge Los Angeles*, and *Curve Magazine*. The main branch of the **Los Angeles Convention and Visitors Bureau**

is in Downtown, and it offers multilingual assistance. Their visitors' guide gives listings of restaurants, hotels, shops, and attractions. There is also a 24-hour events hotline. The city's two other main information centers are the **West Hollywood Conventions & Visitors Bureau** and the **Beverly Hills Visitors' Bureau**. In addition, **www.yelp. com** and **www.la.com** are useful sources of information.

## BUYING TICKETS

The simplest source of tickets to concerts, plays, and sports events in LA is **Ticketmaster**. You can order the tickets online using a credit card, or visit one of their centers at a branch of Wherehouse Music or a Macy's department store (see p168). If you want to avoid their service charges, try calling the venues direct. Other agencies include **Tickets LA**, **Prestige Tickets**, and **Los Angeles Times Tickets**. Theater productions and times are available by calling **LA Stage Alliance**'s information line.

## DISCOUNT TICKETS

**Barry's Tickets** promises premium seats for sports, music, and theater events. This service also sells half-price theater tickets online. Most are for short-run shows – don't expect the most popular shows to be discounted.

If you are looking for a bargain and are willing to gamble on the availability of seats a few hours before the show starts, then you can try telephoning the box office direct. Many places offer last minute "rush" discounts on unsold seats for performances.

Students who hold a valid ISIC card (see p620) may be able to get discounts to some concerts and plays. The best spots to try are those affiliated with Los Angeles's universities, such as UCLA's Geffen Playhouse (see p174).

LACMA (see pp114–17), a venue for free concerts

Hollywood Bowl, one of LA's premier concert venues *(see p111)*

## FREE EVENTS

Most of the areas within Los Angeles have local festivals, particularly in the summer, which feature food, live music, arts, and crafts. Contact the **LA Department of Cultural Affairs** for details. On Thursday nights in the summer, Santa Monica Pier has concerts featuring a variety of music styles *(see pp78–9)*.

Also in the summer, the LA Philharmonic allows visitors to listen to its midday concert rehearsals at the Hollywood Bowl *(see p111)*. Some of Los Angeles's museums do not charge entrance fees. They include the California Museum of Science and Industry *(see p165)*, Travel Town in Griffith Park *(see p150)*, and the J Paul Getty Museum *(see pp82–5)*. Los Angeles County Museum of Art *(see pp114–17)* hosts concerts of jazz and chamber music on Fridays and Sundays in the museum plaza.

## FACILITIES FOR THE DISABLED

As elsewhere in California *(see p620)*, almost all clubs, movies, and theaters in LA are wheelchair accessible and will provide special seating. Most establishments also have parking and toilets designed to facilitate the needs of people with disabilities.

Information about disabled access at events and attractions can be found on the Los Angeles Convention and Visitors Bureau's website.

Detail on a LA theater

The **Los Angeles County Commission on Disabilities** can provide advice on transportation and equipment rental. **Travelers Aid International** operates a useful website called USTravAbility, with links to many resources for disabled travelers throughout the United States.

**LA Tourist** is a website with information on and links to most Los Angeles attractions, including whether or not they are wheelchair-accessible, have assisted-listening systems, sign-language interpreters, ramps, elevators, and handicapped parking.

Art Deco façade of Hollywood's Pantages Theater *(see p108)*

# DIRECTORY

## USEFUL NUMBERS

**Beverly Hills Visitors Bureau**
239 S Beverly Dr, Beverly Hills, CA 90212. *Tel (310) 248-1015.*
www.beverlyhillschamber.com

**Hollywood Conventions & Visitors Bureau**
6801 Hollywood Blvd, Hollywood, CA 90028.
*Tel (323) 467-6412.*
www.lacvb.com

**LA Department of Cultural Affairs**
201 N Figueroa St, Suite 1400, Los Angeles, CA 90012.
*Tel (213) 202-5500.*
www.culturela.org

**Los Angeles Convention and Visitors Bureau**
685 S Figueroa St, Los Angeles, CA 90017. *Tel (213) 689-8822.*
www.discoverlosangeles.com

## TICKET AGENCIES

**Barry's Tickets**
*Tel (866) 708-8499.*
www.barrystickets.com

**LA Stage Alliance**
*Tel (213) 614-0556.*
www.lastagealliance.com

**Los Angeles Times Tickets**
*Tel (866) 215-8463.*
www.tickets.latimes.com

**Prestige Tickets**
*Tel (888) 595-6260.*
www.prestigetickets.com

**Ticketmaster**
*Tel (213) 381-2000.*
www.ticketmaster.com

## FACILITIES FOR THE DISABLED

**LA Tourist**
www.latourist.com

**Los Angeles County Commission on Disabilities**
500 W Temple St, Room 1350, Los Angeles, CA 90012.
*Tel (213) 974-1053, (213) 974-1707 TDD.*

**Travelers Aid International**
1612 K St, NW, Suite 206, Washington, DC 20006.
www.ustravability.org

# Entertainment Venues

As befits a city of its size and reputation, LA has a vast range of entertainment spots. Sophisticated restaurants, concert venues, and lounges are found throughout the city. Downtown's Grand Avenue is the main cultural corridor, and is graced by the prestigious Museum of Contemporary Art and by the Music Center *(see p125)*. Hollywood and West Hollywood abound with historic movie houses, theaters, and celebrity-owned nightclubs such as The Viper Room *(see p102)*. By day, visitors can join a TV studio audience or watch a game at one of the major sports arenas. Almost every weekend, a vibrant themed festival takes place somewhere in the city.

The famous Rooftop Bar at the Standard Downtown Hotel

## BARS

From traditional, old-school watering holes to the latest and trendiest hot spots, LA's diverse bar scene is always expanding. Enjoy yourself, but be aware of rigorously enforced anti- drinking and-driving laws when planning your itinerary for the evening.

At **Musso and Frank Grill**, a historic Hollywood cornerstone, the cocktails and decor remain almost unchanged since the time when renowned author William Faulkner drank here. **Beauty Bar**, with its faux

Hotel Casa del Mar's luxurious and popular lobby lounge, Veranda.

beauty salon look, attracts those who like a martini with their manicure. Top DJs spin here weekly. Specialty bars also abound. The kitschy yet hip **El Carmen** serves more than 270 kinds of tequila along with authentic Mexican bar fare. European-style gastro-pub **Father's Office** in Santa Monica has 36 artisan beers on tap and a wonderful choice of estate wines. It serves some of the most outstanding bar snacks in town. **Tom Bergin's Tavern** is a traditional Irish pub, with veteran bartenders who prepare the best Irish coffee in town. For star sightings, try **Polo Lounge** at Beverly Hills Hotel, or **Windows Lounge** at Four Seasons Hotel. Both venues cater to tycoons, the very well-heeled, and celebrities. **Rooftop Bar** at Standard Downtown combines panoramic skyscraper views, with alfresco lounging all year long. The bar is gently lit by lights from

**THE COMEDY STORE**

Club sign on Sunset Boulevard

the office towers nearby, while an outdoor fireplace keeps the rooftop warm. Another intimate and elegant bar is Hotel Casa del Mar's lobby lounge, **The Veranda**, which is cosily furnished with plush leather couches, and offers picturesque ocean views.

## CLUBS

Trends change rapidly in LA's dynamic club scene, so check local listings to stay up-to-date. Also, be prepared to show ID, since the 21-and-over drinking law is strictly enforced.

For the best clubbing action in LA, head to Hollywood. **The Avalon** is one of the oldest and most beloved clubs in the area, often attracting world-famous DJs and performers. It also houses the stylish Spider Club, an intimate VIP lounge. **Geisha House** is an Oriental-themed club that offers full restaurant service along with a thriving party scene. Be ready to pay a hefty cover charge. For clubbing with a twist, try **CineSpace**, which shows films on screens placed throughout the lounge.

In Santa Monica, **Zanzibar** has the hippest DJs and decor. For rock and indie music, **Spaceland** and **Hotel Cafe** are best, often featuring live gigs by up-and-coming bands. West Hollywood, with its sizeable gay population, has many discos such as **The Factory** for a fun night out. Both **The Mayan** and **The Conga Room** are hot venues for salsa, merengue, and rock en español music. For ample laughs, visit one of LA's many comedy clubs. Talented unknowns, as well as major names, perform at **The Comedy Store**, **Hollywood Improv**, and **Laugh Factory**.

## MOVIE THEATERS

Most visitors do not spend a lot of time watching movies in LA, even though current releases and countless classics are always being shown. The movie palaces themselves, however, draw huge crowds, with Grauman's Chinese and El Capitan theatres *(see p110)* being the best known.

Multiplexes, such as **The Grove**, **ArcLight Cinemas**, and **Loews Universal Cineplex 20** offer state-of-the-art entertainment. Built as a silent film palace in 1922, **The Egyptian Theatre** is old Hollywood at its best, run by American Cinematheque, it now shows a mix of cult and international films. For a nostalgia trip, visit **Silent Movie Theatre**, which shows classics from the 1920s. Screenings here are frequently accompanied by charming musical performances.

## STUDIO TOURS AND TV SHOWS

Several of LA's television and film studios offer behind-the-scenes tours as well as tickets to tapings of popular shows. In the high-tech studios of **CBS-TV**, sitcoms and game shows are taped before live audiences. For tickets, write about six weeks before your trip, specifying the date and show you want to see. Audience members must understand and speak English. During production season, July through March, check the **TV Tickets** website for entrance to dozens of shows.

In Burbank *(see pp144–5)*, **NBC-TV** offers tickets to *The Tonight Show* and a tour of the studios. The **Warner Bros** tour is probably the truest look at modern-day film-making – the deluxe tour includes lunch at the studio commissary. Visitors on the **Paramount Studios** *(see p113)* tour must be at least 12 years old. Show tickets are also available.

## THEATER

With hundreds of professional plays staged each year, there is something for everyone in Los Angeles. Downtown's Music Center *(see p125)* is home to two of the city's leading theaters for drama – **Mark Taper Forum** and **Ahmanson Theatre**. Ahmanson and Pantages *(see p118)* in Hollywood attract the big Broadway musicals, while the intimate Mark Taper Forum is known for its experimental drama. Sunset Boulevard's **Kodak Theater** (home to the annual Academy Awards® telecasts) and the new **Nokia Theatre** at LA Live downtown host numerous special events, variety shows, concerts, and dance events. Housed in striking Mediterranean-style theaters, **Geffen Playhouse** and **Pasadena Playhouse** both put on new works as well as old favorites. More alternative productions are performed at the city's smaller spaces, such as **The Actors' Gang** or the innovative **REDCAT Theatre**. In summer, the popular **Theatricum Botanicum** stages Shakespeare's classics in its outdoor amphitheater.

## ROCK, JAZZ, AND BLUES

Still rocking the world, Sunset Strip *(see pp102–104)* boasts the venerable **Whisky A Go-Go**. A rock'n'roll legend since the time it hosted performances by The Doors, it carries on the tradition by featuring gigs by many established artists. Nearby, perennial favorite **The Roxy** may be somewhat cramped, but that does not deter the big names in rock from performing there. **The Viper Room**, with its line-up of promising new bands, also remains hugely popular with the young Hollywood crowd.

Roxy sign on Sunset Boulevard

LA's jazz scene is lively and characterized by cozy joints such as **The Baked Potato**, where there are weekly jam sessions, performances by

**Music Center plaza and fountain leading to Mark Taper Forum**

well-known studio artists, and gourmet baked potatoes on the menu. A refined, classic atmosphere defines the well-respected **Catalina Bar & Grill**, while **Jazz Bakery** offers a rarefied listening experience – there is no club scene, just a focus on the music.

Look for top soul and blues acts in **House of Blues**, and try its "Gospel brunch." The grungy **Troubadour** often hosts promising newcomers, while **McCabe's Guitar Shop** is frequented by musicians for its emphasis on music and performances. The acoustically perfect rooms at **Knitting Factory** present the latest folk and rock acts.

The biggest names perform at LA's arenas, including Staples Center *(see p163)*, Greek Theater *(see p150)*, and Universal Amphitheater *(see p147)*. Expect stratospheric ticket prices and parking charges at these top venues.

**Paramount Studios' famous gates *(see p113)***

## OPERA, DANCE, AND CLASSICAL MUSIC

The **LA Philharmonic**, which winters at the Walt Disney Concert Hall *(see p125)* is a world-class orchestra. During the season, performances range from classical favorites to avant garde, modern works. The Philharmonic's summer home, the idyllic outdoor Hollywood Bowl *(see p111)*, is famous for its magical musical moments, and is a perfect spot for relaxed alfresco picnicking.

The **LA Opera**, under the direction of Plácido Domingo, performs at the Dorothy Chandler Pavilion *(see p125)* between September and June. Chamber groups perform at various places, such as the **Colburn School of Performing Arts**, throughout the city. Colburn also offers a season of free performances, including music, dance, and drama.

Music, dance, and drama enliven Glendale's historic **Alex Theater**. The acoustically outstanding Royce Hall is the main venue at the **UCLA Center for the Performing Arts**. More than 200 performances are featured annually, and offer an eclectic mix of vanguard theater, spoken word, music, and dance, with appearances by many prominent international artists. At the **Ford Amphitheatre**, you can enjoy music, dance, and outdoor film screenings as you feast on a picnic under the stars.

## OUTDOOR ACTIVITIES

Los Angeles's beaches are a great natural resource and offer surfing, swimming, and volleyball. The 27-mile- (43-km-) long beach, with its adjacent bike and skate paths, makes for delightful and invigorating rides. Beachside bike and skate rental outlets are plentiful.

Griffith Park *(see pp150–51)* and Topanga State Park *(see p81)* offer miles of hiking trails. Griffith Park also has horse trails, two golf courses, and two tennis centers. Many city parks have free tennis courts.

Spectator sports include baseball at Dodger Stadium *(see p152)*, professional soccer at the Galaxy's deluxe **Home Depot Center**, and ice hockey and basketball at the Staples Center *(see p163)*. Besides these, you can watch horse racing at the Hollywood Park and **Santa Anita Race-track**, and polo at Will Rogers State Historic Park *(see p81)*.

## CHILDREN'S ENTERTAINMENT

A variety of family-friendly diversions are available in Los Angeles, ranging from the free seaside street theater of the Venice Beach boardwalk to IMAX® movies at the **California Science Center**. During the warmer months, a visit to the beach or the pool is a good idea. The **Under the Sea Indoor Playground** has a turbo slide, games and more. Children can romp in the expanded **Kidspace Children's Museum**, which blends science and fun in hands-on exhibits. An outdoor garden and waterway add much to the visit. Since 1963, **Bob Baker Marionette Theatre** has kept kids spellbound with its traditional puppet theater. Musical theater at **Santa Monica Playhouse** is especially tailored for young audiences.

It is also worth checking newspaper listings pages, which provide details and contact information of upcoming seasonal festivals.

# DIRECTORY

## BARS

**Beauty Bar**
1638 N Cahuenga Blvd.
**Map** 2 C4.
*Tel (323) 464-7676.*
**www**.beautybar.com

**El Carmen**
8138 W 3rd St. **Map** 6 C3.
*Tel (323) 852-1552.*

**Father's Office**
1018 Montana Ave,
Santa Monica.
*Tel (310) 393-2337.*
**www**.fathersoffice.com

**Musso and Frank Grill**
6667 Hollywood Blvd.
**Map** 2 B4.
*Tel (323) 467-7788.*

**Polo Lounge**
Beverly Hills Hotel, 9641
Sunset Blvd. **Map** 5 D2.
*Tel (310) 276-2251.* **www**.
thebeverlyhillshotel.com

**Rooftop Bar**
Standard Downtown Hotel,
550 S Flower St. **Map** 11 D4.
*Tel (213) 892-8080.*
**www**.standardhotels.com

**Tom Bergin's Tavern**
840 S Fairfax Ave. **Map** 7
D4. *Tel (323) 936-7151.*
**www**.tombergins.com

**The Veranda**
Hotel Casa del Mar, 1910
Ocean Way, Santa Monica.
*Tel (310) 581-5533.* **www**.
hotelcasadelmar.com

**Windows Lounge**
Four Seasons Hotel, 300 S
Doheny Drive. **Map** 6 A3.
*Tel (310) 273-2222.*

## CLUBS

**The Avalon**
1735 Vine St. **Map** 2 C4.
*Tel (323) 467-4571.* **www**.
avalonhollywood.com

**The Comedy Store**
8433 W Sunset Blvd.
**Map** 1 A5. *Tel (323) 656-
6225.* **www**.thecomedy
store.com

**CineSpace**
6356 Hollywood Blvd.
**Map** 2 C4.
*Tel (323) 817-3456.*
**www**.cine-space.com

**Conga Room**
LA Live downtown,
800 W Olympic Blvd.
**Map** 10 C5.
**www**.congaroom.com

**The Factory**
652 N La Peer Drive.
**Map** 6 A2. *Tel (310) 659-
4551.* **www**.factorynight
club.com

**Geisha House**
6633 Hollywood Blvd.
**Map** 2 C4.
*Tel (323) 460-6300.*
**www**.dolcegroup.com

**Hollywood Improv**
8162 Melrose Ave.
**Map** 7 D1. *Tel (323) 651-
2583.* **www**.improv.com

**Hotel Cafe**
1623/2 Cahuenga Blvd.
**Map** 2 C4.
*Tel (323) 461-2040.*
**www**.hotelcafe.com

**Laugh Factory**
8001 W Sunset Blvd.
*Tel (323) 656-1336.*
**www**.laughfactory.com

**The Mayan**
1038 S Hill St. **Map** 10
C5. *Tel (213) 746-4287.*

**Spaceland**
1717 Silver Lake Blvd.
*Tel (323) 661-4380.*
**www**.clubspaceland.com

**Zanzibar**
1301 Fifth St,
Santa Monica.
*Tel (310) 451-2221.*
**www**.zanzibarlive.com

# DIRECTORY

## MOVIE THEATERS

### ArcLight Cinemas
6360 W Sunset Blvd.
**Map** 2 C5.
*Tel (323) 464-4226.*
www.arclightcinemas.com

### The Egyptian Theatre
6712 Hollywood Blvd.
**Map** 2 B4.
*Tel (323) 466-3456.*
www.american
cinematheque.com

### The Grove
189 Grove Drive.
**Map** 7 D3.
*Tel (323) 692-0829.*
www.thegrovela.com

### Loews Universal Cineplex 20
100 Universal City Plaza,
Universal City.
*Tel (818) 508-0711.*
www.fandango.com

### Silent Movie Theatre
611 N Fairfax Ave.
**Map** 7 D1.
*Tel (323) 655-2520.*
www.cinefamily.org

## STUDIO TOURS AND TV SHOWS

### CBS-TV
7800 Beverly Blvd.
**Map** 7 D2.
*Tel (323) 575-2624.*
www.cbs.com

### NBC-TV
3000 W Alameda Ave,
Burbank.
*Tel (818) 840-3538.*
www.nbc.com

### Paramount Studios
5555 Melrose Ave. **Map** 8
C7. *Tel (323) 965-1777.*
www.paramount
studios.com

### TV Tickets
www.tvtickets.com

### Warner Bros
3400 Riverside Dr,
Burbank.
*Tel (818) 972-8687.*
http://vipstudiotour.
warnerbros.com

## THEATERS

### The Actors' Gang
9070 Venice Blvd,
Culver City.
*Tel (310) 838-4264.*
www.theactorsgang.com

### Ahmanson Theater, Dorothy Chandler Pavilion, Disney Concert Hall, Mark Taper Forum
135 N Grand Ave.
**Map** 11 E3.
*Tel (213) 972-7211.*
www.musiccenter.org

### Geffen Playhouse
10886 Le Conte Ave.
**Map** 4 A4.
*Tel (310) 208-5454.*
www.geffenplayhouse.com

### Kodak Theater
6801 Hollywood Blvd.
**Map** 2 B4.
*Tel (323) 308-6300.*
www.kodaktheater.com

### Nokia Theatre
776 Chick Hearn Ct.
**Map** 10 C5. *Tel (213)
763-6000.* www.
nokiatheatrelalive.com

### Pasadena Playhouse
39 S El Molino Ave,
Pasadena.
*Tel (626) 356-7529.*
www.pasadenaplay
house.com

### REDCAT Theater
631 W 2nd St.
**Map** 11 D3.
*Tel (213) 237-2800.*
www.redcat.org

### Theatricum Botanicum
1419 Topanga Canyon
Blvd, Topanga.
*Tel (310) 455-2322.*
www.theatricum.com

## ROCK, JAZZ, AND BLUES

### The Baked Potato
3787 Cahuenga Blvd W,
Studio City.
*Tel (818) 980-1615.*
www.thebakedpotato.com

### Catalina Bar & Grill
6725 Sunset Blvd.
**Map** 2 B5.
*Tel (323) 466-2210.*
www.catalinajazzclub.com

### House of Blues
8430 W Sunset Blvd.
**Map** 1 A5.
*Tel (323) 848-5100.*
www.hob.com

### Jazz Bakery
3233 Helms Ave,
Culver City.
*Tel (310) 271-9039.*
www.jazzbakery.org

### Knitting Factory
7021 Hollywood Blvd.
**Map** 2 B4. *Tel (323) 463-
0204.* www.knitting
factory.com

### McCabe's Guitar Shop
3101 Pico Blvd,
Santa Monica.
*Tel (310) 828-4497.*
www.mccabes.com

### The Roxy
9009 W Sunset Blvd.
**Map** 6 A1. *Tel (310)
276-2222.* www.
theroxyonsunset.com

### Troubadour
9081 Santa Monica Blvd.
**Map** 6 A2. *Tel (310)
276-6168.* www.
troubadour.com

### The Viper Room
8852 W Sunset Blvd.
**Map** 6 B1.
*Tel (310) 358-1880.*
www.viperroom.com

### Whisky A Go-Go
8901 W Sunset Blvd.
**Map** 6 B1.
*Tel (310) 652-4202.*
www.whiskyagogo.com

## OPERA, DANCE, AND CLASSICAL MUSIC

### Alex Theater
216 N Brand Blvd,
Glendale.
*Tel (818) 243-2539.*
www.alextheater.com

### Colburn School of Performing Arts
200 S Grand Ave.
**Map** 11 D4.
*Tel (213) 621-2200.*
www.colburnschool.edu

### Ford Amphitheatre
2580 E Cahuenga Blvd.
**Map** 2 B3. *Tel (323) 461-
3673.* www.ford
amphitheater.org

### LA Opera
135 N Grand Ave. **Map** 11
E3. *Tel (213) 972-8001.*
www.laopera.com

### LA Philharmonic
www.laphil.org

### UCLA Center for the Performing Arts
405 Hilgard Ave. **Map** 4
A4. *Tel (310) 825-2101.*
www.uclalive.org

## OUTDOOR ACTIVITIES

### Hollywood Park Track
1050 S Prairie Ave,
Inglewood.
*Tel (310) 419-1500.*
www.hollywoodpark.com

### Home Depot Center
18400 Avalon Blvd, Carson.
*Tel (310) 630-2000.*
www.homedepot
center.com

### Santa Anita Racetrack
285 W Huntington Drive,
Arcadia. *Tel (626) 574-
7223, (800) 574-6401.*
www.santaanita.com

## CHILDREN'S ENTERTAINMENT

### Bob Baker Marionette Theater
1345 W 1st St. **Map** 10
C3. *Tel (213) 250-9995.*
www.bobbaker
marionettes.com

### California Science Center
700 State Drive. *Tel (213)
724-3623.* www.
californiasciencecenter.org

### Kidspace Children's Museum
480 N. Arroyo Blvd,
Pasadena. *Tel (626) 449-
9144.* www.kidspace
museum.org

### Santa Monica Playhouse
1211 4th St, Santa Monica.
*Tel (310) 394-9779.*
www.santamonica
playhouse.com

### Under The Sea Indoor Playground
12211 W Washington Blvd,
No. 120. *Tel (310) 915-
1133.* www.underthesea
indoorplayground.com

# GETTING AROUND LOS ANGELES

The sheer size of Los Angeles – a sprawling 467 sq miles (1,200 sq km) – may seem daunting to navigate. A vast network of freeways *(see pp180–81)* provides an accessible, if sometimes crowded, means of traveling in the area. The fastest method of touring the city is by car, although the public transportation system works well in Downtown Los Angeles and Hollywood. Taxis are usually ordered by telephone. They travel all over town, but can be expensive. Los Angeles has a total of 200 bus lines that run on most of the main streets in the city. LA's growing rail system, the Metro, is useful when exploring the business district. Some neighborhoods are best seen on foot.

**Taxi in Los Angeles**

**Driving toward downtown Los Angeles on the freeway**

## DRIVING

Planning ahead is the key to making sure that driving in Los Angeles is less stressful and not overwhelming. First, refer to the map on pages 180–81 to see which freeway changes or exit you will need. Second, avoid rush hour on the freeways. The peak times are from Monday to Friday, 7am to 9:30am and 4pm to 6:30pm. Carpool lanes are reserved for cars with at least two passengers, and are much faster on the freeways.

When parking, always remember to read the posted signs for limitations and carry plenty of quarters for the parking meters. At night it is safer to valet park.

## WALKING

Even though the city is very spread out, some districts are pedestrian-friendly. Third Street Promenade and the beach and Main Street in Santa Monica *(see pp76–9)* are all pleasant areas for walking. Other areas include: the business district in Downtown Los Angeles *(see pp122–3)*, Old Pasadena *(see p154)*, Melrose Avenue *(see p113)*, the Golden Triangle in Beverly Hills *(see pp90–91)*, and Long Beach's Pine Avenue *(see p132)*. Do not walk alone at night unless the street is well lit and populated.

## CYCLING

The coastal bike path that runs for 25 miles (40 km) beside Santa Monica Bay is the best place to cycle. Other popular areas are Venice Beach, Griffith Park, and the Oceanside Bike Path in Long Beach. Note that bicycles are not allowed on the freeways. The **LA Department of Transportation** provides detailed route maps, and bikes and skates can be rented by the day or hour from **Perry's Café Bike Rentals** along Santa Monica beach and at several pizza stands.

## BUS AND RAIL SYSTEM

Greater LA is served by the **Metropolitan Transportation Authority (MTA)**. Bus stops display a metro sign. Buses run on main thoroughfares: Wilshire Blvd to Santa Monica Beach, Nos. 20 and 720; to Westwood and UCLA, No. 21; Santa Monica Blvd to the beach, No. 4; Sunset Blvd to Pacific Palisades, No. 2. The **DASH** shuttle provides travel within small areas, such as Downtown LA and Hollywood. The **Santa Monica Blue Bus Co.** and **Long Beach Transit** also service those areas.

The Metro light rail and Subway is a rail system that features five separate lines: Red, Purple, Blue, Green, and Gold. These lines serve 70 stations in and around Los Angeles. The rapid bus transit Orange and Silver Lines connects with the suburbs and the Metrolink rail system. The Metrolink is used mainly by commuters and serves Los Angeles and Southern California.

**Cycling through Venice on the bike path**

The Los Angeles rail network is expanding with further Metro light rails planned to create a link between Downtown Los Angeles and Santa Monica.

The Metro system runs between 5am and 12:30am. A weekend service runs on public holidays. Single rides cost $2. A one-week pass is $20 for unlimited rides.

## TAXIS AND LIMOUSINES

Two reliable taxi companies are **Yellow Cab** and the **Independent Cab Co**. Or for a luxurious alternative, rent a limousine from **Limousine Connection** and **Orange County Limo Rental**.

## GUIDED TOURS

Private bus lines such as **Guideline Tours** offer visitors tours around the city and to the major theme parks. You can view the homes of movie stars and local celebrities with **Hollywood Tours** and **Starline Tours**. The popular **Dearly Departed Tours** visits sites of famous crimes and scandals, while **Another Side of LA Tours** offers helicopter flights and Segway tours. If group tours do not appeal, the **LA Conservancy** provides free audio clips for self-guided walking tours of the downtown area of LA's historic district – a great way to view this area.

## DIRECTORY

### CYCLING

**LA Department of Transportation (LADOT)**
100 Main St, CA 90012.
*Tel* (213) 972-4962.
www.ladottransit.com

**Perry's Café Bike Rentals**
1200 Palisades Beach Road,
Santa Monica, CA 90401.
*Tel* (310) 458-3975.

### BUSES AND RAIL SYSTEMS

**DASH**
*Tel* (818) 808-2273.
www.ladottransit.com

**Long Beach Transit**
*Tel* (562) 591-2301.
www.lbtransit.com

**Metropolitan Transportation Authority (MTA)**
*Tel* (800) 266-6883.
www.metro.net

**Santa Monica Blue Bus Co.**
*Tel* (310) 451-5444.
www.bigbluebus.com

### TAXIS AND LIMOUSINES

**Independent Cab Co.**
*Tel* (800) 521-8294.

**Limousine Connection**
*Tel* (800) 266-5466.

**Orange County Limo Rental**
*Tel* (888) 766-7433.

**Yellow Cab**
*Tel* (877) 733-3305.

### GUIDED TOURS

**Another Side of LA Tours**
*Tel* (310) 289-8687.
http://anothersideoflosangeles tours.com

**Dearly Departed Tours**
*Tel* (800) 979-3370.
www.dearlydepartedtours.com

**Guideline Tours**
*Tel* (800) 604-8433.
www.guidelinetours.com

**Hollywood Tours**
*Tel* (800) 789-9575.
www.hollywoodtours.us

**LA Conservancy**
www.laconservancy.org

**Starline Tours**
*Tel* (800) 959-3131.
www.starlinetours.com

## METRO RAIL SYSTEM

North Hollywood
Universal City
Laurel Canyon
Valley College
Woodman
Van Nuys
Sepulveda
Woodley
Wilshire/ Western
Balboa
Reseda
Tampa
Pierce College
De Soto
Canoga
Warner Centre

Hollywood/ Highland
Hollywood/ Vine
Hollywood/ Western
Vermont/ Sunset
Vermont/ Santa Monica
Vermont/ Beverly
Wilshire/ Vermont
37th St/USC
Slauson
Manchester

Memorial Park
Del Mar
Fillmore
Mission
Highland Park
Southwest Museum
Heritage Square
7th Street/ Metro Centre
Westlake/ MacArthur Park
Pico
Grand
San Pedro
Washington
Vernon
Slauson
Florence
Firestone
103rd Street

Lake
Allen
Sierra Madre Villa
Lincoln/ Cypress
Chinatown
Pershing Square
Union Station
Civic Centre
Little Tokyo/ Arts District
Pico/Aliso
Mariachi Plaza
Soto
Indiana
Maravilla
East LA Civic Center
Atlantic

Wilshire/ Normandie

Harbor Freeway
Avalon
Imperial/ Wilmington
Norwalk
Vermont
Crenshaw
Hawthorne
Aviation/ LAX
Mariposa
El Segundo
Douglas
Redondo Beach
Artesia Transit Ctr
Rose-crans
Compton
Del Amo
Wardlow
Willow
Pacific Coast Highway
Pacific
Anaheim
5th Street
1st Street
Transit Mall
Long Beach
Lakewood

### KEY

○ Interchange Station
— Metro Red Line
— Metro Purple Line
— Metro Blue Line
— Metro Green Line
— Metro Orange Line
— Metro Gold Line
— Metro Silver Line

# Los Angeles Freeway Route Planner

A car is essential in Los Angeles and is the quickest way of getting around this vast city. All freeways are numbered but most also have names, such as the Golden State Freeway (I-5). Plan your trip carefully: freeway exits are marked by street name and direction rather than by area. It is advisable not to use the freeways during rush hour (8–9:30am and 4–6:30pm). For more details on getting around LA see pages 178–9.

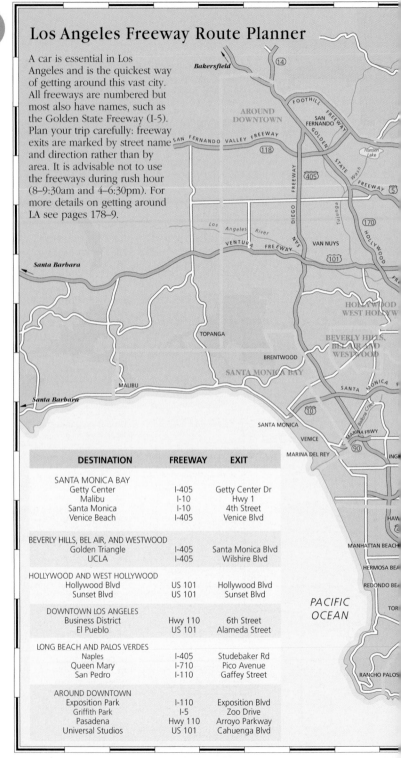

| DESTINATION | FREEWAY | EXIT |
|---|---|---|
| **SANTA MONICA BAY** | | |
| Getty Center | I-405 | Getty Center Dr |
| Malibu | I-10 | Hwy 1 |
| Santa Monica | I-10 | 4th Street |
| Venice Beach | I-405 | Venice Blvd |
| **BEVERLY HILLS, BEL AIR, AND WESTWOOD** | | |
| Golden Triangle | I-405 | Santa Monica Blvd |
| UCLA | I-405 | Wilshire Blvd |
| **HOLLYWOOD AND WEST HOLLYWOOD** | | |
| Hollywood Blvd | US 101 | Hollywood Blvd |
| Sunset Blvd | US 101 | Sunset Blvd |
| **DOWNTOWN LOS ANGELES** | | |
| Business District | Hwy 110 | 6th Street |
| El Pueblo | US 101 | Alameda Street |
| **LONG BEACH AND PALOS VERDES** | | |
| Naples | I-405 | Studebaker Rd |
| Queen Mary | I-710 | Pico Avenue |
| San Pedro | I-110 | Gaffey Street |
| **AROUND DOWNTOWN** | | |
| Exposition Park | I-110 | Exposition Blvd |
| Griffith Park | I-5 | Zoo Drive |
| Pasadena | Hwy 110 | Arroyo Parkway |
| Universal Studios | US 101 | Cahuenga Blvd |

**KEY**
- Freeway
- Other road
- River

# LOS ANGELES STREET FINDER

The key map below shows the areas of LA covered in the *Street Finder*. It includes the city districts of Beverly Hills, Bel Air and Westwood, Hollywood and West Hollywood, and Downtown Los Angeles. All places of interest in these areas are marked on the maps in addition to useful information, such as railroad stations, metro stops, bus terminals, and emergency services. A *Freeway Route Planner* can be found on pages 180 –81. The map refer-

**In-line skater at Venice Beach**

ences given with sights described in the LA section of the guide refer to the maps on the following pages. Map references are also given for entertainment venues *(see p176–7)*, shops *(see p168–9)*, hotels *(see pp524–31)* and restaurants *(see pp568–76)* in LA. Road map references refer to the map inside the back cover. The symbols used for sights and other features on the *Street Finder* maps are listed in the key below.

**KEY TO STREET FINDER**

| | | |
|---|---|---|
| ■ Major sight | ✚ Hospital with emergency room | ═ Pedestrian street |
| ■ Place of interest | ▣ Police station | |
| 🅁 Amtrak station | ⊠ Post office | |
| Ⓜ Metro station | 🅙 Golf course | **SCALE OF MAPS 1–11** |
| 🚌 Bus terminal | ═ Railroad line | 0 meters ────── 500 |
| 🅸 Tourist information | ═ Freeway | 0 yards ────── 500 |

0 kilometers 2

0 miles 2

# SOUTHERN CALIFORNIA

# Southern California at a Glance

Southern California is a region of startling contrasts. Scorching deserts give way to snowcapped mountains, with views of the coast. It is possible to surf in the morning, ski in the afternoon, and play golf in the evening. From San Simeon to San Diego, the coast is lined with resorts, reflecting a shoreline that ranges from rugged bluffs to golden sands. Attractions along the way include historic missions, the charming cities of Santa Barbara and San Diego, and the theme parks of Orange County. Farther inland are two of the most startling desert areas in the United States: Death Valley National Park and the Joshua Tree National Park.

**Santa Barbara Mission** (see pp222–3) *is the most visited mission in the state and is the only one in the chain of missions to have remained in continuous use since it was founded in 1786. The church façade is in Classical style, a theme continued inside the building.*

**SOUTH CENTRAL CALIFORNIA**
*(See pp204–25)*

**LOS ANGELE**
*(See pp59–19*

**Hearst Castle™** (see pp212–15), *on the south central coast, was built by publishing tycoon William R Hearst. In the 1930s and '40s he invited Hollywood stars and royalty here and entertained them lavishly. The Neptune Pool is particularly stunning.*

**ORANGE COU**
*(See pp226–4*

**Mission San Juan Capistrano** *(see pp240–41) in southern Orange County is known as the "Jewel of the Missions." Founded in 1776, its main buildings have been beautifully restored and feature historical exhibits.*

0 kilometers 50

0 miles 50

◁ Joshua trees at dusk in Palm Springs, California

**Death Valley National Park** (see pp290–93) *in the Mojave Desert encompasses one of the hottest places on earth and the lowest point in the Western Hemisphere. Within Death Valley, which is 140 miles (225 km) long, lie dry lake beds, sand dunes, and small outposts built around springs. Despite the harsh conditions, the area is rich in flora and fauna. Sights of historical interest in the park include Scotty's Castle.*

**Joshua Tree National Park** (see pp278–9), *with high and low desert areas, is famed for its distinctive trees. Within easy reach of the city of Palm Springs, it offers superb views of the stark desert landscape with its remarkable rock formations.*

**THE MOJAVE DESERT**
*(See pp280–93)*

**THE INLAND EMPIRE AND LOW DESERT**
*(See pp268–79)*

**SAN DIEGO COUNTY**
*(See pp244–67)*

**Balboa Park** (see pp256–9) *in San Diego was the site of the Panama–Pacific Exposition of 1915. The park is now home to many museums, such as the San Diego Museum of Man, housed in the landmark California Building. The famous San Diego Zoo lies just to the north of Balboa Park.*

# Surfing and Beach Culture

**Bust of Duke Kahanamoku**

If Southern Californians worship at the altars of youth, health, and beauty, then their churches are the beaches. Here, unbelievably beautiful men and women parade their surgically enhanced bodies beneath the ever-present sun. Favorite sports include skating and volleyball, but the ability to look good on a surfboard is the ultimate cool. Surfing was originally practiced by the Hawaiian nobility as a religious ceremony. It was introduced to California by Hawaiian George Freeth in 1907 *(see p66)* and popularized in the 1920s in Waikiki by Olympic swimmer Duke Kahanamoku. In 1961 the Beach Boys released "Surfin'," and the sport took off around the world. Today surf culture is part of the mainstream consciousness. The loose-fitting clothes favored by surfers are reproduced on the catwalk, and surfing slang is used by many who have never been near the beach.

**The Beach Boys** *sang of the joys of surfing despite the fact that none of the group could surf.*

**Films such as** *Gidget (1959),* Ride the Wild Surf *(1964), and* Beach Blanket Bingo *(1965), as well as the documentary* Endless Summer, *helped to establish the cultural allure of surfing. Lengthy beach parties in the style of these films were highly popular during the 1960s.*

## WHERE TO LEARN TO SURF

Beginners are advised to start by body surfing without a board. Boogie boarding, with a half-length board, is also far easier to master than surfing. Beaches with waves that break parallel to the beach (a surf break) are the most suitable. The best beaches on which to learn to boogie board include Santa Monica *(see p65)*, Carpinteria *(p209)*, and Del Mar *(p249)*. Beginners should avoid famous surfing beaches, such as Surfrider *(p64)*, San Clemente *(p230)*, and Huntington *(p230)*, as conditions can overwhelm the inexperienced.

**Boys with boogie boards weighing up the surf**

**Lifeguards** *are stationed on most county and state beaches in California during the summer. Their distinctive gray huts have been made famous throughout the world by the television series* Baywatch. *Always follow their instructions on the beach, and ask if you are in doubt about the tidal conditions.*

A **"tube"** is a cylindrical passage formed when a wave breaks and the crest curls over.

## SURFING HIGHLIGHTS

One exhilarating surfing experience is to "beat the tube." The surfer rides beneath the crest, regulating his speed and position to stay just ahead of the falling wave. If he goes too fast he comes out of the wave; too slowly and he gets knocked off. The wave loses momentum as it nears the shore. At this point the surfer will shoot out of the tube, remaining upright.

**By changing position** a surfer can alter the speed and direction in which he or she is traveling. Crouching lowers the center of gravity and increases stability.

## OTHER BEACH ACTIVITIES

Southern California's spectacular beaches are used by a wide variety of sports enthusiasts. Although the beaches are most popular in summer, activities are enjoyed year-round by hardy souls. Sailing is popular, with thousands of yachts of all sizes harbored in a string of marinas along the coast. Windsurfing and kite flying also take advantage of the prevailing onshore winds. Sea kayakers often explore the rocky coasts of the Channel Islands *(see p224)* and the mainland. Volleyball, once limited to friendly matches, is now a major professional sport with competitions held along the Southern California coast each summer.

**Modern surfboards** are made out of light, man-made materials, such as fiberglass, allowing surfers to reach much higher speeds. Their bright colors make them easy to see in the water.

**The first boards** *came from Hawaii and were called coffin lids because of their distinctive shape. Made out of wood, they were heavy and unwieldy. Early surfboards can be seen at the Lighthouse Surfing Museum in Santa Cruz* (see p507).

**Friendly volleyball game in Santa Monica**

# California Car Culture

**California license plate**

It is difficult to understand Southern California without considering the influence of the car. The introduction of the free-way system in LA in 1940 *(see p54)* spawned an entirely new culture centered around the automobile. Owning a car became integral to the California identity, and the open desert road came to symbolize the free-dom of the state. Customizing automobiles also made the car an art object. Drive-in movies led to the convenience of drive-in banks and fast-food restaurants. But there was a price to pay: smog, the result of car exhaust and sunlight, has become a fact of life in LA. Today, cars have cleaner exhausts, but LA has to cope with some 8 million cars on its increasingly "gridlocked" streets.

**Los Angeles' freeways,** *begun in the 1950s, have expanded into a complex network, linking the city with the rest of the state.*

**Ford Thunderbird emblem**

**The canvas top** could be lowered for sunny weather or raised in rain.

**Chrome** trimmed the backup lights.

**Chrome sidepanel strip**

## BIRTHPLACE OF THE MOTORCYCLE GANG

In the 1950s especially, California was home to rival gangs of "outlaw bikers." The most famous, the Hell's Angels, began with a group of World War II veterans in San Bernardino in 1948. Their notorious reputation was immortalized in the 1953 film *The Wild One* with Marlon Brando. Today, the Hell's Angels have around 1,000 members worldwide, who continue to symbolize defiance of authority.

**Marlon Brando**

**Japanese cars,** *such as those imported through Worldport LA (see p66), continue to be hot competition for American-made automobiles.*

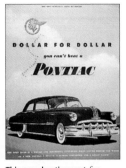

**This car advertisement** *for Pontiac dates from 1950. As automobiles became more of a status symbol, manufacturers competed for customers with increasingly bright ads.*

## WHERE TO SEE CALIFORNIA CAR CULTURE

Californians are very proud of their car culture and history; most towns have a parade or car show featuring vintage, classic, and customized automobiles. For information, inquire at the local visitors' center *(see p619)*. One of the largest automobile events, the Automobile Club of Southern California NHRA drag race, is held each November at the LA County Fairgrounds. There are literally dozens of car shows and races throughout the year, particularly in Southern California, showcasing muscle cars, classics, and collectibles, and specific models, such as the Corvette. California also hosts several famous motor races, such as the Toyota Grand Prix Long Beach in April. There are several world-class automobile museums in the state, including the Petersen Automotive Museum *(p119)* in Los Angeles and the Blackhawk Auto Museum near San Jose *(pp428–9)*.

**Tucker Torpedo, one of the cars on display at the Petersen Automotive Museum in LA**

Chrome door lights were turned on from inside.

The wraparound windshield imitated aircraft designs.

## PINK CADILLAC

With its glamorous design and convertible roof, the 1959 pink Cadillac suited California's image and climate perfectly. However, the car's two-ton weight meant that its steering was heavy, and it soon gave way to more efficient designs.

Chrome bumpers protected the front of the car.

White sidewall tires were a popular option because of their expensive look.

**The Model T Ford** *(affectionately known as the Tin Lizzie) first appeared in 1908. In 1913, Henry Ford introduced the assembly line and cars could be bought for as little as $500. This photograph of a 1924 beachside traffic jam shows that it took only a few years for Californians to become dependent on the car.*

**Recreational vehicles** *(RVs) became popular in the 1960s. Californians could now take to the open road and explore the state's wilderness without leaving any home comforts behind.*

# Deserts and Water Networks

Much of Southern California is desert, and before 1913, migrants to this area depended on wells for their water. The population grew extremely quickly and it soon became necessary to engineer what is now one of the most elaborate water networks on earth. This network has turned parts of what was once inhospitable desert into productive land, and made possible the desert resort of Palm Springs and the huge populations of the Southern Californian cities. However, the South's high rate of water consumption places a great demand on the region's major sources of water: the Colorado River and the Sierra Nevada Mountains.

**The Sacramento/San Joaquin River Delta** supplies water to the farms of the south. At peak times, pumping causes the river to flow in reverse, bringing salt water from San Francisco Bay.

V
NAT

Owen's
Lake

**Owens Lake** *(see p495) lies between the Sierra Nevada Mountains and the Mojave Desert, in Owens Valley. The Los Angeles Aqueduct diverted water from Owens River to LA and the 100-sq mile (260-sq km) lake gradually dried up.*

Cuyama River

California Aqueduct

Los Angeles Aqueduct

• **BAKERSFIELD**

• **SAN LUIS OBISPO**

• **SANTA BARBARA**

SAN GA
MOUN

• **LOS AN**

**The Los Angeles Aqueduct** *made the San Fernando Valley fertile (see p144). Land speculators made their fortunes when the aqueduct was completed in 1914.*

## WILLIAM MULHOLLAND

As head of the Los Angeles city water department, William Mulholland (1855–1935) *(see p144)* and his colleague Fred Eaton designed an aqueduct and a series of tunnels to lead from Owens Valley to LA. Completed in 1914, it cost more than $24 million. By 1929 the supplies were no longer sufficient, and they had to divert water from Mono Basin and the Colorado River, 400 miles (645 km) away.

0 kilometers    75

0 miles    75

## KEY

▨ Populated areas

〜 Rivers

〜 Dry rivers

▭ Canals

▭ Aqueducts

**LOCATOR MAP**

☐ Southern California

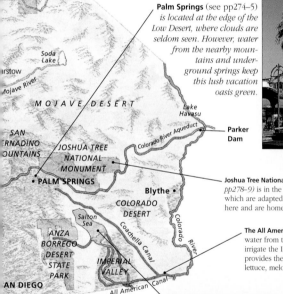

**Death Valley** (see pp290–93) *is so hot, the valley floor shimmers. The tiny amount of rain that falls provides nourishment for the 900 different plant species that live within Death Valley National Park.*

**Palm Springs** (see pp274–5) *is located at the edge of the Low Desert, where clouds are seldom seen. However, water from the nearby mountains and underground springs keep this lush vacation oasis green.*

**Parker Dam**

**Joshua Tree National Monument** *(see pp278–9)* is in the Low Desert. Joshua trees, which are adapted to a dry climate, thrive here and are home to 25 species of birds.

**The All American Canal** brings water from the Colorado River to irrigate the Imperial Valley, which provides the US with year-round lettuce, melons, tomatoes, and peas.

## SOUTHERN CALIFORNIA'S WATER NETWORK

Southern California has two main sources of water: ice-melt from the Sierra Nevada Mountains in the north, brought to LA via the LA Aqueduct, and the Colorado River to the southeast. The Colorado River Aqueduct system carries water 672 miles (1,080 km) from the Parker Dam via 395 miles (635 km) of pipes. Imperial Valley has a network of canals, making it fertile. The same canals irrigate the desert resort of Palm Springs.

**The Salton Sea**, *formed in 1905, is now ravaged by algae; however, a giant restoration project is planned to bring it back to its pristine state (above).*

# SOUTH CENTRAL CALIFORNIA

*S*outh Central California is a land of lonely passes and wooded streams. Broad sandy beaches stretch for miles along the gentle coast with empty, tawny hills as their only backdrop. It is a region of small and friendly towns, scattered farms and vineyards nestled in scenic valleys. Farther inland is Los Padres National Forest, where mountain lions roam freely, and eagles and condors soar overhead.

The region's Spanish heritage is highly visible, and no more so than in Santa Barbara. Here the area's most important garrison and the legendary structure that came to be known as "Queen of the Missions" *(see pp222–3)* can be found. The city's red tile Mission Revival-style architecture *(see p31)* has been imitated throughout the State.

Following the breakup of the wealthy missions during the 1830s, the land was divided into a handful of sprawling ranches, then the 1849 Gold Rush brought an influx of Easterners to California. The newcomers subdivided the large estates and set up small farming communities. They touted the land throughout the world as a "semitropical paradise," where the first season's crops would pay for the cost of the land.

In the early part of the 20th century the Central Coast was a popular vacation destination, drawing thousands of people each summer to seaside towns such as Pismo and Avila Beach. Farther north, at San Simeon, millionaire William Randolph Hearst built his own personal playground, the fabulous private museum now known as Hearst Castle™.

Today, South Central California provides a wealth of activities, from horse-drawn wine-tasting tours in the scenic Santa Ynez valley to relaxation on empty beaches. The more active can try kayaking on the Kern River near Bakersfield. Offshore, the Channel Islands offer a unique view of the area's ecosystems and an opportunity to see the annual passage of the magnificent gray whales. The east of the region is dominated by the Los Padres National Forest, an area of breathtaking beauty with miles of hiking trails and drives through mountain scenery. Here, too, are signs of the Chumash Indians who once lived in thriving communities along the coast. Their enigmatic petroglyphs remain as silent reminders of their presence throughout these hills.

**Seasonal produce on display in Morro Bay**

◁ Fishing off the pier at Pismo Beach

# Exploring South Central California

South Central California's beaches and coastal plains are backed by low rolling hills covered with groves of oak. Beyond this, the Los Padres National Forest has hundreds of miles of mountainous hiking trails. Just north of Santa Barbara, the gentle countryside around Santa Ynez has proved perfect for growing vines. Along the coast of San Luis Obispo County, the seaside towns of Morro Bay and Pismo Beach are known for their fishing and clamming. In the northwest, Hearst Castle is one of California's most popular tourist attractions.

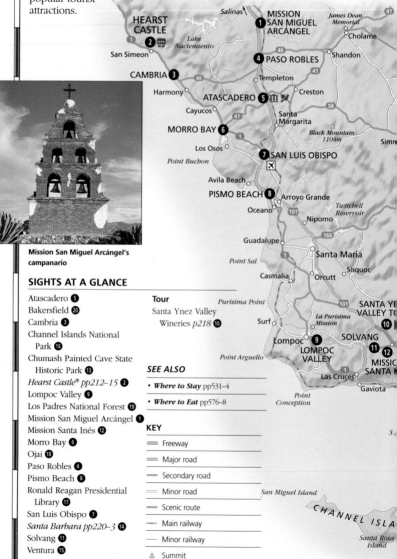

**Mission San Miguel Arcángel's campanario**

## SIGHTS AT A GLANCE

Atascadero **5**
Bakersfield **20**
Cambria **3**
Channel Islands National Park **16**
Chumash Painted Cave State Historic Park **13**
*Hearst Castle* pp212–15 **2**
Lompoc Valley **9**
Los Padres National Forest **19**
Mission San Miguel Arcángel **1**
Mission Santa Inés **12**
Morro Bay **6**
Ojai **18**
Paso Robles **4**
Pismo Beach **8**
Ronald Reagan Presidential Library **17**
San Luis Obispo **7**
*Santa Barbara* pp220–3 **14**
Solvang **11**
Ventura **15**

**Tour**
Santa Ynez Valley Wineries *p218* **10**

### SEE ALSO

• *Where to Stay* pp531–4

• *Where to Eat* pp576–8

### KEY

| | |
|---|---|
| ═══ | Freeway |
| ═══ | Major road |
| ─── | Secondary road |
| ═══ | Minor road |
| ─── | Scenic route |
| ─•─ | Main railway |
| ─── | Minor railway |
| △ | Summit |

Rugged mountains in the vast Los Padres National Forest

## GETTING AROUND

I-101 and Hwy 1 follow the coast, passing through all the major sights. Amtrak runs a daily service, the Coast Starlight, from Los Angeles to San Francisco, stopping at Santa Barbara and San Luis Obispo. Greyhound buses also stop at these cities. There are roads through the Los Padres National Forest to Bakersfield, but the most common driving route to that city is I-5 from LA. Trips to the Channel Islands National Park leave from Ventura and Oxnard.

Stearns Wharf, the recreation pier at Santa Barbara

# California Coastline: South Central

The South Central coast offers miles of accessible, broad, sandy beaches and some of the best surfing in the state. The water here is cooler than the ocean off the Los Angeles to San Diego coast, but these beaches offer privacy and solitude for swimming, sunbathing, and picnicking. The rugged mountain backdrop appears so close you can almost smell the pine and chaparral. Several South Central beaches are within state parks and have hiking and nature trails offering spectacular views. Visit www.parks.ca. gov/parkindex for more details.

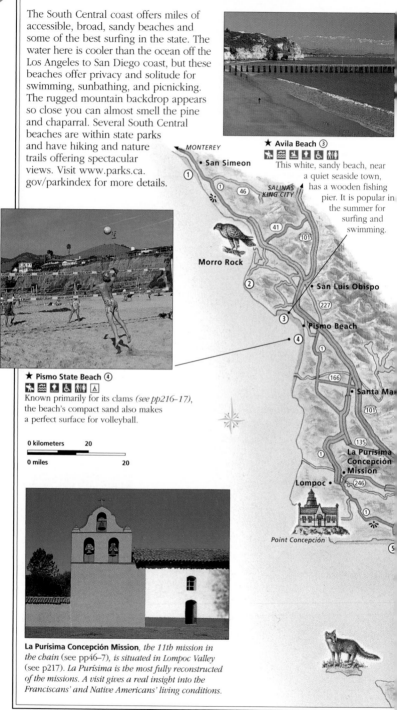

MONTEREY

• San Simeon

SALINAS
KING CITY

Morro Rock

• San Luis Obispo

• Pismo Beach

• Santa Ma

La Purísima
Concepción
Mission

Lompoc •

Point Concepción

★ **Avila Beach** ③
This white, sandy beach, near a quiet seaside town, has a wooden fishing pier. It is popular in the summer for surfing and swimming.

★ **Pismo State Beach** ④
Known primarily for its clams *(see pp216–17)*, the beach's compact sand also makes a perfect surface for volleyball.

0 kilometers     20

0 miles          20

**La Purísima Concepción Mission**, *the 11th mission in the chain (see pp46–7), is situated in Lompoc Valley (see p217). La Purísima is the most fully reconstructed of the missions. A visit gives a real insight into the Franciscans' and Native Americans' living conditions.*

**Morro Rock** *is one of South Central California's most endearing landmarks. Used as a navigation point by the first Spanish explorers, it is best seen at sunrise or sunset (see p216).*

**LOCATOR MAP**

### William R Hearst Memorial State Beach ①

Situated below Hearst Castle® *(see pp212–15)*, this sheltered, crescent-shaped beach is a good spot for a picnic. Boats can be chartered from the pier for deep-sea fishing trips.

### Montana de Oro State Park ②

The rocky beach is backed by 8,000 acres (3,250 ha) of park. Hiking trails wind through the hills and, in winter, monarch butterflies can be seen in the eucalyptus trees.

### ★ East Beach ⑦

This sandy beach stretches for 1.5 miles (2.5 km) from Stearns Wharf, Santa Barbara's fishing pier. Children will enjoy the playground and paddling pool.

### Gaviota State Park ⑤

This 5.5-mile (9-km) beach, in a sheltered cove, has a playground and fishing pier. It adjoins 2,800 acres (1,100 ha) of parkland with hiking trails.

### El Capitan State Beach ⑥

El Capitan is a good place for spotting wildlife, both in the rock pools along the beach and in the woods behind. Gray whales pass close to the shore during the winter.

### Carpinteria State Beach ⑧

Backed by the Santa Ynez Mountains, this sheltered beach is one of the safest and most pleasant places to swim in Southern California.

### Point Mugu State Park ⑩

At the western end of the Santa Monica Mountains, the park is crisscrossed with hiking trails. Dolphins and California sea lions are often seen offshore.

### Leo Carrillo State Beach North ⑪

This stretch of Leo Carrillo State Beach *(see p64)*, which extends across the LA County border, is one of the classic spots for surfing in California.

### ★ San Buenaventura State Beach ⑨

Close to the center of Ventura *(see p224)*, this broad beach is sheltered by the harbor breakwater, making it a good area for swimming.

Los Padres National Forest

④

SANTA BARBARA

• Ojai

⑦

101    33    126

⑧

Ventura

LOS ANGELES

⑨

101

Oxnard •

*Channel Island National Park*

MALIBU

⑩

⑪

### KEY

| | |
|---|---|
| ▨▨▨ | Freeway |
| ▬▬▬ | Major road |
| ═══ | Minor road |
| ⌁ | River |
| ⁂ | Viewpoint |

Arched colonnade at the Mission
San Miguel Arcángel

# Mission San Miguel Arcángel **①**

775 Mission St, San Miguel.
**Road map** B5. **Tel** (805) 467-3256.
🕐 10am–4:30pm daily. 🚹
**www**.missionsanmiguel.org

The Mission complex
is once again open to
the public, following
an extensive renova-
tion program to repair
damage caused by an
earthquake in Decem-
ber 2003. This mission
was the 16th in the
Californian chain *(see
pp46–7)*, and was
founded in 1797 by
Father Fermín de
Lasuén, the successor
to Father Junípero
Serra *(see p46)*. Nine
years later the original church
was destroyed by fire and the
present building, which was
used as a parish church, was
completed in 1819.

The six rooms in the mis-
sion's museum are furnished
as they would have been in
the early 19th century and the
wall decorations in the church
were painted in 1822–3. The
museum has a gift shop and
there is a nice courtyard area.

In addition to growing grain
and raising cattle, the padres
made their own sacramental
wine. Today the surrounding
hills shelter over 30 wineries.

Following secularization in
1834, the mission was used as
a warehouse and bar. In 1928
it was returned to the padres,
and restoration was begun.

# Hearst Castle® **②**

*See pp212–15.*

# Cambria **③**

**Road map** B5. 🏠 *5,000.* 🚌
🚹 *767 Main St.* **Tel** *(805) 927-3624.*
**www**.cambriachamber.org

Situated between rugged
seashore and pine-clad hills,
and handy for Hearst Castle,
Cambria began as a mercury
mining settlement in 1866.
Later it became a center for
dairy farming and lumber
production, and today it is a
popular location for artists
and craftspeople.

The town is divided into two
distinct districts: East Village,
a charming colony of Arts
and Crafts houses *(see p31)*,
and West Village, which is
more modern. Main Street,
which joins the two, is lined
with specialty shops, art
galleries, and
restaurants.

Among the houses
on Hillcrest Drive,
just north of Main
Street, is Nit Wit
Ridge. It was built
by local contractor Art
Beal, who was known
as "Captain Nit Wit."

This whimsical
abode was
fashioned over
six decades, starting
in the 1930s, out of
salvaged material,
from sea shells to old tires.
To the north of the town, on

Statue of St. Michael
the Archangel

Moonstone Drive, is the
Leffingwell Landing, which
offers excellent views of the
surf and occasionally sea lions,
whales, and otters out at sea.
At low tide it is also possible
to climb down to the rock
pools at the bottom of the
cliffs. The area is also well
equipped for picnickers.

# Paso Robles **④**

**Road map** B5. 🏠 *21,000.* 🚌
🚹 *1225 Park St.* **Tel** *(805) 238-0506.*
**www**.pasorobleschamber.com

Paso Robles, or "Pass of the
Oaks," was once part of the
26,000-acre (10,500-ha) El
Paso de Robles ranch. In 1857,
a sulfurous hot spring, long
used by Indians for its curative
powers, was transformed into
a health resort. With the arrival
of the Southern Pacific railroad
in 1886, the town quickly
developed. Today, Paso
Robles is ringed with horse
ranches, vineyards, wineries,
and more than 5,000 acres
(2,000 ha) of almond orchards
that bloom in early spring. The
hot springs have now been
capped – they were polluting
the Salinas River – but the
town still has much to offer.
On Vine Street, between 12th
and 20th streets, are several
restored buildings from the
1890s, including **Call-Booth
House Gallery**. Here works by
mainly local artists are displayed in a Victorian setting.

Some of Paso Robles' many
restaurants are also located in

Nit Wit Ridge in Cambria, made out of junk

*For hotels and restaurants in this region see pp531–4 and pp576–9*

Wine festival event at the Arciero Winery in Paso Robles

19th-century buildings; for instance, Touch of Paso occupies a former post house on the Overland Stage Company route.

The Paso Robles Inn and Gardens, at 1003 Spring Street, stands on the site of the 1860 Hot Springs Hotel. The latter was replaced in 1891 with a three-story redbrick hotel designed by Stanford White. This building in turn was burned down in a fire in 1940. Visitors to the town may wander through the current hotel's landscaped gardens.

There are a number of moderately priced hotels in Paso Robles, which make convenient overnight stops when visiting nearby Hearst Castle®.

Two important events are the California Mid-State Fair – a large agricultural and livestock fair in late July–early August with a reputation for top entertainment – and the Wine Festival in May, during which visitors can sample wines from 90 of almost 200 vineyards in the surrounding area.

**Environs**

Situated 17 miles (27 km) northwest of Paso Robles, off County Road G14, **Lake Nacimiento** is a local recreational spot. Set in a picturesque valley amid pine and oak trees, the lake offers fishing (bass and catfish are often caught here), camping, water sports, and picnicking.

At the second junction of Hwy 46 and Hwy 41, 24 miles (39 km) east of Paso Robles, is the **James Dean Monument**. Set around a tree of heaven, it is a memorial to the

film actor who died here, at the age of 24, when he crashed his silver Porsche 550 Spider on September 30, 1955. A metal plaque gives details of James Dean's short life.

🏛 **Call-Booth House Gallery**
1315 Vine St. **Tel** (805) 238-5473.
◯ *11am–3pm Wed–Sun.*
🔲 *public hols.* 🈂

# Atascadero **⑤**

**Road map** B5. 🏘 *25,300.*
🚌 *San Luis Obispo.* 🚖 *Dial-A-Ride*
*(805 466-7433).* 🚌 ℹ *6904*
*El Camino Real (805 466-2044).*
**www**.atascaderochamber.org

Atascadero, which means "muddy place" in Spanish, was founded in 1913 by the publisher Edward G Lewis, who bought the 23,000-acre (9,300-ha) ranch to build his ideal town. Lewis's headquarters were in an attractive Italian Renaissance-style building, constructed in 1914 for almost half a million dollars. The building used to house the **Atascadero Historical**

**Society Museum**, which contained hundreds of photographs taken by Lewis's official photographer as well as artifacts that belonged to early settlers, but the building was damaged in a major earthquake in late 2003. Portions of the collection are on display at the Colony House until the building is restored.

Unfortunately, Lewis went bankrupt before Atascadero was finished. The town continued to grow steadily from the 1950s, however, as more people were attracted by its rural atmosphere. It was incorporated in 1979.

Today's visitors frequent the town's antique shops, stylish boutiques, and its weekly farmers' market. There is a week-long Colony Days celebration in October, when the town remembers its early history with a parade and other festivities.

Just south of the town, off Hwy 41, Atascadero Park and Lake has pleasant walks and offers fishing, picnic areas, and a children's playground. Next door, the 3-acre (1-ha) **Charles Paddock Zoo**, named after the county park ranger who established the zoo in 1955, houses more than 100 animal species. These include monkeys, meerkats, grizzly bears, a pair of tigers, and a jaguar, which live in settings much like their natural habitats.

🦓 **Charles Paddock Zoo**
9305 Pismo Ave, Atascadero.
**Tel** (805) 461-5080. ◯ *Apr–Oct:*
*10am–5pm; Nov–Mar: 10am–4pm*
🔲 *Thanksgiving, Dec 25* 🈂 🅿
📷 **www**.charlespaddockzoo.org

Ducks swimming on Atascadero Lake

# Hearst Castle® ❷

**Tile detail**

Hearst Castle® perches on a hill above the village of San Simeon. The private play-ground and museum of media tycoon William Randolph Hearst is today one of California's top tourist attractions. Its three guest houses are superb buildings in their own right, but the highlight of the tour is the twin-towered Casa Grande. Designed by the Paris-trained architect Julia Morgan and built in stages from 1922 to 1947, its 115 rooms hold many artworks and epitomize the glamour of the 1930s and 1940s.

**Façade**
*Casa Grande's poured concrete façade is in the Mediterranean Revival style. It is embellished with ancient architectural fragments.*

**Theater**
*The walls of Hearst's private cinema are lined with damask. Lamps held by gilded caryatids light the 50 seats.*

★ **Billiard Room**
*This room features a French early 16th-century millefleurs tapestry.*

## TIMELINE

| | | | | |
|---|---|---|---|---|
| **1865** George Hearst buys 48,000 acres (19,425 ha) of land near San Simeon | **1921** Casa del Mar completed | | *16th-century wooden chest, depicting Christ Meeting St. Peter on the lid* | **1958** Hearst Castle® opens to public |
| | **1924** Casa del Sol completed | | **1951** Hearst dies | |

| 1920 | 1930 | 1940 | 1950 |
|---|---|---|---|

| | | | | |
|---|---|---|---|---|
| **1919** WR Hearst inherits family fortune. Plans a house on "Camp Hill" | **1922** Work begins on Casa Grande | **1935** Neptune Pool completed | | *Classical Greek amphora dating from 3rd century AD* |
| | | **1928** Hearst moves into Casa Grande | **1947** Hearst has heart problems and leaves San Simeon | |

*For hotels and restaurants in this region see pp531–4 and pp576–9*

★ **Gothic Study**
*When in San Simeon, Hearst ran his empire from the Gothic Study. He kept his books behind grilles.*

**VISITORS' CHECKLIST**

750 Hearst Castle Rd. **Road map** B5. *Tel* (805) 927-2020; (800) 444-4445. 🚌 to San Simeon. ⏰ 8am–4pm daily. 🚫 *Jan 1, Thanksgiving, Dec 25.* 🎟 📷 ♿ call ahead. 🅿 📹 obligatory. **www**.hearstcastle.com

**Celestial Suite**
*The two Celestial Suite bedrooms are located high up in the north and south towers. They are linked by a spacious sitting room.*

★ **Assembly Room**
*A 16th-century French fireplace dominates the Assembly Room. Italian choir stalls line the walls, which are hung with Flemish tapestries.*

Main entrance

★ **Refectory**
*Tapestries, choir stalls, and colorful banners cover the walls of the massive dining hall. Its long tables are decorated with silver candlesticks and serving dishes.*

**STAR FEATURES**

★ Assembly Room

★ Billiard Room

★ Gothic Study

★ Refectory

# Exploring Hearst Castle®

Visitors to Hearst Castle® must take one of three guided tours, all of which start from the Visitors' Center. The Grand Rooms' Tour includes the ground floor of the Casa Grande and is recommended for first-time visitors. The two other tours cover the upper floors of the main house, two guest houses, the kitchen, and the wine cellar. During spring and autumn, evening tours of the estate feature actors or "guests" in 1930s costume.

**Statue of Victory**

Hearst's private movie theater. Here, up to 50 guests would watch films. The screen could be removed, revealing a small stage, where famous actors and actresses would sometimes put on plays.

The exquisite indoor Roman Pool, entirely covered in mosaics of hammered gold and Venetian glass, is decor-ated with eight marble statues and was very popular among guests.

The house was continually being developed in accordance with Hearst's ever-changing ideas. One supporting wall was moved at great cost to make room for a bowling alley that was never built. With scores of bedrooms and bathrooms, two pools, and a theater, Casa Grande was a gilded playhouse for all who came here.

**Gold and glass decor of the Roman Pool**

## CASA GRANDE: THE BIG HOUSE

Casa Grande is built from steel-reinforced concrete in order to withstand California's earthquakes. However, it has been designed to look like a masonry cathedral in the Mediterranean Revival style.

Houseguests stayed in one of 36 bedrooms, surrounded by works from the magnate's eclectic art collection. Hearst himself lived in the third-floor Gothic Suite. His bedroom was decorated with a 14th-century Spanish ceiling and a renowned *Madonna and Child* from the School of Duccio di Buoninsegna (c.1255–1318). A sitting room with ocean views linked it to Marion Davies' bedroom.

Across the hall, the Gothic Study housed Hearst's most prized books and manuscripts. It was from this room that he directed his media empire.

The Assembly Room, on the first floor, was designed around a massive 16th-century French fireplace. It came from the d'Anglure family's Château

des Jours in Burgundy. The high-ceilinged Refectory, next door, features a Renaissance dining table, misericord seats, and flagstones from Siena. Guests at Hearst Castle® were required to attend their late evening meals here.

The Billiard Room, with its Spanish Gothic ceiling, showcases an early 16th-century millefleurs tapestry of a stag hunt. Adjoining this room is

## THE GROUNDS AND NEPTUNE POOL

Hearst transformed the rocky California hillside into a veritable Garden of Eden. Fan palms 15 ft (4.5 m) high and Italian cypresses were hauled up the dirt road at great expense, and thousands of flowers were planted each year.

Massive loads of topsoil were brought up to create flower-beds for the 127 acres (51 ha) of gardens. Five greenhouses supplied colorful plants

### WILLIAM RANDOLPH HEARST

The son of a multimillionaire, WR Hearst (1863–1951) was an ebullient personality who made his own fortune in magazine and newspaper publishing. He married Millicent Willson, an entertainer from New York, in 1903. On his mother's death in 1919, Hearst inherited the San Simeon property. He began to build the castle and grounds as a tribute to his mother. On moving in, he installed his mistress, actress Marion Davies. The couple entertained royally at San Simeon over the next 20 years. When Hearst suffered problems with his heart in 1947, he moved to a house in Beverly Hills, where he died in 1951.

**Portrait of WR Hearst, age 31**

throughout the year. To hide the water resevoirs on a distant hill, 6,000 Monterey pines were planted in holes blasted out of the rock. Many varieties of fruit trees were planted on the estate, providing an abundance of fresh fruit.

Ancient and modern statues were collected to adorn the terraces. Among the finest are four statues of Sekhmet, the Egyptian goddess of war. The oldest works at San Simeon date from 1350–1200 BC.

The *pièce de résistance* of the grounds is the 104-ft- (32-m-) long Neptune Pool. Made in white marble, it is flanked by colonnades and features Roman architectural elements and a temple façade. The latter is made from ancient columns and decorated with authentic friezes. The statues around the pool were carved in the 1920s by Charles-George Cassou, a Parisian sculptor.

A great lover of the outdoors, Hearst had a 1-mile- (1.6-km-) long pergola so that he could ride in all weathers. Two tennis courts were also constructed above the indoor Roman Pool.

Hearst had a private zoo on "Camp Hill." The remains of enclosures, where lions, bears, elephants, pumas, and leopards were once kept can still be seen. Giraffes, ostriches, zebras, and even a baby elephant were free to wander the grounds.

## JULIA MORGAN

Julia Morgan, the architect of San Simeon, was 47 when she began her 30-year collaboration with Hearst. One of the first women graduates of engineering at the University of California, Berkeley, Morgan was the first woman to receive a certificate in architecture from the Ecole Nationale et Spéciale des Beaux-Arts in Paris. She was a multitalented architect and artist – she designed almost every aspect of Hearst Castle®, from tiles and windows to swimming pools and fountains – and a rigorous supervisor of the project's many contractors and artisans. Her relationship with Hearst was based on mutual respect but was often tempestuous. After spending long hours together finalizing a plan, Hearst would often telegraph Morgan with changes.

**Julia Morgan (1872–1957)**

**Tiered façade of Casa del Sol**

## THE GUEST HOUSES

Until the mid-1920S, when Casa Grande became ready for occupancy, Hearst lived in the 19-room Casa del Mar, the largest of the three guest houses. He enjoyed his years in the smaller house, but on viewing the completed Casa Grande admitted, "If I had known it would be so big, I would have made the little buildings bigger." The "little buildings," however, are mansions in their own right.

Casa del Sol is built on three levels and has 18 rooms. It features views of the sunset and has a broad terrace with a tall fountain topped with a cast bronze copy of *David* by Donatello. The smallest of the houses, Casa del Monte, faces the hills and has ten rooms.

**Neptune Pool, flanked by colonnades and Roman architectural elements**

Fishing boats encircling Morro Rock in Morro Bay

# Morro Bay ➏

**Road map** B5. 🏠 *10,000.*
🚌 *Dial-A-Ride (805) 772-2744.* 📠
🛈 *845 Embarcadero Rd, Suite D (805
772-4467).* www.morrobay.org

This seaside port was
founded in 1870 to ship
produce from the area's cattle-
ranching and dairy-farming
businesses. Today, tourism
has become the town's main
industry, and the waterfront is
lined with galleries, shops, an
aquarium, and seafood restaurants. Whale-watching trips,
bay cruises, and a commercial
fishing fleet also operate from
here. A redwood stairway, celebrating the town's 100th birth-
day, descends from a stone
pelican at clifftop level down
to the Embarcadero where a
giant chessboard sports redwood pieces up to 33 inches
(84 cm) tall. The view from
Black Hill Lookout is worth
the hike from the parking lot
to the top of the mountain.
The bay's principal feature
is Morro Rock, a dome-shaped
576-ft- (175-m-) high volcanic
peak – one of nine in the area.
Named "El Moro" by Juan Rodríguez Cabrillo (João Rodrigues
Cabrilho) in 1542, who thought
it resembled a Moor's turban,
it was connected to the mainland by a causeway in 1933.
Between 1880 and 1969 it was
used as a quarry, and a million
tons of rock were blasted away
for breakwater construction.
Today, Morro Rock is a wildlife preserve housing nests of
peregrine falcons, while Coleman Park, at the rock's base,
is a highly popular fishing spot.

# San Luis Obispo ➐

**Road map** B5. 🏠 *43,000.* ✈ *San
Luis Obispo.* 🚌 🚆 🛈 *811 El Capitan
Way, Suite 200, (805) 541-8000.*
www.sanluisobispocounty.com

This small city, situated in
a valley in the Santa Lucia
Mountains, developed around
the **Mission San Luis Obispo
de Tolosa**. The mission was
founded on September 1, 1772,
by Father Junípero Serra
*(see p46)*. Fifth in the chain
of 21 missions built by the
Franciscan Order, and one of
the wealthiest, it is still in use
as a parish church. Beside the
church, the mission's museum
displays Chumash Indian artifacts, such as baskets, vessels,
and jewelry; the padre's bed;
and the mission's original altar.
In front of the church is
Mission Plaza, a landscaped
public square bisected by a
tree-lined creek. During the
1860s, bullfights and bear-
baiting took place in the park;
today it is the site of many of

the city's less bloody events.
Just west of the plaza, at 800
Palm Street, is the Ah Louis
Store. Founded in 1874 by a
Chinese cook and railroad
laborer *(see pp50–51)*, it
became the center of a
then thriving Chinatown, and
was a post office, bank, and
general store. It is now a gift
shop, but is open on an
irregular schedule.

🏠 **Mission San Luis Obispo
de Tolosa**
751 Palm St. **Tel** *(805) 781-8220.*
⏱ *9am–5pm weekdays.*
🚫 *public hols.*

# Pismo Beach ➑

**Road map** B5. 🏠 *8,700.* ✈ *San
Luis Obispo.* 🚆 *San Luis Obispo.* 📠
🛈 *581 Dolliver St (805) 773-4382.*
www.pismochamber.com

Pismo Beach is famous for the
Pismo clam. At the turn of the
century up to 40,000 clams
were harvested per day. In
1911 harvesters were limited

Pismo Beach, backed by rolling hills

to 200 clams per person; now, a fishing license is required and there are strict size and quantity restrictions. A clam festival is held in autumn.

The town's beach *(see p208)* stretches south for 8 miles (13 km) to the Santa Maria River. It offers campsites, boating, fishing, and picnic facilities. The sand is firmly compacted, so cars can go onto the beach via ramps at Grand Avenue in Grover Beach and Pier Avenue in Oceano. Extensive sand dunes shelter birdlife, sagebrush, wildflowers, verbena, and other seashore plants along with the occasional foxes, rabbits and coyotes. Shell mounds in the dunes, especially near Arroyo Grande Creek, identify sites where Chumash Indians once lived.

During the 1930s and 1940s the dunes were the center of a cult of artists, nudists, and mystics. Filmmakers have also been drawn to these sands, which have been compared to the Sahara Desert. One of the many movies made here is *The Sheik* (1921) starring Rudolph Valentino *(see p112)*.

## Lompoc Valley ❾

**Road map** B5. ✈ *Santa Barbara.* 🚌 *Lompoc.* 🛈 *111 S I St, Lompoc (805) 736-4567.* **www**.lompoc.com

Lompoc Valley is one of the world's major producers of flower seed. The hills and flower fields surrounding the valley are a blaze of color between late spring and midsummer. Among the varieties grown are marigolds, sweet peas, asters, lobelia, larkspur,

### DUNE ECOLOGY

Coastal dunes are the product of wind and, surprisingly, plants. Just above the high-tide line, dry sand is stabilized by sea lettuce. Behind it, beach grass and silver lupine trap more sand, creating small hummocks held in place by the plants' roots. Lupine compost mixes with the sand to produce soil, allowing other plants, such as dune buckwheat and haplopapus, to move in and overcome the lupine itself. Eventually, ice plant, verbena, and morning glory take root in the sandy soil. The plants provide food and protection for a broad range of insects and animals, from sand wasps and beetles to Jerusalem crickets and tiny mice. Most beach wildlife depends on the dew that drops from these plants into the sand below. If part of the fragile plant cover is destroyed by storms, high winds, or people, sand is dispersed farther inland, and a new dune is formed.

**Ice plant growing among the coastal sand dunes**

nasturtiums, and cornflowers. A map of the flower fields in the area is distributed by the town of Lompoc's Chamber of Commerce. The Civic Center Plaza, between Ocean Avenue and C Street, has a display garden in which all the many flowers are identified.

**La Purísima Concepción Mission**, 3 miles (5 km) northeast of the town, was the 11th mission to be founded in California. It was declared a State Historic Park during the 1930s. The early 19th-century buildings have now been authentically reconstructed, and the complex and grounds provide a real insight into the missionary way of life.

Visitors to the mission are able to view the priests' living quarters, furnished with authentic pieces, in the elegant residence building. The simple, narrow church is decorated with colorful stencilwork. In the adjacent workshops, cloth, candles, leather goods, and furniture were at one time produced for the mission.

La Purísima's gardens have been faithfully restored. The varieties of fruit, vegetables, and herbs that are grown here were all common in the 19th century. Visitors can also view the system that provided the mission with water.

🛈 **La Purísima Concepción Mission**
2295 Purísima Rd, Lompoc. **Tel** (805) 733-3713. 🕘 *9am–5pm daily.* 🚫 *Jan 1, Thanksgiving, Dec 25.* 🎫

**La Purísima Concepción Mission in Lompoc Valley**

# Tour of the Santa Ynez Valley Wineries ❿

Santa Ynez Valley is one of the newest and most distinctive wine regions in the state. The area experiences coastal fog, which produces microclimates according to shifts in altitude and distance from the sea. The area also has a longer growing season than Northern California. These unique conditions, coupled with varied soils, produce a selection of classic grape varieties.

**Local wine**

## TIPS FOR DRIVERS

*Tour length:* 30 miles (48 km).
*Stopping-off points:* Los Olivos Café (see p576) is an award-winning place to stop for lunch or dinner. Most wineries have picnic areas, where you can enjoy a local wine with your meal.

**Fess Parker Winery ⑤**
Pinot Noirs, Syrahs, and Rieslings are produced at ex-actor Fess Parker's winery. Tastings are available in an attractive building in scenic Foxen Canyon.

**Brander Vineyard ⑥**
Established in 1975, Brander offers award-winning Sauvignon Blancs and other wines in a French-style building overlooking the vineyards.

**Firestone Vineyard ③**
The largest producer in the region presents distinctive Cabernet Sauvignons, Chardonnays, and Merlots in a large tasting room adjoining the winery.

**Curtis Winery ④**
The specialty here is Rhone Varietal and Syrahs, to be enjoyed in a tasting room adjoining the cellar.

**Gainey Vineyard ①**
Distinctive wines are offered for tasting in a Spanish-style ranch building.

**Santa Ynez ②**
Among the vineyards and wineries surrounding this town is the Sunstone Vineyard and Winery.

SUNSTONE VINEYARDS AND WINERY

## KEY

▬▬ Tour route

═══ Other roads

0 kilometers 2

0 miles 2

SANTA MARIA

Foxen Canyon Road

Zaca Station Road

Alamo Pintado Creek

Figueroa Mountain Road

• Los Olivos

101

154

246

BAR

Mission Santa Inés church façade and campanile

# Solvang ⑪

**Road map** C5. 👥 5,000. ▦
🛈 1639 Copenhagen Dr. **Tel** (800) 468-6765. **www**.solvangusa.com

This Scandinavian-style town was established in 1911 by a group of Danish educators. They paid $360,000 for 9,000 acres (3,650 ha) of land on which to build a Danish colony and school. The original schoolhouse, a two-story frame structure on Alisal Road is today the the Bit o' Denmark Restaurant. Solvang's Bethnania Lutheran church, built in 1928 to a traditional Danish design, has a model sailing ship hanging from its ceiling. Visitors can tour the town in a horse-drawn streetcar, the *honen* (hen), and see windmills, roofs with wooden storks, and gas streetlights. Restaurants serve *aebleskiver* (a type of Danish pancake), during the town's Danish Days festival (see p38).

**Statue of the Madonna**

# Mission Santa Inés ⑫

1760 Mission Dr, Solvang.
**Road map** C5. **Tel** (805) 688-4815.
◯ 9am–5pm daily. ⬤ Easter, Thanksgiving, Dec 25. 📷 🚻 ♿
**www**.missionsantaines.org

Founded on September 17, 1804, Santa Inés was the 19th in the chain of California missions (see pp46–7). In 1812 an earthquake destroyed the larger part of the church. It was rebuilt with 5-ft- (1.5-m-) thick walls and rededicated five years later. Before secularization in 1834 the mission was prosperous, with a herd of 12,000 cattle; afterward, it fell into disrepair and most of the Native Americans left. In 1843, the mission became the site of the state's first seminary. Restoration work began after World War II, including the campanile (financed by WR Hearst, see p214) and the church sanctuary. The mission also has a small museum, with period furnishings, parchment books, the vestments worn by early priests, and original murals by Native Americans. There is a landscaped garden.

# Chumash Painted Cave State Historic Park ⑬

Painted Cave Road. **Tel** (805) 733-3713. ▦ from Santa Barbara. Parking limited to 2 vehicles. **www**.parks.cal.gov

In the Santa Ynez Mountains, 8 miles (13 km) northwest of Santa Barbara, are a number of remote and scattered caves with Chumash drawings. The most famous example is a 20 by 40 ft (6 by 12 m) cave just off Hwy 154. Inside, an egg-shaped cavity, covered in small ocher scratchings, is protected by a metal screen.

Some caves have primitive drawings that resemble lizards, snakes, and scorpions, executed in red, black, or white paint. Tribes are known to have traded different pigments with each other. Some experts believe the drawings are symbolic of the Chumash religion; others think they are random, with no significant meaning.

Native American paintings in the Chumash caves

## MONARCH BUTTERFLIES

Each year millions of monarch butterflies migrate from the western US and Canada to winter in Southern and Central California and Mexico. Starting their journey in October and November, the butterflies cover up to 80 miles (130 km) a day at speeds approaching 30 mph (50 km/h). Along the central coast, they usually settle in eucalyptus groves. After the mating season in January and February, the butterflies attempt the journey back to their summer habitat. In season they can often be seen around Montana de Oro State Park (see p209), Pismo Beach, and Ventura.

**Monarch butterfly**

# Street-by-Street: Santa Barbara ⓮

Santa Barbara is a Southern Californian rarity: a city with a single architectural style. Following a devastating earthquake in 1925, the center was rebuilt according to strict rules that dictated Mediterranean-style architecture. The city was founded as a Spanish garrison in 1782 – four years before Santa Barbara Mission (*see pp222–3*). During the 19th century Santa Barbara was a quiet pueblo, home to only a few hundred families and a center for the nearby cattle ranches. Remarkably, about a dozen adobes from that era have survived. Today, Santa Barbara is a favorite resort community with sand beaches, fine cafés and restaurants, boutiques, and art galleries.

**Fountain outside the County Courthouse**

**To Santa Barbara Mission**

FIGUEROA STREET

ANACAPA ST

CAR...

## ★ Museum of Art
*This outstanding regional art collection includes Asian art, antiquities, American art, prints, drawings, and photography. In the 19th-century French section is Jules Bastien-Lepage's The Ripened Wheat (1884).*

## ★ County Courthouse
*The 1929 Spanish Colonial-style courthouse is still in use. It is decorated with Tunisian tiles and wrought-iron metalwork. Murals by DS Groesbeck in the Mural Room depict California history (see p42). There are panoramic views from the clock tower.*

**KEY**

– – –  Suggested route

**STAR SIGHTS**

★ County Courthouse

★ Museum of Art

★ Presidio

**Paseo Nuevo**
*This colorful outdoor shopping and dining center complements an older arcade on the opposite side of State Street.*

For hotels and restaurants in this region see pp531–4 and pp576–9

**★ Presidio**
*Santa Barbara's Presidio was built in 1782 by the Spanish. It was the last in a chain of four fortresses erected along the California coast.*

## VISITORS' CHECKLIST

**Road map** C5. 🔼 *90,200.*
✈ *Santa Barbara Airport, 8 miles (13 km) N of Santa Barbara.* 🚌 *34 W Carrillo.*
🚉 *Stearns Wharf.* **Visitors' Center** *1 Garden St, (805) 965-3021.*
**www.**santa barbaraca.com
**Museum of Art Tel** *(805) 963-4364.* ◯ *11am–5pm Tue–Sun.*
🏛 **County Courthouse Tel** *(805) 962-6464.* ◯ *daily.* ● *Dec 25.*
🏛 **Presidio Tel** *(805) 946-9719.* ◯ *10:30am–4:30pm daily.* 🅿
🌐 **www**.sbthp.org **Santa Barbara Historical Museum Tel** *(805) 966-1601.* ◯ *10am–5pm Tue–Sat, noon–5pm Sun.*
**Donation.** 🅿 🌐 **www.**santabarbaramuseum.com

**The Cañedo Adobe** once housed soldiers and families from the Presidio.

**El Cuartel** is the Presidio's family living quarters.

**Lobero Theatre**
*This graceful 1924 building stands on the site of the city's original theater, which was built in 1873 by Jose Lobero, an Italian musician.*

**Historical Museum**
*The Historical Museum's collections are housed in two adobe buildings. Among the many artifacts is a statue of the 4th-century martyr St. Barbara.*

To East Beach

| 0 meters | 100 |
|---|---|
| 0 yards | 100 |

# Santa Barbara Mission

**Franciscan friar**

Labeled the "Queen of the Missions," Santa Barbara is the most visited mission in the state. Founded in 1786 on the feast day of St. Barbara, it was the tenth mission built by the Spanish *(see pp46–7)*. After the third adobe church on the site was destroyed by an earthquake in 1812, the present structure took shape and was completed in 1820. Its twin towers and mix of Roman, Moorish, and Spanish styles served as the main inspiration for what came to be known as Mission Style *(see p30)*. The mission was again hit by an earthquake in 1925, damaging the towers and façade of the church. These sections were repaired but, because of a chemical reaction between the alkalies and aggregates in the cement, the entire front had to be rebuilt in 1953, following the original design. Santa Barbara is the only California mission to have been in continuous use since it was founded.

**Central Fountain**
*Palm trees tower above a central fountain in the Sacred Gardens.*

**A missionary's bedroom** has been furnished as it would have been in the early 1800s.

**Entrance**

**Arcaded Corridor**
*An open corridor fronts the museum rooms. Originally the living quarters, these now display a rich collection of mission artifacts.*

**Kitchen**
*The kitchen has been restored to show the typical cooking facilities of the early 1800s. Most of the food eaten was produced on the mission, which had fields and livestock.*

**STAR FEATURES**

★ Church

★ Main Façade

★ Sacred Gardens

**★ Sacred Gardens**
*The beautifully landscaped Sacred Gardens were once a working area for Native Americans to learn Western trades. Workshops and some living quarters were located in the surrounding buildings.*

**VISITORS' CHECKLIST**

2201 Laguna St. **Tel** (805) 682-4713. 🚌 22. ⬚ 9am–5pm daily. 🈂️ ✝️ 7:30am Mon–Sat; 4pm Sat; 7:30am, 9am, 11am Sun. 📷 ♿ 🛍️

**★ Church**
*The narrow church has a Neo-Classical interior. Imitation marble columns and detailing have been painted on the walls and doorways. The wooden reredos, replaced after the 1915 earthquake, has carved wooden statues.*

**The side chapel**, next to the altar, is dedicated to the Blessed Sacrament.

**The width of the nave** was determined by the height of the trees used as cross beams.

**The cemetery garden** contains the graves of some 4,000 Native Americans as well as friars.

**★ Main Façade**
*The church's Classical façade was designed by Padre Antonio Ripoll. Ripoll admired the Roman architect Vitruvius Pollio (working around 27 BC) and drew heavily on his ideas when building the church.*

San Buenaventura Mission's church in Ventura

## Ventura **⑮**

Road map C5. 🏠 102,000. 🚃 🛈 101 S California St, Suite C. **Tel** (805) 648-2075. **www**.ventura-usa.com

All that remains of the **San Buenaventura Mission**, founded in 1782 and completed in 1809, is a church with a courtyard garden and tiled fountain. A museum at the mission details the buildings of the original complex.

Two mid-19th-century adobe houses survive in the city. The tiny **Ortega Adobe** reveals the harsh living conditions many experienced at that time. In contrast, the Monterey-style *(see p30)* **Olivas Adobe** is a two-story ranch hacienda, furnished in period style, with rose and herb gardens.

Today Ventura is largely an agricultural center. Ventura Harbor Village has shops, restaurants, a merry-go-round, and a community theater. Harbor fishing charters, and whale-watching cruises, as well as boats to the Channel Islands National Park depart from here. You can also rent fishing equipment and kayaks.

🏛 **San Buenaventura Mission**
211 E Main St. **Tel** (805) 643-4318. ◯ daily. ● Jan 1, Easter, Thanksgiving, Dec 25. **www**.san buenaventuramission.org

🏛 **Ortega Adobe**
215 W Main St. **Tel** (805) 648-2075. ◯ daily. ● Jan 1, Easter Sun, Labor Day, Thanksgiving, Dec 25.

🏛 **Olivas Adobe**
4200 Olivas Park Drive. **Tel** (805) 658-4785. **Grounds** ◯ daily. **House** ◯ Sat & Sun. ● Jan 1, Easter, Thanksgiving, Dec 25.

## Channel Islands National Park **⑯**

Road map C6. 🚃 Ventura. 🚃 **Visitors' Center** 1901 Spinnaker Dr, Ventura. **Tel** (805) 658-5730. ◯ daily. 🚢 Island Packers, 1867 Spinnaker Drive (805 642-1393). **www**.nps.gov/chis

The islands of Santa Barbara, Anacapa, San Miguel, Santa Cruz, and Santa Rosa together make up the Channel Islands National Park, a series of volcanic islands unpopulated by humans. Access to the islands is strictly monitored by park rangers, who issue landing permits from the Visitors' Center. Camping is allowed on all the islands, but visitors must make reservations at least two weeks in advance. They must also bring all their own food and water supplies, because there are none available on any of the five islands.

Depending on the island and the time of year, lucky visitors may spot dolphins, gray whales, and California brown pelicans on the passage across the Santa Barbara Channel. Wildlife on the small, picturesque islands is plentiful and includes cormorants, sea lions, elephant seals, and gulls.

Day trips to Anacapa, the nearest island to the mainland, offer an insight into this unique coastal ecosystem. Even more can be learned, however, by taking one of the various guided walks, conducted by

California brown pelican

park rangers, on all the islands. Visitors must stay on the designated trails, and pets are not allowed.

The rock pools on all of the islands are rich in marine life, and the kelp forests surrounding the islands provide shelter for more than 1,000 plant and animal species.

The islands' many sea caves make sea-kayaking a unique and exciting experience. The snorkeling and scuba diving in this area are superb.

## Ronald Reagan Presidential Library **⑰**

40 Presidential Drive, Simi Valley. Road map C5. **Tel** (800) 410-8354. ◯ 10am–5pm daily. ● Jan 1, Thanksgiving, Dec 25. 🎦 ♿ **www**.reagan.utexas.edu

President Reagan's papers are all archived in this Mission Revival-style structure. The library features a permanent exhibition documenting the life of Reagan and his wife, Nancy. There are also temporary exhibitions of gifts, costumes, works of art, and other objects related to his eight-year tenure in the White House, including a large piece of the Berlin Wall with its original graffiti. There is also an exact full-size replica of the Oval Office. In the Air Force One Pavilion, visitors can board the aircraft which was used by six presidents from 1973 to 2001.

**Reconstruction of the Oval Office at the Reagan Presidential Library**

**Mission Revival arcade on Main Street, Ojai**

# Ojai ⑱

**Road map** C5. 🏠 *8,000.* 🚌 🚆
🛈 *150 W Ojai Ave.* **Tel** *(805) 646-8126.* **www**.ojaichamber.org

Founded in 1874, this town was originally called Nordhoff after the author Charles Nordhoff, who wrote a book promoting California in the 1870s. In 1917 the town was renamed Ojai, a Chumash Indian word for moon, a reference to the crescent-shaped valley where the town lies.

Ojai's Mission Revival arched arcade was funded by Edward J Libby, a glass-manufacturing millionaire, and was designed in 1917 by Richard Requa. Its tower was modeled on a campanile in Havana, Cuba. The arcade fronts two blocks of shops on the main street.

Barts Corner bookshop at No. 302 West Matilija Street has 25,000 volumes, many of which are outdoors. Late-night readers can browse and then pay for their finds through a slot in the door. Spiritual groups have been going on retreats in the Ojai Valley since the 1920s. Today several religious organizations and boarding schools are based here.

# Los Padres National Forest ⑲

**Road map** C5. 🚌 *Santa Barbara.* **Visitors' Center** ⭕ *8am–4:30pm Mon–Fri.* **Tel** *(805) 968-6640.* **www**.fs.fed.us/r5/lospadres

Los Padres National Forest covers almost 2 million acres (810,000 ha) of terrain that varies from desert to pine-clad mountains with peaks as high as 9,000 ft (2,700 m). Black bears, foxes, deer, and mountain lions are among the animals found here. Birds include golden eagles and giant condors. The latter are North America's largest birds with a wingspan of 9 ft (3 m).

Coastal redwood trees grow on the lower slopes, and the higher elevations are thick with firs, bristling with pine cones. Temperatures in the summer can be scorching, and there is very little, if any, rain here between May and October.

The forest is crisscrossed by hundreds of miles of hiking trails for experienced hikers, but there are few roads. Hwy 33 and Hwy 150 are two exceptions. Hwy 154 crosses one corner as it runs between Santa Ynez (*see p218*) and Santa Barbara (*see pp220–23*). On the way, it passes over Cold Spring Arch Bridge.

Scattered within Los Padres National Forest are 88 camp sites. Activities include fishing, horseback riding, and, on Mount Pinos, skiing.

# Bakersfield ⑳

**Road map** C5. 🏠 *384,000.* 🚌
🛈 *515 Truxton Ave.* **Tel** *(866) 425-7353.* **www**.visitbakersfield.com

Bakersfield was named after Colonel Thomas Baker, a settler who planted a field of alfalfa here. The shrub fed the animals of early travelers who rested here before crossing the Tehachapi Mountains, the "border" that divides Northern and Southern California.

The town can be reached on the I-5 from San Francisco, before the ascent up Grapevine Canyon to LA. It can also be reached from Santa Maria or Ojai through the Los Padres National Forest.

Bakersfield's modern history began with the discovery of gold in the 1850s and several oil strikes in the following decades. Many people from Mediterranean countries settled on the fertile land, bringing agriculture to the area.

Today it is among the fastest growing cities in California, but still manages to retain a rural feel and is a recognized center for country music. There are also fine antique shops. The **Kern County Museum** has historical and oil industry exhibits. On the outskirts of Bakersfield is the Kern River for rafting and kayaking (*see p612*). Lake Isabella, 40 miles (65 km) east of the city, is a center for water sports.

🏛 **Kern County Museum**
*3801 Chester Ave.* **Tel** *(661) 852-5000.* ⭕ *10am–5pm Mon–Sat, noon–5pm Sun.* ⬤ *Jan 1, Thanksgiving, Dec 24, 25, 31.* 🖼
**www**.kcmuseum.org

**Cold Spring Arch Bridge, Los Padres National Forest**

# ORANGE COUNTY

*A century ago Orange County lived up to its name. This dry, sunny land, which stretches from the Santa Ana Mountains to the beautiful Pacific coastline, was indeed scattered with orange orchards and farms. Today, the region is a mass of freeways and suburban housing. Visitors to the county can explore a wide range of museums, sites of historical interest, and entertainment complexes.*

In the mid-1950s, the roads leading to the county's theme parks still passed through extensive orange groves. At that time, Disneyland was attracting its first enthusiastic crowds, and a local boy called Richard Nixon had become Vice President of the US. Today, orange groves have given way to urban development and fruit crate labels have become collectors' items. More than three million people live here, enjoying perennial sunshine and a high standard of living.

The coastline of Orange County is lined with wide, sandy beaches and a succession of legendary surfing haunts, marinas, and artists' enclaves. In the affluent coastal towns, few visitors can resist the temptation to seek out a clifftop bar and watch the sun set.

Inland lies a variety of cultural sights. Mission San Juan Capistrano, founded in 1776, is a reminder of the days of the Spanish Franciscan settlers. The Bowers Museum of Cultural Art in Santa Ana houses superb examples of the art of indigenous peoples from all around the world. At Yorba Linda, the impressive Richard Nixon Library and Birthplace commemorates the life of Orange County's most famous son.

Orange County is the entertainment capital of California. For visitors seeking family fun and roller-coaster thrills, there are the homey Knott's Berry Farm, America's oldest theme park, and the fantasy kingdom of Disneyland, which is, as the saying goes, "the most famous people-trap ever built by a mouse."

Reflecting Pool at the Richard Nixon Library and Birthplace

◁ Log Ride at Knott's Berry Farm theme park

# Exploring Orange County

Much of Orange County's 798-sq mile (2,050-sq km) area is covered with sprawling urban communities linked by ever-busy freeways. Anaheim, home of Disneyland®, is its second largest city, after Santa Ana. The popular Knott's Berry Farm® theme park lies a few miles northwest at Buena Park, and together these cities form the tourist capital of the county. Most of the coastline is built-up, but its communities have more variety and character than those around the theme parks. Inland, open spaces can be found where the county's eastern region encompasses part of the vast Cleveland National Forest and the Santa Ana Mountains.

Catalina Island's Two Harbors

### SEE ALSO

• **Where to Stay** pp534–5

• **Where to Eat** pp579–81

La Habra
Los Angeles
La Mirada
Brea
**RICHARD NIXON LIBRARY AND BIRTHPLACE** ❸
Long Beach
La Palma
Fullerton
**KNOTT'S BERRY FARM® & SOAK CITY USA** ❷
Anaheim
**DISNEYLAND® RESORT** ❶
**CRYSTAL CATHEDRAL** ❹
Garden Grove
Orange
Westminster
**BOWERS MUSEUM OF CULTURAL ART** ❺
Seal Beach
Santa Ana
Sunset Beach
*Bolsa Chica State Beach*
Fountain Valley
**HERITAGE MUSEUM OF ORANGE COUNTY** ❻
**Huntington Beach**
Costa Mesa
*Huntington State Beach*
Newport Beach
Balboa Island
*Corona del Mar State Beach*
Crystal Cove
*Gulf of Santa Catalina*

*San Pedro Channel*
*Silver Peak 550m*
Two Harbors
*Black Jack Mountain 610m*
*Whitleys Peak 648m*
❽
**CATALINA ISLAND**   Avalon

| 0 kilometers | 5 |
| 0 miles | 5 |

### KEY

═══ Freeway

═══ Major road

─── Secondary road

──── Minor road

─·─ Main railway

─── Minor railway

△ Summit

**Enormous Crystal Cathedral at Garden Grove, south of Anaheim**

## SIGHTS AT A GLANCE

Bowers Museum of
Cultural Art **5**

*Catalina Island pp242–3* **8**

Crystal Cathedral **4**

*Disneyland® Resort
pp232–5* **1**

Heritage Museum of Orange
County **6**

*Knott's Berry Farm® and Soak
City pp236–7* **2**

*Mission San Juan Capistrano
pp240–41* **7**

Richard Nixon Library and
Birthplace **3**

### GETTING AROUND

Interstate-5 is a major north–
south artery, which links Los
Angeles and San Diego. New
express toll lanes now operate
in an effort to eliminate traffic
jams. The more scenic Hwy 1,
the Pacific Coastal Highway,
unites the coastal resorts. Amtrak
*(see p630)* and Metrolink commuter trains run south from Los
Angeles. Stops include San Juan
Capistrano and Anaheim. Most
bus routes are designed to meet
the needs of local commuters,
but shuttle vans and tour buses
offer quick connections to the
theme parks and to Los Angeles.
Ferries to Catalina Island run
daily in summer, but travelers
should check schedules in
winter. Crossings from the
mainland to Avalon or Two
Harbors take about an hour.

# Orange County Coastline

Orange County's coast is Southern California at its most classic. The northern shoreline is flat and low-lying. South of the Balboa Peninsula, the coast features scenic cliffs and sheltered coves. Multi-million dollar homes, luxury marinas, constant sports activity, and a fashionable lifestyle reflect the wealth and vitality of its communities.

LOS ANGELES

Huntington Harbor

Hunting Beach

**The Balboa Pavilion**
*opened in 1905 as a terminal for the Pacific Electric Red Car Line from LA. Stars of the Big Band era, such as Count Basie, played here in the 1930s and 1940s. Today the wooden pavilion is a restaurant and center for sightseeing cruises around Newport Harbor.*

★ **Huntington State Beach** ③

California's Surf City USA®, Huntington Beach has a surfing museum, international competitions, and waters full of surfers whose exploits can be watched from the long pier.

**Upper Newport Bay Ecological Preserve** *is a 750-acre (300-ha) wedge of coastal wetland providing a refuge for wildlife and migratory birds. Facilities in the preserve include a bike path, fishing, and guided tours on foot and by kayak.*

**KEY**

| | |
|---|---|
| | Freeway |
| | Major road |
| | Minor road |
| | River |
| ☼ | Viewpoint |

**Seal Beach** ①

This is a quiet, 1-mile (1.6-km) long beach with level sand and some surfers. The wooden pier is popular with anglers. A walk along its 1,865-ft (570-m) length offers views northward to the high-rise buildings of Long Beach *(see pp132–3)*.

**Bolsa Chica State Beach** ②

The name Bolsa Chica means "little pocket" in Spanish. Flat, wilderness sands, oil extractors, and the protected wetlands of the 300-acre (120-ha) Bolsa Chica Ecological Reserve give this beach a unique atmosphere.

**Newport Beach** ④

Famous for its million-dollar homes and lifestyles to match, Newport Beach boasts a 3-mile (5-km) stretch of wide sand and two piers. Fresh fish, caught by the historic Dory fishing fleet, is sold beside Newport Pier at the northern end of the beach.

**Aliso Beach** ⑦

At the mouth of Aliso Creek lies this small, sandy beach. The 620-ft- (190-m-) long concrete pier is used by anglers. At the southern end of the beach is a marine life refuge with beds of giant kelp offshore.

**Doheny State Beach** ⑧

This sandy beach and marine life refuge is close to the mouth of San Juan Creek. The beach attracts a typically Southern Californian mix of swimmers, surfers, bird-watchers, anglers, cyclists, and campers.

**San Clemente State Beach** ⑨

The hillside community of San Clemente has a narrow, sandy beach at its foot. Near the railroad station there is a municipal pier. Farther south, the 100-acre (40-ha) State Beach has landscaped facilities including picnic areas and a camp site.

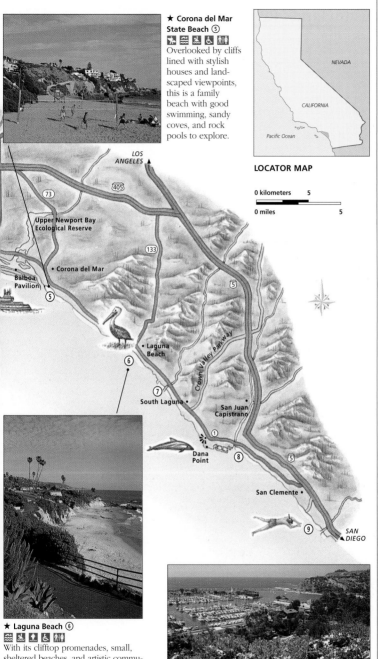

★ **Corona del Mar State Beach** ⑤

Overlooked by cliffs lined with stylish houses and landscaped viewpoints, this is a family beach with good swimming, sandy coves, and rock pools to explore.

**LOCATOR MAP**

0 kilometers 5

0 miles 5

★ **Laguna Beach** ⑥

With its clifftop promenades, small, sheltered beaches, and artistic community, Laguna courts the atmosphere of the Mediterranean Riviera. The ideal spot for a cocktail at sunset, Laguna is famous for its summer arts festival, the Pageant of the Masters *(see p37)*.

**Dana Point** *headland is named after the author Richard Dana, whose 1840 book* Two Years Before the Mast *chronicled the early days of California. A replica of the contemporary brig,* Pilgrim, *is moored in the harbor.*

# Disneyland® Resort ❶

Disney's "Magic Kingdom" in Anaheim is not only the top tourist attraction in California, it is part of the American Dream. Now encompassing the original Disneyland® Park, Disney's California Adventure™ Park, and Downtown Disney®, plus three enormous hotels, the Resort has become the model for theme parks around the globe. Visitors to "The Happiest Place on Earth" find fantasy, thrill rides, glittering shows, and shopping in a brightly orchestrated land of long lines, fireworks, and Mickey Mouse, which is as American as apple pie.

### Exploring the Resort

Spread over 85 acres (34 ha), the original Disneyland® Park is divided into eight theme areas, known as "lands." Transportation around the park is provided by the Disneyland® Railroad and monorail. Disney's California Adventure™ Park has four theme areas *(see p235)*. Smaller in area than Disneyland® Park, Disney's California Adventure™ Park is easily covered by walking. This newest venture into nostalgia, impeccably executed in superb and stunning Disney-style, is suited to the interests and tastes of the whole family. In the heart of the Resort, between the two theme parks, lies Downtown Disney®. This lively area is full of restaurants, shops, and various innovative entertainment venues.

It takes at least three days to make the best of a visit, now that the Resort has grown so large. A joint ticket *(see p233)* can be bought for all the theme parks; it provides access to all the rides and shows, and includes a park map, and a schedule of the day's events. Both parks stay open late in the evening during the peak seasons; and the **Fireworks Show** that takes place in Disneyland® is well worth losing a little sleep for.

## MAIN STREET, U.S.A.®

This spotlessly clean, colorful street lined with turn-of-the-century buildings welcomes visitors to Disneyland®. The Town Square, near City Hall, is a good place to view the daily parade, which features cheerfully waving Disney characters and scenes from many of Disney's most famous movies. This is only one of the places where guests can meet and talk with many of the famous Disney cartoon characters. If you're lucky, you can find ample opportunities here for photographs and videos.

**City Hall** offers maps, dining and entertainment schedules, and general information about the park, while the **Main Street Cinema** screens early Disney silent films. Main Street itself has a large selection of attractions, shops, and places to eat.

## TOMORROWLAND®

Visions of the future inspire the attractions here, which change regularly to keep ahead of technology and still retain a sense of fantasy. One of the first attractions in 1955 was **Autopia**, now completely redesigned and updated to take guests into a parallel universe from a car's point of view. The track winds through Tomorrowland® and Fantasyland®.

### Buzz Lightyear Astro Blasters

An interactive experience in which guests pilot their own Space Cruisers.

### Finding Nemo Submarine Voyage

A truly unique experience where visitors go underwater accompanied by Nemo and his friends.

### Star Tours©

Designed in collaboration with the *Star Wars©* genius, George Lucas, the use of flight-simulator technology makes this one of the most realistic rides in the park. The attraction recently added Odysseys in 3-D, with more than 50 story combinations.

### Space Mountain®

A hands-down Disneyland® favorite and updated for the Millennium, this attraction provides a high-speed roller-coaster ride, 118 ft (36 m). Conducted almost entirely in darkness, the ride has meteoric flashes, celestial showers, and space-age music. Not suitable for very young children.

---

### TOP 5 ATTRACTIONS

★ Pirates of the Caribbean®

★ Indiana Jones™ Adventure

★ It's a Small World

★ Soarin' Over California

★ Star Tours®

---

### SHOPPING

The Disneyland® shops, particularly those along Main Street, U.S.A.®, are often busy late in the day, especially at closing time. If you can, it is worth making your purchases earlier in the day and then collecting them later from the Redemption Center. Although many of the goods on sale in the theme park bear the faces of Disney characters, each of the eight lands adds its own variations to what is on offer to buy. In Adventureland®, for example, you can buy Indiana Jones-style clothing, and Native American crafts are on sale in Frontierland®. The largest of all the shops within the Magic Kingdom® is the Emporium in Main Street, U.S.A.®. If you are looking for Disney® characters or Disney merchandise, this is the first place to go.

Fairytale façade of Sleeping Beauty Castle in Fantasyland®

## VISITORS' CHECKLIST

1313 Harbor Blvd, Anaheim.
**Tel** (714) 520-5060. 🏢 (714)
781-4565. ✈ from LAX.
🚌 435. ◯ Jun–Aug: 8am–midnight daily; Sep–May: 9am–6pm
daily. 📷 ⊙ 🚻 🎁 🍴 ⫶
🌐 www.disneyland.com

and canal boats to the Mad Hatter's giant spinning teacups. There are almost twice as many attractions to enjoy here as in most of the other lands, and the constant crowds illustrate the enduring appeal of this area.

### Matterhorn Bobsleds

This historic attraction and park icon has been providing "icy" roller-coaster rides since 1959. A copy of the famous peak near Zermatt in Switzerland, the Matterhorn Mountain towers 147 ft (45 m) above the park. Bobsleds carrying four passengers climb to the mountain's snow-capped summit, then drop into a steep, high-speed descent, zooming in and out of the hollow peak, passing glacier caves and waterfalls as they go. At the end of the trip, riders in the front seats are splashed as the sleds careen into a pond.

### It's a Small World

This show features dolls inspired by favorite Disney characters, but dressed in costumes from around the world. Colorful boats transport passengers through the attraction, which features nearly 300 singing-and-dancing Audio-Animatronics dolls, all in national costume.

### MICKEY'S TOONTOWN®

All of Disney's favorite animated characters reside here. This is where visitors are most likely to find Mickey, Goofy, and other well-known characters having their pictures taken with guests.

The most popular celebrity residences are Mickey's house and Minnie's cottage, where subtle touches typify Disney's legendary attention to detail. Most of the attractions in this area are geared toward kids from age three up. **Chip 'n Dale Treehouse**, is in a giant Redwood, and the bustling interactive downtown area offers gentle excitement for this younger set.

**Roger Rabbit's Car Toon Spin** is Toontown®'s largest and most popular attraction. It's spinning cars provide a madcap taxi drive through a surreal cartoon world fraught with near-misses.

### FANTASYLAND®

Dominated by the pink and gold towers of **Sleeping Beauty Castle** and a replica of the **Matterhorn**, Fantasyland® is a shrine to children's dreams and adult nostalgia. Nursery heroes such as Peter Pan, Dumbo, and Snow White provide the themes for gentle fairytale rides in vehicles that range from flying galleons

### TICKETS AND TIPS

A basic one-day ticket to Disneyland® or Disney's California Adventure™ Park covers admission and most rides and attractions. Parking is extra, as are food and arcades. Multiday tickets for two to six days and Annual Passports allow unlimited admission and access to rides and attractions. Fastpass lets guests obtain a voucher with a computer-assigned boarding time for specific attractions or rides. This eliminates waiting in long lines. You can also save time at the front gate by buying your tickets in advance at any Disney Store or online at www.disneyland.com. To help you plan your day, there is updated information on showtimes, waiting times, and ride closures at the information board at the end of Main Street, U.S.A®, opposite the Plaza Pavilion, and on the website.

**Mark Twain Riverboat navigating the Rivers of America**

## FRONTIERLAND®

This area is inspired by the adventurous days of the Wild West. Skirt-lifting song and dance take place on the **Golden Horseshoe** stage featuring Billy Hill and the Hillbillies. Every weekend at night the spectacular **Fantasmic!** show with fireworks, sound effects, and live performers light up the

### DOWNTOWN DISNEY®

Located between the entrances to Disneyland® park and Disney's California Adventure™ Park, Downtown Disney® is a lively walking street, offering guests some 300,000 sq ft (27,870 sq m) of innovative restaurants, shops, and entertainment venues. The fact that this area has no admission fee makes Downtown Disney® one of the more popular – but crowded – spaces. A 12-screen AMC Theatre®, ESPN Zone™, and a LEGO Imagination Center® are the top attractions here. The snack shops, top-notch restaurants, plus a vast range of retail and specialty shops and a travel center, create a total Disney experience.

skies above Frontierland®. The **Mark Twain Riverboat** offers visitors a 15-minute cruise on a paddle-wheel boat. While it crosses the Rivers of America, look out for the plastic moose and deer. Take time to visit the scary new **Pirate's Lair** on Tom Sawyer Island.

Thrill-seekers love the **Big Thunder Mountain Railroad** roller-coaster ride. Open ore trucks set off from the 1880s mining town of Big Thunder without a driver. The runaway train then speeds through the cavernous interior of Big Thunder Mountain, narrowly escaping boulders and waterfalls. Remember that this ride has height and age restrictions.

## CRITTER COUNTRY

Built in a rustic style, based on the rugged American Northwest, Critter Country is a 4-acre (1.6-ha) area next to New Orleans Square. Home of Splash Mountain®, one of the most popular attractions in Disneyland®, and a quiet restaurant, the Hungry Bear.

### Splash Mountain®

This is a winding, watery ride in hollowed-out logs. Brer Rabbit and Brer Fox are among the furry, singing characters from the 1946

film *Song of the South*, who inhabit the mountain through which the ride passes. The ride culminates in a plummet down a steep waterfall. As on the Matterhorn ride, people in the front seats will get wet.

### Davy Crockett's Explorer Canoes

Groups can take to the water and row downriver frontier-style. Guides provide lessons and ensure safety.

### The Many Adventures of Winnie the Pooh

The world's most beloved bear and his stalwart friends go on a hunt for honey.

## NEW ORLEANS SQUARE

This charming town square is modeled on the French Quarter in New Orleans, as it was in that city's heyday in the 19th century. The buildings have wrought-iron balconies and house interesting French-style shops.

### The Haunted Mansion®

Some of the visitors to this attraction, which promises 999 "ghosts and ghouls," are now so familiar with its introductory commentary that they join in as they descend into its spooky world of mischievous spirits and grave-diggers. The holographic figures, including a talking woman's head in a crystal ball, are very realistic. This show, which took 15 years to plan, has decor inspired by Tim Burton's *The Nightmare Before Christmas*. The show is exclusive to Disneyland® in California and is lovely and cool inside on hot afternoons.

### Pirates of the Caribbean®

This show provides a floating ride through a yo-ho-ho world of ruffians and wenches who have been empowered with the gifts of song, dance, and heavy drinking by Audio-Animatronics. This technique, which brings toy figures to life using electronic impulses to control their sounds and actions, was perfected at Disneyland®. Characters from the popular movie have been added to the show.

## ADVENTURELAND®

The exotic atmosphere in Adventureland® offers dark, humid waterways lined with tropical plants. This is the smallest, but perhaps the most adventuresome, "land" in the park. **The Enchanted Tiki Room** showcases mechanical singing birds in a zany, musical romp through the tropics.

### Indiana Jones™ Adventure

Inspired by the 1982 film trilogy, passengers set off on a jeep-style drive through the Temple of the Forbidden Eye.

Theatrical props and scenery, a realistic soundtrack, sensational film images, and the physical sensation of a roller coaster make this the ultimate experience created by Disneyland® to date.

### Jungle Cruise

This safari-style boat ride through a jungle forest full of rampant apes and bloodthirsty headhunters is narrated by a real-life captain, who tells his captive audience terrible but amusing jokes during the ride through steamy waterways.

### Tarzan™'s Treehouse

A climb-up, climb-through experience, starring Tarzan and Jane, with an interactive and musical play area at the base of the tree.

# Disney's California Adventure™ Park

Disney's California Adventure™ Park is adjacent to Disneyland® and built on 55 acres (22 ha) of the old parking lot. Disney's California Adventure™ Park is divided into "lands," each offering themed experiences that celebrate the California dream. The emphasis here is on adults and older teens, but there are still plenty of rides and attractions that appeal to all ages. Together with the original Disneyland® Park, Disney's California Adventure™ Park adds to the Disney legend.

## HOLLYWOOD PICTURES BACKLOT

The Backlot offers a great tongue-in-cheek view of the motion-picture industry. There are two blocks of façades and fakery, giving the visitor a Disney-eye view of Hollywood. Other attractions include **The Twilight Zone Tower of Terror™**, with a 13-story elevator drop, and **Monsters Inc. Mike and Sulley to the Rescue**, where visitors race around Monstropolis on a mission to return Boo home safely.

## GOLDEN STATE

A tribute to the state's topography and agriculture, the rock-carved Grizzly Peak stands as the landmark icon of Disney's California Adventure™ Park. The centerpiece ride is **Soarin'™ Over California**, a simulated hang-glider ride that portrays the beauties of California's varied landscape on a huge wrap-around screen. There is no narrative, but guests can feel the wind currents and smell the scent of orange blossoms as they soar 40 feet (12 m) aloft. **Grizzly River Run** will cool you down on a summer's day as you run the rapids on a rubber raft. **Bug's Land** features bug rides for children and a 3-D film starring Flik from *A Bug's Life*.

## PARADISE PIER

Lower key than the thrill rides in the original park, Paradise Pier is the place where roller coasters and Ferris wheels rule. **California Screamin'** roller coaster, the giant **Mickey's Fun Wheel**, **Games of the Boardwalk**, and **King Triton's Carousel** are reminiscent of seaside boardwalk amusement parks of years ago.

**Grizzly River Run is California Adventure™ Park's signature attraction**

# Knott's Berry Farm® and Soak City ❷

Knott's Berry Farm® has grown from a 1920s boysenberry farm to a 21st-century multi-day entertainment complex. America's first theme park offers more than 165 different rides and attractions, but its main charm lies in its emphasis on authenticity. The Old West Ghost Town at the heart of the

Statues of cowboys on a Ghost Town bench

park has original ghost town buildings and artifacts. Located in Buena Park in Orange County, 6 miles (10 km) from Disneyland®, Knott's offers five themed areas, dozens of live-action stages, thrill rides, shopping and dining, and a full-service resort hotel.

## GHOSTRIDER

*Built in 1998, this mega-woodie has risen to the top of the "best coaster ride" list. With an initial drop of 108 ft (33 m) at speeds approaching 60 mph (97km/b), the 2.5-minute ride is a must for every visitor to the Old Ghost Town.*

## OLD WEST GHOST TOWN

This 1880s Goldrush town has authentic century-old buildings. An 1880 steam train, the **Ghost Town & Calico Railroad**, circles the park, and a genuine **Butterfield Stagecoach** takes passengers on a trip into the past.

The **Gold Trails Hotel and Mercantile**, a restored Kansas school-house, and the **Western Trails Museum** are chock full of Wild West memorabilia. Visitors can join a line-dance at **Calico Square**. The **Timber Mountain Log Ride** floats visitors through a real 1880s sawmill before plunging down a waterfall. At the heart of Ghost Town, the **Ghostrider** roller coaster towers over the park. **Silver Bullet** is Knott's first suspended coaster with spirals and corkscrews, and the **Pony Express** offers a horseback relay at speeds never imagined in the Old West.

Largest wooden coaster in the United States at 118-ft (36-m) high

4,533-ft (1,382-m) long track

An 1880 steam engine transports visitors around the park

## CAMP SNOOPY

Inspired by the majestic High Sierra, Camp Snoopy's six-acre (2.4-ha) wonderland is an interactive participatory children's paradise. There are over 30 kid-tested attractions and pint-sized rides, hosted by the beloved Peanuts characters Snoopy, Lucy, and Charlie Brown. Children under 12 delight in the **Timberline Twister** roller coaster, the Red Baron's airplanes, and an old-fashioned Ferris wheel, where parents and kids can see wonderful views. The **Charlie Brown Speedway** appeals to little stock-car enthusiasts and their parents. **Woodstock's**

**Airmail** is a child-sized version of Supreme Scream℠. Kids of all ages will want to come aboard **Lucy's Tugboat**, take a spin on **Sierra Side-winder**, or watch a show at the **Camp Snoopy Theatre**.

Kids get behind the wheel at the Charlie Brown Speedway

## FIESTA VILLAGE

Celebrating California's Spanish legacy, Fiesta Village offers a collection of south-of-the-border adventures and high-energy thrills. **Casa Arcada** challenges the whole family to the latest video technology, while a ride on the world's oldest **Dentzel Carousel** is a pleasant nostalgic treat. Two large roller coasters, the family-pleasing **Jaguar** and, for the more adventurous fun-seeker, **Montezooma's Revenge** provide the thrills.

**Supreme Scream**<sup>SM</sup>, a
vertical ascending and
descending thrill ride

## INDIAN TRAILS

Intricate arts and crafts of Native Americans from the Pacific Northwest, Great Plains, Southwest, and Far West are showcased in this area. Totem poles and tepees from the Navajo, Cherokee, and Chumash tribes seen throughout Indian Trails were built to convey the beauty and diversity of Native American culture. Through participatory learning adventures and exquisite artworks, visitors will understand how the people lived, and how their beliefs, climate, and environment influenced their daily lives.

## THE BOARDWALK

A continuous beach party is the theme here, where everything centers around Southern California's seaside culture. Beachside concessions and the most radical thrill rides rule: **Supreme Scream**<sup>SM</sup> simulates a rocket launch while the **Perilous Plunge** and **Xcelerator** are not for the nervous. Then, relax and take in a big-stage show at the **Charles M. Schulz Theater**.

## WILD WATER WILDERNESS

Experience the magic of the 1900s river wilderness with a raging white-water river, soaring geysers, and a giant waterfall – **Bigfoot Rapids** will fulfill your wildest dreams. The multi-sensory **Mystery Lodge** celebrates Native American culture, complete with an Indian storyteller, music, and dance.

The **Ranger Station** has a resident naturalist who makes friends with Sasquatch, the California High Sierra creature also known as Bigfoot.

## SOAK CITY

Southern California's newest water adventure park has 21 awesome water rides – all themed to the 1950s and 1960s surfing culture.

Adjacent to Knott's main park, and separately gated, Soak City serves up 13 water-logged acres (5.3 ha), replete

with tube and body slides, surfing pipelines, a six-lane super slide, and **Tidal Wave Bay**, a special pool with gentle to moderate wave action. **Gremmie Lagoon** is a wet kid's playground with hands-on fun. **Pacific Spin**, the newest attraction, drops riders into a 75-ft (22-m) tunnel.

All rides have age and height requirements. Men's and women's changing rooms and lockers are also available.

## KNOTT'S BERRY FARM® RESORT HOTEL

Under this umbrella are Southern California's three finest entertainment venues: Knott's Berry Farm® Theme Park, Soak City, and the Knott's Berry Farm® Resort Hotel. Guests in the 321-room hotel can stay in Snoopy-themed suites and take advantage of the pools, sports facilities, fitness center, and children's activity area. Family-friendly restaurants such as Amber Waves add to the festive atmosphere. There are, of course, special rates for frequent guests, value-added packages.

**Spectacular water rides at Soak City**

**House in which Richard Nixon was born**

## Richard Nixon Library and Birthplace ❸

**Road map** D6. 18001 Yorba Linda Blvd. **Tel** *(714) 993-5075*. 🚊 *to Fullerton.* ⭕ *10am–5pm Mon–Sat, 11am–5pm Sun.* ⭕ *Thanksgiving, Dec 25.* 📷 ♿ 📷
**www**.nixonfoundation.org

The life and achievements of the Republican politician Richard Nixon, president of the United States from 1969 to 1974, are celebrated in this museum and archive. In the immaculately landscaped grounds is the simple wooden house where the former president was born in 1913. Nearby are a Reflecting Pool and the graves of Nixon and his wife, Pat, marked by matching black granite tombstones.

In the museum, a walk-through exhibit provides a chronological account of Nixon's rise and fall, emphasizing his role as a peacemaker and international statesman. The Foreign Affairs gallery has a reconstruction of a Chinese pavilion housing an exhibit on Nixon's 1972 state visit to China. There is also a replica of St. Basil's Cathedral in Moscow, with a display on Nixon's trip to the Soviet Union that same year.

Don't miss the World Leaders' Room, where statues of famous politicians are surrounded by some of the many gifts that Nixon received while in office, such as a 6th-century BC statue of the goddess Isis from Anwar Sadat of Egypt, a Sonia Delaunay painting from Georges Pompidou of France,

and a malachite jewelry box from Leonid Brezhnev of the Soviet Union.

Historic items exhibited in other galleries include a three-billion-year-old lump of rock from the moon, a 12-ft (3.5-m) section of the Berlin Wall, and dresses worn by the First Lady. Visitors are able to eavesdrop on the infamous "Watergate Tapes," which led to Nixon's resignation. In the Presidential Forum, a touch-screen exhibit using archive footage allows visitors to put questions to the late president. In additional galleries changing exhibitions are held. These cover popular

aspects of US presidential history, such as the visits paid to the White House by such pop stars as Elvis Presley.

## Crystal Cathedral ❹

12141 Lewis St, Garden Grove. **Tel** *(714) 971-4000.* 🚌 *45 N.* ⭕ *Mon–Sat.* ♿ 📷 🕐 *9:30am, 11am, 6:30pm Sun.*
**www**.crystalcathedral.org

Constructed from an elaborate maze of white steel trusses covered with more than 10,000 panes of silvered glass, the Crystal Cathedral is a shimmering monument to the television-led evangelism that enthralls millions of Americans today. The cathedral, which can comfortably hold almost 3,000 worshipers, is the pulpit from which R Schuller and the pastors broadcast the famous "Hour of Power" service live on Sundays.

Everything about this unique cathedral is large – music is provided by one of the biggest pipe organs in the world, and there is a 15-ft (4.6-m-) wide color video screen. A huge glass door

**Vast interior of the Crystal Cathedral in Garden Grove**

opens during the Sunday services, to enable the drive-in congregation outside to listen to the service without leaving their cars. The memorial cemetery has a capacity of 10,000.

Designed in 1980 by Philip Johnson, the star-shaped cathedral is both a spiritual shrine and an architectural wonder. Beside the building is a 236-ft (72-m) steeple, added in 1990 and adorned with polished stainless-steel prisms.

The cathedral represents the culmination of a lengthy evangelical crusade that began in 1955 when the indefatigable Dr. Schuller Senior started preaching in a nearby drive-in theater. Today the church has many followers in the US, Canada, and Australia.

Worshipers come from afar to attend pageants performed at Christmas and Easter, featuring such things as human "angels" flying from the ceiling and live animals portraying scenes from the Bible. There are free tours from 9am to 3:30pm daily, except Sundays.

## Bowers Museum of Cultural Art ⑤

2002 N Main St, Santa Ana. **Road map** D6. **Tel** (714) 567-3600. 🚊 to Anaheim. 🚌 45 S. ⏰ 10am–4pm Tue–Sun. ⏰ Jan 1, Jul 4, Thanksgiving, Dec 25. 🎟 ♿ 📷 (Sat–Sun). **www**.bowers.org

The Bowers has long been considered to be Orange County's leading art museum. Its serene Mission-style buildings house rich permanent collections and high-profile temporary exhibitions. There is a stylish California café and a shop packed with ethnic crafts and art books.

The museum was founded in 1932. Its display of African masks, collected by Paul and Ruth Tishman and now on long-term loan from the Disney Corporation, is reason enough for a pilgrimage. Other galleries, with exhibitions of treasures from the pre-colonial cultures of Southeast Asia, Oceania, Mexico, and Native

**Entrance arch leading to the Bowers Museum of Cultural Art**

America, reflect the museum's commitment to art of indigenous peoples. Fascinating examples of their crafts illustrate both the religious beliefs and the daily lives of these people. The upstairs galleries, decorated with 1930s murals and plaster work, cover the mission and rancho periods of California and Orange County history (see pp46–7). One block away, a former bank has been converted into the companion **Kidseum**, where kids can enjoy arts-related activities and can try on masks and costumes from all over the world.

**Mayan statuette (AD 800–950), Bowers Museum**

🏛 **Kidseum**
1802 N Main St, Santa Ana. **Tel** (714) 480-1520. ⏰ 10am–3pm Tue–Fri, 11am–3pm Sat & Sun. 🎟 ♿

## Heritage Museum of Orange County ⑥

3101 W Harvard St, Santa Ana. **Road map** D6. **Tel** (714) 540-0404. 🚊 to Anaheim. 🚌 45 S. ⏰ 1–5pm Fri, 11am–3pm Sun. ⏰ Jan 1, Easter Sun, Thanksgiving, Dec 25. 🎟 ♿ 📷 **www**.heritagemuseumoc.org

Victorian times in Orange County are brought to life in this curious three-story mansion, built in 1898 by a civil engineer, Hiram Clay Kellogg.

Fascinated by ships, Kellogg incorporated several nautical design features into his Santa Ana residence. The oval, cabinlike dining room has an oak and walnut floor, laid in strips to resemble a ship's deck. Some of the drawers in the built-in wooden cabinets can also be opened from the kitchen, on the other side of the wall. Clusters of fruit are painted on the ceiling, and the room is overlooked by an elegant circular staircase with a mastlike central pillar.

The mansion now houses an exciting and child-friendly museum, which is also of historic and architectural interest to adults. Young visitors are given the opportunity to dress up in genuine antique clothing and experience life as it was at the turn of the century.

Upstairs, rooms are furnished with antique school desks, dolls' houses, and period games. In the master bedroom, now the textile room, a treadle sewing machine and spinning wheel are on display. Downstairs, you can investigate such instruments as a stereoscope and a hand-crank telephone, and see the old-fashioned kitchen that has an icebox and butter churn. Next door is an 1899 ranch house, carriage barn, and water tower. There is also an orchard of orange trees – now a rare sight in the county.

**Implements for orange cultivation at the Heritage Museum Orange County**

# Mission San Juan Capistrano ❼

**Statue of St. John of Capistran**

This beautiful "Jewel of the Missions" was founded in 1776, and its chapel is the only surviving building in California in which the famous Father Junípero Serra *(see p46)* preached. One of the largest and most prosperous in the whole chain, the mission was crowned by a Great Stone Church, completed in 1806. Six years later this was destroyed by an earthquake, leaving a ruined shell set amid a rambling complex of adobe and brick buildings. A restoration program, ornamental gardens, and many historical exhibits now enable visitors to imagine the mission's former glory.

**★ Padres' Living Quarters**
*The fathers of Mission San Juan Capistrano lived in sparsely furnished rooms and slept on hard plank beds. Visitors enjoyed more comfortable accommodation.*

**The kitchens** have corner ovens and displays of utensils.

**A domed hut**, built from wooden poles, resembles the traditional dwellings of Native American villages at the time of the mission.

**Sacred Garden Bells**
*The original four bells from the Great Stone Church now hang in the wall of a small garden. The larger pair date from 1796.*

## STAR FEATURES

★ Courtyard Gardens

★ Padres' Living Quarters

★ Serra's Chapel

**Junípero Serra**
*A statue of Father Serra and a Native American boy stands in a corner of the gardens.*

## VISITORS' CHECKLIST

26801 Ortega Hwy, San Juan
Capistrano. **Road map** D6.
**Tel** (949) 234-1300. 8:30am–
5pm daily. Good Fri pm,
Thanksgiving, Dec 25. www.missionsjc.com

### ★ Courtyard Gardens

*This courtyard was at the heart of mission
life. Surrounded by cloisters, it still has a
fountain at its center and is today graced
by mature trees and beautiful gardens.*

**The Bodega**, or
warehouse, where tallow,
grains, woolens, and
hides were stored.

### Cloisters

*Covered walkways with
arches frame the mission's
central courtyard. With their
tiled walls, the cloisters provide a cool, shaded place in
which to stroll or sit and
contemplate the gardens.*

### ★ Serra's Chapel

*Built from cherry
wood and covered
with gold leaf, the 300-
year-old altar in the
mission's chapel was
brought from Barcelona,
Spain, in 1906.*

### SWALLOWS AT THE MISSION

Every spring thousands of migrating swallows return to San
Juan Capistrano from South America. Their annual arrival is
celebrated with a festival held on March 19, St. Joseph's
Day (see p36). The birds have been nesting
in the tiled roofs and adobe walls of the
mission for more than two centuries.
They use mud pellets to build enclosed
nests, in which four or five eggs are
incubated. When autumn comes, the
swallows fly south again.

**Migratory swallow at the mission**

**Ruins** are all that remain of
the cruciform Great Stone
Church, which was destroyed
in an earthquake in 1812.

# Catalina Island ❽

Just 22 miles (50 km) from the mainland, Catalina Island is the most accessible of California's Channel Islands. It was named Santa Catalina by the Spanish explorer Sebastián Vizcaíno when he landed here in 1602 on the feast day of St. Catherine of Alexandria. Much of the island's mountainous landscape remains unspoiled, and it has long been a favorite weekend and vacation destination.

Catalina's main town is the virtually traffic-free port of Avalon. The biggest buildings were constructed by the chewing-gum millionaire William Wrigley, Jr., who bought the island in 1919. Today most of Catalina's 76 sq miles (200 sq km) are owned by the Santa Catalina Island Conservancy, which preserves the island's natural beauty.

**Two Harbors**
*This low-lying isthmus backed by two bays is a popular anchorage for yachts. Facilities include a camp site, diving center, and general store.*

West End

Two Harbors

Catalina Harbor

Little Harbor Road

Airport-in-the-Sky and Nature Center

Empire Landing Road

Little Harbor

BLACK JACK MOUNTAIN

Middle Canyon Trail

BULLRUSH CANYON

**Little Harbor**
*This out-of-the way spot located on the island's west shore has a sheltered cove with a beach and a scenic harbor. There are also several hiking trails and a good camp site.*

**Black Jack Mountain,** which rises to 2,006 ft (610 m), is the second-highest mountain on Catalina Island and was mined in the 1920s for lead, zinc, and silver.

## CATALINA WILDLIFE

Over the centuries, Catalina has become a sanctuary for plants and animals that have died out on the mainland. Rare ironwood and mahogany trees and the highly poisonous wild tomato are among eight endemic plants surviving on the island. Distinctive animal subspecies have also evolved, such as the small gray Catalina fox and the beechey ground squirrel. Some animals brought to the island by early settlers have now turned wild, including goats, pigs, and deer. Catalina even has a population of bison, ferried over in 1924 for a film shoot and never rounded up.

**One of the island's wild bison**

*For hotels and restaurants in this region see pp534–5 and pp579–81*

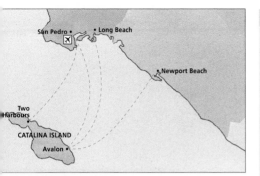

## VISITORS' CHECKLIST

**Road map** C6. 🏘 *3,500.*
🛩 **Island Express Helicopter Service** *(310) 510-2525 from San Pedro & Long Beach to Avalon.* 🚢 **Catalina Express** *(310) 519-1212,; (800) 618-5533 from San Pedro to Avalon or Two Harbors year-round.* **Catalina Passenger Service** *(800) 830-7744 from Newport Beach to Avalon.* **www**.catalinainfo.com
🛈 *Foot of Green Pleasure Pier, Avalon (310 510-1520).*
🎭 *Catalina Arts Festival (mid-Sep).* **www**.visitcatalina.org

**★ Avalon Casino**
*Guided tours can be taken of this 1929 Art Deco jewel, which was never a gambling venue but was once a famous spot for big bands and is now lovingly restored.*

**Avalon Museum** is on the casino's lower floor. This historical museum shows how the island has been variously used for ranching, mining, tourism, and as a film location.

### KEY

| | |
|---|---|
| ═══ | Minor road |
| ═══ | Road in poor condition |
| ▪ ▪ ▪ | Trail |
| ▪ ▪ ▪ | Trans Catalina Trail (TCT) |
| 〜 | River |
| 🛪 | Airport |
| ⛴ | Ferry service |
| 🛈 | Tourist information |
| ✲ | Viewpoint |

0 kilometers 5
0 miles 2

**Lovers Cove Marine Reserve** is visited by glass-bottomed boats that reveal the colorful marine life existing around Catalina.

**Seal Rocks** tours can be booked through four fishing charter companies, from which colonies of migratory sea lions can be seen.

**★ Avalon Bay**
*About 3,000 people live in Avalon, which has a pier, restaurants, and hotels. Locals travel around in golf carts, which visitors can rent.*

**★ Wrigley Memorial & Botanical Gardens**
*This 38-acre (15-ha) park honoring William Wrigley, Jr. has an imposing memorial and a collection of plants endemic to Catalina.*

### STAR SIGHTS

★ Avalon Bay

★ Avalon Casino

★ Wrigley Memorial & Botanical Gardens

# SAN DIEGO COUNTY

I n San Diego in 1769, the Spanish friar Junípero Serra laid down the first link in the chain of 21 missions that underpins the modern state of California (see pp46–7). Blessed with a near-perfect climate and a magnificent natural harbor, his settlement has now become the eighth largest city in America. San Diego County has much to offer visitors, with its Pacific coastline, inland forests, and extensive state parks.

San Diego's character has always been determined by the sea. In the 19th century, gold prospectors, hide dealers, and whalers sailed into San Diego Bay. The United States Navy arrived in 1904, starting an enthusiastic courtship that has made San Diego the largest military establishment in the world. Aircraft carriers are a common sight in the bay, but so are cruise ships, fishing boats, yachts, and pleasure craft. San Diego is a city of sports and leisure – three times host to the Americas Cup, home of the Padres baseball team and the Chargers football team. There are plenty of opportunities for surfing, sailing, golf, and water sports.

First-time visitors are always surprised by the sense of space and how much there is to enjoy. Most have heard of San Diego Zoo and the SeaWorld marine park, but few realize that San Diego is a fast-growing city, with shimmering new skyscrapers soaring beside the waterfront. Culturally, San Diego is rapidly gaining prestige, as the many museums and arts venues of Balboa Park flourish.

North of the city the rugged Pacific Coast is lined with affluent beachside communities and wildlife preserves. Inland lie small towns, surrounded by peaceful countryside and fertile farmland. Deep forests and several state parks make the interior of San Diego County a paradise for hikers and campers escaping the frantic pace of city life. To the east, the region becomes increasingly mountainous, giving way to desert landscapes. And to the south, just a short train ride away from San Diego, is the Mexican border town of Tijuana.

Bazaar del Mundo in San Diego Old Town

◁ Marina in San Diego Bay, with the skyscrapers of Downtown in the background

# Exploring San Diego County

Covering more than 4,000 sq miles (10,350 sq km), San Diego County has a coastline of rocky cliffs, sandy beaches and wetlands, and a spacious, mountainous hinterland. The Anza-Borrego Desert *(see pp276–7)* forms a natural boundary to the east. San Diego city lies close to the border with Mexico, exploiting a large bay protected by two peninsulas. Stunning beaches and plentiful opportunities for leisure activities are the main attractions along the Pacific shoreline. A drive inland takes the visitor to the tranquillity of the Cleveland National Forest and the wilderness of state parks, such as Palomar Mountain and Cuyamaca Rancho.

Cuyamaca Rancho State Park landscape

## SEE ALSO

- *Where to Stay* pp536–8

- *Where to Eat* pp581–4

Shelter Island yacht harbor in San Diego Bay

△ *Margarita Peak*
972m

*Los Angeles*

Riverside

Rain

Fallbrook

15

Camp Pendleton

Bonsal

MISSION SAN
LUIS REY
🛈 ⑧ 76

Oceanside

Vista

LEGOLAND ⑦

Carlsbad

San
Marcos

78

5

Leucadia

Escc

Encinitas

Cardiff-by-the-Sea

Rancho
Santa Fe

Solana Beach

Del Mar

*Torrey Pines State Beach*

805

LA JOLLA ⑤

52

*Pacific Beach*

SA
DE

MISSION BAY ④

SEAWORLD ③

*Ocean Beach*

Old To

SAN DIEGO ①

Coronado

Natior
C

*Point Loma*

*Silver Strand
- Beach* 75

CHULA VIST
NATUR
CENTE

**KEY**

| | |
|---|---|
| ▬▬ | Freeway |
| ▬▬ | Major road |
| ▬ | Secondary road |
| ═ | Minor road |
| ▬ | Scenic route |
| ▬ | Main railway |
| ─ | Minor railway |
| ▬▬ | International border |
| △ | Summit |

## SIGHTS AT A GLANCE

**Cabrillo National Monument
in San Diego**

**Surfers at Swami's Beach near Encinitas**

## GETTING AROUND

The main transportation routes run from north to south – the coastal I-5 and Amtrak railway line both provide a fast connection with Los Angeles via the Orange County coast *(see p230)*. The scenic Coaster train route serves stations between San Diego and Oceanside. A car is essential for exploring the county's inland areas. Within San Diego itself, public transportation is a viable option for the visitor *(see p266)*. The city has a comprehensive bus network, and the two lines of the efficient San Diego Trolley system extend east to El Cajon and south to the Mexican border.

# San Diego County Coastline

Stretching from Orange County to the Mexican border, the coastline of San Diego County has 70 miles (112 km) of lovely sandy beaches, cliffs, coves, and seaside resorts. The beach culture is sophisticated, and the sports activity is frenzied. Peace can be found at Batiquitos Lagoon, Torrey Pines State Preserve, and the Chula Vista Nature Center

**Sign at entrance to Swami's Beach**

*(see p264),* which are all sanctuaries for coastal wildlife. At Carlsbad, Legoland® California is a 128-acre family theme park for youngsters aged 2–12, with a castle, miniature lego cities, and an amusement park.

**Batiquitos Lagoon** *lies between South Carlsbad and Leucadia State Beaches. Habitats include upland, intertidal, and open water, with abundant varieties of fish, saltwater plants, and birds such as the protected least tern and the snowy plover.*

**The Del Mar Racetrack** *was made famous in the 1930s by the singer Bing Crosby and other Hollywood stars. Its annual meetings remain a high point of the social calendar. San Diego's County Fair takes place at the adjacent fairground every June, and the racing season runs from late July to mid-September.*

**Torrey Pines State Reserve** *and Santa Rosa Island (see p224) are the only two places in the world where the Torrey Pine, or Pinus torreyana, survives. A remnant of pre-Ice Age forests, this tree is well adapted to this area's dry, sandy environment.*

## KEY

| | |
|---|---|
| ▰▰ | Freeway |
| ▬ | Major road |
| ▭ | Minor road |
| ≈ | River |
| ❋ | Viewpoint |

0 kilometers 5

0 miles       5

★ **San Onofre State Beach** ①

🚶 🏖 🏊 ⛵ 🚻 🏕 ♨

Although close to the coastal San Onofre nuclear power plant and the vast Camp Pendleton military base, this popular beach is worth visiting to see serious California surfers in action.

**Swami's Beach** ③

🚶 🏖 🚻

This surfing beach is named after the founder of the Self-Realization Fellowship Temple, which overlooks the shore.

**Cardiff State Beach** ④

🚶 🏖 🏊 ♿ 🚻 🏕 ♨

On the south side of Encinitas, Cardiff offers swimming, surfing, and fine popular camp sites, as well as ocean-front dining on Restaurant Row at its north end.

**Torrey Pines State Beach** ⑥

🚶 🏖 🏊 ⛵ 🚻 ♨

This beach is popular for picnics and swimming. Just to the south is the Torrey Pines State Preserve, where several cliff-top hiking trails among the pine trees offer views over the ocean.

**Mission Beach** ⑨

🚶 🏖 🏊 ⛵ 🚻

This is the liveliest beach in San Diego with plenty of opportunity for people-watching, plus the fairground attractions of Belmont Park *(see p261).*

**Ocean Beach** ⑩

🚶 🏖 🏊 ⛵ ♿ 🚻

Ocean Beach's T-shaped pier, popular with pelicans, has good views of the coastline.

**Silver Strand Beach** ⑫

🚶 🏖 🏊 ⛵ ♿ 🚻 🏕 ♨

This long, thin beach is sandwiched between areas of land reserved for naval training. It takes its name from the silvery shells in its sand.

### ★ Oceanside ②
🎿 ⛱ ⚓ 🏄 ♿ 🚻
Dating from 1988, the 1,954-ft (596-m) long pier on this sandy beach is the longest wooden pier on the United States west coast. The beach is ideal for surfing, and the town has an interesting surfing museum.

### ★ Del Mar ⑤
🎿 ⛱ ⚓ 🏄 ♿ 🚻
This resort supplements beach activities with horseracing, ballooning, and fairs, along with shopping and dining at Del Mar Plaza.

**LOCATOR MAP**

### ★ La Jolla ⑦
🎿 ⛱ ⚓ ♿ 🚻
La Jolla Shores is a 1.6-km-(1-mile-) long beach with excellent sand and activities but can be crowded in the summer. La Jolla Cove lies within an underwater ecological preserve, open for snorkeling and scuba-diving. The town of La Jolla (see p261) has many upscale shops and restaurants.

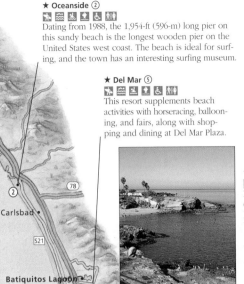

Carlsbad •

S21

**Batiquitos Lagoon** •

Encinitas •

**Del Mar Racetrack**

S21

**Torrey Pines State Reserve** •

### ★ Pacific Beach ⑧
🎿 ⛱ ⚓ 🏄 ♿ 🚻
This busy beach is graced by the bustling wooden Crystal Pier. It is a good place from which to fish or watch surfers in action.

**Mission Bay**

**SAN DIEGO**

Point Loma •

### ★ Coronado Beach ⑪
🎿 ⛱ ⚓ 🏄 ♿ 🚻
Crowned by the Hotel del Coronado (see p255) and offering wide sands and views across the bay, this is one of San Diego's most romantic beaches.

San Diego Bay

Chula Vista •

TIJUANA

# San Diego

Shaped like a hook and protected by the peninsula of Coronado (see p255), the 22 sq miles (57 sq km) of San Diego Bay form a natural deep-water harbor around which the second largest city in California has grown. Discovered in 1542 by the explorer Juan Rodríguez Cabrillo (João Rodrigues Cabrilho), colonization did not follow until 1769.

**Tiles in Santa Fe Depot**

In that year, the founding father of the mission chain, Junípero Serra, arrived in the region as part of a military expedition to secure Alta California (the part of California north of the Baja Peninsula) for Spain. Its commanders built a presidio and mission near the San Diego River, an area now known as Old Town (see pp254–5).

**Shops in Seaport Village**

## Exploring Downtown San Diego

The growth of modern San Diego began in the 1870s, when Alonzo Horton, a San Francisco businessman, began to develop the town's waterfront areas. He laid down the grid of streets of the Gaslamp Quarter (see pp252–3), which, along with the Westfield Horton Plaza shopping center, has become the centerpiece of San Diego's rejuvenated Downtown district.

The city's main street is Broadway, punctuated at its western end by the **Santa Fe Depot**. The towers and brightly tiled interior of this Spanish Colonial-style railroad station date from 1915. It was built to impress visitors to the Panama-Pacific Exposition in Balboa Park (see pp256–7).

Since the 1980s, Downtown San Diego has become the site of an ongoing architectural competition. The tallest building in San Diego, the 34-story **America Plaza**, near the Santa Fe Depot, was built in 1991. On the waterfront, the galleon-like **San Diego Convention Center** overlooks San Diego Bay.

The promenades and piers of the **Embarcadero** waterfront pathway provide an introduction to San Diego's role as a major commercial and military port. At the northern end are the Maritime Museum's historic ships. A short stroll south is **Broadway Pier**, where visitors can join a harbor excursion. **Seaport Village**, a shopping and dining complex, has views across to the aircraft carriers of the **North Island United States Naval Air Station**.

**🚇 Westfield Horton Plaza**
Broadway, G St, 1st & 4th Aves.
**Tel** (619) 239-8180. ◯ daily.
⬤ Easter, Thanksgiving, Dec 25.
**www**.westfield.com
This innovatively designed shopping center has been a catalyst in the regeneration of Downtown San Diego. The plaza is painted in festive pastel shades and built on interlocking levels lined with 120 shops, department stores, and cafés. Visitors can enjoy some evening shopping close to the Gaslamp Quarter restaurants.

**Three of the levels in the Westfield Horton Plaza shopping center**

## 🏛 Maritime Museum

1492 North Harbor Drive. **Tel** (619) 234-9153. ⏲ 9am–8pm daily, 9pm in summer. 📷 **www**.sdmaritime.com
The *Star of India*, an 1863 merchantman, and the San Francisco Bay passenger ferry, the *Berkeley* (1898), are moored here. Alongside them are the steam yacht *Medea* (1904) and the *HMS Surprise*, a replica of an 18th-century frigate from the film *Master and Commander*.

## 🏛 Museum of Contemporary Art

1001 & 1100 Kettner Blvd. **Tel** (858) 454-3541. ⏲ 11am–5pm Thu–Tue. ⏲ Jan 1, Dec 25. **www**.mcasd.org
This two-story museum is the Downtown counterpart of the museum of the same name in La Jolla *(see p261)*. The museum comprises two buildings, directly across from each other. The four galleries display changing exhibitions of new work by living artists, and selections from the museum's large permanent collection.

### VISITORS' CHECKLIST

**Road map** D6. 🏚 1,300,000.
✈ Lindbergh Field Airport, 3707 N Harbor Drive.
🚃 1050 Kettner Blvd.
🚌 120 West Broadway.
ℹ 1040 1/3 West Broadway.
🎭 Street Scene Festival (Aug).
**www**.sandiego.org

## 🚲 Little Italy

Between W Laurel St and W A St, Pacific Hwy and Front St. ℹ (619) 233-3898. **www**.littleitalysd.com
Little Italy, sometimes known as Middletown, was originally a fishing neighborhood but has now become gentrified, although it retains its bohemian character. Italian restaurants, hip cafés, family-owned boutiques, and art galleries line the streets, and festivals related to Italian culture are held throughout the year.

The hip Little Italy area

## 🏛 The New Children's Museum

200 W Island Ave. **Tel** (619) 233-8792. ⏲ 10am–4pm Mon, Tue, Fri & Sat, 10am–6pm Thu, noon–4pm Sun. 📷 **www**.thinkplaycreate.org
This state-of-the-art museum was designed by Rob Wellington Quigley and is a premier family attraction. Children of all ages explore their creativity with hands-on projects.

Taking part in one of the many activities at The New Children's Museum

0 kilometers 1
0 miles 1

**Key to Symbols** *see back flap*

# A Walk through the Gaslamp Quarter

During the boom years of the 1880s, the 16 blocks of San Diego's Gaslamp Quarter became known as the "Stingaree." It was an area notorious for prostitution, gambling, and drinking, where naïve customers could easily be "stung" by confidence tricksters. In spite of police clampdowns in the following decades and the growth of a close-knit Asian community, its streets remained in decline until the 1970s, when moves were made to revive its fortunes and protect its wealth of historic buildings. In 1980, the area was designated a National Historic District. As a result, the Gaslamp Quarter has emerged as the new heart of San Diego. It is now renowned as a place to shop, dine, and dance. Visitors can also admire the period buildings, ranging from a pie bakery and a hardware store to ornate office blocks and a Victorian hotel. The district is particularly attractive at night, when it is illuminated by graceful gaslamps that line its pavements.

One of the quarter's street lamps

**VISITORS' CHECKLIST**

Broadway & 4th–6th Aves. **Road map** D6. 🚌 1. 🚢 Bayside. ℹ 410 Island Ave (619) 233-4692. **www**.gaslampquarter.org

**Old City Hall**
*This 1874 Italianate office building once housed the entire city government.*

**The Lincoln Hotel** at No. 536 was built in 1913. Its architecture is influenced by Chinese style.

**The Backesto Building** office block at No. 614 dates from 1873.

**FIFTH AVENUE WEST SIDE** ▸▸▸▸▸▸▸▸▸▸▸▸▸▸▸▸▸▸▸▸▸▸▸▸▸▸▸▸▸▸▸▸▸▸▸▸▸▸▸

**★ Louis Bank of Commerce**
*Constructed in 1888, this was the first granite building in the city and housed the Bank of Commerce for just 5 years. It also housed an oyster bar and a brothel.*

**The Marston Building**
*This retail outlet on the corner of 5th Avenue and F Street dates from 1881. It was built by civic leader George Marston as a department store. The structure was remodeled in 1903 following fire damage.*

**FIFTH AVENUE EAST SIDE** ▸▸▸▸▸▸▸▸▸▸▸▸▸▸▸▸▸▸▸▸▸▸▸▸▸▸▸▸▸▸▸▸▸▸▸▸▸▸▸

**KEY**

▸▸▸▸▸▸ West side walking north

◂◂◂◂◂◂ East side walking south

**Llewelyn Building**
*Dating from 1877, this structure housed a shoe store until 1906 and then a succession of hotels.*

**The Gaslamp Quarter at night**
*In the evening the streets of the Gaslamp Quarter bustle with people eating and drinking in its many restaurants and bars, or simply strolling around.*

0 meters 10

0 yards 10

★ **Yuma Building**
*Built in 1886, this commercial property was one of the first brick buildings in Downtown. In 1915, the Yuma Building housed the first brothel to be closed down during a police raid of the red-light district.*

**STAR SIGHTS**

★ Louis Bank

★ Yuma Building

**Wyatt Earp**
*Lawman Wyatt Earp ran the Oyster Bar on Fifth Avenue in the late 1800s. In order to distance themselves from the "Stingaree," the area's more respectable businesses moved north of Market Street.*

# Beyond Downtown

Four miles (6.5 km) north of the present Downtown lies the area now known as Old Town. Here, visitors can see San Diego's earliest buildings, many of which have been restored to their original state, and explore the fascinating Junípero Serra Museum. To the west of Old Town, the coast runs south to the end of the Point Loma Peninsula. From here, visitors have magnificent views of the Pacific Ocean and the city's waterfront across the bay. South of Point Loma, Coronado, with its numerous luxury hotels and popular sandy beaches, enjoys a privileged location at the end of a low-lying peninsula thrusting into San Diego Bay.

Victorian house in Heritage Park

Interior of Mason Street School in Old Town

## Exploring Old Town

Until the 1870s the city of San Diego was centered around the presidio, the site of the original Spanish military outpost, in an area now known as Old Town. Today more than 20 historic buildings from this period have been restored or re-created to form the **Old Town San Diego State Historic Park**. At its center lies the grassy Plaza where parades and fiestas still take place. The **Robinson-Rose Building** at the western end of the Plaza now serves as the park's headquarters and visitors' center.

Other buildings of historical interest include the **Colorado House** and **Mason Street School**, which dates from 1865. Mexican themes are evoked in the vibrant **Fiesta de Reyes** shopping center *(see p266)* in the north corner of the Plaza.

Old Town San Diego spreads far beyond the official limits of the park. Constructed in 1856, **Whaley House** at No. 2482 San Diego Avenue was the first two-story brick building in California and once functioned as a courthouse.

## 🏛 Junípero Serra Museum

2727 Presidio Drive. **Tel** *(619) 297-3258.* ⬜ *10am–5pm Sat & Sun.* 🎟

Crowning Presidio Park, the whitewashed Junípero Serra Museum was built in 1929 in the Spanish Revival style *(see p31)* and is named after the founder of California's mission chain. Overlooking the San Diego River, the park occupies the site of the presidio fort and mission, which were built by the Spanish in 1769. The ruins of the presidio are still being explored by a team of archaeologists, and some of their finds, from fine china to cannonballs, can be seen in the museum. Its displays cover San Diego's early days and the city's successive Native American, Spanish, Mexican, and American residents. Of particular interest is a didactic painting *La Madre Santísima de la Luz*, painted in Mexico by Luis Mena (c.1760), depicting Native Americans kneeling before the Virgin Mary. The painting is a rare surviving artifact from the time of the first mission, which moved to San Diego de Alcalá in 1774 *(see p260)*. Exhibits upstairs describe the first Spanish expedition to California, daily life in the presidio, and the changing face of San Diego.

## 🏚 Heritage Park

2450 Heritage Park Row. **Tel** *(858) 565-3600.* ⬜ *daily.* ⬤ *Thanksgiving, Dec 25.* **www**.sdparks.org

On the east side of Old Town Heritage Park is a collection of immaculately restored Victorian buildings from all over the city

Junípero Serra Museum in Old Town San Diego

## Casa de Estudillo

Old Town State Historic Park.
*Tel* (619) 220-5422. 10am–5pm
daily. Jan 1, Thanksgiving, Dec 25.
**Donation.**
Of the original adobe and
wooden buildings in Old
Town San Diego State
Historic Park, this is one of
the most impressive. It was
constructed by the commander
of the presidio, José María de
Estudillo, in 1829. The house
has 13 rooms built around an
internal courtyard and has
been refurnished in the
Mexican-California style.

## Seeley Stables

Old Town State Historic Park.
*Tel* (619) 220-5422. daily. Jan
1, Thanksgiving, Dec 25. **Donation**.
The museum housed in this
reconstructed stable displays
a collection of horse-drawn
carriages and stagecoaches,
as well as some interesting
Wild West memorabilia.

### Exploring Point Loma

The 156-acre (63-ha) **Cabrillo
National Monument** park
straddles the southern part of
the Point Loma Peninsula. The
monument was named after
the Portuguese explorer Juan
Rodríguez Cabrillo (also
known as João Rodrigues
Cabrilho) *(see p46)*, the first
European to step ashore in
California in 1542. His statue
appropriately overlooks the
ships passing in and out of
San Diego Bay.

Between late December and
the end of February the nearby
Whale Overlook is a popular
place from which to watch
enormous gray whales under-
taking their annual southward
migration. Visitors can also follow the 2-mile (3-km) Bayside
Trail around the Point, with the
aid of a highly informative
leaflet, and visit rock pools
on its western shore.

## Cabrillo National Monument Visitor Center

Tip of Point Loma Peninsula. *Tel* (619)
557-5450. 9am–5pm daily.
www.nps.gov/cabr
This excellent visitors' center
near the park entrance has a
small museum. A film recounts
Juan Rodríguez Cabrillo's
800-mile (1,300-km) voyage
along the California coast.

**Old Point Loma Lighthouse**

## Old Point Loma Lighthouse

Cabrillo National Monument
Park. *Tel* (619) 557-5450.
9am–5pm daily.
The lighthouse, a short walk
south from the Cabrillo statue,
sent its first beams into the
night in 1855 and operated for
36 years. Although its tower
is usually closed to the public,
lower rooms recreate the lighthouse keepers' living quarters
as they were in the 1880s.

### Exploring Coronado

The city of Coronado, at the
head of a 4,100-acre (1,650-ha)
peninsula in the middle of
San Diego Bay, is moneyed
and self-confident. Businessman Elisha Babcock, Jr. bought
the land in 1885 and set out
to develop a world-class
resort. Coronado now boasts
San Diego's most exclusive
homes, boutiques, hotels, and
restaurants. Its Pacific shore is
lined by a stunning beach *(see
p249)*, which is dominated at
its southern end by the landmark Hotel del Coronado.

## Coronado Ferry

1050 N Harbor Drive. *Tel* (619) 234-
4111. daily. www.sdhe.com
Until the opening of the San
Diego–Coronado Bay Bridge
in 1969, the ferry provided
the area's principal link with
the mainland, a service that
has been revived for the benefit of both tourists and locals.

The 15-minute trip between
the Broadway Pier on the
Embarcadero, or the San Diego
Convention Center, and the
Ferry Landing Marketplace is
breathtaking at dusk when the
sun illuminates the skyscrapers
of Downtown. From the Ferry
Landing, visitors can take a
bus or walk along Orange
Avenue to the Pacific shore.

## Hotel del Coronado

1500 Orange Ave, Coronado.
*Tel* (619) 435-6611, (800) 468-
3533. daily.
www.hoteldel.com
Opened in 1888 and given
National Historic Landmark
status in 1977, the "Del" *(see
p536)* is a lovingly preserved
grand Victorian seaside hotel.
It was built using both
architects and labor from the
railroads – a heritage that is
most obvious in the domed
ceiling of the Crown Room,
which is built from sugar pine
without a single nail. The list
of illustrious guests who have
stayed here is impressive –
presidents from Franklin D
Roosevelt to Bill Clinton, film
stars from Marilyn Monroe to
the *Baywatch* belles. The
hotel has been the setting for
several films, including *Some
Like It Hot*, the 1959 classic
starring Marilyn Monroe, Jack
Lemmon, and Tony Curtis.

**Impressive turrets and gables of the exclusive Hotel del Coronado**

# Balboa Park and San Diego Zoo

**Statue of El Cid in Balboa Park**

Named after the Spanish explorer who first set eyes on the Pacific Ocean in 1513, Balboa Park was founded in 1868. Its beauty owes much to the dedicated horticulturalist Kate Sessions who, in 1892, promised to plant trees throughout its 1,200 acres (485 ha) in exchange for renting space for a nursery. In 1915 the park was the site of the city's Panama-California Exposition (see p349), a world's fair celebrating the opening of the Panama Canal. Several of the Spanish Colonial-style pavilions built in that year survive along El Prado (the park's main street), and the animals gathered for the exhibition formed the nucleus from which San Diego Zoo has grown (see p259). Twenty years later the organizers of the California-Pacific International Exposition added more exhibition spaces around Pan-American Plaza. All these buildings now form a rich concentration of museums and performance venues.

**Plaza de Panama**
*This plaza in the center of the El Prado thoroughfare was at the heart of the Panama-California Exposition.*

Skyfari

**★ San Diego Museum of Man**
*This historical museum is housed in the 1915 California Building. Designed in Spanish Renaissance style, its façade is decorated with statues representing famous Californians.*

Old Globe Theater

El Prado

San Diego Automotive Museum

**Air and Space Museum**
*A child looks at the Apollo 9 exhibit in this museum devoted to the history of flight.*

## STAR SIGHTS

- ★ California Building/San Diego Museum of Man

- ★ San Diego Museum of Art

- ★ San Diego Zoo

Pan-American Plaza

Spreckels Organ Pavilion

Park Tram

0 meters          100

0 yards          100

## VISITORS' CHECKLIST

Park Blvd, Laurel & 6th Sts. **Road map** D6. 🚌 7. **Visitors' Center**, 1549 El Prado, **Tel** (619) 239-0512. 🕐 9:30am–4:30pm daily. 🚫 Jan 1, Thanksgiving, Dec 25. www.balboapark.org **Spreckels Organ Pavilion** (free concerts 2–3pm Sun; Jun–Sep: 7:30pm Mon). **San Diego Zoo Tel** (619) 231-1515. 🕐 early Sep–Jun: 9am–4pm daily; Jul–Aug: 9am–6pm daily. 🚫 📷 🏪 🚻 ♿ 🖥 www.sandiegozoo.org

Tour bus

San Diego Zoo entrance

Timken Museum

**★ San Diego Zoo**
*Orangutans are among the 4,000 animals that live in the well-kept enclosures of this world-famous zoo.*

Casa del Prado

San Diego Natural History Museum

**Botanical Building**
*Constructed from thin strips of redwood, this shaded sanctuary is full of tropical and subtropical plants.*

**★ San Diego Museum of Art**
*A café and sculpture garden stand next to the principal art museum in the park. Both North American and European works are exhibited.*

Reuben H Fleet Science Center

Casa de Balboa

de na

# Exploring Balboa Park and San Diego Zoo

Topiary elephant at zoo entrance

Balboa Park, located at the heart of San Diego, is one of the city's most popular attractions. On the weekend, its pleasant, lush grounds and traffic-free promenades are crowded with strollers, joggers, cyclists, and street artists. In between museum tours, visitors can picnic in one of the shady picnic groves or play ball games on the grassy lawns. Just to the north of the museums and recreation grounds of Balboa Park lies San Diego Zoo, where 800 species from all over the world are housed in enclosures designed to resemble as closely as possible their natural habitat.

Sunday afternoon street entertainers in Balboa Park

## 🏛 San Diego Museum of Man

1350 El Prado. **Tel** (619) 239-2001.
⬜ 10am–4:30pm daily. 🌑 Jan 1, Thanksgiving, Dec 25. 🖼
www.museumofman.org

The landmark pavilion of the Panama-California Exposition of 1915 (see p256), also known as the California Building, houses an anthropological museum on the early history of mankind. Exhibits cover topics such as the cultures of ancient Egypt and the Mayans, and Native American crafts.

## 🏛 San Diego Museum of Art

1450 El Prado. **Tel** (619) 232-7931.
⬜ 10am–5pm Tue–Sat (to 9pm Thu in summer), noon–5pm Sun.
🌑 Jan 1, Thanksgiving, Dec 25.
🖼 www.sdmart.org

This museum's large, varied art collection is boosted by a pro-gram of special exhibitions. European and American art from 1850 to the 20th century is shown in the first-floor galleries, along with exhibits

Ornate Colonial-style façade of the San Diego Museum of Art

from southern Asia, Japan, and China. The displays on the second floor feature work from 1300 to 1850, including *Coronation of the Virgin* (1508), by Luca Signorelli.

*Portrait of a Gentleman* (1634) by Frans Hals in the Timken Museum

## 🏛 Timken Museum of Art

1500 El Prado. **Tel** (619) 239-5548. ⬜ 10am–4:30pm Tue–Sat, 1:30–4:30pm Sun. www.timkenmuseum.org

Opened in 1965, the Timken exhibits a few exquisite works in an inviting space. On display are works by European mas-ters such as Frans Hals (1581/5–1666), François Boucher (1703–70), and Paul Cézanne (1839–1906). The Timken also has works by 19th-century American artists, including *The Yosemite Fall* (1864) by Albert Bierstadt, and a collection of Russian icons.

## 🏛 Museum of Photographic Arts

1649 El Prado. **Tel** (619) 238-7559.
⬜ 10am–5pm Tue–Sun (to 9pm Thu). 🌑 Dec 25. 🖼 www.mopa.org

This museum is located on the main floor of the ornate Casa de Balboa. It specializes in high-quality traveling exhibitions that demonstrate the art and power of photography. There is also a good bookstore.

## 🏛 San Diego History Center

1649 El Prado. **Tel** (619) 232- 6203.
⬜ 10am–5pm Tue–Sun. 🌑 Jan 1, Thanksgiving, Dec 24 & 25. 🖼
www.sandiegohistory.org

The museum showcases the region's unique and colorful history, exhibiting artifacts, costumes, textiles, art, furni-ture, and photographs. The Research Library has extensive archives of maps, architectural drawings, and one of the largest collections of photo-graphs in the western US.

## 🏛 Reuben H Fleet Science Center

1875 El Prado. **Tel** (619) 238-1233.
⬜ 10am; closing times vary.
🖼 call ahead for IMAX® show times.
www.rhfleet.org

The big attraction here is the vast dome of the IMAX® cinema in the Space Theater, where films about the world around us are projected onto an enormous tilting screen. Planetarium shows are also staged.

The complex is open some evenings and has a Science Center with over 100 hands-on exhibits that demonstrate the laws of science. There is also a café, and a shop selling books, games, and puzzles.

## 🏛 San Diego Natural History Museum

1788 El Prado, Balboa Park.
**Tel** (619) 232-3821. ⬜ 10am–5pm
daily. ⬤ Jan 1, Thanksgiving, Dec 25.
🖥 www.sdnhm.org

The museum was founded in 1874 and is an active research institution, dedicated to understanding the evolution and diversity of the Southern California-Baja California region. It features giant-screen films and a variety of programs for visitors of all ages. It is the oldest scientific institution in Southern California.

## 🏛 San Diego Air and Space Museum

2001 Pan American Plaza. **Tel** (619) 234-8291. ⬜ 10:30am–4:30pm daily (to 5:30pm in summer).
⬤ Jan 1, Thanksgiving, Dec 25. 🖥 www.aerospacemuseum.org

The Air and Space Museum covers five centuries of aviation history, demonstrating the remarkable progress of flight. It has more than 60 aircraft and space vehicles on display (including both original and full-scale reconstructions of the aircraft). The "Apollo 9 Has Landed" exhibit features the only Apollo Command Module flown in space on display west of the Rockies.

**A 1948 Tucker Torpedo from the Automotive Museum's collection**

## 🏛 San Diego Automotive Museum

2080 Pan American Plaza. **Tel** (619) 231-2886. ⬜ 10am–5pm daily.
⬤ Jan 1, Thanksgiving, Dec 25. 🖥 www.sdautomuseum.org

Dream cars and motorcycles from both the United States and Europe shine on in this unashamedly nostalgic museum. Because most of the cars are privately owned, the collection is constantly changing, but gleaming paintwork and whitewall tires are guaranteed.

## SAN DIEGO ZOO

San Diego Zoo is one of the best-known zoos in the world, famous both for its conservation programs and as a highly educational source of family entertainment. With some 4,000 animals dispersed over 100 acres (40 ha), the best introduction is to take the 35-minute narrated bus tour that covers most of the zoo. The aerial Skyfari ride, which offers a trip across the south of the park in gondola cars 180 ft (55 m) up, is also rewarding. After these, visitors can track down their favorites in the animal world by following the paths and moving walkways. There is also a Children's Zoo, and in summer the zoo is open for nocturnal exploration.

### FINDING THE ATTRACTIONS

① Flamingo Lagoon
② Reptile House
③ Children's Zoo
④ Petting Paddock
⑤ Insect House
⑥ Wegeforth Bowl
⑦ Tiger Trail
⑧ Scripps Aviary
⑨ Monkey Trail
⑩ Absolutely Apes
⑪ Owen's Rain Forest Aviary
⑫ Sun Bear Forest
⑬ Panda Canyon
⑭ Wings of Australasia
⑮ Gorilla Trophies
⑯ Hippo Trail
⑰ Lost Forest
⑱ Ituri Forest
⑲ Eagle Trail
⑳ Elephant Odyssey
㉑ Hunte Amphitheatre
㉒ African Rock Kopje Exhibit
㉓ Urban Jungle
㉔ Outback

**Sichuan takin calf resting in San Diego Zoo**

Interior of the church at the Mission San Diego de Alcalá

## Mission San Diego de Alcalá ❷

10818 San Diego Mission Rd, San Diego. **Road map** D6. *Tel* (619) 281-8449. 🚌 13, 20. ⭕ 9am–4:45pm daily. 🏛 Jan 1, Thanksgiving, Dec 25. **Donation**. ✝ daily. ♿ www.missionsandiego.com

Originally located at what is now the Junípero Serra Museum in Presidio Park *(see p254)*, San Diego's mission was moved to Mission Valley in 1774. The land surrounding the new site was more fertile and had a larger population of potential Native American converts. The name Diego refers to St. Didacus, born in Alcalá, Spain, in 1400.

The first mission in the California chain *(see pp46–7)* is today engulfed by freeways and urban development, but its harmonious buildings and gardens retain an atmosphere of peace. Early this century, the complex was restored to its appearance of 1813. The church retains some original materials, such as the timbers over its doorways, the floor tiles, and the adobe bricks in the baptistry. In the garden stands the Campanario (bell tower), and a statue of St. Francis. A small museum honors the state's first Christian martyr, Padre Luis Jayme, who was murdered

when a gang of 600 Native Americans attacked the newly established mission in 1775.

## SeaWorld ❸

500 SeaWorld Drive. **Road map** D6. *Tel* (800) 257-4268. 🚌 9. ⭕ daily. 🏞 ♿ 📷 www.seaworld.com

In this state famous for its theme parks, the great lure of San Diego's SeaWorld is the chance to get close to many ocean creatures. Opened in 1964, the marine park now covers 150 acres (60 ha) of Mission Bay and provides its visitors with entertainment for a full day. A good starting point is the five-minute ride up the Skytower, a 320-ft (98-m) column with panoramic views.

**Statuette at San Diego de Alcalá**

Another view is offered by the 100-ft- (30-m-) high Bayside Skyride in the park's northwest corner, where gondola cars take you in a 0.5-mile (1-km) loop over the waters of Mission Bay.

The stars of SeaWorld are its performing whales and dolphins. One show reveals the intelligence of dolphins and pilot whales, while another demonstrates the virtuosity of killer whales. Among the other attractions in the park are pools with sharks, otters, and turtles, freshwater aquariums, and opportunities to feed killer whales and seals and to touch rays and starfish. Kids will particularly enjoy cavorting with Sesame Street characters, an aquatic adventure park, and its largest attraction, Journey to Atlantis. It includes a wet and wild thrill ride that ends with a 60-ft (18-m) plunge and a negative G-force drop.

There is also a more serious side to SeaWorld – its staff are devoted to animal rescue and rehabilitation and take in an average of one sick or abandoned animal per day. The park also runs education and conservation programs.

## Mission Bay ❹

**Road map** D6. 🚌 *from Downtown Mission Bay.* **Visitors' Center** *Tel* (619) 276-8200. ⭕ 9am–5pm Mon–Sat, 9:30am–4:30pm Sun. www.sandiego.gov

Mission Bay park is an area of 4,200 acres (1,700 ha) entirely given over to public recreational use. San Diegans come

Killer whales performing acrobatic feats for the crowds at SeaWorld

Sailing on the peaceful waters of Mission Bay

here to keep fit and relax in the well-tended parkland. The area was once a marsh, but systematic dredging and landscaping, begun in the 1930s, transformed it. The San Diego River has been corralled into a channel to the south, creating beaches, water-sports centers, and islands. Although the main attraction in Mission Bay is SeaWorld, visitors can also enjoy kite-flying, volleyball, golf, and cycling. Along the shoreline, swimming, fishing, and sailing take place.

In the southwest corner of the bay is Mission Beach (see p248), one of the most lively beaches in San Diego County. Lovers of traditional seaside amusements will enjoy the beachfront **Belmont Park**. Its Giant Dipper dates from 1925.

### 🎢 Belmont Park
3146 Mission Blvd.
**Tel** (858) 228-9283. 🗓 daily.
**www**.belmontpark.com

## La Jolla ❺

**Road map** D6. 🏠 *32,000*.
🚌 *from San Diego*. ℹ️ *7966 Herschel Ave (858) 454-5718*.
**www**.lajollabythesea.com

The origin of the name La Jolla (which is pronounced "La Hoya") is the subject of an on-going debate – while some people believe it to come from the Spanish *la joya*, meaning "jewel," others claim it was inspired by a Native American word, with the same pronunciation, which means "cave." Located 4 miles (6 km) north of San Diego's Mission Bay, La Jolla is an elegant, upscale coastal resort set amid beautiful cliffs and coves (see p249). Its pretty streets are lined with gourmet chocolatiers, designer clothes shops, and top-name jewelers. San Diegans and tourists alike have come to enjoy the many art galleries and the chic restaurants promising a

"Mediterranean" view. A companion to the museum in Downtown San Diego (see p251), La Jolla's **Museum of Contemporary Art** occupies a prime oceanfront location. It displays works from its permanent collection of post-1950 art and houses a bookstore, café, and sculpture garden.

The town is also home to the University of California at San Diego and to the famous **Salk Institute for Biological Studies**, founded in 1960 by Dr. Jonas Salk, who developed the polio vaccine. Overlooking Scripps Beach is the Scripps Institution of Oceanography, with its magnificent **Birch Aquarium at Scripps**. The aquarium provides an insight into the fascinating world of oceanography, with exhibits, interactive displays, and feeding shows in the kelp tank. In the aquarium, visitors can observe sea life from the waters of the north Pacific as well as the tropics, including an Alaskan giant octopus.

### 🏛 Museum of Contemporary Art
700 Prospect St. **Tel** (858) 454-3541.
🗓 11am–5pm Thu–Tue. 🔴 Wed, Jan 1, Thanksgiving, Dec 25. 🌐
**www**.mcasd.org

### 🏫 Salk Institute for Biological Studies
10010 N Torrey Pines Rd. **Tel** (858) 453-4100. 🗓 Mon–Fri. 🔴 public hols. 🌐 noon. **www**.salk.edu

### 🐠 Birch Aquarium at Scripps
2300 Expedition Way. **Tel** (858) 534-3474. 🗓 9am–5pm daily.
🔴 Jan 1, Thanksgiving, Dec 25. 🌐
**www**.aquarium.ucsd.edu

Beautiful rocky shoreline of La Jolla Cove

# San Diego Wild Animal Park ❻

Hwy 78, 15500 San Pasqual
Valley Rd. **Tel** (760) 747-8702.
🚍 *Escondido.* ⬜ *daily.* 🖼 ♿ 🎫
www.sandiegozoo.org

A rural counterpart to San
Diego Zoo *(see p259)*, this
wildlife park displays an
encyclopedic variety of birds
and mammals in its 1,800
acres (730 ha) of carefully
landscaped grounds. Opened
in 1972, the park was conceived as a breeding sanctuary
for the world's endangered
species and has remained at
the forefront of the conservation race. As well as caring
for its 3,200 residents, the
park exchanges animals with
zoological institutions around
the world, with the ultimate
goal of releasing endangered
species back into the wild.
Among the program's success
stories is that of the California
condor, a species once close
to extinction.

A good way to begin
a visit is to take the Journey
Into Africa tour. This
25-minute, 2-mile (3-km)
guided ride through African
habitats visits giraffes, rhinos,
and gazelles. It also stops at
a waterhole where there are
herons, ostriches, and many
other birds. Another great trip
is the Tethered Balloon Safari
which rises to about 400 ft
(120 m) and offers a
panoramic view of the whole
animal park including lions,
giraffes, zebras, and cheetahs.

**Visitors enjoy the California Coast Cruise boat ride at Legoland®**

For many, the big animals,
such as elephants, lions, and
rhinos, are the stars. However,
the park's various simulated
natural environments, such as
the Australian Rainforest and
the Hidden Jungle, are also
engrossing, and the Petting
Kraal is popular with children.
Before visiting the Wild Animal
Park, it is worth finding out
the times of daily events.

Nairobi Village is a 17-acre
(7-ha) area, where the park's
amphitheaters and most of
its facilities are to be found.
Its many shops sell Africa-
related books and souvenirs.

# Legoland® ❼

1 Legoland Drive, Carlsbad.
**Road map** D6. **Tel** (760) 918-5346.
🚍 *S Carlsbad.* ⬜ *daily, but check
website.* ♿ www.legoland.com

This unusual 128-acre (744-ha)
park is aimed mainly at families
with children and offers more
than 60 rides, shows, and

attractions such as an aquarium
with a Lego-voyage to the
ocean's depths, and a water
park. For younger visitors, the
DUPLO section showcases
African wildlife such as giraffes
and lions made of bricks.

The main attraction is the
display of seven miniature
areas of the United States,
created using more than
20 million Lego bricks.

Other areas of the park
include Land of Adventure,
transporting the visitor to
1920s Egypt, with rides
such as Pharaoh's Revenge.

# Mission San Luis Rey ❽

Hwy 76 (Mission Ave), Rancho
del Oro Drive, San Luis Rey.
**Tel** (760) 757-3651. 🚍 *from San
Diego.* ⬜ *10am–4pm daily.*
**Donation.** www.sanluisrey.org

One of the largest and most-
prosperous estates in the
California mission chain

**Animals roaming around freely in the San Diego Wild Animal Park**

**Façade of Mission San Luis Rey**

*(see p46)*, San Luis Rey de Francia was founded by the Spanish priest Padre Fermín Lasuén in 1798. The mission was named after the canonized 13th-century French king, Louis IX, and owed much of its success to the cooperation of the local Luiseño Indians. More than 3,000 Native Americans lived and worked in Mission San Luis Rey. They kept livestock and cultivated crops such as grain and fruit. The majority of the mission's remaining buildings benefited from a long period of restoration in the early 20th century. Visitors are guided first to a **museum** outlining the history of the mission and the surrounding area. Of the vestments and religious artifacts on display, several have survived only because, after the church was secularized in 1833, some of its treasures were hidden by the Christian Native Americans. Their families returned the artifacts to the mission only when it was designated a Franciscan monastery in 1893.

**statue in the church**

The church at San Luis Rey has a cruciform shape as at San Juan Capistrano *(see p241)*, but was the only one in the chain with a domed wooden ceiling. The wooden pulpit is original, and the painted designs are based on surviving stencils. The mission still functions as a church and retreat, and in its grounds are a partly restored laundry area, a cemetery, and California's oldest pepper tree, brought from Peru in 1830.

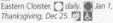

### 🏛 Museum

Eastern Cloister. ◯ daily. ● Jan 1, Thanksgiving, Dec 25. 🖼 ♿

## Palomar Observatory ❾

**Road map** D6. 🚌 *from Julian.*

At the summit of Palomar Mountain is the surreal-looking white dome of the **Palomar Observatory**. Operated by the California Institute of Technology, this internationally renowned observatory first opened in 1948. It houses a computer-controlled Hale telescope with a 200-inch (510-cm) mirror capable of studying areas of the universe that are more than a billion light years away. From 1948 to 1956, the observatory's Oschin telescope was used to photograph the entire night sky. A second survey began in 1985 and lasted until 2000, producing digital images. Currently, the Oschin is conducting a fully automated, wide-field survey of the sky as part of the Palomar Transient Factory systematic exploration project.

The observatory is now home to five telescopes that are used for a wide variety of astronomical research. Recent discoveries have included a new star orbiting the Big Dipper's Alcor, found in 2009, and a novel type of supernova first seen in 2011. Tours of the observatory cover historical and current scientific research, with an emphasis on the Hale Telescope.

Visitors are not permitted to look through the 540-ton telescope; however, an exhibition area and photo gallery explain how it functions.

### 🏛 Palomar Observatory

35899 Canfield Rd, Palomar Mountain. **Tel** *(760) 742-2119.*
◯ 9am–3pm daily. ● Dec 24 & 25.
🎁 10am–4pm Sat & Sun.

**Dome of the Palomar Observatory at sunset**

## Julian ⑩

**Road map** D6. 🏠 2,000. 🚌 from San Diego. ℹ 2129 Main St (760 765-1857). **www**.julianca.com

When San Diegans want to go for a pleasant drive or spend a romantic weekend in the "back country," they often head for the mountain town of Julian. Gold was discovered here in 1870, and the restored 19th-century wooden buildings that line the main street help to re-create the atmosphere of those pioneer days.

Today tourists rather than gold-diggers flock here. In autumn, the "Apple Days" of October attract hundreds of visitors, who come to taste Julian's famous apple pie and buy rustic souvenirs in the quaint gift shops. The delightfully cluttered **Julian Pioneer Museum** is packed with curiosities and photographs evoking the town's history. Visitors can also venture inside an original gold mine at the **Eagle and High Peak Mines**.

For visitors wishing to stay overnight, there are plenty of homey hotels and bed-and-breakfast accommodation both in and around the town (see p536).

🏛 **Julian Pioneer Museum**
2811 Washington St. **Tel** (760) 765-0227. ☐ Apr–Nov: Fri–Sun; Dec–Mar: Sat & Sun. 📷

🚇 **Eagle and High Peak Mines**
C St. **Tel** (760) 765-0036. ☐ daily, but call ahead. ● Jan 1, Easter Sun, Thanksgiving, Dec 25. 📷

## Cuyamaca Rancho State Park ⑪

**Road map** D6. 🚌
ℹ (760) 765-3020. ☐ daily. **www**.parks.ca.gov

Only an hour's drive east of San Diego, Cuyamaca Rancho State Park is a place to get away from it all. Almost half of its 25,000 acres (10,100 ha) are an officially designated wilderness that is home to skunks, bobcats, coyotes, mule deer, and mountain lions.

As well as horseback riding, camping, and mountain biking facilities, there are 130 miles (210 km) of hiking trails in the park. The Cuyamaca Peak Trail is an arduous but rewarding ascent by paved fire road. From the summit, hikers can enjoy fine views of the forested hills of northern San Diego County as far as Palomar Mountain (see p263).

At the northern end of the park lies the Stonewall Gold Mine. Once a 500-strong prospectors' town, it yielded over two million dollars' worth of gold in the 1880s.

*Apple pie store sign in Julian*

ℹ **Park Headquarters and Museum**
12551 Hwy 79. **Tel** (760) 765-0755. ☐ daily. ● public hols.

## Lake Morena Park ⑫

**Road map** D6. 🚌 from San Diego. **Tel** (619) 579-4101.

This lush, oak-shaded park surrounding a large fishing lake forms an oasis in the dry

**Shores of Lake Morena**

southeastern corner of San Diego County. The park covers 3,250 acres (1,300 ha) of land. For those who come to fish or simply enjoy a peaceful afternoon on the lake, rental boats are available.

## Chula Vista Nature Center ⑬

100 Gunpowder Point Dr. **Road map** D6. **Tel** (619) 409-5900. 🚌 E St, Bay. ☐ 10am–5pm daily. ● public hols. 📷 🚻 **www**.chulavistanaturecenter.org

This remarkable zoo and aquarium beside San Diego Bay provides an opportunity to observe the wildlife of California's coastal wetlands. A free bus takes visitors to the Nature Center from a parking lot located by I-5, and from the San Diego Trolley Station.

Here visitors can learn about the fragile environment of the 316 acres (130 ha) of protected land. Birds that can be seen all year round include herons, ospreys, and kestrels.

## Tijuana River National Estuarine Research Reserve ⑭

301 Caspian Way. **Road map** D6. **Tel** (619) 575-3613. ☐ 10am–5pm Wed–Sun. ● Jan 1, Thanksgiving, Dec 25. **www**.trnerr.org

Encompassing 2,500 acres (1,010 ha) of coastal wetlands, this estuary is an important breeding, nesting, and feeding ground for over 370 species of native and migratory birds.

**Horseback riding in the Cuyamaca Rancho State Park**

*For hotels and restaurants in this region see pp536–8 and pp581–4*

# Tijuana ⑮

**Carved wooden Mexican bird**

Thousands of Americans have traditionally visited Tijuana to enjoy its inexpensive shopping and lively nightlife. Reports of violence between rival drug cartels since 2008–9 and increased border controls has, however, seen a decline in visitor numbers. Greater services and discounts are now on offer to attract tourists back. Contact the San Diego tourist office about any travel warnings before visiting.

**LOCATOR MAP**

— International border

— San Diego Trolley line

▢ Mexico

### Exploring Tijuana

The border city of Tijuana is hardly representative of the fabled Mexico of Mayan art and Spanish colonial architecture, but it is interesting as a hybrid frontier town.

The city's futuristic **Centro Cultural Tijuana** was built on the banks of the Tijuana River in 1982. This cultural center has an OMNIMAX theater, where films about Mexico are shown on a giant tilting screen.

**Sociedad de Historia de Tijuana** is a cultural area with a museum, gallery, library, and computer center.

Most visitors come to shop and party – Tijuana has long been popular with young Americans taking advantage of laws permitting anyone over 18 to drink alcohol.

The best shopping is in the quiet bazaars situated in the lively Avenida Revolución. Painted pottery, leather boots, silver jewelry, and tequila are some favorite buys. Tourists are encouraged to barter with the merchants.

**Bottles of liqueur on sale in a street bazaar in Tijuana**

English-speaking staff at the **Tijuana Convention and Visitor's Bureau** can provide maps and free advice.

🏛 **Centro Cultural Tijuana**
Paseo de los Héroes. *Tel* 011-52 (664) 687-9600, (664) 687-9635.
◯ daily. 🎫

ℹ **Tijuana Convention and Visitor's Bureau**
Ave Revolución (between 3rd & 4th).
*Tel* 011-52 (664) 685-3117, (888) 775-2417 (from USA), (888) 025-0888 (from Mexico).
◯ daily. **Tourist Assistance Hotline** dial 078.
**www**.seetijuana.com

## TIPS FOR TRAVELERS

***Getting there:*** *Since the San Diego Trolley (see p266) runs as far as the international border, the cheapest and simplest way to cross the border into Tijuana is on foot. Take a southbound trolley to San Ysidro and follow the crowds across the pedestrian bridges and walkways that lead to the city. You can also take a bus from San Ysidro across the border to downtown Tijuana, or book an excursion through the Tijuana Convention and Visitor's Bureau. Those taking a car or a motorcycle will need Mexican vehicle insurance. This is inexpensive and is available at the border.*

***Visas:*** *Travel requirements change frequently and it is best to check on the latest documentation needed to cross the border before you travel. Citizens of the United States need a passport or a government-issued Nexus Card for re-entry into the US. Citizens of Australia, Canada, and the United Kingdom require passports but not visas to enter Mexico, unless they are planning to remain in the country for longer than six months. When crossing the border, non-American nationals must present a completed Mexican Tourist Card, which may be obtained directly at the port of entry. For further information, contact the Mexican consulate in your home country before departure. All travelers must ensure that they meet visa requirements.*

***Currency:*** *Visitors on a short trip will rarely need to change money since US dollars and major credit cards are widely accepted.*

**Façade of the Centro Cultural Tijuana**

# PRACTICAL INFORMATION

S an Diego is an easy city to get to know, with a clean, efficient public transit system and a welcoming attitude toward visitors. The regeneration of the city's heart is evident in the growing number of shops, restaurants, and nightspots around Westfield Horton Plaza (see p250) and the Gaslamp Quarter (see pp252–3). A variety of public transportation penetrates this Downtown area, where there are all the shops and entertainment spots you would expect in a vibrant California city. There are also regular connections to Old Town, Balboa Park, Coronado, and the Mexican border, while the best way to enjoy the waterfront of the Embarcadero (see p250) is on foot. Tourist information is available from excellent visitors' centers located in Westfield Horton Plaza and Balboa Park, as well as in Coronado.

Jessop's Clock in Horton Plaza

---

Passengers boarding a San Diego bus

## GETTING AROUND

The three lines of the **San Diego Trolley**, the city's streetcar system, link Old Town East to Santee, and south to Downtown and the Mexican border. Another line links Downtown to Santee. Trolleys run every 15 minutes during the day and operate until around 1am. A comprehensive bus network runs throughout the city. The **Flagship San Diego Harbor Excursion** offers a regular service to the Coronado Peninsula (see p255). Maps, timetables, and special one- to four-day Day Passes, valid for unlimited travel on

any bus, trolley, or ferry, can be obtained from the **Transit Store**. **Old Town Trolley Tours** offer regular guided tours visiting all the principal sights.

The city's **Amtrak** station is housed in the beautiful Santa Fe Depot in Downtown. **San Diego International Airport** is located 3 miles (5 km) northwest of Downtown. Buses, taxis, and rental cars are all available from the airport.

The **Balboa Park Tram** provides free rides around the cultural park (see pp256–7). All along San Diego Bay, the **San Diego Water Taxi** takes visitors to points of interest around the shoreline.

San Diego is also a bicycle-friendly city, well served with bike paths and bike rental shops. There is a gentle route from Mission Beach to La Jolla (see p261), offering fine ocean views. Bikes can be carried on trolleys and buses for a small fee. Bicycle taxis are also widespread in the Downtown area.

It is generally safe to walk around the areas to the north and west of Downtown, even at night. However, the areas to the south of Downtown and, particularly, to the east of the Gaslamp Quarter are best avoided after dark.

Mexican-style shopping in the Bazaar del Mundo

## SHOPPING

If you intend to visit Tijuana (see p265), avoid doing too much shopping before you go, since bargain goods are the main reason for crossing the border. The Fiesta de Reyes in Old Town San Diego (see p254) also has plenty of Mexican crafts and souvenirs.

**Westfield Horton Plaza** is the city's most colorful shopping center and can meet most tourists' needs, while the Paladion next door sells couture clothing. The oceanfront Seaport Village complex (see p250) is a good place to buy souvenirs and gifts to take home. Farther up the coast,

A San Diego Trolley, offering a fast, frequent service to the Mexican border

**Attractive shopping area of Seaport Village, on the waterfront**

Prospect Street in La Jolla has a selection of elegant stores. Del Mar and Carlsbad also have a good mix of boutiques, antique shops, and art galleries.

There are several factory outlet centers in San Diego County, where outlet stores sell well-known brand-name goods at considerably reduced prices (see p607). The Las Americas Factory Outlet Center, located just before the Mexican border crossing in San Ysidro, is one of the largest and best in the region, with more than 120 factory outlet stores. Ask at the information desk in the large parking lot for a sheet of discount tokens, which allow you to obtain further reductions of up to 15 percent in many of the shops.

Here, as throughout the state, major credit cards are accepted, and the hours of most shops are 10am–6pm Monday to Saturday, with some stores open on Sundays as well. A local sales tax of 8.5 percent applies to all purchases. This is automatically added to the advertised price of the goods when you pay for them.

## ENTERTAINMENT

San Diego has a reputation for its cultural energy and has its own symphony orchestra, opera, and repertory theater companies. Listings of all the current cultural events can be found in the *San Diego Union-Tribune* and a range of free tourist magazines. *The Reader*, available free in cafés, bars, and bookstores, is a good weekly source for finding out about poetry readings, live music, and the alternative

arts. Tickets for all these events can be bought from the **Times Arts Tix** office in Westfeld Horton Plaza.

The Gaslamp Quarter (see pp252–3) is the best area to go to for good restaurants and nightclubs. The nearby Lyceum and Spreckels theaters have regular stage performances. In Balboa Park, the Old Globe Theater (see p256) stages award-winning shows and is one part of a three-stage performing arts complex.

Like most Californians, San Diegans are also avid sports fans – the Chargers football team play in Mission Valley, and the Padres baseball team play downtown at Petco Park. If, however, you prefer participating in sports to watching them, Mission Bay (see pp260–61) offers a wide range of water sports, as well as beach games such as volleyball. San Diego County also has 90 excellent golf courses – ask at hotels or at local visitors' centers for information.

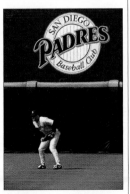

**San Diego's own baseball team, the Padres**

## DIRECTORY

### GETTING AROUND

**Amtrak**
Santa Fe Depot, 1050 Kettner Blvd. *Tel* (800) 872-7245.
www.amtrak.com

**Balboa Park Tram**
*Tel* (619) 239-0512. www.
balboapark.org/maps/tram.php

**Flagship San Diego Harbor Excursion**
1050 N Harbor Dr. *Tel* (619) 234-4111. www.flagshipsd.com

**Metropolitan Transit System (MTS)**
1255 Imperial Ave, #1000.
*Tel* (619) 233-3004.
http://transit.511sd.com

**Old Town Trolley Tours**
4010 Twiggs St. *Tel* (619) 298-8687. www.trolleytours.com

**San Diego International Airport**
Lindbergh Field. *Tel* (619) 400-2400. www.san.org

**San Diego Trolley**
[f] (619) 595-4949.
www.sdmts.com/trolley

**San Diego Water Taxi**
*Tel* (619) 235-8294.
www.flagshipsd.com

**Transit Store**
102 Broadway. *Tel* (619) 234-1060.
www.sdmts.com

### SHOPPING

**Westfield Horton Plaza**
G St & 1st Ave. *Tel* (619) 239-8180. www.westfield.com

### ENTERTAINMENT

**Times Arts Tix**
Broadway Circle, Horton Plaza.
*Tel* (619) 238-0700.
www.sandiegoperforms.com

### TOURIST INFORMATION

**Balboa Park**
1549 El Prado. *Tel* (619) 239-0512. www.balboapark.org

**Coronado**
1100 Orange Ave.
*Tel* (619) 437-8788.
www.coronadovisitorcenter.com

**San Diego Visitors Bureau**
West Broadway at Harbor Dr.
*Tel* (619) 236-1212.
www.sandiego.org

# THE INLAND EMPIRE
# AND LOW DESERT

*The Inland Empire and Low Desert landscape is one of the most varied in California. The countryside changes from pine forests, cooled by gentle breezes, to searing desert. The contrast can be startling: passengers taking the Palm Springs Aerial Tramway make the transition between these two ecosystems in ten minutes.*

The Anza-Borrego Desert State Park was the forbidding entry point to California for tens of thousands of hardy miners and settlers coming overland in the 1850s. Thirty years later communities in the northwest of the region, known as the Inland Empire, were transformed from a small collection of health resorts into the heart of a veritable economic empire based on the navel orange. The thick-skinned seedless Brazilian fruit, which traveled well, came to represent the sweet and healthy promise of California for millions of Americans. Many of the Victorian mansions built by citrus millionaires are still standing in the towns of Redlands and Riverside, but most of the fragrant orange groves have disappeared under asphalt and urban sprawl. Today Riverside is practically a suburb of Los Angeles.

At the heart of this region is Palm Springs, a favorite weekend retreat for Angelenos seeking relaxation and the desert sun. Just under two hours drive from LA, it has luxurious hotels, verdant golf courses, and a record number of pools and tennis courts.

Lying to the east of Palm Springs is the Joshua Tree National Park. This is a land of hot, dry days, chilly nights, tumbleweed, and creosote bushes. The stark and silent beauty of the rocky landscape evokes images of desperados, hardy pioneers in covered wagons, and leather-clad high plains drifters – visions of the Wild West of so many novels and films.

When the desert becomes too hot, travelers can escape to one of the mountain resorts. The Rim of the World Tour is a spectacular drive in the heart of the San Bernardino Mountains.

Western film set in Pioneertown, near Yucca Valley

◁ Joshua tree silhouetted against the barren desert landscape

# Exploring the Inland Empire and Low Desert

The Inland Empire is a region of vast scenic and climatic contrasts. In the northwest is the San Bernardino National Forest, with its cool mountain air and breathtaking views. Farther south lies the sun-baked Coachella Valley, ending in the steamy Salton Sea. Palm Springs, the largest of the desert resorts, is flanked by the stark Joshua Tree National Park and the alpine community of Idyllwild. The forbidding Anza-Borrego Desert State Park, in the southwest of the region, is the gateway to San Diego County.

Adelanto
Victorville
Pinon Hills
Phelan
Hesperia
Lucerne Valley
Wrightwood
Mount San Antonio 3067m
Lake Arrowhead
Big Bear Lake
Big Bear City
Crestline
Running Springs
Pion
RIM OF THE WORLD TOUR
Los Angeles
Rialto
San Bernardino
YUCCA VA
Ontario
Redlands
Yucaipa
San Gorgonio 3505m
Chino
Rubidoux
RIVERSIDE
Beaumont
Dese Hot Spring
Corona
Moreno Valley
Banning
Perris
Hemet
San Jacinto Peak 3293m
PALM SPRINGS
Sun City
Mountain Center
Idyllwild
Lakeland Village
PALM PINES HIGHW
Murrieta
Murrieta Hot Springs
Temecula
San Diego
Aguanga
Oak Grove
Ranchita
Julian

A wild bighorn sheep in the
Anza-Borrego Desert State Park

## SEE ALSO

- **Where to Stay** pp538–40
- **Where to Eat** pp584–6

View across Desert Dunes golf course, near Palm Springs

## KEY

▬ Freeway

▬ Major road

▬ Secondary road

▬ Minor road

— Scenic route

— Main railway

— Minor railway

▬ State border

▬ International border

△ Summit

**For additional map symbols** *see back flap*

**Wind turbines in the Coachella Valley**

### GETTING AROUND

The easiest way to explore the desert areas is by car. The I-10 crosses the Inland Empire and Low Desert from east to west. Palm Springs, 107 miles (170 km) southeast of LA and 120 miles (190 km) northeast of San Diego, has a Greyhound bus terminal, an Amtrak station, and an airport, and is a good base for exploring the region.

0 kilometers    20

0 miles          20

# Rim of the World Tour ❶

From San Bernardino this invigorating drive winds across the forested San Bernardino Mountains, offering spectacular views of the desert beyond. The altitude provides for distinct seasons, with warm, pine-scented air in the summer and brisk, cool days in the winter, when the snow-covered mountain trails are perfect for cross-country skiing. The tour passes through the resorts beside Lake Arrowhead and Big Bear Lake, both favorite destinations for those wanting to escape the heat and smog of LA. In Redlands visitors are offered a sense of the area's heady Victorian past, and yet another pleasure: the sweet smell of orange groves.

San Bernardino Mountain landscape

**Big Bear Lake** ③
A popular resort area, Big Bear Lake offers a range of sports including fishing, sailing, swimming, and, in the winter, skiing. Its two commercial centers are Big Bear City, to the east, and Big Bear Village, to the south.

**Heaps Peak Arboretum** ④
A one mile (1.6 km) nature trail winds through this wooded hillside, planted with native and other trees. Species include dogwoods, Jeffrey pine, ponderosa pine, black oaks, live oaks, and white fir.

**Children's Forest** ⑤
Located in the San Bernardino National Forest, Children's Forest aims to educate on forest ecology and involve youngsters in regeneration work.

**Lake Arrowhead** ⑥
Lake Arrowhead Village, on the south shore, offers shops, restaurants and accommodation in both hotels and log cabins. Trips up the lake aboard the *Arrowhead Queen* also begin here. The north shore is almost exclusively residential.

**Redlands** ①
This town is famous for Victorian mansions, buil the end of the 19th cent those who made their fo growing navel oranges p50). Among the finest Kimberly Crest House a Gardens, the Morey Mai and the Edwards Mansio

**Ornate Mission Inn in Riverside**

38

②

lometers            10

iles          5

**Y**

Tour route

Other roads

## Riverside ②

**Road map** D6. 300,000. 3750 University Ave, (951) 222-4700.
www.exploreriverside.com

Some of the most elegant architecture in Southern California is to be found in Riverside. During the late 19th century, the town was the center of California's citrus industry and by 1905 it had the highest per capita income in the US. One of the two original orange trees responsible for this great success was planted in 1875 by Eliza and Luther Tihbetts (see p50). The same orange tree is still thriving in a small park at the intersection of Magnolia and Arlington avenues.

Riverside's **Mission Inn Hotel & Spa**, built in 1876 as a 12-room adobe house, was expanded early in the 20th century into a 275-room hotel (see p540). Architecturally, this ornate hotel is an unusual mixture of Mission Revival, Moorish, and Oriental styles, with flying buttresses, spiral staircases, and gargoyles. The **Riverside Metropolitan Museum** has exhibits on the town's history and Native American culture.

**Pot at Hi-Desert Nature Museum**

🏨 **Mission Inn Hotel & Spa**
3649 Mission Inn Ave. **Tel** (951) 784-0300. www.missioninn.com

🏛 **Riverside Metropolitan Museum**
3580 Mission Inn Ave. **Tel** (951) 826-5273. 10am–5pm daily.

## Yucca Valley ③

**Road map** D5. 44,000. 56711 Twenty-nine Palms Hwy, (760) 365-6323. www.yuccavalley.org

Yucca Valley is a small town located west of the Joshua Tree National Park (see pp278–9). On a hillside, the **Desert Christ Park** has more than 40 statues depicting the life of Jesus, sculpted by Antone Martin in the 1950s. The town's **Hi-Desert Nature Museum** has various exhibits on the region's geology, crafts, flora, and fauna. **Pioneertown**, 4 miles (6 km) northwest of Yucca Valley, is a hamlet built in 1947 as a Western film set.

🌵 **Desert Christ Park**
End of Mohawk Trail. **Tel** (760) 364-0469. daily.

🏛 **Hi-Desert Nature Museum**
57090 Twenty-nine Palms Hwy. **Tel** (760) 369-7212. 10am–5pm Tue–Sun. public hols.

**Statue of Christ at the Antone Martin Memorial Park**

# Palm Springs ❹

**Popcorn in Ruddy's**

The Coachella Valley has been inhabited for 10,000 years, but it was only in 1853 that a government survey party came across a grove of palm trees surrounding a mineral pool bubbling up out of the desert sand. The area's first hotel was constructed in 1886, and by the turn of the century the city of Palm Springs was a thriving health spa. In the 1920s and 1930s the area become a fashionable winter resort, colonized by the rich and famous.

### Exploring Palm Springs

The postwar building boom (*see p54*) brought rapid hotel and residential development to Palm Springs. Drawn by the city's growing popularity, developers later began opening up the empty desert lands eastward along the Coachella Valley. From 1967 to 1981, the resort cities of Cathedral City, Rancho Mirage, Palm Desert, Indian Wells, and La Quinta shot up between Palm Springs and the date-growing center of Indio, 22 miles (35 km) away. Desert Hot Springs, a spa just northeast of Palm Springs, also became a popular vacation destination. The extraordinary proliferation of luxury golf courses dates from this period (*see p277*).

These towns are now gathered under the umbrella of Palm Springs Desert Resorts, and people often refer to all of them as Palm Springs. Palm Desert, the most citified and home of luxury shopping, has long outstripped the actual town of Palm Springs in population, and these days the most luxurious resort hotels and estates are found in Indian Wells, Rancho Mirage, and La Quinta. An infinite choice awaits the millions of visitors who come to swim, golf, play tennis, relax, and enjoy the lifestyle, when they're not browsing through resale shops or playing the slot machines in the valley's casinos.

Still, the city of Palm Springs with its long history of Hollywood glamor retains its attraction. Many celebrities still keep homes there, and several companies offer guided tours to point out their houses.

**Old Shredded Wheat advertisement from Ruddy's in Village Green**

### 🏛 Village Green Heritage Center

221 S Palm Canyon Drive.
*Tel* (760) 323- 8297. ⬜ *call for hours.* ⬤ *public hols.* 🚶 *walking tours available 9:45am Wed–Sat from McCallum Adobe.*

This quiet enclave, in the heart of Palm Springs' shopping district, contains four historical buildings. Palm Springs' first white resident, John Guthrie McCallum, built the McCallum Adobe in 1884. Originally it stood near the Indian village of Agua Caliente, the site of the natural hot springs that inspired the town's name. The house was moved to its present location during the 1950s.

The Cornelia White House (1893) is built partly out of

railroad ties. It is furnished with antiques dating from Palm Springs' pioneer era.

The heritage of the area's Cahuilla people is related through artifacts and photographs in the Agua Caliente Cultural Museum. There is also a collection of antique baskets that were handcrafted by Native American weavers.

Also in the Village Green Heritage Center is Ruddy's 1930s General Store Museum. Once the town's only druggist, Ruddy's is an immaculate and well-stocked replica of a Depression-era shop. Authentically packaged goods range from licorice to shoelaces.

### 🌊 Knott's Soak City

1500 Gene Autry Trail. *Tel* (760) 327-0499. ⬜ *Mar–early Sep: daily; Sep–Oct: Sat & Sun.* ⬤ *public hols.* 💻 www.knotts.com

This state-of-the-art water park covers 16 acres (6.5 ha). Designed to evoke southern California beaches, the park boasts a variety of water rides and attractions, including an exciting 70-ft (20-m) free-fall slide and a 600-ft (180-m) artificial "river" for riding inflated inner tubes. There are special slides and pools for young children, like Kahuna's Beach House, which includes slides, hose jets, and water curtains. California's largest wave-action pool creates artificial waves suitable for surfing and boogie boarding. Surfboards and inner tubes can be rented from the park on either an hourly or a daily basis.

**Kahuna's Beach House water ride for young children at Knott's Soak City**

**Palm Springs Aerial Tramway ascending to the Mountain Station**

## 🚡 Palm Springs Aerial Tramway

1 Tram Way. **Tel** (760) 325-1391.
⬜ daily. 🖥 **www**.pstramway.com
The Aerial Tramway's two
revolving Swiss-built cars, each
holding 80 passengers, are one
of Palm Springs' most popular
attractions. The trams depart
from Valley Station, situated
6 miles (10 km) northwest of
Palm Springs. The 2.5-mile
(4-km) trip at a maximum
angle of 42° takes about 10
minutes and ascends 5,900 ft
(1,790 m) over spectacular
scenery to the Mountain Station
in the Mount San Jacinto State
Park and Wilderness Area.

Passengers travel through
five distinct ecosystems,
ranging from desert to alpine
forest, which is akin to
traveling from Mexico to
Alaska. The temperature
changes dramatically during
the journey. The heat of the
valley floor sometimes differs
as much as 40°F (4°C) from
the temperature at the peak,
so dress appropriately.

At the top there are 54 miles
(85 km) of hiking trails, one
of which leads to Idyllwild
(see p276). The Adventure
Center is open in the winter,
with rentals available for cross-
country skiing. There are also
camp sites and picnic areas.

Observation decks perched
on the edge of the 8,500-ft-
(2,600-m-) high lookout offer
views of the Coachella Valley,
Palm Springs, and the San
Bernardino Mountains. On a
very clear day, it is possible
to see for 50 miles (80 km) to
the Salton Sea (see p277).

Both stations have gift
shops, cocktail lounges, and
snack bars. The Mountain
Station also has a cafeteria
and a fine dining restaurant.

## 🏛 Palm Springs Art Museum

101 Museum Drive. **Tel** (760) 332-
4800. ⬜ 10am–5pm Tue, Wed & Fri–
Sun, noon–8pm Thu. ● Mon & public
hols. 🖥 **www**.psmuseum.org
The Palm Springs Art Museum
focuses on painting and
sculpture dating from the
19th century to the present
day. Native American art,
Mesoamerican artifacts, and
photography are on display
too. The museum also houses
the extensive William Holden
Collection, a gift from the
estate of the late actor.

The adjoining Annenberg
Theater is a 433-seat center
for the performing arts, which
features cabaret, pop, and
contemporary entertainers, as
well as dance, comedy, and
theater. The lush gardens are
enhanced by fountains and
demonstrate that the desert
need not be a barren place.

A trail leads out from the
museum and enables visitors
to explore the flora and fauna
of this desert region. The
2-mile (3-km) Museum Trail
climbs 800 ft (244 m) up into
the Mount San Jacinto State
Park. It joins the Lykken Trail
at Desert Riders Overlook
(a viewpoint from which to
look out across Palm Springs
and the Coachella Valley).

**VISITORS' CHECKLIST**

**Road map** D6. 🏔 42,000.
✈ Palm Springs International Airport, 1 mile (1.5 km) NE of Downtown. 🚉 Indio. 🚌 3111 N Indian
Ave. 🛈 2901 N Palm Canyon Dr;
(800) 927-7256, (760) 778-8418.
🎬 Palm Springs International
Film Festival (early–mid-Jan).
**www**.visitpalmsprings.com

The Lykken Trail then
continues for another 4 miles
(6 km) to the mouth of the
Tahquitz Canyon (see p276).

**Exhibition inside the Palm Springs
Art Museum**

## PALM TREES

Only one palm variety in Palm Springs is native to
California, the desert fan palm (*Washingtonia filifera*),
which crowds the secluded mountain oases. Unlike other
palm varieties, the dead fronds do not drop off the trunk
but droop down to form a "skirt" that provides a shelter
for wildlife.

Date palms (*Phoenix dactylifera*) were introduced from
Algeria in 1890 as an experiment. A mature date palm can
produce up to 300 lb (135 kg) of dates a year. An annual
ten-day National Date Festival in Indio features a cornu-
copia of dried and fresh dates (see p39).

**Date palm grove in the Coachella Valley**

## ⚜ Indian Canyons

*38–520 S Palm Canyon Dr.* **Tel** *(760) 323-6018.* ☐ *Oct–Jul: 8am–5pm daily; Jul–Sep: 8am–5pm Fri–Sun.* 🖼
www.indian-canyons.com

Approximately 5 miles (8 km) south of Palm Springs are four spectacular natural palm oases, set in stark, rocky gorges and surrounded by barren hills. Clustered along small streams fed by mountain springs, Murray, Tahquitz, Andreas, and Palm canyons are located on the land of the Agua Caliente Cahuilla people. Rock art and other traces of the area's early inhabitants can still be seen.

The 15-mile- (24-km-) long Palm Canyon is the largest of the gorges and contains many wild California fan palm trees and indigenous flora and fauna. Refreshments are available near the parking lot and from here it is a short but steep walk down to the main trail. There are also picnic tables beside a stream *(see p275)*.

**Desert fan palm oasis in the Indian Canyons**

## ⚜ The Living Desert, A Zoo and Botanical Garden

*47–900 Portola Ave, Palm Desert.* **Tel** *(760) 346-5694.* ☐ *daily.* ⬤ *Dec 25.* 🖼 www.livingdesert.org

The Living Desert is a well-designed zoo and botanical garden representing the desert environments of North America and Africa. The park covers 1,200 acres (485 ha), but most of its major attractions can be seen in half a day. Broad paths lead visitors through 40 different gardens and 60 animal exhibits. The zoo houses 500 wild animals, and of special interest are golden eagles, mountain lions, a large

**Flowering ocotillo in the Living Desert Wildlife and Botanical Park**

selection of nocturnal creatures, and a jaguar exhibit. The property also features various hiking trails, live animal shows, a model train exhibit, and camel rides. On winter days, walking through the park is a pleasure. During the summer, temperatures can exceed 100°F (37°C), so morning visits are recommended.

## Palms to Pines Highway ❺

**Road map** D6.
www.palmspringsusa.com

One of the most interesting drives in Southern California begins at the junction of Hwy 111 and Hwy 74 in Palm Desert. As you climb Hwy 74, you gradually leave behind the desert ecosystem with its palms, creosote, and desert ironwood trees and move into mountain scenery, made up of pines, juniper, and

mountain mahogany. The view from Santa Rosa Summit, just under 5,000 ft (1,500 m) high, is spectacular. Continue northwest on Hwy 74 to Mountain Center and the lush meadows of Garner Valley.

At Mountain Center, take Hwy 243 to the picturesque alpine village of Idyllwild, with its many restaurants, lodges, and camp sites. The renowned Idyllwild School of Music and the Arts holds regular classical music concerts during the summer. More active visitors can follow one of the many surrounding hiking trails, for which maps are available at the Ranger Station. One 8-mile (13-km) trek leads to the Mountain Station of the Palm Springs Aerial Tramway *(see p275)*. This provides the quickest way back to the desert floor. Mule-pack rides may be available in the summer, and during the winter months there is cross-country skiing.

## Anza-Borrego Desert State Park ❻

*200 Palm Canyon Drive.*
**Road map** D6. ☷ *Escondido.*
**Visitors' Center Tel** *(760) 767-4205.* ☐ *daily year-round.*
www.parks.ca.gov

Starting with the Gold Rush of 1849 *(see pp48–9)*, the Southern Emigrant Trail, the only all-weather land route into California, brought tens of thousands of miners and early settlers through the Anza-Borrego Desert. Today, this former overland gateway is a remote and pristine park,

**Picturesque mountain town of Idyllwild**

**Badlands in the Anza-Borrego Desert State Park**

offering a rare insight into a unique desert environment.

The desert's well-equipped visitors' center is in Borrego Springs. This is the only significant town in the otherwise undeveloped park. Nearby, the leisurely 1.5-mile (2.5-km) Palm Canyon Nature Trail leads to an oasis where the endangered bighorn sheep can occasionally be seen.

The Box Canyon Historical Monument is 31 miles (50 km) southwest of the visitors' center on County Road S2. Here you can view the old road once used by those miners who braved the desert climate on their way to the goldfields, which lay 500 miles (800 km) to the north.

The Anza-Borrego Desert is inhospitable for most of the year. Between March and May, however, following the winter rains, the burning land bursts into life. Cacti and desert flowers such as brittle-bush, desert poppies, and dune primroses produce a riot of color.

The desert's geology is as fascinating as its ecosystem. Over the millennia, a network of earthquake faults lifted and tilted the ground. Winter rains then carved through the shattered landscape, leaving multi- colored "layer-cake" bluffs, steep ravines, and jagged canyons such as the famous Borrego and Carizzo Badlands.

Much of the Anza-Borrego State Park, including its well-kept camp sites, is easily accessible via 100 miles (160 km) of surfaced and scenic highways. However, four-wheel drive vehicles are recommended for use on the park's 500 miles (800 km) of unsurfaced roads.

Drivers of standard vehicles should contact the visitors' center in advance to check on current road conditions.

## Salton Sea ⑦

**Road map** E6. 🚊 *Mecca.* 🚌 *Indio.* **Visitors' Center** ***Tel*** *(760) 393-3052.* ◯ *daily.* **www**.desertusa.com/salton

This manmade phenomenon has an interesting history, though for the next few years, you may choose not to visit unless interested in ecological reclamation.

Once a vibrant recreational area, the Salton Sea is currently experiencing rising salinity and selenium levels and is bogged down with algae in summer. Something of an ecological disaster, both fish and birds in adjoining marshland are fast disappearing. Governmental agencies have been working on restoration plans; however, no firm timetable has of yet been announced.

California's largest lake, the Salton Sea was created by accident in 1905 when the Colorado River flooded and flowed into a newly dug irrigation canal leading to the Imperial Valley. It took a team of engineers two years to stem the flow. By then, however, a 35-mile (55-km) inland sea had formed in the Salton Sink, 230 ft (70 m) below sea level.

On the east side of the sea there are hiking trails and camp sites set within the State Recreation Area. There is also a visitors' center.

### DESERT GOLF

Thanks to irrigation with water supplied from underground sources, Palm Springs is now known as the golf capital of the United States. There are more than 100 courses in the region, most of which belong to private clubs or are attached to resorts or hotel complexes. Some courses are rugged, while others are more lush. Among the professional golf events held in the area each year are the Bob Hope Classic in January and the Women's Kraft Nabisco Golf Championship in late March to early April. A number of courses are open to the public, including the Desert Dunes course, noted for adding the desert terrain to its challenging layout. In the summer it is best to tee off early in the morning. November and December offer better value and cooler weather. Most courses are closed in October for reseeding.

**Tahquitz Creek Golf Resort in Palm Springs**

# Joshua Tree National Park

**National park sign**

The Joshua Tree National Park was established in 1944 to preserve the groves of the unusual, spiny-leaved Joshua tree. The species was reportedly named in 1851 by early Mormon travelers, who saw in the twisted branches the upraised arms of the biblical Joshua. This large member of the agave family is unique to the area and can grow up to 30 ft (9 m) tall, living for 250–300 years. The 790,000-acre (319,700-ha) park offers uncommon vistas of the stark Californian desert, with its astounding formations of pink and gray rocks and boulders. A climber's paradise, Joshua Tree is also a fascinating area for hikers, who can discover lost mines, palm oases, and in the spring, a wealth of desert flowers. The Visitors' Center provides the latest weather report.

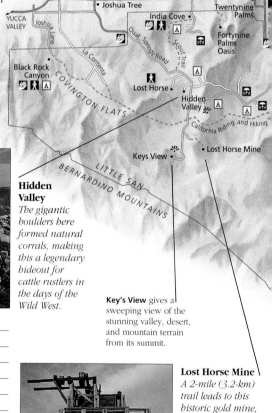

**Joshua Trees**
*Large groves of Joshua trees thrive in the higher, wetter, and somewhat cooler desert areas of the park's western half.*

**Hidden Valley**
*The gigantic boulders here formed natural corrals, making this a legendary hideout for cattle rustlers in the days of the Wild West.*

**Key's View** gives a sweeping view of the stunning valley, desert, and mountain terrain from its summit.

**Lost Horse Mine**
*A 2-mile (3.2-km) trail leads to this historic gold mine, which was discovered by a cowboy searching for his lost horse. More than $270,000 in gold was extracted during the mine's first decade of operation.*

**KEY**

| | |
|---|---|
| ▬▬ | Freeway |
| ▬ | Major road |
| ▬ | Minor road |
| ▬ | Unsurfaced road |
| - - - | Hiking trail |
| — | National Park boundary |
| 🚶 | Ranger station |
| 🅲 | Fee station |
| Ⓐ | Campsite |
| ⛟ | Picnic area |
| 🌿 | Viewpoint |

## DESERT WILDLIFE

Despite the harshness of the arid desert environment, a variety of animals thrives here. In many cases, they have adapted to cope with lack of water. The kangaroo rat gets both its food and water from seeds alone, while its very large hind feet enable it to travel over the hot sand. Powerful legs, rather than wings, also serve the roadrunner, which gets its moisture from insects and small prey. The jackrabbit is born with a full coat of muted fur to camouflage it from large predators such as the coyote, bobcat, and eagle.

**Coyote, wily denizen of the desert**

## VISITORS' CHECKLIST

**Road map** D5. 🚌 *Desert Stage Lines from Palm Springs to Twentynine Palms.* 🏛 **Oasis Visitors Center** 74485 National Park Drive, Twentynine Palms. **Tel** (760) 367-5500. ⬡ daily. ⬡ Dec 25. **www**.nps.gov/jotr

0 kilometers 10

0 miles 10

**The arid wilderness** of the Colorado Desert *(see p203)* occupies the park's eastern half. This inhospitable region is difficult to reach.

PINTO MOUNTAINS

COXCOMB MOUNTAINS

PINTO BASIN

...la ...us ...den

Pinto Basin Road

HEXIE MOUNTAINS

Cottonwood 🥾
Cottonwood Spring ⛺

...ONWOOD ...AINS

Lost Palms Oasis

EAGLE MOUNTAIN

ALM ...RINGS

BLYTHE

**Lost Palms Oasis**
*A 4-mile (6.4-km) trail leads through attractive desert scenery to the largest group of palms in the park. It is one of the few areas where water occurs naturally near the surface.*

**Cottonwood Spring** is a man-made oasis of palms and cottonwood trees that attracts desert birds. There is a visitors' center nearby.

**Cholla Cactus Garden**
*A dense concentration of cholla cacti are the focal point of a short nature trail featuring desert flora and fauna. But beware – the cactus's fluffy fingers are really sharp spines.*

# THE MOJAVE DESERT

The Mojave Desert is the state's greatest secret, all too often missed by travelers who zoom through it on the interstate highway. The desert is a harsh environment – Death Valley is one of the hottest places in the United States. But this dry region supports a surprising amount of plant life and for a few weeks each year, when the wildflowers appear amid the arid rocks, it becomes hauntingly beautiful.

The Mojave Desert was a year-round overland gateway to California for much of the 19th century. Trappers, traders, and early settlers traveled hundreds of miles along the Old Spanish Trail from Santa Fe in New Mexico to Los Angeles. Passing through the towns of Barstow and Tecopa, the journey across the vast desert was both demanding and dangerous.

In the 1870s, gold, silver, borax, and various other precious minerals were discovered in the region, attracting large numbers of miners. Instant cities such as Calico sprang up, but when the mines became exhausted, many of the settlements were abandoned. In 1883 commercial mining became more viable when the Santa Fe Railroad was completed. Towns located along the route prospered, and the human population of the Mojave Desert increased.

In the early 20th century a new breed of desert lovers emerged. Jack Mitchell settled in the empty expanses of the East Mojave Desert in the 1930s and turned the spectacular Mitchell Caverns into a popular tourist destination. Death Valley Scotty was another desert enthusiast. He spent much of his life in a castle built in the 1920s by his friend, Albert Johnson, near the hottest and lowest point in the western hemisphere. Death Valley National Park now attracts thousands of visitors each year, who come to explore the area's wealth of historical landmarks and impressive natural sights.

The main draw of the Mojave Desert region today, however, is Nevada's Las Vegas, a five-hour drive from Los Angeles. This center of entertainment and gambling is proof that people are still trying to strike it rich in the desert.

**Death Valley's Moorish-style Scotty's Castle**

◁ **Desert shrubs in Death Valley**

# Exploring the Mojave Desert

Most of the Mojave Desert is at an altitude of over 2,000 ft (600 m). It has cold winters and baking-hot summers. Many of the region's rivers and lakes are dry during the summer but are prone to flash floods. The desert is home to an array of plant species and a range of animals, from tortoises to foxes, which have evolved to survive in this climate. Barstow, the largest town in the Mojave region, caters to travelers to and from Las Vegas. The northern Mojave is dominated by the Death Valley National Park. To the east lie the resorts of Lake Havasu.

**Premises of a 19th-century ore smelter in Calico Ghost Town**

## SIGHTS AT A GLANCE

Barstow **3**
Calico Ghost Town **4**
Cinder Cone National Natural Landmark **6**
*Death Valley National Park pp290–93* **9**
Edwards Air Force Base **2**
Kelso Dunes **5**
Lake Havasu **7**
Las Vegas **8**
Red Rock Canyon State Park **1**

## KEY

━━━ Freeway

━━━ Major road

━━━ Secondary road

═══ Minor road

━━━ Scenic route

━━━ Main railway

╌╌╌ Minor railway

━━━ State border

△ Summit

## SEE ALSO

• *Where to Stay* p540–41

• *Where to Eat* p586–7

0 kilometers 25

0 miles 25

**Map labels:** Oasis, Deep Springs, 168, Las Chance Range, Salime Range, Eureka Dunes, Scotty's Castle, Daylight, DEATH VALLEY NATIONAL PARK **9**, Mono Lake, Lone Pine, Stovepipe Wells, 136, Keeler, Towne Pass 1511m, Owens Lake, Panamint Springs, 190, Cartago, Olancha, Darwin, Telescope Peak 3368m, Haiwee Reservoir, 395, Panamint Valley, Dunmovin, China Lake Naval Weapons Centre, Coso Junction, Argus Range, Little Lake, Pearsonville, Pioneer Point, 178, China Lake, Searles Dry Lake, Inyokern, Trona, Ridgecrest, Straw 1602m, 14, 395, RED ROCK CANYON STATE PARK **1**, Cantil, Koehn Dry Lake, China Lake Naval Weapons Centre, Bakersfield, California City, Mojave, North Edwards, Harper Lake, CALICO, Edwards, EDWARDS AIR FORCE BASE **2**, 58, Hinkley, BARSTOW **3**, 14, Rogers Dry Lake, 395, Hodge, Dag, Los Angeles, Helendale, 15, Adelanto, Victorville, Apple V, San Bernardino, 18

**Sand dunes north of Furnace Creek in the Death Valley National Park**

### GETTING AROUND

I-15 crosses the region. It links San Diego to Las Vegas, Nevada, via San Bernardino. This route follows the northern border of the East Mojave National Preserve, and I-40 skirts its southern border. The main south-north route across the desert is Hwy 127, from which Hwy 190 branches out, crossing the Death Valley National Park from southeast to southwest. In the west, US Hwy 395 leads south to LA. For safety reasons, it is vital that visitors to the desert obey posted signs and do not stray from main roads. Always carry water, a jack, a usable spare tire, a cell phone, and stay close to your vehicle if you break down. There is no public access to the area's clearly marked military zones (*see p284*).

**Stunning colors of Red Rock Canyon**

# Red Rock Canyon State Park ❶

**Road map** D5. 🚌 *from Mojave, Ridgecrest.* **Visitors' Center Tel** *(661) 946-6092.* ☐ *daily.* www.parks.ca.gov

Alternate layers of white clay, red sandstone, pink volcanic rocks, and brown lava are spectacularly combined in Red Rock Canyon. This beautiful state park is situated in the El Paso Mountains, which lie at the southern end of the Sierra Nevada Mountains. Like the High Sierras *(see p484)*, Red Rock Canyon is the product of plate movements that pushed up the bedrock approximately 3 million years ago. The western side of the canyon slopes gently upward in stark contrast to the high, abrupt cliffs on its eastern side, which have been carved and crenellated by water and wind.

Three major desert ecozones overlap here, providing a wealth of plant and animal life. Eagles, hawks, and falcons nest in the cliffs. Coyotes, kit foxes, bobcats, and various reptiles, such as the desert iguana, are common. The landscape has been used as the backdrop for countless Westerns, advertisements, and science-fiction films, making it oddly familiar to many visitors.

# Edwards Air Force Base ❷

**Road map** D5. **Tel** *(661) 277-1110.* 🚌 *from Mojave, Rosamond.* ☐ *Mon–Fri.* ● *public hols.* 📷 ♿ 🎥 *1st & 3rd Fri of month – by appt only.* www.edwards.af.mil

While it is famous around the world as the site of the West Coast space shuttle landings,

Edwards Air Force Base has been steeped in the history of America in flight since 1933. The 65-sq-mile (168-sq-km) flat expanse of Rogers Dry Lake provides an enormous natural runway that is perfect for emergency landings. The area's year-round fine and clear weather adds to its suitability for aircraft testing and the training of test pilots. It was here that the very first jet-propelled aircraft was tested in 1942. Here, too, Captain Chuck Yeager became the first to break the sound barrier on October 14, 1947, in

**Space shuttle Atlantis landing at Edwards Air Force Base**

a Bell XS-1 rocket plane. Fifty pilots still graduate each year from the Test Pilot School.

Edwards offers free guided tours of its NASA Dryden Flight Research Center and the space Aeronautics Center, by reservation (30 days in advance). Tours include a video on the history of aeronautics research and a visit to a hangar.

# Barstow ❸

**Road map** D5. 🏠 *24,000.* 🚌 🚊 *681 North First Ave (760 256-8617).* www.barstowchamber.com

During the 19th century, this was a small settlement that served farmers as well as immigrants and miners on the Old Spanish Trail *(see p281)*. In 1886 the new Barstow–San Bernardino rail line opened, linking Kansas City with the Pacific Coast. Barstow's original railroad station, the Casa del

---

## THE MILITARY IN THE MOJAVE

The United States government has set aside vast areas of the Mojave Desert for military use. All such areas are strictly off-limits to civilians. During World War II, the Desert Training Center covered 17,500 sq miles (45,300 sq km) and was used by General Patton to train his forces. Today, smaller military preserves include the China Lake Weapons Center, northeast of Mojave, which is used for live bombing and artillery testing. North of Barstow, the Fort Irwin National Training Center (NTC), which covers more than 1,000 sq miles (2,600 sq km), is an important US Army installation. The NTC has a population of 22,000, including civilian workers. Its desert terrain was used to prepare troops for the Gulf War in 1990–91, and is one of the main US training areas for tanks and weapons.

**T-38 Talon high-altitude jet trainer at Edwards Air Force Base**

---

Restored and reconstructed buildings in Calico Ghost Town

Desierto, has been restored. From 1937 to the late 1950s, Barstow was an important town along Route 66, the only surfaced road from Chicago to the West Coast. The town is best known today as being the midway point on I-15 between Los Angeles and Las Vegas. To the 41 million people who make this journey each year, it is a convenient stopping-off point. But many also come here in search of the precious minerals and gemstones to be found in the surrounding desert.

The **Desert Discovery Center**, in Barstow, has informative indoor displays on the Mojave Desert's flora and fauna. Maps of the area and hotel and restaurant information are available.

**🏛 Desert Discovery Center**
831 Barstow Rd, Barstow.
*Tel* (760) 252-6060. ⬜ 11am–4pm
Tue–Sat. ⬛ Jan 1, Dec 25, public
hols. **http://**discoverytrails.org

## Calico Ghost Town ❹

**Road map** D5. *Tel* (800) 862-5426. 🚌 Yermo. ⬜ 9am–5pm daily.
⬛ Dec 25. 🈯 🅰 **http://**cms.
sbcounty.gov/parks/Parks.aspx

Calico Ghost Town, 11 miles (18 km) east of Barstow, is a late 19th-century mining town, which is part-authentic and part-reconstruction. Silver was found in the Calico Mountains on March 26, 1881, and soon hundreds of miners arrived. Some of the veins they struck were so rich that they produced 25 lb (11 kg) of silver per ton. Two years later, borax was discovered 3 miles (5 km) east of Calico, and the town's prosperity seemed assured. During the 1880s, Calico boasted a population of 1,200

**A flint tool from the Early Man Site**

but after the price of silver fell and the equally valuable borax gave out, the miners left. By 1907, Calico was a ghost town.

Walter Knott, founder of Knott's Berry Farm® *(see p236),* began the restoration process in the 1950s. Calico's isolation and desert setting reinforce the sense of a rough old mining town. Many of the original buildings remain, and visitors can take a ride in a mine train or explore tunnels in Maggie Mine, one of the most famous silver mines on the West Coast. Shows and tours are also held, including mock "shoot-outs," which are staged on the main street daily.

### Environs
About 10 miles (16 km) west of Calico lies the **Calico Early Man Site**. At this archaeological site, thousands of 100,000-year-old stone tools have been discovered. They were made by North America's earliest known inhabitants, who once lived in this area. The renowned archaeologist and paleontologist Dr. Louis Leakey was director of the site from 1964 to 1972.

**🏛 Calico Early Man Site**
Off I-15 & Minneola Rd.
*Tel* (760) 252-6000. ⬜ 12:30–
4:30pm Wed, 9am–4:30pm Thu–
Sun. ⬛ Jan 1, Jul 4, Dec 25. 🈯

Casa del Desierto, Barstow's historic railroad station

Mesquite mud flats in Death Valley National Park *(see pp290–93)* ▷

## Kelso Dunes ❺

**Road map** E5. 🚃 *Baker.* **Tel** *Mojave National Preserve (760) 252-6100.* ⭕ *daily.* **www.**nps.gov/moja

Kelso Dunes tower more than 600 ft (160 m) above the desert floor. Situated in the Mojave National Preserve, the dunes are formed from grains of golden rose quartz that have been blown from the Mojave River basin, 35 miles (56 km) to the west. Known as the "singing" dunes, they emit buzzing and rumbling sounds caused by the upper layers of sand sliding down the face of the dune, producing vibrations that are then amplified by the underlying sand.

**The desert floor with the Kelso Dunes in the background**

## Cinder Cones National Natural Landmark ❻

**Tel** *(760) 252-6100.* ⭕ *open daily.* **www.**nps.gov/moja

The 32 cinder cones silhouetted against the horizon of Mojave National Preserve

**Looking inside a lava tube at Cinder Cones**

**The original London Bridge, now located in Lake Havasu City**

were designated a National Natural Landmark in 1973. The hills of red and black volcanic rocks, and the black basalt lava flows surrounding them, are the result of volcanic activity that occurred about 7.6 million years ago. Cinder cones are formed when small streams of scorching lava are spewed through the cooler air, making the lava solidify and preserving small pockets created by escaping gases.

The light, cratered rocks created by the eruption accumulated around the vent to create captivating conical hills. The lava that did stream out across the desert ground created spectacular lava tubes, or tunnels.

The cinder cones that remain today form a serene landscape that tourists can either hike to or view from Kelbaker Road. The lava tube can also be entered, although it is not maintained by the National Park Service, and cell phone service is unreliable, so visitors are advised to speak with park rangers for seasonal safety recommendations.

## Lake Havasu ❼

**Road map** E5. 🚃 *Las Vegas.* **Tel** *(928) 453-3444.* **www.**golakehavasu.com

Lake Havasu is a 46-mile (74-km) long reservoir, which was created in 1938 when the Colorado River was blocked by the Parker Dam *(see p203)*. Lake Havasu City, a resort town on the border between California and Arizona, was developed by the millionaire Robert McCulloch in the 1960s. McCulloch imported the historic London Bridge stone-by-stone to the newly created development. The bridge spans the Bridgewater Channel, which was dredged especially for it and leads from Lake Havasu to Thomson Bay.

The lake itself lies within a National Wildlife Refuge, which is frequented by bird-watchers and anglers. There are many camp sites and marinas that offer houseboats, boats, and water-sports equipment for rent. Several short boat tours around the lake are available. A daily three-hour excursion to Topock Gorge, at the northern end of Lake Havasu, offers a more leisurely introduction to this rugged desert setting.

### Environs

Off Hwy 95, 20 miles (32 km) south of Lake Havasu City, lies the Colorado River Indian Reservation. Here, visitors can admire a collection of giant prehistoric figures, carved out of the rocks that form the desert floor. In both human and animal form, it is not known whether the figures were made for religious or artistic reasons.

# Las Vegas

Las Vegas is in Nevada, 45 miles (72 km) from the California border. With the construction of the Hoover Dam in the 1930s, it grew into a major city. Gambling was legalized in Nevada in 1931. In 1946 the Flamingo Hotel and Casino were built on the outskirts on what is known as "The Strip." Similar places soon sprang up, and Las Vegas became a 24-hour oasis of gambling and entertainment.

**One of the city's many neon signs**

**Las Vegas "Strip" at dusk**

### Exploring Las Vegas

The gambling capital of the world, Las Vegas is fast becoming the restaurant and theater capital, too. Famed New York, San Francisco, and LA restaurateurs continue to open branches of their establishments along the Strip. Broadway hit musicals and Cirque de Soleil productions (and its famed girlie extravaganzas) keep theaters filled.

After a failed experiment in attracting families with children, Las Vegas has returned to its old Sin City image.

### VISITORS' CHECKLIST

**Road map** E4. 🚶 600,000.
✈ McCarran Int. Airport, 4 miles (6.5 km) S of Las Vegas. 🚌 200 S Main St. 🚉 1 Main St. 🚏 3150 Paradise Rd (702 892-0711).
**www**.lvcva.com **TI Hotel and Casino** 3300 Las Vegas Blvd. **Tel** (702) 894-7111. **Mirage Hotel and Casino** 3400 Las Vegas Blvd. **Tel** (702) 791-7111. **Luxor Las Vegas** 3900 Las Vegas Blvd. **Tel** (702) 262-4000. **Venetian Hotel and Casino** 3355 Las Vegas Blvd. **Tel** (702) 414-1000. **Wynn Las Vegas** 3131 Las Vegas Blvd. **Tel** (702) 770-7000.

This colorful city has about 2 million permanent residents, with its own museums and cultural institutions. However, it is the 37 million tourists a year who continue to fuel the amazing development of the US's gambling capital.

Hotels here provide more than food, lodging, and casinos. They are architectural marvels and offer some of the best free entertainment in town. T I (the Treasure Island Hotel) stages mock sea battles between pirate ships. Next door is the Mirage Hotel with its exploding volcano out front. The Luxor, built on the same scale as the pyramids of Egypt, houses the largest atrium in the world, complete with animatronic camels, Egyptian decor and high-tech laser shows. The nearby Venetian Hotel offers gondola rides on its own grand canal, while the Wynn has its own golf course.

### 🏛 Stratosphere Tower

2000 Las Vegas Blvd S.
**Tel** (702) 380-7777.
At 1,149 ft (350 m), Stratosphere Tower is the tallest freestanding observation tower in the United States. At the top there is an incomparable view of Las Vegas from two observation decks (the views are best seen at night), a revolving restaurant and cocktail lounge, and three wedding chapels. The world's highest roller-coaster ride has been replaced by the three highest thrill rides in the world.

### 🏛 Fremont Street Experience

Bordered by Charles & Stewart Sts.
**Tel** (702) 678-5777. ◯ daily.
Las Vegas's first gaming license was issued on Fremont Street in the 1930s. Over the years, this downtown area became known as "Glitter Gulch," due to its profusion of neon signs and lights. Now five blocks of Fremont, stretching from Main Street to Las Vegas Boulevard, have been transformed into the Fremont Street Experience – a covered pedestrian promenade. Casinos line the street. A spectacular light and sound show is held each night, using over 12 million LED lights.

### Environs

Lake Mead, which lies 25 miles (40 km) east of Las Vegas, was created by the construction of Hoover Dam, completed in 1936. The lake extends 110 miles (175 km) and has more than 500 miles (800 km) of shoreline. Scuba-diving, boating, water-skiing, and fishing facilities are all available. There are daily tours of the 726-ft- (220-m-) high dam and a visitors' center with exhibits on the region's natural history. The Valley of Fire State Park, 55 miles (88 km) northeast of Las Vegas, has stunning orange sandstone formations. Petroglyphs and other remains of an ancient Native American civilization can still be seen. Red Rock Canyon (not the same as the park on *page 284*), 15 miles (24 km) west of Las Vegas, has 3,000-ft- (900-m-) high escarpments and ridges, and trails for all levels of hikers.

**Stratosphere Tower**

# Death Valley National Park 9

Throughout the summer months, Death Valley National Park has the highest mean temperature of anywhere on the planet. This is a land·of wrenching extremes, a sunken trough in the earth's crust that reaches the lowest point in North America. The valley is guarded on both sides by ranges of rugged mountains. The range on the western side soars 11,000 ft (3,350 m) to form razor-sharp peaks. Even though it is inhospitable for half the year, Death Valley is also a place of subtle colors and polished canyons, of burning salt flats and delicate rock formations. It is now one of the most unique and popular tourist destinations in the state of California.

### Central Death Valley
Furnace Creek, with its various provisions and accommodation centers, is located in the heart of Death Valley. Many of the most impressive sights in the park are within easy reach of this visitors' complex.

### Salt Creek
Salt Creek supports the hardy pupfish. Endemic to Death Valley, the pupfish can live in water almost four times as salty as the sea and withstand temperatures of up to 111° F (44° C). The fish attract other wildlife, including great blue herons. Wooden walkways allow visitors to explore this unique site without disturbing the fragile habitat.

### ⌂ Borax Museum
Furnace Creek Ranch.
**Tel** (760) 786-2345. ◻ daily.
Borax was discovered in Death Valley in 1873, but mining did not begin until the 1880s when crystallized borate compounds

**Ruins of the Harmony Borax Works processing plant**

were taken to the Harmony Borax Works to be purified. They were then loaded onto wagons and hauled by teams of 20 mules the 165 miles (265 km) to Mojave Station. Each team of mules pulled two wagons carrying up to 10 tons of borax each. The wagons carried their heavy mineral loads from 1883 to 1888.

Used for producing glass that is heat-resistant, borax is more commonly used today as an ingredient in washing powder
The Borax Museum has displays of mining tools and transport machinery used at the 19th-century refinery. On Hwy 190, 1 mile (1.5 km) north of the Death Valley Visitor Center the eerie ruins of the Harmony Borax Works can still be seen.

### ⌂ Furnace Creek Visitor Center
Rte 190, Furnace Creek.
**Tel** (760) 786-3200. ◻ daily.
🖳 www.nps.gov/deva
Interesting exhibits and a 20-minute film explain the natural and human history of Death Valley. Evening park-ranger programs and guided walks are available.

### Furnace Creek
At Furnace Creek, millennia of flash floods have carved a natural gateway into Death Valley through the hills to the east. The springs here have drawn Shoshone Indians for thousands of years. Today, the same abundant springs make Furnace Creek a desert oasis and the de facto center of Death Valley. Shaded by date-bearing palms are restaurants and motels. The world's lowest golf course is also here, lying at 214 ft (65 m) below sea level. The Furnace Creek Inn (*see p541*), a four-star hotel built in the 1920s, sits above the valley on a small mesa.

**Historic Inn at Furnace Creek, set in spectacular surroundings**

*For hotels and restaurants in this region see pp540–42 and pp586–7*

Salt formations at the Devil's Golf Course

## Southern Death Valley

Some of the valley's most breathtaking natural features are to be found in this area south of Furnace Creek.

### Golden Canyon

Just over 3 miles (5 km) south of Furnace Creek on Hwy 178, a 1-mile (1500-m) hike leads into Golden Canyon. The mustard-colored walls, after which the canyon was named, are best seen in the afternoon. Native Americans used the red clay at the canyon mouth for ceremonies. The layers of rock were originally horizontal, but geological activity has tilted them to a 45° angle.

A paved road once led into the Golden Canyon, but it was washed out by a sudden storm in 1976. The battered state of the few remaining stretches of the road demonstrate the sheer power of fast-flowing water.

### Devil's Golf Course

This expanse of salt pinnacles is located 12 miles (19 km) south of Furnace Creek, off Hwy 178. Until about 2,000 years ago, successive lakes covered this area. When the last lake evaporated, it left behind alternating layers of salt and gravel, at least 1,000 ft (305 m) deep and covering 200 sq miles (520 sq km). As surface moisture continued to evaporate, ridges and spires of crystallized salt formed. The ground is now 95 percent salt. Visitors can hear the salt expand and contract during changes of temperature. New crystals (with a whiter hue) are constantly forming.

### Badwater

Temperature increases as elevation decreases, so the air at Badwater can reach 120° F (49° C). With the ground temperature 50 percent higher than the air temperature, it really is possible to fry an egg on the ground here. Rain is very rare, although flash flooding, caused by rainstorms, is common. In spite of its inhospitable environment, Badwater is home to several species of insect and to the endemic Badwater snail.

### Northern Death Valley

This area includes Ubehebe Crater (see p292), where only a few tourists venture, despite the beauty of the landscape. Scotty's Castle, which has more visitors per year than any other sight in the park, is also here.

### Scotty's Castle

Hwy 267. *Tel* (760) 786-2392.
**Castle** daily. **Grounds** daily. **www**.nps.gov/deva
Albert Johnson began work on his "Death Valley Ranch" in 1922 after rejecting an original design by Frank Lloyd Wright. Materials were hauled from a railroad line 20 miles (32 km) away. When work ended in 1931 the castle covered more than 30,000 sq ft (2,800 sq m). Johnson died in 1948. "Death Valley Scotty" (see p292), who lent his name to Johnson's ranch, was allowed to remain there until his death in 1954.

### Western Death Valley

Sand dunes cover 15 sq miles (39 sq km) on this side of the park, not far from the second-largest outpost in Death Valley, Stovepipe Wells (see p292).

### Sand Dunes

A walk along the 14 sq miles (36 sq km) of undulating sand dunes, north of Stovepipe Wells, is one of the greatest experiences of Death Valley. Shifting winds blow the sand into the classic crescent dune configuration. Mesquite trees dot the lower dunes. A variety of wildlife feeds on the seeds of these trees, such as kangaroo rats and lizards. Included among the region's other, mainly nocturnal, creatures are the rattlesnake, the chuckwalla lizard, and the coyote.

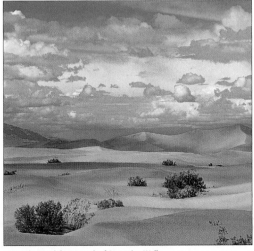

Impressive sand dunes north of Stovepipe Wells

# A Tour of Death Valley

The Native Americans called the valley Tomesha, referring to the ochre-colored rock in the surrounding hills. The valley is also the site of the highest recorded temperature in the United States: 134° F (57° C) in the shade, in July 1913. Death Valley stretches for some 140 miles (225 km) north to south and was once an insurmountable barrier to miners and emigrants. The valley and surrounding area were declared a National Park *(see pp290–91)* in 1994. It is now accessible to visitors, who can discover this stark and unique landscape by car and by taking short walks from the main roads to spectacular viewpoints. However, this remains the California desert at its harshest and most awe-inspiring.

### Scotty's Castle ⑧

This incongruous Moorish-sty castle was commissioned by Albert Johnson at a cost of $2 million. However, the public believed it belonged to Walter Scott, an eccentric prospector. The house remained unfinishe after Johnson lost his money i the Wall Street Crash of 1929. 1970 the building was bought by the National Park Service, who now hold hourly guided tours of the interior *(see p291*

### Ubehebe Crater ⑦

This is one of a dozen volcanic craters in the Mojave area. The Ubehebe Crater is at least 2,000 years old. It is more than 900 yds (800 m) wide and 500 ft (150 m) deep.

## DEATH VALLEY SCOTTY

Walter Scott, would-be miner, beloved charlatan, and sometime performer in Buffalo Bill's Wild West Show, liked to tell visitors to his home that his wealth lay in a secret gold mine. That "mine" was, in fact, his friend Albert Johnson, a Chicago insurance executive, who built the castle where Scott lived and received visitors. Built during the 1920s by European craftsmen and local Native American labor, the castle represents a mixture of architectural styles and has a Moorish feel. Scott never owned the land or the building, and Johnson paid all his bills. "He repays me in laughs," said Johnson. Although Scott died in 1954, the edifice is still known as Scotty's Castle.

### Stovepipe Wells ⑥

Stovepipe Village, founded in 1926, was the valley's first touri resort. According to legend, a lumberjack traveling west struc water here and stayed. An old stovepipe, similar to the ones that were then used to form th walls of wells, marks the site.

Grandiose Scotty's Castle

## KEY

| | |
|---|---|
| ▬▬ | Tour route |
| ═══ | Other roads |
| ℹ | Tourist information |
| 🚶 | Ranger station |
| ⛽🍴 | Gas station |

**Zabriskie Point** ②
Made famous by Antonioni's 1960s film of the same name, Zabriskie Point offers views of the multicolored mud hills of Golden Canyon *(see p291)*. The spot was named after a former general manager of the borax operations in Death Valley *(see p290)*.

## TIPS FOR DRIVERS

***Tour length:*** *236 miles (380 km).*
***When to go:*** *The best time to visit is October to April, when temperatures average 65° F (18° C). May to September, when the ground temperature can be extremely hot, should be avoided. Try for an early start, especially if you are planning to take any hikes. Always wear a hat and use plenty of sunblock.*
***Precautions:*** *Check the weather forecast before you leave and always carry water, a map, a first aid and snake-bite kit, a cell phone, a jack, and a spare tire. Remain near your vehicle if you break down. If you plan to travel in remote areas, inform someone of where you are going and when you plan to return. The area is not suitable for rock climbing. Do not feed wild animals or reach into burrows or holes.*
***Stopping-off points:*** *Furnace Creek Ranch, Furnace Creek Inn, Stovepipe Wells Village (see p541), and Panamint Springs are the only lodging and eating places in the park. Shoshone, Amargosa, and Tecopa, outside the park, also have motels.*
***Emergency:*** *Phone park rangers on 911 or (760) 786-3200.*
*www.nps.gov/deva*

**Furnace Creek** ①
The springs here are one of the few freshwater sources in the desert. They are thought to have saved the lives of hundreds of gold prospectors crossing the desert on their way to the Sierra foothills. The full-service visitors' complex here *(see p290)* is the valley's main population center.

**Dante's View** ③
At 5,475 ft (1,650 m), the view takes in the entire valley floor and is best seen in the morning. The name of the viewpoint was inspired by Dante's *Inferno*. In the distance is Telescope Peak in the Panamint Range.

190

Wax Museum •

**Death Valley Museum and Visitor Center**

Golden Canyon

► DEATH VALLEY JUNCTION

190

Furnace Creek Wash

Devil's Golf Course

TECOPA HOT SPRINGS

178

**Badwater** ④
Badwater *(see p291)* is the lowest point in North America. It lies 282 ft (85 m) below sea level and is one of the world's hottest places. The water is not poisonous, but it is unpalatable, filled with sodium chloride and sulfates.

**Artist's Palette** ⑤
These multicolored hills of cemented gravels were created by mineral deposits and volcanic ash. The colors are at their most intense in the late afternoon sun.

0 kilometers 10

0 miles 10

# SAN FRANCISCO AND THE BAY AREA

# San Francisco and the Bay Area at a Glance

San Francisco is a compact city and much of the central area can be explored on foot. The many hills give rise to some strenuous climbing, but are useful landmarks for orientation and offer superb views. A rich ethnic mix adds a distinctive character to the city's many neighborhoods. The smaller cities of Oakland and Berkeley on the East Bay are reached via the Bay Bridge, while to the north, Golden Gate Bridge links the peninsula to the Marin Headlands and the Point Reyes National Seashore. To the south are the colonial city of San Jose and rugged stretches of coastline inhabited by a variety of flora and fauna.

**LOCATOR MAP**

San Francisco & the Bay Area

***Golden Gate Bridge***
*Built in 1937, the bridge is as much a part of the landscape as the craggy Marin Headlands and the idyllic bay* (see pp380–81).

GOLDEN GATE PARK
AND THE PRESIDIO
*(see pp364–81)*

***Palace of Fine Arts***
*Built for the Panama-Pacific Exposition of 1915, this Neo-Classical monument was fully restored in 1962* (see p349).

◁ Golden Gate Bridge over a foggy San Francisco Bay

**BAY AREA**
*pp410-31*

San Francisco

0 kilometers 25

0 miles 25

**Coit Tower**
*The 1933 tower is floodlit at night (see p343).*

FISHERMAN'S WHARF AND NORTH BEACH
*(see pp332–43)*

CHINATOWN AND NOB HILL
*(see pp324–31)*

PACIFIC HEIGHTS AND THE CIVIC CENTER
*(see pp346–53)*

DOWNTOWN
*(see pp310–23)*

HAIGHT ASHBURY AND THE MISSION
*(see pp354–63)*

**Chinatown Gateway**
*This elaborate gate is the entrance to the city's historic Chinatown (see p328).*

**Mission Dolores**
*The oldest building in San Francisco is one of the 21 Franciscan missions in California (see p361).*

**City Hall**
*The building is the city's most imposing structure, with a vast rotunda displaying a wealth of architectural detail (see p353).*

0 kilometers 2

0 miles 2

# The Shape of San Francisco

**San Francisco road sign**

San Francisco, with its estimated 43 hills, sits at the tip of a peninsula, surrounded by the Pacific Ocean to the west and San Francisco Bay to the east. To the north, linked by the Golden Gate Bridge, are the rugged Marin Headlands and the protected wildlife area of the Point Reyes Peninsula. The Diablo Coast Range, with the 3,850-ft (1,170-m) Mount Diablo at its heart, forms a mountainous backdrop to the heavily populated cities of Richmond, Oakland, and Berkeley in the East Bay, and divides the region from the flat plains of the Central Valley. To the south, the coastal mountains enclose the industrial Silicon Valley and run along the coastline toward Big Sur.

*Vallejo*
*This town, in the north of the bay, is home to Six Flags Discovery Kingdom wildlife park and oceanarium, which includes dolphin displays* (see p415).

Ferries

*Sausalito*
*This former fishing community, across the Golden Gate Bridge, is lined with Victorian houses looking out toward the bay* (see p414).

RICHM⬤
RICHM
BRIDG
TIBURON
29
37
101
SONOMA MOUNTAINS
MOUNT TAMALPAIS

*POINT REYES NATIONAL SEASHORE*

PACIFIC OCEAN

***Point Reyes Peninsula***
*The rugged coastline of the peninsula, situated on the San Andreas Fault and only partly attached to the mainland, is abundant with wildlife and is a very productive dairy farming community* (see p414).

**The Marin Headlands**
are part of the Golden Gate National Recreation Area. These green hills and quiet beaches offer perfect relaxation away from the city, with hiking, fishing, and birdwatching opportunities (see pp416–17).

**Downtown**
One of the major financial districts in the United States is located in San Francisco's Downtown area. Its skyline is dominated by the Transamerica Pyramid (see pp310–23).

**Livermore**
This rural community is home to the world's largest wind farm, making use of the area's strong winds to produce natural energy (see p426).

**Berkeley** includes the University of California at Berkeley campus, once known for its radicalism (see pp418–21).

**The Diablo Coast Range** separates the East Bay from the Central Valley. Mount Diablo is at the heart of the range (see p426).

AY BRIDGE

**SAN MATEO BRIDGE**

(84)

Golden Gate Bridge

**GOLDEN GATE NATIONAL RECREATION AREA**

**SAN BRUNO MOUNTAINS**

**…eland**
…busy city has a multicultural …ilation and many historic landmarks. …linked to San Francisco by the Bay …ge (see pp422–5).

**San Jose** was originally a Spanish colonial city and preserves its history. It is still home to a large Mexican–American population (see pp428–9).

**Palo Alto**
This town was built up specifically to serve the Stanford University campus, which was created by railroad baron Leland Stanford in 1891 (see p427).

# Victorian Houses in San Francisco

Italianate
window

Despite earthquakes, fires, and the inroads of modern life, thousands of ornate, late- 19th-century houses still line the streets of San Francisco. In fact, in many neighborhoods they are by far the most common type of houses. Victorian houses are broadly similar, in that they all have wooden frames, elaborately decorated with mass-produced ornamentation. Most were built on narrow plots to a similar floor plan, but they differ in the features of the façade. Four main styles prevail in the city, although in practice many houses, especially those constructed in the 1880s and 1890s, combine aspects of two or more styles.

Detail of Queen Anne-style gateway at Chateau Tivoli

## GOTHIC REVIVAL (1850–80)

Gothic Revival houses are the easiest to identify, as they always have pointed arches over the windows and sometimes, over the doors. Other features are pitched gabled roofs, decorated verge-boards (again, with pointed arch motifs), and porches that run the width of the building. The smaller, simpler houses of this type are often painted white, rather than the vibrant colors of later styles.

**No. 1111 Oak Street** *is one of the city's oldest Gothic Revival buildings. Its front garden is unusually large.*

**The pitched roof** over the main façade often runs lengthwise, allowing the use of dormer windows.

**A gabled roof** with ornate verge-boards is the clearest mark of Gothic Revival.

**Gothic porch with cross bracing at No. 1978 Filbert Street**

**Full-width porches** are reached by a central stair.

**Balustrades** on the porch betray the Deep South origins of the style.

## ITALIANATE (1850–85)

Italianate houses were more popular in San Francisco than elsewhere in the US, perhaps because their compact form was suited to the city's high building density. The most distinctive feature of the style is the tall cornice, usually with a decorative bracket, which adds a palatial air even to modest homes. Elaborate decoration around windows and doors is also typical of the style.

**No. 1913 Sacramento Street** *displays a typical formal Italianate façade, modeled on a Renaissance palazzo. The wood boarding is made to look like stone.*

**Tall cornices**, often with decorative brackets, conceal a pitched roof.

**Imposing entrance with Italianate porch**

**Symmetrical windows** are capped by decorative arches.

**Neo-Classical doorways**, sometimes with ornate pedimented porches, are a typical Italianate touch.

## STICK (1860–90)

This architectural style, with its ungainly name, is perhaps the most prevalent among Victorian houses in the city. Sometimes also called "Stick–Eastlake" after London furniture designer Charles Eastlake, this style was intended to be more architecturally "honest." Vertical lines are emphasized, both in the wood-frame structure and in ornamentation. Bay windows, false-gabled cornices, and square corners are key identifying features.

*No. 1715–17 Capp Street is a fine example of the Stick–Eastlake style, with a plain façade enlivened by decorative flourishes.*

**Gabled roof with Eastlake windows at No. 2931 Pierce Street**

**Wide bands of trim** often form a decorative truss, emphasizing the underlying structure of Stick houses.

**Decorative gables** filled with "sunburst" motifs are used on porches and window frames.

**Adjoining front doors** can be protected by a single projecting porch.

## QUEEN ANNE (1875–1905)

The name "Queen Anne" does not refer to a historical period; it was coined by the English architect Richard Shaw. Queen Anne houses combine elements from many decorative traditions but are marked by their towers, turrets, and large decorative panels on wall surfaces. Many of the houses display intricate spindle-work on balustrades, porches, and roof trusses *(see pp30–31)*.

**Palladian windows** were used in gables to give the appearance of an extra floor.

**Queen Anne gable filled with ornamental panels at No. 818 Steiner Street**

**Queen Anne turret topped by a finial at No. 1015 Steiner Street**

**Round, square, and polygonal turrets and towers** are typical of Queen Anne-style houses.

**Gable pediments** hold ornamental windows and decorative panels.

**The curved window frame** is not itself characteristic of Queen Anne style, but many houses include features borrowed from other styles.

**The asymmetrical façade** *of No. 850 Steiner Street, together with its eclectic ornament, is typical of a Queen Anne house. Such features are often painted in various bright colors.*

### WHERE TO FIND VICTORIAN HOUSES

# San Francisco's Cable Cars

The cable car system was launched in 1873, and its inventor Andrew Hallidie rode in the first car. He was inspired to tackle the problem of transporting people up the city's steep slopes after witnessing a bad accident, when a horse-drawn tram slipped down a hill, dragging the horses with it. His system was a success, and by 1889 cars were running on eight lines. Before the 1906 earthquake *(see pp52–3)*, more than 600 cars were in use. With the advent of the internal combustion engine, cable cars became obsolete, and in 1947 attempts were made to replace them with buses. After a public outcry the present three lines, using 17 miles (25 km) of track, were retained.

**Cable car traffic lights**

**The Cable Car Museum** *garages the cars at night, and is a repair shop, museum, and powerhouse for the entire cable car system (see p331).*

Bell

POWE[

**The gripman** *has to be strong, with good reflexes. Only a third of candidates pass the training course.*

Sand box

Grip handle

Center plate and jaws grip the cable

Emergency brake

Wheel brake

Cable

## HOW CABLE CARS WORK

Engines in the central powerhouse wind a looped cable under the city streets, guided by a system of grooved pulleys. When the gripman in the cable car applies the grip handle, the grip reaches through a slot in the street and grabs the cable. This pulls the car along at a steady speed of 9.5 mph (15.5 km/h). To stop, the gripman releases the grip and applies the brake. Great skill is needed at corners where the cable passes over a pulley. The gripman must release the grip to allow the car to coast over the pulley.

**Cable car grip mechanism**

Grip handle

Destination board

Wooden beams

Grip crotch

Brake lever

Side seating

Cable car floor

Paving stones

Yoke

POWELL and MARKET
AQUATIC PARK
MARITIME MUSEUM
HYDE and BEACH
FISHERMANS WHARF

**Hatch House** *is the name given to a four-story house that needed to be moved in its entirety in 1913. Herbert Hatch used a system of jacks and hoists to maneuver the house across the cable car line without causing any cessation of the service.*

**A cable car celebration** *was held in 1984 after a two-year-long system refurbishment. Each car was refitted, and all lines were replaced with reinforced tracks. The system should now work safely for the next 100 years.*

**A cable car bell-ringing contest** *is held at Union Square every July, when conductors ring out their most spirited rhythms. On the street, the bell signals a warning to other traffic.*

Brake block       Brake shoe

**The original** *San Francisco cable car, tested by Hallidie on Clay Street on August 2, 1873, is on display in the Cable Car Museum (see p331). The cable car system has remained essentially unchanged since its invention.*

**Rebuilding the cable cars** *has to be done with attention to historical detail, since they are designated historic monuments.*

### ANDREW SMITH HALLIDIE

Andrew Smith was born in London in 1836 and later adopted his uncle's surname. He trained as a mechanic, emigrated to San Francisco in 1852, and formed a company that made wire rope. In 1873 he tested the first cable car, which soon became profitable by opening the hills of the city to development.

# San Francisco's Best: Museums and Galleries

Museums and galleries in the city range from the encyclopedic de Young museum and the Legion of Honor, to the contemporary art of the Museum of Modern Art and its neighbor, the Yerba Buena Center for the Arts. There are several excellent science museums, including the Exploratorium and the California Academy of Sciences. Other museums celebrate the city's heritage, including its ancestral Native American culture, and the people and events that made the city what it is today.

**The Exploratorium** *is one of the best science museums in the US. Here visitors experiment with Sun Painting, a feast of light and color. (See p349.)*

**Legion of Honor** *houses a collection of ancient art through to the Middle Ages and the 19th century, including* Sailboats on the Seine *(c.1874) by Claude Monet. (See pp374–5.)*

**de Young** *museum (see p367) has collections of American art, as well as art from Central and South America, the Pacific Islands, and Africa. It also has textiles and collections of ancient art and 20th-century European art.*

*Golden Gate Park and the Presidio*

*Pacific and t
C*

0 kilometers        2

0 miles        1

**The California Academy of Sciences** *incorporates a planetarium, a natural history museum, and an aquarium in a superbly refurbished building in Golden Gate Park. (See pp370–71).*

**The Chinese Historical Society** *administers one of the city's smallest museums. Inside is a unique collection that details the history of California's Chinese communities and their participation in the development of the state. Included among the exhibits is this magnificent dragon's head. (See p330.)*

**Fort Mason Museums** *house ethnic culture artifacts. Muto by Mimo Paladino (1985) is one of the many exhibits. (See pp350–51.)*

**Wells Fargo History Museum** *is a small gallery that displays the colorful history of California, from the early days of the Gold Rush. This bronze stagecoach (1984) is by M Casper. (See p314.)*

*Fisherman's Wharf and North Beach*

*Chinatown and Nob Hill*

*Downtown*

*ght Ashbury the Mission*

**San Francisco Museum of Modern Art** *is a highly regarded showcase of 20th-century art. The museum was designed by architect Mario Botta. Back View by Philip Guston (1977) is in the permanent collection. The displays are often rotated. (See pp318–19.)*

**Yerba Buena Center for the Arts** *is a gallery that displays diverse works of contemporary art. These change regularly, since there is no permanent collection here. (See pp322–3.)*

**The Asian Art Museum,** *loacted in a beautiful 1917 Beaux Arts building, was once the Old San Francisco Main Library. (See p352.)*

# San Francisco's Murals

San Francisco is proud of its reputation as a culturally rich and cosmopolitan city, qualities evident in the vivid elaborate murals that decorate walls and fences in several areas of the city. Many were painted in the 1930s, and many more in the 1970s, with some appearing spontaneously while others were commissioned. One of the best is the *Carnaval Mural* on 24th Street in the Mission District *(see p362)*; further examples are shown here.

**Mural at Balmy Alley**

**503 Law Office at Dolores and 18th streets**

## PAST AND PRESENT

Some of the best examples of San Francisco's historical mural art can be found inside Coit Tower, where a series of panels, funded during the Great Depression of the 1930s by President Roosevelt's New Deal program, is typical of the period. Many local artists participated in creating the work, and themes include the struggles of the working class and the rich resources of California. The city has since been decorated with a number of modern murals, most notably by the Precita Eyes Mural Arts Studio, as well as many others.

**Detail from Coit Tower mural focuses on California's rich resources**

**Coit Tower mural showing life during the Depression years**

**Precita Eyes Mural Arts Association** *is a community-based organization that seeks to promote the mural arts through collaborative projects. They also sponsor new murals by established artists and run lively mural tours around San Francisco.*

**Mosaic mural (2007) by Precita Eyes, Hillcrest school**

**Balloon Journey, Precita Eyes**

**This mural** *was designed and painted by AYPAL (Asian Pacific Islander Youth Promoting Advocacy and Leadership) students in 2007, in association with Precita Eyes. The association runs a number of community and youth workshops, which produce between 15 and 30 new murals every year. Visitors can see examples of these throughout the Bay Area.*

**Stop the Violence at 1212 Broadway #400, Oakland**

## LIFE TODAY

Life in the modern metropolis is one of the major themes of mural art in San Francisco, as much now as it was in the 1930s. In the Mission District particularly, every aspect of daily life is illustrated on the walls of banks, schools and restaurants, with lively scenes of the family, community, political activity and people at work and play. The Mission District contains around 200 murals, many painted in the 1970s, as part of a city program that paid young people to create works of art in public places. The San Francisco Arts Commission continues to foster this art form.

Golden Gate Bridge

Palace of Fine Arts

Cable car

BART

Tourists

**This Balmy Alley mural** *is a view of the city as tourists see it. The alley, in the Mission District, is decorated with numerous vivid murals, first painted by local children, artists and community workers in the 1970s. The works are now a major attraction.*

**The Learning Wall, Franklin St.,** depicts education and art

*Positively Fourth Street,* a weathered mural at Fort Mason

## THE MULTICULTURAL CITY

San Francisco's heritage of diversity and tolerance comes alive in the murals that enliven its ethnic neighborhoods. In Chinatown, Chinese-American artists evoke memories of the "old country." The Mission District is filled with art, some of it politically inspired, celebrating the struggles and achievements of its Mexican and Latin American population.

Mexican American dancer

American Indian drummer

Caucasian bass player

African American maracas player

**Multicultural San Francisco** *is celebrated at Park Branch Library in Haight Ashbury.*

**Mural in Washington Street** encapsulating life in China

### WHERE TO FIND THE MURALS

# The 49-Mile Scenic Drive

Official sign

Linking the city's most intriguing neighborhoods, fascinating sights and spectacular views, the 49-Mile Scenic Drive (79 km) provides a splendid overview of San Francisco. Keeping to the well-marked route is easy – just follow the blue-and-white seagull signs. Some of these are hidden by overhanging vegetation, so you need to be alert. Set aside a whole day for this trip; there are plenty of places to stop to take photographs or admire the views.

**The Palace of Fine Arts and the Exploratorium ②**
*The grand Neo-Classical building and its modern science museum stand near the entrance to the Presidio.*

**Stow Lake ⑤**
*There is a waterfall and a Chinese pavilion on the island in this picturesque lake. Boats can be rented.*

Queen Wilhelmina Tulip Garden

**Sutro Tower ⑧**
*This distinctive orange and white tower is visible from all over the city.*

0 kilometers 2

0 miles 1

**KEY**

— 49-Mile Scenic Drive

❇ Viewpoint

Five-tiered pagoda in Japantown

**Coit Tower** ⑳
*Overlooking North Beach, Telegraph Hill is topped by this tower, which has fine murals and an observation deck.*

**Marina Green** ㉓
*This is an excellent vantage point from which to view or photograph Golden Gate Bridge.*

**Grace Cathedral** ⑱
*This impressive cathedral, based on Notre Dame in Paris, dominates the summit of the city's steepest hill, Nob Hill.*

## TIPS FOR MOTORISTS

**Starting point:** Anywhere. The circuit is designed to be followed in a counterclockwise direction starting and ending at any point.
**When to go:** Avoid driving during rush hours: 7–9am, 4–7pm. Most of the views are as spectacular by night as by day.
**Parking:** Use the parking lots that are situated around the Financial District, the Civic Center, Japantown, Nob Hill, Chinatown, North Beach, and Fisherman's Wharf. Elsewhere, street parking is usually easily available.

## FINDING THE SIGHTS

# DOWNTOWN
# SAN FRANCISCO

**M**ontgomery Street, now right in the heart of the Financial District, was once a street of small shops, where miners came to weigh their gold dust. Wells Fargo built the city's first brick building on the street during the Gold Rush *(see pp48–9)*. Today, old-fashioned

Motif on
Union Bank

banks stand in the shadow of modern skyscrapers. Union Square is the city's main shopping district and has a wealth of fine department stores. SoMa (South of Market) has become the city's "artists' quarter," with its old warehouses converted into studios, bars, and avant-garde theaters.

## SIGHTS AT A GLANCE

### Historic Streets and Buildings
California Historical Society **12**
Ferry Building **10**
Jackson Square Historic District **2**
Merchant's Exchange **7**
Old Mint **25**
Pacific Exchange **8**
Powell Street Cable Car Turntable **23**
Union Bank **6**

### Shops
Crocker Galleria **18**
Gump's **19**
Union Square Shops **22**
Westfield San Francisco Centre **24**

### Modern Architecture
Bank of America **4**
Embarcadero Center **1**
Rincon Center **11**
Transamerica Pyramid **5**
*Yerba Buena Gardens pp322–3* **14**

### Theaters
Theater District **21**

### Hotels
The Palace **16**

### Museums and Galleries
Contemporary Jewish Museum **17**
Museum of Cartoon Art **15**
*Museum of Modern Art pp318–9* **13**
Wells Fargo History Museum **3**

### Parks and Squares
Justin Herman Plaza **9**
Union Square **20**

## GETTING THERE

All streetcar, cable car, and BART lines, and most ferries and bus lines, converge at some point on Market Street – the heart of this section. From Market Street, bus lines reach all parts of the district.

0 meters    400
0 yards     400

### KEY

| | Street-by-Street map *See pp312–3* |
| Cable car terminus |
| BART station |
| Ferry terminus |

◁ **A view of downtown San Francisco at night**

# Street-by-Street: Financial District

San Francisco's economic engine is fueled predominantly by the Financial District, one of the chief commercial centers in the US. It reaches from the imposing modern towers and plazas of the Embarcadero Center to staid Montgomery Street, called the "Wall Street of the West." All the principal banks, brokers, and law offices are situated within this area. The Jackson Square Historical District, north of Washington Street, was once the heart of the business community.

**★ Embarcadero Center**
*The center houses commercial outlets and offices. A shopping arcade occupies the first three tiers of the towers* ❶

**Hotaling Place** is a narrow alley known for its many excellent antique shops.

**Jackson Square Historic District**
*This district, more than any other, recalls the Gold Rush era* ❷

Bus stop (No. 41)

WASHINGTON STREET

BATTERY STREET

SACRAMENTO STREET

SANSOME STREET

MONTGOMERY STREET

**★ Transamerica Pyramid**
*This 853-ft (260-m) skyscraper is now the tallest on the city's skyline* ❺

**The Golden Era Building** was built during the Gold Rush and housed the paper *Golden Era*, for which Mark Twain wrote.

**Union Bank**
*This enormous bank is guarded by fierce stone lions carved by sculptor Arthur Putnam* ❻

**Merchant's Exchange**
*Paintings of shipping scenes line the walls* ❼

**Wells Fargo History Museum**
*An old stagecoach, evoking the Wild West days, is one of the exhibits in this transportation and banking museum* ❸

**Bank of America**
*There are fine views from the 52nd floor of this important banking institution* ❹

0 meters 100
0 yards 100

*For hotels and restaurants in this region see pp542–9 and pp587–95*

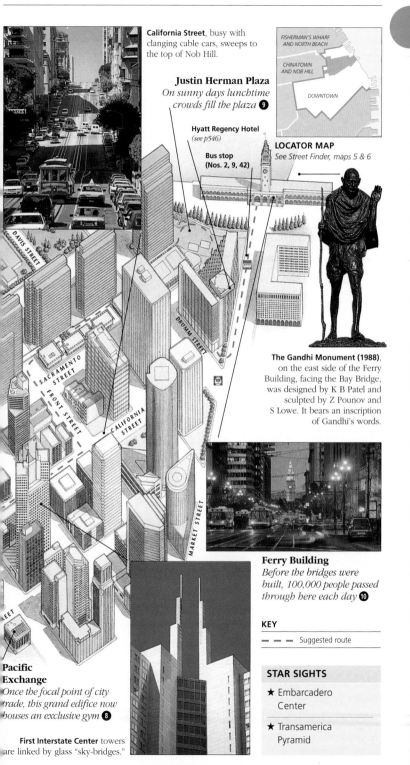

**California Street**, busy with clanging cable cars, sweeps to the top of Nob Hill.

**Justin Herman Plaza**
*On sunny days lunchtime crowds fill the plaza* ❾

**Hyatt Regency Hotel**
(see p546)

**Bus stop**
(Nos. 2, 9, 42)

FISHERMAN'S WHARF
AND NORTH BEACH

CHINATOWN
AND NOB HILL

DOWNTOWN

**LOCATOR MAP**
*See Street Finder, maps 5 & 6*

DAVIS STREET

SACRAMENTO STREET

FRONT STREET

DRUMM STREET

CALIFORNIA STREET

MARKET STREET

**The Gandhi Monument (1988)**,
on the east side of the Ferry Building, facing the Bay Bridge, was designed by K B Patel and sculpted by Z Pounov and S Lowe. It bears an inscription of Gandhi's words.

**Ferry Building**
*Before the bridges were built, 100,000 people passed through here each day* ❿

**KEY**

— — — Suggested route

**Pacific Exchange**
*Once the focal point of city trade, this grand edifice now houses an exclusive gym* ❽

**First Interstate Center** towers are linked by glass "sky-bridges."

**STAR SIGHTS**

★ Embarcadero Center

★ Transamerica Pyramid

## Embarcadero Center ❶

**Map** 6 D3. *Tel* (415) 772-0700.
🚌 1, 42. 🚊 J, K, L, M, N.
🚋 California St. See **Shopping**
p382–7 and **Where to Stay** p545.
www.embarcaderocenter.com

Completed in 1981 after a
decade of construction, San
Francisco's largest redevelop-
ment project stretches from
Justin Herman Plaza to
Battery Street. Office workers
and shoppers use its open
spaces to relax in the sun and
eat their lunch. Five high-rise
towers reach 35 to 45 stories
above the landscaped plazas
and elevated walkways.
   Adjacent to the fourth tower
of the Embarcadero Center is
the swanky Hyatt Regency
Hotel (see p545), whose
interior is just waiting to be
admired. Its 17-story atrium
contains an immense sculpted
globe by Charles Perry,
entitled *Eclipse*. Also housed in
the center is a cinema screen-
ing an impressive array of
independent and foreign films.

Lobby of the Hyatt Regency Hotel at the Embarcadero Center

**Hotaling Place in Jackson Square**

## Jackson Square Historic District ❷

**Map** 5 C3. 🚌 12, 15, 42, 83.

Renovated in the early 1950s,
this neighborhood contains
many historic brick, cast-iron,
and granite façades dating
from Gold Rush days. From
1850 to 1910 it was known as
the Barbary Coast, notorious
for its squalor and the crude-
ness of its inhabitants. The

old Hippodrome theater at
No. 555 Pacific Street contains
bawdy relief sculptures in the
recessed front, which recall
the risqué shows that were
performed there. Today the
buildings are used as showrooms, law offices, and fine
antique shops; the best ones
can be seen in Jackson Street,
Gold Street, Hotaling Place,
and Montgomery Street.

## Wells Fargo History Museum ❸

420 Montgomery St. **Map** 5 C4.
*Tel* (415) 396-2619. 🚌 1, 12, 15,
42. 🚊 Montgomery St. ⏰ 9am–
5pm Mon–Fri. ⬤ public hols. ♿ 📷
www.wellsfargohistory.com

Founded in 1852,
Wells Fargo & Co.
became the greatest
banking and trans-
portation company in
the West and was
influential in the
development of the
American frontier.
   The company moved
people and goods from
the East to the West Coast,
and between the mining
camps and towns of
California. It also
transported gold from
the West Coast to the

**Black Bart, the poet bandit**

East, and delivered mail,
placing mailboxes in
convenient locations to enable
the messengers to sort letters
en route. The Pony Express
was another mail venture in
which Wells Fargo & Co.
played a major role.
   The splendid stagecoaches
on display are famous, particularly for the legendary stories
of their heroic drivers and the
bandits who robbed them. The
best-known bandit was Black
Bart, who left poems at the
scene of his crimes. He stalk-
ed the many lonely roads from
Calaveras County up to the
Oregon border from 1875
to 1883. In one holdup he
mistakenly left behind
his handkerchief. Its
distinctive laundry mark
revealed him as min-
ing engineer Charles
Boles (see p479).
   Museum visitors
can experience
how it felt to sit for
days in a jostling
stagecoach, and listen
to the recorded diary
of an immigrant called
Francis Brocklehurst.
Exhibits include Pony
Express mail, photo-
graphs, early checks,
and gold nuggets from
the famous 1849
Gold Rush.

# Bank of America 4

555 California St. **Map** 5 C4.
**Tel** (415) 433-7500 (Carnelian
Room). 🚌 1, 15. 🚋 California St.

The red granite-clad building
housing the headquarters of
the Bank of America opened
in 1972. Its 52 floors make it
the tallest skyscraper in San
Francisco, and incredible
views from the Carnelian
Room on the 52nd floor show
the fascinating workings of
city life. The Bank of America

was originally the Bank of
Italy, which was founded by
AP Giannini in San Jose *(see
pp428–9)*. It built up a huge
clientele early in the 20th
century by catering to immigrants and investing in the
booming farmlands and small
towns. In the great fire of
1906 *(see pp52–3)*, Giannini
personally rescued his bank's
deposits, carrying them to
safety by hiding them in fruit
crates, so there were sufficient
funds for the bank to invest
in the rebuilding of the city.

*Transcendence* by Masayuki Nagari
(1972) at the Bank of America

# Transamerica Pyramid 5

600 Montgomery St. **Map** 5 C3.
🚌 1, 15, 42. ⬜ 8:30am–4:30pm
Mon–Fri (lobby only). ⬤ public hols.
♿ **www**.thepyramidcenter.com

Capped with a pointed
spire on top of its
48 stories, the pyramid
reaches 853 ft (260 m)
above sea level. It is the
tallest and most widely
recognized building in
the city, and although
San Franciscans disliked
it when it opened in
1972, they have since
accepted it as part of
their city's skyline.
   Designed by William
Pereira & Associates, the
pyramid houses over
1,500 office workers on
a site that is historically
one of the richest in the
city. The Montgomery
Block, which contained
many important offices
and was the largest
building west of the
Mississippi, was built
here in 1853. In the
basement was the
Exchange Saloon,
which was frequented
by Mark Twain/
Samuel Clemens. The
Financial District was
extended south in
the 1860s, and artists
and writers took up
residence in the
Montgomery Block.
The Pony Express
terminus, marked
by a plaque, was
opposite, at
Merchant Street.

**The spire** is hollow, rising 212 ft (64 m) above the
top floor. Lit from inside, it casts a warm, yellow
glow at night. Its purpose is purely decorative.

**The vertical wings** *of the
building rise from the middle of
the ground floor and extend
beyond the frame, which tapers
inward. The eastern wing houses
18 elevator shafts, and the
western wing houses a smoke
tower and emergency stairs.*

**The observation
deck** *is situated on the
ground floor. Here, a
bank of monitors
provides visitors with
views beamed down
from four cameras
that revolve at the
apex of the spire.*

**Earthquake protection** *is
ensured by white precast
quartz aggregate, interlaced
with reinforcing rods at
four places on each floor,
that cover the exterior of the
pyramid. Clearance
between the panels allows
for lateral movement in
case of an earthquake.*

**The shape** *of the
building tapers so that it casts
a smaller shadow than a
conventional design.*

**The 3,678 windows**
take cleaners an entire
month to wash.

**The foundations** rest on a steel and
concrete block, sunk 52 ft (15.5 m)
into the ground and designed to
move with earth tremors.

# Union Bank ⑥

400 California St. **Map** 5 C4.
***Tel*** *(415) 705-7142.* 🚌 *1, 42.*
🚋 *California St.* **Museum of
Money of the American West**
⏱ *9am–5pm Mon–Fri.*
⚫ *public hols.* ♿

William Ralston and Darius
Mills founded this bank in
1864. Ralston, known as
"the man who built San
Francisco," invested profitably
in the Comstock mines *(see
p49).* He used the bank and
his personal fortune to finance
many civic projects in San
Francisco, including the city's
water company, a theater, and
the Palace Hotel *(see p547).*
When economic depression
struck in the 1870s, Ralston's
empire collapsed.

The present colonnaded
building was completed in
1908. In the basement, the
Museum of Money of the
American West displays gold,
coins, old banknotes, and dia-
grams of the Comstock mines.

**Neo-Classical façade of the
Union Bank**

# Merchant's Exchange ⑦

465 California St. **Map** 5 C4.
***Tel*** *(415) 421-7730.* 🚋 *Montgomery
St.* 🚌 *1, 4, 10, 15.* ⏱ **Banking
Hall** *9am–5pm Mon–Fri.* **Lobby**
*24 hours Mon–Fri.* ♿ **www**.
merchantsexchangebuilding.com

The exchange, designed by
Willis Polk in 1903 survived the
great fire of 1906 with little
damage *(see pp52–3).* Inside,
William Coulter seascapes line
the walls, depicting epic maritime scenes from the age of
steam and sail. This was the
focal point of San Francisco's
commodities exchange in the
early 20th century, when

look-outs in the tower relayed
news of ships arriving from
abroad. Now dwarfed by
skyscrapers, it once dominated the skyline.

# Pacific Exchange ⑧

115 Sansome St. **Map** 5 C4. 🚌 *3,
4, 15, 42.* ⚫ *closed to the public.*
**www**.pacific.ex.com

This was once America's
largest stock exchange outside New York. Founded in
1882 it occupied these buildings, which were remodeled
in 1930 by Miller and Pflueger
from the existing US Treasury.
The monumental granite
statues that flank the Pine
Street entrance were sculpted
by Ralph Stackpole, also in
1930. The building is now
closed, its once-frantic
trading floor silent due to
the emergence of electronic
and Internet trading.

# Justin Herman Plaza ⑨

**Map** 6 D3. 🚌 *many buses.* 🚋 *F, J,
K, L, M, N.* 🚋 *California St.*

Popular with lunchtime
crowds from the nearby
Embarcadero Center *(see
p314),* this plaza is best
known for its avant-garde
Vaillancourt Fountain,
built in 1971 by the
Canadian artist Armand
Vaillancourt. The fountain
is modeled from huge
concrete blocks, and
some people find it
ugly, especially when
it is allowed to run
dry during times of
drought. However,
you are allowed to
climb on and through
it, and with its
splashing pools and
columns of falling
water, it is an
intriguing public work
of art when function-
ing as intended.

The area is often
rented out to musicians
during the lunch hour –
the popular rock
band U2 performed a

**The Vaillancourt Fountain in
Justin Herman Plaza**

lunchtime concert here in
1987, after which they spray-
painted the fountain.

# Ferry Building ⑩

Embarcadero at Market St. **Map** 6 E3.
🚌 *many buses.* 🚋 *F, J, K, L, M, N.*
🚋 *California St.* **www**.
ferrybuildingmarketplace.com

Constructed between 1896
and 1903, the Ferry Building
survived the great fire of 1906
thanks to fireboats pumping
water from the bay. The clock
tower is 235 ft (71 m)
high, inspired by the
Moorish bell tower of
Seville Cathedral, Spain. In
the 1930s over 50 million
passengers a year passed
through the building –
many were travelers from
the transcontinental railroad terminal in Oakland
others were commuters
using the 170 daily
ferries between the
city and their homes
across the bay. With
the opening of the
Bay Bridge in 1936
*(see pp422–3),* the
Ferry Building
ceased to be the
city's main entry
point. Today it house
restaurants and shops
A few ferries still cross
the bay, to Larkspur,
Tiburon, and Sausalito
in Marin County *(see
pp414–15),* Alameda
and Oakland in the
East Bay *(see pp422–
3),* and Vallejo in the
North Bay *(see p298)*

**The clock tower on
the Ferry Building**

Rincon Annex mural depicting the Spanish discovery of San Francisco

## Rincon Center ⑪

**Map** 6 E4. 🚌 14.
See **Shopping** pp382–5.

This shopping center, with its soaring atrium and its 90-ft (27-m) fountain, was added on to the old Rincon Annex Post Office Building in 1989. The Rincon Annex dates from 1940 and is well known for its murals by the Russian-born artist Anton Refregier, showing aspects of the history of San Francisco. Some of the works depict harsh images of important events and people of the city, which caused much controversy when first shown.

## California Historical Society ⑫

678 Mission St. **Map** 6 D5. **Tel** (415) 357-1848. 🚇 Montgomery St. ◯ noon–4:30pm Wed–Sat (Library closed Sat). 🅿 🔲 www.california historicalsociety.org

The California Historical Society is dedicated to preserving and interpreting Californiana. The Society offers a reference and research library, museum galleries, and a well-stocked bookstore. There is also an impressive photographic collection, more than 900 oil paintings and watercolors by American artists, and a unique costume collection.

## Museum of Modern Art ⑬

See pp318–19.

## Yerba Buena Gardens ⑭

See pp322–3.

Cartoon art on a US stamp

## Museum of Cartoon Art ⑮

655 Mission St. **Tel** (415) 227-8666. ◯ 11am–5pm Tue–Sun. 🅿 🔲 www.cartoonart.org

Founded in 1984, this is the only museum of original cartoon art on the West Coast. The 10,000 pieces in the collection date from the 18th century to the present day and include the original artwork for such well-known cartoon characters as Popeye, Charlie Brown, L'il Abner, Little Orphan Annie, and Walt Disney's numerous creations. The museum also includes a children's area and offers fun cartooning classes for children and adults.

## The Palace ⑯

2 New Montgomery St. **Map** 5 C4. **Tel** (415) 512-1111. 🚌 7, 8, 9, 21, 31, 66, 71. 🚃 J, K, L, M, N.
See **Where to Stay** p546.
www.sfpalace.com

The original Palace Hotel was opened by William Ralston, one of San Francisco's best-known financiers, in 1875. It was the most luxurious of San Francisco's early hotels, with 7 floors, 700 windows, an inner courtyard, and exotic international decor. It was regularly frequented by the rich and famous. Among its patrons were the actress Sarah Bernhardt and writers Oscar Wilde and Rudyard Kipling. The celebrated tenor Enrico Caruso was a guest at the hotel at the time of the earthquake of 1906 when the hotel, like much of the city, caught fire. It was rebuilt shortly after under the direction of the architect George Kelham, and reopened in 1909. The Garden Court glass dome contains about 63,000 pieces of iridescent glass and totals 12,000 sq ft (1,115 sq m), making it one of the largest expanses of colored glass on Earth.

The Garden Court at the Sheraton Palace Hotel

# San Francisco Museum of Modern Art ⓫

This dramatic museum forms the nucleus of San Francisco's reputation as a leading center of modern art. Created in 1935 with the aim of displaying works from 20th-century artists, it moved into its new quarters in 1995. The focus of Swiss architect Mario Botta's modernist building is the 125-ft (38-m) cylindrical skylight, which channels light down to the first-floor atrium court. The museum has over 26,000 works of art in its collection and 50,000 sq ft (4,600 sq m) of gallery space on four floors. It offers a dynamic schedule of changing exhibits from around the world.

*Zip Light* (1990) by Sigmar Willnauer

**Personal Values**
*Belgian Surrealist René Magritte created this late masterpiece in 1952. It features his use of everyday objects in strange and often unsettling surroundings, all painted in a realistic style.*

★ **No. 14, 1960**
*This oil on canvas was painted by Mark Rothko, a leading Abstract Impressionist. It is one of the most beautiful and hypnotic works from the artist's oeuvre.*

## MUSEUM GUIDE
*The museum shop, auditorium, café, and special events space are on the first floor. On the second floor is the Koret Visitor Education Center and galleries devoted to works from the museum's collection of painting, sculpture, architecture, and design. Photography and special exhibitions are displayed on the third floor, with media arts, special exhibitions, and a sculpture terrace on the fourth floor. The fifth floor galleries feature contemporary works of paintings and sculpture from the museum's collection.*

**The Nest**
*Louise Bourgeois created this spidery sculpture in 1994, at the age of 83. The elongated forms are typical of her work.*

125-ft- (38-m-) tall cylindrical skylight

Second floor

Auditorium

First floor

Main entrance

Emergency staircase

### KEY TO FLOOR PLAN
- Painting and sculpture
- Architecture and design
- Photography and works on paper
- Media arts
- Koret Visitor Education Center
- Special exhibitions
- Non-exhibition space

Fifth floor

★ **California Art**
*This 1861 photographic albumen print of Bridalveil Fall, Yosemite Valley, by Carleton E Watkins is a highlight of the collection.*

Fourth floor

Rooftop Sculpture Garden

Third floor

Atrium

**Blossoms in the Night**
*This 1930 work is by the Swiss artist Paul Klee – an inventive modernist linked to the Blaue Reiter movement, who made his name in Germany before World War II.*

**Koret Visitor Education Center**
*This educational facility offers drop-in events as well as a full list of programs. Art activities are also available for children.*

**Country Dog Gentlemen**
*Bay Area artist Roy De Forest painted this fantasy of a universe guarded by animals in 1972.*

## STAR EXHIBITS

★ No. 14, 1960

★ California Art

**Central plaza of the Crocker Galleria**

# Contemporary Jewish Museum ⑰

736 Mission St. **Tel** (415) 655-7800. 5, 6, 7. J, K, L. 1–8pm Thu, 11am–5pm Fri–Tue. www.thecjm.org

Housed in a building designed by Daniel Libeskind, this museum has wide-ranging exhibitions that celebrate and explore Judaism. These include hands-on activities, art, historical objects, film, and music.

# Crocker Galleria ⑱

Between Post, Kearny, Sutter, and Montgomery Sts. **Map** 5 C4. **Tel** (415) 393-1505. 2, 3, 4. J, K, L, M, N. See **Shopping** pp382–5.

The Crocker Galleria was built in 1982. Inspired by Milan's Galleria Vittorio Emmanuelle, the building features a central plaza under an arched atrium. More than 50 shops and restaurants are housed here, with displays promoting the best of European and American designers.

# Gump's ⑲

135 Post St. **Map** 5 C4. **Tel** (800) 882-8055. 2, 3, 4, 30, 38, 45. J, K, L, M, N. Powell–Mason, Powell–Hyde. 10am–6pm Mon–Sat. See **Shopping** pp382–5. www.gumps.com

Founded in 1861 by German immigrants who were once mirror and frame merchants, this indigenous San Francisco department store has now become a local institution.

Gump's houses the largest collection of fine china and crystal in the United States, by prestigious designers such as Baccarat, Steuben, and Lalique. The store is also celebrated for its oriental treasures, furniture, and rare works of art. The Asian art is particularly fine, especially the jade collection, which enjoys an international reputation. In 1949 Gump's imported a great bronze Buddha and presented it to the Japanese Tea Garden (see pp366–7).

Gump's has a very refined atmosphere and is often frequented by the rich and famous. It is renowned for its extravagant window displays.

# Union Square ⑳

**Map** 5 C5. 30, 38, 45. J, K, L, M, N, T. Powell–Mason, Powell–Hyde.

Union Square was named after the big, pro-Union rallies held here during the Civil War of 1861–5. The rallies galvanized popular support for the Northern cause, which was instrumental in bringing California into the war on the side of the Union. The original churches, gentlemen's clubs, and the synagogue have been replaced by shops and offices. This green square, lined with palm trees, is at the heart of the shopping district and marks the edge of the Theater District. On the west side is the luxurious Westin St. Francis Hotel (see p548). In the center, a bronze statue of the Goddess of Victory stands at the top of a 90-ft (27-m) Corinthian column. Sculpted by Robert Aitken in 1903, it commemorates Admiral Dewey's victory at Manila Bay during the Spanish-American War of 1898.

# Theater District ㉑

**Map** 5 B5. 2, 3, 4, 38. Powell–Mason, Powell–Hyde. See **Entertainment** pp388–91.

Several theaters are located near Union Square, all within a six-block area. The two largest are on Geary Boulevard, the Curran Theater, designed in 1922 by Alfred Henry D Jacobs, which imports Broadway shows, and the Geary Theater, with its Edwardian façade. The Geary Theater is now home to the American Conservatory Theater (ACT), which shows classical and contemporary pieces. The city has a fine reputation for the variety of performances it offers and has always attracted great actors. Isadora Duncan, the innovative 1920s dancer, was born nearby at No. 501 Taylor Street, which is now marked by a plaque.

# Union Square Shops ㉒

**Map** 5 C5. 30, 38, 45. J, K, L, M, N, T. Powell–Mason, Powell–Hyde. See **Shopping** pp382–5.

Many of San Francisco's largest department stores can be found here, including Macy's, Saks Fifth Avenue, and

**Department stores overlooking Union Square**

Rotating a cable car on the Powell Street Turntable

## Westfield San Francisco Centre ㉔

Fifth St and Market St. **Map** 5 C5.
*Tel* (415) 512-5245. 🚌 5, 7, 8, 9, 14,
21, 71. 🚋 J, K, L, M, N. 🚃 Powell–
Mason, Powell–Hyde. ◻ 10am–
8:30pm Mon–Sat, 10am–7pm Sun.
See **Shopping** pp382–5.

Located in the heart of San
Franciso, near Union Square,
the Westfield San Francisco
Centre integrates the existing
San Francisco Centre with the
adjacent former Emporium
department store building
whose dome dates back to
1904 and is the centerpiece of
the project. The mall features
more than 200 shops, restaurants, and cafés, along with
San Francisco's largest day
spa and a Century 9 cinema.

## Old Mint ㉕

Fifth St and Mission St. **Map** 5 C5.
*Tel* (415) 537-1105. 🚌 14, 14L, 26,
27. 🚋 J, K, L, M, N. ◻ by appointment only. **www**.sfhistory.org

San Francisco's Old Mint
produced its last coins in
1937. It was built of granite in
the Classical style by AB Mullet
between 1869 and 1874, hence
its nickname, the "Granite
Lady." Its windows were forti-
fied by iron shutters and its
basement vaults impregnable.
The building was one of the
few to survive the 1906 earthquake (see pp52–3). Following
partial restoration in 1972, the
eastern part of the building
opened to the public for
special events. Plans are
under way to convert The
Mint into a history
museum.

Gump's. The Neiman Marcus
store, at the request of San
Franciscans, has preserved
the 1900 rotunda and skylight
from the City of Paris. The
latter was the city's most
elegant store at the end of the
19th century but was demolished in 1982. As well as the
larger stores, the area houses
many antiquarian bookshops
and smaller boutiques. The
Circle Gallery Building, at
140 Maiden Lane, is a contemporary art gallery. Designed
by Frank Lloyd Wright in
1947, it was the precursor to
his Guggenheim Museum in
New York (see p33).

## Powell Street Cable Car Turntable ㉓

Hallidie Plaza, Powell St at Market St.
**Map** 5 C5. 🚌 many buses. 🚋 J, K,
M, N. 🚃 Powell–Mason, Powell–Hyde.

The Powell–Hyde and the
Powell–Mason cable car lines
are the most spectacular
routes in San Francisco. They
start and end their journeys
to Nob Hill, Chinatown, and
Fisherman's Wharf at the
corner of Powell Street and
Market Street. Unlike the
double-ended cable cars that
are found on the California
Street line, the Powell Street
cable cars were built to move
in one direction only – hence
the need for a turntable at the
end of each line.

After the last passengers
have disembarked, the car is
pushed onto the turntable
and rotated manually by the
conductor and gripman. The
next passengers for the return
journey wait for the half-circle
to be completed amid an ever-
moving procession of street
musicians, local shoppers,
and office
workers.

The impregnable "Granite Lady" Old Mint

# Yerba Buena Gardens 🄸

The construction of the Moscone Center, San Francisco's largest venue for conventions, heralded the start of ambitious plans for Yerba Buena Gardens. New housing, hotels, museums, galleries, shops, restaurants, and gardens have now been built to rejuvenate a once-depressed area. Access the center from Yerba Buena Lane, home to retail shops and a museum.

★ **Yerba Buena Center for the Arts**
*The center is an arts forum, with galleries and regular screenings of contemporary films.*

**Esplanade Gardens**
*Visitors can wander along the paths or relax on benches.*

**The Martin Luther King Jr. Memorial** has words of peace in several languages.

**Children's Creativity Museum**
*This museum is located at the Yerba Buena Children's Garden. It has an ongoing program of events and provides opportunities for youngsters and artists to collaborate in the design and creation of anything from airplanes, robots, and futuristic buildings to mosaics and sculptures.*

## STAR SIGHTS

★ Yerba Buena Center for the Arts

★ San Francisco Museum of Modern Art

## MOSCONE CENTER

Engineer TY Lin found an ingenious way to support the rooftop garden above this huge underground hall without a single interior column. The bases of the eight steel arches are linked, like an archer's bow strings, by cables under the floor. By tightening the cables, the arches exert enormous upward thrust.

### Yerba Buena Center for the Arts Theater

*Performing arts reflecting San Francisco's cultural diversity are presented in the 755-seat indoor theater. There is also an outdoor theater.*

## VISITORS' CHECKLIST

Mission, 3rd, Folsom, and 4th Sts. **Map** 5 C5. 978-2787. 9, 14, 15, 30, 45, 76. J, K, L, M, N. **Children's Creativity Museum** 820-3349. 11am–5pm Wed–Sun (Tue–Sun in the summer). Dec 25. SF Museum of Modern Art (see pp120–24). www.yerbabuenagardens.com

**Yerba Buena Center for the Arts Gallery** noon–5pm Tue, Wed, Fri–Sun (8pm Thu). public holidays. (free first Tue of month).

**North entrance to Moscone Center**

**East Garden**

★ **San Francisco Museum of Modern Art**
This privately funded museum is opposite Yerba Buena Gardens.

**South entrance to Moscone Center**

**Moscone Ballroom** is part of San Francisco's extensive convention facilities. It is available for large conferences and symposia.

**The children's garden** has imaginative play equipment in a pleasant outdoor setting.

**Bowling Center**

**Ice-skating rink**

**Entrance foyer**

**Ballroom**

**Exhibition hall**

**Ground-level rooftop**

**Base of supporting arch**

# CHINATOWN AND NOB HILL

T he Chinese settled around Portsmouth Square during the 1850s; wealthy San Franciscans moved further up Nob Hill where there was more room to build. Today the district recalls the atmosphere of a typical village in Guangdong, although the architecture, customs, and public events are distinctly American hybrids on a Cantonese theme. This densely populated neighborhood has been called the "Gilded Ghetto," because its colorful façades and lively markets stand in contrast to a harsher world where the poor live in undesirable conditions. Nob Hill is San Francisco's most celebrated hilltop, famous for its cable cars, plush hotels, and views. In the late 19th century, the "Big Four," who built the first transcontinental railroad, were among its richest tenants. In 1906, the earthquake and fire *(see pp52–3)* leveled all but one of these houses, but today's luxury hotels still recall the opulence of the Victorian era *(see pp544)*.

Chinese symbol outside the Bank of America

## SIGHTS AT A GLANCE

### Historic Streets and Buildings
Chinatown Alleys ⑤
Chinatown Gateway ①
Grant Avenue ⑥
Nob Hill ⑩

### Galleries and Museums
Cable Car Museum ⑪
Chinese Historical Society of America ⑨

Pacific Heritage Museum ⑧

### Churches and Temples
Grace Cathedral ⑫
Kong Chow Temple ③
Old St. Mary's Church ②
Tien Hau Temple ④

### Parks and Squares
Portsmouth Square ⑦

## KEY

▨ Street-by-Street map
  *See pp326–7*

🚋 Cable car turntable

0 meters    500
0 yards     500

## GETTING THERE
Visit on foot if possible. Car drivers can sometimes park in one of the Nob Hill hotel garages, under Portsmouth Plaza, or at St. Mary's Square in Chinatown. All cable car lines go to Nob Hill and Chinatown.

◁ Colorful oriental architecture along Chinatown's streets

# Street-by-Street: Chinatown

Grant Avenue is the Chinatown for tourists, with dragon lampposts, Chinese pagoda-style roofs, and neighborhood hardware stores selling everything from kites to cooking utensils. Locals shop on Stockton Street, where boxes of vegetables, fish, and other produce spill over onto crowded sidewalks. In the alleys in between, look for temples and family-run restaurants.

**A street lamp in Chinatown**

★ **Chinatown Alleys**
*Authentic sights and sounds of the Orient echo in these busy alleys* **5**

Ross Alley

JACKSON STREET

WASHINGTON STREET

**Chinese Historical Society of America**
*The society's collection of historical artifacts, documents, and photographs is exhibited here* **9**

**Kong Chow Temple**
*Fine Cantonese wood carvings are a feature of this temple* **3**

POWELL STREET

SACRAMENTO STREET

**Tin How Temple**
*This was founded in 1852 by Chinese people grateful for their safe arrival in San Francisco* **4**

CALIFORNIA STREET

GRANT

STOCKTON

**The Bank of Canton** was home to Chinatown's telephone exchange until 1946. The operators spoke five Chinese dialects.

## STAR SIGHTS

★ Chinatown Alleys

★ Chinatown Gateway

★ Grant Avenue

**Cable Cars** run down two sides of Chinatown and are an essential part of the area's bustling atmosphere. Any of the three lines will take you there.

BUSH STR

0 meters    100
0 yards     100

For hotels and restaurants in this region see pp542–9 and pp587–95

**Portsmouth Square**
*Laid out in 1839, this was the social center for the village of Yerba Buena. Today it is a place for children and players of cards and mahjong* **7**

**LOCATOR MAP**
*See Street Finder, map 5*

**KEY**

– – – Suggested route

★ **Grant Avenue**
*In the 1830s and early 1840s this was the main thoroughfare of Yerba Buena* **6**

**The Chinese Culture Center**
contains an art gallery and a small crafts shop. It sponsors a lively program of lectures and seminars.

To buses nos. 30, 45

**Pacific Heritage Museum**
*Housed in an elegant building below the Bank of Canton, this small museum has fine exhibitions of Asian art, which are regularly changed* **8**

KEARNY STREET

CLAY STREET

**Old St. Mary's Church**
*The clock tower of this church, built while the city was still in its infancy, bears an arresting inscription* **2**

SON.OBSERVE THE TIME AND FLY FROM EVIL.ECC.IV.23.

PINE STREET

**St. Mary's Square** is a quiet haven in which to rest.

To bus nos. 31, 38

★ **Chinatown Gateway**
*Also known as the "Dragons' Gate," this marks Chinatown's south entrance* **1**

# Chinatown Gateway ❶

Grant Ave at Bush St. **Map** 5 C4.
🚌 2, 3, 4, 15, 30, 45.

This ornate portal, opened in 1970, was designed by Clayton Lee as an arch over the entrance to Chinatown's main tourist street, Grant Avenue. It was inspired by the ceremonial entrances of traditional Chinese villages. The three-arched gateway is capped with green roof tiles and a host of propitiatory animals, all of glazed ceramic. The gate was erected by an American institution, the Chinatown Cultural Development Committee. The materials were donated by Taiwan (Republic of China).

It is guarded by two stone lions that are suckling their cubs through their claws, in accordance with ancient lore. Once through the gate, visitors can buy antiques, embroidered silks, and gems, though prices can be aimed at tourists.

**Stone lions decorating the Chinatown gateway**

# Old St. Mary's Cathedral ❷

660 California St. **Map** 5 C4. **Tel** (415) 288-3800. 🚌 1, 8, 15, 30, 45. 🚋 California St. ⛪ 7:30am, noon Mon–Fri, noon, 5pm Sat, 8.30am, 11am Sun. 🌐 www.oldsaintmarys.org

San Francisco's first Catholic cathedral, Old St. Mary's, was consecrated on Christmas Day 1854 as the seat of the Roman Catholic bishop of the Pacific Coast. Until 1891 it served a largely Irish congregation, when the new St. Mary's Cathedral was built on Van Ness Avenue. Because of the unavailability of the right building materials in California, the bricks and iron for the church were imported from the East Coast, while the granite foundation stones came from China. The clock tower of the church bears a large inscription, "Son, observe the time and fly from evil," said to have been directed at the brothels that stood across the street. It was one of the few buildings to remain unharmed by the 1906 earthquake and retains its original foundations and walls. The graceful interior, with stained-glass windows and a balcony, was completed in 1909.

**Entrance to Old St. Mary's Church below the clock tower and its inscription**

# Kong Chow Temple ❸

4th floor, 855 Stockton St. **Map** 5 B4. **Tel** (415) 788-1339. 🚌 30, 45. 🕙 10am–4pm daily. **Donation**. ♿

From the top floor above the district's post office, the Kong Chow Temple looks out over Chinatown and the Financial District. Although the building itself dates from only 1977, the Taoist temple was founded in 1857 and the altar and statuary are thought to form the oldest Chinese religious shrine in the country. One altar was handcarved in Guangzhou (Canton), and shipped here in the 19th century. The main shrine is presided over by a carved wooden statue of Kuan Di, also dating from the 19th century. He is the deity most often found in shrines in Cantonese cities.

Kuan Di is also frequently seen in the city's Chinatown

**Carved statue of Kuan Di inside the Kong Chow Temple**

*For hotels and restaurants in this region see pp542–9 and pp587–95*

district: his highly distinctive face looks down from Taoist shrines in many of the area's restaurants. He is typically depicted holding a large sword in one hand and a book in the other. These are symbols of his unswerving dedication to both the martial and the literary arts.

## Tien Hau Temple ❹

Top floor, 125 Waverly Pl. **Map** 5 C3. **Tel** (415) 986-2520. 🚎 1, 15, 30, 45. ⭕ 9am–4pm daily. **Donation**.

This unusual temple is dedicated to Tien Hau, the Queen of Heaven and protector of seafarers and visitors, and is the oldest operating Chinese temple in the United States. The sanctuary was originally founded in 1852 by Day Ju, one of three Chinese immigrants who were the first to land in San Francisco. The temple was designed in 1911 and is now situated at the top of three steep, wooden flights of stairs, which are considered to place it closer to heaven. The narrow space is filled with the smoke from both incense and burned paper offerings, and is brightly decorated with hundreds of gold and red lanterns. It is lit by red electric light bulbs and burning wicks floating in oil. Gifts of fruit lie on the carved altar in front of the wooden statue of the temple's namesake deity.

**The impressive façade of the Tien Hau Temple on Waverly Place**

**A view along Chinatown's main street, Grant Avenue**

## Chinatown Alleys ❺

**Map** 5 B3. 🚎 1, 30, 45.

Contained within a busy neighborhood, the Chinatown Alleys are situated between Grant Avenue and Stockton Street. These four narrow lanes intersect at Washington Street within half a block of each other. Of these, the largest is Waverly Place, known as the "Street of Painted Balconies" for reasons that are apparent to every passerby. Its other nickname, "15 Cents Street," derives from the cost of a haircut by the Chinese barbers trading here at the turn of the century. Nearby, Sun Yat-sen spent many years in exile at No. 36 Spofford Alley.

The alleys contain many old buildings, as well as traditional shops and restaurants. There are also atmospheric, old-fashioned herbalist shops, displaying elk antlers, sea horses, snake wine, and other exotic wares in their windows. Numerous small restaurants, above and below street level, serve cheap and delicious home-cooked food.

## Grant Avenue ❻

**Map** 5 C4. 🚎 1, 30, 45. 🚋 California St.

Grant Avenue is historically important for being the first street of Yerba Buena, the village that preceded San Francisco. A plaque at No. 823 marks the site of the first dwelling, a canvas tent that was erected on June 25, 1835. By 1836 the tent was replaced with a wooden structure and by 1837 with an adobe house. The street was then named Calle de la Fundacíon, the "Street of the Foundation."

An estimated 25,000 Chinese arrived in San Francisco during the Gold Rush era (see pp48–9). They settled in this area on the undesirable lower east slopes of Nob Hill, which were too steep for horse-drawn carriages. In 1885 the street was renamed Grant Avenue, in memory of Ulysses S Grant, the US president who died that year.

Most of the buildings on Grant Avenue were built after the 1906 earthquake in an Oriental Renaissance style. They now form the main tourist street in Chinatown.

**Portsmouth Plaza, at the hub of Chinatown life**

## Portsmouth Square **7**

**Map** 5 C3. 🚋 1, 15.

San Francisco's original town square was laid out in 1839. It was once the social center for the village of Yerba Buena. On July 9, 1846, just after US rebels in Sonoma had declared California's independence from Mexico *(see pp464–5)*, Marines raised the American flag above the plaza, officially seizing the port as part of the United States. Two years later, Sam Brannan announced the discovery of gold in the Sierra Nevada Mountains *(see pp48–9)* here. In the 1850s the area was the hub of this new dynamic city, but in the 1860s the business district shifted to flatlands reclaimed from the bay and the plaza declined in civic importance.

Today Portsmouth Square is the social center of Chinatown. Children play, people practice *t'ai chi* or gather in the evening to play cards.

## Pacific Heritage Museum **8**

608 Commercial St. **Map** 5 C3. **Tel** (415) 399-1124. 🚋 1, 15. ⬜ 10am–4pm Thu–Sat, except public hols. ♿ www.ibankunited.com

The museum building is as elegant as the changing collections of Asian arts displayed inside. It is a synthesis of two buildings. The US Sub-Treasury was erected here in 1875–77 by William Appleton Potter, on the site of the city's first mint. Old coin vaults can

still be seen in the basement. In 1984 the 17-story Bank of Canton headquarters were built above the Treasury, incorporating the old façade and basement.

## Chinese Historical Society of America **9**

965 Clay St. **Map** 5 C3. **Tel** (415) 391-1188. 🚋 1, 30. 🚋 Powell St. ⬜ noon–5pm Tue–Fri, 11am–4pm Sat. ⬤ public hols. 🚫 📷 free 1st Thu every month. **www**.chsa.org

Among the exhibits in this museum are a ceremonial dragon costume and a "tiger fork." This triton was wielded in one of the battles during the reign of terror known as the Tong Wars. The tongs were rival Chinese clans who fought over the control of gambling and prostitution in the city in the late 19th century. Other objects, documents and photographs illuminate the daily life of Chinese immigrants in San Francisco. There is a yearbook of the neighborhood written in Chinese, and the original Chinatown telephone directory.

The contribution of the Chinese to California's development was extensive despite the antagonism and poor treatment they encountered. Chinese workers made the perilous voyage to

**Dragon's head in the Historical Society**

California in their thousands to find gold and escape the economic difficulties of their homeland. Rich merchants used them as cheap labor in the gold mines, and later they were used to build the western half of the transcontinental railroad *(see pp50–51)*. They also constructed dikes in the Sacramento River delta, were pioneers in the fishing industry, and planted the first vines in many of California's early vineyards.

## Nob Hill **10**

**Map** 5 B4.

Nob Hill is the highest summit of the city center, rising 338 ft (103 m) above the bay. Its steep slopes kept prominent citizens away until the opening of the California Street cable car line in 1878. The rich then flocked to build homes here, including the "Big Four" railroad barons *(see pp472–3)*. Its name is thought to come from the Hindi word *nabob*, meaning governor. Sadly, all the mansions were burned down in the fire of 1906 *(see pp52–3)*, except the home of James C Flood, now the Pacific Union Club. Nob Hill still attracts the affluent to its splendid hotels, which benefit from spectacular views of the city.

**A panoramic view of the city from a penthouse bar on Nob Hill**

# Cable Car Museum ⓫

201 Mason St. **Map** 5 B3. *Tel (415)* 474-1887. 🚌 1, 12, 30, 45, 83. 🚋 Powell–Mason, Powell–Hyde. 🕐 10am–6pm daily. 🚫 Jan 1, Thanksgiving, Dec 25. 🔲 mezzanine only. **Video show.** 📷 www.cablecarmuseum.org

This is both a museum and the powerhouse of the cable car system (*see pp302–3*).

Anchored to the floor are the wheels that wind the cables through the system of channels and pulleys beneath the city's streets. You can observe them from the mezzanine, then walk downstairs to see under the street. The museum also houses an early cable car and specimens of the mechanisms that control the movements of individual cars. The cable car system is the last of its kind in the world.

**The entrance to the Cable Car Museum**

# Grace Cathedral ⓬

1100 California St. **Map** 5 B4. *Tel (415)* 749-6300. 🚌 1. 🚋 California St. 🕐 7am–6pm Mon–Fri, 8am–6pm Sat, 7am–7pm Sun. ✝ Choral evensong 5:15pm Thu, 3pm Sun; Choral Eucharist 8:30am, 11am Sun. 🔲 📷 1–3pm Mon–Fri, 11:30am–1:30pm Sat, 12:30–2pm Sun. 📷 www.gracecathedral.org

Grace Cathedral, designed by Lewis P Hobart, is the main Episcopal church in San Francisco. Building started in 1928, but it was not completed until 1964. Despite its modern construction, the building is inspired by Notre Dame in Paris, using traditional materials. The leaded windows were designed by Charles Connick, using the blue glass of Chartres as his inspiration. The rose window is made using 1-inch- (2.5-cm-) thick faceted glass, which is illuminated from inside the building at night. Other windows were executed by Henry Willet and Gabriel Loire. These include depictions of modern heroes such as Albert Einstein and astronaut John Glenn. Objects in the cathedral include a 13th-century Catalonian crucifix and a 16th-century Brussels tapestry. The entrance doors are cast from molds of Ghiberti's "Doors of Paradise," made for the Baptistry in Florence. There is an outdoor terrazo-stone labyrinth and an indoor one made of limestone.

**Cast figure from the main entrance**

**The New Testament Window**, made in 1931 by Charles Connick, is placed on the south side of the church.

**The Rose Window** was made in Chartres by Gabriel Loire in 1964.

**The Carillon Tower** houses 44 bells made in England in 1938.

**The Chapel of Grace**, funded by the Crocker family, has a 15th-century French altarpiece.

**The Doors of Paradise** are decorated with scenes from the bible and portraits of Ghiberti and contemporaries.

**Entrances**

# FISHERMAN'S WHARF AND NORTH BEACH

Fishermen from Genoa and Sicily first arrived in the Fisherman's Wharf area in the late 19th century and founded the San Francisco fishing industry. The district has slowly given way to tourism since the 1950s, but brightly painted boats still set out from the harbor on fishing trips early each morning. To the south of Fisherman's Wharf lies North Beach, sometimes known as "Little Italy." This lively part of the city has an abundance of delis, bakeries, and cafés, from which you can watch the crowds. It is home to many Italian and Chinese families, with a sprinkling of writers and bohemians; Jack Kerouac (see pp26–7), among others, found inspiration here.

**Fisherman's Wharf entrance sign**

## SIGHTS AT A GLANCE

**Museums and Galleries**
The Beat Museum ⑬
Ripley's Believe It Or Not!
Museum ⑤
San Francisco Art Institute ⑩
San Francisco Maritime
National Historic Park ⑧
USS *Pampanito* ③
Wax Museum ④

**Historic Streets and Buildings**
*Alcatraz Island pp338–9* ①
Lombard Street ⑨
Pier 39 ②
Vallejo Street Stairway ⑪

**Shopping Centers**
The Cannery ⑥
Ghirardelli Square ⑦

**Restaurants and Bars**
Club Fugazi ⑫

**Parks and Gardens**
Levi's Plaza ⑰
Telegraph Hill ⑯
Washington Square ⑭

**Churches**
Saints Peter and
Paul Church ⑮

## KEY

- Street-by-Street map
  See pp334–5
- Cable car turntable
- Ferry terminal
- Historical trolley line

**0 meters                    500**
**0 yards                      500**

## GETTING THERE

The Powell–Hyde cable car line goes to Ghirardelli Square and Russian Hill. The Powell–Mason line passes through North Beach, to Fisherman's Wharf and Pier 39. Many buses run through the district.

◁ **View of Fisherman's Wharf and Alcatraz Island from the Powell–Hyde cable car**

# Street-by-Street: Fisherman's Wharf

Italian seafood restaurants have now replaced fishing as the primary focus of the Fisherman's Wharf local economy. Both the expensive restaurants and the cheap outdoor crab pots serve San Francisco's celebrated Dungeness crab, in season from November to June. As well as sampling the seafood, visitors also enjoy taking in the many shops, museums, and other attractions for which Fisherman's Wharf is noted.

★ **USS _Pampanito_**
*A tour gives an idea of the hardships endured by sailors in this World War II submarine* ❸

**Fishermen's and Seamen's Chapel**

**Fisherman's Wharf** is now a street lined with seafood restaurants and crab stands.

**Fish Alley** is where the morning's catch is landed and prepared.

T A Y L O R   S T R E E T

J E F F E R S O N

J O N E S   S T R E E T

To Powell–Hyde cable car turntable (1 block)

**The Cannery**
*Once a fruit cannery, the building was converted to a mall, with restaurants, fine shops, and museums* ❻

**Sea lions basking on Pier 39's** docks delight tourists, but are a pest for boat owners. They arrive here around January.

0 meters          100

0 yards           100

**LOCATOR MAP**
See Street Finder, map 5

San Francisco Bay

FISHERMAN'S WHARF AND NORTH BEACH

CHINATOWN AND NOB HILL

DOWNTOWN

**Wax Museum**
*Almost 300 life-size wax figures of past- and present-day personalities greet visitors to this museum* ❹

**Red and White Fleet ferry tickets** (p399)

**Blue and Gold Fleet ferry tickets** (p399)

E M B A R C A D E R O

POWELL STREET

E E T

**Bus stop (No. 32)**

**Historic Trolley Line** features restored, colorful streetcars that ran in most United States cities from the 1930s.

**Ripley's Believe It or Not! Museum**
*This is a selection of the cartoonist's strange collection of curiosities and odd facts* ❺

**★ Pier 39**
*A collection of restaurants, shops, and amusements, set against a backdrop of spectacular bay views, is one of the city's more popular attractions* ❷

**KEY**

━ ━ ━  Suggested route

**STAR SIGHTS**

★ Pier 39

★ USS *Pampanito*

# Alcatraz Island ❶

See pp338–9.

# Pier 39 ❷

**Map** 5 B1. 🚌 25. ⭕ 10am–10pm
daily (but hours can vary).
See **Shopping** pp382–5.

Refurbished in 1978 to resemble a quaint wooden fishing village, this 1905 cargo pier now houses tourist shops and specialty stores on two levels.
The pier's street performers and amusements are popular and appealing, particularly to families with children. You can ride on the two-level carousel, or brave the Turbo Ride, a roller-coaster simulator where a film gives the illusion of speed and danger.
A sensational multi-media show called the San Francisco Experience takes visitors through a whirlwind historical tour of the city, complete with Chinese New Year celebrations and an earthquake.

**USS *Pampanito*'s torpedo room**

# USS *Pampanito* ❸

Pier 45. **Map** 4 F1. **Tel** (415) 775-1943. 🚌 8X, 47. � F. ⭕ 9am–6pm daily (stays open late some days; call ahead to check). 📷 📹
www.maritime.org

This World War II submarine fought in, and survived, several bloody battles in the Pacific, sinking six enemy ships and severely damaging others. Tragically for the Allies, two of its fatal targets were carrying British and Australian prisoners of war. The *Pampanito* managed to rescue 73 men, however, and carry them to safety in the US. A self-guided tour of the ship

takes visitors from stern to bow and includes visits to the torpedo room, the claustrophobic galley, and officers' quarters. In the days when the USS *Pampanito* was in service, it had a crew of 10 officers and 70 enlisted seamen.

# Wax Museum ❹

145 Jefferson St. **Map** 5 B1.
📞 (800) 439-4305. 🚌 32. 🚃 F.
⭕ 10am–9pm daily. 📷 📹 ♿
limited. **www**.waxmuseum.com

One of the world's largest and most absorbing collections of life-size wax figures is displayed here. All aspects of life and history are displayed here, from the gruesome Chamber of Horrors to the inspiring Hall of Religions and the Library of US Presidents. In the Palace of Living Art, world-famous portraits are rendered in wax, and there is a *Titanic* exhibit in the Lower Lobby.
A gallery of wax figures includes such diverse personages as members of the British Royal Family, Elvis Presley, Beethoven, Neil Armstrong, Marilyn Monroe, and Martin Luther King, Jr. The building is also home to the Rainforest Cafe with its waterfall and theme shops.

# Ripley's Believe It Or Not! Museum ❺

175 Jefferson St. **Map** 4 F1.
**Tel** (415) 205-9850. 🚌 32. 🚃 F.
⭕ Sep–May: 10am–10pm Sun–Thu,
10am–midnight Fri & Sat; Jun–Aug:
9am–11pm Sun–Thu, 9am–midnight
Fri & Sat. 📷 ♿ **www**.ripleys.com/
sanfrancisco

Californian native Robert L Ripley was an illustrator who collected peculiar facts and artifacts and earned his fame from syndicating his celebrated US newspaper cartoon strip, called "Ripley's Believe It Or Not!" Among the 350 oddities on display are a cable car built of 275,000 matchsticks, a two-headed calf, tombstones with wry epithets, and a life-size replica of a man with two pupils in each eyeball.

**The two-level Venetian Carousel on Pier 39**

## The Cannery ❻

801 Leavenworth St. **Tel** (415) 771-
112. **Map** 4 F1. 🚌 19, 30.
🚋 Powell–Hyde. ⏰ 10am–6pm Mon–
at, 11am–6pm Sun. ⊘ Thanksgiving,
Dec 25. ♿ **www**.thecannery.com
See **Shopping** pp382–5.

The interior of this 1907
fruit-canning plant was
redeveloped in the 1960s. It
now incorporates footbridges,
rambling passages, and sunny
courtyards, with restaurants
and shops selling clothing,
collector dolls, and Native
American arts and crafts.

Jack's Cannery Bar boasts
a massive oak-paneled long
hall, as well as a finely carved
fireplace, both of which were
brought from Europe to the
United States by William
Randolph Hearst in the
1920s. Of particular note is
the incredible 13th-century
Moorish ceiling (installed on
the third floor), which came
from the Palacio de Altamira
in Toledo, Spain.

Ghirardelli Square

## Ghirardelli Square ❼

900 North Point St. **Tel** (415) 775-5500.
**Map** 4 F1. 🚌 19, 30, 47, 49. 🚋 F.
🚋 Powell–Hyde. **www**.ghirardellisq.
com See **Shopping** pp382–5.

This former chocolate factory
and woolen mill is the most
attractive of the city's many
refurbished sites, with elegant
shops and restaurants. The
clock tower and roof sign
from the original building
still remain. The Ghirardelli
Chocolate Manufactory on the
plaza houses old chocolate-
making machinery and sells
the confection, but the chocolate bars are now made in
San Leandro, across the bay.

Fountain Plaza is a colorful
focal point for shoppers, at
any time of day and evening.

## San Francisco Maritime National Historic Park ❽

900 Beach St at Polk St. **Map** 4 F1.
**Museum Tel** (415) 447-5000.
🚌 19, 30, 47. 🚋 Powell–Hyde.
⏰ 10am–4pm daily. 🎟 pier.
♿ pier and museum. 🎦 **Lectures,
maritime demonstrations,
activities.** 💻 www.nps.gov/safr

Resembling a beached ocean
liner, the 1939 Aquatic Park
Bathhouse building first
housed the Maritime Museum
in 1951. On display is
a collection of ship
models, vintage
nautical instru-
ments, paintings,
and photographs
illustrating local
nautical history.

Hyde Street Pier

In the lobby, visitors to the
museum can also see colorful,
historical murals depicting the
underwater world. Moored
at the nearby Hyde Street
Pier is the US's largest
collection of National Historic
Landmark ships. Among the
most spectacular is the 1886
*Balclutha*, a three-masted
square-rigger that rounded
Cape Horn 17 times. Also
at the pier is the 2,320-ton
side-wheel ferryboat, *Eureka*,
built in 1890 to ferry trains
between Hyde Street Pier
and the counties north of San
Francisco Bay. It carried 2,300
passengers and 120 cars and
was the largest passenger
ferry of its day. In summer,
the 1891 *Alma* offers 3-hour
sailing ranger tours.

### BALCLUTHA

*This ship is the star of Hyde
Street Pier. Launched in
1886, she sailed twice
a year between
Britain and Cali-
fornia, trading
wheat for
coal.*

Mainmast

Mizzenmast

Foremast

Quarterdeck

Bowsprit

# Alcatraz Island ❶

Alcatraz means "pelican" in Spanish and refers to the first inhabitants of this rocky, steep-sided island. Lying 3 miles (5 km) east of the Golden Gate, its location is both strategic and exposed to ocean winds. In 1859, the US Army established a fort here that guarded San Francisco Bay until 1907, when it became a military prison. From 1934 to 1963, it served as a maximum-security Federal Penitentiary. In 1969 the island was seized by members of the Native American Movement (*see p56*) claiming it as their land. They were expelled in 1971, and Alcatraz is now part of the Golden Gate National Recreation Area.

**Badge on entrance to cellhouse**

★ **Cell Block**
*The cell house contains four cell blocks. No cell has an outside wall or ceiling. The dungeonlike foundation of the prison block shares the original foundation of the old military fortress.*

**Alcatraz Island from the Ferry**
*"The Rock" has no native soil. Soil was shipped from Angel Island to make garden plots.*

**The officers' apartments** stood here.

**Military parade ground**

**Barracks buildings**

| 0 meters | 75 |
| 0 yards | 75 |

**KEY**

– – – Suggested route

**The Warden's House** was fire damaged during the 1969–71 siege.

**Alcatraz Pier**
*Most prisoners took their first steps ashore here; no other wharf served the steep-sided island. Now visitors alight at this pier.*

---

**STAR SIGHTS**

★ Cell Block

★ Exercise Yard

---

*For hotels and restaurants in this region see pp542–9 and pp587–95*

★ **Exercise Yard**
*Meals and walks around the exercise yard were the highlights of a prisoner's day. The walled yard featured in films made at the prison.*

**VISITORS' CHECKLIST**

Map 6 F1. *Tel* (415) 981-7625 or online for tickets and schedules. **Night tours** (Thu–Mon) call (415) 561-4926. from Pier 33. daily. Jan 1, Dec 25. in places, but difficult. free with ticket. **No restaurant or café**. www.alcatrazcruises.com

**Metal detectors** checked prisoners when they passed to and from the dining hall and exercise yards.

**The Military Dorm** was built in 1933.

**The Military Morgue** is tiny and cramped, and is not open to the public.

**Prison workshops**

**Alcatraz Hospital Wing**

**Water tower**

**The Information Center** is in the old barracks.

**Rose Terrace**

**The Officers' Row Gardens**

**The officers' club**, dating from the days of Fort Alcatraz, was a military store that also served as a recreation center.

## FAMOUS INMATES

### Al Capone
The Prohibition gangster, "Scarface" Capone was actually convicted in 1934 for income tax evasion! He spent much of his five-year sentence on Alcatraz in an isolation cell, and left the prison mentally unstable.

### Robert Stroud
The original *"Birdman of Alcatraz"* spent all of his 17 years on The Rock in solitary confinement.

**Carnes, Thompson, and Shockley**
In May 1946, prisoners led by Clarence Carnes, Marion Thompson, and Sam Shockley overpowered guards and captured their guns. The prisoners failed to break out of the cell house, but three inmates and two officers were killed in what became known as the "Battle of Alcatraz." Carnes received

an additional life sentence, and Shockley and Thompson were executed at San Quentin prison for their part in the insurrection.

### Anglin Brothers
John and Clarence Anglin, together with Frank Morris, chipped through the walls of their cells, and hid the holes with cardboard grates. Leaving dummy heads in their beds, they made a raft to enable their escape and were never caught. Their story was dramatized in the film *Escape from Alcatraz* (1979).

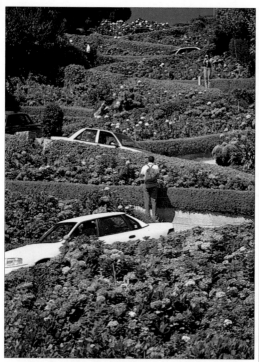

Cars negotiating the steep and crooked section of Lombard Street

## Lombard Street ❾

**Map** 5 A2. 🚌 *45.* 🚃 *Powell–Hyde.*

Banked at a natural incline of 27°, this hill proved too steep for vehicles to climb. In the 1920s the section of Lombard Street close to the summit of Russian Hill was revamped and the severity of its gradient was lessened by the addition of eight curves.

Today it is known as "the crookedest street in the world." Cars can travel downhill at a speed of only 5 miles per hour (8 km/h), while pedestrians use steps. There are spectacular views of San Francisco from the summit.

## San Francisco Art Institute ❿

800 Chestnut St. **Map** 4 F2.
***Tel*** *(415) 771-7020.* 🚌 *30.* **Diego Rivera Gallery** ⬜ *9am–5pm daily.*
⬛ *public hols.* ♿ *partial.* 🔲 🖥

San Francisco's Art Institute dates from 1871 and once occupied the immense

# A 30-Minute Walk through North Beach

Settlers originally from Chile, and more recently Italy, have brought their enthusiasm for nightlife to North Beach, earning this quarter its vibrant reputation. Its café-oriented atmosphere has long appealed to bohemians, particularly the 1950s Beat Generation *(see pp26–7)*.

### The Beat Neighborhood
Start the walk from the southwest corner of Broadway and Columbus Avenue at City Lights Bookstore ①. Owned by Beat poet Lawrence Ferlinghetti, City Lights was the first bookshop in the US to sell paperbacks exclusively. The author Jack Kerouac, a friend of Ferlinghetti, coined the word "Beat," later referred to as "Beatnik."

One of the most popular Beat bars was Vesuvio ②, south of City Lights, across Jack Kerouac Alley. Welsh poet Dylan Thomas was a patron here, and it is still a favorite with

**Jack Kerouac**

poets and artists. From here travel south to Pacific Avenue, cross to the opposite side of Columbus Avenue and walk back toward Broadway, stopping at Tosca ③. The walls of this bar and café display murals of Tuscany, and a jukebox plays selections from Italian opera. A few steps north bring you to Adler Alley. Specs ④, a lively bar filled with memorabilia of the Beat era, is at No. 12. Walking back to Columbus Avenue, turn right into Broadway and at the corner of Kearny Street cross over to Naked Lunch ⑤.

**Columbus Café** ⑪

### The Strip
Naked Lunch, the inheritors of Enrico's Sidewalk Café's fêted space, is the best place from which to watch the action on The Strip ⑥, a stretch of Broadway noted for its "adult entertainment." At the junction with Grant Avenue is the former Condor Club ⑦, where the world's first topless stage show was performed in June 1964.

wooden mansion built for the family of railroad baron Mark Hopkins on Nob Hill (see p330), which burned down in the fire of 1906 (see pp52–3). Today it is housed in a Spanish Colonial-style building that was constructed in 1926, complete with cloisters, a courtyard fountain, and bell tower. A modern extension was added at the rear of the building in 1969. The Diego Rivera Gallery, named after the famous Mexican muralist, sits to the left of the main entrance.

The Institute holds temporary exhibitions of works, from contemporary photography to design and technology.

Diego Rivera's *Making of a Fresco* (1931), San Francisco Art Institute

## Vallejo Street Stairway ⑪

Mason St and Jones St. **Map** 5 B3.
🚌 30, 45. 🚋 *Powell–Mason.*

The steep climb from Little Italy to the summit of Russian Hill reveals some of the best views of Telegraph Hill, North Beach, and the bay. The street gives way to steps at Mason Street, which climb up through Ina Coolbrith Park.

Above Taylor Street, there are lanes, with several Victorian houses (see pp300–301). At the crest of the hill is one of the rare parts of the city not destroyed in the earthquake of 1906 (see pp52–3).

## Club Fugazi ⑫

678 Beach Blanket Babylon Blvd.
**Map** 5 B3. **Tel** (415) 421-4222.
🚌 15, 30, 45. 🕐 *Wed–Sun.*
See *Entertainment* pp390–95.
**www**.beachblanketbabylon.com

Built in 1912 as a North Beach community hall, the Club

Fugazi is the venue for the musical cabaret *Beach Blanket Babylon*. This is a lively show that has been running for more than two decades and has become an institution among San Franciscans. It is popular with locals and tourists, and is famous for its outrageous songs and the bizarre hats often worn by the performers.

## The Beat Museum ⑬

540 Broadway **Map** 5 C3. **Tel** (800) 537-6822. 🕐 *10am–7pm daily.* 🌐
**www**.thebeatmuseum.org

Celebrating the Beat Movement of 1950s San Francisco (see p27), this "museum" showcases everyone and everything linked to the phenomenon. With references galore to Allen Ginsberg's *Howl* poem, including a warning of an emergency exit that will "howl" if opened, the museum's collection features letters, photos, magazine and newspaper clippings, books, and album covers.

### Upper Grant Avenue

Turn right into Grant Avenue where you will find The Saloon ⑧ with its original 1861 bar. On the corner of Vallejo Street is Caffè Trieste ⑨, the oldest coffee house in San Francisco, and a

genuine Beat rendezvous since 1956. Very much a part of Italian-American culture, it offers live opera on Saturday afternoons. Follow Grant Avenue north past the Lost and Found Saloon ⑩, now a blues club but formerly the Coffee Gallery, another of the Beat haunts. Turn left at Green Street and look for Columbus Café ⑪, whose exterior

Vesuvio, a popular Beat bar ②

walls are decorated with attractive murals. Turning left again at Columbus Avenue, follow this main street of North Beach south past many more Italian coffee houses, to return to your starting point.

### TIPS FOR WALKERS

***Starting point:*** Corner of Broadway and Columbus Avenue.
***Length:*** 1 mile (1.6 km).
***Getting there:*** Muni bus No. 15 runs along Columbus Avenue.
***Stopping-off points:*** All the bars and cafés mentioned are worth visiting for a drink and the atmosphere. Children are not usually allowed in bars.

**KEY**

•• Walk route

| 0 meters | 200 |
| 0 yards | 200 |

The façade of Saints Peter and Paul Church, Washington Square

has an Italianesque façade, with a complex interior notable for its many columns and ornate altar. There are also statues and mosaics illuminated by stained-glass windows. The concrete and steel structure of the church, with its twin spires rising over the surrounding rooftops, was completed in 1924.

Cecil B DeMille filmed the workers laying the church's foundations and used the scene to show the building of the Temple of Jerusalem in his film *The Ten Commandments*, made in 1923.

The church is sometimes referred to as the Fishermen's Church (many Italians once earned their living by fishing), and there is an annual mass and procession from Columbus Avenue to Fisherman's Wharf to celebrate the Blessing of the Fleet in October. Masses in the church can still be heard in Italian and Cantonese.

## Telegraph Hill 🖲

Map 5 C2. **Coit Tower** Telegraph Hill Blvd. **Tel** (415) 362-0808. 🚌 39. ◻ 10am–6:30pm daily. 🏛 🅰 murals only. 📷

Originally called Alta Loma by the Mexicans, then Goat Hill after the animals that grazed on its slopes, Telegraph Hill was renamed in 1850 after the semaphore installed on its crest. This alerted the city's merchants to the arrival of ships through the Golden Gate. On the eastern side,

## Washington Square 🖳

Map 5 B2. 🚌 15, 30, 39, 45.

The square consists of a simple expanse of lawn, surrounded by benches and trees, set against the twin towers of Saints Peter and Paul Church. It has an almost Mediterranean atmosphere, appropriate for the "town square" of Little Italy. Near the center of the square stands a statue of Benjamin Franklin. A time capsule was buried under the statue in 1979 and is scheduled to be reopened in 2079. It is said to contain some Levi's jeans, a bottle of wine, and a poem written by Lawrence Ferlinghetti, one of San Francisco's famous Beat poets *(see pp26–7)*.

## Saints Peter and Paul Church 🖳

666 Filbert St. **Map** 5 B2. **Tel** (415) 421-0809. 🚌 8X, 30, 39, 45. ◻ 7:30am–4pm Mon–Fri, 7:30am–6pm Sat & Sun. 🛉 call or check website for mass times. 🅰 **www. stspeterpaul.san-francisco.ca.us**

Still known by many as the Italian Cathedral, this large church is situated at the heart of North Beach, and many Italians find it a welcome haven when they first arrive in San Francisco. It was here that the local baseball hero, Joe Di Maggio, was photographed after his marriage to the actress Marilyn Monroe in 1957, although the actual wedding ceremony was held elsewhere. The building, designed by Charles Fantoni,

**Coit Tower mural showing Fisherman's Wharf in the 1930s**

**Steps at the bottom of Filbert Street leading up to Telegraph Hill**

which, until 1914, was regularly dynamited to provide rocks for landfill and paving, the hill falls away abruptly to form steep paths, bordered by leafy gardens.

The western side slopes more gradually into the area known as "Little Italy," around Washington Square, although in recent years the city's Italian population has begun to settle in the Marina District. In the past the hill has been a neighborhood of immigrants living in wooden cabins, and of struggling artists, who appreciated the panoramic views. These days, however, the quaint pastel clapboard homes are much sought after, and this is one of the city's prime residential areas.

Coit Tower was built in 1933 at the top of 284-ft- (86-m-) high Telegraph Hill, with funds left to the city by Lillie Hitchcock Coit, an eccentric San Franciscan pioneer and philanthropist. The 210-ft (64-m) reinforced concrete tower was designed as a fluted column by the architect Arthur Brown. When floodlit at night, its glow can be seen from most of the city's eastern half. The encircling view around the North Bay Area from the observation platform (reached by an elevator) is quite spectacular.

In the lobby of the tower are absorbing murals (*see pp306–7*). These were sponsored in 1934 by a government-funded program designed to keep artists in employment during the Great Depression. Twenty-five

artists worked together on the vivid portrait of life in modern California. Scenes range from the busy streets of the city's Financial District (with a robbery in progress) to factories, dockyards, and the Central Valley wheat fields. There are a number of fascinating details – a car crash, a family of immigrants encamped by a river, newspaper headlines, magazine covers, and book titles. There is a sense of frustration, satire, and whimsy in the pictures. Various political themes also feature. Many of the faces in the paintings are those of the artists and their friends, along with local figures such as Colonel William Brady, the caretaker of Coit Tower. The work's political subject matter caused some public controversy and delayed its official unveiling.

On the eastern side of Telegraph Hill the streets become steep steps. Descending from Telegraph Hill Boulevard,

Filbert Street is a rambling stairway, constructed of wood, brick, and concrete, where rhododendron, fuschia, bougainvillea, fennel, and blackberries thrive.

## Levi's Plaza ⑰

**Map** 5 C2. 🚌 42.

This square is where the headquarters of Levi Strauss & Co., the manufacturers of blue jeans, can be found. The square was landscaped by Lawrence Halprin in 1982, with the intention of recalling the company's long history in the state. The plaza is studded with granite rocks and cut by flowing water, thus symbolizing the Sierra Nevada canyon scenery in which the miners who first wore the jeans worked. Telegraph Hill in the background adds a more natural mountainous element.

---

### LEVI STRAUSS AND HIS JEANS

**Levi Strauss**

First manufactured in San Francisco in the days of the Gold Rush (*see pp48–9*), denim jeans have had a great impact on popular culture, and they are just as fashionable today as they were when they first appeared. One of the leading producers of jeans is Levi Strauss & Co., founded in the city in the 1860s.

The company's story started in 1853, when Levi Strauss left New York to establish a dry goods business with his brother-in-law in San Francisco. In the 1860s, though still primarily a seller of dry goods, he pioneered the use of a durable, brown, canvaslike material to make work trousers, sold directly to miners. In the 1870s his company began to use metal rivets to strengthen the stress points in the garments, and demand increased. The company then expanded, and early in the 20th century it moved to 250 Valencia Street in the Mission District. Levi's jeans are now an institution, and are produced, sold, and worn all over the world. The company that was first founded by Levi Strauss is still owned and managed by his descendants.

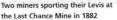

**Two miners sporting their Levis at the Last Chance Mine in 1882**

# PACIFIC HEIGHTS AND THE CIVIC CENTER

Pacific Heights is an exclusive neighborhood, rising 300 ft (90 m) above the city. After cable cars linked it with the city center in the 1880s, it quickly became a desirable place to live, and fine Victorian houses now line its streets. To the north of Broadway, the streets drop steeply down to the Marina District, with its smart shops, fashionable cafés, and two prestigious yacht clubs. To the south of Pacific Heights is the Civic Center, which was built after the earthquake of 1906. It includes some of the best Beaux-Arts architecture in the city and was declared a historic site in 1987. The Civic Center is perhaps one of the most elegant city complexes in the US.

Fort Mason logo

## SIGHTS AT A GLANCE

**Historic Streets and Buildings**
Alamo Square **18**
Asian Art Museum **14**
Bill Graham Civic Auditorium **15**
City Hall **16**
Cow Hollow **9**
Fort Mason **7**
Haas-Lilienthal House **1**
Octagon House **10**
Palace of Fine Arts and the Exploratorium **5**
Spreckels Mansion **2**
University of San Francisco **19**

**Shopping Areas**
Chestnut Street **8**
Fillmore Street **11**
Hayes Valley **17**

**Modern Architecture**
Japantown **12**

**Churches**
St. Mary's Cathedral **13**

**Parks and Gardens**
Alta Plaza **4**
Lafayette Park **3**
Marina Green **6**

**GETTING THERE**
Muni buses 1 and 12, and the California Street cable car serve the Pacific Heights area. The Civic Center BART/Muni station on Market Street is two blocks east of City Hall. Buses 5, 8, and 19 all travel into the Civic Center.

### KEY

- Street-by-Street map *See pp346–7*
- Cable car terminus
- BART station
- Streetcar terminus

◁ **View from Alamo Square across the Civic Center toward the Financial District**

# Street-by-Street: Pacific Heights

The steep blocks between Alta Plaza and Lafayette Park are set in the heart of the exclusive Pacific Heights district. The streets here are quiet and tidy, lined with stylish apartment blocks and palatial Victorian houses. Some of these date from the late 19th century, while others were built after the great earthquake and fire of 1906 *(see pp52–3)*. To the north of this area, the streets drop steeply down toward the residential Marina District and offer outstanding views of San Francisco Bay. Wander through the two large landscaped parks and past the luxurious gardens of the private mansions in between, then visit one of the many fashionable bars, cafés, and restaurants along Fillmore Street.

**The Webster Street Row houses** have been declared a historic landmark. They were built for a middle-class clientele in 1878 and have since been restored to their original splendor.

**Washington Street** lies to the east of Alta Plaza. Here the Victorian houses, built in various architectural styles, fill an entire block.

### ★ Alta Plaza
*Set aside as a public park in the 1850s, this hilltop green space has a playground, tennis courts, and spectacular views of San Francisco* ❹

To bus no. 12

WEBSTER STREET

FILLMORE STREET

STEINER STREET

| 0 meters | | 100 |
| 0 yards | | 100 |

**KEY**

— — — Suggested route

**STAR SIGHTS**

★ Alta Plaza

★ Spreckels Mansion

### Haas-Lilienthal House
*Furnished in Victorian style, this mansion is the head-quarters of San Francisco Architectural Heritage* ❶

**LOCATOR MAP**
*See Street Finder, maps 3, 4*

To bus nos. 47, 76

**No. 2151 Sacramento Street** is an ornate French-style mansion. A plaque commemorates a visit by the author Sir Arthur Conan Doyle in 1923.

**Lafayette Park**
*This quiet park offers good views of the Victorian houses that surround it* ❸

**★ Spreckels Mansion**
*This impressive limestone building, constructed on the lines of a French Baroque palace, has been home to best-selling novelist Danielle Steele since 1990* ❷

**No. 2004 Gough Street**, one of the more elaborate Victorian houses in Pacific Heights, was built in 1889.

The Haas-Lilienthal House, a Queen Anne mansion from 1886

# Haas-Lilienthal House ❶

2007 Franklin St. **Map** 4 E3. **Tel** (415) 441-3004. 🚌 1, 19, 27, 47, 49, 83. ⏰ noon–3pm Wed & Sat, 11am–4pm Sun (times may vary so call ahead). 🎟 🌐 www.sfheritage.org/haas-lilienthal-house

This attractive Queen Anne-style mansion (see pp300–301) was built in 1886 for the rich merchant William Haas. Alice Lilienthal, his daughter, lived here until 1972, when it was given to the Foundation for San Francisco's Architectural Heritage. It is the only intact private home of the period in San Francisco, now open as a museum, and it is complete, with authentic furniture. A fine example of an upper-middle-class Victorian home, it has elaborate wooden gables and luxurious ornamentation.

A display of photographs in the basement describes the history of the building and reveals that this grandiose house was modest in comparison with some of the mansions destroyed in the great fire of 1906 (see pp52–3).

# Spreckels Mansion ❷

2080 Washington St. **Map** 4 E3. 🚌 1, 47, 49. ⚫ to the public.

Dominating the north side of Lafayette Park, this imposing Beaux-Arts mansion is sometimes known as the "Parthenon of the West." It was built in 1912 for the flamboyant Alma de Bretteville Spreckels and her husband, Adolph, heir to the sugar fortune of Claus Spreckels (see p348). The house contains 26 bathrooms, and a large swimming pool in which Alma Spreckels swam daily until the age of 80. Her love of French architecture inspired the design. The architect of Spreckels mansion was George Applegarth, who in 1916 also designed the California Palace of the Legion of Honor in Lincoln Park (see pp374–5). The Palace was donated to the city by the Spreckelses in 1924.

Today Spreckels Mansion is privately owned. It occupies a block of Octavia Street, which is paved and landscaped in a similar style to curvy Lombard Street (see p340).

**Façade of the impressive Spreckels Mansion**

# Lafayette Park ❸

**Map** 4 E3. 🚌 1, 12.

One of San Francisco's prettiest hilltop gardens, Lafayette Park is a leafy green haven of pine and eucalyptus trees, although its present tranquillity belies its turbulent history. Along with Alta Plaza and Alamo Square (see p353) the land was set aside in 1855 as a city-owned open space. Then squatters and others, including a former City Attorney, laid claim to the land and began to build their houses on it. The largest of these houses remained standing at the center of the hilltop park until 1936, the squatter who had built it refusing to move. It was finally demolished after the city authorities agreed to swap it for other land on nearby Gough Street. Steep stairways now lead to the summit of the park and its delightful views.

In the streets surrounding Lafayette Park there are a number of other palatial Victorian buildings. Particularly ornate examples are situated along Broadway, Jackson Street, and Pacific Avenue going east–west, and Gough, Octavia, and Laguna streets going north–south.

# Alta Plaza ❹

**Map** 4 D3. 🚌 1, 3, 12, 22, 24.

Situated in the center of Pacific Heights, Alta Plaza is a landscaped urban park, where the San Franciscan elite come to relax. The stone steps rising up from Clay Street on the south side of the park offer good views of Haight Ashbury (see pp354–63), the Fillmore district, and Twin Peaks (see p363). The steps may be familiar to film buffs – Barbra Streisand drove down them in *What's Up Doc?* There are also tennis courts and a playground.

From the north side of the park some splendid Victorian mansions are visible, including Gibbs House, at No. 2622 Jackson Street, built by Willis Polk in 1894. Smith House, at No. 2600 Jackson Street, was

**Relaxing in the peaceful Alta Plaza park**

one of the first houses in San Francisco to be supplied with electricity in the 1890s.

# Palace of Fine Arts and the Exploratorium ⑤

3601 Lyon St. **Map** 3 C2. **Tel** (415) 561 0360. ▦ 22, 28, 29, 30, 43, 45, 47, 49. ◯ 10am–5pm Tue–Sun. ● Mon, Thanksgiving, Dec 25. ◱ (free first Wed of month). ♿ **Tactile Dome Tel** (415) 561-0362 (reservations). **www**.exploratorium.edu

Sole survivor of the many grandiose monuments built as part of the 1915 Panama-California Exposition, the

Palace of Fine Arts is a Neo-Classical folly. It was designed by the architect Bernard R Maybeck, who drew inspiration from the drawings of the Italian architect Piranesi and by the painting *L'Isle des Morts* by Swiss artist, Arnold Böcklin. Originally built of wood and plaster, the Palace eventually began to crumble, until one concerned citizen began to raise funds for its reconstruction in 1959. It was restored to its original splendor between 1962 and 1968 using reinforced concrete.

The central feature is the rotunda, perched on the edge of a landscaped, swan-filled lagoon. Its dome is decorated with allegorical paintings, all of which depict the defense of art against materialism. On top of the many Corinthian columns are nymphs with bent heads – symbolic of the "melancholy of life without art."

The Palace's auditorium can hold up to 1,000 spectators, while an elongated industrial shed inside the Palace houses the Exploratorium, one of the most entertaining science museums in the United States. Established in 1969 by the physicist Frank Oppenheimer (whose brother Robert helped to develop the atom bomb), it is filled with more than 400 interactive exhibits, exploring

the world of science and the senses. In the exhibits, divided between two floors, visitors can learn about living systems, sound and listening, electricity and magnetism, color and perception, kinetic motion, and more. Displays invite visitors to experience a subway ride as if they were hard of hearing, to monitor their blood pressure as they tell a lie, and to harvest their own cheek cells and compare them with those of a tomato or potato. The Tactile Dome offers a sensory journey taken in total darkness.

The gardens form a relaxing and attractive backdrop to this imitation Roman ruin, which is a firm favorite with San Francisco residents.

**The world of science explained in the Exploratorium**

**Classical rotunda of the Palace of Fine Arts**

## PANAMA-CALIFORNIA EXPOSITION

In 1915 San Francisco celebrated its successful recovery from the 1906 earthquake and fire with a monumental fair. Officially, it was intended to celebrate the opening of the Panama Canal, and was designed to be the most splendid world's fair ever held. Its grand structures were indeed described by one highly enthusiastic visitor as "a miniature Constantinople."

The halls and pavilions of the fair were constructed on land reclaimed from San Francisco Bay, on the site of today's Marina District. They were donated by all the states and by 25 foreign countries, and lined a concourse 1 mile (1.6 km) long. Many of the buildings were based on such architectural gems as a Turkish mosque and a Buddhist temple from Kyoto. The brilliant Tower of Jewels, at the center of the concourse, was encrusted with glass beads and lit by spotlights. To the west stood the beautiful Palace of Fine Arts, which visitors reached by gondola across a landscaped lagoon.

# Marina Green **6**

**Map** 4 D1. 🚌 22, 28, 30.

A long thin strip of lawn running the length of the Marina District, Marina Green is popular with kite-flyers and picnickers, especially on the Fourth of July, when the city's fireworks display can be seen from here. Paths along the waterfront are the city's prime spots for cyclists, joggers, and skaters. Golden Gate Promenade leads from the west end of the green to Fort Point, or you can turn east to the Wave Organ at the end of the harbor jetty.

# Chestnut Street **8**

**Map** 4 D1. 🚌 22, 28, 30, 43.

The main shopping and night-life center of the Marina District, Chestnut Street has a varied mix of movie theaters, markets, and restaurants, catering more to the local residents than to visitors. The strip stretches just a few blocks from Fillmore Street west to Divisadero Street, after which the neighborhood becomes residential in character.

# Cow Hollow **9**

**Map** 4 D2. 🚌 22, 41, 45.

Cow Hollow is a shopping district along Union Street. It is so called because it was used as grazing land for the city's dairy cows up until the 1860s. It was then taken over for development and turned into a residential neighborhood. In the 1950s the area became fashionable, and chic boutiques, antique shops, and art galleries took over the old neighborhood stores. Many of these are in restored 19th-century buildings, lending an old-fashioned air to the district, in stark contrast to the sophistication of the merchandise on display.

Union Street itself has more than 300 boutiques, and open-air arts, crafts, and food fairs are held regularly in the area.

**View from Fillmore Street, overlooking Cow Hollow**

# Fort Mason **7**

**Map** 4 E1. 📞 (415) 441-3400.
**Events** 441-3400. 🚌 22, 28, 30, 42, 43. ♿ partial. www.fortmason.org

Fort Mason reflects the military history of San Francisco. The original buildings were private houses, built in the late 1850s, which were confiscated by the US Government when the site was taken over by the US army during the American Civil War (1861–5).

The Fort was an army command post until the 1890s. It later housed refugees whose homes had been destroyed in the 1906 earthquake *(see pp52–3)*. During World War II, it was the embarkation point for around 1.6 million soldiers.

The Fort was converted to peaceful use in 1972 although some of the white-painted mid-19th-century buildings still house military personnel. Other buildings, however, are open to the public. These include the original barracks, and the old hospital, which

Herbst Pavilion
Festival Pavilion
Museo ItaloAmericano
Magic Theatre
Greens Restaurant
City College of San Francisco Art Campus
Entrance
Young Performers Theatre
San Francisco Maritime Museum Library
Great Meadow

# Octagon House ⓾

2645 Gough St. **Map** 4 E2. **Tel** (415) 441-7512. 🚌 41, 42, 45, 47, 49. ◯ noon–3pm on second Sun and second and fourth Thu of the month, except Jan. **Donation**. 🚫 ♿ limited.

Built by William C McElroy in 1861, the Octagon House, with its eight-sided cupola, is a well-preserved example of a house style that was once popular throughout the United States. Now run by the Colonial Dames of America, the ground floor has been opened up into one large room, and this and the first floor house a small but engaging collection of decorative arts as well as historic documents of the Colonial and Federal periods of the United States. Among the exhibits are furniture, paintings, porcelain, silver, pewter, samplers, playing cards from the American Revolutionary era, and signatures of 54 of the 56 signatories to the Declaration of Independence.

Octagon House's cupola ensures sunlight in each room

# Fillmore Street ⓫

**Map** 4 D4. 🚌 1, 2, 3, 4, 22, 24.

Fillmore Street managed to survive the 1906 earthquake and fire virtually intact, so for several years afterward it was forced to serve as the civic heart of the ruined city. Government departments, as well as several independent businesses, were housed in local shops, homes, and even churches. Today the main commercial district linking Pacific Heights and the Civic Center is located here, from Jackson Street to the outskirts of the Japan Center (see p352) around Bush Street. This area is filled with fine bookstores, fashionable restaurants, and exclusive boutiques.

San Francisco Fisherman's Wharf Hostel

Fort Mason Officers' Club

🛈 ♿

Chapel

Visitors' Center

Golden Gate National Recreation Area headquarters

Meta III (1985) by Italo Scanga at Museo ItaloAmericano Chapel

serves as a Visitors' Center and as the headquarters of the Golden Gate National Recreation Area (GGNRA). Besides being rich in history and culture, Fort Mason offers some of the city's finest views, looking across the bay toward Golden Gate Bridge (see pp380–81) and Alcatraz Island (see pp338–9). Starting from the west gate of the Fort, Golden Gate Promenade winds eastward to Aquatic Park and then to Fisherman's Wharf (see pp334–5).

## Fort Mason Center

Part of the Fort is now occupied by one of San Francisco's major art complexes. The Fort Mason Center houses over 25 cultural organizations, which include art galleries, museums, and theaters, such as the Cowell Dance Theater and the Bayfront Theater, home to BATS Improv. Italian and Italian-American

artists display their works at the Museo ItaloAmericano. The Magic Theater is an experimental theater, and the Young Performers Theater is a playhouse for children. The Maritime Library holds a wonderful collection of books, oral histories, and ships' plans. The Maritime Museum itself is located near Fisherman's Wharf (see p337)

The Fort Mason Center produces a monthly calendar of current events. Call the Events Line or visit their website for more information.

The SS Balclutha, at Hyde Street Pier, part of the Maritime Museum

**The pagoda in Japantown's Peace Plaza**

## Japantown @

Geary, Post, Fillmore & Laguna Sts.
**Map** 4 E4. ⬛ 2, 3, 4, 38. 🕐 10am–6pm daily. **www**.sfjapantown.org

The Japan Center was built as part of an ambitious 1960s scheme to revitalize the Fillmore District. Many blocks of aging Victorian houses were demolished and replaced by the Geary Expressway and the large shopping complex of the Japan Center. The neighborhood, now known as Japantown, has been the heart of the Japanese community for some 75 years.

At the heart of the complex, and centered upon a five-tiered, 75-ft (22-m) concrete pagoda, is the remodeled Peace Plaza. Taiko drummers and others perform here at the Cherry Blossom festival each April. Each side of the pagoda is a mall with shops, sushi bars, bathhouses, and *Shiatsu* massage centers, all modeled on Tokyo's Ginza district. One of the city's best movie theaters, the Sundance Kabuki Cinema *(see pp390–91)*, is also here. More Japanese shops line the open-air mall across Post Street, flanked by twin steel sculptures by Ruth Asawa.

## Cathedral of St. Mary of the Assumption @

1111 Gough St. **Map** 4 E4.
**Tel** (415) 567-2020. ⬛ 38.
🕐 8:30am–5pm Mon–Fri,
9am–5:30pm Sat, 9am–5pm Sun.
✝ 6:45am, 8am, 12:10pm Mon–Fri,
6:45am, 8am, 5:30pm Sat, 7:30am,
9am, 11am, 1pm (in Spanish) Sun.
♿ **www**.stmarycathedralsf.org

Situated at the summit of Cathedral Hill, St. Mary's is one of San Francisco's most prominent architectural land-marks. Designed by Pietro Belluschi and Pier Luigi Nervi, it was completed in 1971.

The four-part arching paraboloid roof stands out like a white-sailed ship. The 200-ft (60-m) high concrete structure, which seems to hover effort-lessly above the nave, supports the cross-shaped stained-glass ceiling. A canopy of aluminum rods sparkles above the altar.

## Asian Art Museum @

200 Larkin St. **Map** 4 F5.
**Tel** (415) 581-3500. ⬛ 5, 8, 19, 21,
26, 31, 47, 49. 🚇 F, J, K, L, M, N.
🕐 10am–5pm Tue–Sun (9pm Thu).
⬤ public hols. 🆓 free
1st Sun every month.
♿ 🎧 📷 📹
**www**.asianart.org

The Asian Art Museum is located in a building that was the crown jewel of the Beaux Arts movement. The former Main Library, built in 1917, underwent seismic strength-ening and the original space has been reused to create the largest museum outside Asia devoted purely to Asian art. The museum's holdings include 17,000 art objects spanning 6,000 years of history and representing

more than 40 Asian nations. Among the highlights is a gilt-bronze Buddha, one of the oldest Chinese Buddhas in the world. The museum also offers a diverse range of programs for all ages.

## Bill Graham Civic Auditorium @

99 Grove St. **Map** 4 F5. **Tel** (415)
624-8900. ⬛ 5, 8, 19, 21, 26, 47,
49. 🚇 J, K, L, M, N.

Designed in Beaux-Arts style by architect John Galen Howard, the city's Civic Auditorium was opened in 1915 and has since become one of San Francisco's major performance venues. It was inaugurated by the French pianist and composer Camille Saint-Saëns. The building was completed along with City Hall, during the architectural renaissance that followed the great earthquake of 1906 *(see pp52–3)*. It was built, together with the adjoining Brooks Exhibit Hall, beneath the Civic Center Plaza.

The civic auditorium now serves as the city's main conference center, and seats 7,000 people. In 1964 its name was changed in honor of Bill Graham *(see p349)*, the local rock music impresario.

**Grand staircase in the Asian Art Museum**

The imposing façade of City Hall in San Francisco's Civic Center

# City Hall **16**

1 Dr. Carlton B. Goodlett Pl. **Map** 4 F5. **Tel** (415) 701-2311. 🚌 3, 5, 6, 9, 19, 21, 47, 49, 71. 🚃 J, K, L, M, N. 🕙 8am–5pm Mon–Fri. ♿ ✔ **www**.sfgov.org

City Hall, completed in 1915, just in time for the Panama-Pacific Exposition (*see p349*), was designed by the architect Arthur Brown at the height of his career. Its grand Baroque dome was modeled after St. Peter's Basilica in Rome and is higher than that of the United States Capitol in Washington, DC.

The renovated building stands at the heart of the Civic Center complex, and is a magnificent example of the Beaux-Arts style. Allegorical figures evoking the city's Gold Rush past fill the pediment above the Polk Street entrance, which leads into the rotunda, one of the city's finest interior spaces.

# Hayes Valley **17**

**Map** 4 E5. 🚌 21, 22.

Situated west of City Hall, these few blocks of Hayes Street have become one of San Francisco's trendier shopping districts. After US 101 highway was damaged in the 1989 Loma Prieta earthquake (*see p505*) the road was demolished. The former

highway had previously divided Hayes Valley from the wealthy power-brokers and theatergoers who frequented the rest of the Civic Center. A small number of adventurous cafés and restaurants, such as Ivy's and Mad Magda's Russian Tea Room, had already established themselves alongside Hayes Street's second-hand furniture and reject shops. Today an influx of art galleries, interior design shops, trendy cafés, and unique boutiques has made the area noticeably more stylish.

View from Alamo Square toward the Downtown skyscrapers

# Alamo Square **18**

**Map** 4 D5. 🚌 21, 22.

The most photographed row of Victorian houses in the city lines the eastern side of this sloping green square. It is set

225 ft (68 m) above the Civic Center, offering great views of City Hall and the Downtown skyscrapers. The square was laid out at the same time as the beautiful squares in Pacific Heights, but it developed later, with speculators building nearly identical houses.

The "Six Sisters" Queen Anne-style houses built in 1895 at 710–20 Steiner Street on the east side of the square appear on numerous postcards of San Francisco. The city has now declared the area to be a historic district.

# University of San Francisco **19**

2130 Fulton St. **Map** 3 B5. **Tel** (415) 422-5555. 🚌 5, 31, 33, 38, 43. 🕙 8am–5pm Mon–Fri. **www**.usfca.edu

Originally founded in 1855 as St. Ignatius College, the University of San Francisco (USF) remains a Jesuit-run institution, though classes are now coeducational and non-denominational. The landmark of the campus is the St. Ignatius Church, completed in 1914. Its buff-colored twin towers are visible from the western half of San Francisco, especially when lit up at night. The campus and the surrounding residential area occupy land that was once San Francisco's main cemetery district, on and around Lone Mountain.

# HAIGHT ASHBURY AND THE MISSION

**Figure from Mission Dolores**

To the north of Twin Peaks – two windswept hills rising 900 ft (274 m) above the city – lies Haight Ashbury. With its rows of Victorian houses *(see pp300–301)*, it is mostly inhabited by the wealthy middle classes, although this is where thousands of hippies lived in the late 1960s *(see p359)*. The Castro District, to the east, is the center of the city's gay community. Well known for its hedonism in the 1970s, the area has become far quieter in recent years, although its cafés and shops are still lively. The Mission District, even farther east, was first founded by Spanish monks *(see pp46–7)* and is home to many Latin Americans.

## SIGHTS AT A GLANCE

### Historic Streets and Buildings
Castro Street **8**
Clarke's Folly **15**
Dolores Street **10**
Haight Ashbury **2**
Lower Haight Neighborhood **5**
Noe Valley **14**
(Richard) Spreckels Mansion **3**

### Churches
Mission Dolores **9**

### Landmarks
Sutro Tower **18**

### Parks and Gardens
Buena Vista Park **4**
Corona Heights Park **6**
Dolores Park **11**
Golden Gate Park Panhandle **1**
Twin Peaks **16**
Vulcan Street Steps **17**

### Museums and Galleries
Carnaval Mural **13**
Mission Cultural Center for the Latino Arts **12**

### Theaters
The Castro Theatre **7**

### KEY

▦  Street-by-Street map See pp356–7

🚇  BART station

🚊  Streetcar terminus

0 meters    750
0 yards    750

### GETTING THERE
The Muni N streetcar serves Haight Ashbury, the J streetcar serves the Mission, and all other lines serve the Castro Street station. Bus 33 links all three neighborhoods.

◁ **Street scene in Haight Ashbury**

# Street-by-Street: Haight Ashbury

Stretching from Buena Vista Park to the
flat expanses of Golden Gate Park, Haight
Ashbury was a place to escape to from
the city center in the 1880s. It then developed into a residential area, but between
1930 and 1960 it changed dramatically
from a middle-class neighborhood to the
center of the "Flower Power" world, with
a free clinic to treat hippies without
medical insurance. It has now settled
into being one of the liveliest and most
unconventional places in San Francisco,
with an eclectic mix of people, excellent
book and music shops, and good cafés.

**Haight Ashbury**
*In the 1960s, hippies met at this crossroads,*
*which gives the area its name* ❷

**Golden Gate Panhandle**
*This thin green strip runs west*
*into the heart of Golden*
*Gate Park* ❶

**Cha Cha Cha** is one of the
liveliest places to eat in
San Francisco, serving
Latin American food in a
series of small dishes
*(see p594).*

To bus nos. 7, 33

## STAR SIGHTS

★ Buena Vista Park

★ (Richard) Spreckels
   Mansion

**The Red Victorian Bed
& Breakfast**, a relic of
the 1960s hippie era,
caters to a New Age
clientele, with health
food and rooms with
transcendental themes
*(see p548).*

**No. 1220 Masonic Avenue** is one of many ornate Victorian mansions built on the steep hill that runs down from Golden Gate Park Panhandle to Haight Street.

**LOCATOR MAP**
*See Street Finder, map 10*

**KEY**

– – – Suggested route

★ **(Richard) Spreckels Mansion**
*This grand home at No. 737 Buena Vista Avenue was built in 1887* ❸

OAK STREET

LYON STREET

CENTRAL STREET

BUENA VISTA WEST

★ **Buena Vista Park**
*Through its mass of twisting, matted trees, this dramatic park offers magnificent views over the city* ❹

| 0 meters | 100 |
| 0 yards | 100 |

To bus no. 37

## Golden Gate Park Panhandle ❶

**Map** 9 C1. 🚌 6, 7, 21, 43, 66, 71.

This one-block-wide and eight-block-long stretch of parkland forms the narrow "Panhandle" to the giant rectangular pan that is Golden Gate Park (see pp366–9). It was the first part of the park to be reclaimed from the sand dunes that rolled across west San Francisco, and its eucalyptus trees are among the oldest and largest in the city.

The Panhandle's winding carriage roads and bridle paths were first laid out in the 1870s, and the upper classes came here to walk and ride. They built large mansions on the outskirts of the park, many of which can still be seen today. In 1906 the Panhandle was used as a refuge for families made homeless by the earthquake (see pp52–3). Today the old roads and paths are frequented regularly by large crowds of joggers and cyclists.

The Panhandle is still remembered for its "Flower Power" heyday of the 1960s. The era's young hippies flocked to the park to listen to impromptu free concerts held here by the new psychedelic bands from Haight Ashbury. The area is still a popular spot for the city's street musicians and hippie guitarists.

**Junction of Haight and Ashbury streets**

## Haight Ashbury ❷

**Map** 9 C1. 🚌 6, 7, 33, 37, 43, 66, 71. 🚋 N.

Taking its name from the junction of two major streets, Haight and Ashbury, this district contains alternative bookshops, large Victorian houses, and numerous cafés. Following the reclamation of Golden Gate Park (see pp366–9) and then the opening of a large amusement park called The Chutes, the area was rapidly built up in the 1890s as a middle-class suburb – hence the dozens of elaborate Queen Anne-style houses (see pp300–301) lining its streets. The Haight district survived the 1906 earthquake and fire (see pp52–3), and then experienced a brief boom, which was followed by a long period of decline.

After the tram tunnel underneath Buena Vista Park was completed in 1928, the middle classes began their exodus to the suburbs in the Sunset. The area reached its lowest ebb in the years after World War II. The big Victorian houses were divided into apartments and low rents attracted a disparate population. By the 1960s the Haight had become host to a bohemian community that was a hotbed of anarchy. A component of this "hippie scene" was the music of rock bands such as the Grateful Dead, but the area stayed fairly quiet until 1967. Then the "Summer of Love," fueled by the media, brought some 75,000 young people in search of free love, music, and drugs, and the area became the focus of a worldwide youth culture.

The Haight retains its radical atmosphere, but now there are problems with crime, drugs, and homelessness. However, from the cafés to the second-hand clothing shops, it still offers an "only in San Francisco" experience.

**Late-Victorian mansion built for Richard Spreckels**

## (Richard) Spreckels Mansion ❸

737 Buena Vista West. **Map** 9 C2. 🚌 6, 7, 37, 43, 66, 71. ⬤ to the public.

This house should not be confused with the grander Spreckels Mansion situated on Washington Street (see p348). It was, however, also built by the millionaire "Sugar King" Claus Spreckels, for his nephew Richard. The elaborate Queen Anne-style house (see pp300–301), built in 1887, is a typical late-Victorian Haight Ashbury home. It was once a guesthouse, whose guests included the acerbic journalist and ghost-story writer Ambrose Bierce, and the adventure writer Jack London, who wrote White Fang here in 1906 (see p26). The house is now in private hands.

## Buena Vista Park ❹

**Map** 9 C1. 🚌 6, 7, 37, 43, 66, 71.

Buena Vista Park rises steeply 570 ft (174 m) above the geographical center of San Francisco with views over the Bay Area. First landscaped in 1894, it is a pocket of land left to nature. Numerous overgrown and eroded paths wind up from Haight Street to the crest, but there is a paved route from Buena Vista Avenue. It is best to avoid the park at night.

# Lower Haight Neighborhood

**Map** 10 D1. 6, 7, 22, 66, 71. K, L, M.

Halfway between City Hall and Haight Ashbury, and marking the southern border of the predominantly African-American Fillmore District, the Lower Haight is an area in transition. Unusual art galleries and boutiques, including the Used Rubber USA shop, which sells clothes and accessories made entirely of recycled rubber, began to open here in the mid-1980s. These were in addition to the inexpensive cafés, bars, and restaurants serving a bohemian clientele already in business in the area. This combination has created one of the most lively districts in San Francisco.

As in nearby Alamo Square (see p353), the Lower Haight has dozens of houses known as "Victorians" (see pp300–301) built from the 1850s to the early 1900s, including the picturesque cottages such as the Nightingale House at No. 201 Buchanan Street, built in the 1880s. The 1950s public housing blocks have discouraged wholesale gentrification. The area is safe during the day but, like Alamo Square, it can seem threatening after dark.

**Sign from Cha Cha Cha restaurant on Mission Street** (see p593)

# Corona Heights Park

199 Museum Way. **Map** 9 D2.
**Tel** (415) 554-9600. 24, 37.
Randall Museum. L, M.
10am–5pm Tue–Sat. public hols. limited. donation.
**www.**randallmuseum.org

Corona Heights Park is a dusty and undeveloped rocky peak. Clinging to its side is

**View from Corona Heights across the Mission**

the unusual Randall Museum for children, with an extensive menagerie of rabbits, owls, snakes, and other animals, many of which children can handle and stroke. The emphasis of the museum is on participation, with many hands-on exhibits and workshops. Children also enjoy climbing on the craggy outcrops in the park. Corona Heights was gouged out by brick-making operations in the 19th century. It was never planted with trees, so its red rock peak has great views over the city. There is a good view of the winding streets of Twin Peaks (see p363).

## THE SOUNDS OF 1960S SAN FRANCISCO

During the late 1960s, and most notably during the 1967 "Summer of Love," young people from all over the country flocked to the Haight Ashbury district. They came not just to "turn on, tune in, and drop out," but also to listen to bands such as Janis Joplin's Big Brother and the Holding Company, Jefferson Airplane, and the Grateful Dead, all of whom emerged out of a thriving music scene. They established themselves at the city's new music venues.

**Premier music venues**
The Avalon Ballroom on Van Ness Avenue first opened in 1968 and was the most significant venue. Run by Chet Helms and the Family Dog collective, the Avalon pioneered the use of colorful psychedelic posters by designers such as Stanley Mouse and Alton Kelly (see pp440–41).

Fillmore Auditorium, facing the Japan Center (see p352) and a former church hall, was taken over by impresario Bill Graham in 1965, after whom the Civic Auditorium (see p352) is named. He put unlikely pairs such as Miles Davis and the Grateful Dead on the same bill, and brought in big-name performers from Jimi Hendrix to The Who. The Fillmore Auditorium was damaged in the 1989 earthquake but has recently reopened.

By the time Bill Graham died in 1992 he had become the most successful rock music promoter in the US.

**Janis Joplin (1943–70), hard-edged blues singer**

# The Castro Theatre ❼

429 Castro St. **Map** 10 D2. **Tel** 621-6120. 🚌 8, 24, 33, 35, 37. 🚋 F, K, L, M. **www**.thecastrotheatre.com
See **Entertainment** pp390–91.

Completed in 1922, this brightly lit neon marquee is a Castro Street landmark. It is the most sumptuous and best preserved of San Francisco's neighborhood film palaces, and one of the first commissions of the architect Timothy Pflueger. With its Arabian Nights interior, complete with a glorious Wurlitzer organ that rises from the floor between the screenings, it is well worth the price of admission. The ceiling of the auditorium is cast in plaster and resembles the interior of a large tent, with imitation swathes of fabric, rope, and tassels. The theater seats 1,500 and shows mainly revival classics.

**Historic and ornate Castro Theatre**

# Castro Street ❽

**Map** 10 D2. 🚌 8, 24, 33, 35, 37. 🚋 F, K, L, M.

The hilly neighborhood around Castro Street between Twin Peaks and the Mission District is the heart of San Francisco's high-profile gay and lesbian community. Focused on the intersection of Castro Street and 18th Street, the self-proclaimed "Gayest Four Corners of the World" emerged as a homosexual nexus during the 1970s. Gays of the Flower Power generation moved into this predominantly working-class district and began restoring Victorian houses and setting up businesses. They also opened gay bars such as the Twin Peaks Tavern on the corner of Castro Street and 17th Street. Unlike earlier bars, where lesbians and gays hid in dark corners out of public view, the Twin Peaks installed large windows. Though the many shops and restaurants attract all kinds of people, the area's openly homosexual identity has made it a place of pilgrimage for gays and lesbians. Still the world's largest gay community, it symbolizes for this minority group a freedom not often found in cities elsewhere.

One of the city's first openly gay politicians, Harvey Milk was known as the Mayor of Castro Street before his assassination on November 28, 1978. He and Mayor George Moscone were killed by an ex-policeman, whose lenient sentence caused rioting in the city. Milk is remembered with a plaza outside the Muni stop on Market Street and a candlelit procession from Castro Street to City Hall every year.

Over a quarter of a million people come to the area for the Castro Street Fair, which is held each October. Arts, crafts, beer, food, and music are all provided, and proceeds go towards helping the local community.

**AIDS Memorial Quilt on display in Washington, DC in 1992**

## THE NAMES PROJECT

The NAMES Project's AIDS Memorial Quilt was conceived by San Francisco gay rights activist Cleve Jones, who organized the first candlelit procession on Castro Street for Harvey Milk in 1985. Jones and his fellow marchers wrote the names of all their friends who had died of AIDS on placards, which they then taped to the San Francisco Federal Building. The resulting "patchwork quilt" of names inspired Jones to create the first panel for the AIDS Memorial Quilt in 1987. Public response to the quilt was immediate – both in the US and across the world. It is now made up of over 60,000 panels, some sewn by individuals and others by "quilting bees" – friends and relatives who have come together to commemorate a person lost to AIDS. All panels are the same size – 3 by 6 ft (90 by 180 cm) – but each is different: the design, colors, and material reflect the life and personality of the person commemorated. In 2002 the Memorial Quilt moved from its base in San Francisco to permanent headquarters in Atlanta, Georgia.

# Mission Dolores ❾

16th St and Dolores St. **Map** 10 E3.
📞 621-8203. 🚌 22. 🚊 J.
🕐 9am–5pm (to 4pm in winter).
⬤ Thanksgiving, Dec
25. 📷 🅿 ♿ 🎦
**www.**mission
dolores.org

Preserved intact
since it was built in
1791, Mission Dolores
is the oldest building
in the city and an
embodiment of
San Francisco's
religious Spanish colonial
roots (see pp46–7). The
mission was founded by
Father Junípero Serra and
is formally known as the
Mission of San Francisco

**Figure of saint in
the mission**

de Asis. The name Dolores
reflects its proximity to *Laguna
de los Dolores* (Lake of Our
Lady of Sorrows), an ancient
insect-plagued swamp.
The building is modest
by mission standards,
but its 4-ft (1.2-m-)
thick walls have sur-
vived the years
without serious
decay and Native
American paintings
adorn the ceiling.
There is a fine
Baroque altar and
reredos, and a
display of histori-
cal documents in
the small museum.
Most services are
now held in the
basilica, built next

to the mission in 1918. The
cemetery contains graves of
San Franciscan pioneers. A
statue marking the mass grave
of 5,000 Native Americans,
most of whom died in measles
epidemics in 1804 and 1826,
was later stolen. All that now
remains is a pedestal, reading
"In Prayerful Memory of our
Faithful Indians."

**The painted and gilded
altarpiece** *was imported from
Mexico in 1780.*

**The statue** of Father Junípero Serra
is a copy of the work of local
sculptor Arthur Putnam.

**The ceramic mural** was created by
Guillermo Granizo, a native San
Francisco artist.

**Museum and
display**

**The ceiling** paintings
are based on original
Ohlone designs using
vegetable dyes.

**Entrance for
the disabled**

**The mission
cemetery** originally
extended across
many streets. The
earliest wooden
grave markers have
disintegrated, but
the Lourdes Grotto
commemorates the
forgotten dead.

**Statue of Our Lady
of Mount Carmel**

**The mission
façade** has four
columns which
support niches
for three bells,
inscribed with their
names and dates.

**Entrance
and gift
shop**

Spanish-American War memorial on Dolores Street

## Dolores Street ⑩

**Map** 10 E2. 🚌 8, 22, 33, 48. 🚃 J.

Lined by lovingly maintained late Victorian houses (see pp300–301) and an island of palm trees, this street is one of the city's most attractive public spaces. The broad street runs parallel to Mission Street, forming the western border of the Mission District. It starts at Market Street, where a statue honoring soldiers of the Spanish-American War is over-whelmed by the Old Mint.

Mission High School, with the white walls and red tile roof typical of Mission-style architecture (see p30), and Mission Dolores (see p361) are both situated on Dolores Street. The street ends in the Noe Valley district.

## Dolores Park ⑪

**Map** 10 E3. 🚌 22, 33. 🚃 J.

Originally the site of San Francisco's main Jewish cemetery, Dolores Park was transformed in 1905 into one of the Mission District's few large open spaces. Ringed by Dolores, Church, 18th, and 20th streets, it is situated high on a hill with an excellent view of the city center.

Dolores Park is very popular during the day with tennis players, sunbathers, and dog walkers, but after dark it can draw drug dealers. Above the park to the south and west, the streets rise so steeply that

many turn into pedestrian-only stairways. Some of the city's finest Victorian houses can also be seen here.

## Mission Cultural Center for Latino Arts ⑫

2868 Mission St. **Map** 10 F4. **Tel** (415) 821-1155. 🚌 14, 26, 48, 49. 🚃 J. Gallery. ⏰ 10am–5pm Tue–Fri, 10am–6pm Sat. ♿ **www**.missionculturalcenter.org

This dynamic arts center, part-ly funded by the city, offers music and dance classes, con-certs, theater, two art galleries, and a silk-screen print shop for the local Latino community. It also hosts the district's Day of the Dead (see p38) celebration.

**Detail from the Carnaval Mural**

## Carnaval Mural ⑬

24th St and South Van Ness Ave. **Map** 10 F4. 🚌 12, 14, 48, 49, 67. 🚃 J.

One of the many brightly painted murals on the walls of the Mission District, the Carnaval Mural celebrates the diverse people who come together for the Carnaval festival (see p36). This annual spring event is the highlight of the year.

Guided tours of the other murals, some with political themes, are given by civic organizations. There is also an outdoor gallery with murals in Balmy Alley (see pp306–7).

## Noe Valley ⑭

🚌 24, 35, 48. 🚃 J.

Noe Valley is often referred to as "Noewhere Valley" by its residents, who remain determined to keep it off the tourist map. It is a pleasant, comfortable neighborhood, largely inhabited by young professionals. Its spotless streets and safe atmosphere seem at odds with the sur-rounding, densely populated Mission District.

The area was named after its original land-grant owner, José de Jesús Noé, justice of the peace of Yerba Buena, the Mexican village that eventually grew into San Francisco. The valley was first built up during the 1880s after a cable car line over the steep Castro Street hill was completed. The low rents attracted mostly working-class Irish families. Then, like so many other areas of San Francisco, this once blue-collar district underwent gentrification in the 1970s, raising the value of the properties and resulting in today's engaging mix of boutiques, bars, and restaurants. The Noe Valley Ministry, found at No. 1021 Sanchez Street, is a late 1880s Presbyterian church in the "Stick Style" (see pp300–301), the most prevalent architectural style in the city, with its emphasis on vertical lines. The ministry was converted into a community center in the 1970s.

**Victorian façade of the Noe Valley Ministry on Sanchez Street**

**Nobby Clarke's Folly**

## Clarke's Folly **⑮**

250 Douglass St. **Map** 10 D3. 🚌 8, 33, 35, 37, 48. ⬤ to the public.

This resplendent white manor house was at one time set in its own extensive grounds. It was built in 1892 by Alfred Clarke, known locally as Nobby. Clarke had worked for the San Francisco Police Department at the time of the Committee of Vigilance in 1851, when a group of local citizens attempted to control the city's growing lawlessness (see pp48–9). The house is said to have cost $100,000 to build, a huge sum in the 1890s.

Although it is now surrounded by other buildings, the house is a fine example of Victorian domestic architecture. The turrets and the gabled roof are typical of the Queen Anne style, while the shingled walls and front porch adopt the elements of Eastlake architecture (see pp300–301).

Today the house is divided into private apartments.

## Twin Peaks **⑯**

**Map** 9 C4. 🚌 33, 36, 37.

These two hills were first known in Spanish as El Pecho de la Chola, the "Bosom of the Indian Girl." They lie at the heart of San Francisco, and reach a height of 900 ft

(274 m) above sea level. At the top there is an area of parkland with steep, grassy slopes, from which incomparable views of the whole of San Francisco can be enjoyed.

Twin Peaks Boulevard circles both hills near their summits; there is a parking lot and viewing point that overlooks the city. Those who are prepared to climb up the steep path to the very top on foot can leave the crowds behind and get a breathtaking 360-degree view.

Twin Peaks are the only hills in the city left in their original state. The residential districts on the lower slopes have curving streets that wind around the contours of the hills, rather than the grid system that is more common in the rest of San Francisco.

## Vulcan Street Steps **⑰**

Vulcan St. **Map** 9 C2. 🚌 37.

Apart from a tiny figure of Spock standing on a mail-box, there is no connection between the cult television program Star Trek and this block of houses climbing between Ord and Levant Streets. However, the Vulcan Steps do feel light years away from the busy Castro District below. The small, picturesque gardens of the houses spill out and soften the edges of the steps, and a canopy of pines muffles the city sounds. There are great views of the Mission District and the southern waterfront.

## Sutro Tower **⑱**

**Map** 9 B3. 🚌 36, 37. ⬤ to the public.

Marking the skyline like an invading robot, Sutro Tower is 970 ft (295 m) high. It was named after the local philanthropist and landowner Adolph Sutro, and it carries antennae for the signals of most of San Francisco's TV and radio stations. Built in 1973, it is still much used, despite the rise of cable networks. The tower is visible from all over the Bay Area, and sometimes seems to float above the summer fogs that roll in from the sea. On the north side of the tower there are dense eucalyptus groves, first planted in the 1880s by Adolph Sutro.

**View of the city and of Twin Peaks Boulevard from the top of Twin Peaks**

# GOLDEN GATE PARK AND THE PRESIDIO

The spectacular Golden Gate Park is one of the world's largest urban parks, created in the 1890s out of sandy wasteland. It houses three museums and a range of sports facilities. Land's End, the city's wildest region and scene of many shipwrecks, is accessible from the park.

**Cannon from the Presidio**

To the north of Golden Gate Park, the Presidio, overlooking San Francisco Bay, was established as an outpost of Spain's New World empire in 1776, and for many years was a military base. In 1993 it became a National Park, and visitors can now stroll through its acres of woodland full of wildlife.

## SIGHTS AT A GLANCE

### Historic Streets and Buildings
Clement Street ⑫
*Golden Gate Bridge pp380–81* ⑱
Presidio Officers' Club ⑭

### Parks and Gardens
Bison Paddock ⑧
Conservatory of Flowers ⑤
Japanese Tea Garden ③
Queen Wilhelmina Tulip Garden ⑨
San Francisco Botanical Garden at Strybing Arboretum ⑥
Shakespeare Garden ②
Stow Lake ⑦

### Museums and Galleries
*California Academy of Sciences* ①
de Young ④
Fort Point ⑰
*Legion of Honor pp374–5* ⑩
Presidio Visitor Center ⑮
The Walt Disney Family Museum ⑯

### Churches and Temples
Holy Virgin Cathedral ⑪
Temple Emanu-El ⑬

0 kilometers  1
0 miles  0.5

## GETTING THERE

For Golden Gate Park, take buses 5, 7, 21, 71, or 73, or the N streetcar. The Presidio is best seen by car, but Muni bus 29 stops at the main sights, bus 43 serves the eastern end, and bus 28 the northern boundary.

### KEY

⬛ Street-by-Street map
*See pp366–7*

⬛ The Presidio
*See pp376–7*

◁ **Golden Gate Bridge from Fort Point**

# Street-by-Street: Golden Gate Park

Golden Gate Park is 3 miles (5 km) long and almost 1 mile (1.6 km) across. It stretches from the Pacific Ocean to the center of San Francisco, forming an oasis of greenery and calm in which to escape from the bustle of city life. Within the park an amazing number of activities are catered to, both sporting and cultural. The landscaped area around the Music Concourse, with its fountains, plane trees, and benches, is the most popular and developed section.

**Lamp in the Japanese Tea Garden**

Here you can enjoy free Sunday concerts at the Spreckels Temple of Music. A total of three museums stand on either side of the Concourse, and the Japanese and Shakespeare gardens are within walking distance.

**★ de Young**
*This museum showcases collections from around the world. Exhibits include this mahogany chest, made in Philadelphia in 1780* ❹

**The Great Buddha** reaches almost 11 ft (3 m) in height.

**★ Japanese Tea Garden**
*This exquisite garden, with its well-tended plants and pretty lake, is one of the most attractive parts of the park* ❸

**KEY**

– – – Suggested route

| 0 meters | 80 |
| 0 yards | 80 |

**STAR SIGHTS**

★ de Young

★ Japanese Tea Garden

**Shakespeare Garden**
*This tiny garden holds more than 150 species of plants, all mentioned in Shakespeare's poetry or plays* ❷

…e statue of the *Apple Cider …ess*, by sculptor Thomas …ields-Clarke, is …e of the few …onuments to …rvive from …e California …idwinter …ir of …94.

**LOCATOR MAP**
See Street Finder, map 7 & 8

THE PRESIDIO

Pacific Ocean

GOLDEN GATE PARK

**The Music Concourse** is the venue for summer concerts.

**California Academy of Sciences**
*This extraordinary venue contains a rainforest and nearly 40,000 animals* ❶

# California Academy of Sciences ❶

See pp370–71.

# Shakespeare Garden

Music Concourse, Golden Gate Park. **Map** 8 F2. 🚌 44.

Gardeners here have tried to cultivate all the plants mentioned in Shakespeare's works. Relevant quotations are inscribed on plaques set in the wall at the back of the garden. A 19th-century bust of the playwright is kept in a box opened only occasionally.

# Japanese Tea Garden ❸

Music Concourse, Golden Gate Park. **Map** 8 F2. **Tel** (415) 752-4227. 🚌 5, 38, 44. ◯ Mar–Oct: 9am–6pm daily; Nov–Feb: 9am–4:45pm daily. 🈸 🔲 🗍

Established by the art-dealer George Turner Marsh for the 1894 California Midwinter Fair, this garden is very popular. A Japanese gardener, Makota Hagiwara, was later contracted to tend it. He and his family maintained and expanded the garden until 1942, when they were interned during World War II. The best time to visit is when the cherry trees blossom in April.

# de Young ❹

50 Hagiwara Tea Garden Drive, Golden Gate Pk. **Map** 8 F2. **Tel** (415) 750-3600. ◯ 9:30am–5:15pm Tue–Sun. 🈸 (free first Tue of month.) 🔥 www.deyoungmuseum.org

Founded in 1895, the de Young houses one of the city's finest art collections. In 1989 the original building was too damaged by an earthquake to be saved. The collection is now housed in an exciting, purpose-built, state-of-the-art facility. The museum contains a broad range of American art, as well as extensive pre-Columbian-American, African, and Oceanic works.

## Conservatory of Flowers ❺

100 John F Kennedy Drive, Golden Gate Park. **Map** 9 A1. **Tel** (415) 831-2090. 🚌 33, 44. 🕐 10am–4:30pm Tue–Sun. 🎟 (free 1st Tue of the month.) 🎞 📷 ♿ limited. 🏪 www.conservatoryofflowers.org

This ornate greenhouse, inspired by the one in London's Kew Gardens, is the oldest building in the park. A property developer, James Lick, imported the frame from Ireland, but died before its erection in 1879. Ferns, palms, and orchids thrived for over a century until a hurricane in 1995 largely destroyed the conservatory. San Franciscans campaigned for its repair, and it reopened in 2003.

## San Francisco Botanical Garden at Strybing Arboretum ❻

9th Ave at Lincoln Way, Golden Gate Park. **Map** 8 F2. **Tel** (415) 661 1316. 🚌 44, 71. 🕐 Apr–Oct: 9am–6pm daily; Nov–Mar: 10am–5pm daily. 🎟 📷 ♿ 🕐 1:30pm daily. 🏪 www.sfbotanicalgarden.org

On display in the Botanical Garden are 7,500 species of plants, trees, and shrubs from

**Garden of Fragrance in the Strybing Arboretum**

around the world. There are Mexican, African, South American, and Australian gardens, and one that is devoted entirely to native California plants. Well worth a visit is the enchanting Moon-Viewing Garden. It exhibits Far Eastern plants in a naturalistic setting. Both medicinal and culinary plants are grown in the Garden of Fragrance, which is designed for blind plant-lovers. Here the emphasis is on the senses of taste, touch, and smell, and all the plants are identified in Braille.

Another area, with a stream winding through it, is planted with indigenous California redwood trees. This re-creates the flora and the atmosphere of a northern Californian coastal forest. There is also a New World Cloud Forest, with

flora from the mountains of Central America. Surprisingly, all these gardens thrive in the Californian fogs.

There is a small shop selling seeds and books, as well as the Helen Crocker Horticultural Library, which is open to the public. A flower show and plant sale is held every spring.

## Stow Lake ❼

Stow Lake Drive, Golden Gate Park. **Map** 8 E2. 🚌 28, 29. 🖥 ♿

In 1895, the President of the Park Commission, WW Stow, ordered the construction of this artificial lake, the largest in the park. It was created encircling Strawberry Hill (named after the wild fruit that once grew here), so that the summit of the hill now forms an island in the lake. It is linked to the mainland by two stone-clad bridges. Stow Lake's circular stream makes an ideal course for rowing laps from the boathouse, although the tranquil atmosphere makes leisurely drifting seem more appropriate. A Chinese pavilion on the island's shore was a gift to San Francisco from its sister city in Taiwan, Taipei. The red and green pavilion arrived in San Francisco by ship in 6,000 pieces and then was reassembled on the island.

**Chinese moon-watching pavilion on Stow Lake**

*For hotels and restaurants in this region see pp542–9 and pp587–95*

The millionaire railway baron Collis Porter Huntington *(see pp50–51)* donated the money in 1894 to create the reservoir and the waterfall that cascades into Stow Lake. These are known as Huntington Falls. Damaged in the 1906 earthquake *(see pp52–3)*, it was restored in the 1980s and is now one of the park's most attractive features.

## Buffalo Paddock ❽

John F Kennedy Drive, Golden Gate Park. **Map** 7 C2. 🚌 *5, 29.*

The shaggy buffalo grazing in this specially designed paddock are the largest of all North American land animals. Immediately recognizable by their short horns and humped backs, buffaloes are the symbol of the American plains, and are more properly known as the American bison.

This paddock was opened in 1892, with the aim of protecting the species, then on the verge of extinction. The first herd, however, brought in from Wyoming, all died of a tuberculosis epidemic and had to be replaced. In 1902 William Cody, the American scout and showman "Buffalo Bill," traded one of his bulls for one from the Golden Gate Park herd. Both parties thought that they had rid themselves of an aggressive beast, but Cody's newly purchased bull jumped a high fence once it was back at his encampment and escaped. According to one newspaper, the *San Francisco Call*, it took 80 men to recapture it.

Queen Wilhelmina Tulip Garden and the Dutch Windmill

## Queen Wilhelmina Tulip Garden ❾

**Map** 7 A2. 🚌 *5, 18.* **Windmill** ♿

This garden was named after the Dutch Queen Wilhelmina, and hundreds of tulip bulbs are donated each year by the Dutch Bulb Growers' Association. In the spring, the area is carpeted with the flowers in full bloom. The Dutch Windmill, near the northwest corner of Golden Gate Park, was built in 1903. Its purpose, along with its companion, the Murphy Windmill, erected in the park's southwest corner in 1905, was to pump water from a source underground, in order to irrigate the park. The increasing volume of water required – about 5 million gallons, or 230 million liters per day – soon made the windmills obsolete, and they are no longer in use.

### JOHN MCLAREN

Although Golden Gate Park was designed by William Hammond Hall, the park's current status owes the most to his successor, John McLaren.

McLaren was born in Scotland in 1846 and studied botany before emigrating to California in the 1870s. He succeeded Hall as administrator in 1887 and devoted the rest of his life to the park.

An expert landscape gardener and botanist, McLaren succeeded in importing exotic plants from all over the world and making them thrive, despite the poor soil and foggy climate. He planted thousands of trees and chose the right shrubs to make sure the park was in full bloom all year long.

John McLaren Lodge, a sandstone villa situated on the park's east side, was built in 1896 as a home for McLaren and his family. As McLaren lay dying in 1943, he requested that the cypress tree outside the lodge be lit with Christmas lights, and his request was granted, despite a wartime blackout being in force. The tree is still referred to as "Uncle John's Christmas Tree" and is lit every December in his honor. He is buried in a tomb in the San Francisco City Hall. Golden Gate Park still remains true to his vision – a place in which to escape from city life.

**Buffalo in the Buffalo Paddock**

# California Academy of Sciences 🟊

The California Academy of Sciences has moved back to its permanent, refurbished home in Golden Gate Park. The building, housing Steinhart Aquarium, Morrison Planetarium, and the Kimball Natural History Museum, combines innovative green architecture with flexible exhibition spaces. A large piazza is at the heart of the building, with excellent views overlooking Golden Gate Park.

**A penguin in the African Hall**

A 2.5-acre (1-ha) living roof covers the building

## MUSEUM GUIDE

*Steinhart Aquarium displays are spread throughout the museum, but most of the tanks can be found in the basement beneath the Piazza. An auditorium above the café holds traveling exhibits as well as special performances and programs. The back of the building holds the museum's collection of over 26 million scientific specimens along with staff offices and research laboratories.*

The Swamp

Coral Reef Tank

Sharks

**Morrison Planetarium**
*State of the art exhibits and digital technology transform the ceiling here into a night sky.*

## KEY TO FLOOR PLAN

- ☐ African Hall
- ☐ Kimball Natural History Museum
- ☐ Morrison Planetarium
- ☐ Rainforests of the World
- ☐ Steinhart Aquarium
- ☐ Aquarium Tanks
- ☐ Non-exhibition space

**Tusher African Center**
*Realistic models of animals from Africa's deserts and savannas are displayed here, in lifelike dioramas.*

**★ Steinhart Aquarium**
*The world's deepest living coral reef display, a two-story Swamp, Discovery Tidepool, and hundreds of "jewel" tanks showcase the stunning diversity of aquatic life.*

...azza (more
...einhart Aquarium
...hibits one floor
...low)

## VISITORS' CHECKLIST

55 Concourse Dr. **Map** 8 F2.
*Tel* (415) 379-8000. ☐
9:30am–5pm Mon–Sat (until 9pm Thu), 11am–5pm Sun. ⊠
(free third Wed of every month.)
🚻 ♿ 🛄 📷 🖥 For more information, visit **www**.calacademy.org

**California Coast Tank**
*Critters that live in the cold waters of California, like this hermit crab, can be found in this section.*

**Tyrannosaurus Rex Skeleton**
*This gigantic predator was the most powerful carnivore ever to walk the earth.*

**★ Rainforests of the World**
*This four-story exhibit offers a vertical journey through four different rainforest habitats. Real macaws and other exotic birds live in the canopy of this exhibit.*

## STAR EXHIBITS

★ Rainforests of the World

★ Steinhart Aquarium

Golden Gate Bridge from Lincoln Park golf course ▷

# Legion of Honor ⓾

Inspired by the Palais de la Légion d'Honneur in Paris, Alma de Bretteville Spreckels built this museum in the 1920s to honor Californian soldiers who died in World War I, and to promote French art in California. Designed by the architect George Applegarth, it contains paintings by Monet, Rubens, and Rembrandt, more than 70 sculptures by Rodin, and over 4,000 years of ancient art. The Achenbach Foundation for Graphic Art, a famous collection of graphic works, occupies part of the gallery.

**Old Woman**
*French artist Georges de la Tour painted this female portrait in about 1618.*

**Florence Gould Theater**

**The Porcelain Gallery**
contains figurines, china, and other pieces dating from the 18th century.

**Stairs down from first floor**

**Virgin and Child**
*This oil-on-panel by the Flemish artist Dieric Bouts dates from the 15th century. It forms part of a series of four panels titled* Life of the Virgin.

## STAR FEATURES

★ The Thinker by Auguste Rodin

★ Waterlilies by Claude Monet

### VISITORS' CHECKLIST

34th Ave & Clement, Lincoln Park. **Map** 1 B5. **Tel** *(415) 750-3600.* 🚌 *18.* ⬜ *9:30am– 5.15pm Tue–Sun.* ⬤ *public hols.* 🆓 *(free 1st Tue of every month.)* ♿ 📷 📹 ⬛
**www**.legionofhonor.org

**The Tribute Money** *(1612)*
*The use of primary colors in this oil-on-canvas is typical of the Flemish artist Peter Paul Rubens.*

**The Impresario**
*In this portrait from around 1877, artist Edgar Degas emphasizes the subject's size by making him appear too large for the frame.*

### GALLERY GUIDE

*The museum's permanent collection of European and ancient art is displayed throughout the galleries on the first floor. Works are arranged chronologically, from the medieval period, left of the main entrance, through the Renaissance, and on to the 20th century. Temporary exhibitions, graphic art, and the porcelain collection are on the lower level.*

**Entrance**

★ **Waterlilies**
*Claude Monet's work from between 1914 and 1917 is one of a series depicting the lily pond in his gardens in Giverny, near Paris.*

★ **The Thinker**
*An original bronze casting of Rodin's* Le Penseur *(1904) is at the center of the colonnaded Court of Honor. It is one of 11 castings of the statue in collections around the world.*

### KEY TO FLOOR PLAN

| | |
|---|---|
| ⬜ | Permanent displays |
| ⬜ | Achenbach Foundation Library |
| ⬜ | Porcelain gallery |
| ⬛ | Theater storage |
| ⬜ | Special Exhibitions |
| ⬜ | Non-exhibition space |

# The Presidio

**Presidio Park sign**

The winding roads and lush green landscaping of the Presidio belie its long military history. This prominent site has played a key role in San Francisco's growth, and it has been occupied longer than any other part of the city. Remnants of its military past, including the well-preserved barracks, artillery emplacements, and cannons, can be seen everywhere, and there are many hiking trails, bike paths, beaches, and restaurants. The coastal path in Crissy Field is one of the most popular walks in the city. The Golden Gate Bridge crosses the bay from the northwest corner of the Presidio to Marin County.

**Fort Point**
*This impressive brick fortress, now a national historic site, guarded the Golden Gate during the Civil War of 1861–5* **16**

**★ Golden Gate Bridge**
*Opened in 1937, the bridge has a single span of 4,200 ft (1,280 m)* **17**

**Mountain Lake** is a large spring-fed lake and a popular picnic spot. The original Presidio was established nearby in 1776 to defend the bay area and Mission Dolores *(see p361)*.

**Crissy Field** was reclaimed from marshland for the 1915 Panama-Pacific Exposition *(see p351)*. It was used as an airfield from 1919 to 1936 and has been restored.

**LOCATOR MAP**
*See Street Finder, map 2 & 3*

**The Military Cemetery** holds the remains of almost 15,000 American soldiers killed during several wars.

**The Tidal Marsh** is part of the restoration of the Presidio area at Crissy Field.

**Arguello Gate**
*This decorative gate with its military symbols marks an entrance to the former army base, now a national park, open to the public.*

**★ Presidio Visitor Center**
*The visitor center on Moraga Avenue is in the Main Post area of the Presidio.*

**STAR SIGHTS**

★ Golden Gate Bridge

★ Presidio Visitor Center

| 0 meters | | 500 |
| 0 yards | | 500 |

# Holy Virgin Cathedral **⓫**

6210 Geary Blvd. **Map** 8 D1. 📞 (415) 221-3255. 🚌 2, 29, 38. 🕐 9:30–11:30am Tue & Wed. ✝ 8am, 6pm Mon–Sat, 7:30am, 9:45am, 6pm Sun.

Shining gold onion-shaped domes crown the Russian Orthodox Holy Virgin Cathedral of the Russian Church in Exile, a startling landmark in the suburban Richmond District. Built in the early 1960s, it is generally open to the public only during services. In contrast to those of many other Christian denominations, the services in this cathedral are conducted with the congregation standing, so there are no pews or seats.

The cathedral and the many Russian-owned businesses surrounding it, such as the lively Russian Renaissance restaurant, are situated at the heart of San Francisco's extensive Russian community (*see p35*). This has flourished since the 1820s, but it reached its highest population when immigrants arrived after the Russian Revolution of 1917. It boomed again in the late 1950s and late 1980s.

# Clement Street **⓬**

**Map** 1 C5. 🚌 2, 28, 29, 44.

This is a bustling main thoroughfare of the otherwise sleepy Richmond District. Bookshops and small boutiques flourish here, and the inhabitants of the neighborhood meet together in a lively mix of bars, fast-food cafés, and ethnic restaurants. Most of these are patronized more by locals than by tourists.

Clement Street is surrounded by an area known as New Chinatown, home to more than one-third of the Chinese population of San Francisco. As a result, some of the city's best Chinese restaurants can be found here, and the emphasis in general is on Far Eastern cuisine (*see p590–91*).

The area is also known for the diversity of its restaurants, and Peruvian and French establishments, among others, flourish here. The street stretches from Arguello Boulevard to the north/south cross-streets that are more commonly known as "The Avenues." It ends near the Legion of Honor (*see pp374–5*).

Interior of Temple Emanu-El, showing the Holy Ark

# Temple Emanu-El **⓭**

2 Lake St. **Map** 3 A4. **Tel** (415) 751-2535. 🚌 1, 33. 🕐 8:30am–5:30pm Mon–Thu (to 4:30pm Fri; to 7:30pm first Fri of month). ✡ 5:30pm, 7:30pm Fri, 10:30am Sat (call to verify times). 🚫 during services. ♿ www.emmanuelsf.org

After World War I hundreds of Jews from Russia and Eastern Europe moved into the Richmond District and built major religious centers. Among these is the Temple Emanu-El, its dome inspired by that of 6th-century Hagia Sophia, Istanbul.

The temple was built in 1925 for the longest established congregation of Jews in the city, founded in 1850. The architect was Arthur Brown, who also designed City Hall (*see p352*). The temple is an architectural hybrid: Mission style (*see pp30–31*), Byzantine ornamentation and Romanesque arcades.

# Presidio Officers' Club **⓮**

50 Moraga Ave. **Map** 3 A2. **Tel** (415) 561-2582. 🚌 29. 🕐 9am–5pm daily. 🔴 some public hols.

Looking out across the original parade grounds of the Presidio, the Officers' Club was built in the Spanish Mission style (*see pp30–31*). Although it dates from the 1930s, it was carefully built around the adobe (sun-dried brick) remains of the original 18th-century Spanish fort. Private events and public exhibitions are held here.

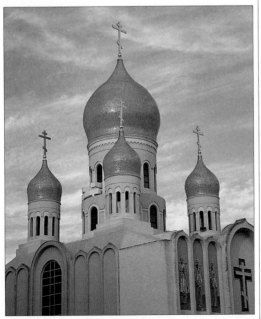

**The Russian Orthodox Holy Virgin Cathedral**

# Presidio Visitor Center **⑮**

Temporarily in 105 Montgomery. **Map** 3 A2. **Tel** (415) 561-4323. ◯ 10am–4pm Thu–Sun. **www**. presidio.gov or **www**.nps.gov/prsf

Due to current renovation in the Presidio area, the Presidio Visitor Center now serves as the gateway not only to the Presidio, but also to Fort Point Historic Site, Crissy Field, and Battery Chamberlain. Temporarily housed in a brick 1890s soldiers' barracks, the center houses exhibits showcasing the history of the Presidio. Displays focus on eyewitness accounts of the Presidio's evolution, from small, frontier military outpost to a major metropolis.

Two small cabins behind the Old Post Hospital *(see p377)* are representative of the hundreds of shelters set up here after the earthquake of 1906 *(see pp52–3)*.

# The Walt Disney Family Museum **⑯**

104 Montgomery St. **Map** 3 A2. **Tel** (415) 345-6800. ◯ 10am–6pm Wed–Mon. ● Jan 1. 🎟 www.waltdisney.org

Walt Disney is most often associated with the characters he created, from Mickey Mouse to Goofy, but less is known about Disney himself. This museum focuses on the life

**Golden Gate Bridge, seen from Fort Point**

and times of Walt Disney using photographs, documents, animation art, and an impressive range of interactive exhibits.

# Fort Point **⑰**

Long Ave & Marine Drive. **Map** 2 E1. 🏢 (415) 556-1693. ◯ 10am–5pm Fri–Sun (call for extra days open in summer). 📷 ♿ partial. www.nps.gov/fopo

Completed by the US Army in 1861, this fort was built both to protect San Francisco Bay from military attack and to defend ships carrying gold from the Californian mines *(see pp48–9)*. It is only the third system fort constructed along the Pacific coastline and is a classic example of a pre-Civil War

brick-and-granite fortress. The building soon became obsolete when new rifled artillery came into use and its 8-ft- (2-m-) thick brick walls were not strong enough to stand up to continued bombardment. It was closed in 1900.

The fort's brickwork vaulting is unusual for San Francisco and may have saved the fort from collapse in the 1906 earthquake *(see pp52–3)*. It was nearly demolished in the 1930s to make way for the Golden Gate Bridge, but it survived and is a good place from which to view the bridge. Restored in the 1970s, the fort now houses a museum displaying military uniforms and arms. Cannon-loading demonstrations and tours are available.

**Cannon near the Old Post Hospital on the grounds of the Presidio**

## A HISTORY OF THE PRESIDIO

In 1776 José Joaquín Moraga, one of the first Spanish settlers, founded a presidio. His aim in erecting this camp of adobe buildings on the edge of San Francisco Bay was to defend the Mission

**The Presidio in the 19th century**

Dolores *(see p361)*. Following Mexican independence from Spain, the site remained the northernmost fort of the short-lived republic until the United States took it over in 1847. The Presidio was used for military purposes until 1990.

From the 1850s to the 1930s, the adobe buildings were replaced, first with wooden barracks, and later with concrete Mission- and Georgian-style cottages for the officers and their families. These buildings remain.

The site covers 1,400 acres (567 ha), and its landscaped forests of eucalyptus and cypress trees are not found on any other army base in the world. The Presidio has now been declared an historic site and is a protected member of the Golden Gate National Recreation Area (GGNRA).

# Golden Gate Bridge ⑱

Named after that part of San Francisco Bay called "Golden Gate" by John Frémont in 1844, the bridge opened in 1937, connecting the city with Marin County. It took just over four years to build at a cost of $35 million. Breathtaking views are offered from this spectacular, world-famous landmark, which has six lanes for vehicles plus a free pedestrian walkway. It is the world's third largest single-span bridge and, when it was built, it was the world's longest and tallest suspension structure.

**Bridge builder wearing protective mask**

**The twin steel towers** rise to a height of 746 ft (227 m) above the water. The towers are hollow.

**Catching the Hot Rivets**
*Working in gangs of four, one man heated the rivets and threw them to another, who caught them in a bucket. The other two fastened sections of steel with the hot rivets.*

**The Foundations**
*The foundations of the twin towers are a remarkable feat of engineering. The south pier, 1,125 ft (343 m) offshore, was sunk 100 ft (30 m) into the sea bed.*

Pier base

Fender

Reinforcing iron frame

**The roadway** is 220 ft (67 m) above water 318-ft (97-m) deep

**Toll Booths**
*As many as 600 cars an hour cross through the 14 toll booths at the Golden Gate Bridge during the rush hour. Tolls are collected in the southbound direction only.*

### The Roadway
*The original steel-supported concrete roadway was constructed from the towers in both directions, so that weight on the suspension cables was evenly distributed.*

### Joseph Strauss
*Chicago engineer Joseph Strauss is officially credited as the bridge's designer, and he led the opening ceremony in April 1937. He was assisted by Leon Moisseiff and Charles Ellis. Irving F Morrow acted as consulting architect.*

**The length** of the bridge is 1.7 miles (2.7 km), the span is 4,200 ft (1,280 m), and the roadway is 220 ft (67 m) above the water.

**View from Vista Point**
*The best view of both the bridge and the San Francisco skyline is from the Marin County side.*

### THE BRIDGE IN FIGURES

• Every year more than 40 million vehicles cross the bridge; every day about 118,000 vehicles use it.
• The original coat of paint lasted for 27 years, needing only touch-ups. From 1965 to 1995, a crew stripped off the old paint and applied a more durable coating.
• The two great 7,650-ft (2,332-m) cables are more than 3 ft (1 m) thick, and contain 80,000 miles (128,744 km) of steel wire, enough to circle the earth at the equator three times.
• The volume of concrete poured into the piers and anchorages during the bridge's construction would be enough to lay a 5-ft (1.5-m-) wide sidewalk from New York to San Francisco, a distance of more than 2,500 miles (4,000 km).
• The bridge can withstand 100 mph (160 km/h) winds.
• Each pier has to withstand a tidal flow of more than 60 mph (97 km/h), while supporting a 44,000-ton steel tower.

**Painting the bridge**

# SHOPPING IN SAN FRANCISCO

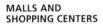

Shopping in San Francisco is much more than simply making a purchase, it's a whole experience that allows a glimpse into the city's culture. It is the diversity of San Francisco that makes buying anything here an adventure. An enormous range of goods is available, from the practical to the more eccentric, but you can take your time in choosing, since browsers

*Clock over entrance to Tiffany's*

are generally made to feel welcome, particularly in the many small specialty shops and boutiques of the city. If you want convenience, the numerous shopping centers and department stores are excellent. For those in search of local color, every neighborhood shopping district has a charm and personality of its own, with each reflecting a different aspect of the city.

## MALLS AND SHOPPING CENTERS

In contrast to a great many suburban shopping malls, those of San Francisco have character, and one or two of them are of considerable architectural interest. The Embarcadero Center *(see p314)* has more than 125 shops, in an area covering eight blocks. Ghirardelli Square *(see p337)* was a well-known chocolate factory from 1893 until 1953. It now houses more than 50 shops and several restaurants, overlooking San Francisco Bay.

The Westfield San Francisco Centre *(see p321)* has nine levels and more than 200 shops. Pier 39 *(see p336)* is a marketplace on the waterfront, with restaurants, a double-decker Venetian merry-go-round, a marina, and many specialty boutiques. In the Cannery *(see p337)*, located at Fisherman's Wharf, you will find a variety of charming small shops. The beautiful Crocker Galleria *(see p320)* is one of the city's most

**Emporio Armani**

spectacular malls, with three floors set under a high glass dome built around a bright central plaza.

The Japan Center *(see p352)*, complete with pagoda, offers exotic foods, goods, and art from the East, as well as a Japanese-style hotel and traditional baths. The Rincon Center *(see p317)*, with a 90-ft (27-m) water column at its center, is an Art Deco haven for shopping and eating.

## DEPARTMENT STORES

Most of San Francisco's major department stores are in or near Union Square. They are huge retail stores that offer their customers an outstanding selection of goods and services.

The **Bloomingdale's** chain opened its West Coast flagship store in San Francisco in late 2006 and is now the country's second-largest "Bloomies." The emphasis is on upscale fashion, as well as luxury accessories and housewares.

**Macy's** stocks an enormous range of goods and has a number of extra amenities, including currency exchange and an interpreting service. The men's department is particularly extensive.

**Neiman Marcus** is another stylish emporium. The huge stained-glass dome in its Rotunda Restaurant was part of the original building and is well worth coming to see.

**Nordstrom**, known for its fashion and shoes, is often called the "store-in-the-sky"; it is located in the top four floors of the innovative San Francisco Shopping Center.

**Flags flying in front of the pagoda at the Japan Center**

## SHOPPING AROUND UNION SQUARE

Serious shoppers should concentrate on the blocks bordered by Geary, Powell, and Post Streets, and on the surrounding blocks between Market and Sutter Streets. Here luxurious shops and inexpensive boutiques sell everything from designer bed linens to snow-globe souvenirs. Exclusive hotels, chic restaurants, and colorful flower stalls all add to the fashionable atmosphere.

## SHOPS FOR A GOOD CAUSE

San Franciscans take great pleasure in shopping for a good cause. All purchases made at **The Pirate Store** benefit 826 Valencia, a non-profit organization dedicated to helping 6- to 18-year-olds with their writing skills, and to assisting teachers

Flower stall on Union Square

in creating curricula that will inspire their students to write. The **Warming Hut Bookstore** offers eco-conscious gifts. Proceeds benefit environmental education at the Crissy Field Center. All the profits that are made at **Under One Roof** benefit the various groups set up to help combat AIDS. **Patagonia** offers plenty of outdoor gear made of recycled fibers. They also have fundraisers and donate clothes to non-profit groups.

## SOUVENIRS

Many souvenirs, such as T-shirts, keyrings, and mugs are decorated with motifs symbolizing San Francisco in **Only in San Francisco** and the **Cable Car Store**. Souvenir and novelty hats are available at **Krazy Kaps**, while the store entrances on Grant Avenue *(see p329)* and Fisherman's Wharf *(see pp334–5)* are lined with baskets filled with bargain gifts.

## BEST BUYS

Gourmet shoppers should look for seafood, one of the city's specialties. Wine from the Napa Valley *(see pp462–3)* is another good buy, as is the city's famous Ghirardelli chocolate. You will find blue jeans at competitive prices, also vintage clothing, ethnic art, books, and records particularly in the Mission District and the Haight-Ashbury.

## SHOPPING TOURS

Some tour companies may be able to arrange private shopping tours with a personalized guide service. The San Francisco Travel Association can provide information. Also, Macy's offers a VIP shopping day with shopping assistance and discounts.

## MUSEUMS

Museum shopping offers exquisite gifts to suit all budgets. Among the city's best are the **Academy Store** in the California Academy of Sciences *(see p320)*, the **Museum Store** at the Legion of Honor, *(see pp374–5)*, the **San Francisco MOMA Museum Store** *(see pp318–19)* and **The Asian Art Museum Store** *(see p352)*.

Grant Avenue, Chinatown

# DIRECTORY

**Academy Store**
California Academy of Sciences, Golden Gate Park, 55 Concourse Dr. **Map** 8 F2. **Tel** *(415) 933-6154.* **www**.calacademy.org

**The Asian Art Museum Store**
200 Larkin St. **Map** 4 F5. **Tel** *(415) 581-3600.* **www**.asianart.org

**Bloomingdale's**
845 Market St. **Tel** *(415) 856-5300.*

**Cable Car Store**
Pier 39. **Map** 5 B1. **Tel** *(415) 989-2040.*

**Krazy Kaps**
Pier 39. **Map** 5 B1. **Tel** *(415) 296-8930.*

**Macy's**
Stockton & O'Farrell Sts. **Map** 5 C5. **Tel** *(415) 954-6271.*

**Museum Store**
Legion of Honor, Golden Gate Park. **Map** 1 B5. **Tel** *(415) 750-3677.* **www**.deyoungmuseum.org

**Neiman Marcus**
150 Stockton St. **Map** 5 C5. **Tel** *(415) 362-3900.*

**Nordstrom**
San Francisco Shopping Center, 865 Market St. **Map** 5 C5. **Tel** *(415) 243-8500.*

**Only in San Francisco**
Pier 39. **Map** 5 B1. **Tel** *(415) 397-0143.*

**Patagonia**
700 North Point St. **Map** 5 A2. **Tel** *(415) 771-2050.*

**The Pirate Store**
826 Valencia St. **Map** 10 F2. **Tel** *(415) 642-5905.*

**San Francisco MOMA MuseumStore**
Museum of Modern Art, 151 Third St. **Map** 6 D5. **Tel** *(888) 357-0037.* **www**.sfmoma.org

**San Francisco Travel Association**
900 Market St. **Tel** *(415) 391-2000.*

**Under One Roof**
518A Castro St. **Map** 10 D3. **Tel** *(415) 503-2300.*

**Warming Hut Bookstore**
983 Marine Dr at Long Ave. **Map** 2 F2. **Tel** *(415) 561-3043.*

# San Francisco Specials

Entrepreneurial spirit in San Francisco is strong and innovative, and the city's sophisticated image is very much deserved. Whether it is a small souvenir, a designer outfit, an antique, or a mouthwatering snack that is required, visitors will never be disappointed amid the shops and markets of San Francisco. The city is also home to many dedicated "foodies," gastronomes whose liking for fine wine and gourmet meals have resulted in unusual and delicious grocery stores. All this creates an environment that makes shopping in San Francisco an exciting experience.

Ghirardelli Square, home to San Francisco's famous chocolate

## SPECIALTY SHOPS

If you are looking for whimsical art – either to wear or to display – head to **Kati Koos: A Gallery with Tongue in Chic**. Since Gold Rush days, **Malm Luggage**, a family-owned and operated shop for luggage, briefcases and small leather goods, has kept its reputation for excellence. You can describe the city's attractions on a designer card from **Flax Art and Design**, a sixty-year-old business offering a huge selection of handmade papers and artists' tools. **Comix Experience** sells a

The colorful exterior of Flax Art and Design on Market Street

large selection of comics and graphic novels. Exquisite Italian ceramics (majolica) are on display at **Biordi Art Imports** in North Beach, where handpainted dishware, vases, and platters are for sale. Those who would like to experience the authentic atmosphere of Chinatown will find it at **Ten Ren Tea Company** of San Francisco. At **Golden Gate Fortune Cookies**, descendants of Chinese immigrants allow their customers to taste samples before buying the San Francisco fortune cookies that were a Chinatown invention.

## FOOD AND WINE

From abalone to zucchini, and from fresh California produce to imported specialty foods, the gourmet grocery **Whole Foods** carries a wide variety of items. **Williams-Sonoma** has jams, mustards, and gifts. **David's** is known for its lox (smoked salmon), bagels, and deli sandwiches. The Italian **Molinari Delicatessen** is famous for its fresh ravioli and tortellini, ready to throw into a saucepan. **Lucca Ravioli Company** has a friendly staff, who make their pasta on the premises. **Pasta Gina** caters to the young, fashionable crowd with freshly prepared pasta, pesto, and other sauces. It is well worth going to Chinatown (*see pp316–17*) for Far Eastern food products and produce. At **Casa Lucas Market** you will find a variety of Spanish and Latin American food specialties. A baguette of fresh sourdough bread from **Boudin Bakery** is a long-standing addiction with locals

Fig jam, Williams-Sonoma

and a tradition with visitors. **Boulangerie** brings Paris to San Francisco, with some of the best bread in the city. **Cheese Plus** sells fine cheeses and gourmet food items. Chocoholics are catered to at San Francisco's own **Ghirardelli Chocolate Factory**. San Franciscans are coffee connoisseurs, and there are many specialty houses. **Caffè Trieste** is the city's oldest coffee house and sells a range of custom-roasted and blended coffees, and a variety of brewing equipment. **Caffè Roma Coffee Roasting Company** and the **Graffeo Coffee Roasting Company** both sell excellent beans. The staff at the **California Wine Merchant** makes good recommendations and are

Caffè Trieste on Vallejo Street is a North Beach landmark

very knowledgeable about their affordable wines. The **Napa Valley Winery Exchange** features selections from the many Californian wineries, including the smaller local producers.

Locally grown fruit and vegetables arrive by the truckload at the regular farmers' markets in the center of the city. Stalls are erected for the day, and the farmers sell their goods directly to the public. The **Heart of the City** is open 7am to 5pm on Wednesdays, and to 5:30pm on Sundays. **Ferry Plaza Farmers' Market** is held Tuesdays and Thursdays (10am–2pm) and Saturdays (8am–2pm). Chinatown's produce stores have the feel of an exotic farmers' market and are open every day.

## BOOKS, MUSIC, ART, AND ANTIQUES

Independent bookstores have had a hard time in recent years, with the closure of some landmark stores. **Modern Times**, which depends heavily on its local membership, carries a wide selection of best-sellers and classics as well as unusual specialties. Beats once talked about the country's emerging 1960s social revolution at the **City Lights Bookstore** *(see pp330–31)*, which stays open late and is a famous San Francisco institution. **Green Apple Books & Music** has new and used books, and is open until 10:30pm, or 11:30pm on Fridays and Saturdays. **Adobe Book Shop** offers eccentric and rare books at discount prices. **William Stout Architectural Books** stocks books on art, architecture, furniture and interior design, and graphic and industrial design.

A wide selection of music is offered at various branches of **Rasputin Music** and **Best Buy**. More obscure music can usually be found at **Recycled Records**. **Amoeba Music** has the largest selection of CDs and tapes in the country. It has 500,000 titles, both new

Pinot Noir, a popular wine of the region

and secondhand, including jazz, international blues, and rock music. A music collector's paradise, this is the place to go if you are looking for hard-to-find music at low prices. All types of sheet music and books of collections can be found at the **Music Center of San Francisco**. Art lovers will find something to their liking in the city's hundreds of galleries. The **John Berggruen Gallery** has the city's largest collection of works by both emerging and more established artists. **The Fraenkel Gallery** is known for its collection of 19th- and 20th-century photography. **Xanadu Gallery & Folk Art International** has masks, textiles, sculptures, and jewelry.

Jackson Square is San Francisco's main area for antiques *(see p304)*. **49 Geary Street** is a veritable treasure-trove for art collectors, housing 20 galleries and four rare book shops. **Lang Antiques** has all kinds of antique jewelry. **Dragon House** sells Oriental antiques and fine art, while antique books, prints, and maps can be found at **Prints Old & Rare** – although you will need to make an appointment.

## CLOTHING

San Francisco designer shops include **Diana Slavin** for classics, **Joanie Char's** for sportswear, and **Wilkes Bashford** for up-and-coming designs. **MAC** or Modern

Appealing Clothing, sources one-third of its menswear as well as womenswear from San Francisco designers. For discount designer clothes, head to the trendy SoMa district. Yerba Buena Square contains several kinds of outlets, including **Burlington Coat Factory**. Here you can find discounted lines from many local designers. **Georgiou Retail** showcases classic styles made from natural fibers. **Jeremy's** in SoMa's swish South Park area, discounts formal clothing and designerwear for both men and women.

The Wasteland on Haight Street, a treasure of vintage garments

**Buffalo Exchange** offers secondhand clothing with a history. **The Wasteland** in the Haight-Ashbury District is known for its vintage clothes. **La Rosa Vintage** stocks a collection of hand-picked items, while **Clothes Contact** sells vintage clothes by the pound.

**Brooks Brothers** is well known for its conservative men's suits and button-down shirts. Fashionable outdoor clothing is available from **Eddie Bauer**. For men's

City Lights Bookstore *(see p330)* on Columbus Avenue

designer brands, sportswear, shoes, and accessories with a European influence, try **Rolo**. Many of the world's famous names in fashion are in San Francisco, including **Chanel** and **Gucci**. **Salvatore Ferragamo** is in Union Square. **Prada** is famous for its extra-fine merino wool and cashmere clothes. **Marc Jacobs** carries men's and women's clothing, as well as high-end accessories. **Banana Republic** and **Guess** are well known for stylish, wearable clothes. **Loehmann's** sells designer clothing from New York and Europe at a discount. **Urban Outfitters** has chic new clothes, and **Sui Generis illa Boutique** carries stylish, gently used designer clothing. **Original Levi's Store** has been in business since 1853,

offering a broad range of clothes, all of which can be worn with their famous jeans *(see p343)*.

**Small Frys** is the locals' favorite for cotton children's clothes. Top-quality footwear is available at **Kenneth Cole**. Best names in comfort are at **Ria's**, including Clarks, Ecco, Dansko, Timberland, and Sebago. **Nike Town** is a megastore for sneakers, and **DSW Shoe Warehouse** offers discounted shoes.

## TOYS, GAMES, AND GADGETS

Inside Exploratorium, San Francisco's fascinating science museum, is the **Exploratorium Store**. The store stocks a wide variety of science books, kits,

and games that make learning fun for children of all ages.

At **Puppets on the Pier** new owners are given puppetry lessons in the shop. **Jeffrey's Toys** is an unassuming downtown shop packed with action figures, stuffed animals, games, and the latest in practical joke technology. **The Chinatown Kite Shop** takes shopping to new heights, displaying an extraordinary assortment of flying objects. These range from traditional to World Champion stunt kites, all making attractive souvenirs. In **Brookstone** even the adult who has everything, is sure to be intrigued by the high-tech wizardry of the gadgets and electronic goods on sale.

# DIRECTORY

## SPECIALTY SHOPS

**Biordi Art Imports**
412 Columbus Ave.
**Map** 5 C3.
*Tel (415) 392-8096.*

**Comix Experience**
305 Divisadero St.
**Map** 10 D1.
*Tel (415) 863-9258.*

**Flax Art and Design**
1699 Market St.
**Map** 10 F1.
*Tel (415) 552-2355.*

**Golden Gate Fortune Cookies**
56 Ross Alley.
**Map** 5 C3.
*Tel (415) 781-3956.*

**Kati Koos: A Gallery with Tongue in Chic**
500 Sutter St.
**Map** 5 B4.
*Tel (415) 362-3437.*

**Malm Luggage**
1425 Bush St.
**Map** 5 C4.
*Tel (415) 673-2286.*

**Ten Ren Tea Company of San Francisco**
949 Grant Ave.
**Map** 5 C3.
*Tel (415) 362-0656.*

## FOOD AND WINE

**Boudin Bakery**
4 Embarcadero Center.
**Map** 6 D3.
*Tel (415) 362-3330.*

**Boulangerie Bay Bread**
2325 Pine St. **Map** 4 D4.
*Tel (415) 440-0356.*

**Caffè Roma Coffee Roasting Company**
526 Columbus Ave.
**Map** 5 B2.
*Tel (415) 296-7942.*

**Caffè Trieste**
601 Vallejo St.
**Map** 5 C3.
*Tel (415) 982-2605.*

**California Wine Merchant**
2113 Chestnut St.
**Map** 4 D2.
*Tel (415) 567-0646.*

**Casa Lucas Market**
2934 24th St.
**Map** 9 C3.
*Tel (415) 826-4334.*

**Cheese Plus**
2001 Polk St.
**Map** 5 A3.
*Tel (415) 921-2001.*

**David's**
474 Geary St.
**Map** 5 A5.
*Tel (415) 276-5950.*

**Ferry Plaza Farmers' Market**
1 Ferry Building.
**Map** 6 D3.
*Tel (415) 291-3276.*
www.ferrybuildingmarket
place.com

**Ghiradelli Chocolate Factory**
Ghirardelli Square.
**Map** 4 F1.
*Tel (415) 474-3938.*
44 Stockton St.
**Map** 5 C1.
*Tel (415) 397-3030.*

**Graffeo Coffee Roasting Company**
735 Columbus Ave.
**Map** 5 B2.
*Tel (415) 986-2420.*

**Heart of the City Farmers' Market**
1182 Market Street,
No. 415.
**Map** 10 A1.
*Tel (415) 558-9455.*

**Lucca Ravioli Company**
1100 Valencia St.
**Map** 10 F3.
*Tel (415) 647-5581.*

**Molinari Delicatessen**
373 Columbus Ave.
**Map** 5 C3.
*Tel (415) 421-2337.*

**Napa Valley Winery Exchange**
415 Taylor St.
**Map** 5 B5.
*Tel (415) 771-2887.*
www.nvwe.com

**Pasta Gina**
741 Diamond St.
**Map** 10 D4.
*Tel (415) 282-0738.*

**Whole Foods**
1765 California St.
**Map** 4 F4.
*Tel (415) 674-0500.*

**Williams-Sonoma**
340 Post St.
**Map** 5 C4.
*Tel (415) 362-9450.*

## BOOKS, MUSIC, ART, AND ANTIQUES

**49 Geary St**
49 Geary St.
**Map** 5 C5.
*Tel (415) 986-5826.*

**Adobe Bookshop**
3166 16th St.
**Map** 10 E2.
*Tel (415) 864-3936.*

# DIRECTORY

**Amoeba Music**
1855 Haight St.
Map 9 B1.
Tel (415) 831-1200.

**Best Buy**
1717 Harrison St.
Map 6 D5.
Tel (415) 626-8700.

**City Lights Bookstore**
261 Columbus Ave.
Map 5 C3.
Tel (415) 362-8193.

**Dragon House**
455 Grant Ave.
Map 6 C4.
Tel (415) 421-3693.

**Fraenkel Gallery**
49 Geary St.
Map 5 C5.
Tel (415) 981-2661.

**Green Apple Books & Music**
506 Clement St.
Map 3 A5.
Tel (415) 387-2272.

**John Berggruen Gallery**
228 Grant Ave.
Map 5 C4.
Tel (415) 781-4629.

**Lang Antiques**
323 Sutter St.
Map 5 C4.
Tel (415) 982-2213.

**Modern Times**
29/9 24th St.
Map 10 E4.
Tel (415) 282-9246.

**Music Center of San Francisco**
2nd Floor, 207 Powell St.
Map 5 B1.
Tel (415) 781-6023.

**Prints Old & Rare**
580 Crespi Drive, Pacifica, California.
Tel (650) 355-6325.

**Rasputin Music**
69 Powell St.
Map 5 B5.
Tel (800) 350-8700.

**Recycled Records**
1377 Haight St.
Map 9 C1.
Tel (415) 626-4075.

**William Stout Architectural Books**
804 Montgomery St.
Map 5 C3.
Tel (415) 642-5905.

**Xanadu Gallery & Folk Art International**
Frank Lloyd Wright Bldg, 140 Maiden Lane.
Map 5 B5.
Tel (415) 392-9999.

## CLOTHING

**Banana Republic**
256 Grant Ave.
Map 5 C4.
Tel (415) 788-3037.

**Brooks Brothers**
150 Post St.
Map 5 C4.
Tel (415) 397-4500.

**Buffalo Exchange**
1555 Haight St.
Map 9 C1.
Tel (415) 431-7733.
1210 Valencia St.
Map 10 F4.
Tel (415) 647-8332.

**Burlington Coat Factory**
899 Howard St.
Tel (415) 495-7234.

**Chanel Boutique**
156 Geary St. Map 5 C5.
Tel (415) 981-1550.

**Clothes Contact**
473 Valencia St.
Map 10 F2.
Tel (415) 621-3212.

**Diana Slavin**
3 Claude Lane.
Map 5 C4.
Tel (415) 677-9939.

**DSW Shoe Warehouse**
111 Powell St. Map 5 B5.
Tel (415) 445-9511.

**Eddie Bauer**
3251 20th Ave.
Map 8 E2.
Tel (415) 664-9262.

**Georgiou Retail**
925 Bryant St.
Tel (415) 554-0150.

**Gucci**
240 Stockton St.
Map 5 C5.
Tel (415) 392-2808.

**Guess**
865 Market St, Suite 206.
Map 5 C5.
Tel (415) 495-0200.

**Guys and Dolls**
4100 24th St.
Map 10 E4.
Tel (415) 285-7174.

**Jeremy's**
2 South Park St.
Map 5 C4.
Tel (415) 882-4929.

**Joanie Char**
537 Sutter St.
Map 5 B4.
Tel (415) 399-9867.

**Kenneth Cole**
865 Market St.
Map 5 C5.
Tel (415) 227-4536.

**La Rosa Vintage**
1711 Haight St.
Map 9 C1.
Tel (415) 668-3744.

**Loehmann's**
222 Sutter St.
Map 5 C4.
Tel (415) 982-3215.

**MAC**
1833 Union St. Map 5 B1.
Tel (415) 771-6113.

**Marc Jacobs**
125 Maiden Lane.
Map 5 C4.
Tel (415) 362-6500.

**NikeTown**
278 Post St.
Map 5 C4.
Tel (415) 392-6453.

**Original Levi Store**
300 Post St, Union Square.
Map 5 C5.
Tel (415) 501-0100.

**Prada**
201 Post St.
Map 5 C4.
Tel (415) 848-1900.

**Ria's Shoes**
301 Grant Ave.
Map 5 C4.
Tel (415) 834-1420.

**Rolo**
2351 Market St.
Map 10 D2.
Tel (415) 431-4545.

**Salvatore Ferragamo**
233 Geary St.
Map 5 C5.
Tel (415) 391-6565.

**Small Frys**
4066 24th St.
Map 10 D4.
Tel (415) 648-3954.

**Sui Generis illa Boutique**
2265 Market St.
Map 10 D2.
Tel (415) 437-2265.

**Urban Outfitters**
80 Powell St.
Map 5 B5.
Tel (415) 989-1515.

**The Wasteland**
1660 Haight St.
Map 9 B1.
Tel (415) 863-3150.

**Wilkes Bashford**
375 Sutter St.
Map 5 C4.
Tel (415) 986-4380.

## TOYS, GAMES, AND GADGETS

**Brookstone**
865 Market St.
Map 5 C5.
Tel (415) 546-6667.

**Chinatown Kite Shop**
717 Grant Ave.
Map 5 C3.
Tel (415) 989-5182.

**Exploratorium Store**
Marina Blvd and Lyon St.
Map 3 C2.
Tel (415) 561-0393.

**Jeffrey's Toys**
685 Market St.
Map 5 C5.
Tel (415) 243-8697.

**Puppets on the Pier**
Pier 39.
Map 5 B1.
Tel (415) 781-4435.

*Many of the listings have multiple branches. Shops will be happy to provide information of their nearest branch.*

# ENTERTAINMENT IN SAN FRANCISCO

San Francisco has prided itself on being the cultural capital of the West Coast since the city first began to prosper in the 1850s, and the entertainment offered is generally of high quality. The performing arts complex of the Civic Center, opposite the City Hall, is the principal venue for classical music, opera, and ballet. A vital part of the city's cultural life is the highly rated Center for the Arts Theater at Yerba Buena Gardens. Many international touring shows can be seen here.

**Beach Blanket Babylon**
(see p341)

There are numerous repertory movie theaters offering filmgoers a wide range of programs, but theater, except for some of the "alternative" venues, is not the city's strongest suit. Popular music, in particular jazz and blues, is where San Francisco really excels, and you can hear good bands for the price of a drink or at the street fairs and music festivals that are held during the summer months. Facilities are also available for a wide variety of sports, from cycling to golf, tennis, and sailing.

## INFORMATION SOURCES

Complete listings of what's on and where are given in the *San Francisco Chronicle* and *Examiner* newspapers. The *Chronicle*'s Sunday edition is very useful. Other good sources are the free weekly newspapers, such as the *San Francisco Weekly* (available in kiosks, cafés, and bars) or the *San Francisco Bay Guardian*. These give both listings and reviews, especially of live music, films, and nightclubs.

Visitors planning farther in advance will find the *San Francisco Book* very helpful. This is published twice yearly by the **San Francisco Travel Association** and is available free at the **Visitor Information Center** at Hallidie Plaza or for

$2 if mailed out. You can also phone the visitors' bureau's Events Line for recorded information. Numerous free magazines for visitors are available, as well as calendars of events. Among these are *Key This Week San Francisco* and *Where San Francisco*.

## BUYING TICKETS

The main source for tickets to concerts, theater, and sporting events is **Ticketmaster**, which has a virtual monopoly on ticket sales, running an extensive charge-by-phone operation with outlets in the Tower and Wherehouse record shops *(see pp608–9)* all over Northern California. There is a "convenience charge" of

**Storefront of San Francisco ticket agency**

about $4 per ticket. An alternative to Ticketmaster is to buy directly from the box offices, though many of these are only open just before the start of evening performances.

To see productions by the reputable San Francisco Symphony, Ballet, and Opera companies, advance planning is essential. All have subscription programs, which are useful if you are planning to stay in the city for a lengthy period of time.

There are only a few ticket agencies in San Francisco, and they mostly specialize in selling limited seats at marked-up prices. They are all listed in the Yellow Pages of the telephone directory, found in most public pay phones. Ticket scalpers are invariably found outside sold-out events, offering seats at extortionate prices. If you are willing to bargain (and risk missing the start of the game or the opening act) it is often possible to get a good deal this way.

**Front entrance of the War Memorial Opera House**

**Outdoor chess, popular in Portsmouth Plaza, Chinatown**

## DISCOUNT TICKETS

Discount tickets for some selected events are available from **TIX Bay Area**, offering half-price seats from a booth on the east side of Union Square (see p320). Tickets are sold starting at 11am, on the day of the performance only. Occasionally, there are also some half-price tickets available on weekends for those events that are taking place on the following Sunday and Monday.

TIX Bay Area is also a full-service Ticketmaster outlet selling full-price tickets for advance sales. It is open on Tuesdays, Wednesdays, Thursdays, and Fridays from 11am to 6pm; on Saturdays from 10am to 6pm; and from 10am to 3pm on Sundays.

## FREE EVENTS

In addition to San Francisco's many ticket-only events, a number of free concerts and performances are regularly staged all over the city. Many of these take place during the day and outdoors in the summer; they can offer a welcome change of pace from the usual standard fare.

The San Francisco Symphony (see pp390–91) gives just one of the many musical performances in a series of free Sunday concerts from mid-June through August at Stern Grove, south of the Sunset District.

The San Francisco Opera stages a free full-scale performance in Golden Gate Park as a key event in the opera's first week of the season. Sponsored by the *San Francisco Chronicle*, this attracts 20,000-plus people each year. "Opera in the Park" is another popular annual event held in Dolores Park, which also plays host to the San Francisco Mime Troupe. In the summer, Golden Gate Park is the place to be for the Shakespeare Festival and Comedy Celebration Day.

From May through October, Yerba Buena Gardens puts on popular and operatic music series, cultural festivals, dance performances, and more. Throughout the year dozens of free festivals and celebrations, such as Chinese New Year, provide plenty of fun.

## FACILITIES FOR THE DISABLED

California is a national leader in providing facilities for the handicapped. Most theaters and concert halls in San Francisco are therefore fully accessible and have open areas set aside for wheelchair-users. Some smaller venues may require the use of special entrances, or elevators to reach the upper tiers. Many movies offer amplifying head-phones. Contact the theaters to be sure of their facilities.

**The Presidio Cinema**

## DIRECTORY

### USEFUL ADDRESSES

**Information Center**
900 Market St, Hallidie Plaza.
*Tel* (415) 391-2000.
www.sfvisitor.org

**Events Line (24-hour)**
(415) 391-2001 (English).
(415) 391-2003 (French).
(415) 391-2004 (German).
(415) 391-2122 (Spanish).

**Stern Grove**
*Tel* (415) 252-6252.
www.sterngrove.org

### TICKET AGENCIES

**Ticketmaster**
Charge-by-phone.
*Tel* (800) 745-3000.
www.ticketmaster.com

**TIX Bay Area**
Union Sq, Powell St.
*Tel* (415) 433-7827.
www.theatrebayarea.org

**AT&T Park, home of the San Francisco Giants (see pp392–3)**

# Entertainment Venues

With a variety of entertainment options, San Francisco is one of the most enjoyable cities in the world. Whatever your cultural preferences, what you see here is sure to be good. Besides housing the West Coast's best opera and ballet companies, it has a highly regarded symphony orchestra. The city also offers a wide range of jazz and rock music, diverse theater companies, and specialty movie houses. For the sports fan there are also plenty of opportunities to both watch and take part.

The ultramodern Louise M Davies Symphony Hall

## FILM AND THEATER

San Francisco has an avid film-going community. The city's newest multi-media experience is the **AMC Loews Metreon**, a 15-screen complex plus IMAX with shops, restaurants, special programs, and other attractions.

The landmark Castro Theatre

One of the city's best movie houses is the **Sundance Kabuki Cinemas**, an eight-screen complex in the Japan Center (see p352), which also hosts the **San Francisco International Film Festival** each May. Other popular venues for first-run films include the **Bridge Theatre**

and the **Embarcadero Center Cinema**, which excels at indie films. Main venues for first-run foreign films are the **Clay Theatre** in Pacific Heights, the Civic Center's **Lumiere**, and **Opera Plaza Cinema**. The **Castro Theatre** (see p360) shows Hollywood classics and other revivals, with a film program that changes daily.

Many residents of San Francisco show apparent disdain for the international commercial successes, which explains why theater has a lower profile here than in other large cities. Mainstream theaters, which host a range of touring Broadway productions as well as those by local companies, are concentrated in the Theater District (see p320). Three of the largest theaters are the **Golden Gate Theater**, the **Curran Theater**, and the **Orpheum Theater**, all part of the Best of Broadway performance series. The **Children's Creativity Museum** stages both student and professional productions, while musicals and comedy are staged at **The Marsh**. The most respected major company is the **American Conservatory Theater (ACT)**. Its longtime home, the landmark Geary Theater, has now

reopened after renovations following the 1989 earthquake (see pp24–5). A variety of plays are performed during its October to May season.

## OPERA, CLASSICAL MUSIC, AND DANCE

The main season of the **San Francisco Opera** runs from September to December; tickets can cost more than $100, but there is a summer season, with less expensive tickets.

The main venue for opera, classical music, and dance is the Civic Center performing arts complex on Van Ness Avenue. The **Louise M Davies Symphony Hall** located here is now San Francisco's principal location for fine classical music performances, and home to the highly regarded **San Francisco Symphony**, which performs up to five concerts a week during its winter season. Guest conductors, performers, and touring orchestras perform additional special concerts. Next door to the Opera House, the **Herbst Theatre** also hosts recitals by prominent performers.

In addition to these big events, there are numerous less formal recitals and concerts in the Bay Area. The **Philharmonia Baroque Orchestra**, a period instrument ensemble, plays at various sites around the city, while the historic **Old First Presbyterian Church** has a series of chamber music and individual recitals on Friday nights and Sunday afternoons.

The Geary Theater (see p310)

In addition to educating the gifted musicians of tomorrow, the **San Francisco Conservatory of Music** hosts a plethora of classical performances, from faculty recitals to one-act operas, and the perenially popular Midsummer Mozart series. **Grace Cathedral** is a particularly striking setting for choral church music. The choir sings at Evensong on Thursdays at 5:15pm, while Choral Eucharist is celebrated on Sundays at 11am.

Founded in 1933, the **San Francisco Ballet** is the oldest professional ballet company in the US. Its season of classical and new works runs from February to April. There are performances by local talent which take place at the intimate **Theater Artaud** and the **ODC Performance Gallery**, both located in the Mission District. The Yerba Buena Center for the Arts *(see pp322–3)* is home to the LINES Contemporary Ballet, while **Zellerbach Hall** across the Bay in Berkeley attracts the area's best touring productions.

Slim's, one of San Francisco's best rock venues

## ROCK, JAZZ, AND BLUES

Two of the best rock clubs to hear live music are **Slim's** and **Bimbo's 365 Club**. Bimbo's hosts rock, jazz, country, and R&B – and attracts a similarly diverse crowd. Slim's is a bit more upscale, tending to feature established performers in its comfortable 436-seat room. Another popular place is the **Fillmore Auditorium**, which is the legendary birthplace of psychedelic rock during the 1960s *(see p359)*.

There are a number of excellent places to hear live jazz in the city. The entertainment is usually free, if you buy dinner or drinks. For traditional Dixieland in an informal (and free) setting,

visit the amiable **Gold Dust Lounge**, just off Union Square. Also try the piano bars located in downtown restaurants and hotels. For an interactive music experience, check out **Dueling Pianos at Johnny Foley's**, where two pianists square off while working the crowd and playing requests. **SFJazz** is located in a state-of-the-art center built solely for, and dedicated to, jazz. The $50-million center hosts 200 performances per year, and it is the venue for some of SFJazz's signature activities, such as the annual SFJazz Festival *(see p38)* and SFJazz Hotplate. Many jazz fans plan trips to San Francisco to coincide with the world-famous **Monterey Jazz Festival**, which is held every September in Monterey *(see p38)*. Monterey is 2 hours south of San Francisco. Live blues is played somewhere in town every night of the week, in bars such as **The Saloon** and the **Boom Boom Room**. Lou's Pier 47, on Fisherman's Wharf, has one or more blues bands on the bill almost every day, with special shows on weekends. The award-winning **Biscuits and Blues** has local blues spotlights on weekdays and special shows on weekends.

## CLUBS

Most of the larger clubs are located in the industrial South of Market (SoMA) area, and

Banner for the Jazz Festival *(see p34)*

run from around 9pm until 2am. A few clubs stay open all night, especially on weekends, but all places stop serving alcohol at 2am. Always bring valid ID to prove you are over 21 or you will not be admitted. One of San Francisco's popular clubs is **DNA Lounge** on 11th Street, with its multiple dance floors, flashy decor, great sound system, and fashionably mainstream clientele. R&B, hip-hop, and jazz are played at **Nickie's BBQ** in Haight Ashbury. To dance to tunes spun by some of the best DJs in San Francisco, head to the **Chambers Eat & Drink**.

Check out **330 Ritch Street** for house music, goth, Brit pop, mod, Indie, R&B, and hip-hop. Some of the most popular clubs are primarily, though rarely exclusively, gay. These include **The Endup** and **Club Hide**, which has square dancing every night.

Piano bars all have nightly live music that you can enjoy for the price of a drink. One of the best is the beautiful Art Deco-style **Top of the Mark** at the top of the Mark Hopkins InterContinental Hotel. Another good rooftop piano bar is **Grandviews at the Hyatt** on the 36th floor of Union Square's Grand Hyatt Hotel. **Playbar**'s cocktail lounge with its Victorian-style interior serves up plenty of

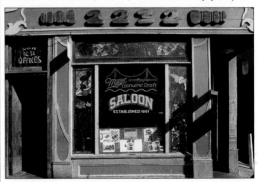

The Saloon on Grant Avenue, North Beach

house and techno music. The **Tonga Room** in the Fairmont Hotel is an elaborate cocktail bar where you can dance or just listen to jazz with a simulated rainstorm every half-hour.

Check local newspapers for comedy club listings. Some of the best stand-up comedy shows take place at **Bourbon Street Bar N Grill**, as well as at **The Marsh** in the Mission and **Cobb's Comedy Club** in Fisherman's Wharf. **Kimo's** features drag, cabaret, and comedy shows every week.

## SPORTS AND OUTDOOR ACTIVITIES

San Franciscans are sports enthusiasts, and there are plenty of activities to suit every taste. Popular spectator sports include football, baseball, and basketball. The home ground of the **San** **Francisco 49ers** is Candlestick Park; the **Oakland Raiders** play at Oakland-Alameda County Coliseum. Local colleges, including the **University of California at Berkeley** (see p418) and **Stanford University** (see p427), also have good football teams. Two professional baseball teams play in the Bay Area: the National League **San Francisco Giants** play their home games at the stadium at AT&T Park; the American League **Oakland Athletics** also play at the Oakland-Alameda Coliseum, just across the bay in Oakland. The Bay Area's only NBA basketball team is the **Golden State Warriors**, who play at the Oracle Arena.

Large business hotels usually have health club facilities on the premises. Those that do not usually have an agreement with a private club that gives short-term membership to hotel guests. If neither of these options is available, choose from the upscale **San Francisco Bay Club**, near the Financial District, the **Pacific Heights Health Club**, or the **24-Hour Fitness Center**.

Golfers have a range of courses to choose from, including the municipal links in **Lincoln Park** and **Golden Gate Park**, and the beautiful **Presidio Golf Course**. The Presidio and Golden Gate Park area is also ideal for cycling. Rental shops here include **Stow Lake Boat & Bike Rentals**. In North Beach, **Blazing Saddles** also rents bikes. Most of the public swimming pools are on the suburban fringes; contact the **City of San Francisco Recreation and Parks District**. To swim in the chilly ocean, head out to China Beach, the only safe beach in the city.

# DIRECTORY

## FILM AND THEATER

**AMC Loews Metreon**
101 Fourth St.
**Map** 5 C5.
**Tel** (415) 369-6201.
www.westfield.com

**American Conservatory Theater (ACT)**
Geary Theater,
415 Geary St.
**Map** 5 B5.
**Tel** (415) 749-2228.

**Bridge Theatre**
3010 Geary Blvd.
**Map** 3 B5.
**Tel** (415) 267-4893.

**The Castro Theatre**
429 Castro St.
**Map** 10 D2.
**Tel** (415) 621-6120.

**Children's Creativity Museum**
221 4th St.
**Map** 5 C5.
**Tel** (415) 820-3320.

**Clay Theatre**
2261 Fillmore St.
**Map** 4 D3.
**Tel** (415) 267-4893.

**Curran Theatre**
445 Geary St.
**Map** 5 B5.
**Tel** (415) 551-2000.

**Embarcadero Center Cinema**
Embarcadero Center.
**Map** 6 D3.
**Tel** (415) 267-4893.

**Golden Gate Theatre**
1 Taylor St.
**Map** 5 B5.
**Tel** (415) 551-2000.

**Lumiere**
1572 California St.
**Map** 4 F3.
**Tel** (415) 267-4893.

**The Marsh**
1062 Valencia St.
**Map** 10 F3.
**Tel** (415) 826-5750.
www.themarsh.org

**Opera Plaza Cinema**
601 Van Ness Ave.
**Map** 4 F5.
**Tel** (415) 267-4893.
www.landmark
theatre. com

**Orpheum Theatre**
1192 Market St.
**Map** 4 F5.
**Tel** (415) 551-2000.

**San Francisco Film Society International Film Festival**
**Tel** (415) 561-5000.
www.sffs.org

**Sundance Kabuki 8**
1881 Post St.
**Map** 4 E4.
**Tel** (415) 929-4650.

## OPERA, CLASSICAL MUSIC, AND DANCE

**Grace Cathedral**
1100 California St.
**Map** 5 B4.
**Tel** (415) 749-6300.
www.gracecathedral.org

**Herbst Theatre**
401 Van Ness Ave.
**Map** 4 F5.
**Tel** (415) 392-4400.

**LINES**
26 Seventh St.
**Map** 5 C5.
**Tel** (415) 863-3040.

**Louise M Davies Symphony Hall Box Office**
201 Van Ness Ave.
**Map** 4 F5.
**Tel** (415) 864-6000.

**ODC**
351 Shotwell St.
**Map** 10 F3.
**Tel** (415) 863-6606.

**Old First Presbyterian Church**
1751 Sacramento St.
**Map** 4 F3.
**Tel** 474-1608.
www.oldfirstconcerts.org

**Philharmonia Baroque Orchestra Box Office**
180 Redwood St,
Suite 200.
**Map** 4 F5.
**Tel** (415) 252-1288.

**Project Artaud**
499 Alabama St.
**Tel** (415) 621-4240.

**San Francisco Ballet**
455 Franklin St. **Map** 4 F4.
**Tel** (415) 865-2000.
www.sfballet.org

**San Francisco Conservatory of Music**
50 Oak St. **Map** 10 F1.
**Tel** (415) 503-6231.

# DIRECTORY

**San Francisco Opera**
301 Van Ness Ave.
**Map** 4 F5.
*Tel (415) 864-3330.*

**San Francisco Symphony**
201 Van Ness Ave.
**Map** 4 F5.
*Tel (415) 864-6000.*

**Zellerbach Hall**
UC Berkeley.
*Tel (415) 642-9988.*

## ROCK, JAZZ, AND BLUES

**Bimbo's 365 Club**
1025 Columbus Ave.
**Map** 5 A2.
*Tel (415) 474-0365.*
www.bimbos365club.com

**Biscuits and Blues**
401 Mason St.
**Map** 5 B5.
*Tel (415) 292-2583.*

**Boom Boom Room**
1601 Fillmore St.
**Map** 10 F2.
*Tel (415) 673-8000.*

**Dueling Pianos at Johnny Foley's**
243 O'Farrell St.
**Map** 5 B5.
*Tel (415) 954-0777.*

**Fillmore Auditorium**
1085 Geary at Fillmore St.
**Map** 4 D4.
*Tel (415) 346-6000.*
www.thefillmore.com

**Gold Dust Lounge**
247 Powell St.
**Map** 5 B5.
*Tel (415) 397-1695.*

**Lou's Pier 47**
300 Jefferson St.
**Map** 5 B1.
*Tel (415) 771-5687.*

**Monterey Jazz Festival**
2000 Fairgrounds Rd at Casa Verde, Monterey.
*Tel (831) 373-3366.*
www.montereyjazz festival.org

**Rrazz Room**
222 Mason St.
**Map** 5 B5.
*Tel (415) 394-1189.*

**The Saloon**
1232 Grant Ave.
**Map** 5 C3.
*Tel (415) 989-7666.*

**SF Jazz Center**
Franklin and Fell St.
**Map** 10 E1.
*Tel (866) 920-5299.*

**Slim's**
333 11th St. **Map** 10 F1.
*Tel (415) 255-0333.*
www.slims-sf.com

## CLUBS

**330 Ritch St**
330 Ritch St.
*Tel (415) 541-9574.*

**Bourbon Street Bar N Grill**
2765 Clayton Rd.
*Tel (925) 676-7272.*

**Chambers Eat & Drink**
601 Eddy St.
**Map** 5 A5.
*Tel (415) 829-2316.*

**Club Hide**
280 7th St.
*Tel (415) 621-1197.*

**Cobb's Comedy Club**
The Cannery at Beach St, 915 Columbus Ave. **Map** 5 A1. *Tel (415) 928-4320.*

**DNA Lounge**
375 11th St.
*Tel (415) 626-1409.*

**The Endup**
401 6th St.
*Tel (415) 646-0999.*

**Grandviews**
Grand Hyatt Hotel 36th floor, 345 Stockton St. **Map** 5 C4.
*Tel (415) 398-1234.*

**Kimo's**
1351 Polk St.
**Map** 4 F4.
*Tel (415) 885-4535.*

**The Marsh**
1062 Valencia St.
**Map** 10 F3.
*Tel (800) 838-3006.*

**Nickie's**
466 Haight St.
**Map** 10 E1.
*Tel (415) 255-0300.*

**Playbar**
101 6th St.
**Map** 5 C5.
*Tel (415) 512-7529.*

**Tonga Room**
950 Mason St.
**Map** 5 B4.
*Tel (415) 772-5278.*

**Top of the Mark**
Mark Hopkins InterContinental Hotel, 1 Nob Hill. **Map** 5 B4.
*Tel (415) 616-6916.*

## SPORTS AND OUTDOOR ACTIVITIES

**Blazing Saddles**
1095 Columbus Ave.
**Map** 5 A2.
*Tel (415) 202-8888.*
One of seven branches.
www.blazingsaddles.com

**Golden Gate Park**
(Municipal 9 hole).
**Map** 7 B2.
*Tel (415) 751-8987.*
www.parks.sfgov.org

**Golden State Warriors**
Oracle Arena.
*Tel (888) 479-4667.*
www.nba.com/warriors

**Lincoln Park**
300 34th Ave.
**Map** 1 C5.
*Tel (415) 221-9911.*

**Oakland Athletics, Oakland Raiders**
Oakland-Alameda County Coliseum.
*Tel (510) 864-5000.*
www.raiders.com

**Pacific Heights Health Club**
2356 Pine St. **Map** 4 D4.
*Tel (415) 563-6694.*
www.phhcsf.com

**Presidio Golf Course**
300 Finley Rd. **Map** 3 A3.
*Tel (415) 561-4661.*

**Recreation and Parks District**
Golden Gate Park, 501 Stanyan St.
*Tel (415) 831-2700*

**San Francisco 49ers**
Candlestick Park.
*Tel (415) 464-9377.*
www.49ers.com

**San Francisco Bay Club**
150 Greenwich St.
**Map** 5 C2.
*Tel (415) 433-2200.*
www.sfbayclub.com

**San Francisco Giants**
AT&T Park.
*Tel (415) 972-2000.*
www.sfgiants.com

**Stanford University Athletics**
Stanford University.
*Tel (650) 723-4591.*

**Stow Lake Boat & Bike Rentals**
Golden Gate Park.
**Map** 8 E2.
*Tel (415) 752-0347.*

**UC Berkeley Golden Bears**
UC Berkeley.
*Tel (800) 462-3277.*

# San Francisco's Bars

San Francisco has been a drinkers' town ever since the heady days of the Gold Rush (see pp48–9), when there was a saloon for every 50 residents. The bawdy public houses of the mid-19th century no longer exist. Instead, today, you can drink with a view; grab a local brew; sip an elegant, sweet cocktail in a chic lounge; sample a fine local country vintage wine; mingle with cheering local fans at a sports bar; see satellite-broadcast matches from Europe and soak up charm and an occasional concert at an Irish Bar. Alternatively, you can observe how a notable segment of San Francisco's population parties at a gay bar.

## ROOFTOP BARS

Those with a head for heights and a craving to be above the hills can visit the bars at the top of the towers in the city center. Grand Hyatt's **Grandviews**, **The View** at Marriott Hotel, and **Top of the Mark** at the Mark Hopkins, all offer splendid views and evening jazz along with dance music. **Cityscape**, on the 46th floor of the Hilton Hotel, has no pillars to obstruct the view. For those who want Mediterranean tapas with their city views, the Mission's **Medjool Restaurant/Lounge** will fit the bill.

## BEER BARS

For a more down-to-earth experience, visit one of the city's many beer bars, popular gathering places for the after-work crowd and weekend revelers. The best of these specialize in beers brewed by West Coast breweries, including San Francisco's fine Anchor Steam and Liberty Ale.

One of the best, the English **Mad Dog in the Fog**, is situated on Haight Street. **Magnolia Pub & Brewery**, in a 1903 Haight Victorian, retains its original wooden bar and name from ex-dancer, Magnolia Thunderpussy. **Thirsty Bear Brewing Company**, known for tapas; **The City Beer Store & Tasting Bar**, where drinkers can peruse bottles as they sip from fine brews; and the upscale **Gordon Biersch Brewery Restaurant**, all make their own excellent beer on the premises. At the Pacific Ocean edge of Golden Gate Park, **Beach Chalet**'s brews combine with fine views.

## COCKTAIL BARS

Traditional cocktail bars, with a chatty bartender holding court in front of rows of gleaming bottles, are great fun in San Francisco, and there are plenty of venues to choose from.

Singles often drink at **Harry Denton's Starlight Room**, and those in the need-to-be-seen crowd are in the Clift Hotel **Redwood Room**, with a backlit bar and upper tier cocktail prices. A lively bohemian crowd can be found along Columbus Avenue at **Specs'**, **Tosca Café**, and **Vesuvio** – a one-time beatnik hangout where a popular house drink is the Jack Kerouac (rum, tequila, orange/cranberry juice, and lime). Banquettes, cocktail tables, and Rat Pack-era decor mix with a relaxed North Beach crowd at **Tony Nik's Café**.

Across town in the Mission District, **Elixir** is a neighborhood bar with darts, and a wooden back-bar in a Victorian building that once had a bootblack on the premises. For a swinging night of live music and potent cocktails, head to **Bimbo's 365 Club** in North Beach. **Buena Vista Café** is the 1952 birthplace of Irish Coffee and serves 2,000 glasses a day. **Minx** showcases San Francisco at its most bizarre and fun, with a taxidermied raccoon to greet guests. **Chambers Eat & Drink** is a groovy, glam-rock bar and gastropub, with cool cocktails, leather sofas, and neon lights. In other bars, such as **Café du Nord**, in a former Prohibition speakeasy, and the award-winning **Biscuits and Blues**, live jazz is available.

## WINE BARS

With the proximity to Northern California Wine Country, the **Ferry Plaza Wine Merchant Bar**, surrounded by artisan cheesemakers and bakers, is a fine spot to sample wines.

Champagne and candlelight create the atmosphere of the **Bubble Lounge**. On weekdays **Barrique** caters to Financial District workers who seek the true experience of "barrel sampling." **Ma'velous** harnesses the combined culinary resources of California to offer an establishment, specializing in both the finest roasted coffees and boutique wines. Nearby, the well-reputed **Press Club**, in a cozy underground space beneath the Four Seasons Hotel, spotlights two wineries a month. Further north, **Corkage Sake & Wine Shop** caters to lovers of wines from across the globe.

## THEMED BARS

One of the best spots to connect with local passion is **Knuckles Sports Bar**, with over 24 televisions for live broadcasts. Bring your own food or snacks to the drinks-only **The Greens Sports Bar**. **Edinburgh Castle Pub** offers indie music complete with fish 'n' chips, darts, and pool. Good Irish cheer and ample Guinness are quaffed at **The Irish Bank** and **The Chieftain**.

## GAY BARS

Watering holes popular with the gay, lesbian, bisexual, and transgendered range from leather, biker, latex, and fetish-specialized to bars favored simply because the clientele is predominantly of one type. The Castro, SoMa, and Mission Districts are magnet areas. **Daddy's 440**, in the Castro, draws a Levi's and leather crowd. **AsiaSF** and **EndUp** keep drinks flowing with the dancing. In a city where few lesbian bars have survived, **Wild Side West** keeps the party going. **Divas Nightclub & Bar** is a well-known transgendered spot.

# DIRECTORY

## ROOFTOP BARS

### Cityscape Bar & Restaurant
46th floor, Hilton Hotel, 333 O'Farrell St.
**Map** 5 B5.
*Tel (415) 771-1400.*

### Grandviews
Grand Hyatt Hotel
36th floor, 45 Stockton St.
**Map** 5 C4.
*Tel (415) 398-1234.*

### Medjool Restaurant/Lounge
2522 Mission St.
**Map** 5 C5.
*Tel (415) 550-9055.*

### Top of the Mark
19th floor,
Mark Hopkins
InterContinental Hotel,
1 Nob Hill.
**Map** 5 B4.
*Tel (415) 616-6916.*

### The View
39th floor, Marriott Hotel,
55 4th St.
**Map** 5 C5.
*Tel (415) 896-1600.*

## BEER BARS

### Beach Chalet
1000 Great Hwy.
**Map** 7 A2.
*Tel (415) 386-8439.*
www.beachchalet.com

### The City Beer Store & Tasting Bar
1168 Folsom St.
*Tel (415) 503-1033.*

### Gordon Biersch Brewery Restaurant
2 Harrison St.
**Map** 6 E4.
*Tel (415) 243-8246.*

### Mad Dog in the Fog
530 Haight St.
**Map** 10 E1.
*Tel (415) 626-7279.*

### Magnolia Pub & Brewery
1398 Haight St.
**Map** 9 C1.
*Tel (415) 864-7468.*
www.magnoliapub.com

### Thirsty Bear Brewing Company
661 Howard St.
**Map** 6 D5.
*Tel (415) 974-0905.*
www.thirstybear.com

## COCKTAIL BARS

### Bimbo's 365 Club
1025 Columbus Ave,
North Beach.
**Map** 5 B2.
*Tel (415) 474-0365.*

### Biscuits and Blues
401 Mason St.
**Map** 5 B5. **Tel** 292-2583.
www.biscuitsand
blues. com

### Buena Vista Café
2765 Hyde St.
**Map** 4 F1.
*Tel (415) 474-5044.*
www.thebuenavista.com

### Café du Nord
2170 Market St.
**Map** 10 D2.
*Tel (415) 861-5016.*
www.cafenord.com

### Chambers Eat & Drink
601 Eddy St.
**Map** 5 A5.
*Tel (415) 8829-2316.*

### Elixir
3200 16th St.
at Valencia St.
**Map** 10 F2.
*Tel (415) 552-1633.*
www.elixirsf.com

### Harry Denton's Starlight Room
450 Powell St.
**Map** 5 B4.
*Tel (415) 395-8595.*
www.harrydenton.com

### Minx
827 Sutter St.
**Map** 5 B4.
*Tel (415) 779-6469.*

### Redwood Room
Clift Hotel, 495 Geary St.
**Map** 5 B5.
*Tel (415) 929-2372.*
www.clifthotel.com

### Specs' Twelve Adler Museum Café
12 William Saroyan Alley.
**Map** 5 C3.
*Tel (415) 421-4112.*

### Tony Nik's Café
1534 Stockton St.
**Map** 5 B2.
*Tel (415) 693-0990.*

### Tosca Café
242 Columbus Ave.
**Map** 5 C3.
*Tel (415) 986-9651.*

### Vesuvio
255 Columbus Ave.
**Map** 5 C3.
*Tel (415) 362-3370.*
www.vesuvio.com

## WINE BARS

### Barrique
461 Pacific Ave.
**Map** 5 C3.
*Tel (415) 421-9200.*

### Bubble Lounge
714 Montgomery St.
**Map** 5 C3.
*Tel (415) 434-4204.*
www.bubblelounge.com

### Corkage Sake & Wine Shop
1302 Fulton St.
**Map** 4 D5.
*Tel (415) 567-6503.*

### Ferry Plaza Wine Merchant & Wine Bar
One Ferry Building,
Shop 23.
**Map** 6 E3.
*Tel (415) 391-9400.*

### Ma'velous
1408 Market St.
**Map** 10 D2.
*Tel (415) 626-8884.*

### Press Club
20 Yerba Buena Lane.
**Map** 5 C5.
*Tel (415) 744-5000.*

## THEMED BARS

### The Chieftain
198 5th St.
*Tel (415) 615-0916.*
www.thechieftain.com

### Edinburgh Castle Pub
950 Geary Blvd.
**Map** 5 A5.
*Tel (415) 885-4074.*

### The Greens Sports Bar
2339 Polk St.
**Map** 5 A3.
*Tel (415) 775-4287.*

### The Irish Bank
10 Mark Ln
(off Bush St).
**Map** 5 B4.
*Tel (415) 788-7152.*
www.theirishbank.com

### Knuckles Sports Bar
555 North Point St.
**Map** 5 A1.
*Tel (415) 486-4376.*

## GAY BARS

### 440 Castro
440 Castro St.
**Map** 10 D3.
*Tel (415) 621-8732.*
www.the440.com

### AsiaSF
201 9th St.
**Map** 11 A2.
*Tel (415) 255-2742.*

### Divas Nightclub & Bar
1081 Post St.
**Map** 4 F4.
*Tel (415) 474-3482.*

### The Endup
401 6th St.
*Tel (415) 646-0999.*

### Wild Side West
424 Cortland Ave.
**Map** 10 F5.
*Tel (415) 744-5000.*

# GETTING AROUND
# SAN FRANCISCO

San Francisco occupies a compact area, making it a sightseer's dream. Many of the sights featured on visitors' itineraries are only a short walk from each other. Cycling is also a popular way to travel around. The public transportation system is easy to use and efficient. Bus routes crisscross town and pass many attractions. MUNI Metro streetcars and BART lines serve downtown as well as the suburbs and outlying neighborhoods. Taxis are reasonably priced and recommended for trips after dark in certain areas. They can be hailed on the street or booked in advance by telephone. And, of course, no one can resist a cable car ride over the city's famed hills. Passenger ferries and boat trips run regularly east and north across the bay. If driving in San Francisco see page 633 for details on the city's parking laws.

**Do not cross the street**

**You may cross the street**

## WALKING

The best way to explore San Francisco is on foot. The main tourist areas are within 15 to 20 minutes of each other when walking at an average speed. The hills can be a struggle, but the views over the city and the bay make them well worth the climb.

Most road intersections are marked with a green and white sign bearing the name of the cross street, or names are imprinted in the concrete pavement at street corners.

Vehicles are driven on the right-hand side of the road and are allowed to turn right on a red light if the road is clear, so be careful when crossing at traffic lights. Never rely solely on a pedestrian "Walk" signal.

Jaywalking is common but illegal and crossing a street when the "Don't Walk" signal is showing can result in a hefty fine. Wait for the "Walk" signal and proceed with caution. Pedestrian lights countdown to show how much time you have to cross.

## TAXIS

Taxis in San Francisco are licensed and operate 24 hours a day. You can catch a cab at a taxi stand, call for a pick-up, or hail a cab when its rooftop sign is illuminated.

There is a flat fee ($3.50) for the first mile (1.6 km). This increases by about $2.25 for each additional mile or 45 cents a minute while waiting at an address or in heavy traffic. Add a 15 percent tip onto the fare.

## CYCLING

Cycling is a popular way to get around San Francisco. It is possible to find cycle lanes avoiding hills along the waterfront. Bikes can be rented from $30 a day or $130 a week from hire outlets. Buses are equipped to carry bikes strapped to the front of the bus. A bike sharing scheme is to be introduced, with bikes stationed all over the city. A 30-minute ride will be free of charge or pay to ride longer.

## OTHER WAYS TO GET AROUND

Pedicabs and horse-drawn carriages can be found on The Embarcadero, especially near Fisherman's Wharf (*see pp334–5*). Small, two-seater

**A pedicab – an increasingly popular way of seeing the sights**

go karts are available to rent throughout the city as well, through **GoCar**. The small cars can drive up to 60 mph (97 kmh) and are pre-programmed with tours and GPS systems to guide you around the city. If you don't feel like driving, a fleet of motorized cable cars dash around the city giving guided tours of all the sights, allowing you to hop-on and off. Sight-seeing bus tours are offered as half- or full-day trips.

## DIRECTORY

### TAXIS

**Black & White Checker**
*Tel* (415) 285-3880.

**DeSoto**
*Tel* (415) 970-1300.

**Fog City Cab**
*Tel* (415) 282-8749.

**Yellow Cab**
*Tel* (415) 626-2345.

### CYCLING

**Bay City Bike**
2661 Taylor St, Fishermans Wharf.
**Map** 4 F1.
*Tel* (415) 346-2453.
**www**.baycitybike.com

**Blazing Saddles**
2715 Hyde St. **Map** 5 A1.
*Tel* (415) 202-8888.
**www**.blazingsaddles.com

### OTHER WAYS TO GET AROUND

**GoCar**
*Tel* (800) 914-6227.
**www**.gocartours.com

# Traveling by Bus and MUNI Metro Streetcar

San Francisco Municipal Railway (MUNI) is the organization that runs the city's bus, cable car, and light rail systems. You can use one interchangeable pass – MUNI Passport – to travel on MUNI buses, MUNI Metro streetcars (electric trams), the F Market & Wharves historic streetcar line, and the three cable car lines. Buses and streetcars serve most tourist attractions and all neighborhoods.

## FARES AND TICKETS

Buses, streetcars, and the metro cost $2 per ride. Since the **MUNI** system has phased out paper tickets, visitors now need to buy either a Clipper card or Limited Use MUNI tickets. The Clipper card is a reloadable fare card that is accepted on all MUNI vehicles, as well as on BART, AC Transit, Caltrain, SamTrans, VTA, and Golden Gate Transit and Ferry. It can be bought at BART and MUNI stations, as well as at many stores and costs $5. Visitors can buy a Limited Use MUNI Ticket from machines in MUNI stations for use on MUNI only. Senior citizens over 65 and children aged five to 17 years pay reduced fares. Kids under five travel free.

A MUNI Passport, valid for one, three, or seven days, allows unlimited travel on buses, streetcars, and cable cars. It is available from information kiosks at San Francisco International airport, the **San Francisco Travel Association**, and the cable car ticket booths at Powell & Market and Hyde & Beach Streets.

**CityPass** (see p619) is another option. For $69 ($39 for kids), you get unlimited MUNI and cable car rides, plus entry to five attractions including the SF Museum of Modern Art.

MUNI Metro streetcar, with its distinctive red and silver cars

## BUSES AND MUNI METRO STREETCARS

Buses stop only at their designated bus stops every two or three blocks. The route number and the destination are found on the front and side of each bus. Those route numbers followed by a letter (L, EX, A, etc.) are limited-stop or express services.

Bus stops have signs displaying the MUNI logo. The walls of the shelter list the route numbers of buses that stop there, and provide route maps and frequency guides. On boarding, put the exact change in the fare box or show your MUNI Passport to the driver. To indicate that you want to get off at the next stop, pull the cord that runs along the windows or inform the driver. The "Stop Requested" sign above the front window will light up.

MUNI Metro streetcars and BART trains (see p398) share four of the seven underground stations along Market Street, marked by orange, yellow, and white illuminated signs. Once inside, look for the separate "MUNI" entrance.

To travel west of the city, choose "Outbound"; to travel east, choose "Downtown." Electronic signs indicate which streetcar is about to arrive. Doors open automatically unless you're at a low-level or street-level station, in which case just push on the low bar beside the door. Stops above ground level are identified by an orange-and-brown flag or a yellow band around a pole, marked "MUNI" or "Car Stop." Streetcar stops are wheelchair accessible and ramps are provided to board.

## SIGHTSEEING BY BUS

The following are some popular bus routes for visitors: Route 38 runs to Japantown and the hills above Ocean Beach; Golden Gate Park (see pp366–9) is on Routes 5, 21, 28, 29, 44, 71, and N. For Chinatown and Nob Hill (see pp324–31) take Routes 1, 9X, 12, 15, 30, 45. For Haight Ashbury (see pp354–63) take Route 6, 7, 33, 37, 43, 71; Mission District is on Routes 14, 18, 22, 24, 33, 48, J. The rest of the Bay Area (see pp410–31) can be reached in about 30 to 45 minutes.

## DIRECTORY

### MUNI INFORMATION

*Tel* (415) 673-6864.
**www**.sfmta.com

**City Pass**
*Tel* (888) 330-5008.
**www**.citypass.com

**San Francisco Travel Association**
Hallidie Plaza. **Map** 5 C5.
*Tel* (415) 391-2000.
**www**.511.org

Destinations are shown on the front and side of the bus

# Traveling by Cable Car, BART, and Ferry

San Francisco's cable cars are world-famous
(see pp302–3) and every visitor will want to ride
one at least once. San Francisco peninsula and the
East Bay are linked by BART (Bay Area Rapid Transit),
a 104-mile (114-km) light rail system with a high-speed,
efficient fleet of trains, all wheelchair accessible. Boats
and passenger ferries are also a favorite way to see
the city's shoreline and to get around.

**Nob Hill, where the Powell and California lines cross**

**The thrilling descent down Hyde Street to the bay**

### USING THE CABLE CARS

The city's cable car service operates 6:30am–12:30am daily with special schedules at weekends. There is a flat fare of $6 for a single trip with a discount for seniors and the disabled between 9pm–7am. Kids of four and younger travel free. A $14 All-Day Passport gives you unlimited cable-car rides, plus unlimited MUNI streetcar and bus rides. There are also three-day and seven-day unlimited tickets ($21 and $27 respectively).

Cable cars are reliable and run at 15-minute intervals. To catch a cable car, you should be prepared to jump on board quickly. Stops are marked by maroon signs that display the outline of a cable car in white, or by a yellow line painted on the road at right-angles to the track.

If you have not purchased a MUNI Passport (see p397), you can buy a ticket or a one-day pass from the conductor. Tickets are collected once you board. MUNI passes, souvenir tickets, and maps are available at kiosks at Powell and Market streets and at Hyde and Beach streets, or at the San Francisco Travel Association (see p397). Cable cars run along three routes. The name of the line is displayed on the front, back, and sides of every car. The Powell–Hyde line is the most popular, starting at the Powell and Market turntable (see p321) and ending on Hyde Street, near Aquatic Park. The Powell–Mason line also begins at Powell and Market streets and ends at Bay Street. Sit facing east on the Powell lines and you will see the best sights as you travel. The California line runs from the base of Market Street, then through part of the Financial District and Chinatown, ending at Van Ness Avenue.

The city's hills present no problem to the cable cars and they tackle precipitous slopes effortlessly. The most thrilling descent is the final stretch of the Powell–Hyde line as it dips from Nob Hill to the bay.

Commuters also use cable cars, so try to avoid traveling during the rush hours 7am to 9:30am Mon–Fri and 4pm to 6:30pm Mon–Fri.

### TRAVELING SAFELY IN A CABLE CAR

If there is not a crowd, you can sit or stand inside, sit outside on a bench, or stand on a side running board. If you choose the latter, hold on tightly to the "hang on" poles that are provided.

Try not to get in the way of the gripman; he needs plenty of room to operate the grip lever. This off-limits area is marked by yellow lines on the floor. Use caution while on board. Passing other cable cars is exciting, but don't lean out too far because they get very close to one another. Be careful when boarding or getting off, as cable cars often stop at intersections, where you have to maneuver between the car and other vehicles.

### FERRY SERVICES AND BAY TRIPS

Residents of the Bay Area adore their ferries, and they are used as much by local commuters as they are by tourists. Although these ferries do not provide audio tours to point out and describe the sights, they are a less expensive option than sightseeing cruises.

The Ferry Building (see p316) is the terminal for Golden Gate Ferries. Bay sightseeing cruises from Fisherman's Wharf are

Bell ———                     Destination board ———

Side seating |          Running board          Gate

**A San Francisco cable car**

## MAKING A JOURNEY BY BART

**The BART logo**

BART trains operate daily from early morning until midnight. During rush hours, 7am to 9am and 4pm to 7pm, they run at nearly full capacity. The trains are clean, well kept, and the service is highly efficient.

BART trains run each day from the International Terminal of San Francisco International Airport (SFO) into the heart of the city every 15–20 minutes. These trains stop at four central stations, all underneath Market Street – Civic Center, Powell, Montgomery, and Embarcadero. It costs $8.50 each way and takes 30 minutes. All eastbound trains stop at downtown

### BART ROUTE MAP

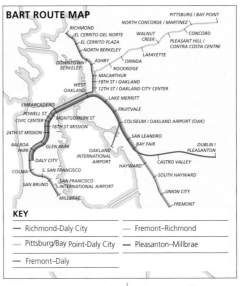

**KEY**

— Richmond-Daly City

— Pittsburg/Bay Point-Daly City

— Fremont–Daly

— Fremont–Richmond

— Pleasanton–Millbrae

SF stations before heading for the East Bay via a dark, 4-mile (6-km) underwater tunnel. Transfers in the East Bay are best done at MacArthur and

19th Street Oakland stations. Clipper cards *(see p397)* can be reloaded at the machines in all stations.

operated by **Blue & Gold Fleet** and **Red & White Fleet**. Excursions offered include Angel Island and towns that lie on the north shore of the bay *(see pp414–15)*. **Alcatraz Cruises** operates tours of Alcatraz island *(see pp338–9)*. There are also combined boat and bus tours to Six Flags Marine World and Muir Woods *(see p414)*.

You can dine and dance aboard one of several cruisers that ply the bay's waters. **Hornblower Dining Yachts** offer lunch on Friday, brunch

on weekends, and dinner daily on their cruises. Choose a bayside table for a spectacular view of the waterfront during your meal. The **Oceanic Society** offers trips with an onboard naturalist around the Farallon Islands, which lie 25 miles (40 km) off the coast of San Francisco *(see pp412–13)*. Whale-watching expeditions off the city's west coast *(see p614)* are also available, but you should check with individual operators for seasonal details.

## DIRECTORY

### CABLE CARS

**Cable Car Museum**
*(see p331)*

### FERRIES

**Alcatraz Cruises**
*Tel (415) 981-7625.*
**www**.alcatrazcruises.com

**Blue & Gold Fleet**
Pier 39. **Map** 5 B1.
*Tel 705-8200.*
**www**.blueandgoldfleet.com

### BAY TRIPS

**Hornblower Dining Yachts**
Pier 3. **Map** 5 C1.
*Tel (888) 467-6256.*
**www**.hornblower.com

**Oceanic Society**
*Tel (415) 441-1106.*
**www**.oceanicsociety.org

**Red & White Fleet**
*Tel (415) 673-2900.*
**www**.redandwhite.com

**Red and white fleet ferry passing under the Golden Gate Bridge**

# SAN FRANCISCO STREET FINDER

Map references given with sights, entertainment venues, shops and Practical Information addresses described in the San Francisco section refer to the maps on the following pages. Map references for hotels and restaurants in the city (see pp542–9 and pp587–95) also apply to these pages.

The key map below shows the area covered by the Streetfinder, including the sightseeing areas and other districts important for restaurants, hotels, and entertainment venues. A large scale map of the city center appears on pages 5 and 6. The symbols used on the Street Finder maps are listed in the key below.

## KEY TO STREET FINDER

| | |
|---|---|
| ▨ | Major Sight |
| ▨ | Places of interest |
| 🚉 | CalTrain station |
| Ⓑ | BART station |
| 🚌 | Long distance bus terminus |
| 🚏 | Streetcar station |
| 🚍 | Bus terminus |
| 🚡 | Cable car terminus |
| ⛴ | Ferry boarding point |
| ℹ | Tourist information office |
| ✚ | Hospital with emergency unit |
| 🏠 | Police station |
| ✝ | Church |
| ✡ | Synagogue |
| ☪ | Mosque |
| 卍 | Buddhist temple |
| 🛕 | Hindu temple |
| ⊠ | Post Office |
| ⛳ | Golf course |
| = | Railroad line |
| ▬ | Freeway |
| <<665 | House number (main street) |

### SCALE OF MAPS 1–4 AND 7–10

| 0 meters | 500 |
|---|---|
| 0 yards | 500 |

### SCALE OF MAPS 5 & 6

| 0 meters | 500 |
|---|---|
| 0 yards | 500 |

*Golden Gate Park and The Presidio*

*Haight and the*

PACIFIC OCEAN

*Land's End*

LINCOLN

PARK

EL CAMINO DEL MAR

Legion of Honor

LEGION OF HONOR DRIVE

LINCOLN PARK MUNICIPAL GOLF COURSE

CLEMENT STREET

Alcatraz
Island

PIER 23

PIER 19

PIER 17

PIER 15

PIER 9

Pier
7

San Francisco
Bay

PIER 5

PIER 3

PIER 1

THE EMBARCADERO

DAVIS STREET

DRUMM STREET

NGTON STREET

EMBARCADERO
PLAZA PARK

MARITIME
PLAZA

arcadero Center

JUSTIN
HERMAN
PLAZA

Hyatt Regency
Hotel

PIER 2

Ferry Building

SAN FRANCISCO OAKLAND BAY BRIDGE

SACENTO
STREET

DAVIS
ST

FRONT
STREET

100
STREET

STEUART STREET

Embarcadero
Station

ast
ange

Amtrak
Terminal
Ticket Office

SPEAR STREET

MAIN STREET

Rincon
Center

MISSION STREET

BEALE STREET

Transbay
Terminal

Folsom
Station

PIER 24

PIER 26

PIER 28

Greyhound
Bus Depot

FREMONT STREET

1ST STREET

HOWARD STREET

ry

MINNA STREET

um

Pacific
Telephone
Building

um of
ern Art

MALDEN
AL

HAWTHORNE STREET

TEHAMA STREET

CLEMENTINA
ST

GUY PL

LANDING

ESSEX ST

FOLSOM STREET

ELMHART PL
ST

HARRISON STREET

1ST STREET

THE EMBARCADERO

PIER 30

PIER 32

PIER 34

c
ion

HAMPTON
PL

DOW PL

VERONICA

BRYANT STREET

RINCON
ST

2ND STREET

Brannan
Station

PIER 36

PIER 38

STREET

HARRISON
STREET

STILLMAN ST

DE BOOM
ST

BRANNAN STREET

# THE BAY AREA

Many of the settlements encircling San Francisco Bay were once summer retreats for the city's residents, but today they are sprawling suburbs or cities in their own right. Two of the most popular destinations in the East Bay are Oakland's museum and harbor and Berkeley's gardens and famous university. Farther south, San Jose has emerged as the region's newest commercial and cultural center, combining the technology of Silicon Valley with fine museums and preserved architecture of its Spanish Colonial past. Smaller towns such as Tiburon, Pescadero, and Sausalito, however, have managed to retain their village atmosphere, despite their closeness to the city. The area also has the advantage of its coastal landscapes: the cliffs of Point Reyes and the Marin Headlands, with their abundance of wildlife, offer perfect afternoon retreats away from the metropolis.

**Detail from
Sather Gate, Berkeley**

## SIGHTS AT A GLANCE

### Historic Towns
Benicia **7**
Berkeley **9**
Livermore **13**
Oakland **10**
Pescadero **16**
San Jose **17**
Sausalito **4**
Tiburon **5**

### Theme Parks
Six Flags
    Discovery Kingdom **6**

### Historic Buildings
Filoli **15**
Stanford University **14**
Tao House **11**

### Parks and Beaches
John Muir National Historic
    Site **8**
Marin Headlands **3**
Mount Diablo State Park **12**
Muir Woods and Beach **2**
Point Reyes National
    Seashore **1**

0 kilometers   25

0 miles                     25

### KEY
Central San Francisco
Urban areas
✈ Airport
Ⓡ Amtrak station
Major road
Minor road

# The Bay Area Coastline

The coastline around San Francisco varies a great deal, its rugged cliffs alternating with sandy beaches. Since the ocean water hovers around 60° F (15° C) all year, nobody swims or surfs without a wet suit, but for sunbathing or aimless beachcombing strolls, the Bay Area beaches are hard to beat. Much of the coast is protected by a series of state and federal parks, such as the Point Reyes National Seashore (see p406), the Marin Headlands section of the Golden Gate National Recreation Area (pp416–17), and the many state beaches that line the southern coast.

**Pacifica** *was once the agricultural outpost of Mission Dolores* (see p361). *The two-story Sanchez Adobe in the town now houses a museum of 19th-century farming equipment.*

**★ Point Reyes National Seashore** ①

This protected stretch of land is noted for its diverse eco-systems and its 360 species of birds *(see p414)*.

**Bolinas** ②

Following the Gold Rush *(see pp48–9)*, Bolinas became a summer haven for San Franciscans, and some Victorian buildings still survive. The town is also a winter home to monarch butterflies.

**Marin Headlands** ④

The Marin Headlands benefit from stunning views of San Francisco as well as a wilderness rife with diverse birdlife *(see pp416–17)*.

**Treasure Island** ⑥

At the center of the Bay Bridge *(see pp416–17)*, the island was the site of the 1939 World's Fair. Connected to Yerba Buena Island, Treasure Island is now a residential community.

**Fort Funston** ⑦

The bluff overlooking this beach, which is also used as an observation site, is a favorite launch site for professional and amateur hang gliders.

**Colma** ⑧

This unusual town consists almost entirely of cemeteries, containing the graves of former San Franciscans and Bay Area residents. Cemeteries are prohibited within the city of San Francisco.

**Pillar Point Harbor** ⑨

This is the only naturally protected harbor located between San Francisco and Santa Cruz. In the late 19th century it was used as a whaling station.

**★ Farallon Islands** ⑫

Twenty-seven miles (44 km) west of Point Bonita, the islands are the most important nesting site for sea birds and stopover point for migratory birds in California. They are also a breeding ground for elephant seals. There is no public access.

**Muir Woods National Monument** *is the last remaining redwood forest in the Bay Area. The others were cut down for lumber during the 19th century (see p414).*

SANTA
Tomales Road
Point Reyes
Station
Sir Francis

**Mount Tamalpais**, *reaching a height of 2,604 ft (794 m), is the habitat of various flora and fauna, including the rarely sighted mountain lion. The Mountain Theater is set in a natural bowl overlooking the bay.*

**LOCATOR MAP**

**★ Muir Beach ③**

Redwood Creek drains down from Mount Tamalpais to the ocean at Muir Beach. It is home to silver salmon and crayfish. South of Muir Beach, Potato Patch Shoal is a low-tide area of turbulence and freak waves.

**★ Point Bonita ⑤**
Point Bonita's lighthouse on this rugged clifftop was the last manually operated lighthouse in the state, only changing to automation in 1980. The lighthouse is reached via a tunnel carved through solid rock or over a surf-lashed bridge.

**★ Half Moon Bay ⑩**

The oldest town in San Mateo County, the area's soil is ideal for growing artichokes, broccoli, and pumpkins. The town holds a pumpkin festival each October in celebration of its prime crop.

**★ Pigeon Point ⑪**

Following numerous shipwrecks in the area, including the *Carrier Pigeon*, which gave the area its name, a 115-ft (35-m) lighthouse was erected in 1872. Sea lions can often be spotted offshore.

0 kilometers 10
0 miles 10

**KEY**

| | |
|---|---|
| | Freeway |
| | Major road |
| | Minor road |
| | River |
| �515 | Viewpoint |

**Dairy farm at picturesque Point Reyes**

# Point Reyes National Seashore **❶**

**Road map** A3. 🚌 *from San Rafael Center (weekends only).* **Bear Valley Visitors' Center** *1 Bear Valley Rd, main entrance to National Seashore, Point Reyes.* **Tel** *(415) 464-5100.* ☐ *9am–5pm Mon–Fri, 8am–5pm Sat & Sun.* **www**.nps.gov/pore

This triangular area of land, only half attached to the San Franciscan coastline, has been gradually drifting northward along the California coast for more than six million years. Situated due west of the San Andreas Fault, the peninsula moved a full 20 ft (6 m) north of the mainland during the 1906 earthquake *(see pp52–3).* A displaced fence

**POINT REYES**
NATIONAL SEASHORE
United States Department of the Interior
National Park Service

**Signpost to Point Reyes**

on the Earthquake Trail near Bear Valley Visitor Center is evidence of its overnight movement. The visitors' center itself contains interesting displays on local geology and geography.

A notable feature of this stretch of coastline is its abundance of wildlife, including a herd of tule elk. The area has cattle and dairy ranches, and three small towns: Point Reyes Station, Olema, and Inverness.

Drake's Bay is named after the English explorer Sir Francis Drake, who is thought to have anchored here in 1579. He named the land Nova Albion and briefly claimed it for England *(see pp46–7).*

# Muir Woods and Beach **❷**

*1 Muir Woods Road.* 🚌 *Mill Valley.* **Visitors' Center** *Hwy 1, Mill Valley.* **Tel** *(415) 388-2595.* ☐ *summer: 8am–8pm, winter: 8am–5pm.* 🏖 *for the woods (beach is free)* **www**.nps.gov/muwo

Nestling at the foot of Mount Tamalpais *(see pp413)* is Muir Woods National Monument, one of the few remaining stands of old-growth coastal redwoods. Before the 19th-century lumber industry flourished, these tall trees (the oldest is at least 1,000 years old) once completely covered the coastal area of California. The woods were named in honor of John Muir, the 19th-century naturalist responsible for turning Yosemite into a national park *(see pp488–91).*

Redwood Creek bubbles out of Muir Woods and makes its way down to the ocean at Muir Beach, a wide expanse of sand popular with beach-combers and picnickers *(see pp412–13).* Along the road to the beach is the incongruous Pelican Inn, a 16th-century-style English inn. It is proud of its traditional English menu, with items such as roast beef, and offers a warm welcome.

Muir Beach is likely to be crowded at weekends, especially during the summer months, but visitors who are prepared to walk for 15 minutes or more along the sand are rewarded with peace and quiet.

# Marin Headlands **❸**

*See pp416–17.*

# Sausalito **❹**

**Road map** inset B. 🏠 *7,060.* 🚗 🚌 🚢 ℹ️ *780 Bridgeway Ave (415 332-0505).* **www**.sausalito.org

In this small town that was once a fishing community, Victorian bungalows cling to steep hills rising from San Francisco Bay. Parallel to the waterfront, Bridgeway Avenue serves as a promenade for the weekend crowds that come to patronize the restaurants and shops and enjoy the views. The **San Francisco Bay Model Visitor Center** is the only operational hydraulic model in the US, which simulates the movement of the tides and currents in San Francisco Bay, and in the bay-delta system.

🏛 **San Francisco Bay Model Visitor Center**
*2100 Bridgeway Ave.* **Tel** *(415) 332-3871.* ☐ *Sep–May: 9am–4pm Tue–Sat; Jun–Aug: 9am–4pm Tue–Fri, 10am–5pm Sat & Sun.* 🌑 *public hols.*

**Harbor scene in Sausalito**

# Tiburon **❺**

**Road map** inset B. 🏠 *8,960.* 🚗 🚌 🚢 ℹ️ *96B Main St. (415 435-5633).* **www**.ci.tiburon.ca.us

The main street of this elegant waterfront town is lined with fashionable shops and restaurants housed in "arks." These unique

**Attractive main street of Tiburon**

buildings are in fact house-boats from the early 20th century that have been pulled ashore and innovatively refurbished. They now stand in what is called "Ark Row."

Less hectic than nearby Sausalito, Tiburon is a good town for walking. Parks are situated along the waterfront from which you can contemplate the bay. A popular spot for hikers and cyclists.

## Six Flags Discovery Kingdom ❻

1001 Fairgrounds Dr. **Road map** inset B. **Tel** (707) 643-6722. 🚌 from San Francisco. ☐ (check website for times). 🎫 ♿ 🛒 **www.** sixflags.com/discoverykingdom

The most unique wildlife park, oceanarium, and theme park in Northern California, Six Flags Discovery Kingdom attracts 1.6 million visitors each year. Its lush 135-acre (55-ha) site is located along I-80 at Hwy 37 on the outskirts of Vallejo. There is equal emphasis on education and entertainment in the park, but the primary attractions are the shows featuring marine mammals. Arenas housing large pools showcase a killer whale, sea lions, and dolphins. In the Shark Experience, visitors enter by way of a transparent tunnel through a tank filled with large sharks and tropical fish.

Land animal attractions include shows featuring Bengal tigers, elephants exotic birds, and tropical butterflies.

## Benicia ❼

**Road map** inset B. 🏛 28,000. 🚌 🚆 ⛴ 🛈 Benicia Chamber of Commerce, 601 1st St (707 745-2120). **www.**visitbenicia.com

Set on the north side of the Carquinez Straits, the narrow waterway through which the Sacramento and the San Joaquin rivers flow from the Sierra Nevada to San Francisco Bay, Benicia is one of California's most historic small towns.

From February 1853 until February 1854, Benicia served as an early state capital. The Greek Revival building that once housed the government has been preserved as a state historic park, complete with many original fixtures and furnishings. Next door to the former capitol, the Fisher-Hanlon House, a former Gold Rush hotel, has also been restored to its original condition as part of **Benicia Capitol State Historic Park**.

At the other end of Main Street from the capitol complex is the Benicia waterfront, where ferries shuttled to Port Costa during the 1850s. The former Benicia Arsenal, which stored army weapons from the 1850s to the 1950s, has been converted into live-work studio spaces.

🏛 **Benicia Capitol State Historic Park**
115 West G St. **Tel** (707) 745-3385. ☐ 10am–5pm Sat & Sun. 🎫

## John Muir National Historic Site ❽

4202 Alhambra Ave, Martinez. **Tel** (925) 228-8860. ☐ 10am–5pm daily. ⬤ Jan 1, Thanksgiving, Dec 25. ♿ 1st floor & grounds only. **www.**nps.gov/jomu

Set amid the suburban neighborhood of Martinez, the John Muir National Historic Site preserves the home where the naturalist and writer lived from 1890 until his death in 1914. The 17-room Italianate house is typical of a late Victorian upper middle class dwelling, conveying little of Muir's simple tastes and back-to-nature inclinations. Only the library, which Muir called his "scribble den," gives a real sense of the man. The house was once surrounded by 2,600 acres (1,052 ha) of fruit trees, only one of which survives. In season, rangers pick fruit for visitors to sample.

The Visitor Center, in keeping with Muir's own values of conservation, has eco-conscious features such as bamboo flooring and a recycled-redwood front desk. The Center includes exhibits on Muir that are used to educate the public about his life and achievements through conservation. There is also information for kids, allowing them to get involved and understand more about being a park ranger.

Nearby are 320 acres (130 ha) of hiking trails, which pass through fruit orchards and wildflower fields. Full Moon walks are also available.

**John Muir (1838–1914)**

# A 90-Minute Walk through the Marin Headlands ❸

At its northern end, the Golden Gate Bridge is anchored in the rolling green hills of the Marin Headlands. This is an unspoiled wild area of windswept ridges, sheltered valleys, and deserted beaches, once used as a military defense post and now part of the vast Golden Gate National Recreation Area. From several vantage points there are spectacular views of San Francisco and vast panoramas of the sea, and, on autumn days, you can see migrating eagles and ospreys gliding past Hawk Hill.

Schoolchildren on a trip to the Marin Headlands

Rodeo Beach ③

## Marin Headlands Visitor Center

Before starting this walk, pause a while at the steepled Visitors' Center ①, which was once the interdenominational chapel for Fort Cronkhite. It has since been refurbished and is now a museum and information center, with a natural history bookshop that specializes in books on birds. Here you can discover the history of the Marin Headlands and see a Coast Miwok Indian shelter. The walk, which will take you around Rodeo Lagoon ②, begins at the gate on the west, ocean side, of the parking lot. Take the path to the left that leads to the sea. This part of the trail is thick with trees and shrubs, including poison oak, of which visitors should be aware. The songs of birds fill the air and around the edges of the lagoon you will see brown pelicans, snowy egrets, and mallards. A 15-minute walk will bring you to the sandy, wind-blown Rodeo Beach ③, and from here you can see Bird Island ④ lying offshore

*MARIN HEADLANDS*
*STATE PARK*
*(GOLDEN GATE NATION*
*RECREATION AREA)*

Cooper's Hawk

⑥ MITCHELL ROAD

⑤

*R o d*
*L a g*

White Egret

③ Rodeo Beach

Herring Gull

*Sm*

Turkey Vulture

④

Bird Island

MENDE

Rodeo Lagoon ②

### KEY

••• Walk route

✴ Viewpoint

🅿 Parking

**Seal at The Marine Mammal Center** ⑦

**Marin Headlands Visitor Center** ①

Horse
Trail

Bike
Trail

**Sign marking a
trail**

path, then turn left at the road that climbs a steep hill to The Marine Mammal Center ⑦. This was used as a missile defense site during the Cold War, but is now run by volunteers who rescue and care for sick or injured marine mammals. Sea lions and seals, including the rare elephant seals,

Cross the bridge, not on the roadway but on the separate footpath at the side. Before the guard rail ends, a path ⑨ plunges to the right into the dense shrubbery. From here, continue up the hill again, via a series of steps that will return you to the path at the end of the Marin Headlands Visitor Center parking lot. Walk across the lot and up the hill to a three-story wooden building, constructed at the turn of the century. This is listed on the National Historic

to the south. Fishing boats may be seen bobbing out at sea, but the beach is mostly empty of people, although sometimes you might see groups of children working on coastal ecology programs. These are run by the Headlands Institute, which is based in the nearby clutch of former army barracks.

### Barracks to The Marine Mammal Center

From the beach, turn inland again as you approach the tip of the lagoon, crossing a wooden footbridge ⑤. Here there are lavatories, and barracks ⑥ housing various offices, among them the Headlands District Office, the Raptor Observatory, and an energy and resources center. Walking past the barracks, continue along the

are examined and treated here in specially designed pens. They are then returned to the sea when they have recovered. You can watch the vets at work and get a close view of the mammals, many of which are orphaned pups. There are also some displays of the marine ecosystem.

### Lagoon to the Golden Gate Hostel

Make your way back down the hill and return to the paved road that runs past Rodeo Lagoon ⑧. There is a separate pathway beside the road for hikers, but you have to climb over a guard rail to get to it. Just before the road crosses a bridge, there is a large bench where you can view the water birds. There are plenty of birds to be seen in this brackish lagoon with its tall grasses.

Registry and has been officers' headquarters, a hospital, and a missile command center. It is now the Golden Gate Hostel ⑩ for travelers. The Marin Headlands also offer a wide range of longer, more challenging walks. Wolf Ridge and Bobcat Trail are two popular routes you may want to try.

### TIPS FOR WALKERS

**Starting point**: The Marin Headlands Visitor Center at Fort Cronkhite.
**Length**: 2 miles (3 km).
**Getting there**: San Francisco MUNI bus 76 leaves from the intersection of Fourth Street and Townsend Street on Sundays and some holidays. **Tel** (415) 673-6864. By car, drive across the Golden Gate Bridge, taking the Alexander Avenue exit. Turn under the freeway, following signs for the Headlands, Fort Cronkhite, and Fort Barry.
**Stopping-off points**: Water is available, but there are no refreshments or restaurants in the Marin Headlands. You will need to bring your own picnic lunch, which can be enjoyed at any number of tables dotted along the trails and the beaches.

---

*Map labels:*

BUNKER ROAD

*fornia
a Lion* ⑧ ROAD

BUNKER ROAD

*Rodeo
Lake*

⑨

P ①

FIELD ROAD

BODSWORTH RD

SIMMONDS RD

ROSENSTOCK RD

⑩

COASTAL TRAIL

*Marin
Headlands
Visitor Center*

0 meters 250

0 yards 250

# Berkeley ⑨

Berkeley began to boom following the earthquake of 1906 (see pp52–3), when many San Franciscans fled their ruined city and settled on the east side of the bay. Berkeley did not really find its own voice, however, until the birth of the Free Speech Movement and the student uprisings against the Vietnam War during the 1960s, earning itself the nickname "Beserkeley." Many stores and market stalls still hark back to the hippie era with their psychedelic merchandise, but in recent years Berkeley has begun to raise its profile. Stylish restaurants and cafés have emerged, as well as a reputation for fine food – it was here that the popular California cuisine was born. Today the city blends idealism and style in unique harmony.

Claremont Resort Hotel

## 🏛 University of California at Berkeley

*Tel (510) 643-7649.* **Phoebe A. Hearst Museum of Anthropology** *Tel (510) 642-3682.* ◯ *10am–4:30pm Wed–Sat, noon–4pm Sun.* ● *public hols.* **Berkeley Art Museum and Pacific Film Archive** *Tel (510) 642-0808.* ◯ *11am–5pm Wed–Sun (to 9pm Fri).* ● *public hols.* 🖼 *(free first Thu of month).* ♿ www.berkeley.edu

The reputation of UC Berkeley for counter-cultural movements sometimes eclipses its academic reputation, yet it is one of the largest and most prestigious universities in the world. Founded in 1868, Berkeley numbers at least ten Nobel laureates among its professors. The campus (see pp420–21) was laid out by the architect Frederick Law Olmsted. There are more than 30,000 students and a wide range of museums and cultural amenities, including the University Art Museum (see p421), Sather Tower (the Campanile), and the Hearst Museum of Anthropology.

Model of DNA at the Lawrence Hall of Science

## 🏛 Lawrence Hall of Science

Centennial Dr, UC Berkeley. *Tel (510) 642-5132.* ◯ *10am–5pm daily.* ● *public hols.* ♿ 🖼 www.lawrencehallofscience.org

Science is fun here. Hands-on exhibits tempt visitors to manipulate a hologram, track earthquakes, or plot stars in the planetarium. There are also changing exhibitions.

At night, the view of the lights around the northern Bay Area from the Hall's plaza is an extraordinary sight.

## 🎾 Claremont Resort Spa and Tennis Club

41 Tunnel Rd, Oakland. *Tel (510) 843-3000, (800) 551-7266.* ♿ www.claremontresort.com

The Berkeley hills form a backdrop to this half-timbered, fairytale castle. The enormous Claremont Resort construction began in 1906 and ended in 1915. In the early years the hotel failed to prosper, partly due to a law that forbade the sale of alcohol within a 1-mile (1.6-km) radius of the UC Berkeley campus. In 1937 an enterprising student actually measured the distance and discovered that the radius line passed through the *center* of the building. The Terrace Bar was opened beyond the line, in the same corner of the hotel that it occupies today.

## 🌺 University of California Botanical Garden

200 Centennial Dr, Berkeley Hills. 📷 *(510) 643-2755.* ◯ *9am–5pm daily.* ● *public hols.* ♿ *limited.* 🖼 *(free first Thu of month).* www.botanicalgarden.berkeley.edu

More than 12,000 species from all over the world thrive in the Mediterranean-style climate of Berkeley's Strawberry Canyon. Although primarily used for research, the collections are arranged in thematic gardens linked by paths. Particularly noteworthy are the Asian, African, South American, European, and California sections. The Chinese medicinal herb garden, the orchid houses, cactus garden, and the carnivorous plants are also well worth a visit.

Wellman Hall on the University of California campus

*For hotels and restaurants in this region see pp549–52 and pp595–7*

## 🍂 Tilden Regional Park

**Tel** (510) 562-PARK. **Steam trains** run 11am–6pm Sat & Sun, and daily during summer. 🎠 **Carousel** ◯ 10am–5pm Sat & Sun, 11am–5pm daily during summer. ● public hols. 🌿 **Botanical Garden** open 8:30am–5pm daily. ♿ limited. **www**.ebparks.org/parks/tilden

Though preserved for the most part in a natural wild condition, Tilden Park offers a variety of attractions. It is noted for the enchantingly landscaped Botanical Garden, specializing in California plants. Visitors can stroll from alpine meadows to desert cactus gardens by way of a redwood glen, and there are guided nature walks. If you have children, don't miss the carousel and the model steam train.

## 🏛 Judah L. Magnes Museum

2911 Russell St, Berkeley. **Tel** (510) 549-6950. ◯ by appointment only. ● Fri, Sat, Jewish and federal hols. 🚫 ♿ in advance. **www**.magnes.org

Located in a rambling old mansion, this is California's largest collection of art and historical artifacts pertaining to Jewish culture from ancient times to the present day. Among the exhibits are art treasures from Europe, Turkey,

**19th-century Jewish ceremonial dress, Judah L Magnes Museum**

and India, and graphic works and paintings by Marc Chagall, Max Liebermann, and others. There are also mementos of the experience of Jews during the Holocaust, such as a burned Torah scroll rescued from a German synagogue.

Lectures, videos, and temporary exhibitions often enliven the museum's halls.

## 🚋 Telegraph Avenue

Berkeley's most fascinating street is Telegraph Avenue, especially the blocks

between Dwight Way and the University. It has a plethora of coffee houses and cheap eateries, as well as clothing boutiques. The district was the center of student protest during the 1960s. It still swarms with students from dawn to dark, along with street vendors, musicians, protesters, and eccentrics.

## 🚋 Fourth Street

This gentrified enclave north of University Avenue is characteristic of Berkeley's fine craftsmanship and taste. Here you can buy everything from stained-glass windows and furniture, to organically grown lettuce and designer garden tools. There is also a handful of good restaurants (see p595).

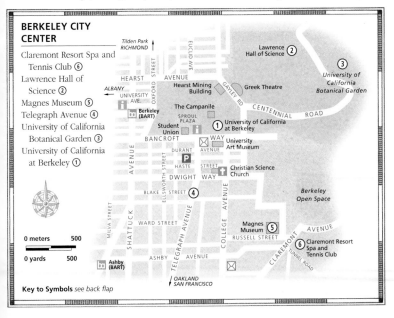

**BERKELEY CITY CENTER**

Claremont Resort Spa and Tennis Club ⑥
Lawrence Hall of Science ②
Magnes Museum ⑤
Telegraph Avenue ④
University of California Botanical Garden ③
University of California at Berkeley ①

0 meters 500
0 yards 500

**Key to Symbols** see back flap

# A 90-Minute Walk around the University of California Campus in Berkeley

This walk concentrates on a distinct area of Berkeley, the famous main campus of the University of California. It allows a stimulating glimpse into the intellectual, cultural, and social life of this vibrant university town (*see pp418–19*).

### West Entrance to Sather Tower

From University Avenue ①, cross Oxford Street and walk along University Drive past the Valley Life Sciences Building ②. Wellman Hall can be seen on the north fork of Strawberry Creek as you follow the road to the right, keeping California Hall ③ on your right. Take a left turn on Cross Campus Road ④. Wheeler Hall lies to the right, and ahead is the main campus landmark, the 307-ft (94-m) tall Sather Tower ⑤. Built by John Galen Howard in 1914, it was based on the campanile in the Piazza San Marco in Venice.

Before visiting the bell tower, go to the Doe Library ⑥ then the AF Morrison Memorial Library ⑦ in the north wing. The adjacent Bancroft Library houses the plate supposedly left by Sir Francis Drake in 1579, when he claimed California for England (*see pp46–7*).

Return to Sather Tower, open 10am–3:30pm Monday to Saturday. There are fine views of the bay from the

top of the tower. Across the way lies South Hall ⑧, the oldest building on campus.

### Hearst Mining Building to the Greek Theater

Continuing north, walk past LeConte Hall then cross over University Drive to the Mining Circle. Here is the Hearst Mining Building ⑨, built by Howard in 1907. Inside are ore samples and pictures of old mining operations. Return to

**Students outside Wheeler Hall on Campus ④**

University Drive, turn left out of East Gate to the Hearst Greek Theater ⑩.

### Faculty Club to the Eucalyptus Grove

Follow Gayley Road, which straddles a major earthquake fault, and turn right down the first path past Lewis Hall and

**Esplanade near Sather Tower ⑤**

| 0 meters | 250 |
|---|---|
| 0 yards | 250 |

**KEY**

- ••• Walk route
- 🚇 BART station
- 🅿 Parking

Hildebrand Hall, then left over a footbridge. The path winds between a log house and the Faculty Club ⑪. This rambling, rustic building was partly designed by Bernard Maybeck and dates from 1903. Faculty Glade ⑫ in front of the club is a favorite picnic and resting place with students and visitors alike.

The path now swings to the right, then sharp left. Take a look at Hertz Hall ⑬, then go down the diagonal walk that passes Wurster Hall to Kroeber Hall. Here you can visit the Hearst Museum of Anthropology (see p418).

Included in the museum are artifacts made by Ishi, the last surviving Yahi Indian who was brought by scientists to live on the campus from 1911 until his death in 1916. Cross Bancroft Way to the Caffè Strada ⑭ and then proceed to the University Art Museum ⑮, which includes Picassos and Cézannes among its exhibits (see p418). Continue along Bancroft Way to Telegraph Avenue ⑯, famous for the student riots of the 1960s and '70s (see p419).

The entrance to the university opposite Telegraph Avenue opens on to Sproul Plaza ⑰, which is often

***Within*** (1969) by A Lieberman at
**UCB Art Museum** ⑮

enlivened by street musicians. Step into the lower courtyard with its modern Zellerbach Hall ⑱, then, noting the state-of-the-art Harmon Gym, pass Alumni House and turn right. Cross over the south fork of Strawberry Creek at Bay Tree Bridge and bear left for the nature area, with some of the world's tallest eucalyptus trees ⑲. The path ends at Oxford Street, near the start of the walk.

### TIPS FOR WALKERS

***Starting point***: *The West Gate at University Avenue and Oxford Street.*
***Length***: *2.5 miles (4 km).*
***Getting there***: *San Francisco–Oakland Bay Bridge, Hwy 80 north, University Avenue exit. By BART, Berkeley stop.*
***Stopping-off points***: *The upscale Caffè Strada, on Bancroft Way, is always crowded with students sipping cappuccinos or eating bagels and cakes. A few steps down the street, in the University Art Museum, is the Café Grace, which looks out on to the sculpture garden. You may want to browse in the bookstores on Telegraph Avenue that also have coffee shops, or try one of the food carts that crowd the entrance to Sproul Plaza. Here you can sample a "smoothie" (blended fruit and ice) or a wide selection of Mexican and Middle Eastern food. In the lower Sproul Plaza of the University, amid a phalanx of bongo drummers, there are several other cafés.*

The Hearst Mining Building around the Mining Circle ⑨

# Oakland ⓪

At one time a small, working-class suburb of San Francisco, Oakland grew into a city in its own right when it became the West Coast terminus of the trans-continental railroad. With access to the town, businesses inevitably boomed, and it soon became one of the largest container ports in the United States. Many of the African-Americans who worked on the railroad then settled in Oakland, later followed by a Hispanic population, giving the city a multicultural atmosphere that continues to this day. Oakland's literary associations, including Jack London and Gertrude Stein, have also enhanced the area as a cultural center.

**VISITORS' CHECKLIST**

**Road map** inset B. 🚗 387,000. ✈ Oakland, 5 miles (8 km) SW of Oakland. 🚆 1245 Broadway St. ℹ 475 14th St (510 874-4800). 🎉 Annual Holiday Parade (1st Sat of Dec).
**www.**oaklandchamber.com

Façade and gardens of the Mormon Temple

### 🔒 Mormon Temple
4776 Lincoln Ave. **Tel** (510) 531-1475. 🚌 Fruitvale, then AC Transit 46 bus. **Visitors' Center** ◯ 9am–9pm daily. **Temple** 🚻 ⬛ ⬛
**www.**ldschurchtemples.com/oakland
Designed in 1963 and built on a hilltop, this is Northern California's only Mormon temple. Its full name is the Oakland Temple of the

Church of Jesus Christ of Latter Day Saints. Floodlit at night, it can be seen from Oakland and San Francisco. The central ziggurat is surrounded by four shorter terraced towers, all clad with white granite and capped by glistening golden pyramids.

From the temple there are magnificent views over the entire Bay Area.

### 🦆 Lake Merritt
Formed when a saltwater tidal estuary was dredged, embanked, and partly dammed, Lake Merritt and its surrounding park form an oasis of rich blue and green in the urban heart of Oakland. Designated in 1870 as the first state game refuge in the US, the lake still attracts migrating flocks of birds. Boats can be rented from two boathouses on the west and north shores, and joggers and cyclists can circle the lake on a 3-mile (5-km) path. The north shore at Lakeside Park has flower gardens, an aviary, and a Children's Fairyland with pony rides, puppet shows, and nursery rhyme scenes.

### 🏛 Jack London Square
Author Jack London, who became famous for his adventure novels *The Call of the Wild* and *White Fang (see pp26–7),* grew up in Oakland in the 1880s and was a frequent visitor to the Oakland waterfront. Today the area

### 🏛 Bay Bridge
**Map** 6 E4

The compound, high-level San Francisco–Oakland Bay Bridge was designed by Charles H Purcell. It has two distinct structures, joining at Yerba Buena Island in the middle of the Bay, and reaches 4.5 miles (7.2 km) from shore to shore. Its completion in 1936 heralded the end of the age of ferry boats on San Fran-

cisco Bay by linking the peninsular city at Rincon Hill to the Oakland "mainland." Train tracks were removed in the 1950s, leaving the bridge for use by more than 250,000 vehicles a day. It is five traffic lanes wide and has two levels. The westbound traffic uses the top deck, eastbound the lower. The eastern cantilever is raised on more than 20

piers, climbing up from the toll plaza causeway in Oakland to 191 ft (58 m) above Yerba Buena Island.

In 1989 the bridge was closed for a month after the Loma Prieta earthquake (see p505) when a 50-ft (15-m) segment disconnected where the cantilever span meets the approach ramp from Oakland. Two suspension spans join at

10 miles (16 km) of cable holding up the bridge

2,310 ft (704 m)

The West Bay Crossing section of Bay Bridge

*For hotels and restaurants in this region see pp549–52 and pp595–7*

**OAKLAND CITY CENTER**

**Key to Symbols** *see back flap*

---

named after him is a bright promenade of shops, restaurants with outdoor tables, and pleasure boats. London's footsteps can be traced to the First and Last Chance Saloon, now sunken with age into the street, and the Yukon cabin occupied by London in 1898.

### 🍴 Old Oakland
**Farmers' Market** *Tel (510) 745-7100.* ☐ *8am–2pm Fri.*

Also known as Victorian Row, these two blocks were erected between the 1860s and 1880s and renovated in the 1980s. Crowds of shoppers visit the Farmers' Market on Fridays at Clay and 9th streets, where

stalls sell fresh produce as well as prepared foods.

At night, try Jesso's Seafood at 901 Washington St. This draws locals and visitors for the live jazz, r&b, and soul music. The second Tuesday of each month is the New Orleans-style party, JesFest. Advance tickets are a must.

---

the central anchorage, which is sunk deeper in the water than that of any other bridge. Now there are plans to completely rebuild the East Bay crossing. Treasure Island, the larger part of Yerba Buena Island, hosted the 1939–40 World's Fair to celebrate the bridge's completion. This small island is now home to small parks and an upscale community.

**East Bay Crossing**

**Central anchorage**

**5-lane double-level roadway**

**Pylons supporting both road decks**

**400 ft (122 m)**

**2,310 ft (704 m)**

# Oakland Museum of California

California's only museum exclusively dedicated to documenting the state's art, history, and environment first opened in 1960 and has undergone a massive, $53 million renovation and expansion. This includes the Art Gallery, History Gallery, and Oak Street entrance, with the Art Gallery offering over 4,000 sq ft (1,219 sq m) of gallery space. Check the website for details of the latest exhibits. Visitors can also enjoy interactive and digital features depicting the many people and stories of California.

**California gold miner's banjo**

**Welcome to California**
*This display celebrates past and present-day life in California.*

**Roof and gardens**

**The Great Hall** is used for special exhibitions and functions.

**Gallery of California Art**
*The modern art in this collection includes* Ocean Park No: 107 *(1978) by Richard Diebenkorn.*

**Level 3**

**Level 2**

**10th Street entrance**

★ **Barry McGee Installation**
*This acrylic assemblage (2010) by San Francisco native Barry McGee reflects his interest in colorful geometric patterns.*

## KEY TO THE OAKLAND MUSEUM LEVELS

☐ Gallery of Californian Art    ☐ Gallery of Californian History

☐ Gallery of Californian Natural Sciences

## VISITORS' CHECKLIST

Oak & 10th Sts. **Road map** inset B.
📞 *(510) 238-2200.*
🚉 *from Lake Merritt.*
⬤ *closed for renovations, check website for details.* 📷 *(free 2nd Sun).* 📷 ♿ 📷 📷 📷
**www**.museumca.org

### California Mud Wagon
*Developed for rural life during the mid-19th century, this multipurpose vehicle could be converted easily from a field wagon to a stylish carriage.*

### Railroad Exhibit
*The construction of the railroad was crucial to the development of California, lifting the state out of isolation.*

## MUSEUM GUIDE
*Level 1 contains the shop and the Natural Sciences Gallery, illustrating the changes in the state's ecology from west to east. Artifacts in the Cowell Hall of California History on level 2 are arranged chronologically. Level 2 has the cafeteria, level 3 the Art Gallery.*

**Level 1**

**Sculpture Gardens**
have outdoor festivals
and are also a popular
spot for picnics.

## STAR EXHIBITS

★ Barry McGee
   Installation

★ Gallery of
   Natural Sciences

### ★Gallery of Natural Sciences
*Explore California's conservation with more than 2,000 different native species and seven major habitats.*

Eugene O'Neill's beautiful Tao House, in Danville

## Tao House ⓫

**Road map** inset B. **Tel** (925) 838-0249. ◯ 10am & 12:30pm Wed–Sun, by reservation only (no booking required on Sat). ♿ ⓘ 10am & 2pm Wed–Fri, Sun. **www**.nps.gov/euon

When the American playwright Eugene O'Neill (1888–1953) won the Nobel Prize for Literature in 1936, he used the stipend to build a home for himself and his wife in the then-rural San Ramon Valley at the foot of Mount Diablo. Tao House, a hybrid of Spanish Colonial and oriental styles, was completed in 1937. Over the next six years O'Neill worked in this house on what is now considered his best work, the semi-autobiographical series of tragic plays, including *The Iceman Cometh*, *A Moon for the Misbegotten*, and *Long Day's Journey Into Night*. In 1944, however, O'Neill was struck down with Parkinson's disease. The remote location of the house and the lack of available nursing staff due to the war forced the disabled O'Neill to abandon his beloved home. He died in a Boston hotel in 1953.

The surrounding valleys have now been developed into suburbs, but Tao House and its beautiful landscaped grounds have been turned into a National Historic Site, operated by the National Park Service. Both have been preserved in the condition the playwright left them in.

**Mask used in O'Neill's stage plays**

## Mount Diablo State Park ⓬

**Road map** inset B. ▭ ▭ Walnut Creek. ⓘ Walnut Creek Visitor Center. **Tel** (925) 837-6119. ◯ 8am–sunset daily. **www**.parks.ca.gov

Rising voluminously over the inland suburbs, the 3,849-ft- (1,173-m-) high Mount Diablo dominates the East Bay region. Its summit offers one of the most impressive panoramas in North America. On a fine and clear day it is possible to see for more than 200 miles (320 km) in each direction, stretching from Mount Lassen (see p453) and the Cascade Mountains in the north to Mount Hamilton in the south, and from the Sierra Nevada mountains in the east to the Farallon Islands (see pp412–13) in the Pacific Ocean to the west. Almost 23,000 acres (9,000 ha) of land surrounding the summit have now been set aside as a state park, and there is a wide range of hiking trails, as well as biking and horseriding. A twisting road takes car drivers within 50 ft (15 m) of the summit. The park's Visitors' Center at the summit offers information on the mountain's fauna and flora, including the wildflowers that cover the mountainside in spring.

## Livermore ⓭

**Road map** inset B. ⛰ 84,000. ▭ ▭ ⓘ 2157 First St. (925 447-1606). **www**.livermorechamber.org

Founded in the 1870s as a cattle-ranching and grape-producing community, Livermore in recent years has grown into an outlying suburb of San Francisco. Still rural in feel and retaining a few ranches and vineyards, the town is now best known as the home of the Lawrence Livermore National Laboratory. This state-of-the-art technology research center is operated by the University of California on behalf of the United States Department of Energy. During the Cold War era the laboratory had primary responsibility for the design of the nation's nuclear weapons arsenal, but today it has diversified into civilian applications.

To the east of Livermore, along I-580 as it climbs over hilly Altamont Pass, are hundreds of shining high-tech windmills. This is the world's largest wind farm, producing natural, nonpolluting energy from the area's constant winds. The windmills are all privately owned and operated, with no

Windmills producing natural energy at Livermore's wind farm

government funding. They consist of two main types: the traditional propeller type, and the more unusual vertical axis windmills, which resemble giant egg-whisks.

# Stanford University ⑭

Junípero Serra St. **Road map** inset B. *Tel* (650) 723-2053. **Visitors' Center** 295 Galvez St. ☐ 8:30am–5pm Mon–Fri, 10am–5pm Sat & Sun. ◑ university hols; call ahead. ⬛ phone (650) 723-2560 for details. **www**.stanford.edu

Among the most pleasant of the Bay Area suburbs, the town of Palo Alto grew up specifically to serve Stanford University, one of the most reputed centers of higher education in the country.

Founded by the railroad tycoon Leland Stanford *(see pp50–51)* in honor of his son who died in 1885 at the age of 16, Stanford University opened in 1891. The campus occupies the former Stanford family farm, covering 8,200 acres (3,320 ha) – larger than the entire downtown district of San Francisco. It was designed in a mixture of Romanesque and Mission styles *(see pp30–31)* by the architect Frederick Law Olmsted, and its sandstone buildings and numerous arcades are capped by red-tiled roofs. At the heart of the university campus is the Main Quadrangle, where the Memorial Church is decorated with a gold-leaf and tile mosaic. Also on the campus is the Cantor Art Center. This small but intriguing museum holds one of the largest collections of sculptures by Auguste Rodin, including the impressive *Gates of Hell*.

# Filoli ⑮

86 Cañada Rd. **Road map** inset B. *Tel* (650) 364-8300, ext 509. ☐ Feb–Oct: 10am–3:30pm Tue–Fri, 10:30am–3:30pm Sat, 11am–3:30pm Sun. ◑ Federal and public hols. ⬛ ⬛ ⬛ **www**.filoli.org

One of the most impressive mansions in Northern California open to the public, the Filoli estate was the home of gold-mining millionaire William Bourn, owner of the Empire Gold Mine *(see p470)*. It was designed in Palladian style by Willis Polk in 1916. The red-brick exterior resembles a Georgian terrace and encloses more than 36,000 sq ft (3,345 sq m) of living space on two fully furnished floors. The house is surrounded by 16 acres (6.5 ha) of formal gardens that provide blooms of varying colors through the year – one million daffodils and 75,000 tulips in spring, roses in summer, and maple leaves in the fall. The estate's name, Filoli, is an acronym for the motto "Fight for a just cause, Love your fellow man, Live a good life."

**Picturesque church in the tiny village of Pescadero**

# Pescadero ⑯

**Road map** inset B. ⬛ 640. ⬛ 235 Main St, Half Moon Bay (650) 726-8380. **www**.hmbchamber.com

Only half an hour's drive from San Francisco to the north and the Silicon Valley *(see p428)* to the south, the tiny town of Pescadero seems light years away from the surrounding modern world.

Pescadero is a sleepy little farming community that produces an abundance of vegetables such as asparagus and pumpkins. It contains little more than a white-washed church (the oldest in the county), a general store, a post office, and the popular Duarte's Tavern *(see p597)* along its two main streets. Its many whitewashed buildings follow a tradition that goes back to the 19th century, when a cargo of white paint was rescued from a nearby shipwreck.

Eight miles (13 km) south of town, the Pigeon Point Lighthouse is well worth a visit. The lighthouse also operates as a hostel *(see pp412–13)*.

**Façade of the Memorial Church at Stanford University**

# San Jose ⑰

The only other original Spanish Colonial town in California after Los Angeles (see pp58–193), San Jose was founded in 1777 by Felipe de Neve and has grown to become the state's third largest city, its population exceeding that of San Francisco. Now the commercial and cultural center of the South Bay and civic heart of the Silicon Valley region, San Jose is a bustling and modern city that has only recently taken action to preserve its history. High-rise offices and high-tech factories now stand on what was only farmland in the 1950s, yet the city's fine museums and historic sites offer genuine attractions to the visitor, despite the suburban sprawl.

**Statue outside the Egyptian Museum and Planetarium**

### Exploring San Jose

San Jose's colonial pueblo was situated on what is now Plaza Park, off Market Street. During 1849–50, California's first State Capitol was located in a hotel on the east side of the plaza, roughly on the site of the present Fairmont Hotel (see p551).

Other historic sites along Market Street include the San Jose Museum of Art and the birthplace of Amadeo P Giannini (see p315).

The well-known Winchester Mystery House (see pp430–31), is located on the town's outskirts.

### 🏛 Peralta Adobe

175 W St John St.
**Tel** (408) 993-8300.
⬜ noon–3:30pm Sat & Sun. ⬛ public hols. 📷
🚹 📷 ♿ first floor only.
One block to the left of Market Street is San

Jose's oldest surviving building, the Peralta Adobe. Built in 1797 it is the sole remnant of the Spanish pueblo. Bars and cafés now surround the area.

### ⛪ Mission Santa Clara de Asis

500 El Camino Real.
**Tel** (408) 554-4023. ⬜ daily.
On the campus of the Jesuit University of Santa Clara, 5 miles (8 km) northwest of downtown San Jose, this mission church is a modern replica of the adobe original, first built in 1777 and reconstructed many times thereafter. Relics on display include bells given to the missionaries by the Spanish monarchy. The gardens adjacent to the church are carefully maintained in their original splendor.

**Mission Santa Clara detail**

### 🏛 Rosicrucian Egyptian Museum and Planetarium

Naglee & Park Aves. **Tel** (408) 947 3600. ⬜ 9am–5pm Mon–Fri (to 8pm Thu), 11am–6pm Sat & Sun. ⬛ Jan 1, Easter Sun, Thanksgiving, Dec 25. 📷
**www**.egyptianmuseum.org
This large museum displays the most extensive collection of ancient Egyptian artifacts west of the Mississippi. Housed in a complex of Egyptian- and Moorish-style buildings, each gallery represents a different aspect of Egyptian culture, from mummies, burial tombs, fertility figures, and canopic jars to domestic implements and children's toys. There are also replicas of the sarcophagus in which Tutankhamun was discovered in 1922, and of the Rosetta Stone.

The museum is operated by a nonsectarian organization known as the Rosicrucian Order, which is dedicated to combining modern science with the ancient wisdoms.

### 🏛 The Tech Museum

201 S Market St. **Tel** (408) 294-8324. ⬜ 10am–5pm Mon–Thu, 10am–9pm Fri–Sun; closing times vary, call ahead to check.
📷 **www**.thetech.org
Located in the heart of San Jose, this fascinating science museum has its eyes set on the future. The Tech Museum is crowded with hands-on exhibits, which encourage visitors of all ages to discover how various technological inventions work. Its main focus is on understanding the workings of computer hardware and software. The IMAX Dome Theater is worth visiting.

---

### SILICON VALLEY

The world-famous center of the computer industry, Silicon Valley covers approximately 100 sq miles (260 sq km) from Palo Alto to San Jose. However, the term refers to myriad businesses rather than to a defined geographical location.

The name, based on the material used in the manufacture of semiconductors, was first used in the early 1970s to describe the area's expanding hardware and software industries. The seeds, however, were sown a decade earlier, at Stanford University and the Xerox Palo Alto Research Center, as well as in the garages of computer pioneers William Hewlett, David Packard, and later Steve Jobs and Stephen Wozniak, who invented the Apple personal computer.

Many world-class high-tech firms are based here, including Intel, Silicon Graphics, and Cisco Systems.

**Silicon chip circuitry**

### 🏛 San Jose Museum of Art

110 S Market St. *Tel* (408) 271-6840.
⬜ 11am–5pm Tue–Sun. 🚫 Jan 1,
Thanksgiving, Dec 25. ⓐ
This small but daring art
museum is known for some
of the Bay Area's most interesting and popular art exhibits.
The permanent collection
focuses on well-known
contemporary California artists.

### 🏛 Children's Discovery Museum of San Jose

180 Woz Way. *Tel* (408) 298-5437.
⬜ 10am–5pm Tue–Sat, noon–5pm
Sun. 🚫 Jan 1, Dec 24–25. ⓐ
**www**.cdm.org
This large purple building,
designed by Mexican architect
Ricardo Legorretta, has interactive exhibits and programs
for all the family. Arts and
technology are featured in
this warm, inviting space.

### 🏛 de Saisset Museum at Santa Clara University

500 El Camino Real. *Tel* (408) 554-
4528. ⬜ call for opening times.
**Donation. www**.scu.edu/desaisset
Next to the Santa Clara Mission,
this museum exhibits artifacts
from the 18th-century mission
and other eras of California
history, along with a collection
of paintings and photographs.

**Trolley car on display at the History San Jose**

### 🏛 History San Jose

1650 Senter Rd. *Tel* (408) 287-
2290. ⬜ noon–5pm Tue–Sun.
🚫 Jan 1, Jul 4, Thanksgiving,
Dec 25. ⓐ 🅿
One mile (1.5 km) southeast
of downtown San Jose, in
Kelley Park, more than two
dozen historic structures of
San Jose have been reassembled into an outdoor museum.
Highlights include a trolley
car, a gas station from the
1920s, and 19th-century
business premises including
a doctor's office, a hotel, and
the original Bank of Italy.
   In the future the museum
aims to have 75 structures,
completing this life-size model
of San Jose as it used to be.

### VISITORS' CHECKLIST

**Road map** inset B. 🏘 846,000.
✈ San Jose International Airport,
2 miles (3 km) NW of San Jose.
🚉 65 Cahill St. 🚌 70 Almeden
St. 🛈 150 W San Carlos St (800
792-4173). 🎭 Tapestry Arts
Festival (Sep). **www**.sanjose.org

### 🎢 California's Great America

4701 Great America Parkway.
*Tel* (408) 988-1776.
⬜ mid-Mar–late May: Sat & Sun;
late May–early Sep: daily. ⓐ
**www**.cagreatamerica.com
The best amusement park
in Northern California packs
a wide variety of attractions
into its 100-acre (40-ha) site.
   The park is divided
into several different areas,
each one designed to evoke
various regions of the United
States. These include Orleans
Place, Yankee Harbor, and
the Yukon Territory. Along
with high-speed roller coasters, such as the Demon and
the Tidal Wave, many rides
incorporate themes from films
and television shows produced by Paramount Studios,
including *Top Gun* and *Star
Trek*. Pop concerts are often
held in the large amphitheater.

**SAN JOSE CITY CENTER**

Children's Discovery
   Museum ⑦
De Saisset Museum ①
Mission Santa Clara de Asis ②

Rosicrucian Egyptian Museum
   and Planetarium ③
San Jose Museum of Art ④
Tech Museum of Innovation ⑤
Winchester Mystery House
   *pp430–31* ⑥

0 kilometers 1
0 miles 0.5

Triton Museum
EL CAMINO REAL
LAFAYETTE STREET
BENTON STREET
Santa Clara University
Mission Santa Clara de Asis ②
De Saisset Museum ①
MARKET STREET
BELLOMY STREET
WASHINGTON ST
ALVISO ST
NEWHALL STREET
WINCHESTER BOULEVARD
NIMITZ FREEWAY
PARK AVENUE
DAVIS STREET
DANA AVENUE
NAGLEE AVENUE
CHAPMAN STREET
HEDDING STREET
THE ALAMEDA
COLEMAN STREET
TAYLOR STREET
STOCKTON AVENUE
OAKLAND
Airport 2 miles (3 km)
880
Municipal Rose Garden
BASCOM AVENUE
HEDDING AVENUE
FOREST AVENUE
STEVENS CREEK BOULEVARD
Rosicrucian Egyptian Museum and Planetarium ③
SAN LEIGH AVENUE
LELAND AVENUE
SCOTT STREET
JUNIPERO SERRA FREEWAY
PARKMOOR AVENUE
SAN CARLOS STREET
MERIDIAN AVE
TRACE AVENUE
AUZERAIS AVE
PARK AVENUE
SAN FERNANDO ST
Amtrak Station
San Jose Arena
GUADALUPE PARKWAY
ALMADEN BLVD
1ST ST
2ND ST
S CLARA ST
MARKET ST
Peralta Adobe
Paramount's Great America Amusement Park
④ San Jose Museum of Art
⑤ The Tech Museum
Children's Discovery Museum ⑦
History San Jose
⑥ Winchester Mystery House
SAN FRANCISCO
280

**Key to Symbols** see back flap

# San Jose: Winchester Mystery House

Winchester Mystery House is a mansion with a remarkable history. Sarah Winchester, heiress of the Winchester Rifle fortune, moved from Connecticut to San Jose in 1884 and bought a small farmhouse. Convinced by a medium that its expansion would exorcise the spirits of those killed by the rifle, she kept builders laboring on the house 24 hours a day, 7 days a week, for 38 years, until her death in 1922. The result is a bizarre complex of 160 rooms, including stairs that lead nowhere and windows set into floors. The house has been refurbished with authentic 19th-century furniture while the Victorian gardens include statues and fountains.

**Stone cherub fountain**

**★ Main Bedroom**
*Sarah Winchester eventually died in her plush bedroom. The flooring is English mitered herringbone. At night she would play the harmonium situated opposite the elaborately carved bed.*

**The Greenhouse** incorporates 13 glass cupolas.

**Tiffany Stained-Glass Window**
*One of a set imported from Vienna, Austria for Mrs Winchester. They depict a lush garden of daisies (her favorite).*

## FACTS AND FIGURES

- The house contains 950 doors, 1,257 windows, 47 fireplaces, 40 bedrooms, and 17 chimneys.
- The number 13 is used superstitiously throughout – 13 bathrooms, 13 windows in a room, and 13 lights in the chandeliers.
- When the top of the house collapsed during the 1906 earthquake, building continued outward rather than upward.
- Mrs. Winchester's height of 4 ft 10 in (147 cm) explains hallways 2 ft (0.6 m) wide and doors only 5 ft (152 cm) high.
- Mrs. Winchester selected a new bedroom out of the 40 in the house each night, to confuse the spirits.

**★ Grand Ballroom**
*This elaborate organ is one of the main features of the Grand Ballroom. Other features include artglass windows, a paneled ceiling, and hand-carved woodwork.*

**Switchback Stairs**
*Each of these 44 steps is only 1.5 inches (3.8 cm) high, and the entire staircase rises only 9 ft (2.7 m) from start to finish. It is thought they were built in this way to ease Sarah Winchester's arthritis.*

**VISITORS' CHECKLIST**

525 S Winchester Blvd.
**Road map** inset B. **Tel** *(408)*
*247-2101.* 🚌 25, 60, 85.
◯ *9am–5pm daily; end
Apr–mid-Jun 9am–5pm
Sun–Thu, 9am–7pm Fri & Sat.*
🚫 *Dec 25.* 📷 🎥 ♿ *gardens
and firearms museum.*
📱 📹 🖥 **www**.winchester
mysteryhouse.com

Tour entrance

**The Winchester Antique Products Museum** contains items, other than rifles, produced by the company, including roller skates, electric irons, and lawn mowers.

**★ Winchester Firearms Museum**
*Included in this extensive display are the Henry Repeating Rifle and the Model 1873, which came to be known as "The Gun that Won the West." Commemorative rifles include the Theodore Roosevelt and the John Wayne.*

**STAR FEATURES**

★ Grand Ballroom

★ Main Bedroom

★ Winchester Firearms Museum

**Stairwell to the Ceiling**
*This stairway leading nowhere is just one of the many unexplained oddities within the house.*

# NORTHERN CALIFORNIA

# Northern California at a Glance

Northern California stretches for more than 500 miles (800 km), from the sparsely populated border with Oregon to the high-tech urban civilization that marks the beginning of Southern California. Vast areas of wilderness cover the region, including volcanic landscapes and dense forests, imposing mountain ranges and rugged coastlines, proudly preserved by a series of national parks. Northern California also has a rich history, from the first European settlers in Monterey to the celebrated Gold Rush of 1849. Its natural beauty is enhanced by equally picturesque and significant towns, including the state's capital, Sacramento.

**THE NORTH**
*(see pp442–65)*

**WINE COUNTRY**
*(see pp454–5)*

**Redwood National Park** (see p450) *is a protected landscape of dense, awe-inspiring redwood forests, including the world's tallest tree, which reaches a height of 368 ft (112 m). The area is perennially popular with anglers, hikers, bird-watchers, and campers.*

**Sonoma** (see pp464–5) *was the site of the Bear Flag Revolt in 1846, when Americans rebelled against Mexican rule and tried to turn California into a republic. The vineyards of Sonoma County and the Napa Valley (see pp462–3), benefiting from good soil and an ideal climate, produce world-class wines.*

**Carmel Mission** (see pp512–13) *was founded in 1770 by Junipero Serra and became the most important of all the 21 Franciscan missions, serving as the administrative center for Northern California. Today, restored to its original splendor, it is considered to be the state's most beautiful church.*

0 kilometers 50

0 miles

◁ Mountains and trees at Old Inspiration Point in the High Sierras in Northern California

**Lassen Volcanic National Park** (see p453) *was formed in 1914, when more than 300 eruptions resulted in a new landscape of mudflows and sulfurous streams heated by molten lava. Mount Lassen, part of the Cascade Mountain Range, is considered to be still active.*

**Sacramento** (see pp472–5) *has been the state capital since 1854, and the Capitol is one of California's finest buildings. Old Sacramento preserves its historic structures from the 1860s and 1870s, when the town was the western terminus of the transcontinental railroad.*

**Yosemite National Park** (see pp488–91) *is an unforgettable wilderness of forests, alpine meadows, breathtaking waterfalls, and imposing granite rocks. In 1864 it became the first protected park in the US.*

D COUNTRY
AND THE
TRAL VALLEY
*(see pp466–81)*

THE HIGH SIERRAS
*(see pp482–97)*

NORTH CENTRAL
CALIFORNIA
*(see pp498–517)*

**Columbia State Historic Park** (see pp480–81) *was once the second largest town in California and is now the best preserved of the old gold mining centers.*

# Wildlife and Wilderness

Eons ago, most of Northern California was under water, until geological forces pushed up the floor of the Central Valley, causing the Pacific Ocean to recede. Diverse terrains and ecosystems then emerged and Northern California is now a land of peaks, canyons, and headlands. Unique flora grows here, such as giant sequoias in the High Sierras *(see pp496–7)* and Monterey cypress trees *(see p511)*. Black bears roam redwood groves and hawks hover above Yosemite Valley *(see pp488–9)*. Legend has it that Bigfoot, America's version of the Yeti, makes his home in these parts. In order to protect this landscape, the environment-friendly Sierra Club began here in 1892 and is still active today.

**Prairie Creek State Park** has a herd of protected Roosevelt elk, which roam the dunes of Gold Bluff Beach.

**Redwood National Park**
(see pp448–9) *contains the world's tallest redwood tree, reaching 368 ft (112 m). These evergreens soak up the winter's heavy rainfall and are kept moist in summer by fogs, which move in from the ocean. Wood-peckers, spotted owls, mule deer, squirrels, and banana slugs frequent the groves.*

**The Sacramento National Wildlife Refuges** protect the many birds that stop off on the Pacific Flyway.

**Point Reyes Peninsula**
(see pp412–13) *is a small "island," almost separated from the mainland by the San Andreas Fault. Its forested ridges, littoral rocks, and rock pools are a prime habitat for crustaceans such as the Pacific rock crab.*

**The Farallon Islands**
(see pp412–13) *are an important breeding ground for sea birds, including the puffin, and elephant seals. Visitors are not per- mitted on the islands.*

**Año Nuevo State Reserve** *(see p504)* is occupied every winter by hundreds of breeding elephant seals.

**The Monterey Peninsula** *(see pp510–11)* is the winter home of the beautiful migratory monarch butterfly.

*Map labels:*

Six Rivers National Forest

Kla Nation

Trinity National Forest

Sha Nati For

Clair Engle Lake

Sha

•Eureka

Klamath River

Black Butte River

**THE NORTH**

Sinkyone Wilderness

Eel River

Mendocino National Forest

Sutte Wild Cac

Clear Lake

**WINE COUNTRY**

Lake Sonoma

L

Bar

Sonoma

San Francisco •

**W BA**

San Jos

E R S

Poir

**KEY**

| | National Park |
| | State Park |
| | National Forest |
| | Wildlife refuge |
| | River |

0 kilometers 25

0 miles          25

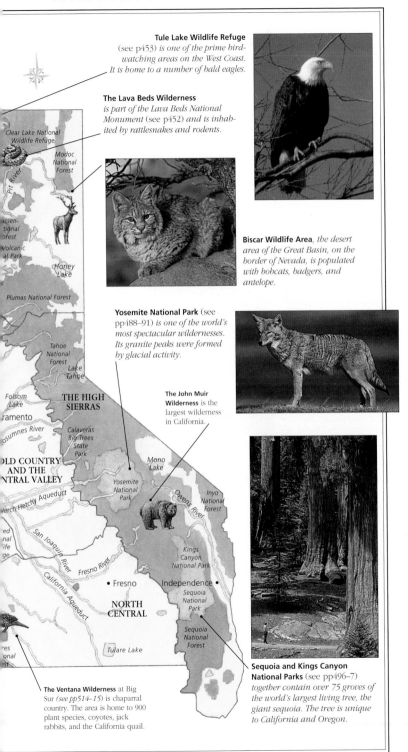

**Tule Lake Wildlife Refuge**
(see p453) *is one of the prime bird-watching areas on the West Coast. It is home to a number of bald eagles.*

**The Lava Beds Wilderness**
*is part of the Lava Beds National Monument* (see p452) *and is inhabited by rattlesnakes and rodents.*

**Biscar Wildlife Area**, *the desert area of the Great Basin, on the border of Nevada, is populated with bobcats, badgers, and antelope.*

**Yosemite National Park** (see pp488–91) *is one of the world's most spectacular wildernesses. Its granite peaks were formed by glacial activity.*

**The John Muir Wilderness** is the largest wilderness in California.

**Sequoia and Kings Canyon National Parks** (see pp496–7) *together contain over 75 groves of the world's largest living tree, the giant sequoia. The tree is unique to California and Oregon.*

**The Ventana Wilderness** at Big Sur *(see pp514–15)* is chaparral country. The area is home to 900 plant species, coyotes, jack rabbits, and the California quail.

Clear Lake National Wildlife Refuge

Modoc National Forest

Pit River

assen tional orest

Volcanic al Park

Honey Lake

Plumas National Forest

Tahoe National Forest

Lake Tahoe

Folsom Lake

ramento

THE HIGH SIERRAS

osumnes River

Calaveras Big Trees State Park

OLD COUNTRY AND THE NTRAL VALLEY

Mono Lake

Yosemite National Park

verch Hetchy Aqueduct

San Joaquin River

ed nal ife ge

Fresno River

California Aqueduct

Owens River

Inyo National Forest

Kings Canyon National Park

• Fresno

Independence •

NORTH CENTRAL

Sequoia National Park

Sequoia National Forest

Tulare Lake

res onal st

# The Wine of Northern California

California is the most important wine-growing area in the United States, producing two-thirds of the nation's wine. More than 635,000 acres (216,140 ha) of the state's land is used for viticulture. Half of the grapes grown here are harvested from the fertile soil of the interior region, particularly the stretch of land bordered by the Sacramento Valley to the north and the San Joaquin Valley to the south. The north coast region accounts for less than a quarter of California's total wine-growing acreage, but many of the country's best Chardonnay, Sauvignon Blanc, Cabernet Sauvignon, and Merlot grapes are grown here. The north coast is also home to most of the state's 3,300 wineries. Chardonnay and Pinot Noir grapes are the mainstays of the central coast region, which extends from the San Francisco Bay Area to Santa Barbara.

**LOCATOR MAP**

☐ Northern California wine region

**Grape harvest at V. Sattui Winery near St. Helena in Napa Valley**

**Late Harvest Zinfandel** *from the Hop Kiln Winery is a red dessert wine made from grapes left on the vine longer than usual to increase their sweetness. The winery is housed in an historic hop kiln barn.*

## THE STORY OF ZINFANDEL

The story of Zinfandel is one of the great success stories of California wine. This versatile grape is thought to have been brought to America from Croatia's Dalmatian coast. Zinfandel arrived in California in the 1850s, and is now the third-leading grape variety in the state. The Zinfandel reds, particularly those from the Dry Creek and Russian River valleys, are now in great demand. Some have oaky flavors, while others have strong, fruity flavors. The rosé White Zinfandel was created by winemakers to use up their surplus red grapes.

**Saintsbury's Vin Gris** *is a Burgundy-style rosé wine, which is made from the juice of Pinot Noir grapes.*

• Fort Bragg

Ukiah •

Healdsburg •

SAN FRANCISCO

## KEY

| | |
|---|---|
| ☐ Lake County | ☐ Carneros Valley |
| ☐ Anderson Valley | ☐ Santa Cruz Mountains |
| ☐ Alexander Valley | ☐ Livermore Valley |
| ☐ Dry Creek Valley | ☐ Lodi Valley |
| ☐ Russian River Valley | ☐ El Dorado Valley |
| ☐ Napa Valley | ☐ Redwood–Ukiah Valley |
| ☐ Sonoma Valley | ☐ San Joaquin Valley |

## KEY FACTS ABOUT CALIFORNIA WINES

**Location and Climate**
California's latitude, proximity to the ocean, and sheltered valleys create a mild climate. Winters tend to be short and mild, while the growing season is long and hot but cooled by summer fogs. Combined with fertile soil, these factors mean that large areas have ideal grape-growing conditions.

**Grape Varieties**
California's most widely planted grape variety is **Chardonnay**, used to make a dry wine with a balance of fruit, acidity, and texture. Other popular whites include **Sauvignon Blanc** (also known as **Fumé Blanc**), **Chenin Blanc**, **Pinot Blanc**, **Gewürztraminer**, and **Johannisberg Riesling**. California's red wines are typically dry with some tannic astringency and include the rich, full-bodied **Cabernet Sauvignon**, **Merlot**, **Syrah**, **Pinot Noir**, and **Zinfandel**.

**Good Producers**
*Chardonnay*: Acacia, Byron, Château Montelena, Ferrari-Carano, Kendall-Jackson, Kistler, Kunde Estate, Sonoma-Cutrer. *Cabernet Sauvignon*: Beaulieu, Beringer, Grgich Hills, Heitz, The Hess Collection, Jordan, Joseph Phelps, Silver Oak, Robert Mondavi, Stag's Leap, Wente, Whitehall Lane. *Merlot*: Clos du Bois, Duckhorn, Frog's Leap, Silverado, Sterling. *Pinot Noir*: Dehlinger, Etude, Gary Farrell, Saintsbury, Sanford. *Sauvignon Blanc*: Duckhorn, Glen Ellen, Kenwood, Matanzas Creek, J Rochioli. *Zinfandel*: Dry Creek, Lake Sonoma, De Loach, Hop Kiln, Ridge, Rosenblum, Sebastiani.

**Good Vintages**
(*Reds*) 2006, 2005, 2004, 2003, 2002, 2001, 2000, 1999, 1998, 1997. (*Whites*) 2006, 2005, 2004, 2003, 2002, 2001, 2000, 1999, 1998, 1997.

**Beaulieu Vineyard's Private Reserve**
*Cabernet Sauvignon is a medium-bodied red wine with ripe cherry and blackcurrant aromas. It has been produced since 1936 and was the first wine in the US to be called Private Reserve.*

**Wente Vineyard's Cabernet Sauvignon** *has ample tannins. The Cabernet grape was brought here from France in the 19th century.*

**Fermentation tanks** *at Sterling Vineyards are typical of the high-tech methods now used.*

# The Bohemian North

Perhaps because the region attracted a wide range of people and enjoyed enormous wealth during the Gold Rush *(see pp48–9)*, Northern California has always tended to be nonconformist and somewhat hedonistic. This has caused some anguish over the years, as charlatans and crackpots have taken advantage of the region's broad-mindedness, but it has certainly made the area a colorful place. During the late 19th century San Francisco's Barbary Coast was home to casinos, opium dens, and brothels *(see p314)*. Utopian communities, organized around humanitarian, religious, or dietary principles, have been another facet of Northern California life. In the 1960s, the area's air of liberality made it a haven for members of the "Make Love, Not War" generation *(see p359)*. It has since attracted everybody from nudists and hot-tub lovers, to religious gurus and the latter-day hippies who helped turn marijuana into a chief crop of Humboldt County.

**Spiritual guidance** *became popular during the 1850s, and 1860s. San Francisco attracted many spiritualist "mediums," who held regular seances. There are still a few spiritualist churches operating in the Bay Area.*

**Sally Stanford**, *born in 1903, was a virtual pariah in Sausalito when she took over the Valhalla (now the Gaylord India), the town's oldest restaurant, in 1950. Local citizens didn't approve of her previous occupation as a San Francisco madam. But Sally's personality eventually won the town over, and she served one term as the town's mayor (1976–8). She died in 1982.*

## UTOPIAN COMMUNITIES

From the 1850s to the 1950s, more Utopian communities were founded in Northern California than in any other place in the nation. William Riker's Holy City was established in 1918 in the Santa Cruz Mountains. Riker, a pro-Nazi and forecaster of apocalypses, called his totalitarian community the "headquarters for the world's perfect government." It eventually died out because the community was celibate.

Fountain Grove was a Utopian outpost north of Santa Rosa, founded in 1875 by New York mystic Thomas Lake Harris. He identified himself with Christ and as a bisexual, "Divine Man-Woman". Under attack for alleged sexual and financial abuses, Harris was forced to close his commune in 1892.

**William Riker**

**Young and old lived** and traveled together in communities.

**Bright colors** and childlike designs were influenced by the lights and patterns experienced during drug-induced hallucinatory "trips."

**Psychedelic Pop Art** *posters of the 1960s were distinctive for their inflated, crammed typeface, developed by artist Wes Wilson.*

## JIM JONES AND THE PEOPLE'S TEMPLE

The Reverend Jim Jones (1931–78) was a popular cult leader in the Bay Area during the 1970s, preaching an amalgam of racial and religious egalitarianism, political empowerment, doomsday visions, and sexual freedom. He was alternately a fundamentalist, supposedly "healing" people through touch, and a modern minister, with his services accompanied by music and dance. But he was also a self-proclaimed messiah. After building up a congregation of some 20,000 at his People's Temple in San Francisco, in 1978 he moved almost 1,000 of them to an isolated agricultural mission in Guyana, South America. After rumors of physical abuse and weapons caches at the colony brought international scrutiny, Jones ordered a mass suicide. Investigators later found hundreds of his followers' corpses in the jungle; they had all drunk a cyanide-laced fruit drink, and the despotic reverend had been shot in the head.

**Jim Jones**

**Hippies from the 1960s**

## PSYCHEDELIA

The term "psychedelic" originally referred to ideas or approaches that were somehow outrageous, non-conformist, or "mind-expanding." But after San Francisco witnessed the opening of the Psychedelic Shop on Haight Street in 1966 *(see p358),* the word became associated with the hallucinatory drugs popular among the region's hippie generation.

Psychedelia then turned into a symbol of an entire lifestyle: young hippie communities rejecting conformity and traveling from one gathering to another on brightly painted buses, taking drugs, and preaching peace.

**The Esalen Institute** (see p515) *became famous in the 1960s as the center of the "human potential movement," a philosophy emphasizing individual responsibility for both the good and bad events in life. Today it is an expensive retreat where former flower children and stressed corporate executives all discuss spiritual insights while reclining in hot springs overlooking the Pacific Ocean.*

# THE NORTH

*anging from deserted beaches strewn with giant driftwood logs to dense forests at the foot of alpine peaks, the far north of California is the state at its most wild and rugged. The landscape is as diverse as any continent – lush redwood groves, the volcanic Cascade Mountains, the arid plains at the edge of the Great Basin – yet all this is confined within one-quarter of the state.*

Native Americans settled in extreme Northern California around 10,000 BC. They coexisted peacefully with each other and with the earth, leaving behind few signs of their existence apart from discarded sea shells and pictographs on cave walls. When the Europeans arrived in the area in the 19th century, things changed swiftly.

The first to come were fur trappers, in search of beavers, sea otters, and other pelts. Soon afterward gold seekers descended upon the region's rivers, hoping for similar riches to those found in the Sierra Nevada *(see pp48–9)*. Some gold was found, but the real wealth was made at the end of the century when lumber companies

began to harvest the forests of coastal redwoods. These giant redwood trees *(Sequoia sempervirens)* are the region's defining feature. The finest forests have been protected by state and national parks and exude a palpable sense of history.

Inland, an even more ancient sight confronts visitors to the strange volcanic areas of Mount Lassen and the Lava Beds National Monument. Millions of years worth of geological activity has formed a stunning landscape that is devoid of civilization.

Far Northern California is sparsely populated, with a few medium-sized towns, such as Redding and Eureka. The prime attractions are natural, and life here, for visitors and residents, revolves around the great outdoors.

Lost Creek in Redwood National Park

◁ Imposing snow-capped peak of Mount Shasta

# Exploring the North

Rugged, wild, and sparsely populated, California's northern extremes have more in common with neighboring Oregon and Washington than they do with the rest of the state. Dense forests of pine, fir, and redwood trees cover more than half the landscape, and two parallel mountain ranges, the Coast Range and, farther inland, the Sierra Nevada Mountains, divide the north into three very different sections. Along the coast, Cape Mendocino makes a good base for exploring the often deserted beaches and coastal redwood groves. Inland, the Sacramento Valley provides access to the beautiful snow-capped Mount Shasta, the volcanic spectacles of Lassen Volcanic National Park, and the Lava Beds National Monument.

**SEE ALSO**

• *Where to Stay* pp552–4

• *Where to Eat* pp598–9

## SIGHTS AT A GLANCE

Patrick's Point State Park in
Humboldt County

## GETTING AROUND

A car is essential for visiting northern California. Two north–south routes run parallel up and down the region, but the only comfortable route through the mountains east–west is Hwy 299. Bisecting the north, I-5 runs through the Sacramento Valley, while to the west US Hwy 101 runs through the lush valleys of the Russian and Eel Rivers. Public transportation is limited to Greyhound buses along the two main highways and around a dozen daily trains through the Sacramento Valley to Seattle.

## KEY

| | |
|---|---|
| ▬ | Freeway |
| ▬ | Major road |
| ▬ | Secondary road |
| ▬ | Minor road |
| ▬ | Scenic route |
| ▬ | Main railway |
| ▬ | Minor railway |
| ▬ | State border |
| △ | Summit |

**Impressive peak of Mount Shasta**

ord

Klamath Falls

Lakeview

Dorris   Tule Lake   **13 TULE LAKE NATIONAL WILDLIFE REFUGES**

Goose Lake

Willow Ranch   Fort Bidwell

orook

v Creek ountain 2387m

Macdoel

*Tule Lake*

*Clear Lake Reservoir*

395

Upper Alkali Lake

Mount Dome 1987m

**14**

Davis Creek   Lake City

ntague

hada

Bray

**LAVA BEDS NATIONAL MONUMENT**   Tionesta

*Modoc National Forest*

299

Cedarville

elle

*Klamath National Forest*

Alturas   *Middle Alkali Lake*

Canby   Eagleville

**12 MOUNT SHASTA**

Eagle Peak 3015m   *Lower Alkali Lake*

Mount Shasta

Bartle   Pondosa   Day   Adin   Likely

ntains

Castella

*Cascade*

Bieber   89   Madeline

Big Bend   McArthur

139

5

Fall River Mills

*ta* *e*   *Pit River*

Lakehead

299   Cassel   Little Valley   Termo   *Observation Peak 2427m*

Hillcrest   Hat Creek   *Lassen National Forest*   Ravendale   *Horse Lake*

89   Old Station

**SHASTA DAM**

Redding   Viola   *Eagle Lake*   44   395

**STA STATE ORIC PARK**

44   *Lassen Peak 3187m*   **15 LASSEN VOLCANIC NATIONAL PARK**

Anderson

Mineral   *Fredonyer Pass 1759m*   Susanville   Johnstonville   *Hot Springs Peak 2341m*

ker

36   Mill Creek   Chester   36   Janesville

36   89   *Lake Almanor*   *Honey Lake*   Milford

Bluff   Dairyville   Canyondam

ed ank   Jonesville   Caribou   Taylorsville   *Plumas National Forest*   Herlong

Lomo   Belden   89   395

5   99

Corning   32   *Dixie Mountain 2539m*   *Adams Peak 2499m*

enta amento   *Chico*   Quincy   Cromberg   Vinton

70   70

Graeagle   Portola

89   Reno

0 kilometers   25

0 miles   25

For additional map symbols *see back flap*

# Redwood National Park ❶

*See pp448–9.*

# Arcata ❷

**Road map** A2. 🏠 16,400. 🚌 *Arcata/Eureka Airport, 8 miles (13 km) N of Arcata.* 🛈 *1635 Heindon Rd (707 822-3619).* **www**.arcatachamber.com

Arcata is a small town and its life revolves around Humboldt State University, in the hills above. Arcata's main square, with palm trees and a statue of President McKinley (1843–1901), is filled with bookstores and cafés. The town is a pleasant base for exploring the redwood region.

The forests east of Arcata are thought to be the stomping grounds of Bigfoot, the US equivalent to Asia's Yeti. No one has yet proved its existence, but footprints larger than those of the biggest bear have been found.

# Eureka ❸

**Road map** A2. 🏠 27,600. 🚌 🛫 *Arcata/Eureka Airport, 15 miles (24 km) N of Eureka.* 🛈 *2112 Broadway (707 442-3738, 800 356-6381).* **www**.eurekachamber.com

Eureka was founded by gold miners in 1850, who were so excited by their find that they

**Ornate Carson Mansion in Eureka**

## REDWOODS AND THE LUMBER INDUSTRY

The tallest tree on earth, the coniferous coastal redwood (*Sequoia sempervirens*) is unique to northern California and southern Oregon, although it is also related to the giant sequoia (*Sequoiadendron gigantea*) of the High Sierras and the *Metasequoia glyptostrobiodes* species, native to China. Redwoods can live for 2,000 years and reach 350 ft (107 m), despite roots that grow up to 200 ft (61 m) horizontally but only 4–6 ft (1–2 m) deep.

The redwood's fast growth and resistance to disease makes it ideal for commercial use. By the 1920s, logging had destroyed 90 percent of the groves. The Save the Redwoods League was formed, buying land now protected in state parks. However, some groves are still owned by lumber companies, and their future is a major issue on both local and national levels.

**Stacked redwood lumber**

proudly named it after the state's ancient Greek motto meaning "I have found it." It has since expanded into the northern coast's largest industrial center, with extensive logging and fishing operations surrounding the state protected natural harbor.

West of US 101, between E and M streets along the waterfront, is Eureka's interesting Old Town. Its restored 19th-century buildings, many with cast-iron façades, are now converted into cafés, bars, and restaurants.

Situated at M and Second streets is the extravagant Victorian architecture of Carson Mansion *(see pp30–31)*. It was built in 1885 for millionaire lumber baron William Carson. Its whimsical Gothic design is enhanced by its redwood construction typical of the area, painted to resemble the more expensive medium of stone. Carson Mansion is now a gentlemen's club and is closed to the general public.

# Samoa Cookhouse ❹

79 Cookhouse Ln & Samoa Rd, Samoa. **Road map** A2. **Tel** (707) 442-1659. ◯ *daily.* ● *Thanksgiving, Dec 25.* ♿ **www**.samoacookhouse.net

The Samoa Cookhouse was built in 1900 as a dining room for workers at the adjacent Louisiana Pacific pulp mill, one of many lumber mills standing on the narrow Samoa Peninsula. It was opened to the public in the 1960s, when automation in the mills had reduced the size of the workforce and the need for on-site dining facilities. The restaurant has retained its rustic decor and its giant-sized portions of traditional American dishes. Antique logging equipment adds to the unique ambience.

# Ferndale ❺

**Road map** A2. 🏠 1,400. 🛫 *Arcata/Eureka Airport, 40 miles (64 km) N of Ferndale.* 🛈 *PO Box 325, Ferndale (707 786-4477).* **www**.victorianferndale.com

Located on a flood plain near the mouth of the Eel River, Ferndale is a pastoral respite from the wilderness of

California's northern coast. The town was founded in 1852 by Danish, Swiss-Italian, and Portuguese immigrants who together established a lucrative dairy industry here. In 1992, Ferndale was hit by one of the most powerful earthquakes in California's recent history, measuring 7.1 on the Richter scale, but damage was limited. Exhibits of the town's history can be seen in the **Ferndale Museum**.

The town is perhaps best known as the host of the annual Kinetic Sculpture Race, during which contestants ride their self-made vehicles from Arcata to Centerville County Beach, outside Ferndale.

**🏛 Ferndale Museum**
Shaw & 3rd St. **Tel** (707) 786-4466.
⏱ Feb–Dec: 11am–4pm Wed–Sat,
1–4pm Sun; Jun–Sep: 11am–4pm
Tue–Sat, 1–4pm Sun. ⬤ Jan.
**www**.ferndale-museum.org

**Gingerbread Mansion, one of Ferndale's Victorian houses**

## Scotia ❻

**Road map** A2. 🏘 2,500. 🚌
✈ Arcata/Eureka Airport, 40 miles
(64 km) N of Scotia. 🚆 715 Wild-
wood Ave (707 764-3436).
**www**.townofscotia.com

The town of Scotia was built in 1887 to house the workers from the **Pacific Lumber Company**'s massive redwood mill, which dominates the south end of town. Palco, as the company is better known, was established in 1869 and owns and manages nearly 200,000 acres (80,000 ha) of prime redwood forest along the banks of the Eel River and its tributaries. Incorporating two sawmills, a school, medical clinics, and housing

**Palco's redwood visitors' center in Scotia**

for nearly 300 lumber employees and their families, Scotia is California's only surviving complete lumber community.

Exhibits on the history of Scotia, and on the redwood lumber industry as a whole, are displayed in a small museum in the center of town, which also dispenses passes for self-guided tours of the lumber mill. Here visitors can see each stage of the milling process: huge logs are debarked by powerful jets of water, sliced by laser-guided saws into lumber, then dried and stacked ready for shipping.

**🏭 Pacific Lumber Company**
125 Main St. **Tel** (707) 764-2222.
⏱ Mon–Fri. 🖥 **www**.palco.com

## Avenue of the Giants ❼

🚌 Garberville. 🛈 Weott (Nov–Apr:
10am–4pm daily; May–Oct: 9am–
5pm daily (707 946-2263).
**www**.avenueofthegiants.net

The world's tallest redwood trees and the most extensive primeval redwood groves stand along the banks of the

Eel River in the impressive 50,000-acre (20,200-ha) Humboldt Redwoods State Park (see p448). The best overall sense of these trees can be seen by driving along the 33-mile (53-km) Avenue of the Giants, a winding two-lane highway running parallel to US 101 through the park. For the best experience, however, leave your car in one of the many parking areas and walk around the groves, taking in the full immensity and magnificence of the trees.

The tallest individual specimen, the 364-ft (110-m) Dyersville Giant, was blown over during a storm in the winter of 1991, but its size is perhaps even more astounding now, lying on its side in Founder's Grove at the north end of the park. Currently the tallest and largest trees stand within the Rockefeller Forest above the west bank of the river.

The visitors' center, halfway along the Avenue of the Giants on US 101, exhibits displays on the natural history of these mighty forests. It also supplies maps and detailed information on the many hiking and camping facilities available within the park.

**Avenue of the Giants, in Humboldt Redwoods State Park**

# A Tour of Redwood National Park ❶

Redwood National Park protects some of
the largest original redwood forests in the
world, stretching along the coastline of
Northern California. Established by
President Johnson in 1968 to promote
tourism to the area, the 58,000-acre
(23,500-ha) park includes smaller areas
that had already been established as
state parks. A tour of the area takes
one full day, although two days
allows time to walk away
from the roads and experience the
tranquillity of these majestic groves.

Fort
Dick•    D4    197
D3
Parkway Drive  ①
②
101
③

**Coastal redwood trees**

**Del Norte Coast Redwood
State Park** ③
This park became the first
protected area in 1926. Part
of the old Redwood High-
way has been maintained as
a hiking trail. In spring, wildflowers cover the hillsides.

**Trees of Mystery** ④
A major tourist attraction of the area is
marked by giant fiberglass statues of the
mythical lumberjack Paul Bunyan and his
ox, Babe. The two characters were popularized in early 20th-century stories about
their journey from Maine to California.

• **Klamath**
④
101

**Tall Trees Grove** ⑤
The world's tallest tree, a
368-ft (112-m) giant, stands
in the aptly named Tall Trees
Grove, at the southern end of
the park. The park provides
a habitat for one of the
world's last remaining herds
of Roosevelt elk.

**Gold Bluffs Beach** ⑥
This 11-mile (18-km)
beach is rated by many
as the most beautiful in
Northern California.

**Humboldt Lagoons State Park** ⑦
Big Lagoon, a freshwater lake
stretching for 3 miles (5 km), and
two other estuaries form Humboldt
Lagoons State Park.

⑥
Davidson Rd
⑤
101
• **Orick**

**Patrick's Point
State Park** ⑧
In winter, the
headlands are a good
place to watch for
migrating gray
whales. Rock pools
abound with smaller
marine life.

**Stone
Lagoon**
⑦

**Big
Lagoon**

0 km    1
0 miles
⑧

### Jedediah Smith Redwoods State Park ①
Found among the 9,200 acres (3,720 ha) of this park are the most awe-inspiring coastal redwoods. The park was named after the fur-trapper Jedediah Smith, the first white man to walk across the US. He explored this region in 1828 *(see p46).*

### Crescent City ②
This northern town is the site of the headquarters and main information center for Redwood National Park.

Y

Tour route

Other roads

### IPS FOR DRIVERS

*our length*: Arcata to Crescent *ity* is 78 miles (125 km). US 101 the quickest route.

*uration of trip*: One could *rive* the entire route in under two *ours* one-way, but to experience more satisfying and relaxing visit the Redwood National Park *ea*, allow at least a full day.

*When to go*: September and *ctober* are ideal months to *avel*. Spring and summer can be *oggy*, but the best flowering *lants* are on view during these *nonths*. Winter is often rainy but best for whale-watching. *ummer* is the prime tourist *eason*, although crowds are *arely* a problem in this remote *rea* of the state.

*Where to stay and eat*: Tourist *ervices* are comparatively few *nd* far between in this region. *however*, there is a limited range *f restaurants* and motels *vailable* in Orick and Klamath, *while* a much wider range of *acilities* is available in Crescent City *ee pp542 & 598)* and Arcata, *outh* of the park *(see p446)*.

*Visitor information*: Crescent *ity Information Center, 111 econd St.* ☐ *Mar–Oct: 9am–pm daily; Nov–Feb: 9am–4pm aily.* ◑ *Jan 1, Thanksgiving, ec 25.* **Tel** *(707) 464-6101.* *www.*nps.gov

**The Lost Coast, near Crescent City**

## The Lost Coast ❽

**Road map** A2. 🚌 *Garberville.* 🛈 *782 Redwood Drive (707 923-2613, 800 923-2613).* **www**.garberville.org

Covering a small section of coastline so craggy and wild that no road could reasonably be built along it, the so-called Lost Coast is the largest remaining stretch of undeveloped shoreline in California. Protected by the government within the Sinkyone Wilderness State Park and the King Range National Conservation Area, the Lost Coast region stretches for more than 40 miles (64 km).

The salmon-fishing port of Shelter Cove, tucked away within a tiny bay, is at the center of the Lost Coast. Its remote location has kept the village small, but it remains a good base for hikers and wildlife enthusiasts. Sixteen miles (25 km) of hiking trails, inhabited only by fauna such as black bears, deer, mink, and bald eagles, run along the clifftops, interspersed with free camp sites. Shelter Cove is accessible only via a winding but well-maintained road.

A good feel for the Lost Coast can be had by taking Hwy 211 west of US 101 and then following the scenic road between Humboldt Redwoods State Park and Ferndale *(see p446)*. This beautiful 50-mile (80-km) road runs to the edge of the Pacific Ocean around Cape Mendocino, the westernmost point on the coast of California.

## Weaverville ❾

**Road map** A2. 🏘 *3,500.* ✈ *Redding Municipal Airport, 40 miles (64 km) E of Weaverville.* 🛈 *215 S. Main St (530 623-6101, 800 487-4648).*

This small rural town, set back in the mountains between the coast and the Central Valley, has changed little in the 150 years since it was founded by gold prospectors.

At the heart of the small commercial district, which boasts the state's oldest drug-store, is the **Jake Jackson Museum and History Center**, which has displays tracing the history of Weaverville and its surrounding gold-mining and lumber region. Adjacent to the museum, the Joss House State Historic Site is the oldest and best-preserved Chinese Temple in the country. Built in 1874, it serves as a reminder of the many Chinese immigrants who arrived in the US to mine gold and stayed in the state as cheap labor building the California railroads *(see pp50–51)*.

North of Weaverville, the Trinity Alps, part of the Salmon Mountain Range, rise up at the center of a beautiful mountain wilderness. They are popular with hikers and backpackers in the summer and with cross-country skiers during the winter months.

🏛 **Jake Jackson Museum and History Center**
780 Main St. **Tel** *(530) 623-5211.* ☐ *Apr: noon–4pm daily; May–Oct: 10am–5pm daily; Nov–Mar: noon–4pm Tue & Sat.* **Donation**.

**Shasta Dam, controlling the North's water supplies**

## Shasta Dam ⑩

🚆 *Redding*. **Redding Convention and Visitors' Bureau** *777 Auditorium Drive.* **Tel** *(530) 225-4100, (800) 874-7562.* **www.**visitredding.org

In order to provide a steady supply of water for agriculture, a cheap source of electricity for manufacturers, prevent flooding in the valley, and offer jobs for workers who had been left unemployed by the downturn in local mining industries, the US government funded the Central Valley Project. This was a network of dams, canals, and reservoirs, set up during the Depression of the 1930s and centered upon the 602-ft- (183-m-) high, 3,460-ft- (1,055-m-) long Shasta Dam. With a spillway three times as high as Niagara Falls, the dam is an impressive civil engineering achievement.

## Shasta State Historic Park ⑪

**Road map** A2. 🚆 *Redding.* **Visitors' Center Tel** *(530) 225-2065.* ⬜ *10am–5pm Wed–Sun.* **www.**parks.ca.gov

During the 1850s, Shasta was one of the largest gold mining camps in the state and the base of operations for prospectors working along the Trinity, Sacramento, McCloud, and Pit Rivers. As the Gold Rush faded, the town faded too, especially after the railroad was rerouted through the town of Redding, 5 miles (8 km) east.

Shasta is now a ghost town, but in the early 1920s the state of California, realizing its historical importance, took over and began to restore it. Numerous old brick buildings are preserved in a state of arrested decay, and the **Shasta Courthouse** has been restored to its original condition. Exhibits at the small visitors' center traces the town's history.

One mile (1.5 km) west of Shasta town, the land around Lake Whiskeytown forms the smallest parcel of the three-part Shasta-Whiskeytown-Trinity National Recreation Area, a forest preserve surrounding the three reservoirs. Lake Shasta is the largest of the three. Trinity Lake is also known as Clair Engle Lake, in honor of the local politician who helped make this ambitious reclamation project a reality. All three lakes are popular with fishermen, water-skiers, houseboat owners, and other recreational users.

### 🏛 Shasta Courthouse and Visitors' Center
Main St. **Tel** *(530) 243-8194.* ⬜ *10am–5pm Wed–Sun.*

## Mount Shasta ⑫

**Road map** B1. 🚉 *Dunsmuir.* 🚌 *Siskiyou.* 🚆 *Shasta.* **Visitors' Center** *300 Pine St.* **Tel** *(530) 926-4865, (800) 926-4865.* ⬜ *daily.* **www.**mtshastachamber.com

Mount Shasta reaches a height of 14,162 ft (4,316 m) and is the second highest of the Cascade Mountains, after Mount Rainier in Washington State. Visible more than 100 miles (160 km) away and usually covered with snow, the summit is a popular destination for mountaineers.

**Mount Shasta, towering over the town of Shasta below**

## Tule Lake National Wildlife Refuges ⑬

**Road map** B1. 🚌 *Klamath Falls.* **Visitors' Center** *4009 Hill Road.* **Tel** *(530) 667-2231.* **www.**stateparks.com/tule_lake.html

Six refuges on both sides of the California–Oregon border form one of the most popular

**Interior of the preserved Shasta Courthouse**

bird-watching spots in the western US. Centering upon Tule Lake and the Lower Klamath River, much of the region has been set aside as wildlife refuges (see pp436–7), popular with bird-watchers. In the fall the refuges attract hundreds of thousands of wildfowl as they migrate south, from Canada to the Central Valley and beyond. Tule Lake is also the winter home to as many as 1,000 bald eagles.

## Lava Beds National Monument **⑭**

**Road map** B1. 🚆 *Klamath Falls.*
**Visitors' Center** *1 Indian Wells.*
**Tel** *(530) 667-8100.* ⬜ *daily.*
**www**.nps.gov/labe

The Lava Beds National Monument spreads over 46,500 acres (18,800 ha) of the Modoc Plateau, the volcanic tableland of northeastern California, and preserves an eerie landscape of lava flows and cinder cones. Beneath the lava beds are more than 500 lava tube caves – cylindrical tunnels created by exposed lava turning to stone.

The greatest concentration of caves can be visited via the Cave Loop Road, 2 miles (3 km) south of the park's visitors' center. From here, a short trail leads down into Mushpot Cave, the only one with lights and a paved floor. The name derives from splatters of lava found near the entrance.

Other caves along the road are also named for their main feature: Crystal Cave contains sparkling crystals, and Catacombs Cave requires visitors to crawl through its twisting passages. To visit any of the caves, wear sturdy shoes, carry a flashlight, and be sure to check first with the visitors' center.

The park is also notable as the site of the Modoc War of 1872–3, the only major war between the US and the Native Americans in California. After being removed from the area to a reservation in Oregon, a group of Modoc Indians returned under the command of Chief Kientpoos, or "Captain Jack." For six months they evaded the US Cavalry, but

**Captain Jack's Stronghold in Lava Beds National Monument**

Captain Jack was eventually captured and hanged, and the rest were forced into a reservation in what is now Oklahoma. Captain Jack's Stronghold is along the park's north border.

## Lassen Volcanic National Park **⑮**

**Road map** B2. 🚆 *Chester, Red Bluff.*
**Visitors' Center** *38050 Hwy 36 East, Mineral, California.* **Tel** *(530) 595-4444.* ⬜ *daily.* **www**.nps.gov/lavo

Prior to the eruption of Mount St. Helens in Washington in 1980, the 10,457-ft (3,187-m) high Lassen Peak was the last volcano to erupt on the mainland United States. In a series of nearly 300 eruptions between 1914 and 1917, Lassen Peak laid waste to 100,000 acres (40,500 ha) of the surrounding land. The area was set aside as Lassen Volcanic National Park in 1916.

The volcano is the southernmost in the Cascade Mountain range and is considered to be still active. Numerous areas on its flanks show clear signs of the geological processes. Bumpass Hell was named

after an early tour guide, Kendall Bumpass, who lost his leg in one of the boiling mudpots in 1865. This boardwalk trail leads past a series of steaming, sulfurous pools of boiling water, heated by molten rock deep underground. Bumpass Hell is one of the park's most interesting stops and is located along Hwy 89, 5 miles (8 km) from the Southwest Entrance Station.

In winter, Hwy 89 across the park is closed because of weather conditions. In summer, the road winds through the park, climbing more than 8,500 ft (2,590 m) high, up to Summit Lake. The road continues across to the Devastated Area, a bleak gray landscape of rough volcanic mudflows, ending at Manzanita Lake in the northwest corner of the park. Here the **Loomis Museum** displays a photographic record of Lassen Peak's many eruptions.

The park contains more than 150 miles (240 km) of hiking trails, including a very steep 2.5 mile (4 km) route up the side of Mount Lassen to the ashen gray summit.

### 🏛 Loomis Museum
Lassen Park Rd, North Entrance.
**Tel** *(530) 595-3399.* ⬜ *late May–Sep (call for opening times).*

**Sulfur springs in Lassen Volcanic National Park**

# THE WINE COUNTRY

*amous throughout the world for its superlative wines, the Wine Country interior has a temperate climate, miles of vine-covered hills, and spectacular architecture. To the west lie the dramatic, rocky landscapes of the Sonoma and Mendocino coastlines. Throughout the region, a wide choice of excellent food and, of course, premium wine is available, making this an ideal place for a relaxing retreat.*

California's wine industry was born in the small, crescent-shaped Sonoma Valley, when, in 1823, Franciscan fathers planted grape vines to produce sacramental wines. In 1857, the flamboyant Hungarian Count Agoston Haraszthy brought winemaking in California to a new level: using imported European grape varieties, he planted the state's first major vineyard at Sonoma's revered Buena Vista Winery *(see p465)*. Haraszthy made a name not only for himself (he is known as the "father of California wine") but also for this previously unrecognized wine-producing region.

Over the years, many wine producers have followed in the count's footsteps, most of them favoring the rich, fertile soil of the Napa Valley. Hundreds of wineries now stand side by side along the length of the valley floor. Most of them offer tours of their facilities and wine tastings. Many are also of architectural interest, including such gems as the Mission-style Robert Mondavi Winery and the white Mediterranean-style Sterling Vineyards, which is perched on a volcanic bluff. Nearby, the stunning modern winery of Clos Pegase is distinguished by rows of imposing russet-and earth-colored columns and towers.

Nestled at the northernmost edge of the Napa Valley is the small town of Calistoga, famous for its restorative mud baths, enormous geysers, and hot mineral-water tubs. West of the valley, the Russian River which is bordered by the Sonoma and Mendocino coastal areas flows into the Pacific Ocean. These wild stretches of shoreline provide perfect opportunities for bird-and whale-watching and beachcombing.

Goat Rock Beach at the mouth of the Russian River

◁ Mustard plants growing in a Napa Valley vineyard in the spring

# Exploring the Wine Country

The sheltered valleys of the coastal ranges provide the best conditions for planting vines, particularly within the Russian River, Sonoma, and Napa valleys. To the west of these famous wine-producing areas, quaint coastal towns, such as Mendocino, Jenner, and Bodega Bay, are surrounded by pristine, secluded beaches and small rock pools. Inland, visitors can explore the ancient redwood groves on foot, horseback, or by train. For those who prefer to have a bird's-eye view of the region, trips are available in hot-air balloons that soar gracefully above the vineyards. A short drive away are several immense state historic parks, with dense forests and unique architecture. Nearby, a wide variety of watersports is offered at Clear Lake, California's largest freshwater lake, and Lake Berryessa, which is the second largest artificial lake in the state.

Gerstle Cove, site of a marine preserve at Salt Point

## GETTING AROUND

The majority of visitors explore the Wine Country and the areas along the Sonoma and Mendocino coasts by car. From San Francisco, Hwy 1 follows the coast; Hwy 101 runs south–north through the center of the region and into Humboldt County. Route 20 links Nevada City and the Wine Country, joining Hwy 101 north of Lake Mendocino. Public transportation services in the area are limited, although bus tours from San Francisco are available, and train tours of the Napa Valley *(see pp462–3)* and of the northern redwood forests *(see p459)* run regularly. The closest international airports are Sacramento, San Jose, San Francisco and Oakland *(see pp628–9).*

### SEE ALSO

- **Where to Stay** pp554–6
- **Where to Eat** pp599–601

### KEY

| | |
|---|---|
| ▬▬ | Freeway |
| ▬▬ | Major road |
| ▬▬ | Secondary road |
| ▬▬ | Minor road |
| ▬▬ | Scenic route |
| ▬▬ | Minor railway |
| △ | Summit |

**Map labels:**

Eureka

LEGGETT VALLEY ❶
Leggett
Cummings
Round In Reser

Rockport
Laytonville
Westport
Branscomb

Inglenook
Cleone

Fort Bragg
Noyo River
Caspar

MENDOCINO ❷
Little River
Comptche

VAN DAMME STATE PARK ❸
Albion
Navarro

Elk
Anderson Val
Phile

Manchester
POINT ARENA LIGHTHOUSE ❹
Point Arena
Garcia River

Anchor Bay
Gualala
Annapolis
Sea Ranch

SALT POINT STATE PARK
FORT R
STATE HISTORIC PA

Coast

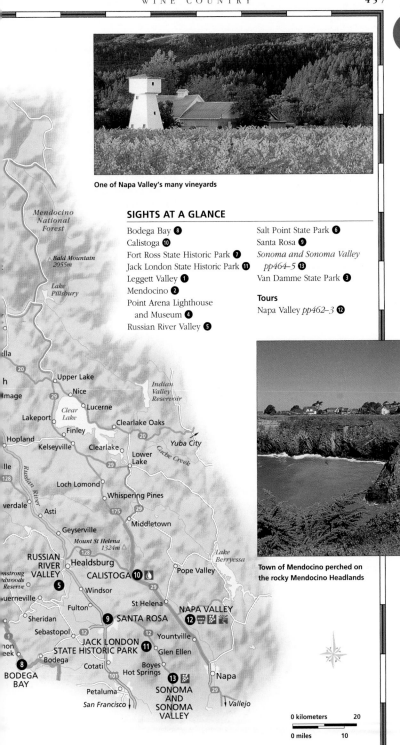

One of Napa Valley's many vineyards

## SIGHTS AT A GLANCE

Town of Mendocino perched on
the rocky Mendocino Headlands

# Leggett Valley ❶

**Road map** A2. 🚌 to Leggett.
ℹ️ 70400 Hwy 101.

This lush, green valley, separated from the Pacific Ocean by the King Mountain Range, is famous in California for its majestic giant redwoods. In the 1930s a hole was cut in the trunk of one enormous redwood to allow motorists to drive through the tree.

Hikers come to Leggett Valley and the surrounding area to enjoy the atmospheric redwood forest trails (part of the forest here was used to film scenes for George Lucas's science-fiction epic, *Star Wars*). The local wildlife population includes raccoons and deer, and golden eagles can often be seen soaring above the trees, searching the forest floor for unsuspecting prey.

South Fork Eel River, which is rich in salmon and steelhead trout, attracts many birds, including herons. The river is also popular with anglers and, in summer, swimmers.

# Mendocino ❷

**Road map** A3. 🏘️ 1,200. 🚌
ℹ️ 2175 Main St, Fort Bragg
(707 961-6300).
**www**.visitmendocino.com

The settlers of this fishing village came to California from New England in 1852. They built their new homes to resemble as closely as possible those they had left behind on the East Coast, with pointed gables and decorative wooden trims. As a result, the Mendocino coastline is often referred to as "California's New England Coast." Perched on a rocky promontory high above the Pacific Ocean, Mendocino has retained the picturesque charm of its days as a major fishing and logging center. Although tourism is now its main industry, the town remains virtually untarnished by commercialism. It is a thriving arts center and has a large number of artists and writers. Visitors can stroll around the many boutiques, book-shops, galleries, and cafés. Those who prefer the attractions of nature can admire the beauty of the heather-covered bluffs, the migrating gray whales, and the stunning ocean vistas.

# Van Damme State Park ❸

Comptche Ukiah Rd. **Tel** (707) 937-5804. 🚌 from Point Arena. ⭘ daily; Apr–Oct: reservations needed for camping. 🎦 ♿ **www**.parks.ca.gov

This beautiful 2,200-acre (890-ha) preserve has some of California's most scenic forest trails, shaded by immense redwoods and giant ferns, and accompanied by meandering creeks. The coastal areas of the park are popular with abalone divers. For visitors who want to enjoy a hike or jog through gorgeous countryside, the

Giant ferns lining the beautiful Fern Canyon Trail in Van Damme State Park

lush Fern Canyon Trail is one of the best in the park, which also has several cycle trails.

Visitors also come to Van Damme to contemplate the peculiar Pygmy Forest, an eerie grove of old, stunted trees. Due to a combination of poor soil and bad drainage, these trees grow no taller than about 4 ft (1.2 m). The Pygmy Forest, 3 miles (5 km) north of the park, is accessible on foot or by car.

# Point Arena Lighthouse and Museum ❹

45500 Lighthouse Rd. **Road map** A3. **Tel** (707) 882-2777, (877) 725-4448. 🚌 from Point Arena. **Lighthouse and Museum** ⭘ 10am–3:30pm daily. 🎦 ♿ museum only. 🎦 **www**. pointarenalighthouse.com

One mile (1.6 km) north of the Point Arena fishing village stands this impressive 115-ft (35-m) lighthouse. Erected in 1870, the original brick building was destroyed in the earthquake of 1906 *(see p24)*. The present reinforced con-crete structure was produced in San Francisco by the Concrete Chimney Company.

A climb up the 145 steps to the top of the lighthouse provides a stunning view of

Mendocino overlooking the ocean from the bay's rocky headlands

the coast – the effort is particularly worthwhile on fog-free days. Tours of the lighthouse (available all year round) offer a chance to see its huge original Fresnel lens close-up. Built in France, it measures over 6 ft (1.8 m) in diameter, weighs more than 2 tons, and floats in a large pool of mercury.

The adjacent fog signal building, which dates from 1869, now houses a museum. Exhibits include compressed-air foghorns and displays on the history of the lighthouse.

**Point Arena Lighthouse overlooking the Pacific Ocean**

# Russian River Valley ❺

🚌 from Healdsburg. 🛈 16209 First St, Guerneville (707 869-9000). www.russianriver.com

Bisected by the Russian River and its tributaries, the area known as the Russian River Valley is so vast that it contains several smaller valleys, some dominated by hillsides planted with grapevines and apple orchards, others by redwood groves, family farms, and sandy river beaches. About 60 wineries, many of which are open for wine tastings, are scattered throughout the valley.

At the hub of the valley is the small town of Healdsburg, where visitors often congregate around the splendid Spanish-style town square, with its shops, cafés, and restaurants.

Southwest of Healdsburg lies the tiny, friendly town of Guerneville, a summertime

## THE SKUNK TRAIN

Since 1885, the Skunk Train has been running from Fort Bragg, a coastal logging town north of Mendocino, into the heart of the redwood groves. Thanks to the odoriferous mix of diesel and gasoline once used to fuel the locomotive, waiting passengers could always smell the train before they could see it, hence its name. Today, locomotive lovers can ride on one of the steam, diesel, or electric trains for a half-or full-day tour through the forests.

**Skunk Train and its smoke cloud**

haven for San Francisco Bay Area residents, particularly gay men and women. Every year in September, Guerneville plays host to the very popular Russian River Jazz Festival at Johnson's Beach. Johnson's is also a good place from which to take a canoe or rafting trip down the gentle Russian River, where turtles, river otters, and great blue herons are often sighted. Hikers and equestrians flock to Guerneville to visit the 805-acre (330-ha) **Armstrong Redwoods State Reserve**, which is the site of one of the few remaining old-growth redwood forests in California. Among the mighty redwoods in the park is a 308-ft (94-m) giant – a 1,400-year-old tree named Colonel Armstrong.

🌿 **Armstrong Redwoods State Preserve**
17020 Armstrong Woods Rd, Guerneville. **Tel** (707) 869-2015, 865-2391. ◯ daily.

# Salt Point State Park ❻

Hwy 1. **Tel** (707) 847-3221, 847-3465. 🚌 from Santa Rosa. ◯ **Visitors' Center** Apr–Oct: 10am–3pm Sat & Sun. 🅿️ ♿ www.parks.ca.gov

Within this forested 6,000-acre (2,400-ha) seaside park are several rocky coves, frequented by abalone divers and surf fishers. Salt Point also includes Gerstle Cove Marine Reserve, where divers admire protected sea anemones, starfish, and various rock fish.

Numerous bridle paths and hiking trails wind through Salt Point's pines, redwoods, and flower-filled meadows. In April and May, the most popular park attraction is the route that leads through the 317-acre (130-ha) Kruse Rhododendron State Reserve, where rhododendrons with pink and purple blooms grow up to 30 ft (9 m).

**Gerstle Cove in Salt Point State Park**

**Cannon on display in front of the Russian Orthodox chapel at Fort Ross**

# Fort Ross State Historic Park ❼

1900 Coast Hwy 1, Jenner. **Road map** A3. *Tel* (707) 847-3286. 🚌 from Point Arena. ⬤ sunrise–sunset daily. **Visitors' Center & Bookstore** 10am–4:30pm daily. ⬤ Thanksgiving, Dec 25. 🎦 ♿ www.parks.ca.gov

On a windswept headland, 12 miles (19 km) north of Jenner, stands the grand Fort Ross State Historic Park. A well-restored Russian trading outpost, the fort was founded in 1812 and was occupied until 1841 (the name "Ross" is a derivative of the Russian word "Rossyia," meaning Russia).

The Russians were the first European visitors to the region, serving as representatives of the Russian-American Company, which had been established in 1799. Although it was the presence of Russian fur hunters in the North Pacific that induced Spain to occupy Alta California in 1769, the Russians never tried to expand their territory in California. After 30 years of peaceful trading, they abandoned the fort.

Built in 1836, the original house of the fort's last manager, Alexander Rotchev, is still intact today, and several other buildings have been painstakingly reconstructed within the wooden palisade. The most impressive structure in Fort Ross is the Russian Orthodox chapel, which was constructed from local redwood in 1824.

Every year, a living history day is held on the last Saturday of July. More than 200 costumed participants re-create life at the outpost in the 1800s.

# Bodega Bay ❽

Hwy 1. 🏠 1,300. 🚌
🛈 850 Hwy 1 (707 875-3866).
www.bodegabay.com

In 1963, the coastal town of Bodega Bay, with its white clapboard houses, appeared in Alfred Hitchcock's classic film, *The Birds*. In the tiny neighboring town of Bodega, visitors can still see the Potter Schoolhouse, which was in the film.

Bodega Head, the small peninsula sheltering Bodega Bay, is one of California's best whale-watching points. Other favorite Bodega Bay pastimes include golfing, bird-watching, digging for clams, and deep-sea fishing. In the evening, visitors can watch the fishing fleets unload their day's catch at Tides Wharf dock on Hwy 1.

**A harbor seal on Goat Rock Beach**

The northern end of Bodega Bay marks the beginning of the Sonoma Coast State Beach, a 10-mile (16-km) stretch of ten beaches, separated by rocky bluffs. At the northernmost tip

of this chain of beaches sits the charming little town of Jenner. Here, the wide Russian River spills into the Pacific Ocean, and hundreds of gray harbor seals bask in the sun and breed on Goat Rock Beach. The most rewarding time to watch the seals is during their "pupping season," which begins in March and lasts until late June.

# Santa Rosa ❾

**Road map** A3. 🏠 136,000.
✈ Sonoma County Airport, 6 miles (10 km) N of Santa Rosa.
🚌 🛈 9 4th St (707 577-8674; 800 404-7673).
www.visitsantarosa.com

Santa Rosa, which is one of the fastest-growing cities in California, is best known for its past and present residents, most notably the horticulturist Luther Burbank (1849–1926). Burbank lived here for more than 50 years and became world famous for creating 800 new plant varieties, including fruits, vegetables, and ornamental flowers. Self-guided tours explore the one-acre (0.5-ha) site of the **Luther Burbank Home and Gardens**, which includes a rose garden, and an orchard. The Victorian garden features plants often found in domestic gardens in the 1880s.

In a restored historical post office dating from 1909 is the Sonoma County museum. It illustrates the history of

**Fishing boats at North Beach Jetty Marina in Bodega Bay**

**Spring flowers in bloom at Luther Burbank Home and Gardens**

Sonoma County through rare historical photographs, documents, and artifacts.

The late Charles Schulz, creator of the "Peanuts" series, was a resident of Santa Rosa. Fans of his cartoon characters can visit **Snoopy's Gallery and Gift Shop**, which stocks the widest range of Snoopy, Charlie Brown, and "Peanuts" products in the world.

🌷 **Luther Burbank Home and Gardens**
204 Santa Rosa Ave. *Tel (707) 524-5445.* **Gardens** ⬜ 8am–5pm daily. **Home** ⬜ Apr–Oct: Tue–Sun. 🟨 www.lutherburbank.org

🏛 **Sonoma County Museum**
425 7th Street. *Tel (707) 579-1500.* ⬜ 11am–5pm Tue–Sun. www.sonomacountymuseum.org

📷 **Snoopy's Gallery and Gift Shop**
1665 West Steele Lane. *Tel (707) 546-3385.* ⬜ 10am–6pm daily. ⚫ public hols. www.snoopygift.com

## Calistoga ⑩

**Road map** A3. 🏘 4,715. 🚌
ℹ 1133 Washington St. (707 942-6333). www.calistogavisitors.com

Visitors have had mineral or mud baths here since this little spa town was founded in the mid-19th century by the state's first millionaire, Sam Brannan (1819–89). Today, crowds are still drawn here by its specialized spa treatments and good Wine Country cuisine. The town also has a range of pleasant accommodations and small boutiques selling everything from handmade soaps to European

home furnishings. Two miles (3 km) north of the town, **Old Faithful Geyser** spouts jets of boiling mineral water 60 ft (18 m) into the sky about once every 40 minutes. To the west lies the **Petrified Forest**. Here hikers can see huge redwoods turned to stone by a volcanic eruption over three million years ago *(see p462)*.

Many visitors who prefer to hike among living redwoods travel east to the Robert Louis Stevenson State Park, where the author of *Treasure Island* and his wife, Fanny Osbourne, spent their honeymoon in 1880 *(see p26)*. Those who climb the 5 miles (8 km) from the park to the summit of the 4,343-ft (1,325-m) Mount St. Helena, the Wine Country's highest peak, are rewarded by a breathtaking view of the vineyards below. To enjoy the view without making the rigorous ascent, it is worth taking a trip in a glider or hot-air balloon. These are available at the gliderport in nearby Calistoga.

🚠 **Old Faithful Geyser**
1299 Tubbs Lane. *Tel (707) 942-6463.* ⬜ daily. 🟨 www.oldfaithfulgeyser.com

🚠 **Petrified Forest**
4100 Petrified Forest Rd. *Tel (707) 942-6667.* ⬜ daily. ⚫ Dec 25. 🟨 ♿ limited. www.petrifiedforest.org

## Jack London State Historic Park ⑪

London Ranch Rd, Glen Ellen.
*Tel (707) 938-5216.* ⬜ **Park** 9:30am–7pm daily (summer), 10am–5pm (winter). **Museum** 10am–5pm daily. ⚫ Jan 1, Thanksgiving, Dec 25. 🟨 ♿ museum only. 🟨 www.parks.ca.gov

In the early 1900s, the world-famous author of *The Call of the Wild*, *The Sea Wolf*, and more than 50 other books *(see p26)* abandoned his hectic lifestyle to live in this tranquil 800-acre (325-ha) expanse of oaks, madrones, California buckeyes, and redwoods. London (1876–1916) aptly named this territory the Beauty Ranch, and it still contains his stables, vineyards, and the cottage where he lived and died. Also here are the eerie ruins of London's dream home, the Wolf House, which was mysteriously destroyed by fire just before its completion. The park is ideal for a quiet picnic and a hike.

After London's death, his widow, Charmian Kittredge (1871–1955), built a magnificent home on the ranch, called the House of Happy Walls. The house is now a museum displaying London memorabilia. The author's writing desk and early copies of his work are exhibited.

**Old Faithful Geyser spurting hot water into the sky**

# Napa Valley Tour ⑫

Statue at Clos Pegase

The sliver of land known as Napa Valley is 35 miles (56 km) long and lies at the heart of Northern California's wine industry. More than 350 wineries are scattered across its rolling hillsides and fertile valley floor, some dating from the early 19th century. Most of the wineries hug the scenic Silverado Trail and Hwy 29, two major arteries that run the length of the valley and through the towns of Yountville, Oakville, Rutherford, St. Helena, and Calistoga *(see p461)*. Many of Napa Valley's popular wineries offer visitors free tours of their facilities, while some charge a small wine-tasting fee.

**Sterling Vineyards ⑦**
An aerial tramway provides access to this large, white, Mediterranean-style winery, which is perched on a hill overlooking the valley and vineyards.

**Clos Pegase ⑥**
Renowned architect Michael Graves designed this Post-Modern winery, which is well known for its distinctive art collection and fine wines.

**Petrified Forest ⑤**
This forest is the home of the largest petrified trees in the world *(see p461)*.

**Bale Grist Waterwheel ④**
Built in 1846, this waterwheel still grinds grain into meal and flour on weekends.

**Robert Mondavi Winery ③**
Beautiful sculptures and paintings are on display throughout this huge, Mission-style winery. Guided tours are available year-round.

## FOOD AND WINE IN THE NAPA VALLEY

In addition to a number of superior wines, the Wine Country is well known for its fresh produce and prestigious chefs. Produce stalls and farmers' markets line the valley roads, selling organic vegetables and fruit and freshly squeezed juices. Restaurants in most small towns serve excellent meals, prepared with the freshest ingredients. Classic Wine Country cuisine includes dishes such as Sonoma leg of lamb with fresh mint pesto, creamy risotto with artichoke hearts and sun-dried tomatoes, wild-mushroom sauté in herb-garlic phyllo pastry, and Sterling salmon sautéed and served with a Pinot Noir sauce.

Restaurant terrace at Domaine Chandon in Yountville

**KEY**

▬ Tour route
— Other roads
☀ Viewpoint

**Napa Valley vineyard in the late-afternoon sunlight**

### TIPS FOR DRIVERS

*Tour length:* 40 miles (64 km),
including the scenic Petrified
Forest detour.
*Stopping-off points:* There
are several bed-and-breakfast inns
and hotels in the towns of
St. Helena and Calistoga. For an
excellent meal, visit Domaine
Chandon, Boudon Restaurant,
or Mustards Grill in Yountville;
Tra Vigne or Brava Terrace in
St. Helena (see also pp599–600).

**Napa Valley Wine Train**
Gourmet Wine Country cuisine
and fine wines are served on this
luxury train (www.winetrain.com)
as it makes a three-hour tour of
the lush Napa Valley.

**Rutherford Hill Winery** ⑧
This contemporary winery
has caves for aging wine.
The caves are carved
half a mile (0.8 km)
into the hillsides.

*Lake*
*Hennessey*

*WINTERS*

*Silverado Trail*

*Conn Creek*

(128)

*therford* •

③

*Oakville*

②

*Napa River*

**Mumm Napa** ⑨
Sparkling wines are made in the
classic tradition at this winery,
which is partly owned by French
champagne producer GH Mumm.

**Yountville** ②
Founded in the
mid-19th century
by pioneer George
Clavert Yount, this
tiny town is now a
popular spot from
which to take a hot-
air-balloon ride over
the Wine Country.

(29)

(1)

*Trancas St*

(121)

**Napa** ①
Napa's streets are lined
with restored buildings
housing restaurants,
stores, and art galleries.

| 0 kilometers | | 5 |
| 0 miles | | 2 |

*VALLEJO*

# Sonoma and Sonoma Valley ⓭

Nestling in the narrow, 17-mile- (27-km-) long Sonoma Valley, cradled by the Mayacama Mountains to the east and by the Sonoma Mountains to the west, are 6,000 acres (2,400 ha) of vineyards. At the foot of the valley lies the tiny town of Sonoma with its 8-acre (3-ha) plaza, a grass-covered town square designed in 1835 by Mexican General Mariano Vallejo (1808–90).

**Bear flag monument**

In the early 1840s, American settlers arriving in the area discovered that land ownership was reserved for Mexican citizens. On June 14, 1846, about 30 armed American farmers took General Vallejo and his men prisoner, seized control of Sonoma, and declared California an independent republic. The rebels' flag was adorned with a red star and stripe and a crude drawing of a grizzly bear. Although the republic was abolished 25 days later, when the United States annexed California (see p47), the state legislature adopted the Bear Flag design as the official California flag in 1911.

Sonoma City Hall at the center of the historic Sonoma Plaza

### 🏠 General Joseph Hooker House

414 1st St East, El Paseo.
**Tel** (707) 938-0510.
◻ 1–4pm Sat–Mon. 🅰 🗹

This 1855 gabled house belonged to Civil War hero "Fighting Joe" Hooker, who later sold it to settlers Pedro and Catherine Vasquez. The house is now the headquarters of the Sonoma League for Historic Preservation. Various historical exhibits and information on Sonoma walking tours are available here.

### 🏠 Toscano Hotel

20 E Spain St. **Tel** (707) 938-5889.
◻ 10am–5pm daily. 🅰 🗹 only.

Located on the north side of the plaza, the restored Toscano Hotel is now a historic monument. The two-story

## Exploring Sonoma

Sonoma's main attractions are its internationally renowned wineries and the attractive area immediately surrounding the Spanish-style **Sonoma Plaza**. The well-shaded plaza is lined with dozens of meticulously preserved historical sites. Many of the adobe buildings around the square house wine shops, charming boutiques, and chic restaurants serving excellent California

and Wine Country cuisine. At the very center of the town's plaza stands the **Sonoma City Hall**, a stone Mission Revival building (see p31) designed in 1908 by the San Francisco architect AC Lutgens. Close to the plaza's northeast corner is the bronze **Bear Flag Monument**, which serves as a memorial to the group of American settlers who rebelled against the ruling Mexican government in 1846.

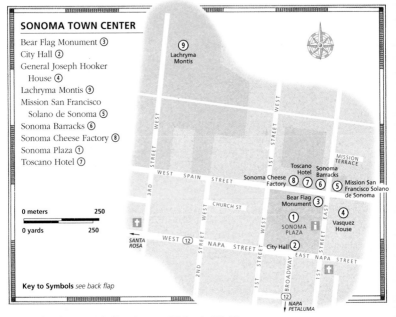

## SONOMA TOWN CENTER

Bear Flag Monument ③
City Hall ②
General Joseph Hooker
  House ④
Lachryma Montis ⑨
Mission San Francisco
  Solano de Sonoma ⑤
Sonoma Barracks ⑥
Sonoma Cheese Factory ⑧
Sonoma Plaza ①
Toscano Hotel ⑦

0 meters 250
0 yards 250

**Key to Symbols** see back flap

wood-frame building dates from the 1850s, when it was used as a general store and library. It was converted into a hotel for gold miners in 1886 and now belongs to the state.

### 🏠 Sonoma Cheese Factory

2 W Spain St. **Tel** *(707) 996-1931, (800) 535-2855.* ☐ *8:30am–5:30pm daily.* **www**.sonomacheesefactory. com

The famous Sonoma Jack cheese has been produced in the enormous vats in this factory since 1931. Visitors can sample the main varieties of the cheese for free and the cheese can be purchased in the factory shop or deli.

### 🏛 Lachryma Montis

W Spain & W 3rd Sts. **Tel** *(707) 938-9559.* ☐ *daily.* ● *Jan 1, Thanksgiving, Dec 25.* 🏷 **www**.napanet.net

Visitors can glimpse the lavish lifestyle of Mexican General Mariano Vallejo by exploring Lachryma Montis, his former home. This Gothic Revival house was built of redwood in 1851. It features an eclectic array of Vallejo memorabilia, which ranges from the general's silver epaulettes and a cattle brand to his favorite books.

The name of the house is Latin for "mountain tear," a reference to a mineral spring on the property.

Lachryma Montis, once home to Mexican General Mariano Vallejo

### 🏛 Mission San Francisco Solano de Sonoma

114 E Spain St. **Tel** *(707) 938-1519.* ☐ *10am–5pm daily.* ● *Jan 1, Thanksgiving, Dec 25.* 🏷

Named after a Peruvian saint, this beautifully restored old mission (commonly called the Sonoma Mission) was the last of the historic chain of 21

Façade of the Mission San Francisco Solano de Sonoma

Franciscan missions built in California *(see p46)*. Father José Altimira of Spain founded the mission in 1823 at a time when California was under Mexican rule. Today, all that survives of the original building is the corridor of Father Altimira's quarters. The present adobe chapel was built by General Vallejo in 1840 to be used by the town's families and soldiers.

### VISITORS' CHECKLIST

**Road map** A3. 🏠 *8,600.* ✈ *Sonoma County Airport, 6 miles (10 km) N of Santa Rosa.* 🚌 *90 Broadway & W Napa Sts, Sonoma Plaza.* ℹ *453 1st St E (707 996-1090); 23750 Arnold Dr (866 996-1090).* **www**.sonomavalley.com

### 🏛 Sonoma Barracks

20 E Spain St. **Tel** *(707) 938-1519.* ☐ *10am–5pm daily.* ● *Jan 1, Thanksgiving, Dec 25.* 🏷

Native American labor was used to build this two-story adobe structure between 1836 and 1840, when it served as the headquarters for General Vallejo and his troops. After the 1846 Bear Flag Revolt, the barracks became an outpost for the United States Army for about a decade. After being purchased by the state in the late 1950s, the building was restored. It is now a California Historical Landmark.

### SONOMA VALLEY WINERIES

The arms of the Sebastiani Vineyards

The Sonoma Valley has a rare perfect combination of soil, sun, and rain for growing superior wine grapes. In 1824, Father José Altimira planted Sonoma's first grapevines, in order to produce sacramental wine for the masses held at the Mission San Francisco Solano de Sonoma. When, in 1834, the ruling Mexican government secularized the mission, General Vallejo replanted grapevines on its land and sold the wine he produced to San Francisco merchants. In 1857, Hungarian Count Agoston Haraszthy *(see p455)* planted the nation's first European varietals at Sonoma's Buena Vista Winery, now the oldest premium winery in the state.

The Sonoma Valley encompasses the Sonoma Valley, Carneros, and Sonoma Mountain wine-growing regions. The climate varies slightly in each region, creating different environments suitable for producing particular grape varieties, including Cabernet Sauvignon and Chardonnay. Today, Sonoma Valley is home to more than 300 wineries, which have 55,000 acres (22,258 ha) of grape plantations.

Some of the valley's most notable wineries are Sebastiani Vineyards, Sonoma's largest premium-variety winery; Benziger Family Winery; Gundlach-Bundschu Winery; and Château St. Jean. Most of the wineries offer picnic areas, though most charge for tastings.

Vineyards in the Sonoma Valley

# GOLD COUNTRY AND THE CENTRAL VALLEY

*L*ocated at the geographical heart of California, the Gold Country is also central to the state's allure as the land of overnight success. Long before the gilded world of Hollywood took shape, this was a real life El Dorado, where a thick vein of solid gold, known as the Mother Lode, sat waiting to be discovered.

The Gold Country is largely rural, despite being the birthplace of modern California with the Gold Rush of 1849 and the designation of Sacramento as state capital.

Before the miners arrived, this quiet region, located on the far fringes of the Spanish colonial empire, was sparsely populated by members of the Miwok and Maidu peoples. With the discovery of gold flakes in January 1848, however, the region turned into a lawless jamboree, and by 1852 an estimated 200,000 men from all over the world were working in the mines. But by 1860 most of the region had fallen silent again, as the mining boom went bust *(see pp48–9)*.

A few years after the Gold Rush, the region experienced another short-lived boom. The transcontinental railroad was constructed through the Sierra Nevada Mountains by low-paid laborers, many of whom were Chinese *(see pp50–51)*. In the early 20th century, the Central Valley became the heart of the state's thriving agricultural industry, which today exports fruit and vegetables worldwide.

Stretching for more than 100 miles (160 km) north to south, the region's landscape is ideal for leisurely hikes or afternoon picnics. The Gold Country also offers one of California's best scenic drives along Hwy 49. The route climbs up and down rocky ridges between pastoral ranch lands, lined with oak trees and crossed by fast-flowing rivers. Many of the picturesque towns it passes through, such as Sutter Creek, have survived unchanged since the Gold Rush.

**Malakoff Diggins Historic Park, preserving the heyday of the Gold Rush**

◁ California State Capitol in Sacramento

# Exploring the Gold Country

The Gold Country ranges from flat delta flood plains to the rugged, river-carved foothills of the Sierra Nevada Mountains. At the heart of the region is Sacramento, the state capital and largest Gold Country city, which has the highest concentration of sights. But the real attraction of this area is in traveling along its many scenic routes. The rural landscape is dotted with small historic towns. Some are still thriving communities, while others are ghostly memorials to their past. The Central Valley, along I-5, is scattered with picturesque farming towns. Larger towns, such as Nevada City and Sutter Creek, make excellent bases for a Gold Country tour, and visitors are welcomed and well taken care of everywhere.

**Impressive State Capitol building in Sacramento**

**Parrots Ferry Bridge over the picturesque New Melones Lake along Hwy 49 in Tuolumne County**

## SIGHTS AT A GLANCE

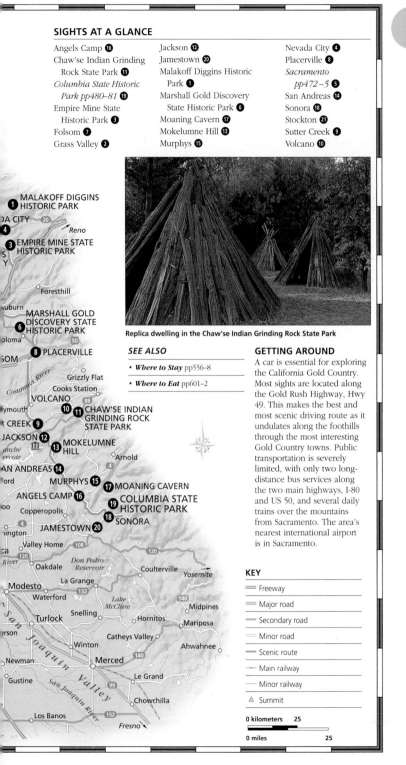

MALAKOFF DIGGINS
① HISTORIC PARK

DA CITY ⑳

④ Reno

③ EMPIRE MINE STATE
HISTORIC PARK
Y

Foresthill

Auburn

MARSHALL GOLD
⑥ DISCOVERY STATE
HISTORIC PARK

oloma

SOM ⑧ PLACERVILLE

Cosumnes River Grizzly Flat

Cooks Station

VOLCANO

lymouth ⑩ ⑪ CHAW'SE INDIAN
GRINDING ROCK
R CREEK ⑨ STATE PARK

JACKSON ⑫

anche ⑬ MOKELUMNE
ervoir HILL

Arnold

AN ANDREAS ⑭

ford

MURPHYS ⑮ ⑰ MOANING CAVERN

ANGELS CAMP ⑯ COLUMBIA STATE
oo ⑲ HISTORIC PARK
Copperopolis ⑱ SONORA

ington JAMESTOWN ⑳

Valley Home

ca Don Pedro
River Oakdale Reservoir Coulterville Yosemite

La Grange

Modesto Lake
Waterford McClure Midpines

Snelling Hornitos Mariposa

Turlock

Catheys Valley Ahwahnee

Winton

erson Merced

Newman Le Grand

Gustine San Joaquin River

Los Banos Chowchilla

Fresno

Replica dwelling in the Chaw'se Indian Grinding Rock State Park

### SEE ALSO

- *Where to Stay* pp556–8

- *Where to Eat* pp601–2

### GETTING AROUND

A car is essential for exploring the California Gold Country. Most sights are located along the Gold Rush Highway, Hwy 49. This makes the best and most scenic driving route as it undulates along the foothills through the most interesting Gold Country towns. Public transportation is severely limited, with only two long-distance bus services along the two main highways, I-80 and US 50, and several daily trains over the mountains from Sacramento. The area's nearest international airport is in Sacramento.

### KEY

| | |
|---|---|
| ▬▬ | Freeway |
| ▬▬ | Major road |
| ▬▬ | Secondary road |
| — | Minor road |
| ▬ | Scenic route |
| –••– | Main railway |
| —— | Minor railway |
| △ | Summit |

0 kilometers    25

0 miles    25

The man-made canyon created by hydraulic mining at Malakoff Diggins

## Malakoff Diggins Historic Park **①**

**Road map** B3. **Tel** (530) 265-2740. 🚌 from Nevada City. ◯ daily. **Museum:** 10am–4pm daily. ● buildings Oct–Apr. 🏛 ♿ 📷 www.parks.ca.gov

As the original gold mining techniques became less rewarding in the late 1850s, miners turned to increasingly powerful and destructive ways of extracting the valuable ore. When the more easily recoverable surface deposits disappeared, the miners began to strip away the soil with powerful jets of pressurized water. Spraying more than 200,000 gal (115,000 liters) of water per hour, the jets washed away entire mountainsides in search of gold, a process known as hydraulic mining. In 1884 the California legislature forbade the dumping of gravel into streams, but huge swathes of land had already been ruined and the rivers had been clogged up with debris *(see pp48–9)*. The largest of these hydraulic mining operations was at Malakoff Diggins, 27 miles (45 km) northeast of Hwy 49, in the mountains above Nevada City. The eroded hillsides created a canyon that now forms an eerily beautiful historic park, with several preserved buildings from the 1870s mining town of North Bloomfield.

## Grass Valley **②**

**Road map** B3. 👥 9,000. 🚗 ℹ 248 Mill St (530) 273-4667. www.grassvalleychamber.com

Long the largest and busiest town in the northern Gold Country, Grass Valley served the Empire Mine and other nearby hard rock gold mines.

In the 1870s and 1880s Grass Valley welcomed workers from the tin mines of Cornwall, England, who were known as "Cousin Jacks." Their expertise enabled the local mines to recover underground ore deposits and so remain in business after the rest of the area had fallen quiet *(see pp48–9)*. Grass Valley also has one of California's best mining museums. The **North Star Mine Powerhouse and Pelton Wheel Museum** is situated in the powerhouse of the former North Star Mine. Surrounding the entrance are the giant Pelton wheels that increased production in the region's underground mines. Displays include a stamp mill (a giant pulverizer used to crush ore), a Cornish pump (used to filter out underground water), and various artifacts relating to the Cornish background of the local miners.

A nugget of gold set inside quartz crystal

**🏛 North Star Mine and Pelton Wheel Museum**
Mill St at Allison Ranch Rd.
**Tel** (530) 273-4255. ◯ May–Oct: 10am–5pm daily. **Donation.**

## Empire Mine State Historic Park **③**

**Tel** (530) 273-8522. 🚌 from Nevada City. ◯ daily. ● Jan 1, Thanksgiving, Dec 25. 🏛 ♿ Grounds & Empire Cottage. 📷 www.parks.ca.gov

One of the longest surviving and most lucrative gold mining operations in the state, the Empire Mine was in business until 1956. It has now been preserved by the state as a historic park. Starting with surface workings in the 1850s, the Empire Mine grew to include 365 miles (585 km) of underground tunnels, from which pure gold estimated at 5.8 million ounces (16.5 million grams) was recovered.

Head frames, which held the mine's elevator shafts and other mining equipment, are scattered over the park's 785 acres (318 ha), but for a real sense of how much money was made here you should visit Empire Cottage.

Designed by San Franciscan architect Willis Polk in 1897 for the mine's owner, William Bourn, the granite and red-brick exterior resembles an English manor house, while the redwood interior gives an air of casual affluence. The gardens next door to the cottage contain nearly 1,000 rose bushes and a large greenhouse.

More exhibits on the history of the Empire Mine and on hard-rock gold mining are on display in the visitors' center, along with samples of the precious metal.

Original stamp mill used to crush ore at the Empire Mine

Firehouse Number 1's façade, a
Nevada City landmark

# Nevada City ❹

**Road map** B3. 🏛 *2,855.* 🚗 🚌
🛈 *132 Main St (800 655-6569).*
**www**.nevadacitychamber.com

With Victorian houses and
commercial buildings lining
its steep streets, picturesque
Nevada City deserves its
reputation as "Queen of the
Northern Mines." Located at
the northern end of the
Mother Lode gold fields,

Nevada City thrived until gold
mining peaked in the 1860s,
then it faded into oblivion.
Nearly a century later, the city
was resurrected as a tourist
destination, with galleries,
restaurants, and inns re-creat-
ing Gold Rush themes.

Hwy 49 takes visitors arriving in Nevada City to the foot
of Broad Street. Looking up
the street, the large building
on the left is the **National
Hotel**. One of the oldest hotels
in California, it first opened in
the mid-1850s *(see p557).*

A block east of the hotel is
**Firehouse Number 1 Museum**,
one of the region's most
photographed façades. Dainty
balconies and a white cupola
decorate the exterior, and
inside, a small museum displays local Maidu
Indian artifacts,
pioneer relics,
including some
relating to the tragic
Donner Party *(see
p486),* and the altar
from a Gold Rush
Chinese temple.
Antique mining
devices are dis-
played in the park

opposite, and several plaques
on the city's walls commemorate events from its past.

Back on Broad Street, the
arcaded brick façade marks
the historic **Nevada Theater**,
which has been in use as a
performance venue since
1865. A block to the south is
the **Miner's Foundry**, an old
metalworks where the innovative Pelton wheel was first
developed and produced.
A block to the north is the
Art Deco façade of the city's
**County Courthouse**, one
of the city's few 20th-century
works of architecture.

🏛 **Firehouse Number
1 Museum**
214 Main St. **Tel** *(530) 265-5468.*
⏰ *times vary, call first.* **Donation**.

Nevada Theater, used as a playhouse since 1865

**NEVADA CITY CENTER**

County Courthouse ③
Firehouse Number 1 ②
First Methodist
   Church ④
National
   Hotel ①

**Key to Symbols** *see back flap*

0 meters  100
0 vards   100

# Street-by-Street: Old Sacramento ❺

**Californian railroad logo**

Covering six blocks between the river and the modern city, Old Sacramento preserves many historic buildings within a precinct of shops, restaurants, and museums. Some of the structures protected here were built to serve the gold miners of 1849 (*see pp48–9*), but most date from the 1860s and 1870s, when Sacramento confirmed its position as the link between rural California and the commercial centers along the coast. The Pony Express and transcontinental railroad both had their western terminus here, with paddle-wheel riverboats providing the connection to San Francisco. A handful of museums trace the area's historic importance, and the riverfront location is ideal for walking and cycling.

**Delta King Riverboat**
*One of the last Sacramento Delta riverboats still afloat, this moored paddle-wheel steamer is now a hotel and restaurant.*

**The former steamboat depot** was the embarkation point for freight bound for San Francisco in the 1860s.

**Old Schoolhouse**
*This one-room building is typical of a 19th-century California schoolhouse.*

0 meters   5
0 yards   5

**Theodore Judah Monument**
*This bas-relief commemorates Theodore Judah, the engineer who planned the transcontinental railroad (see pp50–51).*

FRONT STREET

L STREET

## STAR SIGHTS

★ BF Hastings Building

★ California State Railroad Museum

KEY

– – – Suggested route

The **Discovery Museum**, housed in the city's former municipal buildings, contains memorabilia of Old Sacramento's 19th-century heyday.

### ★ California State Railroad Museum
*Immaculately restored locomotives and train cars are part of this extensive collection.*

### Eagle Theatre
*This is a reconstruction of the original theater, built in 1849 but ruined by a flood in 1850.*

**Visitors' Center**

### Pony Express Monument
*This statue commemorates the 1,966-mile (3,163-km) mail run from Sacramento to St. Joseph, Missouri.*

**CA Military Museum**

**The old fire-house**, built in 1853, was one of the first buildings to be restored.

### ★ BF Hastings Building
*For a sense of what the legal system was like in California's early days, visit the restored chambers of the original Supreme Court, located above a general store.*

# Sacramento: California State Capitol

Standing at the center of a vast, landscaped park, the California State Capitol is Sacramento's primary landmark and one of the state's handsomest buildings. It was designed in 1860 by Reuben Clark and Miner F Butler in grand Greek Revival style, with Corinthian porticos and a tall central dome. The building was completed in 1874 after almost 15 years of construction and expenses totaling $2.5 million. The Capitol was expanded in the 1920s and 1950s and completely renovated and restored in the 1970s. The Governor of California operates from his Capitol office, but the building also stands as a shining example of the Golden State's proud past.

Along with the chambers of the state legislature, which are open to visitors when they are in session, the Capitol serves as a museum of the state's political and cultural history.

**VISITORS' CHECKLIST**

10th St & L St., Capitol Mall, Capitol Park. **Road map** B3.
**Tel** (916) 324-0333. 🚌 from LA & San Francisco. 🚌 30, 31, 36, 38, 61, 62. ◯ 9am–5pm daily.
● Jan 1, Thanksgiving, Dec 25.
🗹 📷 ♿ first floor only. 🅰 🅱
💻 www.capitolmuseum.ca.gov

**★ Capitol Rotunda**
*The impressive rotunda was restored to its original 19th-century splendor in 1975. The copper ball on top of the dome is plated in gold.*

**Original 1860 statuary**

**Entrance**

**The Historic Offices** on the first floor contain a few government offices restored to their turn-of-the-century appearance.

**★ State Senate Chamber**
*The mezzanine gallery is open all year, but it is most interesting when the legislature is in session, making speeches and holding votes on issues of importance.*

**A portrait of George Washington**, the first US president, occupies the focal point on the Chamber wall.

**STAR FEATURES**

★ Capitol Rotunda

★ State Senate Chamber

# 🏛 Crocker Art Museum

216 O St. **Tel** *(916) 808-7000.*
⬜ *10am–1pm Tue & Wed, 10am–9pm Thu, 10am–5pm Fri–Sun.*
● *Jan 1, Thanksgiving, Dec 25.*
🎟 🅿 *(free public hols)*
**www**.crockerartmuseum.org

Founded in 1873, this is the oldest public art museum west of the Mississippi. The collection includes Victorian painting and sculpture from Asia, Europe, and the US, but its real strength is the California art and photography, and the touring shows.

Another prime attraction is the Italianate Victorian building itself, designed by the architect Seth Babson. The gallery includes polychrome tile floors, elaborately carved woodwork, and a graceful central staircase. The Crocker also houses a 125,000-sq-ft (11,610-sq-m) Teel Family Pavilion – a classic, contemporary design that complements the historic structures.

**Foyer of the Crocker Art Gallery**

# 🏕 Sutter's Fort State Historic Park

2701 L St. **Tel** *(916) 445-4422.*
⬜ *10am–5pm daily.* ● *Jan 1, Thanksgiving, Dec 25.* 🎟
**www**.parks.ca.gov

Now somewhat marooned amid the suburban streets of the modern state capital, Sutter's Fort in its heyday was one of the most important and populous sites in early California history.

Established by John Sutter in 1839, the fort became the cultural and economic center of northern California in the years leading up to the Gold Rush. Apart from the 21 Spanish missions along the coast, it was the only Anglo-European settlement in California. Throughout the 1840s, new immigrants following the overland trails from the eastern states stopped here for the fort's blacksmith shop, grain mill, and many other facilities.

**Reconstructed 19th-century kitchen at Sutter's Fort**

The three-story central building is all that survives of the original fort. The rest of the complex has been reconstructed to give a picture of frontier life. A courtyard, surrounded by 18-ft (5.5-m) walls, houses various historical exhibits along a self-guided audio tour. These include a prison, a bakery, and a blacksmith's. This is one of the few official sites in California where the Mexican flag still flies.

# 🏛 State Indian Museum

2618 K St. **Tel** *(916) 324-0971.*
⬜ *10am–5pm daily.* ● *Jan 1, Thanksgiving, Dec 25.* 🎟
**www**.parks.ca.gov

This area of California was once occupied by the Maidu people. This small but fascinating museum, set in a park adjacent to Sutter's Fort, explores the different Native American cultures that existed in the state before the 16th-century arrival of the first Europeans *(see pp44–5)*. Displays of handicrafts focus on the beautiful reed baskets that held both a practical and spiritual value to the Indians, and a series of dioramas recreate the look and feel of tribal reservations. Slide shows, tape recordings, and films document other aspects of tribal culture, from language to agricultural skills.

Special programs, generally held on weekends, celebrate the survival of ancient Native American ways of life into the present day.

---

## JOHN SUTTER

The story of the early California entrepreneur John Sutter is a classic real-life rags to riches to rags adventure. Following bankruptcy in his native Switzerland, Sutter emigrated to California in 1839. Only a year after his arrival, he was granted a 50,000-acre (20,000-ha) tract of land by the Mexican government, which he patriotically named New Helvetia (New Switzerland). In 1843 Sutter went into debt once again in order to buy Fort Ross on the northern coast from its Russian owners *(see p460)*. For the next five years his land and wealth made him virtual lord and master over most of northern California.

However, the discovery of gold flakes by his employee James Marshall at his mill in 1848 *(see p470)* spelled the end of his vast empire. Thousands of miners swarmed to the region and almost immediately took over his land. Sutter spent the rest of his life in Washington, DC, hoping for compensation from the US government, but he died almost penniless in 1880.

**John Sutter (1802–80)**

Reconstructed Sutter's Mill, where gold was first discovered

# Marshall Gold Discovery State Historic Park ❻

310 Back St, Coloma. **Road map** B3.
**Tel** (530) 622-3470. 🚌 from
Placerville. ⭘ 8am–sunset daily.
⬤ Jan 1, Thanksgiving, Dec 25. 🎫
🚹 📷 www.parks.ca.gov

Covering some 250 acres
(101 ha) along the banks of
the American River, this
peaceful state park protects
and interprets the site where
gold was first discovered in
January 1848. James Marshall
spotted shiny flakes in the
water channel of a sawmill he
and his fellow workmen were
building for John Sutter (see
p475), and the rest is history.

Within a year, some 10,000
miners had turned Coloma
into a thriving city, but with
news of even richer deposits
elsewhere the boom went
bust as quickly as it began,
and little remains from this era.

A reproduction of Sutter's
Mill stands on the original site,
and a statue of James Marshall
sits on a nearby hill to mark
the spot where he is buried.
The park's visitors' center includes the small **Gold Country
Museum** with Native American artifacts, films, and other
displays on the discovery of
gold, as well as memorabilia
relating to James Marshall.

🏛 **Gold Country Museum**
1273 High St, Auburn. **Tel** (530)
889-6500. ⭘ 10am–4pm daily (to
3pm Sep–Mar). ⬤ Jan 1, Thanksgiving, Dec 25. 🎫 www.placer.ca.gov

# Folsom ❼

**Road map** B3. 🏘 46,000. 🚌
🚹 200 Wool St (916 985-2698).
www.folsomchamber.com

Folsom is now a pleasant
Sacramento suburb, despite
being the site of the state
penitentiary made famous by
Johnny Cash's 1970s song
"Folsom Prison Blues."

It played an important role
as the last station on the Pony
Express and transcontinental
railroad. Folsom is now one
of the few remaining transcontinental railroad sites, as
documented in the local
**Folsom History Museum**.
Antique shops line the Wild
West-style Sutter Street, set
amid boxcars and other
railroad memorabilia.

At the foot of Riley Street,
behind Folsom Dam, there is
also a large lake, which is a
popular summer vacation spot
for boating and fishing.

🏛 **Folsom History Museum**
823 Sutter St. **Tel** (916) 985-2707.
⭘ 11am–4pm Tue–Sun.
⬤ public hols. **Donation**.
www.folsomhistorymuseum.org

# Placerville ❽

**Road map** B3. 🏘 15,000. 🚌
🚹 542 Main St (530 621-5885).
www.eldoradocounty.org

During the Gold Rush,
Placerville was a busy supply
center for the surrounding
mining camps. Still located on
one of the main routes to

Sacramento, Placerville has
retained its importance as
a transportation center,
although the stagecoaches
have long since given way to
cars and trucks along US 50.

The downtown business
district preserves a handful of
historic structures and sites,
but the best sense of Placerville's past comes from the
**Placerville History Museum**
on Main Street and the **El
Dorado County Historical
Museum**. The displays range
from old mining equipment
and a replica of a 19th-century
general store to artifacts from
the Chinese settlement and
other local historical exhibits.

🏛 **El Dorado County
Historical Museum**
104 Placerville Dr. **Tel** (530 )621-
5865. ⭘ 10am–4pm Wed–Sat,
noon–4pm Tue & Sun. ⬤ public
hols. **Donation**.

Gold Rush general store in
Placerville's El Dorado Museum

# Sutter Creek ❾

**Road map** B3. 🏘 2,000. 🚌
🚹 71-A Main St. (209 267-1344).
www.suttercreek.org

Named after John Sutter
(see p475), Sutter Creek is
one of the prettiest Gold
Country towns, full of antique
shops and whitewashed
country inns. It grew up
around 1860 to service the
Old Eureka Mine, which was
owned by Hetty Green, re-
putedly the "Richest Woman
in the World."

Leland Stanford, one of the "Big Four" railroad barons (*see pp50–51*), made his fortune in Sutter Creek. He put $5,000 into the town's Lincoln Mine, which turned into a multimillion-dollar investment. He used the money to become a railroad magnate and then, governor of California.

An attractive drive in the region is along Sutter Creek Road to Volcano, past remains of former mining equipment.

## Volcano ⑩

**Road map** B3. 🏚 *150.* 🚌 ℹ *115 Main St, Jackson (209 223-0350).* **www**.amadorcountychamber.com

For a taste of the Gold Rush without the tourist trappings, visit Volcano, a picturesque ghost of a mining town containing a wealth of historic sights.

During the Gold Rush, the town had an unusual reputation for sophistication and culture, creating the state's first library and its first astronomical observatory. The old jail, stagecoach office, brewery, and a cannon dating from the Civil War are among the preserved buildings and artifacts on display around the four-block town. The most attractive Victorian building is the former historic **St. George Hotel**, covered with Virginia creeper.

Springtime visitors to the region should also follow the signs to Daffodil Hill, 3 miles (5 km) north of Volcano, when more than 300,000 naturalized daffodil bulbs come into full bloom on the hillside.

🏨 **St. George Hotel**
16104 Main St, off Volcano Rd.
**Tel** (209) 296-4458.
**www**.stgeorgehotel.com

## Indian Grinding Rock State Historic Park ⑪

🚌 *from Sacramento.* 🚗 *from Sacramento.* 🚗 *from Jackson.* **Tel** *(209) 296-7488.* ℹ *14881 Pine Grove, Volcano Rd.* 🕐 *11am–3pm Mon–Fri, 10am–6pm Sat & Sun.* **www**.parks.ca.gov

Tucked away amid the oak trees in the hills above Jackson, this 136-acre (55-ha) park protects one of the largest and most complete Native American sites in the country. The area was once home to the Miwok people and the park is dedicated to their past and future. The aim of this comprehensive museum is to increase understanding of Native American life, centering on the Californian foothill peoples. Exhibits include an array of basketry, dance regalia, and ancient tools.

Hundreds of mortar holes form the main focus of the park. These limestone pockets were formed by generations of Miwok Indians grinding meal from acorns. There are also many rock carvings and replica Miwok dwellings.

**St. Sava's Serbian Orthodox Church outside Jackson**

## Jackson ⑫

**Road map** B3. 🏚 *3,500.* 🚌 ℹ *115 Main St (209 223-0350).* **www**.amadorcountychamber.com

Located at the crossroads of two main Gold Rush trails, Jackson was once a bustling gold mining community and has continued to thrive as a commercial center and lumber mill town since 1850.

The town center features a number of old Gold Rush buildings, but the most interesting stop is the **Amador County Museum**, located on a hill above the town. Here visitors can view working models of stamp mills (*see p470*) and a variety of other old mining equipment.

North of the town, in a small park off Hwy 49, are the massive tailing wheels from the Kennedy Mine, one of the deepest in the US. Reaching 58 ft (18 m) in diameter, these wheels were used to dispose of leftover rocks after the gold had been extracted. St. Sava's Serbian Orthodox Church, built in 1894 with a delicate white steeple, is also in the park. It is a testament to one of many cultures that contributed to the history of the Gold Country.

🏛 **Amador County Museum**
225 Church St, Jackson.
**Tel** *(209) 223-6375.*
🕐 *10am–4pm Wed–Sun.*
🚫 *public hols.* **Donation.**

**Replica of a Miwok ceremonial roundhouse in Chaw'se State Park**

**Headstone on "Moke Hill"**

## Mokelumne Hill ⑬

**Road map** B3. 👥 *1,200.*
ℹ️ *1192 S Main St, Angels Camp (209 736-0049; 800 225-3764).*
**www**.visitcalaveras.org

Bypassed by Highway 49, Mokelumne Hill is one of the most intriguing old Gold Country towns. A handful of old buildings, including the Hotel Leger and the old Wells Fargo stagecoach station, form a one-block business district. But the sleepy ambience of "Moke Hill," as it is commonly known, belies the town's unsavory and violent history.

Although much of the town has fallen into picturesque decay, during the Gold Rush era the hotels and saloons were packed with rowdy miners, whose drunken fights resulted in an average of one killing per week. Many of the victims ended up in the hill-top Protestant Cemetery – a short walk to the west of town. Here the multilingual headstones are now all that remain of the international population who came here in search of gold.

## San Andreas ⑭

**Road map** B3. 👥 *1,500.* ℹ️ *1192 S Main St, Angels Camp (209 736-0049).* **www**.visitcalaveras.org

San Andreas is now a small, bustling city, home to the Calaveras County government. During the Gold Rush era,

however, it was a gritty mining camp, originally built in 1848 by Mexicans who were later forcibly removed by white Americans after rich deposits of gold were found *(see pp48–9).* In 1883 the legendary outlaw Black Bart was captured here.

Very little now remains from the Gold Rush days, although San Andreas does house one of the Gold Country's best museums, the **Calaveras County Historical Museum**, in the old courthouse just north of Hwy 49. Along with exhibits tracing gold mining history from 1848 to the 1930s, the collection includes Miwok Indian artifacts and the courtroom where Black Bart was tried and convicted. His prison cell during the trial, situated behind the museum, is now surrounded by a pleasant, if somewhat incongruous, garden of indigenous plants and trees.

🏛 **Calaveras County Museum & Archives**
30 N Main St. **Tel** *(209) 754-1058.*
⏰ *10am–4pm daily.* ⬤ *Jan 1, Thanksgiving, Dec 25.* 🈳

## Murphys ⑮

**Road map** B3. 👥 *2,000.* ℹ️ *1192 S Main St, Angels Camp (209 736-0049).* **www**.visitcalaveras.org

With mature sycamores, elms, and locust trees lining its quiet streets, Murphys is among the prettiest towns in the southern Gold Country. It offers a quiet break from the frantic tourism of many of the

other Mother Lode towns and sights in the area.

Having played host to such luminaries as Ulysses S Grant, Mark Twain, and Will Rogers, the restored Murphys Hotel, built in 1855, is now the town landmark. Across the street, the **Old-Timers' Museum** houses a quirky collection of Gold Rush memorabilia. The outside wall displays a series of humorous plaques detailing the town's history.

🏛 **Old-Timers' Museum**
450 Main St. **Tel** *(209) 728-1160.*
⏰ *11am–4pm Fri–Sun.* ⬤ *Jan 1, Thanksgiving, Dec 25.* 🈳

## Angels Camp ⑯

**Road map** B3. 👥 *3,000.*
ℹ️ *1211 S Main St (209 736-0049).*

Angels Camp is a former gold mining town that was best known as the real-life location of Mark Twain's classic short story "The Celebrated Jumping Frog of Calaveras County" *(see pp26–7).* Today the town has grown into a commercial center for the surrounding area.

A few historic structures, including the Angels Hotel where Twain heard the story of the jumping frog, still line the steep streets of the compact downtown area, which comes alive every May for a popular reenactment of the frog-jumping competition.

Two huge 19th-century locomotives stand on Hwy 49 in front of the **Angels Camp Museum**, which contains a standard array of old mining

**Picturesque main street of the gold mining town, Angels Camp**

equipment. There is also a large collection of Indian artifacts and exhibits on Mark Twain and the jumping frog.

### 🏛 Angels Camp Museum

753 S Main St. **Tel** (209) 736-2963. ◯ Mar–mid-Nov: 10am–4pm Thu–Mon; mid-Nov–Feb: 10am–4pm Sat & Sun. ● Thanksgiving, Dec. 🖾

## Moaning Cavern ⑰

5350 Moaning Cave Rd, Vallecito. **Tel** (209) 736-2708, (866) 762-2837. ◯ daily. 🖾 www.caverntours.com

One of the largest limestone caverns in the area, Moaning Cavern took its name from the groaning sound emitted by the wind flowing out of the entrance. Unfortunately the sound was destroyed when the cavern was enlarged to improve public access. Guided tours, lasting about an hour, focus on the main "room," which is about 165 ft (50 m) high. Visitors can descend into the caves using the stairs or, if they dare, by rappelling down a rope.

Nineteenth-century St. James Episcopal Church in Sonora

A guided tour of Moaning Cavern

## Sonora ⑱

**Road map** B3. 🏠 5,000. 🚌
🛈 222 S. Shepherd St (209) 532-4212. www.sonoraca.com

Outstripping Columbia (see pp480–81) for the seat of county government during the Gold Rush, Sonora is now the Tuolumne County seat and a busy commercial center and logging town. Its sedate main street shows little sign of the town's once-violent reputation during the second half of the 19th century. Many of its historic buildings have been preserved, including the St. James Episcopal Church on Washington Street. There are also a number of interesting Victorian houses.

Sonora's old jail was built in 1857 and renovated after being destroyed by fire in 1866. It is now home to the **Tuolumne County Museum and History Center**. It houses a collection of Gold Rush artifacts, including gold nuggets and a number of 19th-century photographs.

### 🏛 Tuolumne County Museum and History Center

158 W Bradford Ave. **Tel** (209) 532-1317. ◯ 10am–4pm Mon–Fri, 10am–3:30pm Sat. ● Jan 1, Dec 25.

### BLACK BART

Famous for his politeness to his victims and his habit of leaving doggerel poetry at the scene of his crimes, the outlaw known affectionately as Black Bart has become one of the state's best-loved legends.

After holding up stagecoaches between 1877 and 1883, he was caught when the laundry mark on his handkerchief was traced to San Francisco. Black Bart turned out to be Charles Boles, a mining engineer.

After being tried and convicted in San Andreas, he spent five years in San Quentin prison. He disappeared from public view after his release in 1888.

The outlaw Black Bart

# Street-by-Street: Columbia State Historic Park ⑲

**Stagecoach schedule sign**

At the height of the Gold Rush, Columbia was one of the largest and most important towns in the Gold Country. Most of California's mining camps were abandoned; they quickly disintegrated and disappeared after the gold ran out in the late 1850s. Unusually, Columbia remained active. It was proudly kept intact by its remaining residents until 1945, when the California government turned the entire town into a state historic park. A few of the buildings have been reconstructed, but the majority of them have been preserved in their original state.

**The Chinese Herb Shop** contains traditional medicines brought to the state by Chinese immigrants.

**City Hotel**

**Johnson's Livery Stable**
*Several old-style wagons are housed here.*

PACIFIC STREET

JACKSON STREET

MAIN STREET

COLUMBIA STREET

BROADWAY

STATE STREET

Old jail

Museum

FULTON STREET

WASHINGTON STREET

★ **Wells Fargo Express Office**
*This stagecoach office was the center of the town's transportation network.*

**Matelot Gulch Miners Supply**
*Visitors are sold pans of sand and gravel here so that they can try panning for gold themselves.*

## VISITORS' CHECKLIST

Hwy 49. **Road map** B3. 🛈 22708 Broadway (209) 588-9128. 🚉 🚌 **Wells Fargo Express Office** ◯ 10am–4pm daily (Jun–Aug until 6pm). ● Thanksgiving, Dec 25. 🔲 **Columbia Schoolhouse** ◯ 10am–4pm daily (Jun–Aug until 6pm). ● Thanksgiving, Dec 25. 🔲 www.parks.ca.gov

★ **Columbia Schoolhouse**
*The building was last used as a school in 1937, but in 1960 it was restored with the help of funds raised by California schoolchildren.*

| 0 meters | 100 |
|---|---|
| 0 yards | 100 |

**KEY**

– – – Suggested route

### STAR SIGHTS

★ Columbia Schoolhouse

★ Wells Fargo Express Office

**Historic antique store, The Emporium, on Main Street, Jamestown**

## Jamestown ❷⓿

**Road map** B3. 🏙 2,300. 🚌 🛈 222 South Shephard St, Sonora (209 532-4212). www.jamestown-ca.com

Jamestown was home to the largest gold mine in operation until 1993. Some of the historic town was destroyed by fire in 1966, but Main Street still has many picturesque buildings.

**Railtown 1897 State Historic Park**, north of downtown, preserves the steam locomotives and historic carriages of the Sierra Railroad. Rides are offered on weekends (April to October).

🏛 **Railtown 1897 State Historic Park**
5th Ave & Reservoir Rd. **Tel** (209) 984-3953. ◯ daily. ● Jan 1, Thnksg, Dec 25. **Donation**.

## Stockton ❷❶

**Road map** B3. 🏙 250,000. 🚌 🛈 445 W Weber Ave, Suite 220 (877) 778-6258 www.visitstockton.org

Stockton is an inland port and a transportation hub for Central Valley farms. It is set on the eastern edge of the delta at the confluence of the Sacramento, American, and San Joaquin Rivers. Stockton's history is told at the Haggin Museum, which includes Native American crafts, 19th-century storefronts and works by Renoir. It also traces the development by a local inventor of the Caterpillar track.

🏛 **Haggin Museum**
1201 n Pershing Ave. **Tel** (209) 462-4116. ◯ Wed–Sun, 1:30–5pm. ● Jan 1, Dec 23–25, 30, 31. 🔲 (free 1st Sat every month).

### JOAQUIN MURIETA: THE CALIFORNIA BANDIT

Little documentary evidence exists about Joaquin Murieta, the Gold Country criminal portrayed as everything from a 19th-century Gold Rush Robin Hood to a murderous outlaw.

His legend can be traced to the writer John Rollins Ridge, who published a novel called *The Life and Adventures of Joaquin Murieta, Celebrated California Bandit* in 1854. Ridge drew on the criminal exploits of five outlaws, all named Joaquin. The Governor of California offered a $1,000 reward for the capture of any of these men. In 1853 a man named Harry Love delivered the head of one Joaquin Murieta, which had been pickled in a glass jar. Ridge's novel was published the following year, and the Murieta legend was born.

# THE HIGH SIERRAS

F orming a towering wall along the eastern side of central California, the densely forested Sierra Nevada mountains rise to over 14,000 ft (4,270 m) and include many of the most impressive peaks in the mainland United States. Known as the High Sierras, these rugged mountains make up one of the state's most popular recreation areas, preserved by a series of splendid national parks.

The most popular High Sierras destination is Yosemite National Park, one of the world's most spectacular natural sights. Waterfalls, ranging from delicate cascades to raging torrents, drop steeply down the granite walls of this alpine valley. Rock-climbers, photographers, and sightseers come from all over the globe to experience the park first-hand. South of Yosemite, the Sequoia and Kings Canyon National Parks preserve more of the state's high country scenery, including groves of sequoia, the tallest living trees on earth.

To the north, Lake Tahoe has been a year-round recreational haven for over a century. It offers hiking, camping, and water sports on one of the bluest bodies of water in the US. In winter, the region becomes a skier's paradise, with many Olympic-class resorts.

East of the Sierra Nevada's granite spine lies a less-visited but equally compelling region. The ghost town of Bodie is preserved as it was when gold miners abandoned it in 1882. Nearby, Mono Lake is an eerie sight of limestone towers and alkaline water. The eastern slope of the High Sierras merits exploration, including the 14,500-ft (4,420-m) Mount Whitney, the highest peak on the US mainland, and the bristlecone pines of the White Mountains, some of which are more than 4,000 years old.

**Bodie State Historic Park, a preserved ghost town to the east of the Sierras**

◁ Imposing granite peak of Half Dome in Yosemite National Park

# Exploring the High Sierras

The highest peaks, the tallest trees, and some of the most impressive natural scenery in the United States are found in California's Sierra Nevada. This region includes one of the best-known wonders of the world, Yosemite National Park, as well as countless other remarkable examples of nature's prowess. North of Yosemite, the emerald waters of Lake Tahoe are set within an alpine valley at the highest point of the High Sierras, while to the south stand the immense groves of Sequoia and Kings Canyon National Parks.

Other than the resorts encircling Lake Tahoe, there are no large towns in the High Sierras. East of the mountains, however, near the shores of the eerily beautiful Mono Lake, the best ghost town in the state, Bodie, is immaculately preserved.

## SIGHTS AT A GLANCE

## HOW THE SIERRAS WERE MADE

The Sierras were formed 3 million years ago when a giant granite batholith (igneous rock), approximately 6 miles (10 km) deep, lifted up the earth's surface and tilted it from a tectonic "hinge" beneath California's Central Valley. The effects of this uplift are most clearly visible on the steep eastern slopes, typical of mountains on the earth's faults. The western slopes are more gradual, made up of sedimentary, volcanic, and metamorphic rock, mixed together over the epochs.

**Granite peaks of the High Sierras**

Jagged peaks on eastern slopes

Gradual western slopes

Block forced down

Eroded material

Batholith

Block uplifted to form mountain range

**Yosemite Valley in Yosemite National Park**

## GETTING AROUND

There are no roads across the mountains for more than 150 miles (240 km) between Yosemite and Kings Canyon, so it is essential to plan your route well ahead. Most visitors approach the mountains from the west, on the highways climbing up from the San Joaquin Valley. The eastern face of the High Sierras, Bodie, and Mono Lake can all be reached via Hwy 395 through Owens Valley. Public transportation is limited, but there is a daily bus service from Merced to Yosemite National Park.

**Delta Riverboat on Lake Tahoe**

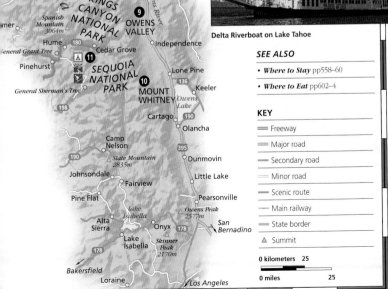

eville
Walker

*Mount Patterson*
△ *3558m*
*Devils Gate*
*2292m*

**5** **BODIE STATE HISTORIC PARK**
Bodie

*Excelsior Mountain*
△ *3794m*

**6** **MONO LAKE**

ITE
NAL
RK **4**
ite
*Tioga Pass*
*3031m*
**120**
Benton
**6**

*Mount Ritter*
*4010m*
ed Peak
74m **7** Mammoth Lakes
**DEVIL'S POSTPILE**
**395**

**WHITE MOUNTAINS**
**8**
Chalfant
Rovana
Mono Hot Springs
Bishop
**395**

*Mount Humphreys*
*4263m*
Big
Pine
Big
Creek

**KINGS CANYON NATIONAL PARK**
*Spanish Mountain*
*3064m*
**9** **OWENS VALLEY**
mer

Hume
**180**
Independence
General Grant Tree
Cedar Grove
Pinehurst **11**
▲ ✕ ◆
**SEQUOIA NATIONAL PARK**
General Sherman's Tree
**10** **MOUNT WHITNEY**
Lone Pine
**136**
Keeler
*Owens Lake*
**198**
Cartago
**190**
Olancha

Camp Nelson
**395**
△ *Slate Mountain*
*2835m*
Dunmovin
Johnsondale
Fairview
Little Lake
Pine Flat
Pearsonville
*Lake Isabella*
*Owens Peak*
*2577m*
Alta Sierra
Onyx **178** *San Bernadino*
**178**
Lake Isabella
*Skinner Peak*
*2170m*

*Bakersfield*
Loraine
*Los Angeles*

### SEE ALSO

• *Where to Stay* pp558–60
• *Where to Eat* pp602–4

### KEY

═══ Freeway
═══ Major road
─── Secondary road
─── Minor road
─── Scenic route
─── Main railway
─── State border
△ Summit

0 kilometers  25
0 miles  25

# Donner Memorial State Park ❶

*Tel (530) 582-7892.* ☐ *call for hours.* ⬛ *Truckee.* ⬛ *Truckee.* www.parks.ca.gov

This tranquil 350-acre (140-ha) park, to the south of I-80, marks the site of one of the most tragic episodes of the United States frontier era.

In the winter of 1846–7 a group of 89 California-bound emigrants from Independence, Missouri, were trapped by heavy snowfall. Known as the Donner Party because two of the families shared that surname, the group was one of the many wagon trains bound for the West Coast from the Midwest, along the Oregon Trail. Halfway into their journey, the Donner families, and another family headed by James Reed, decided to leave the established trail and try a shortcut recommended by the contemporary adventurer Lansford Hastings. This turned out, however, to be a far more difficult route, and added three weeks to what was already an arduous journey. The Donner

Party finally arrived at the eastern foot of the Sierra Nevada Mountains in October 1846, having lost the majority of their cattle and belongings.

After resting for a week they were caught by an early winter storm east of Truckee. A few members decided to struggle on foot across the snowy mountains to seek help from Sutter's Fort *(see p475)*, but the rest of the party, now trapped by the heavy snow and with insufficient supplies, were forced to resort to cannibalism in order to survive. By the time rescuers were able to reach them in mid-February 1847, 42 of the 89 pioneers had already died.

A statue of this heroic pioneering family, standing atop a 22-ft (6.7-m) pedestal indicating the depth of the snow they encountered, now marks the site. The park's **Emigrant Trail Museum** details the Donner Party's story, as well as describing the natural history of the High Sierras.

🏛 **Emigrant Trail Museum**
12593 Donner Pass Rd. *Tel (530) 582-7892.* ☐ *9am–4pm daily.* 🚫 *Jan 1, Thanksgiving, Dec 25.*

Façade of the 19th-century Old Truckee Jail, now a museum

# Truckee ❷

**Road map** B3. 🏚 *13,000.* 🚉 ⬛ ℹ *10065 Donner Pass Road.* **Tel** *(530) 587-2757.* **Tel** *(530) 546-5253 winter weather hotline.* www.truckee.com

One of the highest and coldest towns in California, Truckee is thought to have gotten its name when a native Paiute greeted the first white Americans with "Trokay," meaning "peace."

Truckee is situated along the main highway (I-80) and rail route across the Sierra Nevada Mountains. Its history as a transportation center goes back to 1863, when it was founded as a changeover point for railroad crews along the transcontinental railroad *(see pp50–51)* The Southern Pacific Depot still serves rail and bus passengers as well as operating as a visitors' center.

Much of the town's Wild West character and history as a lumber center survives, especially along Commercial Row in the heart of town, where a line of old brick and wooden buildings faces the tracks. Many of these have now been converted into atmospheric shops, restaurants, and cafés.

Another evocative survivor of the town's past is the **Old Truckee Jail**, built in 1875. It is a small museum depicting the wilder side of frontier life. Located only 25 miles (40 km) from Lake Tahoe, Truckee is also a popular historical base for winter skiers and summer hikers.

🏛 **Old Truckee Jail**
Jibboom & Spring Sts. *Tel (530) 582-0893.* ☐ *Jun–Aug: 11am–4pm Sat & Sun.* 🚫 *public hols.* 📷

## SKIING AROUND LAKE TAHOE

The peaks surrounding Lake Tahoe, particularly on the California side, are famous for their ski resorts. The world-class Alpine Meadows and Squaw Valley are where the Winter Olympics were held in 1960. The largest ski area, Heavenly Valley, is above the city of South Lake Tahoe, with many more around the lake and at Donner Pass, west of Truckee, along I-80. There are also cross-country ski areas with groomed trails. The Lake Tahoe area receives more than 10 ft (3 m) of snow each winter and is the state's major center for winter recreation from November to March.

Skiing at Lake Tahoe's Alpine Meadows resort

# A Tour of Lake Tahoe ❸

The most beautiful body of water in California, Lake Tahoe is 1,645 ft (501 m) at its deepest point and is surrounded by forested peaks. The area began to develop as a tourist resort after the construction of the first road in 1915 made it more accessible. Casinos opening on the Nevada border in the 1930s and the Winter Olympics in 1960 further increased its popularity.

View of Lake Tahoe from Heavenly Valley

*RENO*

*TRUCKEE*

267

431

**Crystal Bay** ④

28

89

• **Tahoe City**

28

*CARSON CITY*

50

• **Tahoma**

• **Glenbrook**

89

5

50

3

**Tahoe Village**

2

207

1

6

50

*Fallen Leaf Road*

*Pioneer Trail Road*

89

**Ponderosa Ranch** ④
Near the northeast shore of the lake, this ranch was formerly an amusement park based on the cult 1960s Wild West TV show, *Bonanza*.

**Cave Rock and Cave Rock Tunnel** ⑤
Lake Tahoe's east shore is so rugged that part of the highway is tunneled through solid granite.

**Stateline** ⑥
Situated on the border of California and the more liberal state of Nevada, Stateline is the main gambling town of the Lake Tahoe region.

**DL Bliss State Park and Ehrman Mansion** ③
A popular picnic area surrounds Ehrman Mansion, built in 1903 and now a visitors' center.

## TIPS FOR TRAVELERS

*Tour length*: 65 miles (105 km).
*Getting there*: I-80 and US 50 are open all year-round. Amtrak trains operate to Truckee. Grey-hound buses and limited flights from San Francisco and Oakland serve South Lake Tahoe.
*When to go:* Peak tourist seasons are July, August, and winter, when the ski resorts are open. Spring and autumn are less crowded, but some facilities may be closed.
*Where to stay and eat:* Contact Lake Tahoe Visitors' Authority.
*Tourist information:* Lake Tahoe Visitors' Authority, South Lake Tahoe. *Tel* (800) 288-2463.
www.visitinglaketahoe.com

**South Lake Tahoe** ①
The largest town in the area, South Lake Tahoe caters for visitors to Nevada's casinos.

**Emerald Bay State Park and Vikingsholm** ②
The beautiful inlet of Emerald Bay is the most photographed part of the lake. Vikingsholm, built as a summerhouse in the 1920s, is an incongruous reproduction of an old Nordic castle.

0 kilometers          10

0 miles                    10

## KEY

▬▬▬ Tour route

═══ Other roads

⁂ Viewpoint

# Yosemite National Park ❹

A wilderness of evergreen forests, high meadows, and sheer granite walls, much of Yosemite National Park is accessible only to experienced hikers or horseback riders. The spectacular Yosemite Valley, a good base from which to explore the park, is easily reached by car and there are 200 additional miles (320 km) of paved roads providing access to more remote areas. Soaring cliffs, plunging waterfalls, gigantic trees, rugged canyons, mountains, and valleys all combine to lend Yosemite its incomparable beauty.

**Yosemite Museum**
*The history of the Miwok and Paiute people is displayed here, along with works by Yosemite artists.*

**Lower Yosemite Falls**
*Yosemite Creek drops 2,425 ft (740 m), to form the highest waterfall in the US (see p490).*

**Ahwahnee Hotel**
*Rustic architecture, elegant décor, and beautiful views make this hotel one of the most renowned in the country (see p491).*

**Yosemite Chapel** *(1879) This tiny wooden church is all that is left of Yosemite's 19th-century Old Village.*

Valley Visitor Center

To Upper Yosemite Falls

Yosemite Creek

Yosemite Falls Trail

Yosemite Village

Sunnyside

Northside Drive

Yosemite Lodge

Merced River

Southside Drive

Sentinel Creek

Four-Mile Trail

Lower River

Upp

Stairca Falls

**SENTINEL ROCK** ▲ **7,038 ft (2,145 m)**

Sentinel Falls

**Sentinel Dome** can be reached on foot from the valley floor. The trail continues to Glacier Point.

**Mirror Meadow**
*Park rangers no longer interfere with nature by dredging the lake, so the water at the foot of Half Dome is now silting up and forming a meadow (see p491).*

## VISITORS' CHECKLIST

Road map C3. ℹ PO Box 577, Yosemite. 🔣 (209) 372-0200. 🚂 from Merced. 🚌 Yosemite Valley. 🚍 from Merced. ○ daily. 🎟 📷 ♿ 🚻 📵 🍴 🏪
**www.nps.gov/yose**

### KEY

━━ Major road

══ Minor road

‐ ‐ Paths and trails

- - Shuttle bus

✕✕ Bike route

〜 Rivers

🅿 Parking

⛽ Gas station

🅰 Camping

🍽 Picnic area

ℹ Tourist information

☀ Viewpoint

**Washington Column**

**NORTH PINES**

**OWER PINES**

Tenaya Creek

**UPPER PINES**

Merced River

**Half Dome**
*A formidable trail climbs to the top of this cliff, which juts above the valley floor (see p490).*

**Vernal Fall**
*The Merced River pours into its canyon over the 317-ft (97-m) lip of this fall.*

**Merced River**
*This beautiful river can be appreciated along both the Mist Trail and the Panorama Trail. Anglers enjoy fishing for brown trout in its waters.*

0 meters 1000
0 yards 1000

# Exploring Yosemite National Park

Some of the world's most beautiful mountain terrain is protected within the 1,170 sq miles (3,030 sq km) of Yosemite National Park. Hundreds of thousands of visitors descend upon the park each year to admire its breathtaking views, formed by millions of years of glacial activity. Each season offers a different experience, from the swelling waterfalls of spring to the rustic colors of autumn. The summer months are the most crowded, but during the snowbound winter months several roads are inaccessible. Bus tours and well-maintained cycle paths, hiking trails, and roads are all aimed at leading visitors from one awe-inspiring panoramic scene to another.

**Upper Yosemite Falls, swollen with ice-melt in the spring**

## Half Dome

Eastern end of Yosemite Valley.
⬜ *daily.*

Standing nearly 1 mile (1.6 km) above the valley floor, the silhouette of Half Dome has become a symbol of Yosemite. Its curved back rises to a wave-like lip, before dropping vertically to the valley below.

Geologists believe that Half Dome is now three-quarters of its original size, rather than a true half. It is thought that as recently as 15,000 years ago, glacial ice floes moved through the valley from the Sierra crest, scything off rock and depositing it downstream.

The 8,840-ft (2,695 m) summit of Half Dome offers an unsurpassed view of the valley. Follow the 9-mile (14-km) trail from Happy Isles trailhead to reach the peak.

## Yosemite Falls

North Yosemite Valley. ⬜ *daily.*
Yosemite Falls are the highest waterfalls in North America and tumble from a height of 2,425 ft (740 m) in two great leaps, Upper Yosemite and Lower Yosemite Falls. One of the most recognizable features of the park, the cascades are visible all over the valley.

The top of Upper Yosemite Falls, by far the longer and more elegant of the pair, can be reached via a strenuous 7-mile (11-km) round-trip trail. The Lower Falls are easier to visit, via a short trail that starts next to Yosemite Lodge and frames an unforgettable view of both falls.

As with all the park's waterfalls, Yosemite Falls are at their peak in May and June, when the winter snows melt and fill the creek to capacity. Conversely, by September the falls often dry up and disappear altogether, their presence marked only by a dark stain on the granite wall.

## Vernal and Nevada Falls

Eastern end of Yosemite Valley.
⬜ *daily.*
A popular half-day hike in Yosemite National Park is the Mist Trail, which visits these two waterfalls.

The first fall visited on this 7-mile (11-km) round-trip is Vernal Fall, which plunges 320 ft (95 m) and spreads its spray across the trail. The trail then continues for 2 miles (3 km) to the top of Nevada Falls, which drops an impressive 595 ft (180 m). At the top of Nevada Falls the Mist Trail joins the John Muir Trail, which runs around the back of Half Dome all the way south to the summit of Mount Whitney (*see p495*).

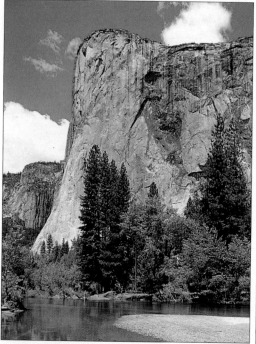

**Sheer drop of El Capitán**

*For hotels and restaurants in this region see pp558–60 and pp602–4*

### 🔆 Glacier Point

Glacier Point Rd. ◯ *May–Oct: daily.*
The great Yosemite panorama
can be experienced from
Glacier Point, which rests on
a rocky ledge 3,215 ft (980 m)
above the valley floor. Most
of the waterfalls and other
features of Yosemite Valley
are visible from here, but the
dominant feature is Half Dome.
The panorama also includes
much of the surrounding
landscape, a beautiful area of
alpine peaks and meadows.

Glacier Point can be reached
only during the summer. The
road is blocked by snow
during winter at Badger Pass,
which was developed in 1935
as California's first commercial
ski resort. Another summer
route is the Four-Mile Trail,
which begins at the western
side of the valley. Summer
bus services also allow hikers
to ride up to Glacier Point
then hike down to the valley.

### 🔆 Mariposa Grove

**Visitors' Center** Hwy 41, South
Entrance. ◯ *mid-May–Oct: daily.*
At the southern end of Yosemite, this beautiful grove was
one of the main reasons the
park was established. More
than 500 giant sequoia trees
can be seen here, some of
which are more than 3,000
years old, 250 ft (75 m) tall
and more than 30 ft (9 m) in
diameter at their base. A series
of hiking trails winds through

Tunnel View, looking across Yosemite Valley

the grove, and open-air trams
make a 5-mile (8-km) circuit
along roads constructed
during the early years of
Yosemite tourism.

### 🔆 Tunnel View

Hwy 41 overlooking Yosemite Valley.
◯ *daily.*
One of the most photographed
views of Yosemite can be had
from this lookout on Hwy 41
at the western end of the valley. Despite the name, which
is taken from the highway tunnel that leads to Glacier Point
Road, the view is incredible,
with El Capitán on the left,
Bridalveil Fall on the right
and Half Dome at the center.

### 🔆 El Capitán

Northwestern end of Yosemite Valley.
◯ *daily.*
Standing guard at the western
entrance to Yosemite Valley,
the granite wall of El Capitán
rises more than
4,500 ft (1,370 m)
from the valley
floor. The world's
largest exposed
rock, El Capitán is
a magnet to rock-
climbers, who
spend days on its
sheer face to reach
the top. Less ad-
venturous visitors
congregate in the
meadow below,
watching the rock-
climbers through
binoculars.

Named by US
soldiers, who in
1851 were the first
white Americans
to visit the valley,
El Capitán is the
Spanish phrase
for "captain."

### 🔆 Tuolumne Meadows

Hwy 120, Tioga Rd.
◯ *Jun–Sep: daily.*
In summer, when the snows
have melted and the wild-
flowers are in full bloom,
the best place to experience
the striking beauty of the
Yosemite landscape are these
sub-alpine meadows along
the Tuolumne River. Located
55 miles (88 km) from
Yosemite valley via Tioga Pass
Road, Tuolumne Meadows
are also a base for hikers setting off to explore the area's
many granite peaks and trails.

Black-tailed deer roaming
Yosemite's meadows

### 🏨 Ahwahnee Hotel

Yosemite Valley. **Tel** (866) 875-8456.
◯ *daily. See **Where to Stay** p560.*
www.yosemitepark.com
A building that comes close
to matching Yosemite's natural
beauty, the Ahwahnee Hotel
was built in 1927 at a cost of
$1.5 million.

It was designed by Gilbert
Stanley Underwood, who
used giant granite boulders
and massive wood timbers to
create a rustic elegance that is
in tune with its surroundings.
The interior of the Ahwahnee
Hotel also emulates the natural setting, decorated in a
Native American style. A few
Native American arts and crafts
are on display in the lobbies.
The hotel also has a high-
quality restaurant *(see p604).*

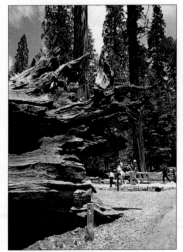

Giant sequoia trees in Mariposa Grove

Sierra Nevada, near Lone Pine ▷

Ghostly wooden buildings in Bodie State Historic Park

# Bodie State Historic Park ❺

**Road map** C3. 🏚 10. 🚌 from Bridgeport. ℹ End of Hwy 270 (760 647-6445). ◷ 8am–6pm daily. www.parks.ca.gov

High up in the foothills of the eastern Sierra Nevada, Bodie is the largest ghost town in California.

Now protected as a state historic park, Bodie was, during the second half of the 19th century, a bustling gold mining town, with a population that topped 8,000 in 1880. Named after the gold prospector Waterman S Bodey, who first discovered placer deposits (surface gold) here in 1859, Bodie boomed with the discovery of hard rock ore in the mid-1870s. Soon many different mines had been established in the area, but it all came to an end when the gold ran out in 1882. Later, a series of fires destroyed much of the town. Only the Standard Mine remained in business, but it closed in 1942 because of a wartime ban on mining.

The state acquired the entire town in 1962, and has maintained the 170 buildings in a condition of "arrested decay." The result is an evocative experience of empty streets lined by deserted wooden buildings. The Miners' Union Hall has been converted into a visitors' center and museum.

# Mono Lake ❻

**Road map** C3. 🚆 Merced. ℹ Hwy 395 & 3rd St (760 647-6595). www.monolake.org

One of the strangest looking places in the United States, and possibly one of the oldest lakes in the world, Mono Lake is a 70-sq mile (180-sq km) body of alkaline water at the eastern foot of the Sierra Nevada Mountains, set between two volcanic islands. The lake has no natural outlet, but evaporation in the summer heat combined with water diversion to LA has caused it to shrink to one-fifth of its original size. The result is extremely brackish water, three times saltier than sea water. It has also exposed a number of contorted tufa spires. These were formed when calcium from underground springs came into contact with carbonates in the lake water, forming limestone. The tufa formations once sat under water, but are now arrayed along the lakeside.

In recent years, Mono Lake has also been the subject of a heated political and environmental debate, part of an ongoing battle over water rights. The City of Los Angeles purchased a large amount of land in the eastern Sierras and Owens Valley in 1905, and began diverting the streams and rivers through a system of aqueducts to LA in 1941. This has accelerated the lake's shrinkage and put local wildlife, particularly the state's large seagull population, which breeds on the lake's islands, in danger (see pp202–3). In 1994 the California State Government ruled that LA must preserve the lake and its surrounding ecosystem at 6,392 ft (1,950 m) above sea level.

Tufa spires rising out of Mono Lake

*For hotels and restaurants in this region see pp558–60 and pp602–4*

# Devil's Postpile National Monument **7**

**Road map** C4. **Tel** (760) 934-2289.
🚌 *shuttle from Mammoth Mountain Inn.* ◯ *mid-Jun–Sep: daily.* 🏵 ♿
📷 www.nps.gov/depo

On the west of the Sierra Nevada crest, but most easily accessible from the eastern resort of Mammoth Lakes, Devil's Postpile National Monument protects one of the most impressive geological formations in the state.

A wall of basalt columns, in varying geometrical shapes, predominantly pentagons and hexagons, cover a 545 sq yard (652 sq m) area. More than 60 ft (18 m) tall, they rise 7,560 ft (2,320 m) above sea level. The columns were formed around 100,000 years ago, when molten lava cooled and fractured. Set at the heart of an 800-acre (320-ha) park, they resemble a tiled floor seen from above. The monument is covered in snow most of the year and is only accessible in summer via shuttle bus. Rainbow Falls, 2 miles (3 km) from the Postpile, are named after the refraction of sunlight in their spray.

# White Mountains **8**

ℹ️ *798 N Main St, Bishop (760 873-2500).*

Rising along the eastern side of Owens Valley, the White Mountains, at 12,000 ft (3,660 m), are almost as high but far drier than the 13,000-ft (3,960-m) parallel range of Sierra Nevada. Lack of water has kept the peaks rugged and largely free of vegetation, but the few trees that do survive here, the bristlecone pines *(Pinus aristata)*, are among the oldest living things on earth.

These gnarled pine trees seem to thrive on the adverse conditions, which batter them into strange, contorted shapes. The species is found only on the lower slopes of the White Mountains and on a few of the mountains in neighboring Nevada. Extremely slow

Bristlecone pines on the slopes of the White Mountains

growing, they seldom reach more than 50 ft (15 m) in height, despite living for more than 4,000 years – 1,000 years longer than the oldest sequoia tree *(see pp496–7).*

# Owens Valley **9**

🚌 *Lone Pine.* ℹ️ *126 S Main St, Lone Pine (760 876-4444).* www.lonepinechamber.org

Owens Valley has more in common with Nevada than with the rest of California. It is sparsely populated but ruggedly beautiful, the valley being wedged between the White Mountains and the Sierra Nevada. Once covered with farms and ranches, the land here was bought secretly in 1905 by agents working for the City of Los Angeles. Los Angeles needed to secure a

water supply, and the aqueducts still drain the valley, destroying local agriculture.

In 1942 a detention camp was established at Manzanar for 10,000 Japanese-Americans, who were deemed a threat to national security and imprisoned for the duration of World War II. Exhibits on this and other aspects of Owens Valley can be seen at the **Eastern California Museum**, in the town of Independence.

🏛 **Eastern California Museum**
155 N Grant St, Independence.
**Tel** (760) 878-0364. ◯ *10am–5pm daily.* ⬤ *Jan 1, Easter Sun, Thanksgiving, Dec 25.* **Donation.**
www.inyocounty.us

# Mount Whitney **10**

**Tel** (760) 876-6200. 🚌 *Merced.*

The highest peak in the lower 48 states of the US, Mount Whitney rises to a height of 14,496 ft (4,420 m), forming a sheer wall above the town of Lone Pine. A steep 11-mile (18-km) trail leads from Whitney Portal Road to the summit, offering a panorama over the High Sierras. A permit is required to hike the trail. The mountain, named in honor of the geologist Josiah Whitney, was first climbed in 1873.

Mount Whitney borders the beautiful Sequoia National Park *(see pp496–7),* and the surrounding alpine meadows are ideal for backpacking in the summer months.

Owens Valley, backed by the White Mountains

# Sequoia and Kings Canyon National Parks ⓫

**Sequoia National Park sign**

These twin national parks preserve lush forests, granite peaks, and glacier-carved canyons. Breathtaking scenery complements a habitat rich with wildlife. The parks embrace 34 separate groves of the giant sequoia tree, the earth's largest living species. America's deepest canyon, the south fork of the Kings River, cuts a depth of 8,200 ft (2,500 m) through Kings Canyon. Along the eastern boundary of Sequoia is Mount Whitney *(see p495)*, the highest summit on the US mainland.

Roads serve the western side of the parks; the rest is accessible only to hikers or with rented pack-trains of horses or mules. Winter visitors can ski cross-country over both marked and unmarked trails.

**Road "tunnel" formed by a felled giant sequoia in Sequoia National Park**

**General Grant Tree**
*The third-largest sequoia is known as the "Nation's Christmas Tree."*

Wilsonia •

180

Cedar Brook

Redwood Mountain Grove

North Fork Kaweah River

Redwood Creek

M465

SEQUOIA NATIONAL PARK

Yucca Creek

**KEY**

▬ Major road

▬ Minor road

- - ▸ Paths and trails

— National Park boundary

〰 River

▨ Skiing

Ⓐ Camping

⛩ Picnic area

ℹ Tourist information

☀ Viewpoint

**Big Stumps**
*The sequoia's unyielding nature makes it uneconomical for lumber, as these tall stumps, left by loggers in the 1880s, prove.*

### Moro Rock

*A staircase carved into the rock takes visitors to the top of this granite monolith and affords a 360° view of the High Sierras and the Central Valley.*

### General Sherman's Tree

*The world's largest living thing is 275 ft (84 m) tall, with a trunk measuring 36 ft (11 m) around its base. The tree still grows 0.4 inches (1 cm) every ten years.*

**Tharp's Log**, a hollowed-out sequoia, was home to Hale Tharp, a 19th-century farmer who was introduced to the area by Native Americans.

### Crescent Meadow

*An array of sequoias border this area, which is more of a marsh than a meadow and too wet at its heart for the trees to survive.*

…stal Cavern, one of … few caves open to visitors, …lled with stalagmites and stalactites.

**Giant Forest** contains one of the largest groves of living sequoias in the world.

| 0 kilometers | 2 |
| 0 miles | 2 |

# NORTH CENTRAL CALIFORNIA

With a rugged shoreline rising from the Pacific Ocean and dense forests covering coastal mountains, North Central California marks the visual transition between the north and south of the state. The landscape holds an embarrassment of riches, with golden beaches, splendid wilderness, and inland valleys that include some of the world's most productive agricultural regions.

The natural beauty of the area, combined with a wealth of cultural history, makes this one of the state's most engaging regions. Native Americans lived along the coast and in the inland valleys for centuries prior to the arrival of Europeans in the 17th century. More than a century later the first European settlement was established at Monterey on June 3, 1770, marking the beginning of today's California. Monterey remained the capital of Upper California until the United States took formal control in 1848. The city still retains a unique character, with its many historic buildings now protected and restored.

North central California has also inspired some of the state's most significant literature, from the poetry of Robinson Jeffers to the novels of Nobel prize-winner John Steinbeck. Many of the world's best photographers, including Ansel Adams and Edward Weston, have lived and worked here.

For all its culture and history, the region also abounds in recreational activities. Visitors can enjoy the historic amusement park at Santa Cruz, play golf on the world-famous courses at Pebble Beach, or simply walk around the many nature preserves, including the state's most beautiful stretch of coastline, Big Sur.

Writer John Steinbeck's house in Salinas

◁ Bixby Creek Bridge on Coastal Hwy 1 at Big Sur

# Exploring North Central California

Monterey, the Spanish colonial capital of
California, is at the heart of north central California
and the best base from which to explore the region.
The wealthy resorts of Pacific Grove and Carmel
stand on a rugged peninsula just south of the town.
Farther south is the wildest length of coastline in the
state, Big Sur, where otters and whales can be
spotted offshore. To the north is Santa Cruz, a lively
beach town, backed by densely forested mountains.
Inland, the Salinas and San Joaquin valleys give a
taste of California's productive agricultural areas.

**Pfeiffer Burns State Park at Big Sur**

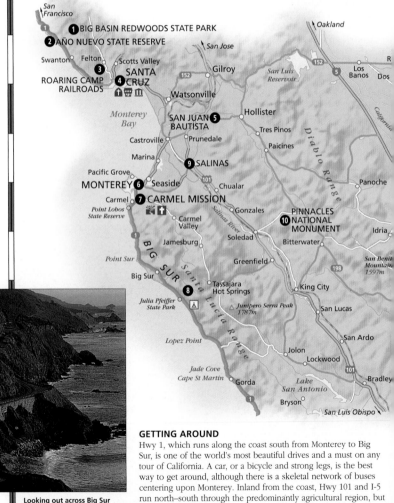

**Looking out across Big Sur
along Hwy 1**

### GETTING AROUND

Hwy 1, which runs along the coast south from Monterey to Big
Sur, is one of the world's most beautiful drives and a must on any
tour of California. A car, or a bicycle and strong legs, is the best
way to get around, although there is a skeletal network of buses
centering upon Monterey. Inland from the coast, Hwy 101 and I-5
run north–south through the predominantly agricultural region, but
there are very few roads between the coast and inland valleys.

**For additional map symbols** *see back flap*

## SIGHTS AT A GLANCE

**Elephant seals at the Año Nuevo State Reserve**

### KEY

| | |
|---|---|
| ▬ | Freeway |
| ▬ | Major road |
| ▬ | Secondary road |
| ▭ | Minor road |
| ▬ | Scenic route |
| ▬ | Main railway |
| ▭ | Minor railway |
| △ | Summit |

*Yosemite*

Oakhurst

Coarsegold

*Modesto*

Raymond

O'Neals

Chowchilla

Auberry

Prather

Berenda

Friant

Tollhouse

Madera

Trimmer

*Pine Flat Lake*

Ripperdan

Clovis

*Kings River*

Piedra

baugh

Biola

⑪ 🏛 FRESNO

Mendota

Dunlap

Kerney Park

Sanger

Pinehurst

San Joaquin

Easton

Orange Cove

Badger

Helm

Selma

Caruthers

Kingsburg

Cutler

Cantua Creek

Laton

Traver

Woodlake

Three Rivers

Ivanhoe

Visalia

Lemoncove

⑫ ⓘ HANFORD

Lemoore

Exeter

Huron

Guernsey

Tulare

Lindsay

Milo

Coalinga

Stratford

Plainview

Strathmore

Springville

Corcoran

Tipton

Poplar

Porterville

Kettleman City

Pixley

Avenal

California Hot Springs

*Colonel Allensworth State Historic Park*

Earlimart

Ducor

Allensworth

White River

*Los Angeles*

*Bakersfield*

0 kilometers   20

0 miles   20

# The North Central Coastline

The beaches of north central California are varied, from long, thin stretches to tiny coves at the foot of coastal bluffs. In summer, sun-worshipers and volleyball players congregate on the sands, and while the water is generally too cold for swimming, surfers don wet suits to brave the chilly waves. With almost no commercial developments along this stretch of coastline, these beaches are also ideal for leisurely walks, searching for driftwood or seashells. You may also catch a glimpse of the area's abundant wildlife, which ranges from shore birds and tidepool-dwellers to elephant seals and migrating gray whales.

SAN FRANCISCO
PACIFICA

① ①

⑨
• Boulder Creek

Scotts
Valley

⑨

Sa
Cr

Wilder Ranch State Park •

②

**Moss Landing** *is a colorful harbor and the home port for most of Monterey Bay's commercial fishing boats. It has many good seafood restaurants along its wharves.*

0 kilometers 5

0 miles 5

★ **Santa Cruz Beach** ③
With free volleyball courts and barbecue pits backed by the popular Boardwalk Amusement Park *(see p506)*, this broad golden expanse is the area's most popular beach.

**Lighthouse Field State Beach** ②
This rugged 36 acres (14 ha) of shoreline is well suited to surfing or simply admiring the sculpted 40-ft (12-m) sand-stone headlands. It is also a good place to spot sea otters, brown pelicans, and the occasional whale offshore.

**Capitola Beach** ④
A wooden railway trestle bridges the small creek that meets the ocean at this sandy beach. Next to the beach is Capitola Wharf, with restaurants, shops, and observation decks. The Capitola Bluffs are an important paleontological site, and the prehistoric shells can be seen at low tide.

**Marina State Beach** ⑤
Backed by sand dunes, this beach was once a part of a US Army base and is now part of a university campus.

**Waddell Creek Beach** ①
This golden strand of beach is part of the Big Basin Redwoods State Park *(see p504)* and is a favorite spot for picnickers, anglers, and windsurfers.

**KEY**

| | |
|---|---|
| Freeway |
| Major road |
| Minor road |
| River |
| Viewpoint |

**Wilder Ranch State Park**, *at the northern edge of Santa Cruz, is a historic coastal dairy farm. Complete with ranch house and barns dating from the 1890s, it has been preserved as a state park.*

**LOCATOR MAP**

**Elkhorn Slough**, *halfway along Monterey Bay, is one of the prime bird-watching areas along the North Central coastline.*

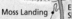

Aptos
Capitola
Watsonville
Moss Landing • Elkhorn Slough
SALINAS
Marina
Seaside
Monterey •
Carmel •

★ **Asilomar State Beach** ⑦

This broad, rocky beach is an ideal place for watching migrating gray whales as they pass offshore every winter on their way south.

★ **Lovers' Point** ⑥

Originally called Lovers of Jesus Point, the headlands form a natural amphitheater that was used for religious revivals in the 1880s. It is one of the few sandy beaches on the northern Monterey Peninsula.

★ **Carmel City Beach** ⑧

Bright white sand and brilliant blue water are the distinguishing characteristics of this long beach, which sits at the foot of central Carmel's popular shopping and restaurant district (see p510).

N JOSE

SAN LUIS OBISPO

Elephant seals ashore at Año Nuevo State Reserve

# Big Basin Redwoods State Park ❶

🖼 Santa Cruz, Boulder Creek Golf Course. **Visitors' Center** 21600 Big Basin Way, Boulder Creek. **Tel** (831) 338-8860. ☐ **Park** 6am–10pm daily. **www**.parks.ca.gov

In 1900 a group of environmentalists formed the Sempervirens Club with the aim of preventing the logging of redwoods. This resulted in Big Basin Redwoods State Park, California's first state park, being established in 1902. It covers 16,000 acres (6,475 ha) and protects the southernmost groves of the coastal redwood tree (see p446) and forests of Douglas fir and other conifers. It is also home to wildlife such as black-tailed deer and the mountain lion.

Trails lead through redwood groves to the park's many waterfalls, including the popular Berry Creek Falls. There are also more than 100 miles (160 km) of other routes, including the Skyline-to-Sea Trail, which drops down to the Pacific Ocean at Waddell Creek (see pp502–3).

# Año Nuevo State Reserve ❷

**Road map** B4. 🖼 Santa Cruz, Waddell Creek. 🛈 (650) 879-2025, 879-0227 (recorded info). ☐ daily. **www**.parks.ca.gov

The Año Nuevo State Reserve, 60 miles (96 km) north of Monterey, has as its main point of interest the breeding grounds of the Northern

elephant seal, one of the world's most fascinating creatures. A short stretch of sandy beach and a small offshore island are populated each winter by hundreds of these giant mammals, which arrive here from all over the Pacific Ocean to mate and give birth.

Elephant seals were hunted almost to extinction in the 19th century because of their valuable oil-bearing blubber. A few survivors found refuge off the coast of Mexico and made their way back to California in the 1950s. The first pups were born at Año Nuevo in 1975. There are now some 120,000 elephant seals off the coast of California.

The seals are named after the dangling proboscis of the male, which can reach 20 ft (6 m) in length and weigh upward of 2 tons. Ungainly on land, elephant seals can perform incredible feats in the sea – remaining under water for up to 20 minutes at a time and diving more than 4,000 ft (1,220 m) beneath the surface. Each December, the male seals

arrive here and begin the battle for dominance, engaging in violent fights. Only a handful of the most powerful males are able to mate, but one male can father pups with as many as 50 different females in one season. After spending most of the year at sea, the females arrive in January to give birth to young conceived the previous winter. Mating follows soon after, although conception is delayed for up to four months while the female recovers from giving birth.

The name Año Nuevo ("New Year") was given to the island by explorer Sebastián Vizcaíno, who sailed past the area on January 1, 1603 (see pp46–7). The park is open all year, but during the winter when the elephant seals are present, visitors are allowed only on guided tours. Tickets are available through the California State Parks reservation service, DestiNet (see p610).

# Roaring Camp Railroads ❸

**Tel** (831) 335-4400. 🖼 Santa Cruz. ☐ Jan–Mar: Sat & Sun. ● public hols. 🎫 ♿ 📷 11am, 12:15pm, 2pm. **Santa Cruz Big Trees Railroad Tel** (831) 355-4484. ☐ call for times. 🎫 ♿ 📷 **www**.roaringcamp.com

High up in the Santa Cruz Mountains, near the town of Felton, a pair of historic logging railroads have been kept in operation as the focus of a family-orientated theme

Roaring Camp and Big Trees Railroad

**Façade of Mission San Juan Bautista**

park devoted to the late 19th-century and early 20th-century lumber industry. Between January and March, a narrow-gauge train departs on a weekend 6-mile (10-km) round-trip through the adjacent forests of Henry Cowell Redwoods State Park. From April to December, the traditional-gauge Big Trees, Santa Cruz, and Pacific Railroad, sets off from Roaring Camp on an hour-long trip through the mountains and down to Santa Cruz. There is a three-hour stopover, during which passengers can enjoy the beach and Boardwalk Amusement Park before the return journey *(see pp506–7)*. The trip can also be taken as a round-trip from Santa Cruz.

## Santa Cruz ❹

*See pp506–7.*

## San Juan Bautista ❺

**Road map** B4. 🚶 *1,650.* 🚌 *from Hollister.* 🛈 *650 San Benito St, Hollister (831) 637-5315.* **www**.sanbenitochamber.com

For a quick insight into California's multifaceted history, there is no better place than San Juan Bautista. This small town has retained its rural character, despite being a mere 30 miles (48 km) from the heart of the high-tech Silicon Valley *(see p428)*.

The main attraction of the town is Mission San Juan Bautista, which stands to the

west of the central plaza. The largest of the missions built during Spanish colonial rule, it is also the only one to have aisles along the nave. Alfred Hitchcock used the mission's façade for the final scenes of

**El Camino Real sign**

his film *Vertigo*. The adjacent monastery has been converted into a museum, displaying mission artifacts and photographs of the town at various

stages of development. On the north side of the church there is a cemetery, next to which a faint trail marks the historic route of El Camino Real. This 650-mile (1,050-km) path linked the 21 California missions, all within a day's journey of their nearest mission *(see pp46–7)*. By coincidence, this trail also follows the San Andreas Fault, the underlying source of all California's earthquakes *(see pp24–5)*. A seismograph on the edge of the town's plaza monitors tectonic activity.

The east and south sides of the plaza are lined by three historic buildings, all of which have been preserved as part of San Juan Bautista State Historic Park. The Plaza Hotel incorporates part of the original barracks built in 1813. The town's stables now house antique carriages and stagecoaches, and Castro House was owned by Patrick Breen, a survivor of the tragic Donner Party *(see p486)*.

---

### THE LOMA PRIETA EARTHQUAKE

The powerful tremor that rocked San Francisco on October 17, 1989 had its epicenter beneath Loma Prieta, a hill between Santa Cruz and San Juan Bautista. Although the international media concentrated on the extensive damage caused in and around San Francisco, the worst damage occurred in Santa Cruz and the surrounding communities, where a number of homes and commercial buildings were destroyed. Approximately 40 businesses were forced to relocate to tentlike temporary buildings occupying three full blocks. The downtown district of Santa Cruz was a vast building site until the end of 1994. The majority of the damaged structures have now been repaired or replaced, but empty lots still remain where buildings once stood.

**Destruction caused by the Loma Prieta earthquake**

# Santa Cruz ❹

Perched at the northern tip of Monterey Bay, Santa
Cruz is a composite of small-town California, with an
agricultural rather than suburban feel. Its surrounding
farmland forms a broad shelf between the bay and the
densely forested Santa Cruz Mountains that rise to the
east. These mountains separate Santa Cruz from
the urban Silicon Valley *(see p428)* and, along with the
scenic coastline, provide residents and visitors with an
easy access to nature. The city's past is preserved in a
replica 18th-century mission and in the excellent local
history museum. The large University of California
campus in the town, attracting students and professors
from all over the world, also gives Santa Cruz a
cosmopolitan and erudite character.

**Reconstructed façade of Santa
Cruz Mission**

### Exploring Santa Cruz
The downtown, which
centers on Pacific Avenue, is
875 yards (800 m) inland.
Much of this area was badly
damaged by the Loma Prieta
earthquake *(see p505)*, but
the city has recovered swiftly,
with many good bookstores,
art galleries, and cafés lining
the streets. The
historic core of
the city,
including
the remains
of the 1791
Mission Santa
Cruz, is on a hill
to the northeast of the town.

**Detail of the Giant
Dipper**

The highlight of Santa Cruz
is the waterfront, including the
Boardwalk Amusement Park
and scenic West Cliff Drive
that runs along the coast.

### 🎡 Santa Cruz
### Beach Boardwalk
400 Beach St. **Tel** *(831) 423-5590.*
⭕ *call ahead for opening times.*
www.beachboardwalk.com
The last surviving old-style
amusement park on the West
Coast, the Santa Cruz Beach
Boardwalk offers a variety of

attractions and games lined up
along the beachfront. Visitors
can wander freely, deciding
which of the rides to try. The
main attraction is the Giant
Dipper roller coaster, built in
1924 by Arthur Looff and now
a National Historic Landmark.
The car travels along the
1-mile (1.6-km) wooden track
at 55 mph (88 km/h).
The carousel nearby
features horses
and chariots hand-
carved by Looff's
father, craftsman Charles
Looff, in 1911. The ride is
accompanied by a
100-year-old pipe organ. The
park also has 27 more
modern rides and an Art
Deco dance hall.

### 🏛 Mission Santa Cruz
Emmet & High Sts. **Tel** *(831) 426-*
*5686.* ⭕ *10am–4pm Tue–Sat,*
*10am–2pm Sun.* **Donation**.
On top of a hill overlooking
the town, Mission Santa Cruz
was founded on September 25,
1791 by Father Lasuén, as the
12th Franciscan mission in
California. The buildings were
completed three years later.

The mission was never a great
success, however, due to earthquakes, poor weather, and its
isolated location, all of which
have eliminated any remains of
the original structure. A park
outlines the site, and a 1931
replica of the mission has been
constructed. This houses a
small museum.

### 🏛 Museum of Art & History
### at the McPherson Center
705 Front St. **Tel** *(831) 429-1964.*
⭕ *11am–5pm Tue–Sun (11am–6pm
1st Fri of every month & free entry).*
⬤ *Jan 1, Thanksgiving, Dec 25.* 🖼
www.santacruzmah.org
One positive development to
arise out of the rubble of the
1989 Loma Prieta earthquake
was this 20,000 sq ft (1,858
sq m) cultural center, which
opened in 1993 to house the
local art and history galleries.
The Art Gallery shows works
primarily by north central
artists depicting the local landscape. The History Gallery
includes a series of displays
tracing the development of
Santa Cruz County, from the
pre-colonial and mission eras
through to the present day.

Also in the History Gallery
are exhibits detailing the
region's agricultural and
industrial heritage, with
photographs of late 19th-cen-
tury and early 20th-century
farms and logging operations.
The museum also incorpo-
rates the adjacent Octagon
Gallery that was completed
in 1882 as the County Hall
of Records.

**Giant Dipper roller coaster in the Boardwalk Amusement Park**

Eroded archway at the Natural Bridges State Beach

### 🏖 Natural Bridges State Beach

2531 W Cliff Dr. **Tel** *(831) 423-4609.*
⏰ *daily.* 🏛 **Visitors' Center** *end of
W Cliff Drive.* ⏰ *8am–sunset daily.*
Natural Bridges State Beach
takes its name from the picturesque archways that were
carved into the cliffs by the
ocean waves. Two of the three
original arches collapsed but
one still remains, through
which waves roll into a small
sandy cove. The park also preserves a eucalyptus grove and
a nature trail, showing all the
stages in the life cycle of the
monarch butterfly *(see p219).*

### 🏛 Santa Cruz Surfing Museum

Lighthouse Point, 701 W Cliff Drive
**Tel** *(831) 420-6289.* ⏰ *winter: noon–
4pm Thu–Mon; summer: 10am–5pm
Wed–Mon.* ● *public hols.* **Donation**.
www.santacruzsurfingmuseum.org
In a lighthouse overlooking
the region's main surfing area,
this museum has artifacts from
every era of Santa Cruz surfing.
The sport was brought to the
state from Hawaii to promote
tourism. It evolved into a truly
Californian pursuit with the
music of the Beach Boys in the
1960s *(see pp56–7).* The surfboards range from the redwood planks of the 1930s to
today's high-tech laminates.

### 🏖 Mystery .Spot

465 Mystery Spot Rd.
**Tel** *(831) 423-8897.* ⏰ *daily.*
🏛 www.*mysteryspot.com*
Two miles (3 km) east of
Santa Cruz, a redwood grove
has been drawing visitors for
decades due to various
strange events. Balls roll
uphill, parallel lines converge,
and the laws of physics seem
to be suspended. Part tourist
trap, part genuine oddity, the
Mystery Spot has to be seen.

## SANTA CRUZ CITY CENTER

Mission Santa Cruz ⑤
Museum of Art and History at the
    McPherson Center ④
Natural Bridges State Beach ①
Santa Cruz Beach Boardwalk ③
Santa Cruz Surfing Museum ②

0 meters    250
0 yards    250

SAN FRANCISCO
SALINAS
SAN JOSE

Mission ⑤
Santa Cruz

RIVER ST

Mystery
Spot

Museum of Art
and History ④

SOQUEL AVE

BRANCHFORTE AVENUE

CHESTNUT STREET

CABRILLO HIGHWAY

WALNUT AVE

LINCOLN STREET

CENTER STREET

FRONT STREET

PACIFIC AVE

BROADWAY

OCEAN STREET

Greyhound
Bus Station

LAUREL STREET

CALIFORNIA STREET

WASHINGTON STREET

SAN LORENZO BLVD

RIVERSIDE AVE

San Lorenzo

University of California
Santa Cruz

SEASIDE STREET

BAY STREET

CALIFORNIA STREET

3RD ST

2ND ST

MAIN ST

BEACH STREET

3RD ST

Neary
Lagoon
Park

③ Santa Cruz Beach
Boardwalk
Santa Cruz Beach

BELLEVUE ST

YANGLOVE AVE

ALMAR AVENUE

ERRETT
CIRCLE

CALIFORNIA AVENUE

LAGUNA ST

OREGON ST

WEST CLIFF DRIVE

Cowell
Beach

Municipal
Wharf

INGALLS ST

SWIFT STREET

FAIR AVENUE

DELAWARE AVENUE

WOODROW AVE

COLUMBIA STREET

LIGHTHOUSE AVENUE

Steamer Lane
Surfing Area

SWANTON BLVD

ALTA AVENUE

AVENUE

PELTON AVENUE

WEST CLIFF DRIVE

Lighthouse
State Beach

② Santa Cruz
Surfing Museum

① Natural Bridges
State Beach

**Key to Symbols** *see back flap*

# Street-by-Street: Monterey ❻

The Spanish explorer, Sebastián Vizcaíno, landed here in 1602 and named the bay after his patron, the Count of Monterrey. But it was not until the Spanish captain Gaspar de Portolá (1717–1784) and Father Serra *(see pp46–7)* landed here in 1770 and established a church and presidio that the garrison grew into a pueblo. Monterey served as the capital of California until 1848. After the Gold Rush *(see pp48–9)* the city lost its status to San Francisco and settled into the role of a hardworking fishing port, market town, and military base.

Today, visitors come to tour the historic sites, dine on seafood at Fisherman's Wharf, and attend the annual jazz festival.

**California's First Theater**
*Built in 1847 as a boarding house, it became a theater in 1848.*

**★ Colton Hall**
*The California State Constitution was first signed here in 1849. The hall now houses a museum commemorating the event.*

**Larkin House**
*Thomas Larkin, an East Coast merchant, built this house in 1832. The architecture has become representative of Monterey style (see pp30–31).*

FRANKLIN STREET

PIERCE STREET

PACIFIC STREET

JEFFERSON STREET

CALLE PRINCIPAL

MUNRAS

**The Sherman Quarters** were General Sherman's military base from 1847–1849.

**The Cooper-Molera Complex** combines a garden, a carriage display and personal mementos of three generations of the Cooper family, who occupied the house between 1832 and 1900.

| STAR SIGHTS |
| --- |
| ★ Colton Hall |
| ★ Fisherman's Wharf |

0 meters 100
0 yards 100

**KEY**

– – – Suggested route

*For hotels and restaurants in this region see pp560–61 and pp604–5*

### VISITORS' CHECKLIST

**Road map** B4. 🚶 35,000.
✈ Monterey Peninsula Airport.
🚌 Tyler, Pearl & Munras Sts, (831)
899-2555. ℹ 380 Alvarado St.
(831 648-5360). 🎷 Monterey
Blues Festival (Jul); Monterey Jazz
Festival (Sep); Laguna Seca Races
(May–Oct). www.montereyinfo.org

★ **Fisherman's Wharf**
*Once the center of the fishing and whaling
industries, the area is now known for its
shops, seafood restaurants, and markets.*

**Custom House**
*This old government
building is preserved
as it was in the
1830s and 1840s.*

**Old Whaling Station**
*Mementos of the Monterey whaling
industry are displayed in the house.
The paving outside the building
was made using whale bones.*

**Robert Louis Stevenson
Silverado Museum**
*Robert Louis Stevenson lived here in
1879. The house is now a museum.*

**The Royal Presidio Chapel**,
built 1791–4, is the town's
oldest surviving building.

# Exploring The Monterey Peninsula

Writers and artists have long extolled the spectacular coastline of the Monterey Peninsula. Its granite rocks have been cut into rugged coves and jutting points by the ocean. Forests of Monterey cypress and pine trees, wintering grounds of the monarch butterfly, cover the inland area. Otters and sea lions swim in the kelp forests beyond the shore. The peninsula is home to three main towns: Monterey, the capital of Spanish California *(see pp508–9)*; the former religious retreat, Pacific Grove; and the picturesque village of Carmel-by-the-Sea.

**Marine bird at the Monterey Bay Aquarium**

### ✈ Monterey Bay Aquarium

886 Cannery Row. *Tel (831)* 648-8888. ☐ *daily.* ● *Dec 25.* 🎟
www.montereybayaquarium.org
Monterey Bay Aquarium is one of the largest aquariums in the US, with more than 500 species and tens of thousands of specimens from the Monterey Bay area. Among the exhibits are an enclosed kelp forest, a rock pool, and a live jellyfish display. Visitors are allowed to touch the specimens, including sea stars and bat rays.

A pool connected to the open bay attracts sea otters. The Outer Bay Wing has a huge tank in which the conditions of the ocean are re-created. It contains yellowfin tuna, ocean sunfish, green sea turtles, and barracuda. The Research Institute offers a chance for visitors to watch the marine scientists at work, and the Splash Zone is a hands-on aquarium/museum for kids.

### ▦ Cannery Row

800 Cannery Row.
*Tel (831) 649-6690.* ☐ *daily.*
www.canneryrow.com
This six-block harbor-front street, celebrated by John Steinbeck in his ribald novels

*Cannery Row* and *Sweet Thursday (see p517)*, was once the site of more than 20 fish-packing plants that processed sardines from Monterey Bay. The canneries thrived from the early 20th century, reaching their greatest volume of production in the early 1940s. In 1945 the sardines suddenly disappeared, perhaps as a result of overfishing, and most of the canneries were abandoned, later to be demolished or burned down. The buildings that remain today house an eclectic collection of shops and restaurants. One notable historic building that remains, at No. 800, is the old laboratory of "Doc" Ricketts, noted marine biologist, beer drinker, and best friend of Steinbeck. The building is now a private club.

**Street sign in Cannery Row**

### ▦ Pacific Grove

Forest & Central Aves. *Tel (831)* 373-3304, (800) 656-6650. ☐ *daily.*
● *Jan 1, Thanksgiving, Dec 25.*
www.pacificgrove.org
This sedate town was founded in 1889 as a religious retreat, where alcohol, dancing, and

even the Sunday newspaper were banned. Today it is best known for its wooden houses, many now converted into inns, its beautiful coastal parks, and the monarch butterflies that arrive between October and April *(see p219)*. The annual return of the insects, which are protected by city ordinance, occasions a lively parade.

The Point Pinos Lighthouse was built in 1852 and is now the oldest operating lighthouse in California.

### ▦ Carmel-by-the-Sea

San Carlos, 5th & 6th Sts. *Tel (831)* 624-2522, (800) 550-4333. ☐
*Mon–Sat.* ● *Jan 1, Thanksgiving, Dec 25.* www.carmelcalifornia.org
The varied array of homes in this picturesque village border the steep hillsides down to the ocean. City ordinances restricting streetlights, mail deliveries, and sidewalks gives the town its quaint atmosphere. Art galleries and shops abound along Ocean Ave. The town sponsors an annual playwriting contest, a Bach Festival, and art exhibitions.

### ▦ Carmel River State Beach

Carmelo & Scenic Rds.
This 109-acre (270-ha) state park straddles the mouth of the Carmel River, containing a lagoon and wetland nature preserve for a bountiful population of native and migratory birds. Fishing is permitted on the beach, but swimming is discouraged because of dangerous currents and cold temperatures. The beach is a favorite picnic spot of Carmel residents.

**Point Pinos Lighthouse at Pacific Grove**

*For hotels and restaurants in this region see pp560–61 and pp604–5*

# The 17-Mile Drive

Sightseers may tour the Monterey Peninsula via a toll road, the 17-Mile Drive. The road offers spectacular views of what the area has to offer, including crashing surf, coastal flora, and the Del Monte Forest. The extraordinary beauty of the region has also attracted many wealthy people to build imposing estates and mansions in the area. Most celebrated of all its attractions are the country clubs and championship golf courses.

**Spanish Bay ①**
The shore within this cove at the southern edge of Pacific Grove is a popular picnicking area.

**Spyglass Hill ⑥**
This golf course was named after a location in Robert Louis Stevenson's *Treasure Island*. Stevenson often described the local scenery in his novels.

**Huckleberry Hill ②**
This hill in the Del Monte Forest is popular in the summer with hikers.

## TIPS FOR DRIVERS

**Duration of journey**: 3 hours.
**Entrance**: There is a toll charge for each car. Cycling is free.
**Getting there**: There are four toll gates: 17-Mile Drive, San Antonio Ave, Hwy 1, and SFB Morse Drive. The tour is marked by red and yellow lines.
**When to go**: Summer can be crowded and foggy. In any season, traffic is lighter during the week.
**Where to stay and eat**: Carmel, Monterey, and Pacific Grove have a wide range of hotels and restaurants (see pp560–61 and pp604–5).
**Visitor Information**: Monterey County Convention & Visitors' Bureau, 150 Olivier St. (877) 666-8373. www.montereyinfo.org

**Lone Cypress ⑤**
On a rock overlooking the ocean, this is perhaps the most photographed tree in the world.

**Tor House ④**
This striking rock house was built by the poet Robinson Jeffers between 1918 and 1979.

**Carmel Mission ③**
At one time this beautiful mission was the administrative center for northern California *(see pp512–13)*.

**KEY**

▬▬▬ Tour route

═══ Other roads

▢ Golf courses

| 0 meters | 500 |
| 0 yards | 500 |

# Carmel Mission ❼

**Decorative wall plaque**

Founded in 1770 by Father Junípero Serra (1713–84) and built of adobe brick by Native American laborers, Carmel Mission served as the administrative center for all the Northern California missions. Father Serra resided here until his death and is now buried at the foot of the altar. The mission was secularized and abandoned in 1834, quickly falling into disrepair. Restoration work began in 1924, carefully following the plans of the original mission, and replanting the gardens. The reconstructed living quarters detail 18th-century mission life. The mission still functions as a Catholic church.

**The sarcophagus** depicts Father Serra recumbent in death, surrounded by three mourning padres. It is among the finest of its type in the United States.

**Kitchen**
*This restored room shows the kitchen as it was in missionary days, including the oven brought from Mexico. A section of the original adobe wall can be seen.*

**Bell tower**

**Dining room**

**Statue of Junípero Serra**
*Set within the beautiful front courtyard, a statue of Serra faces the mission church he founded.*

**★ Serra's Cell**
*Father Serra's simple way of life is evident in this sparse, restored cell. The wooden bed, chair, desk, and candlestick were the only pieces of furniture he possessed. He died here in 1784.*

**Façade and front courtyard of Carmel Mission**

## VISITORS' CHECKLIST

3080 Rio Rd, Carmel. **Road map**
B4. **Tel** (831) 624-1271. ☐
9:30am–5pmMon–Sat, 10:30am–
5pm Sun. ● Easter, Thanksgiving,
Dec 24–26. 🖾 ✝ Sun: 7:30am,
9:15am, 11am, 12.45pm. ◎
♿ 🗐 www.carmelmission.org

**Father Serra's** burial place under the altar is marked with a plaque.

**The Chapel Window** is the only place where the original paintwork can still be seen.

**The cemetery** contains the graves of 18th-century missionaries.

**Museum**
*Situated in the old living quarters of the mission, the museum contains several relics belonging to Father Serra.*

**STAR FEATURES**

★ Main Altar

★ Serra's Cell

★ **Main Altar**
*The Gothic arch of Carmel's altar, with its ornate decoration, is the only one of its kind among all the 21 Franciscan missions in California.*

# Big Sur ❽

In the late 18th century, Spanish colonists at Carmel named this stretch of land *El Pais Grande del Sur*, the "big country to the south," and the coastline of Big Sur has been attracting hyperbole ever since. The novelist Robert Louis Stevenson called it "the greatest meeting of land and sea in the world," and the 100 miles (160 km) of breathtaking mountains, cliffs, and rocky coves still leave visitors grasping for adjectives.

The scenic Hwy 1 was constructed across this rugged landscape during the 1930s, but otherwise Big Sur has been preserved in its natural state. There are no large towns and very few signs of civilization in the area. Most of the shoreline is protected in a series of state parks that offer dense forests, broad rivers, and crashing surf, all easily accessible within a short walk of the road.

Crashing surf and rocky cliffs, typical of the Big Sur coastline

**Point Lobos State Reserve**
*This is the habitat of the Monterey cypress, the only tree to survive the region's mixture of fog and salt spray. Its branches are shaped by the sea winds.*

**Point Sur Lighthouse** sits atop a volcanic cone. It was manned until 1974 but is now automated.

**Nepenthe** is a lovely restaurant hidden from the road by oak trees. It has long been frequented by Hollywood movie stars.

**Bixby Creek Bridge**
*This photogenic arched bridge was built in 1932. For many years it was the world's largest single-arch span, at 260 ft (79 m) tall and 700 ft (213 m) long. Hwy 1 was named the state's first scenic highway here in 1966.*

GARRAPATTA STATE PARK

Little Sur

Coast Rd

Big Sur

Big

**KEY**

| | |
|---|---|
| ═══ | Minor road |
| ▬▬ | Scenic route |
| ▬ ▪ ▬ | Hiking trails |
| ──── | National park boundaries |
| ≈≈ | Rivers and lakes |
| Ⓐ | Camping |
| �018 | Viewpoint |

**Andrew Molera State Park**
*Opened in 1972, this park includes 10 miles (16 km) of hiking trails and 2.5 miles (4 km) of quiet, sandy beach.*

**Julia Pfeiffer Burns State Park**
*A tunnel under Hwy 1, accessible only on foot, leads to the
100-ft (30-m) high bluff from which the McWay Creek
waterfall spills into the Pacific Ocean.*

**VISITORS' CHECKLIST**

**Road map** B4. 🏠 *1,500.* 🚌
*Nepenthe Park.* ℹ️ *(831) 667-21
00.* **www**.bigsurcalifornia.org

**The Esalen Institute** was
set up in the 1960s to hold
New Age seminars. Its hot
springs were first frequented
by Native Americans and
still attract visitors *(see p441).*

**Ventana Wilderness**
*Part of the Los Padres
National Forest, many of
the steep ridges of this
beautiful wilderness are
accessible only to experienced hikers. Camp sites
cover the lower reaches.*

VENTANA
WILDERNESS

Tassajara Creek

Ridge Road

LOS PADRES

NATIONAL FOREST

Big Creek

Lucia

Nacimiento-Ferguson Rd

Los Burros Rd

Plaskett Creek

Alder Creek

Antonio River

Lake San
Antonio

Nacimiento River

Lake Nacimiento

**Jade Cove**
*This beautiful cove can be
reached only by way of a
steep path down the cliff
face. The removal of
jade is prohibited above
the high tide level.*

**San Simeon Point** is
a natural harbor that
was used by William
Randolph Hearst to
ship in materials for his
estate, Hearst Castle™,
on the inland hilltop
*(see pp212–13).*

San Simeon

0 kilometers    10

0 miles    10

**Nobel prize-winning author John
Steinbeck (1902–68)**

# Salinas ❾

**Road map** B4. 🏛 *128,343.* 🚃 🚌
ℹ️ *119 E Alisal St (831 424-7611).*
**www**.seemonterey.com

Situated at the north end of
the predominantly agricultural
Salinas Valley, which stretches
for more than 50 miles (80 km)
between San Francisco and
San Luis Obispo, Salinas is the
region's primary agricultural
center. Vegetable-packing
plants and canneries line the
major highways and railroad
tracks. The region is often
referred to as the "salad bowl
of the nation," its prime
produce being lettuce, as
well as tomatoes and garlic.

The town is perhaps best
known, however, as the
birthplace of the Nobel prize-
winning author John Steinbeck,
who set many of his naturalistic stories here and in the
surrounding area. A selection
of books, manuscripts, photographs, and personal memorabilia relating to the author is on
permanent display in a special
room of the **National Steinbeck
Center Museum**. The library
also supplies information on

Steinbeck-related places to
visit in the area and on the
Steinbeck Festival, held in
Salinas every August.

*Hat in Three Stages of Land-
ing*, a large-scale, bright yellow
steel sculpture of three cowboy hats by the acclaimed Pop
artist Claes Oldenberg, was
erected in the town in the
1970s. It stands, appropriately,
in front of the entrance to the
California State Rodeo. Each
Fourth of July one of the
largest rodeos in the world
is held here.

🏛 **National Steinbeck Center
Museum**
1 Main St. **Tel** *(831) 775-4721.*
◻️ *10am–5pm daily.* ⬤ *public hols.*
♿ **www**.steinbeck.org

# Pinnacles National Monument ❿

500 Hwy 146, Paicines. **Road map**
B4. **Tel** *(831) 389-4485.* 🚃 *King
City & Soledad.* ◻️ *daily.* 📷 ♿
*some trails.* 🌐 **www**.nps.gov/pinn

High in the hills above the
Salinas Valley, 12 miles (20 km)
east of the town of Soledad
on US101, the Pinnacles
National Monument preserves
16,000 acres (6,500 ha) of
a unique volcanic landscape.
A solid ridge of lava flows,
eroded over millions of years
into oddly contorted crags
and spires, runs through the
center of the park, in places
forming cliffs more than
500 ft (150 m) tall. There
are no roads across the park,
but there are many carefully
maintained hiking trails.

One of the most popular and
accessible spots in the park
is the Balconies formation,

reached by a 1.5-mile (2.5 km)
leisurely trail. Here beautiful
red and gold cliffs rise high
above the ground, attracting
rock-climbers, photographers,
and bird-watchers. At the
base of the cliffs, huge
boulders caught between the
narrow canyons have formed
a series of dark talus caves.
These were reputedly used in
the past as outlaws' hideouts.

The park is best visited in
spring, when the temperature
is cool and the wildflowers
are in bloom. Mountain lions,
coyotes, and eagles can
occasionally also be sighted.

**Volcanic crags of the Pinnacles
National Monument**

# Fresno ⓫

**Road map** C4. 🏛 *411,600.*
✈️ *Fresno Air Terminal.* 🚃 🚌
ℹ️ *1550 E Shaw Ave. (559) 981-5500,
(800) 788-0836.* **www**.playfresno.org

Fresno is located at approximately the geographical center
of the state and is its eighth
largest city. It is often referred
to as the "Raisin Capital of the
World" because of its abundant
production of the dried fruit.

**Vegetable pickers and packers in the Salinas Valley**

*For hotels and restaurants in this region see pp560–61 and pp604–5*

Its central position makes a convenient base to make excursions to the High Sierras, Kings Canyon, Sequoia, and Yosemite National Parks *(see pp482–97).*

🏛 **Fresno Art Museum**
2233 N First St.
*Tel (559) 441-4221.*
⏱ *11am–5pm Thu–Sun.*
**www.**fresnoart
museum.org

**Homegrown Fresno raisins**

### Environs
In Kearney Park, 7 miles (11 km) west of Fresno, is **Kearney Mansion**. This elaborate French Renaissance-style house was erected in 1903 by Theodore Kearney, an agriculturalist who helped establish California's raisin industry. The house is now a period museum.

🏛 **Kearney Mansion**
7160 W. Kearney Blvd, Hwy 99.
*Tel (559) 441-0862.* ⏱ *Thu–Sun.*
♿ 🚗 **www.**historicfresno.org

**Colonel Allen Allensworth, resident of Hanford**

## Hanford ⑫

**Road map** C4. 🏘 40,000. 🚉 🚌
ℹ *200 Santa Fe Ave, Suite D (559) 582-5024).* **www.**visithanford.com

One of many medium-sized farming communities in the area, Hanford is significant because of its diverse multi-ethnic heritage. The China Alley neighborhood was once inhabited by one of the largest Chinese communities in California, many of whom worked on the construction of the transcontinental railroad *(see pp50–51).* Located east of the town center, China Alley

surrounds the historic **Taoist Temple**, built in 1893. The temple operated as a hostel for Chinese immigrants and a Chinese school as well as a religious shrine. Downtown Hanford, around Courthouse Square, has a beautiful antique carousel and a number of elegant buildings dating from the late 19th century, now converted into shops and restaurants.

🏯 **Taoist Temple & Museum**
12 China Alley. *Tel (559) 582-4508.*
⏱ *by appointment only.* ♿ 🏠

### Environs
The **Colonel Allensworth State Historic Park** is 30 miles (50 km) south of Hanford. Colonel Allen Allensworth believed his fellow African-Americans could combat racism by building their own future. He ser up a unique farming community in 1908 with a group of African-American families. Memorabilia of this independent community are now on display in the old farmhouses.

🏛 **Colonel Allensworth State Historic Park**
Off Hwy 99 on County Rd J22,
Earlimart. *Tel (661) 849-3433.*
⏱ *daily.* ♿ **www.**parks.ca.gov

---

### JOHN STEINBECK

One of California's most successful 20th-century writers, John Steinbeck (1902–68) was born in Salinas to an established family of farmers and ranchers. When he dropped out of Stanford University *(see p427)*, Steinbeck moved to the Monterey Peninsula in the late 1920s to write fiction. After several attempts he eventually gained a measure of success with the publication of the novella *Tortilla Flat* in 1935. Steinbeck then began a series of short stories and novels, the majority of them focusing on the people and places he knew well in the Salinas Valley and Monterey area. These included some of his greatest work: *Of Mice and Men* (1937), *Cannery Row* (1945), and *East of Eden* (1952).

His best-known work is *The Grapes of Wrath* (1939). The novel fictionalizes the mass westward migration that took place during the Depression of the 1930s, by documenting the struggles of the Joad family as they fled the dust bowl of Oklahoma for the greener pastures of California. It was an immediate bestseller and earned Steinbeck a Pulitzer Prize, although many Californians took its unhappy ending as an insult to their state, and even as Communist propaganda. Steinbeck reacted to this antipathy in 1943 by going to North Africa and becoming a war correspondent. On his return to the United States in 1945 he settled on Long Island, New York. In 1962, he was awarded the Nobel Prize for Literature. Steinbeck is the only American author to have received both the Pulitzer Prize and the Nobel Prize.

He died in New York City on December 20, 1968, but is buried in his hometown, in the Garden of Memories at No. 768 Abbott Street.

**First editions of Steinbeck's most famous works, *Cannery Row* and *The Grapes of Wrath***

---

# TRAVELERS' NEEDS

# WHERE TO STAY

Framed by rugged coastal mountains, lush wooded hills, sophisticated urban centers, and a long stretch of coastline, California is one of the premier vacation destinations in the world. Whether rustic lodges or five-star resorts suit your budget, there is a wealth of options for travelers to the state.

Top hotels can range from film-star luxury to high-tech business centers. Budget accommodations are widespread, from roadside motels to atmospheric inns that offer an insight into the state's history. All accommodations, are however, likely to

offer double beds, bathrooms, and comfortable surroundings. A range of camping facilities is also available for those interested in the great outdoors.

Free magazines containing discount coupons for all sorts of accommodations are available from street distribution bins at freeway rest stops and at car rental centers. Many hotels also offer discounts on reservations during the off season, and it is worth booking ahead to negotiate the rate. The listings on pages 524–66 give full descriptions of quality accommodations throughout the state to suit all budgets.

**Doorman**

## HOTEL CLASSIFICATIONS

The California tourist industry is recognized for its quality lodgings. A guideline of value to travelers is the diamond rating system of the California State Automobile Association. Every lodging, from the most expensive four-diamond hotel to the budget one-diamond motel, is rated for service, cleanliness, and the range of facilities offered.

## HOTELS

In California, hotels come in every shape and size. There are the historic showplaces such as The Sheraton in San Francisco (see p547), the Biltmore in Los Angeles (see p526), and the Ahwahnee in Yosemite National Park (see p560). These were originally built to impress East Coast bankers and prove that the West Coast was worth their investment. There are

also the trendy, visually stunning urban getaways such as the Hotel Triton in San Francisco (see p542) and the Mondrian in West Hollywood (see p531). There are hotels with fashion shops, with corporate conference centers, chandelier ballrooms, or landscaped gardens. There are also small hotels, called "boutique hotels," which have fewer than 100 rooms and the intimate ambience of a bed-and-breakfast.

Several hotels built on American-Indian land have Las Vegas-style casinos attached. Federal and state laws prohibiting casino gambling do not apply to Indian reservations.

No matter the size, you can always count on every hotel having a spacious foyer, a restaurant or café, a pool or exercise room, and a range of services such as laundry, ironing, and in-room video movies. If the hotel does not

**Lounge bar in the exclusive Beverly Wilshire Hotel (see p524)**

have its own exercise facility on-site, there is often an arrangement with a nearby health club that hotel guests can use for a fee. Many city hotels offer maps for joggers, showing the most scenic and safe routes in the area. No-smoking rooms are always available – many hotels have now set aside entire floors for nonsmokers only, and smoke-free hotels are becoming more common.

Rates for hotels range from an inexpensive $75 per night to a moderate $175. Rooms at upscale, well-located hotels can range from $175–$300+. There are some luxury hotels in California, however, be it in Beverly Hills, Big Sur, or Napa Valley, that charge from $300 to $900 a night in season.

**Biltmore Hotel in Los Angeles (see p526)**

Hotels are also subject to city and state taxes, which are 14 percent in San Francisco and Los Angeles. Not included in room rates are additional charges, such as for parking, as well as heavy surcharges for outgoing telephone calls.

## CORPORATE HOTELS

These cater to business travelers by offering weekly and monthly rates. There are also a number of all-suite hotels, with living rooms, in-room computers, and fax connections. Some even have on-site computer centers, providing ample work space. Check the hotel listings on pages 524–66 to see where these services are available.

## CHAIN HOTELS

You can count on good service, moderate prices, and comfortable surroundings at a chain hotel. The popular chains include the **Westin**, **Hilton**, **Sheraton**, **Marriott**, **Ramada**, **Hyatt**, and **Holiday Inn**. Some operate more than one hotel in each city and designate one location as the flagship facility. All chain hotels listed on page 523 have Internet web sites, or you can call the hotel's toll-free number to ask about rates and availability.

Sign over small chain hotel

Chateau Marmont on Sunset Boulevard *(see p530)*

## TIPPING

The hotel porter will often carry your bags to your room on arrival and load up your car on departing. A tip of $2 per bag is fair for this service. If the hotel has valet parking, a tip of 15–20 percent of the parking charge should be given to the driver only when you leave. Room service also requires a 15–20 percent tip. A $10 tip for the maid is acceptable, especially after a long stay.

## RESORTS

Whether a resort has less than 100 rooms or close to 300, the cottages, villas, and grounds are always arranged to encourage privacy. Resorts have all the services of a hotel but are spread over larger grounds.

The key to a quality resort is the range of indoor and outdoor facilities that are offered, be it horseback riding, tennis courts, golf courses, Olympic-size swimming pools, yoga instruction, full-service health spa, or a four-star restaurant. A vacation at a resort is a destination in itself – the natural setting and range of on-site activities will more than hold your attention. Stays in resorts are expensive, but for both relaxation and sports they are worth every penny.

You may want to choose a resort based on location – wine country, oceanside, mountain hideaway, or urban retreat. California has many such hidden treasures, and some of the best are listed on pages 524–66.

San Diego Marriott and Marina Hotel, on San Diego Bay *(see p538)*

Historic Mendocino Hotel *(see p555)*

## MOTELS

Inexpensive roadside motels
sprang up in California in the
1950s, as a product of an
increasingly car-oriented
lifestyle. Motels offer minimal
facilities – double, queen, or
king-size beds, television,
telephone, tea and coffee,
and en-suite bathroom facilities. There is always parking
for cars, and many also have
outdoor swimming pools – a
necessity for travelers in
California's summertime heat.
Some have kitchen facilities,
and most offer non-smoking
rooms. Check with the motel
to see if they allow pets.

There are a number of popular motel chains throughout
the state that have a reputation for clean rooms and
good service at inexpensive
prices. These include **Best
Western**, **Quality Inn**, **Motel 6**,
and **Travelodge**. Rates begin
at around $40 a night.

## HISTORIC INNS

Rich in regional history, these
inns are often all that remain
of late 19th-century buildings
in many of California's small
towns. As well as reflecting
local history, some inns also
have their own story to tell,
having been, perhaps, a
hunting and fishing lodge, a
stern-wheeler riverboat, a
Victorian mansion, or
a hideaway for Hollywood
movie stars in earlier times.
Whatever their heritage, they
all share a unique architecture
and ambience. Many such
inns, built during the era of
railroad expansion in the West,

have achieved protected status
and cannot be demolished or
architecturally altered.

Similar to bed-and-breakfast
hotels in atmosphere, historic
inns are larger, with 20–100
rooms. Most serve compli-
mentary continental breakfast
and afternoon snacks of cakes
or cookies. For more information, contact **California
Historic Country Inns**.

Smaller lodgings, many also
with a claim to historical
significance, may have small,
individual cabins with kitchen
facilities for efficiency accommodations (self-catering).
Rarely do these inns have on-
site restaurants, cafés, or room
service. The majority of them
allow you to bring along pets,
many have outdoor swimming
pools, and larger ones may
also have tennis courts. Check
in advance whether smoking
is allowed in the cabins –
some inns in California now
pride themselves on providing
guests with a completely
smoke-free environment.

## BED-AND-BREAKFAST
## ACCOMMODATIONS

Most bed-and-breakfasts in
California were originally
private homes built many years
ago and which retain the
charm of a bygone era. In
addition to breakfast, afternoon
snacks or evening drinks may
also be available. Prices begin
at $60 upwards a night. Ask
whether the room has its own
bathroom. There is often a
two-night minimum stay,
especially in peak season.
Libraries, living rooms, landscaped gardens, and swimming
pools are common features.
The manager is also often the
owner and can provide details
of local history and sights. See
pages 524–66 for a range of
bed-and-breakfasts, or contact
the **California Association of
Bed-and-Breakfast Inns**.

Casa Laguna Inn in Laguna Beach
*(see p535)*

## ROOMS IN PRIVATE
## HOMES

While many small inns and
lodges may offer kitchen
facilities, there is nothing like
staying in a private home to
get the real flavor of a specific

Deetjen's Big Sur Inn *(see p560)*

**Sweet Dreams Cabin, Tahoe City** *(see p560)*

city or town. There are two ways you can arrange this type of accommodation. The first is to rent an apartment or house from a real estate agency. Every city and town in the state has at least one, if not several, estate agencies that specialize in vacation rental property. These agencies will quote rental rates by the night, week, month, or even longer. Prices per week can range anywhere between $300–$3,000, depending on location and size of the rented property. You will have to pay a cleaning deposit, which is refundable when you leave. For the widest choice of properties, it is best to make reservations at least a month in advance. Contact any town's Chamber of Commerce for details of agencies.

Another option is to arrange a house exchange with a California resident. **Intervac US** is part of a worldwide home exchange network and publishes quarterly directories of people willing to exchange their homes for yours during vacations. Fees to obtain or be listed in this directory range from $65–$85 per year. The network does not match people up; arrangements are made by the individuals.

## YOUTH HOSTELS

This is the least expensive accommodation option in California. Hostels offer clean, modern facilities, often in picturesque locations (such as lighthouses, on national parkland, and mountain hideaways). They usually offer dormitory-style, single-sex sleeping arrangements, though some do have one or two private rooms available for couples. Most hostels also provide kitchen facilities.

Despite the name, youth hostels in the US are not only for the young, as there is no age limit. There are also a number of Elder Hostels, catering to senior citizens who opt for budget travel. Contact **American Youth Hostels** for a full list of accommodations.

## CAMPING, TRAILERS, AND RVS

Campers are always welcome in California's national and state park system *(see p610)*. There is also a large network of privately run camp sites with a range of facilities for trailers and RVs, such as electricity hook-up, water supply, disposal stations, picnic areas, and grocery stores.

**Camping in Yosemite National Park** *(see pp488–9)*

(see p560), (see p610), (see pp488–9)

# DIRECTORY

## CHAIN HOTELS

**Hilton**
**Tel** *(800) 445-8667.*
**www**.hilton.com

**Holiday Inn**
**Tel** *(800) 465-4329.*
**www**.holidayinn.com

**Hyatt**
**Tel** *(888) 591-1234.*
**www**.hyatt.com

**ITT Sheraton/Starwood**
**Tel** *(888) 625-5144.*
**www**.sheraton.com

**Marriott**
**Tel** *(888) 236-2427.*
**www**.marriott.com

**Ramada**
**Tel** *(888) 298-2054.*
**www**.ramada.com

**Westin/Starwood**
**Tel** *(888) 625-5144.*
**www**.westin.com

## CHAIN MOTELS

**Best Western**
**Tel** *(800) 780-7234.*
**www**.bestwestern.com

**Motel 6**
**Tel** *(800) 466-8356.*
**www**.motel6.com

**Quality Inn**
**Tel** *(800) 228-5151.*
**www**.choicehotels.com

**Travelodge**
**Tel** *(800) 578-7878.*
**www**.travelodge.com

## HISTORIC INNS

**California Historic Country Inns**
**www**.californiahistoric
countryinns.com

## BED-AND-BREAKFAST

**California Association of Bed-and-Breakfast Inns**
**Tel** *(800) 373-9251.*

## ROOMS IN PRIVATE HOMES

**Intervac US**
30 Corte San Fernando,
Tiburon, CA 94920. **Tel** *(800)
756-4663.* **www**.intervacus.com

## YOUTH HOSTELS

**American Youth Hostels**
8401 Colesville Rd, Salem Spring,
MD 20910. **Tel** *(310) 495-1240.*

# Choosing a Hotel

The hotels in this guide have been selected across a wide price range for their good value, facilities, and location. These listings highlight some of the factors that may influence your choice. Entries are listed by region, beginning with Los Angeles. For more details on restaurants see pages 568–605.

**PRICE CATEGORIES**
For a standard double room per night in high season, excluding tax and service charges.

⑤ under $100
⑤⑤ $100–$150
⑤⑤⑤ $150–$200
⑤⑤⑤⑤ $200–$250
⑤⑤⑤⑤⑤ over $250

## LOS ANGELES

**AIRPORT Radisson Los Angeles Airport** ⑤⑤⑤
*6225 W. Century Boulevard, 90045* **Tel** *800-395-7046* **Fax** *310-337-6555* **Rooms** *580*  **Road map** *inset A*

Certified as a "Green Seal" eco-friendly hotel, this is the closest hotel to LAX airport. Rooms have free Wi-Fi and there are free airport shuttles, a fitness center, pool, and business services. Well located for sightseeing at the Getty, Santa Monica, and Disneyland®. **www.radisson.com**

**AIRPORT Hilton Los Angeles Airport** ⑤⑤⑤⑤
*5711 W Century Blvd, 90045* **Tel** *(310) 410-4000* **Fax** *(310) 410-6250* **Rooms** *1234*  **Road map** *inset A*

This is one of the world's largest airport hotels. There is a shuttle to the airport, an executive business floor with a private lounge, and a breathtaking lobby with three gardens where guests can relax. All rooms have high-speed Internet access. **www.hilton.com**

**AIRPORT Los Angeles Airport Marriott** ⑤⑤⑤⑤
*5855 W Century Blvd, 90045* **Tel** *(310) 641-5700* **Fax** *(310) 337-5358* **Rooms** *1004*  **Road map** *inset A*

Situated very close to the airport, this full-service property offers spacious rooms complete with state-of-the-art business facilities, including two-line phones, faxes, and wireless Internet access. The excellent guest service is complemented by four restaurants. **www.marriott.com**

**AIRPORT Sheraton Gateway Los Angeles Airport Hotel** ⑤⑤⑤⑤
*6101 W Century Blvd, 90045* **Tel** *(310) 642-1111* **Fax** *(310) 645-1414* **Rooms** *802*  **Road map** *inset A*

Imbued with a resort-style atmosphere, this hotel is close to the airport but you may find it has more of a beach ambience. Business facilities feature wireless Internet access. Good family packages are available. Shula's Steakhouse is worth a visit. **www.sheratonlosangeles.com**

**AIRPORT Westin Los Angeles Airport** ⑤⑤⑤⑤
*5400 W Century Blvd, 90045* **Tel** *(310) 216-5858* **Fax** *(310) 417-4545* **Rooms** *740*  **Road map** *inset A*

Four blocks from the airport, this well-managed hotel offers rooms appointed with the latest business amenities, including high-speed Internet access in all rooms and public spaces. There is a top-notch fitness facility and a good restaurant in the lobby. **www.starwoodhotels.com**

**BEL AIR Luxe Hotel Sunset Boulevard** ⑤⑤⑤⑤
*11461 Sunset Blvd, 90049* **Tel** *(310) 476-6571* **Fax** *(310) 440-0821* **Rooms** *160*  **Road map** *inset A*

Secluded and sophisticated, this luxurious hotel features generously proportioned rooms, with high-speed Internet access and spa-like amenities such as plush bathrobes and expensive soaps. There is a free daily shuttle service to the Getty Museum. Tennis lessons from a professional coach are also available. **www.luxehotelsunsetblvd.com**

**BEVERLY HILLS Hotel Avalon** ⑤⑤⑤⑤
*9400 W Olympic Blvd, 90212* **Tel** *(310) 277-5221* **Fax** *(310) 277-4928* **Rooms** *84*  **Map** *5 F4*

A splendid, mid-20th-century boutique hotel, the Avalon offers friendly service, chic accommodation, and a central location. The atmosphere is calm and serene, and the rooms are equipped with up-to-date features. The restaurant is award winning; dine poolside for a memorable LA experience. **www.avalonbeverlyhills.com**

**BEVERLY HILLS Beverly Hills Hotel and Bungalows** ⑤⑤⑤⑤⑤
*9641 Sunset Blvd, 90210* **Tel** *(310) 276-2251* **Fax** *(310) 887-2887* **Rooms** *204*  **Map** *5 D5*

No detail is too small for the staff at this famed Los Angeles property, set tastefully among lush gardens, and central to all area attractions and several shops. Many rooms have a homey feel, and are spacious with private patios and fully-appointed kitchens. Features include tennis courts and a full-service spa. **www.beverlyhillshotel.com**

**BEVERLY HILLS Beverly Hilton** ⑤⑤⑤⑤⑤
*9876 Wilshire Blvd, 90210* **Tel** *(310) 274-7777* **Fax** *(310) 285-1313* **Rooms** *569*  **Map** *5 E4*

A multi-million-dollar re-modeling injected new life into this stylish LA icon, home to the Golden Globe Awards and Jerry Lewis Telethon. The updated rooms feature fine linen as well as state-of-the-art amenities for business travelers. A great spa and top-notch fitness facilities are available. Pets welcome. **www.beverlyhilton.com**

**Key to Symbols** *see back cover flap*

## BEVERLY HILLS Beverly Wilshire Four Seasons Hotel 🔲 🍴 ≋ 🏋 📺 ♿ 🔲 ⑤⑤⑤⑤⑤

*9500 Wilshire Blvd, 90212 Tel (310) 275-5200 Fax (310) 274-2851 Rooms 395* **Map 5 F4**

This polished hotel offers European charm and style in the heart of Beverly Hills. Accommodation choices include spacious, well-appointed rooms in the historic Wilshire Wing or the contemporary Beverly Wing, which has a clean, modern look. All amenities available, including Internet access. **www.fourseasons.com**

## BEVERLY HILLS Luxe Hotel Rodeo Drive 🔲 🍴 ≋ 📺 ♿ 🔲 ⑤⑤⑤⑤⑤

*360 N Rodeo Dr, 90210 Tel (310) 273-0300, (800) 468-3541 Fax (310) 859-8950 Rooms 88* **Map 5 F3**

Central to world-famous shops, this intimate hotel is charming and well appointed. Many rooms have private sun decks. The location is within walking distance from many attractions, but a town car service is also available. Guests can also make use of the facilities at the hotel's sister property, Sunset. **www.luxehotelrodeodrive.com**

## BEVERLY HILLS Maison 140 🔲 🍴 🏋 📺 ♿ 🔲 ⑤⑤⑤⑤

*140 Lasky Dr, 90212 Tel (310) 281-4000, (800) 670-6182 Fax (310) 281-4001 Rooms 43* **Map 5 D2**

This small, stylish hotel offers upscale luxury at a great price. Rooms are sleek, with touches of Asian flair and retro sophistication. Amenities include high-end linen and bath accessories, as well as high-speed Internet access. There is a popular bar on-site and breakfast is included. **www.maison140beverlyhills.com**

## BEVERLY HILLS Peninsula Beverly Hills 🔲 🍴 ≋ 🏋 📺 ♿ 🔲 ⑤⑤⑤⑤⑤

*9882 S Santa Monica Blvd, 90212 Tel (310) 551-2888 Fax (310) 788-2319 Rooms 193* **Map 5 E4**

The last word in LA luxury for the rich and the famous, this sleek, elegant five diamond hotel pays meticulous attention to detail. Rooms are equipped with every conceivable amenity, including a remote control that operates almost everything. It also has a top-rated spa and restaurant. **www.peninsula.com**

## CENTURY CITY Hyatt Regency Century Plaza Hotel 🔲 🍴 ≋ 🏋 📺 ♿ 🔲 ⑤⑤⑤⑤⑤

*2025 Ave of the Stars, 90067 Tel (310) 228-1234 Fax (310) 551-3355 Rooms 726* **Map 5 D5**

Still enjoying a $70-million upgrade that brought the elegant property to luxurious standards, this local icon has all amenities and has hosted heads of state and Hollywood stars for decades. The rooms are large and feature great city views. The spa and dining facilities are first rate. **www.centuryplaza.hyatt.com**

## CENTURY CITY InterContinental Los Angeles 🔲 🍴 ≋ 🏋 ♿ 🔲 ⑤⑤⑤⑤⑤

*2151 Ave of the Stars, 90067 Tel (310) 284-6500, (877) 270-1390 Fax (310) 277-9438 Rooms 363* **Map 5 E5**

Renowned for its business facilities, this modern hotel features spacious and well-connected rooms, all with a balcony or patio, and including fax machines with private numbers. Extras include a great spa and limousine service for shoppers and theatergoers. **www.intercontinentallosangeles.com**

## DOWNTOWN Best Western Dragon Gate Inn 🔲 🍴 🏋 🔲 ⑤

*818 N Hill St, 90012 Tel (213) 617-3077 Fax (213) 680-3753 Rooms 52* **Map 11 F2**

You will find little more than the basics at this clean, friendly hotel in Chinatown. Rooms are spacious and have data ports and there is an in-room coffee-maker and refrigerator. Its location is convenient to most downtown sights and attractions. Breakfast is included. **www.dragongateinn.com**

## DOWNTOWN Ramada Wilshire Center 🔲 🍴 🏋 ♿ 🔲 ⑤⑤

*3900 Wilshire Blvd, 90010 Tel (213) 736-5222 Fax (213) 736-5038 Rooms 86* **Road map inset A**

Located midtown and within a convenient distance for visiting Hollywood, this tidy, reliable hotel offers great-value rooms featuring comfortable beds and linen, as well as high-speed Internet access. There is a restaurant on-site serving steaks and sandwiches. **www.ramada.com**

## DOWNTOWN Figueroa Hotel 🔲 🍴 ≋ 🏋 🔲 ⑤⑤⑤

*939 S Figueroa St, 90015 Tel (213) 627-8971, (800) 421-9092 Fax (213) 689-0305 Rooms 285* **Map 10 C5**

Quirky and charming, this old but updated hotel, right downtown, blends elements of Southern California, Mexico, and Northern Africa for an eclectic effect. The rooms vary in size and style, but all feature decent amenities and soft linen. The service is excellent. **www.figueroahotel.com**

## DOWNTOWN The Inn at 657 ♿ 🔲 ⑤⑤⑤

*657 W 23rd St, 90007 Tel (213) 741-2200, (800) 347-7512 Rooms 11* **Road map inset A**

An unusual find for LA, this B&B features one- and two-bedroom suites, with garden entrances and pleasant sitting areas. The rooms are comfortable and modestly appointed, most are sunny and bright. The price includes local calls. **www.patsysinn657.com**

## DOWNTOWN Kyoto Grand Hotel and Gardens 🔲 🍴 ≋ 🏋 📺 ♿ 🔲 ⑤⑤⑤

*120 S Los Angeles St, 90012 Tel (213) 629-1200, (888) 354-0831 Fax (213) 622-0980 Rooms 434* **Map 11 E4**

Adjacent to Little Tokyo, this hotel, formerly the New Otani, offers Japanese-style graciousness, and several Japanese dining options. A large traditional garden features waterfalls and foot bridges. There is also a courtesy mini-bus service within downtown, business support services, a health spa, and a fitness center. **www.kyotograndhotel.com**

## DOWNTOWN Miyako Inn and Spa 🔲 🏋 ♿ 🔲 ⑤⑤⑤

*328 E 1st St, 90012 Tel (213) 617-2000, (800) 228-6596 Fax (213) 617-2700 Rooms 174* **Map 11 F4**

Japanese-inspired hospitality in Little Tokyo, this appealing hotel is popular for its extensive list of treatments in the health spa as well as for its lively karaoke lounge. Rooms are outfitted in a simple style and feature most essential amenities. **www.miyakoinn.com**

### DOWNTOWN Millennium Biltmore

$$$$

*506 S Grand Ave, 90071* **Tel** *(213) 624-1011* **Fax** *(213) 612-1545* **Rooms** *683*                          **Map** *11 D4*

An LA icon, the Biltmore has been a popular downtown hotel since 1923. The rooms are tidy, a bit small, but nicely furnished with all amenities. The ornate, Spanish-style lobby is the place to meet and greet. The hotel faces Pershing Square. **www.thebiltmore.com**

### DOWNTOWN Hilton Checkers Hotel

$$$$

*535 S Grand Ave, 90071* **Tel** *(213) 624-0000* **Fax** *(213) 626-9906* **Rooms** *188*                          **Map** *11 4D*

Dating from the 1920s, this luxurious hotel provides top-notch service. Large and relaxing rooms come with marble tubs and sumptuous bath amenities. There is a rooftop swimming pool and deck. The location allows an easy walk to the nearby theaters, nightlife, and convention center. **www.hiltoncheckers.com**

### DOWNTOWN Luxe City Center

$$$$

*1020 S Figueroa Street, 90015* **Tel** *(213) 748-1291* **Fax** *(213) 748-6028* **Rooms** *195*                          **Map** *10 C5*

Looking good since a major top-to-bottom upgrade, rooms at this well-run hotel offer comfortable beds and separate seating areas, as well as complimentary on-site fitness facilities. Across the street from the Staples Center in the LA Live entertainment and shopping district. **www.luxecitycenter.com**

### DOWNTOWN Omni Los Angeles California Plaza

$$$$

*51 S Olive St, 90012* **Tel** *(213) 617-3300* **Fax** *(213) 617-3399* **Rooms** *453*                          **Map** *11 4D*

This appealing, mid-sized hotel is ideally situated for shopping and the music center. Rooms are large, stylish, and cater to the business traveler as well as to the leisure traveler who enjoys comfort. The signature restaurant, Noe, should not be missed. A complimentary car service is available for theatergoers. **www.omnihotels.com**

### DOWNTOWN Los Angeles Athletic Club

$$$$$

*431 W 7th St, 90014* **Tel** *(213) 625-2211* **Fax** *(213) 689-1194* **Rooms** *72*                          **Map** *11 D5*

Originally a private club, this hotel and recreation facility features oversized Victorian-style rooms and suites, with Internet access. Rates include the use of the extensive fitness facility, swimming pool and a Continental breakfast. It is situated close to all downtown attractions. **www.laac.com**

### DOWNTOWN Ritz-Carlton Los Angeles

$$$$$

*900 W. Olympic Boulevard, 90015* **Tel** *213-743-8800* **Fax** *213-743-8801* **Rooms** *123*                          **Map** *10 C5*

This luxury hotel features a lounge, bar, and rooftop pool on the 26th floor. All rooms have city views. The hotel is close to the STAPLES Center, the Nokia Theatre, and an array of restaurants and nightclubs. The main hotel restaurant is WP24, run by celebrity chef Wolfgang Puck. **www.ritzcarlton.com**

### DOWNTOWN Sheraton Los Angeles Downtown

$$$$$

*711 S Hope St, 90017* **Tel** *(213) 488-3500* **Fax** *(213) 488-4110* **Rooms** *485*                          **Map** *11 D4*

Formerly operated by Hyatt, this Financial District hotel was renamed, along with a complete refurbishment and fresh vibrancy. The rooms are large and appointed with business facilities. The lobby lounge is stylish and relaxing. The hotel is linked to the Macy's Plaza shopping complex. **www.starwoodhotels.com**

### GLENDALE Chariot Inn Motel

$

*1118 E Colorado St, 91205* **Tel** *(818) 507-9600, (800) 458-4080* **Fax** *(818) 507-9774* **Rooms** *30*     **Road map** *inset A*

With quiet and comfortable rooms, this no-frills roadside property is located between downtown LA and Pasadena. All rooms are air conditioned and some have whirlpool baths. Amenities include a heated outdoor swimming pool. A Continental-style breakfast is included. **www.chariotinn.com**

### GLENDALE Hilton Glendale Hotel

$$$

*100 W Glenoaks Blvd, 91202* **Tel** *(818) 956-5466* **Fax** *(818) 956-5490* **Rooms** *351*     **Road map** *inset A*

This well-run hotel is conveniently located, with easy freeway access to many points of interest in LA. Rooms offer data ports and other business amenities. There is an on-site swimming pool, as well as a spa, and a full-service fitness center. The staff are friendly and efficient. A courtesy car service is available. **www.hilton.com**

### HOLLYWOOD Hollywood Orchid Suites

$$

*1753 Orchid Ave, 90028* **Tel** *(323) 874-9678, (800) 537-3052* **Fax** *(323) 874-9931* **Rooms** *40*     **Map** *2 B4*

There are few hotels more central to major Hollywood attractions as this converted apartment-hotel, which stands directly behind the famed Chinese Theater. There are two-bedroom suites as well as tidy, well-appointed rooms, some of which come with kitchenettes. **www.orchidsuites.com**

### HOLLYWOOD Beverly Garland's Holiday Inn

$$$

*4222 Vineland Ave, 91602* **Tel** *(818) 980-8000* **Fax** *(818) 766-5230* **Rooms** *255*     **Road map** *inset A*

Located in North Hollywood, close to Universal Studios®, this quiet, family accommodation features rooms with private balconies or patios, as well as an on-site restaurant. Wireless Internet access is available throughout the property. Children under 12 stay and eat free. **www.beverlygarland.com**

### HOLLYWOOD Hollywood Heights

$$$

*2005 N. Highland Avene, 90068* **Tel** *866-696-3157* **Fax** *323-876-3272* **Rooms** *160*     **Map** *2 B4*

Rooms here are retro-modern and simple, with quality linens and Wi-Fi. The location, near the Sunset Strip, makes this convenient for sightseeing, and the restaurant offers a good choice of affordable dining. The hotel staff are friendly and knowledgable. **www.hollywoodheightshotel.com**

**Key to Price Guide** *see p524* **Key to Symbols** *see back cover flap*

### HOLLYWOOD Farmer's Daughter Hotel
⬚ 🍴 ♨ ♿ ⛶    $$$$$

*115 S Fairfax Ave, 90036* **Tel** *(323) 937-3930, (800) 334-1658* **Fax** *(323) 932-1608* **Rooms** *66*    **Map** *2 B4*

Country charm meets urban sophistication at this stylish, fun hotel across from the famous Farmers Market and CBS Studios. The rooms are spacious and comfortable, and fashioned as "his" or "hers". There is a Fusion restaurant in the lobby. **www.farmersdaughterhotel.com**

### HOLLYWOOD Magic Castle Hotel
⬚ 🍴 ♨ ♿ ⛶    $$$$

*7025 Franklin Ave, 90028* **Tel** *(323) 851-0800, (800) 741-4915* **Fax** *(323) 851-4926* **Rooms** *40*    **Map** *2 B4*

This classic Hollywood hotel, close to the Hollywood and Highland Entertainment Center, is renowned for its good value and whimsical castle-like design. Spacious suites and studios have fine amenities and full kitchens. Guests can catch a magic show at the members only Magic Castle next door. **www.magiccastlehotel.com**

### HOLLYWOOD Ramada Hollywood Hotel
⬚ ♨ 🍴 ♿ ⛶    $$$$

*1160 N Vermont Ave, 90029* **Tel** *(323) 315-1800* **Fax** *(323) 660-8069* **Rooms** *130*    **Road map** inset A

This hotel has full amenities, including many family-friendly conveniences, and it offers complete conference facilities. The heart of Hollywood is a short drive from the hotel, and a shuttle service to Universal Studios® is available. **www.hollywoodhotel.net.com**

### HOLLYWOOD The Standard Hotel Hollywood
⬚ 🍴 ♨ ♦ ♿ ⛶    $$$$

*8300 Sunset Blvd, 90069* **Tel** *(323) 650-9090* **Fax** *(323) 650-2820* **Rooms** *163*    **Map** *2 B4*

This Sunset Strip hotel oozes hipness and cutting-edge style, but does not break the bank. Rooms are modestly appointed, but have plenty of flair. Book a "budget" room and save for cocktails in the ultra-chic lounge, or keep an eye out for celebrities in the diner-style restaurant. **www.starwoodhotels.com**

### HOLLYWOOD Hollywood Roosevelt Hotel
⬚ 🍴 ♨ ♦ 🛎 ♿ ⛶    $$$$$

*7000 Hollywood Blvd, 90028* **Tel** *(323) 466-7000* **Fax** *(323) 462-8056* **Rooms** *300*    **Map** *2 B4*

The history and glamor of old Hollywood live on at this refurbished classic, which is enjoying a renaissance in popularity among the young and hip. The hotel features elegant rooms that include cabana-style suites situated around a courtyard pool. Good for celebrity-spotting. **www.hollywoodroosevelt.com**

### HOLLYWOOD Renaissance Hollywood Hotel & Spa
⬚ 🍴 ♨ 🛎 ♿ ⛶    $$$$$

*1755 N Highland Ave, 90028* **Tel** *(323) 856-1200, (800) 769-4774* **Fax** *(323) 856-1205* **Rooms** *637*    **Map** *2 B4*

This centrally located hotel offers rooms with expansive views of surrounding Hollywood. Some have French windows with scenic vistas. Spend an afternoon lounging by the rooftop pool. The hotel is around the corner from Hollywood and Highland Center and other attractions. Try the trendy Twist restaurant. **www.renaissancehollywood.com**

### HOLLYWOOD W Hollywood Hotel and Residences
⬚ 🍴 ♨ 🛎 ♿ ⛶    $$$$$

*6250 Hollywood Boulevard, 90028* **Tel** *323-798-1300* **Fax** *323-798-1305* **Rooms** *305*    **Map** *2 B4*

This hotel at Hollywood and Vine has special amenities to fit in with the glamorous feel. A currency exchange, a 24-hour business center, pet welcome kits, a rooftop pool/lounge/bar and Bliss® spa are all available, as well as different themed restaurants. Rooms are sleek and ultra-modern. **www.whotels.com**

### LONG BEACH Inn of Long Beach
⬚ ♨ ⛶    $

*185 Atlantic Ave, 90802* **Tel** *(562) 435-3791, (800) 230-7500* **Fax** *(562) 436-7510* **Rooms** *50* **Road map** inset A

With a convenient downtown location, and within walking distance from the beach, this pleasant motel has large comfortable rooms. The pool and a generously proportioned enclosed courtyard are great for families. Guests can make free local calls and use the free city shuttle service. **www.innoflongbeach.com**

### LONG BEACH Super 8 Motel
⬚ ♨ ♦ ♿ ⛶    $

*4201 E Pacific Hwy, 90804* **Tel** *(562) 597-7701* **Fax** *(562) 494-7373* **Rooms** *49*    **Road map** inset A

A good budget option for individuals and families, this motel provides clean and comfortable rooms; some come with kitchenettes. It is located close to such attractions as the *Queen Mary* and the aquarium. The service is gracious and accommodating. **www.super8motel.com**

### LONG BEACH Hotel Queen Mary
⬚ 🍴 ♦ ♿ ⛶    $$

*1126 Queen's Hwy, 90802* **Tel** *(562) 435-3511* **Fax** *(562) 437-4531* **Rooms** *365*    **Road map** inset A

Guests booking aboard this restored historic cruise liner are afforded ship tours and treated to a bit of ocean-going history. Rooms are newly refurbished and equipped with select modern amenities. The restaurant and spa facilities are first-rate. The Ghost Tour is a fun diversion. **www.queenmary.com**

### LONG BEACH Hotel Maya
⬚ ♨ ♦ 🛎 ♿ ⛶    $$$

*700 Queensway Dr, 90802* **Tel** *(562) 435-7676* **Fax** *(562) 437-0866* **Rooms** *195*    **Road map** inset A

Expect great value for money at this friendly waterfront hotel. The well-appointed rooms provide free high-speed Internet access. Some rooms feature balconies overlooking the garden or with panoramic ocean views. The hotel is close to local attractions. Breakfast is included. **www.fuegolongbeach.com**

### LONG BEACH Hyatt Regency
⬚ 🍴 ♨ ♦ 🛎 ♿ ⛶    $$$

*200 S Pine Ave, 90802* **Tel** *(562) 491-1234* **Fax** *(562) 983-1491* **Rooms** *528*    **Road map** inset A

With a great harborside location, this corporate-run hotel is popular with conventioneers and business travelers. The recently updated rooms are brightly decorated and have plenty of amenities. Recreational features include a heated outdoor pool and a full-service gym. **www.longbeach.hyatt.com**

### LONG BEACH Renaissance Long Beach Hotel
*111 E Ocean Blvd, 90802* **Tel** *(562) 437-5900* **Fax** *(562) 499-2509* **Rooms** *373*      **Road map** *inset A*

This large hotel is central to downtown and close to the harbor attractions, especially the Aquarium of the Pacific. They have spruced up all guest rooms and public areas, including the installation of high-speed Internet access. On-site amenities include a car reservation desk and two good restaurants. **www.renaissancelongbeach.com**

### MALIBU Casa Malibu Inn on the Beach
*22752 Pacific Coast Hwy, 90265* **Tel** *(310) 456-2219* **Fax** *(310) 456-5418* **Rooms** *21*      **Road map** *inset A*

This small, friendly beachside inn retains some of the old coastal charm. Rooms have a private feel. A few have fireplaces, while many have been updated with tile tubs. Amenities include high-end linen, DVD players, and wireless Internet access. The hotel has a secluded sun deck and its own stretch of beach.

### MALIBU Malibu Beach Inn
*22878 Pacific Coast Hwy, 90265* **Tel** *(310) 456-6444* **Fax** *(310) 456-1999* **Rooms** *47*      **Road map** *inset A*

Intimate, luxurious property overlooking the Pacific, Malibu Beach Inn boasts its own beach. Each room is bright and outfitted with Mission-style decor and comfortable linen. A cottage-like feel prevails, with decks overlooking the water. Wireless Internet throughout the inn. **www.malibubeachinn.com**

### MARINA DEL REY Foghorn Harbor Inn
*4140 Via Marina, 90292* **Tel** *(310) 823-4626* **Fax** *(310) 578-1964* **Rooms** *23*      **Road map** *inset A*

This modest, low-slung hotel near the beach provides exceptional value for its location. Rooms are spacious and comfortably appointed, all with patios or balconies. Amenities include wireless Internet access and complimentary Continental breakfast. The staff are charming and gracious. **www.foghornhotel.com**

### MARINA DEL REY Marina del Rey Hotel
*13534 Bali Way, 90292* **Tel** *(310) 301-1000* **Fax** *(310) 301-8167* **Rooms** *157*      **Road map** *inset A*

Enjoying easy access to the beach and the Marina, this comfortable hotel offers well-appointed rooms with many business traveler amenities. Some of them come with private balconies or patios with water views. There is a relaxing waterfront lounge. A free airport shuttle service is available. **www.marinadelreyhotel.com**

### MONROVIA Doubletree Monrovia
*924 W Huntington Dr, 91016* **Tel** *(626) 357-1900* **Fax** *(626) 359-1386* **Rooms** *171*      **Road map** *inset A*

Located near such attractions as Santa Anita Racetrack and Rose Bowl. Rooms are spacious and nicely appointed, with high-speed wireless Internet in some. Guests are offered discounts to select sights, including Universal Studios® tours. There is a fine dining restaurant. **www.doubletree.com**

### PALOS VERDES The Courtyard by Marriott
*2633 Sepulveda Boulevard, 90505* **Tel** *310-533-8000* **Fax** *310-533-0564* **Rooms** *137*      **Road map** *inset A*

This is a reliable and comfortable hotel, with all the amenities and excellent service expected from a Marriott hotel. All rooms have Wi-Fi, luxury bedding, coffee makers, and pull-out sofas. The large Del Amo Fashion Center Mall is nearby, as is all the action at Redondo Beach Pier. **www.marriott.com**

### PALOS VERDES Terranea Resort
*100 Terranea Way Drive, 90275* **Tel** *310-265-2800* **Fax** *310-265-2700* **Rooms** *582*      **Road map** *inset A*

A luxury resort with a golf course, a spacious spa, restaurants, three pools, boutiques, and hiking trails, this is a self-contained destination with spectacular ocean views. Rooms, bungalows, casitas, and suites have Wi-Fi, and multi-media work stations. **www.terranea.com**

### PASADENA Comfort Inn Eagle Rock
*2300 W Colorado Blvd, 90041* **Tel** *(323) 256-1199* **Fax** *(323) 255-7768* **Rooms** *58*      **Road map** *inset A*

Set in scenic surroundings, with convenient access to Rose Bowl, Comfort Inn is a preferred accommodation option in the area. The no-frills rooms come with some creature comforts, including satellite TV. Good value for families on a budget. Breakfast is included. **www.comfortinn.com**

### PASADENA The Bissell House Bed and Breakfast
*201 Orange Grove Ave, 91030* **Tel** *(626) 441-3535, (800) 441-3530* **Fax** *(626) 441-3671* **Rooms** *5* **Road map** *inset A*

Formerly a private mansion in an area of town known as "Millionaire's Row," the Bissell House is an intimate B&B with historic appeal. Each uniquely decorated room is equipped with Internet access and outfitted with period furnishings and sumptuous linen. **www.bissellhouse.com**

### PASADENA Hilton Pasadena
*168 South Los Robles Ave, 91101* **Tel** *(626) 577-1000* **Fax** *(626) 584-3148* **Rooms** *296*      **Road map** *inset A*

Within walking distance from the downtown area, this business-friendly hotel has updated rooms and public spaces. Bedrooms are comfortably furnished in a traditional style, and there is a fitness room and pool. The Trevos restaurant serves excellent California cuisine. Sightseeing can be organized on request. **www.hilton.com**

### PASADENA Sheraton Pasadena
*303 E Cordova St, 91101* **Tel** *(626) 449-4000, (888) 716-8130* **Fax** *(626) 584-1390* **Rooms** *317* **Road map** *inset A*

This well-run downtown hotel offers many executive-friendly features, including a 24-hour business center. Rooms are spacious and well equipped. Recreational amenities include a complete fitness center and tennis courts. It is connected to the Convention Center. **www.sheratonpasadena.com**

**Key to Price Guide** *see p524* **Key to Symbols** *see back cover flap*

### PASADENA The Westin Pasadena   $$$

*191 N. Los Robles Avene, 91101* **Tel** *626-792-2727* **Fax** *626-792-3755* **Rooms** *350*   **Road map** *inset A*

Located in Old Town near lots of shops and restaurants, this upscale hotel has a 24-hour business center, heated rooftop pool, restaurant, bar, and gift shops. Rooms have coffee makers and mini-bars, luxurious bathrooms, and large flatscreen TVs. **www.starwoodhotels.com**

### PASADENA Langham Huntington Hotel   $$$$

*1401 S Oak Knoll Ave, 91106* **Tel** *(626) 568-3900* **Fax** *(626) 568-3700* **Rooms** *380*   **Road map** *inset A*

With luxury and sophistication at every turn, this hotel offers exemplary service and a secluded location away from the city center. The well-manicured grounds are quiet. The historic building boasts modern amenities in each room, including top-end linen and robes. The full-service spa is a prime attraction. **www.pasadena.langham.hotels.com**

### REDONDO BEACH Portofino Hotel & Yacht Club   $$$$$

*260 Portofino Way, 92077* **Tel** *(800) 468-4292* **Fax** *(310) 372-7329* **Rooms** *161*   **Road map** *inset A*

From the balconies and floor-to-ceiling windows of the rooms of this oceanfront hotel, guests can see pelicans and dolphins, sailboats and sunsets. Rooms have Wi-Fi, and guests get complimentary rentals for beach cruiser bicycles. The Baleen restaurant features a New American menu, rich in fresh local seafood. **www.hotelportofino.com**

### SANTA MONICA Best Western Gateway Hotel   $$$$

*1920 Santa Monica Blvd, 90404* **Tel** *(310) 829-9100* **Fax** *(310) 829-9211* **Rooms** *123*   **Road map** *inset A*

Located in town, this budget-minded hotel has a European atmosphere, enhanced by the multilingual staff. The rooms are basic, yet comfortable, offering Internet access and free local calls. Complimentary services include shuttle transportation to the beach and Third Street Promenade. **www.gatewayhotel.com**

### SANTA MONICA Hotel California   $$$$

*1670 Ocean Ave, 90401* **Tel** *(866) 571-0000, (310) 393-2363* **Fax** *(310) 393-1063* **Rooms** *26*  **Road map** *inset A*

A charming find among the high-end beach resorts in the area, this great-value hotel offers modern comforts and ocean views. Rooms are bright and include elegant linen and Internet access. Located close to the Santa Monica Pier and plenty of beach activities. Breakfast is included. **www.hotelca.com**

### SANTA MONICA Doubletree Guest Suites   $$$$$

*1707 4th St, 90401* **Tel** *(310) 395-3332* **Fax** *(310) 452-7399* **Rooms** *253*   **Road map** *inset A*

A large hotel near the beach, the Doubletree offers spacious two-room suites. Among the up-to-date amenities in each room are high-speed Internet access and two-line telephones. Close to the marina, its location provides easy freeway access. An ideal choice for families with children. **www.doubletree.com**

### SANTA MONICA Fairmont Miramar Hotel & Bungalows   $$$$$

*101 Wilshire Blvd, 90401* **Tel** *(310) 576-7777* **Fax** *(310) 458-7912* **Rooms** *302*   **Road map** *inset A*

Luxurious, fully appointed cliffside hotel, the Fairmont Miramar is a frequent haunt for the rich and famous. The garden bungalows are secluded and private, while there are sweeping ocean views from many rooms. Accommodation amenities are first rate, as are the spa and fitness facilities. **www.fairmont.com**

### SANTA MONICA The Georgian Hotel   $$$$$

*1415 Ocean Ave, 90401* **Tel** *(310) 395-9945* **Fax** *(310) 656-0904* **Rooms** *84*   **Road map** *inset A*

A beautiful bit of seaside luxury can be found at this four-diamond historic property, which features ocean views from most rooms and high-end comfort throughout. The well-preserved property is located close to the beach as well as local restaurants and shops. Pets are welcome. **www.georgianhotel.com**

### SANTA MONICA Huntley Santa Monica Beach   $$$$$

*1111 2nd St, 90403* **Tel** *(310) 394-5454* **Fax** *(310) 458-9776* **Rooms** *209*   **Road map** *inset A*

Here modern features are successfully combined with a stylish old high-rise property, located one block from the beach and close to area shops. Each room comes equipped with a high-speed Internet connection, a plasma TV, and a DVD player. **www.thehuntleyhotel.com**

### SANTA MONICA Loews Santa Monica Beach Hotel   $$$$$

*1700 Ocean Ave, 90401* **Tel** *(310) 458-6700* **Fax** *(310) 458-6761* **Rooms** *342*   **Road map** *inset A*

A personalized service by attentive staff at this four-diamond resort-style hotel makes for a memorable stay. The striking lobby is flanked by towering palm trees. Rooms are sumptuously appointed, affording fabulous ocean views. Full-service fitness center and spa, childcare program, and pet friendly. **www.santamonicaloewshotel.com**

### SANTA MONICA Sheraton Delfina Santa Monica   $$$$$

*530 Pico Blvd, 90405* **Tel** *(310) 399-9344* **Fax** *(310) 399-2504* **Rooms** *308*   **Road map** *inset A*

Recently remodeled and redesigned, this hotel offers the latest amenities in its contemporary guest rooms, including upscale linen and luxury bath soaps. Many rooms have ocean views. On-site features include a state-of-the-art fitness center and wireless Internet access. **www.sheratonsantamonica.com**

### SANTA MONICA Shutters on the Beach   $$$$$

*1 Pico Blvd, 90405* **Tel** *(310) 458-0030* **Fax** *(310) 458-4589* **Rooms** *198*   **Road map** *inset A*

This superb luxury hotel on the beach is renowned as a haunt for celebrities and the well heeled. Renovation has upgraded the rooms as well as the excellent gourmet restaurant and top-rated spa. The hotel offers casual comfort and elegance, plus easy access to the beach. **www.shuttersonthebeach.com**

### UNIVERSAL CITY Sheraton Universal    $$$$

*333 Universal Hollywood Dr, 91608* **Tel** *(866) 716-8130* **Fax** *(818) 985-4980* **Rooms** *436*    **Road map** *inset A*

A Universal City landmark since 1969, the Sheraton stands on the back lot of Universal Studios®. Free high-speed Internet access is available in all rooms. Services include laundry and babysitting. The on-site restaurant, California's, offers contemporary cuisine. A complimentary shuttle service to CityWalk®. **www.sheraton.com/universal**

### UNIVERSAL CITY Hilton Los Angeles Universal City    $$$$$

*555 Hollywood Dr, 91608* **Tel** *(818) 506-2500, (800) 538-8147* **Fax** *(818) 509-2058* **Rooms** *453* **Road map** *inset A*

This large family-friendly hotel is conveniently located directly across from the entrance to Universal CityWalk®. Rooms are equipped with such amenities as Internet access and generously sized closets. There is an on-site fitness and business center. **www.hilton.com**

### VAN NUYS Holiday Inn Express Van Nuys    $$

*8244 Orion Ave, 91406* **Tel** *(818) 989-5010, (800) 315-2621* **Fax** *(818) 909-0408* **Rooms** *132* **Road map** *inset A*

Located ten minutes from Universal Studios® theme park, this convenient, good-value hotel offers spacious rooms with work areas and efficient service. High-speed wireless Internet access in the lobby, a heated pool, and generous breakfasts are some of the amenities provided here. **www.hiexpress.com**

### VENICE The Cadillac Hotel    $$$

*8 Dudley Ave, 90291* **Tel** *(310) 399-8876* **Fax** *(310) 399-4536* **Rooms** *41*    **Road map** *inset A*

There are lovely ocean views from each room at this hip, yet affordable, property, located directly on the famed Venice Beach boardwalk. A trendy vibe pervades the historic hotel, and there is a spa and Internet access. Ideal for a comfortable, no-frills accommodation. Close to restaurants, shops, and nightlife. **www.thecadillachotel.com**

### VENICE BEACH The Venice Beach House    $$$

*15 30th Ave, 90291* **Tel** *(310) 823-1966* **Fax** *(310) 823-1842* **Rooms** *9*    **Road map** *inset A*

This charming historic B&B is located close to the beach. The property is secluded and intimate, and set on well-manicured grounds. With a distinct character and definitive style, each room is uniquely themed, such as the Speedway Room and Olympics Suite. The breakfast is first-rate. **www.venicebeachhouse.com**

### VENICE BEACH The Inn at Venice Beach    $$$$

*327 Washington Blvd, 90291* **Tel** *(310) 821-2557* **Fax** *(310) 827-0289* **Rooms** *43*    **Road map** *inset A*

Bright and cheery rooms are provided at this pleasant inn, located just a block from the famed Venice Beach Boardwalk and adjacent to the yacht harbor. Amenities include free high-speed wireless Internet and a Continental breakfast. The staff are welcoming and attentive. **www.innatvenicebeach.com**

### VENICE BEACH Hotel Erwin    $$$$$

*1697 Pacific Ave, 90291* **Tel** *(310) 452-1111* **Fax** *(310) 452-5479* **Rooms** *115*    **Road map** *inset A*

Ideal for long vacations, the Marina Pacific offers attractive extended-stay rates. Well-maintained rooms and thoughtful amenities like Internet access are provided at this modest hotel on the famed Boardwalk. Suites feature kitchens and fireplaces. Continental breakfast and free local calls. **www.hotelerwin.com**

### VENICE BEACH Su Casa at Venice Beach    $$$$$

*431 Ocean Front Walk, 90291* **Tel** *310-452-9700*    **Rooms** *12*    **Road map** *inset A*

A clean, casual bed and breakfast with an outstanding beach location right on the boardwalk, in the midst of the quirky Venice Beach atmosphere. Modern rooms have free Wi-Fi, HD TV, and kitchenettes. Friendly, accommodating staff. **www.sucasaatvenicebeach.com**

### WEST HOLLYWOOD Best Western Sunset Plaza    $$$$

*8400 Sunset Blvd, 90069* **Tel** *(323) 654-0750* **Fax** *(323) 650-6146* **Rooms** *100*    **Map** *6 C1*

Surprisingly well appointed and elegant for a chain-operated hotel, this property offers attractive guest rooms, with plenty of amenities including Internet access and a central Sunset Strip location. The pool is set in a pleasing garden patio. An elaborate Continental breakfast is served each morning. **www.sunsetplazahotel.com**

### WEST HOLLYWOOD Le Parc Suites    $$$$

*733 N West Knoll Ave, 90069* **Tel** *(310) 855-8888* **Fax** *(310) 659-7812* **Rooms** *154*    **Map** *4 A4*

This stylish hotel is situated off the beaten path in a residential part of town. Rooms are quiet and cozy, with comfortable linen and modern conveniences, including CD players and free Internet access. The secluded grounds feature a lovely pool as well as a full spa and fitness center. **www.leparcsuites.com**

### WEST HOLLYWOOD Andaz West Hollywood Hotel    $$$$$

*8401 Sunset Blvd, 90069* **Tel** *(323) 656-1234* **Fax** *(323) 650-7024* **Rooms** *262*    **Map** *6 C1*

No longer a Hollywood hangout, the Andaz is an upscale, completely renovated version of the old Hyatt, and is aimed at the discerning traveler. The stylish, comfortable rooms are of a high standard, and the hotel prides itself on attention to detail and simple luxury. **www.andaz.com**

### WEST HOLLYWOOD Chateau Marmont    $$$$$

*8221 Sunset Blvd, 90046* **Tel** *(323) 656-1010* **Fax** *(323) 655-5311* **Rooms** *63*    **Map** *1 B5*

Enjoying a well-documented reputation as a celebrity hideaway, Chateau Marmont has standard rooms, suites, and private cottages. All offer home-like and business amenities and top-notch service from the attentive staff. The pool deck has pretty views of the Strip and surrounding valley. Pets welcome. **www.chateaumarmont.com**

**Key to Price Guide** *see p524* **Key to Symbols** *see back cover flap*

### WEST HOLLYWOOD Mondrian Hotel
*8440 Sunset Blvd, 90069* **Tel** *(323) 650-8999* **Fax** *(323) 650-5215* **Rooms** *237*    **Map** *6 C1*

One of the hottest spots on the Strip, stylish Mondrian Hotel features spacious rooms with full kitchens, large work spaces, and dazzling city views. Decor is minimalist, but sleek and classy. The pool and lounge areas are key see-and-be-seen spots. The Asia de Cuba restaurant is wildly popular. **www.mondrianhotel.com**

### WEST HOLLYWOOD Sunset Tower Hotel
*8358 Sunset Blvd, 90069* **Tel** *(323) 654-7100* **Fax** *(323) 654-9287* **Rooms** *74*    **Map** *6 C1*

A beautiful Art Deco hotel, formerly the Argyle, with a rich history in Hollywood, it has elegant, well-equipped rooms, with Internet access, ranging from standard size to gorgeous home-like suites. The pool deck, though small, is popular for celebrity sightings. The restaurant is highly rated. Pets welcome. **www.sunsettowerhotel.com**

### WESTWOOD Royal Palace Westwood Hotel
*1052 Tiverton Ave, 90024* **Tel** *(310) 208-6677* **Fax** *(310) 824-3732* **Rooms** *35*    **Map** *4 A4*

This small hotel is an inexpensive, no-frills option in the heart of Westwood Village, within walking distance of museums, shops, restaurants, and UCLA campus. Rooms are tidy, with balconies or patios. The staff are friendly and courteous. A complimentary breakfast is included. **www.royalpalacewestwood.com**

### WESTWOOD Hilgard House Hotel
*927 Hilgard Ave, 90024* **Tel** *(910) 208-3945, (800) 826-3934* **Fax** *(310) 208-1972* **Rooms** *47*    **Map** *4 A4*

Affordable and cozy, the Hilgard House is situated near the UCLA campus and within walking distance to the Armand Hammer Museum. Some of the sophisticated European-style rooms have Jacuzzis and kitchenettes. Free wireless Internet access and Continental breakfast included. **www.hilgardhouse.com**

### WESTWOOD Palomar
*10740 Wilshire Blvd, 90024* **Tel** *(310) 475-8711, (800) 472-8556* **Fax** *(310) 475-5220* **Rooms** *264* **Road map** *C5*

With a central location, this large, full-service hotel, formerly the Doubletree, is convenient to many local attractions. The updated rooms are well furnished with upscale amenities. There is a lively lounge as well as a gourmet restaurant. Pet friendly. **www.hotelpalomar-lawestwood.com**

### WESTWOOD W Los Angeles Westwood
*930 Hilgard Ave, 90024* **Tel** *(310) 208-8765* **Fax** *(310) 824-0355* **Rooms** *258*    **Road map** *C5*

Sleek and stylish, rooms at this hip hotel are large and equipped with every imaginable amenity. Features include a state-of-the-art spa, two outdoor pools, and the famed "whatever-whenever" service from the polished staff. The high-profile lounge and bar areas enhance the vibrant ambience. **www.starwoodhotels.com**

## SOUTH CENTRAL CALIFORNIA

### BAKERSFIELD Courtyard by Marriott

*3601 Marriott Dr, 93308* **Tel** *(661) 324-6660* **Fax** *(661) 324-1185* **Rooms** *146*    **Road map** *C5*

Clean and modern, this chain hotel is situated near the local airport, and features great amenities for the business traveler, including free high-speed Internet access and large work stations in each room. There is also a hot tub and swimming pool. **www.marriott.com**

### CAMBRIA Burton Inn
*4022 Burton Dr, 93428* **Tel** *(805) 927-5125, (800) 572-7442* **Rooms** *12*    **Road map** *B5*

Set among the shops and galleries of downtown Cambria and nearby Hearst Castle, charming Burton Drive Inn has large rooms and suites and friendly, warm service. The rooms are appointed with period ambience, while bathrooms have spa-like amenities, with luxury soaps and robes. **www.burtoninn.com**

### CAMBRIA Pelican Inn & Suites

*6316 Moonstone Beach Dr., 93428* **Tel** *(800) 966-6490* **Fax** *(805) 927-0218* **Rooms** *24*    **Road map** *B5*

This bright and cheery inn is directly across the street from the boardwalk and famous Moonstone Beach. Many rooms feature balconies looking out towards the ocean. Rooms are spacious and comfortable, and the dining room serves a full, hot breakfast buffet every morning. **www.pelicansuites.com**

### CAMBRIA Best Western Plus Fireside Inn on Moonstone Beach

*6700 Moonstone Beach Dr, 93428* **Tel** *(805) 927-8661, (888) 910-7100* **Fax** *(805) 927-8584* **Rooms** *46* **Road map** *B5*

This romantic oceanside hotel on Moonstone Beach features generously proportioned rooms that possess the essential comforts, and Internet access. Situated close to the village of Cambria, it is convenient for local attractions, including Hearst Castle. **www.bestwesternfiresideinn.com**

### CAMBRIA Cambria Pines Lodge
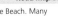
*2905 Burton Dr., 93428* **Tel** *(800) 445-6868* **Fax** *(805) 927-4016* **Rooms** *152*    **Road map** *B5*

This quaint lodge and collection of cottages is surrounded by expansive gardens. A trail in the back of the property makes for a great morning stroll, often interrupted by deer. Rooms are simple and tasteful, with brightly painted walls and crisp white bed covers. **www.cambriapineslodge.com**

### MONTECITO Montecito Inn

*1295 Coast Village Rd, 93108* **Tel** *(805) 969-7854, (800) 843-2017* **Fax** *(805) 969-0623* **Rooms** *61* **Road map** *C5*

Built in 1928 by Charlie Chaplin, Montecito Inn features a complete film library of the legendary actor. It is a comfortable Mediterranean-style hotel with luxurious features and easy beach access. It is fitted with such accessories as flat-screen TVs, Internet access, and large Jacuzzis. Breakfast included. **www.montecitoinn.com**

### MONTECITO San Ysidro Ranch

*900 San Ysidro Lane, 93108* **Tel** *(805) 565-1700* **Fax** *(805) 565-1995* **Rooms** *41*      **Road map** *C5*

An absolutely stunning spot in the mountains above Montecito, San Ysidro Ranch is a treat. Each room is its own little cottage and feature down-feather beds and fireplaces, perfect for a peaceful getaway. The restaurant is outstanding as well, and the below-ground cozy pub serves delicious comfort classics. **www.sanysidroranch.com**

### MORRO BAY Blue Sail Inn

*851 Market Ave, 93442* **Tel** *(800) 971-6910* **Fax** *(805) 772-8406* **Rooms** *48*      **Road map** *B5*

A pleasant hotel in the quaint coastal town of Morro Bay, Blue Sail Inn offers great value. Rooms are individually decorated and come in various sizes. Most of them have private balconies with great views of the bay and its famous rock. Wireless Internet access is available. Breakfast included. **www.bluesailinn.com**

### MORRO BAY Embarcadero Inn

*456 Embarcadero, 93442* **Tel** *(888) 223-5777, (805) 772-2700* **Rooms** *33*      **Road map** *B5*

Situated directly on the working harbor, this friendly inn features rooms facing the water; most have balconies and fireplaces. A new family suite offers groups a chance to stay together. The staff are attentive and efficient, and eager to give advice on recreation choices in the area. **www.embarcaderoinn.com**

### MORRO BAY Inn at Morro Bay

*60 State Park Rd, 93442* **Tel** *(805) 772-5651, (800) 321-9566* **Fax** *(805) 772-4779* **Rooms** *98*      **Road map** *B5*

Charming and luxurious, this French country-style inn is situated in a state park overlooking the bay. Rooms are cozy and contemporary, some featuring fireplaces and all with featherbeds and patios with hot tubs. A good seafood restaurant and spa are on the premises, and there are several golf courses nearby. **www.innatmorrobay.com**

### OJAI Ojai Valley Inn & Spa

*905 Country Club Rd., 93023* **Tel** *(800) 422-6524* **Rooms** *308*      **Road map** *C5*

Once you turn onto the stately, tree-lined driveway, you know you're in for a special experience. Rambling white adobe buildings with red-tile roofs, a golf course that was once a favorite on the Senior PGA tour, and a spa that feels like a secret hideaway. Rooms are fantastic with fireplaces, soft blankets, and fine linens. **www.ojairesort.com**

### PASO ROBLES Paso Robles Inn

*1103 Spring St, 93446* **Tel** *(805) 238-2660, (800) 676-1713* **Fax** *(805) 238-4707* **Rooms** *98*      **Road map** *B5*

A popular destination for over a century, Paso Robles Inn is set in lush grounds that feature gardens, a creek, and natural hot springs. Rooms are basic Mission-style, some featuring a deluxe mineral spa. There is a good steakhouse and a historic ballroom on the property. **www.pasoroblesinn.com**

### PASO ROBLES Hotel Cheval

*1021 Pine St., 93446* **Tel** *(866) 522-6999* **Fax** *(805) 226-9979* **Rooms** *16*      **Road map** *B5*

Hotel Cheval looks like a centuries-old castle, but inside, this pet-friendly hotel features modern rooms, each with its own fireplace and many with private patios and courtyards. The hotel also benefits from a prime downtown location, within walking distance of nearby restaurants, and close to many local wineries. **www.hotelcheval.com**

### SAN LUIS OBISPO Garden Street Inn

*1212 Garden St, 93401* **Tel** *(805) 545-9802* **Fax** *(805) 545-9403* **Rooms** *13*      **Road map** *B5*

Built in a restored 1860 Victorian building, this delightful B&B is set in the central section of downtown San Luis Obispo. The rooms are furnished with antiques and some have a fireplace, a private bath, and Jacuzzi. There is an impressive library on the premises. **www.gardenstreetinn.com**

### SAN LUIS OBISPO The Madonna Inn

*100 Madonna Rd, 93405* **Tel** *(805) 543-9666* **Fax** *(805) 543-1800* **Rooms** *110*      **Road map** *B5*

A tourist attraction in its own right, The Madonna Inn looks more like an amusement park than a hotel, and that's part of the fun. Each room has a theme, ranging from "Antique Cars" to "China Flower," and the grounds are equally over-the-top. The steakhouse and pioneer-themed Copper Café serve meals to visitors and locals. **www.madonnainn.com**

### SAN LUIS OBISPO Apple Farm Inn

*2015 Monterey St, 93401* **Tel** *(800) 255-2040* **Fax** *(805) 546-9495* **Rooms** *104*      **Road map** *B5*

This quaint hotel is utterly charming, with Victorian flair and modern conveniences. Family-friendly, yet perfect for couples, rooms are graciously appointed with sumptuous beds and bath amenities. Grounds feature gardens and large shade trees. Heated pool, Internet access. Choose the Trellis Court rooms for discounted rates. **www.applefarm.com**

### SAN LUIS OBISPO San Luis Creek Lodge

*1941 Monterey St, 93401* **Tel** *(805) 541-1122* **Fax** *(805) 541-2475* **Rooms** *25*      **Road map** *B5*

This small, chic B&B with luxurious, yet affordable, accommodation is provided in three buildings on a campus, away from the traffic on secluded grounds. Rooms are cozy and well appointed, with upscale bedding, microwave and refrigerator. **www.sanluiscreeklodge.com**

**Key to Price Guide** *see p524* **Key to Symbols** *see back cover flap*

## SANTA BARBARA Hotel Santa Barbara $$$

*533 State St, 93101* **Tel** *(805) 957-9300, (800) 549-9869* **Fax** *(805) 962-2412* **Rooms** *75* **Road map** *C5*

Five blocks from the beach, this 1926 hotel retains some of its historic charm. Tidy and well-equipped rooms offer comfortable bedding and Internet access. A light breakfast is included, and seasonal fruit, coffee, tea, and hot chocolate are available 24 hours. **www.hotelsantabarbara.com**

## SANTA BARBARA Old Yacht Club Inn $$$

*431 Corona Del Mar, 93103* **Tel** *(805) 962-1277* **Rooms** *14* **Road map** *C5*

Housed in a charming building, a short walk from the beach, the individually decorated rooms have a yacht club feel to them. Every morning a full gourmet breakfast is served, and wine and cheese is available in the late afternoon on the outdoor deck, weather permitting. **www.oldyachtclubinn.com**

## SANTA BARBARA Hotel Oceana $$$$

*202 West Cabrillo Blvd., 93101* **Tel** *(805) 965-4577* **Fax** *(805) 965-9937* **Rooms** *63* **Road map** *C5*

Right across the street from Santa Barbara's famed pier and beach, Hotel Oceana makes the most of its location with ocean-view rooms, outdoor lounge areas, bright, Mediterranean-inspired decor, and a fleet of shiny beach cruisers for guest use. The cruisers are a great way to get around while you're in town. **www.hoteloceanasantabarbara.com**

## SANTA BARBARA Inn by the Harbor $$$$

*433 W Montecito St, 93101* **Tel** *(805) 963-7851* **Fax** *(805) 962-9428* **Rooms** *42* **Road map** *C5*

Expect affordable grace at this plush hotel located close to the beach. Suites are spacious and have full kitchens; ideal for family stays. Rooms are pleasingly designed in French country decor and feature pine furniture. Amenities include a delicious Continental breakfast, a large sundeck, and heated swimming pool. **www.innbytheharbor.com**

## SANTA BARBARA Santa Barbara Inn $$$$

*901 E Cabrillo Blvd, 93103* **Tel** *(800) 231-0431* **Fax** *(805) 966-6584* **Rooms** *69* **Road map** *C5*

This hotel has location in its favor, close to downtown shops and restaurants, and just across the street from the beach. Modestly appointed rooms feature comfortable beds and enough space for families. Suites are also available. Internet access. **www.santabarbarainn.com**

## SANTA BARBARA White Jasmine Inn $$$$

*1327 Bath St, 93101* **Tel** *(805) 966-0589* **Rooms** *12* **Road map** *C5*

Romantic and cozy, this B&B provides individually themed rooms that are situated in three cottages. Many rooms feature a bedside fireplace, private deck and whirlpool, and a large soaking tub. Breakfast is delivered to the room each morning. **www.whitejasmineinnsantabarbara.com**

## SANTA BARBARA Four Seasons The Biltmore $$$$$

*1260 Channel Dr, 93108* **Tel** *(805) 969-2261* **Fax** *(805) 565-8329* **Rooms** *207* **Road map** *C5*

Exquisite seaside luxury and attention to every detail make this the premier Santa Barbara indulgence. The Spanish Colonial-style property is set elegantly on sprawling grounds, across from the beach and away from town. Rooms are sumptuous and secluded, and come with every amenity. **www.fourseasons.com**

## SANTA BARBARA Simpson House Inn $$$$$

*121 E Arrellaga St, 93101* **Tel** *(800) 676-1280* **Fax** *(805) 564-4811* **Rooms** *15* **Road map** *C5*

The only B&B in North America with the five-diamond distinction, this delightful inn offers generous amenities, top-notch service, and a gorgeous garden setting. Rooms and cottages are elegantly appointed and secluded, though the property is a short walk from restaurants and shops. **www.simpsonhouseinn.com**

## SANTA BARBARA Upham Hotel & Country House $$$$$

*1404 De la Vina St, 93101* **Tel** *(805) 962-0058, (800) 727-0876* **Fax** *(805) 963-2825* **Rooms** *58* **Road map** *C5*

Opened in 1871, the Upham is Southern California's oldest continuously operating hotel. The inn is set on lovely grounds, with a high degree of privacy. Rooms are comfortable and stylishly furnished. Some are cottage-style, and many have fireplaces. **www.uphamhotel.com**

## SANTA PAULA Santa Paula Inn $

*111 N 8th St, 93060* **Tel** *(805) 933-0011* **Fax** *(805) 933-9553* **Rooms** *14* **Road map** *C5*

In a pastoral setting, among lemon and avocado groves, this quaint inn is located only a 10-minute drive from the coast. Rooms are snug and well kept, and feature Jacuzzis, and feather beds and Internet access. Some have kitchenettes. The garden patio offers a tranquil setting for an evening glass of wine. **www.santapaulainn.com**

## SIMI VALLEY Posada Royale $$

*1775 Madera Rd, 93065* **Tel** *(805) 584-6300* **Fax** *(805) 527-9969* **Rooms** *120* **Road map** *C5*

The staff pride themselves on providing personal attention at this comfortable hotel. The guest rooms have upgraded amenities, including two-line telephones and wireless Internet capabilities. Located close to the Ronald Reagan Library and major freeways, there is also a fitness facility and heated pool. **www.posadaroyale.com**

## SOLVANG Hadsten House Inn & Spa $$$$

*1450 Mission Dr., 93463* **Tel** *(800) 457-5373* **Fax** *(805) 688-0026* **Rooms** *75* **Road map** *C5*

An updated motel, Hadsten House features drive-up rooms that have been given a modern design makeover, with wood floors and black, white, and grey furnishings. Rates include breakfast and an evening glass of wine, making this a pleasant, affordable spot from which to explore the area's great wineries and restaurants. **www.hadstenhouse.com**

### SOLVANG Mirabelle Inn      $$$$

*409 1st St, 93463* **Tel** *(800) 786-7925* **Rooms** *10*      **Road map** *C5*

Each unique room in this elegant, European-style inn is decorated with fine antiques and comforts such as featherbeds and upscale linen; some have fireplaces and Jacuzzi tubs. Wine and cheese are served each afternoon. The service is friendly and attentive. **www.solvangstorybook.com**

### SOLVANG Alisal Ranch      $$$$$

*1054 Alisal Rd., 93463* **Tel** *(805) 688-6411* **Fax** *(805) 688-2510* **Rooms** *73*      **Road map** *C5*

Tucked away on several quiet acres, this luxury ranch feels completely away from the world. Alisal takes the "ranch" theme and makes it supremely comfortable, with wood-burning fireplaces, and floor-to-ceiling windows. Breakfast and dinner in the fantastic Ranch Room are included. **www.alisal.com**

## ORANGE COUNTY

### ANAHEIM Anaheim Desert Inn & Suites      $$

*1600 S Harbor Blvd, 92802* **Tel** *(714) 772-5050, (800) 433-5270* **Fax** *(714) 778-2754* **Rooms** *145*   **Road map** *D6*

Across from Disneyland®'s main entrance, this family-friendly hotel offers good value and convenience. Rooms range in size and some sleep eight comfortably. There is a pool and a roof deck outfitted for viewing the park's fireworks each night. It is popular with business travelers too. Breakfast is included. **www.anaheimdesertinn.com**

### ANAHEIM Candy Cane Inn      $$

*1747 S. Harbor Boulevard, 92802* **Tel** *800-345-7057* **Fax** *714-772-5462* **Rooms** *171*      **Road map** *D6*

A clean, friendly hotel, this is great value for families and sightseers, with free parking and frequent shuttles to Disneyland®. This is a Disney vacation on a budget, with large rooms, free Wi-Fi, and kitchenettes. A complimentary breakfast buffet is also served daily. **www.candycaneinn.net**

### ANAHEIM Anaheim Marriott      $$$

*700 W Convention Way, 92802* **Tel** *(714) 750-8000* **Fax** *(714) 750-9100* **Rooms** *1030*      **Road map** *D6*

This huge, convention-style hotel is central to major Anaheim attractions, and features many family-friendly conveniences. Accommodations are spacious and comfortable, and some have views of the Disneyland® Park. Amenities include high-speed Internet access. **www.marriottanaheimhotel.com**

### ANAHEIM Disney®'s Grand Californian Hotel & Spa      $$$$$

*1600 S Disneyland Dr, 92802* **Tel** *(714) 956-6425* **Fax** *(714) 300-7300* **Rooms** *948*      **Road map** *D6*

This magnificent atrium hotel in rustic California Craftsman style is located inside Disney's California Adventure™ Park. Exit the side door and you're in. Besides pools, spa, and all other imaginable amenities, there's an evening kid's club to give parents a carefree night out. Easy walk to the Magic Kingdom®. **www.disneyland.disney.go.com**

### ANAHEIM Disney®'s Paradise Pier Hotel      $$$$$

*1717 S Disneyland Dr, 92802* **Tel** *(714) 956-6425* **Fax** *(714) 776-5763* **Rooms** *481*      **Road map** *D6*

A bright, California beach-themed hotel, the Paradise Pier is located inside Disneyland® Park. The entire property has had its public spaces and recreational amenities re-worked. Rooms are contemporary; some have imposing views of the theme park. There is a full business center on site. **www.disneyland.disney.go.com**

### AVALON Catalina Island Hotel Vista del Mar      $$$$

*417 Crescent Ave, 90704* **Tel** *(800) 601-3836* **Fax** *(310) 510-1452* **Rooms** *15*      **Road map** *C6*

A small and cozy beach hotel, the Vista del Mar stands in a lovely setting, with a picturesque garden courtyard. The rooms are contemporary and bright, and many have fireplaces and ocean views. Freshly-made cookies and milk are offered each night. **www.hotel-vistadelmar.com**

### AVALON Hotel Metropole      $$$$

*Metropole Market Place, Crescent Ave, 90704* **Tel** *(310) 510-1884* **Fax** *(310) 510-2534* **Rooms** *48*   **Road map** *C6*

Experience luxurious comfort in an intimate setting at this chic boutique hotel located near the beach. Rooms are appointed in a modern style, and while most rooms have ocean views, many have fireplaces, Jacuzzis and wireless Internet. Ideal for both romantic and family getaways. **www.hotel-metropole.com**

### COSTA MESA Super 8      $

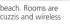

*2645 Harbor Boulevard, 92626* **Tel** *714-545-9471* **Fax** *714-432-8129* **Rooms** *69*      **Road map** *D6*

A good, basic budget motel close to the airport and Newport Beach. There's a pool and Jacuzzi area and complimentary Continental breakfast. Clean, comfortable rooms have free Wi-Fi and large bathrooms. Staff are friendly and helpful. Vacation packages are available including accommodation, car rental, and flights. **www.super8.com**

### COSTA MESA Ayres Hotel & Suites      $$$

*325 Bristol St, 92626* **Tel** *(714) 549-0300, (800) 322-9992* **Fax** *(714) 662-0828* **Rooms** *282*      **Road map** *D6*

Rooms at this charming hotel have boutique appeal and are decorated in French country style. Amenities include complimentary buffet breakfast and evening treats. The property is conveniently located near several local attractions and shops. **www.ayreshotels.com**

**Key to Price Guide** *see p524* **Key to Symbols** *see back cover flap*

## COSTA MESA Residence Inn by Marriott

$$$

*881 W Baker St, 92626 Tel (714) 241-8800 Fax (714) 546-4308 Rooms 144*

The rooms at this friendly hotel have Internet access, and have a residential feel, with kitchenettes and separate living areas. There is a heated pool, whirlpool, and a sports court. There is a social hour, breakfast is included, and pets are welcome. The Residence Inn is close to South Coast Plaza shopping district. **www.marriott.com**

## COSTA MESA Wyndham Orange County

$$$ Road map D6

*3350 Avenue of the Arts, 92626 Tel (714) 751-5100 Fax (949) 751-0129 Rooms 238*

With spacious and superbly appointed rooms, this well-run hotel is located close to the performing arts center and other major attractions. Features include wireless Internet access and cordless phones in each room. The on-site restaurant is a good Italian brasserie. **www.wyndham.com**

## DANA POINT Blue Lantern Inn

$$$$ Road map D6

*34343 Street of the Blue Lantern, 92629 Tel (800) 950-1236 Fax (949) 496-1483 Rooms 29*

Overlooking the harbor, romantic gable-roofed Blue Lantern Inn B&B has luxurious rooms, furnished in country charm, each provided with a fireplace and a jetted tub. The suites offer private decks and spectacular water views. **www.bluelanterninn.com**

## DANA POINT Ritz-Carlton Laguna Niguel

$$$$$ Road map D6

*1 Ritz-Carlton Dr, 92629 Tel (949) 240-2000 Fax (949) 240-0829 Rooms 396*

Set on the bluffs above the shore, this elegant resort-style property offers upgraded guest rooms and public areas. The grounds are spectacular and now have a spa and fitness center. Rooms have balconies and five-star amenities. The on-site restaurant is worth a visit. **www.ritzcarlton.com**

## HUNTINGTON BEACH Shorebreak Hotel

$$$$ Road map D6

*500 Pacific Coast Highway, 92648 Tel 714-916-5253 Fax 714-861-4475 Rooms 196*

Right on the beach and the only hotel in downtown Huntington Beach, this is packed with extras like sunken tubs, luxury linens, complimentary wine hour in the evening, and no fee for pets. The Italian restaurant is highly rated. There's also a 24-hour business center. **www.shorebreakhotel.com**

## HUNTINGTON BEACH The Waterfront Beach Resort

$$$$$ Road map D6

*21100 Pacific Coast Hwy, 92648 Tel (714) 845-8000 Fax (714) 845-8425 Rooms 290*

Among the premier places to stay in Huntington, this full-service, four-diamond Hilton hotel is close to the beach, and features well-appointed guest rooms with upscale bath amenities and plush spa-like robes. The oceanfront suites have wraparound balconies. **www.waterfrontresort.com**

## LAGUNA BEACH The Carriage House

$$$ Road map C5

*1322 Catalina St, 92651 Tel (949) 494-8945 Rooms 6*

Quiet and relaxing, this vintage country inn is housed in a 1920s two-story building and offers spacious rooms and suites just two blocks from the beach. There is a pleasant brick courtyard, wine in the guestrooms, and a family-style breakfast is served in the dining room or out in the courtyard. **www.carriagehouse.com**

## LAGUNA BEACH Casa Laguna Inn & Spa

$$$$ Road map D6

*2510 S Coast Hwy, 92651 Tel (949) 494-2996, (800) 233-0449 Fax (949) 494-5009 Rooms 22*

Though a small-scale B&B, this charming oceanside inn has Mission-style architectural features. Rooms have pillowtop mattresses, sumptuous bath amenities, and Internet access. Service is exceptional. Full gourmet breakfast and afternoon refreshments are served on secluded patios. There is a good view from the restaurant. **www.casalaguna.com**

## LAGUNA BEACH Surf and Sand Resort

$$$$$ Road map D6

*1555 S Coast Hwy, 92651 Tel (949) 497-4477, (888) 869-7569 Fax (949) 494-2897 Rooms 165 Road map D6*

Ranked among top California resorts, this hotel provides contemporary beachfront luxury in each guest room and suite, with large plantation shutters and pleasant views of the water. It has a great location and an excellent restaurant. **www.surfandsandresort.com**

## NEWPORT BEACH Fairmont Newport Beach

$$$$ Road map D6

*4500 MacArthur Blvd, 92660 Tel (949) 476-2001, (800) 441-1414 Rooms 494*

Blending European elegance with Californian flair, this large hotel near the beach has a corporate feel, yet maintains friendly service. Rooms are large and well appointed; some have balconies and ocean views. The business center is equipped with the latest features. Just 5 miles (8 km) from the Pacific Ocean. **www.fairmont.com**

## NEWPORT BEACH Island Hotel

$$$$ Road map D6

*690 Newport Center Dr, 92660 Tel (949) 759-0808, (866) 554-4620 Fax (949) 759-0568 Rooms 295 Road map D6*

A relaxed atmosphere and sophisticated charm are the hallmarks of this high-end hotel, formerly The Four Seasons, one of the top hotels on the coast. Some rooms have great ocean views and have balconies or patios. Located next to Fashion Island Shopping Center. **www.theislandhotel.com**

## SUNSET BEACH Best Western Harbour Inn & Suites

$$ Road map D6

*16912 Pacific Coast Hwy, 90742 Tel (800) 546-4770 Fax (562) 592-3547 Rooms 25*

The hotel's location is just a short walk to the beach and offers spacious rooms with refrigerators and microwave ovens. Each guest room is decorated in one of four unique tropical themes. It is close to many local attractions. A complimentary Continental breakfast is included. **www.bestwestern.com**

## SAN DIEGO COUNTY

### CARLSBAD Pelican Cove Inn
*320 Walnut Ave, 92008* **Tel** *(760) 434-5995* **Rooms** *10*     **Road map** *D6*

Each room at this cozy B&B features a fireplace, feather bed, and private entrance. The hotel can arrange activities for guests, including day spa visits and scenic airplane rides. Enjoy the superb full breakfast in the inside parlor or on the pretty garden-patio. Close to Legoland®. **www.pelican-cove.com**

### CARLSBAD Beach Terrace Inn
*2775 Ocean St, 92008* **Tel** *(760) 729-5951, (800) 433-5415* **Fax** *(760) 729-1078* **Rooms** *48*     **Road map** *D6*

Basic, yet comfortable, this hotel is situated right on the beach. The appealing, one-bedroom suites feature kitchenettes and fireplaces. Most rooms have a private terrace and panoramic ocean views, but a few studio units come without a balcony. There is a pool and spa and breakfast is included. **www.beachterraceinn.com**

### CARLSBAD Carlsbad Inn Beach Resort
*3075 Carlsbad Blvd, 92008* **Tel** *(800) 235-3939, (760) 434-7020* **Fax** *(760) 729-4853* **Rooms** *62*     **Road map** *D6*

This two-story, Tudor-style hotel has some rooms with fireplaces and kitchenettes, plus two-bedroom condos, perfect for families. There's a pool surrounded by a well-manicured lawn above the beach, plus restaurants, beauty spa, and gift shop. Easy walk to little shops and cafés in town. **www.carlsbadinn.com**

### CORONADO Crown City Inn & Bistro
*520 Orange Ave, 92118* **Tel** *(619) 435-3116* **Rooms** *35*     **Road map** *D6*

This charming inn is surrounded by flower gardens and offers modest, clean, and comfortable guestrooms. Kids and pets are welcome, cookies and tea are served in the afternoons, and the on-site restaurant is open for breakfast, lunch, and dinner. Beach bikes and passes for an off-site fitness center are available. **www.crowncityinn.com**

### CORONADO Best Western Suites Hotel Coronado Island
*275 Orange Ave, 92118* **Tel** *(619) 437-1666* **Fax** *(619) 437-0188* **Rooms** *38*     **Road map** *C5*

Centrally located to the beaches, attractions of San Diego, and North Island Naval Air Station, this modern hotel offers spacious, well-equipped guestrooms. In-room amenities include microwave, refrigerator, cable TV, and free high-speed Internet access. Complimentary breakfast is served. **www.bestwestern.com**

### CORONADO Hotel Del Coronado

*1500 Orange Ave, 92118* **Tel** *(619) 435-6611, (800) 468-3533* **Fax** *(619) 522-8262* **Rooms** *757*     **Road map** *D6*

A landmark in San Diego for more than a century, this grand Victorian building is famous for its history. Situated on a stretch of beautiful beach, the hotel offers every amenity. The rooms are modern, and cottages have been added in a section called Beach Villages. Fine spa and superb restaurant. **www.hoteldel.com**

### DEL MAR Del Mar Hilton
*15575 Jimmy Durante Blvd, 92014* **Tel** *(858) 792-5200* **Fax** *(858) 792-9538* **Rooms** *257*     **Road map** *D6*

This Hilton's lobby is magnificent, while the guest rooms either have ocean views or overlook the racetrack across the street. The property is close to the beach, tennis courts, and a golf driving range. A free shuttle service to nearby attractions. **www.sandiegodelmarhilton.com**

### DEL MAR Del Mar Inn
*720 Camino Del Mar, 92014* **Tel** *(858) 755-9765, (800) 451-4515* **Fax** *(858) 792-8196* **Rooms** *80*     **Road map** *D6*

With quiet rooms set among English-style gardens, this quaint property, with a Tudor look, offers comfortable amenities, including some rooms with kitchenettes. The courteous staff serve a morning breakfast to your room and there is an afternoon tea service. Internet access and free local phone calls. **www.delmarinn.com**

### DEL MAR L'Auberge Del Mar Resort & Spa
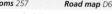
*1540 Camino Del Mar, 92014* **Tel** *(800) 245-9757, (858) 259-1515* **Fax** *(858) 755-4940* **Rooms** *120*   **Road map** *D6*

This elegant, full-service luxury resort has ample recreational amenities, including golf, tennis, and hiking. Spacious, well-furnished rooms have marble baths and private balconies. A small pathway leads from the resort to the beach. There is a great spa on-site. Hotel is within easy reach of San Diego attractions. **www.laubergedelmar.com**

### ENCINITAS Best Western Encinitas Inn & Suites
*85 Encinitas Blvd, 92024* **Tel** *(760) 942-7455* **Fax** *(760) 632-9481* **Rooms** *94*     **Road map** *D6*

Set on a hillside, this well-priced, family-friendly hotel offers clean, comfortable, and spacious rooms, many with ocean views overlooking Moonlight Beach. Free wireless Internet access is provided to guests. The service is prompt and immaculate. Encinitas is close to many San Diego attractions. **www.bwencinitas.com**

### JULIAN The Julian Gold Rush Hotel
*2032 Main St, 92036* **Tel** *(760) 765-0201, (800) 734-5854* **Fax** *(760) 765-0327* **Rooms** *16*     **Road map** *D6*

A well-run, Victorian-era bed and breakfast located in a historic mining town, Julian is great for a romantic getaway. The beautifully restored rooms are furnished with antiques and a fireplace. A special suite for honeymooners is also available here. Within walking distance of gift shops, restaurants, museums, and gold mine. **www.julianhotel.com**

### LA JOLLA La Jolla Beach Travelodge                    $$$

*6750 La Jolla Blvd, 92037* **Tel** *(858) 454-0716* **Fax** *(858) 454-1075* **Rooms** *44*          **Road map** *D6*

Convenience, great value, and friendly staff make this a popular family vacation choice. The two-story motel is located just one block from the beach and a mile from downtown. Guestrooms have free high-speed Internet access, the outdoor pool is heated, and the Continental breakfast is complimentary. **www.travelodge.com**

### LA JOLLA Embassy Suites San Diego–La Jolla                    $$$$

*4550 La Jolla Village Dr, 92122* **Tel** *(858) 453-0400* **Fax** *(858) 453-4226* **Rooms** *340*          **Road map** *D6*

This mid-size, efficiently run hotel is convenient for families and groups. The property features two-room suites, and is close to freeway access, San Diego attractions, and the University of California San Diego campus. Amenities offered include high-speed Internet access and breakfast. **www.embassysuites.com**

### LA JOLLA The Bed and Breakfast Inn at La Jolla                    $$$$

*7753 Draper Ave, 92037* **Tel** *(858) 456-2066, (888) 988-8481* **Fax** *(858) 456-1510* **Rooms** *13*          **Road map** *D6*

An elegant and charming B&B, this historic inn retains its old-world charm while offering the latest in guest comfort. All rooms have individual flair, and many have dazzling ocean views. Staff are friendly and helpful. Good for both business and leisure travelers. One block from the beach. **www.innlajolla.com**

### LA JOLLA La Valencia Hotel                    $$$$$

*1132 Prospect St, 92037* **Tel** *(858) 454-0771* **Fax** *(858) 456-3921* **Rooms** *115*          **Road map** *D6*

Affectionately known as the "pink lady," this venerable luxury hotel is an icon of La Jolla, featuring graciously appointed rooms, with plush bath amenities and sweeping coastal views. The Ocean Villas have private butler service. Wonderful indoor-outdoor gourmet dining. **www.lavalencia.com**

### LA JOLLA San Diego/La Jolla Marriott                    $$$$$

*4240 La Jolla Village Dr, 92037* **Tel** *(858) 587-1414* **Fax** *(858) 546-8518* **Rooms** *360*          **Road map** *D6*

Close to the beach and nearby restaurants, this large hotel features facilities for the business traveler. The generously proportioned rooms are furnished with upscale linen, and have small private balconies. Some offer views of the village and coastline. Pool and tennis. **www.marriott.com**

### RANCHO SANTA FE Rancho Valencia Resort, an Auberge Resort                    $$$$$

*5921 Valencia Circle, 92067* **Tel** *(858) 756-1123* **Fax** *(858) 756-0165* **Rooms** *49*          **Road map** *D6*

Set on an expanse of rolling hills, this resort features an array of activity options, from golf and tennis to hiking. The hacienda-style rooms are spacious and comfortably furnished, offering peaceful seclusion. Some suites have a private pool and Jacuzzi. Magnificent spa. **www.ranchovalencia.com**

### SAN DIEGO Diamond Head Inn                    $

*605 Diamond Street, 92109* **Tel** *858-273-1900* **Fax** *858-273-8532* **Rooms** *21*          **Road map** *D6*

On the boardwalk facing Pacific Beach, this small hotel has simply furnished, clean guest rooms with microwaves and refrigerators. Shops and dining are a short walk away. For those spending the day out sightseeing, it's a real value spot. **www.diamond-head-inn.pacificahost.com**

### SAN DIEGO Best Western plus Cabrillo Garden Inn                    $$

*840 A St, 92101* **Tel** *(619) 234-8477* **Rooms** *30*          **Road map** *D6*

This two-story motel boasts a lush garden area and quiet rooms and is within walking distance of San Diego Copley Symphony Hall, the Gaslamp District, and bus and trolley stops. The guestrooms are equipped with cable TV and high-speed Wi-Fi, and the complimentary full breakfast is better than average. **www.bestwestern.com**

### SAN DIEGO Comfort Inn and Suites Hotel Circle                    $$

*2201 Hotel Circle S, 92108* **Tel** *(619) 881-6800* **Rooms** *192*          **Road map** *D6*

Of the many hotels in this section of town, the Comfort Inn is among the best. Located near sights such as Sea-World® and San Diego Zoo, this family-friendly hotel has rooms with kitchens, outdoor grills near the pool, a spa, and a children's pool. Complimentary full breakfast is provided. Close to the beach. **www.comfortinnhotelcircle.com**

### SAN DIEGO Keating House                    $$

*2331 2nd Avenue, 92101* **Tel** *(619) 239-8585, (800) 995-8644* **Fax** *(619) 239-5774* **Rooms** *9*          **Road map** *D6*

This historic bed and breakfast has been restored to its original Victorian elegance. There is a large foyer with its own fireplace, and also a parlor and dining room. The house is surrounded by lush, tropical grounds, with seating areas in the garden. **www.keatinghouse.com**

### SAN DIEGO Wyndham Garden San Diego                    $$

*3737 Sports Arena Blvd, 92110* **Tel** *(877) 999-3223* **Rooms** *316*          **Road map** *D6*

Ideal for families, this Mission Bay hotel is located near the beach, SeaWorld®, the San Diego Zoo, and more. The grounds are decorated with over 400 palm trees, while the soft blue and beige paint scheme evokes the coastline. On-site currency exchange and shuttles to local attractions are especially convenient. **www.wyndham.com**

### SAN DIEGO Doubletree by Hilton Golf Resort San Diego                    $$$

*14455 Penasquitos Dr, 92129* **Tel** *(858) 672-9100* **Fax** *(858) 672-9187* **Rooms** *174*          **Road map** *D6*

A contemporary hotel located off the I-15 freeway and 25 minutes from downtown. The hotel boasts spacious grounds and an eighteen-hole golf course, as well as tennis courts and a swimming pool. Guestrooms are comfortable with plush-top mattresses, balcony or patio, and high-speed Internet access. **www.doubletree1.hilton.com**

## SAN DIEGO Heritage Park Inn $$$

*2470 Heritage Park Row, 92110* **Tel** *(619) 299-6832, (800) 995-2470* **Fax** *(619) 299-9465* **Rooms** *12* **Road map** *D6*

Housed in a Queen Anne house, this intimate, charming inn is located near the famous San Diego Zoo and SeaWorld®. Rooms are cozy and appointed with period furnishing. Service is friendly and swift. Breakfast and afternoon tea are included. **www.heritageparkinn.com**

## SAN DIEGO Sheraton Mission Valley San Diego Hotel $$$

*1433 Camino Del Rio South, 92108* **Tel** *(619) 260-0111* **Fax** *(619) 497-0853* **Rooms** *260* **Road map** *D6*

A comfortable and convenient hotel located close to the beaches, Qualcomm Stadium, San Diego Zoo, and Mission Valley shopping malls. The well-furnished rooms feature large desks and Internet access. There is a well-equipped fitness facility, as well as an outdoor pool and business center. **www.starwoodhotels.com**

## SAN DIEGO Sommerset Suites Hotel $$$

*606 Washington Street, 92103* **Tel** *619-692-5200* **Fax** *619-692-5299* **Rooms** *80* **Road map** *D6*

Full kitchens, clean rooms with sitting areas, and a trendy Hillcrest location make this a good place for longer stays. It is in between two hospitals so daytime noise can be a nuisance. Amenities include quality linens, a relaxing pool area, and free Wi-Fi. **www.sommersetsuites.com**

## SAN DIEGO Hotel Solamar – A Kimpton Hotel $$$$

*435 6th Ave, 92101* **Tel** *(619) 819-9500, (877) 230-0300* **Fax** *(619) 819-9539* **Rooms** *235* **Road map** *D6*

This stylish hotel near the Petco ballpark and vibrant Gaslamp neighborhood features rooms with the latest in technology and guest comfort. Furnishings are chic and amenities sumptuous. There is a lively lounge on the rooftop. There is a trendy restaurant and bar on-site. Swimming pool and breakfast included. **www.hotelsolamar.com**

## SAN DIEGO San Diego Marriott and Marina $$$$

*333 West Harbor Dr, 92101* **Tel** *(619) 234-1500* **Fax** *(619) 234-8678* **Rooms** *1360* **Road map** *D6*

With convenient access to San Diego waterways, this large, business-friendly hotel has a nautical theme and a bustling lobby. The rooms are spacious and offer lovely views of downtown and the bay. Located within easy walking distance to the Gaslamp Quarter. Free local phone calls. **www.marriott.com**

## SAN DIEGO Beach Cottages $$$$$

*4255 Ocean Blvd, 92109* **Tel** *(858) 483-7440* **Fax** *(858) 273-9365* **Rooms** *78* **Road map** *D6*

This family-run hotel on the beach has been a staple in the area for decades. The accommodations range from basic motel rooms to cottages, with complete kitchens ideal for extended family stays. Several recreational choices are offered, including shuffleboard and beach games. Close to San Diego attractions. **www.beachcottages.com**

## SAN DIEGO The Grant Hotel $$$$$

*326 Broadway, 92101* **Tel** *(619) 232-3121, (866) 837-4270* **Fax** *(619) 239-9517* **Rooms** *210* **Road map** *D6*

In the heart of downtown, this beautiful, historic property features rooms with a period feel, but equipped with modern amenities, including plush bath robes and pillowtop mattresses. The lobby and public areas are opulent and regal. Within walking distance of many shops and restaurants. Internet access. **www.usgrant.net**

## SAN DIEGO Omni San Diego Hotel $$$$$

*675 L St, 92101* **Tel** *(619) 231-6664* **Fax** *(619) 231-8060* **Rooms** *511* **Road map** *D6*

A high-rise hotel near the ballpark and the Gaslamp Quarter, Omni San Diego has sleek rooms with Internet access, flat-screen TVs, and spa-quality bath accessories. Most rooms have great views of the bay or downtown. The Omni has a business center and three restaurants. Pet friendly. **www.omnihotels.com**

# THE INLAND EMPIRE AND LOW DESERT

## BIG BEAR LAKE Big Bear Lake Mallard Bay Resort $

*214 S. Lagunita Lane, 92315* **Tel** *909-866-2526* **Rooms** *16* **Road map** *D6*

Cozy, spotless cabins right on the lake let boaters dock outside their front doors. Volleyball, swimming, shuffleboard horseshoes, and a large fireplace to gather around in the evenings make it a good family spot. Convenient for an array of restaurants, and close to hiking routes. **www.mallardbayresort.com**

## BIG BEAR LAKE Northwoods Resort $$$

*40650 Village Dr, 92315* **Tel** *(909) 866-3121, (800) 866-3121* **Fax** *(909) 878-2122* **Rooms** *147* **Road map** *D5*

The only full-service hotel at Big Bear Lake, Northwoods is at the entrance to Big Bear Village, with shops and restaurants, and close to the lake. The hotel has its own restaurant and lounge with live entertainment. Rooms have Wi-Fi and many have fireplaces. Large swimming pool. Ideal for families. **www.northwoodsresort.com**

## BORREGO SPRINGS Borrego Springs Resort $$

*1112 Tilting T Drive, 92004* **Tel** *760-767-5700* **Fax** *760-767-5710* **Rooms** *100* **Road map** *D6*

Spacious rooms, tennis courts, and outstanding service, as well as an on-site restaurant and bar make this a good place to spend a few quiet nights. Book a tee time at one of three 9-hole courses and some spa services to make the retreat complete. **www.borregospringsresort.com**

**Key to Price Guide** *see p524* **Key to Symbols** *see back cover flap*

### BORREGO SPRINGS Palm Canyon Resort $$

*221 Palm Canyon Dr, 92004* **Tel** *(760) 767-5341* **Fax** *(760) 767-4073* **Rooms** *61* **Road map** *D6*

This casual, western-style resort is located near Anza-Borrego Desert State Park. The guestrooms are spacious and modest; some offer private balconies or patios with desert views. Facilities include an outdoor pool, on-site restaurant, and small gym. Continental breakfast is served on the covered deck. **www.palmcanyonresort.com**

### DESERT HOT SPRINGS Two Bunch Palms Resort & Spa $$$$

*67425 Two Bunch Palms Trail, 92240* **Tel** *(760) 329-8791, (877) 839-3609* **Fax** *(760) 329-1874* **Rooms** *44*

Renowned for its rejuvenating mineral pools, this adults-only oasis getaway offers rooms in casitas, suites, and villas. All rooms are comfortably appointed, while the Casino Dining Room serves good fine dining options. The vast array of spa treatments help the resort maintain a loyal following. **www.twobunchpalms.com**

### IDYLLWILD Creekstone Inn $$

*54950 Pine Crest Ave, 92549* **Tel** *(951) 659-3342, (800) 409-2127* **Rooms** *9* **Road map** *D6*

This quaint, rustic country inn has had incarnations as a restaurant and a general store. It is set at the edge of town and very close to hiking trails and the local wilderness. Most of the uniquely furnished rooms come with fireplaces, while some have Jacuzzis. **www.creekstoneinn.com**

### IDYLLWILD Quiet Creek Inn $$

*26345 Delano Dr, 92549* **Tel** *(951) 659-6110* **Rooms** *10* **Road map** *D6*

Set in 6.5 acres (2.6 ha) of forest alongside Strawberry Creek, Quiet Creek Inn offers comfortable duplex cabins with fireplaces, cotton bed linens, cable TV, and Wi-Fi. The common lounge features complimentary movies, popcorn, hot chocolate, and tea, or you can relax outside by the stream. Pets allowed in some rooms. **www.quietcreekinn.com**

### INDIAN WELLS Hyatt Grand Champions Resort $$$$

*44600 Indian Wells Lane, 92210* **Tel** *(760) 341-1000* **Fax** *(760) 568-2236* **Rooms** *530* **Road map** *D6*

Designed for the golf lifestyle, this resort is set on two famous golf courses (and a tennis center) offering recreation in myriad varieties. The grounds are expansive and well kept. Rooms are spacious and appointed with many modern luxuries. There is a full spa on premises. **www.grandchampions.hyatt.com**

### INDIAN WELLS Indian Wells Resort Hotel $$$$

*76–661 Hwy 111, 92210* **Tel** *(760) 345-6466, (800) 248-3220* **Fax** *(760) 772-5083* **Rooms** *155* **Road map** *D6*

A luxurious desert resort set on a golf course, the Indian Wells offers golf privileges at two courses. Rooms range from small and serviceable to huge and opulent. All feature private balconies or patios and high-speed Internet access. Breakfast is included. **www.indianwellsresort.com**

### INDIO Best Western Date Tree Hotel $$

*81909 Indio Blvd, 92201* **Tel** *(760) 347-3421* **Fax** *(760) 863-1338* **Rooms** *120* **Road map** *D6*

An affordable, well-run hotel situated close to a world-famous golf course, tennis facilities, and local attractions. The immaculate guest rooms are tastefully decorated. The grounds are quiet and feature a full spa and Olympic-size pool. Internet access and a superb Continental breakfast are included. **www.datetree.com**

### PALM DESERT Marriott Desert Springs Resort & Spa $$$$

*74855 Country Club Dr, 92260* **Tel** *(760) 341-2211, (888) 538-9459* **Fax** *(760) 341-1872* **Rooms** *844* **Road map** *D6*

This large, spectacular property has a lake in its atrium lobby – and guests can get around the hotel by boat. The rooms have gorgeous views and are sumptuously appointed, with granite and marble finishes. Recreation includes golf and tennis. Luxury spa and fine dining. **www.desertspringsresort.com**

### PALM SPRINGS Best Western Las Brisas Hotel $$

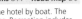

*222 S Indian Canyon Dr, 92262* **Tel** *(760) 325-4372* **Fax** *(760) 329-1371* **Rooms** *90* **Road map** *D6*

This renovated, three-story motel is Mediterranean in style. It is located in town but is within easy reach of the Indian Canyons and the Living Desert Zoo. The guestrooms have refrigerators and are equipped with high-speed Internet access. A complimentary full American breakfast is served. **www.bestwestern.com**

### PALM DESERT Homewood Suites by Hilton Palm Desert $$

*36999 Cook Street, 92211* **Tel** *760-568-1600* **Fax** *760-568-1608* **Rooms** *128* **Road map** *D6*

A well-maintained property near to the main shopping and dining areas, this is a good choice for long stays. Complimentary amenities include Wi-Fi, parking, shopping service, business center, breakfast buffet, and weekday evening receptions. Coin laundry and full kitchens are available. **www.homewoodsuites.hilton.com**

### PALM SPRINGS Palm Court Inn $$

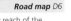

*1983 N Palm Canyon Dr, 92262* **Tel** *(760) 416-2333, (800) 667-7918* **Fax** *(760) 416-5425* **Rooms** *107* **Road map** *D6*

Exceptional value in a great central location can be found at this well-manicured hotel, which features attractive grounds, courteous staff, and rooms with balconies and views of the mountains. Select accommodations have Jacuzzis. Breakfast is included. **www.palmcourt-inn.com**

### PALM SPRINGS Ace Hotel and Swim Club $$$

*701 East Palm Canyon Dr, 92264* **Tel** *(760) 325-9900* **Fax** *(760) 325-7878* **Rooms** *205* **Road map** *D6*

Hip and chic with a retro vibe, this fun boutique hotel runs on solar power. The funky guestrooms are contemporary Americana in style and have great beds and fluffy towels. The deep pool is excellent for serious swimmers while the poolside eatery offers cocktails, fish tacos, and more. **www.acehotel.com**

### PALM SPRINGS Hilton Palm Springs ⬛🍴🏊🏋🎴♿ $$$

*400 E Tahquitz Canyon Drive, 92262* **Tel** *(760) 320-6868* **Fax** *(760) 320-2126* **Rooms** *260* **Road map** *D6*

A downtown hotel, with rooms situated around a large pool. Rooms are spacious and comfortably appointed; many have mountain views and balconies. Amenities include a full spa, fitness facilities, and business center. The Al Fresco is a poolside lounge, while the lovely Terrace Restaurant is an excellent dining choice. **www.hiltonpalmsprings.com**

### PALM SPRINGS The Terra Cotta Inn 🏊♿ $$$

*2388 E Racquet Club Rd, 92262-2629* **Tel** *(760) 322-6059* **Fax** *(760) 322-4169* **Rooms** *17* **Road map** *D6*

This is a clothing-optional resort, which celebrates "naturalism" in an intimate, well-run environment. Rooms are large, basically appointed, and have a microwave and refrigerator. On-site amenities include a pool and barbecue facilities. Spa services are available, and breakfast and Happy Hour are included. **www.sunnyfun.com**

### PALM SPRINGS Villa Royale Inn ⬛🍴🏊🎴♿ $$$

*1620 S Indian Trail, 92264* **Tel** *(760) 327-2314, (800) 245-2314* **Fax** *(760) 322-3794* **Rooms** *31* **Road map** *D6*

An intimate luxury inn with an adults-only environment, Villa Royale Inn provides romantic rooms, each decorated uniquely in the style of a specific European region. Popular with honeymooners, it is set on lovely grounds with a pool and fine-dining restaurant. Breakfast is included. **www.villaroyale.com**

### PALM SPRINGS Hyatt Regency ⬛🍴🏊🏋🎴♿ $$$$

*285 N Palm Canyon Dr, 92262* **Tel** *(760) 322-9000* **Fax** *(760) 322-6009* **Rooms** *197* **Road map** *D6*

This convenient hotel in the middle of town features cozy rooms and a full array of business amenities. The well-appointed one- and two-bedroom suites have balconies affording great desert views. Within walking distance of shops, galleries, and entertainment venues. Putting green and full-service spa. **www.palmsprings.hyatt.com**

### PALM SPRINGS Spa Resort Casino ⬛🍴🏊🎴♿24 $$$$

*401 E Amado Rd, 92262* **Tel** *(888) 999-1995* **Fax** *(760) 325-0688* **Rooms** *228* **Road map** *D6*

Built over hot springs that gave the town its name, this hotel in the city center has a lavish spa and comfortable rooms. A variety of activities are in walking distance, including the hotel's Las Vegas-style casino with live entertainment. **www.sparesortcasino.com**

### PALM SPRINGS Riviera Palm Springs ⬛🍴🏊🏋🎴♿24 $$$$$

*1600 N. Indian Canyon Drive, 92262* **Tel** *(866) 588-8311* **Rooms** *406* **Road map** *D6*

After multi-million-dollar upgrades, this grande dame of the desert sparkles with glamor. Its 24 acres (10 hectares) contain two pools, tennis and volleyball courts, a kids' center, restaurant, bars, a spa, business center, and landscaped grounds. A free trolley bus takes guests downtown. **www.psriviera.com**

### RANCHO MIRAGE Rancho Las Palmas Resort ⬛🍴🏊🏋🎴♿24 $$$

*41000 Bob Hope Dr, 92270* **Tel** *(760) 568-2727, (866) 423-1195* **Fax** *(760) 568-5845* **Rooms** *466* **Road map** *D6*

Rooms at this large, family-friendly hotel have private balconies or patios. The property is well-run and has 25 tennis courts and an exciting water park. There is also a 27-hole golf course. Discounts are offered regularly. **www.rancholaspalmas.com**

### RANCHO MIRAGE Hilton Garden Inn ⬛🍴🏊🎴♿ $$$$$

*71-700 Highway 111, 92270* **Tel** *(760) 776-9700* **Fax** *(760) 776-4110* **Rooms** *120* **Road map** *D6*

Located in the center of Rancho Mirage, this two-story hotel is near the exclusive El Paseo shopping area, as well as evening entertainment and fine dining. Rooms are comfortable with cotton linens, microwave, fridge, and large desk. Hotel amenities include a fitness center, business center, and complimentary parking. **www.hiltongardeninn.com**

### RIVERSIDE Mission Inn Hotel & Spa ⬛🍴🏊🏋🎴♿ $$$$

*3649 Mission Inn Ave, 92501* **Tel** *(951) 784-0300* **Fax** *(951) 683-1342* **Rooms** *239* **Road map** *D6*

An icon of the city, this beautiful hotel dates to 1888 and encompasses an entire block. The property is exquisite, with much of its original Spanish Colonial charm intact. The updated rooms are elegant and appointed with every amenity. A full-service spa and four restaurants complete the scene. **www.missioninn.com**

### TWENTYNINE PALMS Best Western Gardens Hotel 🍴🏊🎴♿24 $$

*71487 Twentynine Palms Hwy, 92277* **Tel** *(760) 367-9141, (800) 780-7234* **Fax** *(760) 367-2584* **Rooms** *83* **Road map** *D5*

Select rooms at this tidy, well-located hotel are beautifully appointed, featuring kitchenettes. Amenities include a pool, hot tub, laundry facilities, free parking, and breakfast. This is a good stop-over for Joshua Tree National Park, which is located just 5 miles (8 kms) away. **www.bestwestern.com**

## THE MOJAVE DESERT

### BARSTOW Super 8 Barstow 🍴🏊♿24 $

*170 Coolwater Lane, 92311* **Tel** *(760) 256-8443* **Fax** *(760) 256-0997* **Rooms** *51* **Road map** *D5*

Decent rooms and friendly staff make this affordable option in the desert worthwhile. Select business amenities include Internet access, fax, and a copying center. Refrigerators and microwaves are available, as is free parking for guests. The Barstow Super 8 is located close to restaurants and shops and Calico Ghost Town. **www.super8.com**

### BARSTOW Comfort Suites

$$

*2571 Fisher Blvd, 92311* **Tel** *(760) 253-3600* **Fax** *(760) 253-3668* **Rooms** *83*      **Road map** *D5*

This hotel is located near historic Route 66. Guests are welcomed into an attractive, two-story lobby and the rooms are well equipped with refrigerator, microwave oven, large plasma TV, and wireless high-speed Internet access. Complimentary full breakfast is offered and the outdoor pool is heated. **www.comfortsuites.com**

### BARSTOW Ramada Inn

$

*1511 E Main St, 92311* **Tel** *(760) 256-5673* **Fax** *(760) 256-5917* **Rooms** *148*      **Road map** *D5*

This updated motor inn is designed in the Mission style. The rooms are no-frills, but clean and comfortable, and feature high-speed Internet access as well as premium television channels. Room service can be ordered from the adjacent restaurants. Close to Calico Ghost Town. **www.ramada.com**

### DEATH VALLEY Amargosa Opera House and Hotel

$

*Death Valley Junction, 92328* **Tel** *(760) 852-4441* **Fax** *(760) 852-4138* **Rooms** *14*      **Road map** *D4*

A quirky hotel in the desert, the Amargosa is a working theater where cabaret shows are performed. Rooms are comfortable, if a bit eccentric, and decorated with fantastical wall murals painted by the proprietor. In keeping with the historic ambience, telephones and televisions are not in the rooms. **www.amargosa-opera-house.com**

### DEATH VALLEY Delight's Hot Springs Resort

$

*368 Tecopa Hot Springs Rd, 92389* **Tel** *(800) 928-8808* **Rooms** *11*      **Road map** *D4*

Renowned for its natural hot springs, this small hotel is within a short drive of Las Vegas, and features motel rooms and cabins with kitchenettes. The unpretentious decor lays emphasis on retaining the old-world charm. The staff are friendly and attentive. Pet friendly. **www.delightshotspringsresort.com**

### DEATH VALLEY Stove Pipe Wells Village

$$

*Hwy 190, Death Valley, 92328* **Tel** *(760) 786-2387* **Fax** *(760) 786-2389* **Rooms** *83*      **Road map** *D4*

Though the guest rooms are well appointed and contemporary, this retreat at an entrance to Death Valley has rustic appeal and is set in a stunning desert landscape. Close to the general store and Big Sand Dunes, with a landing strip close by. Swimming pool. **www.escapetodeathvalley.com**

### DEATH VALLEY Ranch at Furnace Creek

$$$

*Hwy 190, 92328* **Tel** *(760) 786-2345* **Fax** *(760) 786-2514* **Rooms** *224*      **Road map** *D4*

This large cluster of simple but well-kept rooms is just down the hill from Furnace Creek Inn but much more informal and more affordable. It has a swimming pool, a Western saloon, and three restaurants. The resort is especially suited to families with kids. Closed mid-May–mid-Oct. **www.furnacecreekresort.com**

### DEATH VALLEY Furnace Creek Inn

$$$$$

*Hwy 190, 92328* **Tel** *(760) 786-2345* **Fax** *(760) 786-2514* **Rooms** *66*      **Road map** *D4*

A gorgeous oasis in the desert, this historic landmark property has amenities on par with top luxury resorts. Rooms are elegant and sumptuously appointed. Recreational pursuits include swimming in a spring-fed pool, golf, and tennis. Closed mid-May–mid-Oct. **www.furnacecreekresort.com**

### LAKE HAVASU Hidden Palms Resort Condominiums

$

*2100 Swanson Ave, 86403* **Tel** *(928) 855-7144, (800) 254-5611* **Fax** *(928) 855-2620* **Rooms** *22*   **Road map** *E5*

A quiet inn near the lake, the Hidden Palms offers one-bedroom suites with modern furniture, custom cabinetry, and Internet access. Rooms are spacious and appointed with kitchenettes and separate dining areas. Set in a beautiful palm tree landscape, the courtyard is relaxing and idyllic. **www.hiddenpalms.com**

### LAKE HAVASU Quality Inn & Suites

$

*271 S Lake Havasu Ave, 86403* **Tel** *(928) 855-1111* **Fax** *(928) 855-6228* **Rooms** *177*      **Road map** *E5*

This basic one-story motel offers clean, comfortable rooms that are equipped with cable TV, free Wi-Fi, coffee maker, and refrigerator. Other amenities include photocopy and fax services, a guest laundry, a heated pool with sun deck area, and a bar and restaurant. Close to Lake Havasu and shops at the London Bridge. **www.qualityinn.com**

### LAKE HAVASU Hampton Inn

$$

*245 London Bridge Road, 86403* **Tel** *928-855-4071* **Fax** *928-855-2379* **Rooms** *162*      **Road map** *D6*

This clean, comfortable hotel offers rooms with lake views and amenities such as refrigerators and microwave ovens. A hot breakfast bar, coin laundry, ATM, business center, and professional, helpful staff provide good service for visitors. **www.hamptoninn.hilton.com**

### LAKE HAVASU The Nautical Beachfront Resort

$$$

*1000 McCulloch Blvd, 86403* **Tel** *(928) 855-2141, (866) 248-0241* **Fax** *(928) 453-5808* **Rooms** *139*   **Road map** *E5*

This resort-style hotel is set on the lake, and features large rooms in various sizes. Most have private patios, while the suites feature full kitchens. The location offers easy access to water activities. Dock your boat in front of your suite. The hotel has a private guests-only beach. **www.nauticalinn.com**

### MOJAVE Best Western Plus Desert Winds

$

*16200 Sierra Highway Mojave, 93501* **Tel** *(661) 824-3601, (800) 780-7234* **Fax** *(661) 824-3605* **Rooms** *51*  **Road map** *D5*

Rooms are clean, modern, and comfortable at this well-run establishment with friendly staff. Guests can relax by the pool or spa or explore one of the many hiking trails nearby. Rooms have microwaves, and local calls are free. There is a business center, Internet access, and a coin laundry. Breakfast is included. **www.bestwestern.com**

### MOJAVE Days Inn    ⑤

*16100 Sierra Highway, 93501* **Tel** *661-824-2421* **Fax** *661-824-2345* **Rooms** *50*      **Road map** *D6*

Clean, modern rooms with microwaves, refrigerators, coffee makers, and large bathrooms make this one of the best options for a stopover on the way to Death Valley. The staff are friendly and the reasonable rates include a Continental breakfast. **www.daysinn.com**

## SAN FRANCISCO

### CHINATOWN AND NOB HILL Hilton, San Francisco Financial District    ⑤⑤⑤⑤

*750 Kearny St, 94108* **Tel** *(415) 433-6600* **Fax** *(415) 765-7891* **Rooms** *544*      **Map** *5 C3*

With a modern decor and casual residential feel, this Hilton hotel is located near Chinatown and Portsmouth Plaza. There is also a first-class day spa located in the lobby. Cable car lines are just two blocks away. Children under 12, accompanied by an adult, stay free. **www.sanfranciscohiltonhotel.com**

### CHINATOWN AND NOB HILL Orchard Hotel    ⑤⑤⑤⑤

*665 Bush St, 94108* **Tel** *(415) 362-8878, (888) 717-2881* **Fax** *(415) 362-8088* **Rooms** *104*      **Map** *5 C4*

This modern hotel is a short walk from the Powell Street cable car and Union Square. Decor is a blend of traditional and contemporary, and photographs of the city's architecture and scenery decorate the public spaces and rooms. Facilities include a business center, disabled access, free Wi-Fi, and a town car service. **www.theorchardhotel.com**

### CHINATOWN AND NOB HILL The Fairmont San Francisco    ⑤⑤⑤⑤⑤

*950 Mason St, 94108* **Tel** *(415) 772-5000, (800) 441-1414* **Fax** *(415) 772-5013* **Rooms** *591*      **Map** *5 B4*

Famous for its gorgeous lobby and opulent public rooms, the Fairmont is the grandest of all the grand hotels at the top of Nob Hill. It has been much admired since it reopened in 1907, a year after an earthquake and fire ravaged it. The panoramic views are unbeatable. **www.fairmont.com/sanfrancisco**

### CHINATOWN AND NOB HILL Hotel Triton    ⑤⑤⑤⑤⑤

*342 Grant Ave, 94108* **Tel** *(415) 394-0500, (800) 800-1299* **Fax** *(415) 394-0555* **Rooms** *140*      **Map** *5 C4*

Design and media professionals frequent the small but stylish Triton, with a friendly and cheerful ambience. It is just across the street from Chinatown and in the heart of San Francisco's art gallery district. For overseas travelers, foreign newspapers are normally available at the downstairs Café de la Presse. **www.hoteltriton.com**

### CHINATOWN AND NOB HILL Huntington Hotel & Nob Hill Spa    ⑤⑤⑤⑤⑤

*1075 California St, 94108* **Tel** *(415) 474-5400, (800) 227-4683* **Fax** *(415) 474-6227* **Rooms** *135*      **Map** *5 B4*

Built in 1922 as a luxury apartment building, the Huntington was converted into a high-class hotel in 1945. Each of the spacious rooms is individually decorated – many have a wet bar, and some have kitchens. Indulge yourself at the world-famous Nob Hill Spa in the basement and ground floor. **www.huntingtonhotel.com**

### CHINATOWN AND NOB HILL InterContinental Mark Hopkins Hotel    ⑤⑤⑤⑤⑤

*1 Nob Hill, 94108* **Tel** *(415) 392-3434, (800) 946-7621* **Fax** *(415) 421-3302* **Rooms** *380*      **Map** *5 B4*

Located atop Nob Hill, the Mark Hopkins is a 1926 architectural landmark. It stands by its reputation as one of the finest hotels in San Francisco, rich and lavish in style. The Top of the Mark sky lounge, on the 19th floor, offers panoramic views of the city from the peak of Nob Hill. **www.ichotelsgroup.com**

### CHINATOWN AND NOB HILL The Ritz-Carlton San Francisco    ⑤⑤⑤⑤⑤

*600 Stockton St, 94108* **Tel** *(415) 296-7465, (800) 241-3333* **Fax** *(415) 986-1268* **Rooms** *336*      **Map** *5 C4*

Since it opened in 1991, the Ritz-Carlton has been rated one of San Francisco's best hotels. It is housed in an historic Beaux Arts building in an entire block along California Street, near the top of Nob Hill. Service is excellent. There is a four-star dining room and a fitness center. **www.ritzcarlton.com**

### CIVIC CENTER Grove Inn    ⑤⑤

*890 Grove St, 94117* **Tel** *(415) 929-0780, (800) 829-0780* **Fax** *(415) 929-1037* **Rooms** *20*      **Map** *4 E5*

Grove Inn, an Italianate-Victorian B&B, with a good location, dates to the late 1800s. The multilingual hosts have been running the place for over 25 years. The sunny rooms come with a queen-sized bed and Wi-Fi. Rates include a complimentary Continental breakfast. **www.grovinn.com**

### CIVIC CENTER Hotel Metropolis    ⑤⑤

*25 Mason St, 94102* **Tel** *(415) 775-4600, (800) 553-1900* **Fax** *(415) 775-4606* **Rooms** *105*      **Map** *5 B5*

A funky boutique hotel, the Metropolis has a nature theme throughout, with each floor reflecting the elements. All rooms offer amenities, including bars, two-line phones and data ports with voicemail, and free Wi-Fi. **www.hotelmetropolissf.com**

### CIVIC CENTER Phoenix Hotel    ⑤⑤

*601 Eddy St, 94109* **Tel** *(415) 776-1380, (800) 248-9466* **Fax** *(415) 885-3109* **Rooms** *44*      **Map** *4 F4*

This funky two-story motel, in the heart of the Tenderloin District, conjures up images of old Route 66. Grab a drink at the house bar, Chambers, and head out to the courtyard pool to spot celebrities (past guests include Dave Navarro and Linda Ronstadt). The rooms are basic, but great value for a central location. **www.jdvhotels.com**

**Key to Price Guide** *see p524* **Key to Symbols** *see back cover flap*

## CIVIC CENTER Best Western Americana
$$$

*121 7th St, 94103* **Tel** *(415) 626-0200, (800) 444-5816* **Fax** *(415) 863-2529* **Rooms** *143*

Though technically in the trendy South of Market neighborhood, the Americana is a short walk from Union Square. With modern, spacious, and comfortable facilities, the hotel offers free Internet access and free parking, and children under 17 stay free with any paying adult. **www.bestwestern.com**

## CIVIC CENTER Hotel Tomo
$$$

*1800 Sutter St, 94115* **Tel** *(415) 921-4000, (888) 882-8666* **Fax** *(415) 563-1278* **Rooms** *125*     **Map** *4 E4*

Hotel Tomo is perfect for travelers in search of good value, above-average accommodation, and world-class dining just steps from the front door. Located in the heart of Japan Town and close to many good sushi restaurants, it has perfectly acceptable guest rooms. **www.jdvhotels.com**

## CIVIC CENTER Hotel Kabuki
$$$$

*1625 Post St, 94115* **Tel** *(415) 922-3200, (800) 533-4567* **Fax** *(415) 614-5498* **Rooms** *218*     **Map** *4 E4*

Located within the Japan Center complex, the stylish Hotel Kabuki appeals to business travelers as well as regular tourists. Ask for one of the rooms featuring a Japanese steam bath. Japanese rooms with *tatami* mats are also available. The O Izakaya restaurant is just downstairs. Children under 18 stay free. **www.hotelkabuki.com**

## CIVIC CENTER Sleep Over Sauce
$$$$

*135 Gough Street, 94102* **Tel** *(415) 621-0896* **Rooms** *8*     **Map** *3 F5*

The charming Hayes Valley neighborhood, near the symphony and opera halls, museums, and city hall, is the location of this ultra-hip boutique "guest house," above a trendy restaurant and bar. The rooms are small and comfy, and there's business center, and a wood-burning fireplace in the lounge. **www.sleepsf.com**

## DOWNTOWN Taylor Hotel
$

*615 Taylor St, Post St, 94102* **Tel** *(415) 775-0780, (877) 734-6835* **Fax** *(415) 775-6815* **Rooms** *34*     **Map** *5 B5*

A simple, no-frills hotel, ideally located and priced for the budget traveler. The rooms are clean and all have private bathrooms and free wireless Internet access. The staff are always happy to help and advise about any aspect of your stay. A maid service is provided at an extra charge. **www.sanfrancisco-budgethotel.com**

## DOWNTOWN Touchstone Hotel
$$

*480 Geary St, 94102* **Tel** *(415) 771-1600, (800) 620-5889* **Fax** *(415) 931-5442* **Rooms** *42*     **Map** *5 B5*

Just steps from Union Square, Touchstone Hotel is a blend of old-world charm and modern convenience. The hotel is complemented by David's, a famed restaurant/deli/bakery, located right off the lobby, in which hotel guests enjoy a 25 percent discount. Children under 10 stay free. **www.thetouchstone.com**

## DOWNTOWN USA Hostels
$$

*711 Post Street, 94109* **Tel** *(415) 440-5600* **Fax** *(415) 651-8802* **Rooms** *50*     **Map** *5 C4*

Located in an incredible downtown location, and voted "Best Hostel in the US." On offer are individual "privacy pods", and private and multi-guest rooms with en-suite or shared baths, all with microwaves and fridges. There is also a free movie theater, high-speed Internet kiosks, and arranged guided city tours. **www.usahostels.com**

## DOWNTOWN Andrews Hotel
$$$

*624 Post St, 94109* **Tel** *(415) 563-6877, (800) 926-3739* **Fax** *(415) 928-6919* **Rooms** *48*     **Map** *5 B5*

Clean and comfortable rooms are offered in this small, family-owned hotel, located just two blocks away from Union Square. The prices are moderate, and include a complimentary Continental breakfast. An Italian restaurant is situated just off the lobby, and guests are offered a free glass of wine every evening. **www.andrewshotel.com**

## DOWNTOWN Handlery Union Square Hotel
$$$

*351 Geary Street, 94102* **Tel** *(415) 781-7800* **Fax** *(415) 781-0216* **Rooms** *284*     **Map** *5 C4*

In an unbeatable downtown location, this long-time family-owned hotel has comfortable rooms and suites: smaller rooms are in the Historic Section, while over-sized premier rooms have plush amenities and Wi-Fi. Facilities include a pool, a business center, barber shop, restaurant, and bar. Exceptionally helpful staff. **www.sf.handlery.com**

## DOWNTOWN Hotel des Arts
$$$

*447 Bush St, 94108* **Tel** *(415) 956-3232, (800) 956-4322* **Fax** *(415) 956-0399* **Rooms** *51*     **Map** *5 C4*

Hotel des Arts is as much a functioning art gallery as it is a hotel. All of the rooms, painted and decorated by a rotating roster of local artists, makes it one of the most unusual places in the city. Union Square, Chinatown, and the Financial District are close by. **www.sfhoteldesarts.com**

## DOWNTOWN Hotel Diva
$$$

*440 Geary St, 94102* **Tel** *(415) 885-0200, (800) 553-1900* **Fax** *(415) 346-6613* **Rooms** *116*     **Map** *5 B5*

Stepping into Hotel Diva gives one the impression of having wandered into the Museum of Modern Art. The lobby and rooms are whimsically and colorfully decorated and accented by many architectural touches. The tone is hip luxury and the rooms will not disappoint even the most style-conscious traveler. **www.personalityhotels.com**

## DOWNTOWN Hotel Rex
$$$

*562 Sutter St, 94102* **Tel** *(415) 433-4434, (800) 433-4434* **Rooms** *94*     **Map** *5 B4*

This pleasant hotel has rooms painted in rich colors and walls embellished with the works of local artists. A real gem – and the pride of Rex – the downstairs lobby has a dark-hued and cozy library. The lobby bar often hosts literary events and small shows. **www.thehotelrex.com**

## DOWNTOWN Hotel Union Square

$$$

*114 Powell St, 94102* **Tel** *(415) 397-3000, (800) 553-1900* **Fax** *(415) 399-1874* **Rooms** *131* **Map** *5 C5*

Conveniently located two blocks from Union Square, this hotel is ideal for those looking for good value in the heart of San Francisco's shopping hub. Rooms are small and purpose-built, but amenities include free Wi-Fi and on-site currency exchange. **www.personalityhotels.com**

## DOWNTOWN Westin St. Francis

$$$

*335 Powell St, 94102* **Tel** *(415) 397-7000* **Fax** *(415) 774-0124* **Rooms** *1195* **Map** *5 B4*

Since 1904, Union Square's skyline has been defined by the triple towers of Westin St. Francis. Following damage in the earthquake and fire of 1906, the hotel was restored and enlarged. In the 1970s, a 31-story tower, complete with glass elevators, was added onto the back. Best rooms have views of Union Square. **www.westinstfrancis.com**

## DOWNTOWN Grand Hyatt San Francisco

$$$$

*345 Stockton St, 94108* **Tel** *(415) 398-1234, (800) 233-1234* **Fax** *(415) 391-1780* **Rooms** *685* **Map** *5 C4*

The 36-story Grand Hyatt towers over the north side of Union Square, offering great views from all of its rooms. The rooftop Grand View restaurant and lounge have fine views of San Francisco. The location is handy for the Financial District as well as for Union Square shops and theaters. **www.grandsanfrancisco.hyatt.com**

## DOWNTOWN Hilton San Francisco Union Square

$$$$

*333 O'Farrell St, 94102* **Tel** *(415) 771-1400, (800) 445-8667* **Fax** *(415) 771-6807* **Rooms** *1900* **Map** *5 B5*

Filling an entire block just west of Union Square, the city's largest hotel provides excellent views from its 46-story tower. The service, too, matches the establishment's grand scale. The numerous facilities include a heated outdoor swimming pool, a whirlpool, two bars, and health club. **www.hilton.com**

## DOWNTOWN Hotel California

$$$$

*580 Geary St, 94102* **Tel** *(415) 441-2700, (800) 780-7234* **Fax** *(415) 441-0124* **Rooms** *82* **Map** *5 B5*

The Hotel California offers elegance, helpful service, and feather beds with goosedown pillows in all rooms. Each guest is offered a free tequila shot on check-in. Or, if you prefer something more mellow, there is a complimentary wine service every evening from 5pm until 6pm in the hotel lobby. **www.thesavoyhotel.com**

## DOWNTOWN Hotel Carlton

$$$$

*1075 Sutter Street, 94109* **Tel** *(415) 673-0242* **Fax** *(415) 673-4904* **Rooms** *161* **Map** *5 A4*

This European-style, pet-friendly boutique hotel is six blocks from Union Square. The super-friendly staff are helpful and the rooms are modern and comfortable. Hotel Carlton offers a free wine reception, Wi-Fi, car service to the Financial District, and an on-site café. Pay to park across the street. **www.jdvhotels.com**

## DOWNTOWN Hotel Kensington

$$$$

*450 Post St, 94102* **Tel** *(415) 788-6400, (800) 553-1900* **Fax** *(415) 399-9484* **Rooms** *93* **Map** *5 B5*

Located in the 1920s Spanish-Revivalist-style Elks Lodge building, Kensington Park is a comfortable, medium-sized hotel close to Union Square. The lobby is gorgeous, and the nicely furnished rooms are spacious. Evening wine, sherry, and tea are served in the Grand Lobby. Complimentary breakfast. **www.personalityhotels.com**

## DOWNTOWN San Francisco Marriott

$$$$

*55 4th St, 94103* **Tel** *(415) 896-1600* **Fax** *(415) 486-8101* **Rooms** *1,362* **Map** *5 C5*

This 39-story tower is distinctly upscale and is popular with business travelers and for conventions. Families always appreciate the indoor pool and the fact that children under 18, when accompanied by an adult, can stay here free. The hotel also offers four restaurants, a whirlpool, and a spa. **www.marriott.com**

## DOWNTOWN Serrano Hotel

$$$$

*405 Taylor St, 94102* **Tel** *(415) 885-2500, (800) 546-7866* **Fax** *(415) 474-4879* **Rooms** *236* **Map** *5 B5*

This 17-story Spanish-Revivalist-style hotel has convenient access to both Union Square and the Theater District. Each guest room features high ceilings and a warm glow, accented by characteristic Spanish and Moroccan-influenced design. The appealing restaurant is located on the lobby level. **www.serranohotel.com**

## DOWNTOWN Sir Francis Drake Hotel

$$$$

*450 Powell St, 94102* **Tel** *(415) 392-7755, (800) 795-7129* **Fax** *(415) 391-8719* **Rooms** *416* **Map** *5 B4*

A long-established Union Square hotel, Sir Francis Drake glows in Art Deco splendor. It is famed for its Beefeater-uniformed doormen and Harry Denton's Starlight Room, a beautiful rooftop bar. The location on the Powell Street cable car line is unbeatable for access to the Financial District and North Beach. **www.sirfrancisdrake.com**

## DOWNTOWN White Swan Inn

$$$$

*845 Bush St, 94108* **Tel** *(415) 775-1755, (800) 999-9570* **Fax** *(415) 775-5717* **Rooms** *26* **Map** *5 B4*

A small, country-style establishment, the White Swan has rooms with bright floral prints and very comfortable beds. There is also a fireplace that holds a convincing, but artificial, gas-powered open fire. A complimentary gourmet breakfast buffet is served each morning, and wine is offered every evening. **www.jdvhotels.com**

## DOWNTOWN Clift

$$$$$

*495 Geary St, 94102* **Tel** *(415) 775-4700, (800) 697-1791* **Fax** *(415) 441-4621* **Rooms** *373* **Map** *5 B5*

The dramatic Clift is a striking example of modern design, with a lobby created by Phillippe Starck. Each room is elegantly furnished, with all the amenities one would expect from a hotel of this caliber. The downstairs Redwood Room and elegant Velvet Room restaurant are enchanting. **www.clifthotel.com**

**Key to Price Guide** *see p524* **Key to Symbols** *see back cover flap*

### DOWNTOWN Four Seasons Hotel

 $$$$$

*757 Market St, 94103* **Tel** *(415) 633-3000* **Fax** *(415) 633-3001* **Rooms** *277* **Map** *5 C5*

Four Seasons is one of San Francisco's classiest hotels. Spacious and understatedly stylish, each room has cozy sitting areas. The ultra-chic Sports Club/LA is available for guest use. This hotel provides easy access to Union Square, the San Francisco Museum of Modern Art, and the Yerba Buena Center. **www.fourseasons.com**

### DOWNTOWN Galleria Park Hotel

$$$$$

*191 Sutter Street, 94104* **Tel** *(415) 781-3060* **Fax** *(415) 433-4409* **Rooms** *177* **Map** *5 C4*

This upscale, urban-chic boutique hostelry is adjacent to the Crocker Galleria mall and is exceptional value given its location between Union Square and the Financial District. It has a business-oriented atmosphere with access to office supplies, free Wi-Fi, a wine hour, and 24-hour gym. Lively, helpful staff. **www.jdvhotels.com**

### DOWNTOWN Harbor Court Hotel

$$$$$

*165 Steuart St, 94105* **Tel** *(415) 882-1300, (866) 792-6283* **Fax** *(415) 882-1313* **Rooms** *131* **Map** *6 E4*

Housed in what was originally a YMCA building, Harbor Court is the only hotel in San Francisco that is right on the waterfront. Rooms are on the small side, though some have good views of the Bay Bridge. Guests have discounted access to the fitness facilities of the Y gym next door. Nightly wine reception. **www.harborcourthotel.com**

### DOWNTOWN Hotel Frank

$$$$$

*386 Geary St, 94102* **Tel** *(415) 986-2000* **Fax** *(415) 397-2447* **Rooms** *153* **Map** *5 B5*

Built in 1908, the Hotel Frank is located in the heart of Theater District. The entire hotel has been renovated, and all rooms offer amenities such as minibars and in-room safes. All of the rooms have free high-speed wireless Internet access and two have a large patio. **www.hotelfranksf.com**

### DOWNTOWN Hotel Monaco

$$$$$

*501 Geary St, 94102* **Tel** *(415) 292-0100, (800) 214-4220* **Fax** *(415) 292-0111* **Rooms** *201* **Map** *5 B5*

Funky and charming, the Monaco is a few blocks west of Union Square. The guest rooms – a study in pattern and texture – feature many luxurious extras, such as Frette robes, down pillows, and fax machines. The Grand Café is set in a spectacular turn-of-the-19th-century ballroom downstairs. **www.monaco-sf.com**

### DOWNTOWN Hotel Nikko

$$$$$

*222 Mason St, 94102* **Tel** *(415) 394-1111, (866) 898-4128* **Fax** *(415) 394-1106* **Rooms** *534* **Map** *5 B5*

The ultra-modern Nikko caters primarily to business travelers, especially those from Japan. The hotel's excellent fitness center, with its glass-enclosed swimming pool and full range of exercise equipment, is among the best in the city. The lobby-level Anzu restaurant is perfect for drinking or dining. **www.hotelnikkosf.com**

### DOWNTOWN Hotel Vitale

$$$$$

*8 Mission St, 94105* **Tel** *(415) 278-3700, (888) 890-8688* **Fax** *(415) 278-3750* **Rooms** *200* **Map** *6 E4*

The flamboyant Hotel Vitale is the latest and, possibly, the grandest venture from the JDV Hospitality Group. Situated along the Embarcadero, it has all the advantages of a destination resort, in the heart of the city. The guest rooms boast every amenity, and Spa Vitale has stunning views. **www.hotelvitale.com**

### DOWNTOWN Hyatt Regency San Francisco

$$$$$

*5 Embarcadero Center, 94111* **Tel** *(415) 788-1234, (800) 233-1234* **Fax** *(415) 398-2567* **Rooms** *802* **Map** *6 D3*

The Hyatt, built in 1973 around a 15-story atrium lobby, has since had its rooms largely upgraded. Designated mainly for business travelers, the Regency Club floor has a full-time attendant, always on call. This hotel is located next to a shopping center and theater complex. **www.sanfranciscoregency.hyatt.com**

### DOWNTOWN The Inn at Union Square

$$$$$

*440 Post St, 94102* **Tel** *(415) 397-3510, (800) 288-4346* **Fax** *(415) 989-0529* **Rooms** *30* **Map** *5 B5*

In the middle of Union Square, this cozy hotel has the warmth and intimacy of a private apartment. Complimentary Continental breakfast and a newspaper are delivered to your room. Wine and hors d'oeuvres are served in the lobby every evening by the fireplace. **www.unionsquare.com**

### DOWNTOWN Mandarin Oriental

 $$$$$

*222 Sansome St, 94104* **Tel** *(415) 276-9888, (800) 622-0404* **Fax** *(415) 433-0289* **Rooms** *158* **Map** *6 D3*

Particularly convenient for business travelers, Mandarin Oriental is first class in every respect. Some of the Mandarin Rooms have floor-to-ceiling windows, offering magnificent views of San Francisco Bay and the Golden Gate Bridge. Another attraction is the excellent restaurant, Silks, located on the second floor. **www.mandarinoriental.com**

### DOWNTOWN JW Marriott San Francisco

$$$$$

*500 Post St, 94102* **Tel** *(415) 771-8600, (800) 605-6568* **Fax** *(415) 398-0267* **Rooms** *338* **Map** *5 B5*

John Portman was the architect of this beautifully appointed, daringly designed modern hotel, which has an atrium lobby 17 stories high, rising to a rooftop skylight. The public areas are glamorous, and the bedrooms refined and elegant. Business travelers will find the staff extremely helpful. **www.marriott.com/sfojw**

### DOWNTOWN Le Meridien San Francisco

$$$$$

*333 Battery St, 94111* **Tel** *(415) 296-2900, (800) 543-4300* **Fax** *(415) 296-2901* **Rooms** *360* **Map** *6 D3*

Formerly a Hyatt hotel, Le Meridien is small and luxurious. Located next to the Embarcadero Center, it is preferred by business travelers. Visitors can benefit from special rates on weekends. There are also good family deals offering discounts on the price of a second room. **www.lemeridiensf.com**

### DOWNTOWN Palace Hotel ⬛ 🍴 ♨ 🏃 📺 ♿ 🕔 $$$$$
*2 New Montgomery St, 94105* **Tel** *(415) 512-1111, (888) 627-7196* **Fax** *(415) 543-0671* **Rooms** 552   **Map** 5 C4

Early in the 20th century, the Palace was one of the most famous hotels in the world, hosting royalty and heads of state, including President Harding, who died here in his sleep in 1923. Renovated in the late 1980s, it is now known for its glamorous Garden Court, where afternoon tea is served. **www.sfpalace.com**

### DOWNTOWN San Francisco Marriott Union Square ⬛ 🍴 🏃 📺 ♿ 🕔 $$$$$
*480 Sutter St, 94108* **Tel** *(415) 398-8900, (866) 912-0973* **Fax** *(415) 989-8823* **Rooms** 400   **Map** 5 C4

Right on the Powell Street cable car line, the Marriott Union Square contains in-room amenities including high-speed Internet access and coffee makers. The hotel is extremely convenient for business travelers and families. There are two on-site restaurants and a cocktail lounge. **www.marriott.com**

### DOWNTOWN Taj Campton Place ⬛ 🍴 ♿ 🕔 $$$$$
*340 Stockton St, 94108* **Tel** *(415) 781-5555, (866) 969-1825* **Fax** *(415) 955-5536* **Rooms** 110   **Map** 5 C4

The small and elegant Campton Place is situated just off Union Square. It offers plush, well-appointed rooms, good service, and sumptuous public areas. Particularly appealing is the intimate bar off the lobby, and guests can enjoy dinner in the deluxe Campton Place Restaurant. **www.tajhotels.com/camptonplace**

### DOWNTOWN Westin St Francis Market St ⬛ 🍴 🏃 📺 ♿ 🕔 $$$$$
*50 3rd St, 94103* **Tel** *(415) 974-6400, (888) 627-8561* **Fax** *(415) 543-8268* **Rooms** 676   **Map** 5 C5

Views from the floor-to-ceiling windows are breathtaking, looking down over the Yerba Buena complex and the San Francisco Museum of Modern Art. Only a short walk to the Moscone Convention Center, the hotel's location is ideal for business people. **www.westinsf.com**

### FISHERMAN'S WHARF AND NORTH BEACH San Remo Hotel ⑤
*2237 Mason St, 94133* **Tel** *(415) 776-8688, (800) 352-7366* **Fax** *(415) 776-2811* **Rooms** 64   **Map** 5 B2

The only budget hotel in the area, San Remo is a well-maintained Victorian pensione in an Italianate building. It was built in 1906 and has been restored to its original elegance. All the rooms in this non-smoking hotel share bathrooms, with the exception of the rooftop Penthouse. **www.sanremohotel.com**

### FISHERMAN'S WHARF AND NORTH BEACH Ocean Park Motel 🏃 ♿ $$
*2690 46th Avenue, 94116* **Tel** *(415) 566-7020* **Fax** *(415) 665-8959* **Rooms** 24   **Map** 7 B4

A value-priced, 1930s Art Deco gem near Ocean Beach and the zoo, with kitchens, free parking, playground, hot tub, and gardens. Simple, small rooms, some with separate bedrooms and queen beds, fridges, and microwaves. The motel is dog-friendly, with free Wi-Fi and parking. Public transport available close by. **www.oceanparkmotel.com**

### FISHERMAN'S WHARF AND NORTH BEACH Hotel Boheme ⬛ $$
*444 Columbus Ave, 94133* **Tel** *(415) 433-9111* **Fax** *(415) 362-6292* **Rooms** 15   **Map** 5 B3

The stylish and hip Boheme is a homage to the Beat Generation, in the heart of where it all began. Bold color schemes and whimsical touches enhance the hotel's poetic vibe. The rooms are cozy and equipped with free Wi-Fi. Located amid the hustle of North Beach, it is close to many great restaurants and bars. **www.hotelboheme.com**

### FISHERMAN'S WHARF AND NORTH BEACH Suites at Fisherman's Wharf ⬛ 🏃 🕔 $$$
*2655 Hyde St, 94109* **Tel** *(415) 771-0200, (800) 678-3321* **Fax** *(415) 346-8058* **Rooms** 24   **Map** 5 A2

Families and groups tend to stay here, in the city's only all-suite hotel. Business people also come here regularly. Each suite, spacious enough to accommodate four people, has its own kitchen and dining facilities. The hotel is steps away from the Hyde Street cable car. **www.shellhospitality.com**

### FISHERMAN'S WHARF AND NORTH BEACH The Wharf Inn 🏃 $$$
*2601 Mason St, 94133* **Tel** *(415) 673-7411, (877) 275-7889* **Fax** *(415) 776-2181* **Rooms** 51   **Map** 5 B1

This 1960s-style three-story motel is bright, cheerful, and clean. All the rooms are decorated in bold colors, and many feature couches and small sitting areas. The inn is located directly above the bustling Fisherman's Wharf, and offers complimentary parking and free high-speed Internet access. **www.wharfinn.com**

### FISHERMAN'S WHARF AND NORTH BEACH Best Western Tuscan Inn ⬛ 🍴 🏃 ♿ 🕔 $$$$
*425 North Point St, 94133* **Tel** *(415) 561-1100, (800) 648-4626* **Rooms** 221   **Map** 5 B1

This is a spacious and stylish hotel in the middle of Fisherman's Wharf. It is a popular spot for business travelers as well as for visiting film and television crews. Children under 18, accompanied by an adult, stay free of charge. Complimentary wine is served every evening. Free Wi-Fi and free shuttle to the Financial District. **www.tuscaninn.com**

### FISHERMAN'S WHARF AND NORTH BEACH Courtyard by Marriott ⬛ 🍴 🏃 ♿ 🕔 $$$$
*580 Beach St, 94133* **Tel** *(415) 775-3800* **Fax** *(415) 441-7307* **Rooms** 127   **Map** 4 F1

Sitting just one block from Fisherman's Wharf, the Courtyard is great value for its location and amenities. Clean, modern rooms feature high-speed Internet access, and are perfect for both vacationing families and business travelers. **www.marriott.com**

### FISHERMAN'S WHARF AND NORTH BEACH Washington Square Inn 🏃 ♿ 🕔 $$$$
*1660 Stockton St, 94133* **Tel** *(415) 981-4220, (800) 388-0220* **Fax** *(415) 397-7242* **Rooms** 15   **Map** 5 B3

One of the few hotels in the North Beach area, this is the only one facing Washington Square Park, where you can watch people practicing Tai Chi or strolling around the park. Room rates include a complimentary breakfast, though walking to the famous Mamma's Restaurant, just across the street, is a preferred option. **www.wsisf.com**

**Key to Price Guide** *see p524* **Key to Symbols** *see back cover flap*

## FISHERMAN'S WHARF AND NORTH BEACH Hotel Argonaut $$$$$

*495 Jefferson Street, 94109* **Tel** *(415) 563-0800* **Fax** *(415) 563-2800* **Rooms** *252*  **Map** *5 A1*

A nautically-inspired hotel, housed in a vintage brick building right at Fisherman's Wharf. Some rooms have a separate parlor and bedroom, plus spa tubs, and telescopes. Extra-long beds can be arranged for those who need them. There's a free evening wine hour each night and it is very pet friendly. **www.argonauthotel.com**

## FISHERMAN'S WHARF AND NORTH BEACH Hyatt Fisherman's Wharf $$$$$

*555 N Point, 94133* **Tel** *(415) 563-1234, (800) 233-1234* **Fax** *(415) 486-4444* **Rooms** *313*  **Map** *5 A1*

This Hyatt is more family-oriented than the other Hyatt hotels in San Francisco, though it provides service of the same quality. Families are offered a discount on the price of their second room, and there is a heated swimming pool. It is a convenient place for visiting Alcatraz. **www.fishermanswharf.hyatt.com**

## FISHERMAN'S WHARF AND NORTH BEACH The Sheraton $$$$$

*2500 Mason St, 94133* **Tel** *(415) 362-5500, (800) 325-3535* **Fax** *(415) 956-5275* **Rooms** *531*  **Map** *5 B1*

Primarily a family-oriented, tourist hotel, the Sheraton is housed in a large, attractive 1970s building, with all the comforts expected by regular travelers. It provides easy access to Fisherman's Wharf and the ferry that goes to Alcatraz Island. It is also popular with business travelers. Restaurant serves breakfast only. **www.sheratonatthewharf.com**

## HAIGHT ASHBURY AND THE MISSION Red Victorian Bed and Breakfast $$

*1665 Haight St, 94117* **Tel** *(415) 864-1978* **Fax** *(415) 863-3293* **Rooms** *18*  **Map** *9 B1*

The Red Victorian is the ubiquitous Haight Street accommodation, perfect for travelers who want to channel San Francisco in the "Summer of Love." All the rooms are individually themed, with names such as Redwood Forest and Flower Child. No radios or TVs are available, but there is a meditation room. **www.redvic.com**

## HAIGHT ASHBURY AND THE MISSION Stanyan Park Hotel $$

*750 Stanyan St, 94117* **Tel** *(415) 751-1000* **Fax** *(415) 668-5454* **Rooms** *36*  **Map** *9 B2*

Doctors, patients, and patients' families often stay in this lovely Queen Anne-style hotel that enjoys a proximity to the San Francisco Medical Center. The hotel overlooks Golden Gate Park. The rooms are cozy, with decorative fireplaces in many of them. **www.stanyanpark.com**

## HAIGHT ASHBURY AND THE MISSION Willows Inn Bed and Breakfast $$

*710 14th St, 94114* **Tel** *(415) 431-4770, (800) 431-0277* **Fax** *(415) 431-5295* **Rooms** *12*  **Map** *10 E2*

Built in 1903, the Willows is a European-style B&B. Each room comes with a sink, kimono bathrobes, luxury soaps, TV, VCR, and Wi-Fi. Eight private water closets are situated adjacent to the rooms. They also offer a free Continental breakfast, an evening cocktail, and a 24-hour pantry. Geared to the gay and lesbian visitor. **www.willowssf.com**

## HAIGHT ASHBURY AND THE MISSION Inn on Castro $$$

*321 Castro St, 94114* **Tel/Fax** *(415) 861-0321* **Rooms** *10*  **Map** *10 D2*

The Inn on Castro, a fully-restored Edwardian building, blends old and modern, with eclectic flower bouquets and modern art adorning the traditional interiors. It is perfectly poised in the heart of the Castro District, and offers guest suites and self-service apartments. A free Continental breakfast for guest suites. **www.innoncastro.com**

## HAIGHT ASHBURY AND THE MISSION The Parker Guest House $$$

*520 Church St, 94114* **Tel** *(415) 621-3222* **Fax** *(415) 621-4139* **Rooms** *21*  **Map** *10 E3*

A 1909 Edwardian mansion with extensive gardens, The Parker caters to gay clientele. Conveniently located in the Castro District, it is popular with business travelers. Rooms are luxurious. Rates include a deluxe Continental breakfast and an afternoon wine social. **www.parkerguesthouse.com**

## HAIGHT ASHBURY AND THE MISSION The Inn San Francisco $$$$

*943 Van Ness Avenue, 94110* **Tel** *(415) 641-0188, (800) 359-0913* **Rooms** *21*  **Map** *4 E4*

Spared from the great fire of 1906 by a one-block margin, this opulently furnished inn dates to 1872 and takes guests back in time as they enjoy a hearty breakfast in the beautiful double parlor, soak in the eucalyptus-shaded hot tub, and revel in views from the 360-degree sundeck. Wi-Fi and beverages are complimentary. **www.innsf.com**

## PACIFIC HEIGHTS Chateau Tivoli Bed and Breakfast $$$

*1057 Steiner St, 94115* **Tel** *(415) 776-5462, (800) 228-1647* **Fax** *(415) 776-0505* **Rooms** *9*  **Map** *4 D4*

One of San Francisco's "painted ladies," this 100-year-old Victorian house was the center of the 1970s New Age Movement, marked by rebirthing, Reichian release, and nude communal bathing. It has since been restored to its original splendor, with frescoed ceilings, stained-glass windows, and several antiques. **www.chateautivoli.com**

## PACIFIC HEIGHTS Cow Hollow Motor Inn & Suites $$

*2190 Lombard St, 94123* **Tel** *(415) 921-5800* **Fax** *(415) 922-8515* **Rooms** *129*  **Map** *4 D2*

This motel is situated between the fashionable Cow Hollow and Marina Districts of San Francisco, famous for world-class dining and shopping. The rooms here are simple, if slightly outdated, and families traveling with children may enjoy the option to stay in one of the 12 guest suites. **www.cowhollowmotorinn.com**

## PACIFIC HEIGHTS The Greenwich Inn $$

*3201 Steiner Street, 94123* **Tel** *(415) 921-5162* **Fax** *(415) 921-3602* **Rooms** *32*  **Map** *4 D2*

The Greenwich Inn is a basic inn and affordable option for travelers wishing to stay close to San Francisco's Marina District and Presidio Park. The rooms are comfortable, and the staff are friendly. Countless restaurants and shops are within easy walking distance. **www.greenwichinn.com**

## PACIFIC HEIGHTS Marina Inn
$$$

*3110 Octavia St, 94123* **Tel** *(415) 928-1000, (800) 274-1420* **Fax** *(415) 928-5909* **Rooms** *40* **Map** *4 E2*

Well located two blocks from Fort Mason and its grassy park, this low-priced Marina District motel has stunning views of the Bay. It is clean and the staff are friendly, though street noise from Lombard Street can be obtrusive. It is convenient for the Union Street shops and restaurants. **www.marinainn.com**

## PACIFIC HEIGHTS Marina Motel
$$

*2576 Lombard St, 94123* **Tel** *(415) 921-9406, (800) 346-6118* **Fax** *(415) 921-0364* **Rooms** *36* **Map** *4 D3*

Tucked away in a flower-filled Mediterranean courtyard, Marina Hotel enjoys a quiet and private location, close to the neighborhood market, restaurants, and public transport. The Spanish-style building, built in 1939, has bright, airy, and individually decorated rooms, each with a private bathroom. **www.marinamotel.com**

## PACIFIC HEIGHTS Pacific Heights Inn
$$

*1555 Union St, 94123* **Tel** *(415) 776-3310, (800) 523-1801* **Fax** *(415) 776-8176* **Rooms** *40* **Map** *4 E2*

This pleasant, 1960s-era motel is on a quiet block of Union Street, just west of Van Ness Avenue. It is convenient for public transportation and has free on-site parking for guests with their own cars. The restaurants, shops, and bars of the energetic Cow Hollow neighborhood are just a few blocks away. **www.pacificheightsinn.com**

## PACIFIC HEIGHTS The Hotel Majestic
$$$

*1500 Sutter St, 94109* **Tel** *(415) 441-1100, (800) 869-8966* **Fax** *(415) 673-7331* **Rooms** *56* **Map** *4 E4*

One of the few top-notch San Francisco hotels to have survived the 1906 earthquake, the Majestic is an exquisite early 20th-century building in a quiet neighborhood between Pacific Heights and San Francisco Bay. Antique furniture graces the rooms, most of which have canopied beds and fireplaces. **www.thehotelmajestic.com**

## PACIFIC HEIGHTS Jackson Court
$$$

*2198 Jackson St, 94115* **Tel** *(415) 929-7670* **Fax** *(415) 929-1405* **Rooms** *10* **Map** *4 E3*

A stay here makes you feel like turn-of-the-19th-century royalty, as this stunning brownstone, over 100 years old, sits in one of San Francisco's most beautiful neighborhoods. Rooms are simple and elegant, all with TV/VCR combos, hairdryers, and phones. Complimentary Continental breakfast. **www.jacksoncourt.com**

## PACIFIC HEIGHTS Laurel Inn
$$$

*444 Presidio Ave, 94115* **Tel** *(415) 567-8467, (800) 552-8735* **Fax** *(415) 928-1866* **Rooms** *49* **Map** *3 C4*

This quiet, stylish boutique hotel features a hip mid-20th-century style. The comfortable, brightly colored guest rooms come with CD players, VCRs, and writing desks and tables. Complimentary Continental breakfast is provided. The hotel's trendy G Bar is great for a pre-dinner drink. **www.jdvhotels.com**

## PACIFIC HEIGHTS Union Street Inn
$$$

*2229 Union St, 94123* **Tel** *(415) 346-0424* **Fax** *(415) 922-8046* **Rooms** *6* **Map** *4 D3*

When you check into Union Street Inn, you will wish you lived here. Each of the spacious guest rooms is tastefully decorated, and the idyllic back garden is the perfect setting to enjoy a drink at the end of a long day of sightseeing. Two-day minimum stays are required on weekends. **www.unionstreetinn.com**

## PACIFIC HEIGHTS Hotel Drisco
$$$$

*2901 Pacific Ave, 94115* **Tel** *(415) 346-2880, (800) 634-7277* **Fax** *(415) 567-5537* **Rooms** *48* **Map** *3 C3*

Perched at the top of the glamorous Pacific Heights neighborhood, Hotel Drisco offers stately accommodation, perfect for business travelers and tourists. Many rooms feature spectacular views of San Francisco Bay and the Golden Gate Bridge. Complimentary nightly wine service and Continental breakfast. **www.jdvhotels.com**

## PACIFIC HEIGHTS Hotel del Sol
$$$$

*3100 Webster St, 94123* **Tel** *(415) 921-5520, (877) 433-5765* **Fax** *(415) 931-4137* **Rooms** *57* **Map** *4 D2*

Celebrating California's lively culture, this boutique hotel features a playful design with palm trees, hammocks, mosaics, and a pool. The rooms are bright and spacious, with rainbow-colored bedspreads. There are also 10 themed suites. The family suite has bunk beds, board games, and toys. **www.jdvhotels.com**

## PACIFIC HEIGHTS Queen Anne Hotel
$$$$$

*1590 Sutter St, 94109* **Tel** *(415) 441-2828, (800) 227-3970* **Fax** *(415) 775-5212* **Rooms** *48* **Map** *4 E4*

The restored Queen Anne is a beautiful Victorian hotel, built in 1890. Each room is done up differently with antique furniture and authentic decorations. Room rates include Continental breakfast, an afternoon sherry and tea service, and a weekday morning town car available for tourist attractions. **www.queenanne.com**

# THE BAY AREA

## BENICIA Jefferson Street Mansion
$$$$$

*1063 Jefferson St, 94510* **Tel** *(707) 746-0684* **Fax** *(707) 746-1639* **Rooms** *5* **Road map** *inset B*

This Civil War-era military mansion was graciously restored, and serves as an elegant B&B with comfortable accommodations and great food. The rooms are luxurious and appointed with period antiques and upscale bath amenities. The service is also exceptional. **www.jeffersonstreetmansion.com**

## BERKELEY Bancroft Hotel

🔲 $$$

*2680 Bancroft Way, 94704* **Tel** *(510) 549-1000* **Fax** *(510) 549-1070* **Rooms** *22*      **Road map** *inset B*

Located across from the UC Berkeley campus *(see p418)*, this former women's club was designed in the Arts and Crafts style. Beautifully maintained rooms feature the latest amenities, many with large balconies or decks. The property is adjacent to a popular outdoor café, Caffè Strada. Complimentary Continental breakfast. **www.bancrofthotel.com**

## BERKELEY Berkeley City Club

🔲 🚹 🏊 🎦 ⛨ $$$

*2315 Durant Avenue, 94704* **Tel** *(510) 848-7800* **Fax** *(510) 848-5900* **Rooms** *30*      **Road map** *inset B*

A historic landmark designed by Julia Morgan, the architect of Hearst Castle and other iconic buildings in California. This hotel offers, small, period-decor guest rooms, plus a beautiful indoor pool, elegant public rooms, and access to on-site performances and lectures. There is free Wi-Fi, breakfast, and parking. **www.berkeleyhistorichotel.com**

## BERKELEY Hotel Durant

🔲 🚹 ⛨ 🔲 $$$

*2600 Durant Ave, 94704* **Tel** *(510) 845-8981* **Fax** *(510) 486-8336* **Rooms** *143*      **Road map** *inset B*

Situated near the campus, this friendly hotel has European charm and well-appointed rooms, outfitted with linen and such amenities as a business center, high-speed Wi-Fi, and disabled access. The lobby-level restaurant, Henry's, is a local institution and gets very crowded on sporting-event days. **www.jdvhotels.com**

## BERKELEY Rose Garden Inn

⛨ 🔲 $$$

*2740 Telegraph Ave, 94705* **Tel** *(510) 549-2145, (800) 992-9005* **Fax** *(510) 549-1085* **Rooms** *40*    **Road map** *inset B*

A beautiful Victorian inn set in five buildings surrounded by pretty gardens and within walking distance of the campus. Rooms are decorated in a variety of motifs, but all feature comfortable amenities and plenty of space. Complimentary wireless Internet access and full breakfast included. **www.rosegardeninn.com**

## BERKELEY The Claremont Hotel Club & Spa

🔲 🚹 🏊 🎿 🎦 ⛨ 🔲 $$$$$

*41 Tunnel Rd, 94705* **Tel** *(510) 843-3000, (800) 551-7266* **Fax** *(510) 843-3229* **Rooms** *279*    **Road map** *inset B*

A large, historic retreat set in the hills above Berkeley, near the border with Oakland. Facilities include comfortable guest rooms, appointed with all the modern amenities, a large spa, meeting rooms, and children's programs. There are also tennis courts, an outdoor pool, and a good restaurant on the premises. **www.claremontresort.com**

## BOLINAS Smiley's Schooner Saloon and Hotel

⛨ 🔲 $

*41 Wharf Rd, 94924* **Tel** *(415) 868-1311* **Rooms** *6*      **Road map** *inset B*

Set in the charming coastal town of Bolinas, this intimate hotel has Western character and a noisy neighbor in the bar downstairs. Rooms are utterly basic, with no phones or TVs, but the beds are comfortable. The ambience is the main attraction here. They also have a beautiful outdoor sitting area. **www.smileysaloon.com**

## HALF MOON BAY Zaballa House Bed & Breakfast

⛨ $

*324 Main St, 94019* **Tel** *(650) 726-9123* **Fax** *(650) 726-3921* **Rooms** *20*      **Road map** *inset B*

A charming B&B that moves at an easy pace, as is the case with this coastal town. Set in the oldest still-standing house in the city, the structure is completely restored and updated to modern standards. The rooms are neat and comfortable, all have private bathrooms and some have a fireplace. **www.zhousehnb.com**

## HALF MOON BAY Half Moon Bay Inn

🔲 🚹 ⛨ $$$

*401 Main Street, 94019* **Tel** *650-726-1177* **Rooms** *15*      **Road map** *inset B*

A charming boutique hotel in a landmark, 1932 Spanish Revival building with plush amenities including down duvets and pillows. Some rooms and suites have fridges and microwaves, extra beds, and sitting areas. Downstairs, Italia restaurant serves Cal-Ital cuisine. Free Wi-Fi and parking. **www.halfmoonbayinn.com**

## HALF MOON BAY Oceano Hotel and Spa

🔲 🚹 🎦 ⛨ 🔲 $$$$

*280 Capistrano Road, 94019* **Tel** *(650) 726-5400* **Fax** *(650) 726-5402* **Rooms** *95*      **Road map** *inset B*

An upscale hotel at the Half Moon Bay harbor with lovely water views and adjacent to a shopping and restaurant complex. Rooms are spacious and luxurious, and suites have loft bedrooms, fireplaces, kitchens, and living areas. On-site is a full-service spa, health club, restaurant, and bar. Room service is also available. **www.oceanohalfmoonbay.com**

## HALF MOON BAY Mill Rose Inn

🔲 🔲 $$$$$

*615 Mill St, 94019* **Tel** *(650) 726-8750, (800) 900-7673* **Fax** *(650) 726-3031* **Rooms** *6*      **Road map** *inset B*

A friendly, English country-style inn situated near shops and galleries. The rooms are cozy, with fireplaces, period furnishings, and original watercolors. The grounds are delightful, filled with trellised rose bushes. They also offer business facilities. Very popular for weddings and romantic getaways. **www.millroseinn.com**

## HALF MOON BAY Ritz Carlton Half Moon Bay

🔲 🚹 🏊 🎿 🎦 ⛨ 🔲 $$$$$

*1 Miramontes Point Rd, 94019* **Tel** *(650) 712-7000, (800) 241-3333* **Fax** *(650) 712-7831* **Rooms** *261***Road map** *inset B*

Nestled majestically on a bluff overlooking the ocean, this elegant and relaxing resort is one of the top destinations on the North Coast. Rooms are opulently furnished and appointed with luxurious linen and bath amenities. Many have amazing ocean views. They also have a spa, a golf course, and an excellent restaurant. **www.ritzcarlton.com**

## INVERNESS Manka's Inverness Lodge

🚹 $$$$$

*Argyle at Callendar, 94937* **Tel** *(415) 669-1034* **Fax** *(415) 669-1958* **Rooms** *14*      **Road map** *A3*

Supremely alluring, this rustic and secluded inn offers cabin-style accommodation with luxurious beds and stone fireplaces. The property is a former hunting lodge and retains remnants of its history. You can also opt for the boat-house or the annexe. The award-winning restaurant serves local produce and is worth a visit. **www.mankas.com**

### LAFAYETTE Lafayette Park Hotel & Spa

*3287 Mount Diablo Blvd, 94549* **Tel** *(925) 283-3700* **Fax** *(925) 284-1621* **Rooms** *138*          **Road map** *inset B*

This top-rated East Bay property, central to freeway access, features well-appointed rooms, a spa, a fitness center, multiple meeting rooms, and two excellent restaurants. Personal touches here include great service and extremely helpful staff. **www.lafayetteparkhotel.com**

### MENLO PARK Mermaid Inn

*727 El Camino Real, 94025* **Tel** *(650) 323-9481, (800) 237-4622* **Fax** *(650) 323-0662* **Rooms** *39*   **Road map** *inset B*

Mermaid Inn is a friendly, well-run motel near the Stanford University and other Silicon Valley attractions. The property provides basic rooms, with private baths, cable TV, high-speed Internet access; some have kitchenettes. Also offers a heated swimming pool, free parking, and complimentary breakfast. **www.mermaidinnmotel.com**

### MENLO PARK Stanford Park Hotel

*100 El Camino Real, 94025* **Tel** *(650) 322-1234, (866) 241-2431* **Fax** *(650) 322-0975* **Rooms** *163* **Road map** *inset B*

This elegant, European-style hotel is Silicon Valley's only five-star property. Features include well-appointed guest rooms, with top-grade linens and fine furnishings, as well as free coffee and newspaper each morning. There is a pool and fitness center on-site. Also offers conference facilities. **www.stanfordparkhotel.com**

### MILL VALLEY Travelodge

*707 Redwood Hwy, 94941* **Tel** *(415) 383-0340, (800) 578-7878* **Fax** *(415) 381-2132* **Rooms** *48*   **Road map** *inset B*

An efficient, well-operated motor inn near San Francisco, Muir Woods, and Tiburon. The rooms are basic, with facilities such as air conditioning, phones, and TVs, but only some have Jacuzzis. There is an on-site restaurant, and the staff are friendly and attentive. Free parking is also available. **www.travelodge.com**

### MILL VALLEY Acqua Hotel

*555 Redwood Hwy, 94941* **Tel** *(415) 380-0400* **Fax** *(415) 380-9696* **Rooms** *49*          **Road map** *inset B*

Tucked away off the edge of the highway and in the shadows of Mount Tamalpais, this chic hotel is close to San Francisco. Acqua Hotel has an air-and-water theme, and provides modern conveniences with ample style. Rooms are simply appointed, without fuss. Staff are courteous and attentive. Evening wine and cheese. **www.acquahotel.com**

### MOSS BEACH Seal Cove Inn

*221 Cypress Ave, 94038* **Tel** *(650) 728-4114, (800) 995-9987* **Fax** *(650) 728-4116* **Rooms** *10*   **Road map** *inset B*

Each room at this charming, award-winning country inn has a fireplace and a private balcony with spectacular views of the ocean. The grounds are secluded and well maintained, close to the beach and tide pools. Additionals include complimentary breakfast and afternoon tea. **www.sealcoveinn.com**

### MUIR BEACH The Pelican Inn

*10 Pacific Way, 94965* **Tel** *(415) 383-6000* **Fax** *(415) 383-3424* **Rooms** *7*          **Road map** *inset B*

Tucked away in the hills above the ocean, this English-style inn has cozy rooms and a delightful pub, perfect for fog-shrouded afternoons. Each room is uniquely furnished with period accessories and such flourishes as four-poster beds. Some have pleasant views, and all have a private shower. **www.pelicaninn.com**

### OAKLAND Waterfront Hotel

*10 Washington St, 94607* **Tel** *(510) 836-3800, (888) 842-5333* **Fax** *(510) 832-5695* **Rooms** *143* **Road map** *inset B*

Situated among the shops and restaurants of Jack London Square, this full-service hotel has well-appointed rooms, some with balconies and views across the Bay toward San Francisco. Amenities include Wi-Fi, a fitness center, a heated pool, and sauna. The staff are multi-lingual and attentive. **www.jdvhotels.com**

### PRINCETON-BY-THE-SEA Pillar Point Inn

*380 Capistrano Rd, 94081* **Tel** *(650) 728-7377, (800) 623-2661* **Fax** *(650) 726-5402* **Rooms** *11* **Road map** *inset B*

A quaint, comfortable hotel in a charming seaside village. All the rooms are uniquely decorated and feature such comforts as pillowtop beds and fireplaces; most overlook the harbor. They also have on-site parking. **www.oceanohalfmoonbay.com**

### SAN JOSE Hotel De Anza

*233 W Santa Clara St, 95113* **Tel** *(408) 286-1000, (800) 843-3700* **Fax** *(408) 286-0500* **Rooms** *100* **Road map** *inset B*

Located downtown near the convention center, this plush boutique hotel has beautifully appointed rooms and exemplary customer care. Rooms range from standard size to large suites, and all feature upscale amenities, including minibar, and ample work desks. The on-site Italian restaurant is quite good. **www.hoteldeanza.com**

### SAN JOSE Fairmont San Jose

*170 S Market St, 95113* **Tel** *(408) 998-1900, (800) 257-7544* **Fax** *(408) 287-1648* **Rooms** *805* **Road map** *inset B*

This full-service hotel is located in the heart of San Jose's downtown convention and entertainment district. The rooms are spacious and have all the latest amenities, especially catering to business travelers. There is a rooftop pool, a fully-equipped health center, and a good lobby-level restaurant. **www.fairmont.com/sanjose**

### SAN JOSE San Jose Marriott

*301 S Market St, 95113* **Tel** *(408) 280-1300, (800) 314-0928* **Fax** *(408) 278-4444* **Rooms** *506* **Road map** *inset B*

This sleek business-friendly, high-rise hotel is located next to the convention center and within walking distance of downtown restaurants and attractions. The rooms are fully equipped with the latest technology, and many have excellent cityscape views. The street-level restaurant is exceptional. **www.sanjosemarriott.com**

**Key to Price Guide** *see p524* **Key to Symbols** *see back cover flap*

### SAN RAFAEL Panama Hotel
*4 Bayview St, 94901* **Tel** *(415) 457-3993, (800) 899-3993* **Fax** *(415) 457-6240* **Rooms** *14*   **Road map** *inset B*

Reminiscent of the inns of New Orleans or Key West, this charming B&B in the downtown district has well-furnished rooms decorated in different styles, some featuring clawfoot tubs. The staff are friendly and attentive. The restaurant features live jazz on occasion. **www.panamahotel.com**

### SAUSALITO Hotel Sausalito
*16 El Portal, 94965* **Tel** *(415) 332-0700, (800) 442-0700* **Fax** *(415) 332-8788* **Rooms** *16*   **Road map** *inset B*

This 1915 Mission-revival hotel is a landmark inn, with spacious rooms, hand-crafted art and furniture by local artisans, and mosaic tile bathrooms. Some rooms have garden views. There is a complimentary Continental breakfast. **www.hotelsausalito.com**

### SAUSALITO Casa Madrona Hotel & Spa
*801 Bridgeway St, 94965* **Tel** *(415) 332-0502, (800) 288-0502* **Fax** *(415) 331-3125* **Rooms** *63* **Road map** *inset B*

Built on a hillside, this elegant hotel features a mix of rooms, from historic and eclectically decorated, to modern and sleekly furnished. Casa Madrona has a top-notch spa offering various body and holistic treatments, and an excellent Italian restaurant at the lobby level. **www.casamadrona.com**

### SAUSALITO The Inn Above Tide
*30 El Portal, 94965* **Tel** *(415) 332-9535, (800) 893-8433* **Fax** *(415) 332-6714* **Rooms** *29*   **Road map** *inset B*

Set in an out-of-the-way corner of town, this boutique property is nonetheless centrally located to all of the shops and galleries. The inn is perched directly above the water, and each stylish room features balconies with great views of the Bay and San Francisco. Well suited to business travelers. **www.innabovetide.com**

### TIBURON Lodge at Tiburon
*1651 Tiburon Boulevard, 94920* **Tel** *(415) 435-3133* **Fax** *(415) 435-2451* **Rooms** *102*   **Road map** *inset B*

Located a short walk to the bay ferry, shops, and restaurants, this contemporary lodge offers suites with high-tech amenities and room service. Guests can also enjoy relaxing in the small pool, or on the fabulous rooftop terrace, which has outdoor fireplaces. Free Wi-Fi and pet-friendly. **www.thelodgeattiburon.com**

### TIBURON Waters Edge
*25 Main Street, 94920* **Tel** *(415) 789-5999* **Fax** *(415) 789-5888* **Rooms** *23*   **Road map** *inset B*

This upscale hotel offers urban-chic rooms at the ferry dock waterfront, with skylights, fireplaces, and featherbeds. Some rooms also have private balconies, soaking tubs, and bay views. The staff are super-friendly and helpful, plus there's free Wi-Fi, Continental breakfasts, and an evening wine reception. **www.marinhotels.com**

### WALNUT CREEK Marriott Hotel
*2355 N Main St, 94596* **Tel** *(925) 934-2000, (800) 828-5613* **Fax** *(925) 934-6374* **Rooms** *338* **Road map** *inset B*

Situated close to the area freeways and public transit, this full-service hotel is well equipped for the business traveler. Rooms are spacious and nicely appointed, with large work desks. Hotel amenities include a complete fitness center. Also has a games room for children. **www.walnutcreekmarriott.com**

## THE NORTH

### ARCATA Hotel Arcata
*708 9th St, 95521* **Tel** *(707) 826-0217, (800) 344-1221* **Fax** *(707) 826-1737* **Rooms** *32*   **Road map** *A2*

Situated on the town's central square, this friendly historic hotel features comfortable rooms, furnished with clawfoot tubs and period antiques, as well as many modern amenities. The suites are spacious and overlook the square. They also have conference rooms. The staff are friendly. **www.hotelarcata.com**

### ARCATA Best Western Arcata Inn
*4827 Valley W Blvd, 95521* **Tel** *(707) 826-0313, (888) 646-6514* **Fax** *(707) 826-0365* **Rooms** *62*   **Road map** *A2*

A well-operated hotel situated close to many shops and restaurants and several landmarks, including the university. The rooms are clean, and a few guest comforts are offered, including laundry, free high-speed Internet access, and Continental breakfast. The grounds feature a heated indoor pool and a hot tub. **www.bestwestern.com**

### ARCATA Rose Court Cottage Bed & Breakfast
*814 Thirteenth St., 95521* **Tel** *(707) 822-0935* **Rooms** *1*   **Road map** *A2*

A lovely arts & crafts style cottage, with a private courtyard entrance surrounded by flowering rose gardens. Inside, the cottage is decorated with French country flair, complete with a sweet white iron bistro table and antique finishes. A breakfast tray and newspaper are delivered to guests each morning. **www.rosecourtcottage.com**

### AVENUE OF THE GIANTS Miranda Gardens Resort
*6766 Avenue of the Giants, 95569* **Tel** *(707) 943-3011* **Fax** *(707) 943-3584* **Rooms** *15*   **Road map** *A2*

These cozy cottages deep in the Redwoods are laid out in a circle, with a campfire in the middle. Each cottage has a different layout: many include kitchens, some have fireplaces, but all include a patio or deck, about half of which have views of the Redwoods State Park. Breakfast is included in the room rate. **www.mirandagardens.com**

### CRESCENT CITY Anna Wulf House Bed & Breakfast

*622 J St, 95531* **Tel** *(707) 464-5340* **Rooms** *4*

**Road map** *A1*

The 19th-century Anna Wulf House has bright colors and ornate trim outside, with clawfoot tubs and four-poster beds inside. Two suites upstairs share a bathroom, while a third has its own ensuite, and the downstairs William Suite is fully accessible for the disabled. Breakfast is served in either the parlor or the upstairs kitchen. **www.annawulf.com**

### CRESCENT CITY Ocean Front Lodge

*100 A St, 95531* **Tel** *(707) 465-5400* **Fax** *(707) 465-0962* **Rooms** *53*

**Road map** *A1*

This clean and efficiently run property enjoys an incredible location right at the beach, and many of its rooms enjoy similar views from balconies overlooking the rugged surf. Spacious rooms include comfortable beds and complimentary breakfast. There is an indoor pool. The staff are swift and amicable. **www.oceanfrontlodge1.com**

### DUNSMUIR Caboose Motel and Cabins

*100 Railroad Park Rd, 96025* **Tel** *(530) 235-4440* **Fax** *(530) 235-4470* **Rooms** *27*

**Road map** *B2*

Caboose Motel offers lodging that is decidedly unique and quirky. The comfy rooms are built into renovated rail-road cabooses, arranged in a circle around a central swimming pool. The restaurant displays an impressive collection of railroad memorabilia. **www.rrpark.com**

### EUREKA Abigail's "Elegant Victorian Mansion"

*1406 C St, 95501* **Tel** *(707) 444-3144* **Rooms** *3*

**Road map** *A2*

This elegant B&B is situated in a historic Victorian gem – a landmark 1888 structure that has been lovingly preserved and restored. Operated with a friendly touch, the inn has comfortable rooms appointed with period furnishings. Rates include a hearty breakfast. Grounds feature lovely gardens and a croquet lawn. **www.eureka-california.com**

### EUREKA Bayview Motel

*2844 Fairfield St., 95501* **Tel** *(707) 442-1673* **Fax** *(707) 268-8681* **Rooms** *17*

**Road map** *A2*

The Bayview Motel is very clean and affordable. Rooms are large, and have modern amenities such as flatscreen TVs and Wi-Fi, plus the location right off Highway 101 is convenient for those touring the area. The motel's managers are very helpful and friendly. **www.bayviewmotel.com**

### EUREKA Best Western Humboldt Bay Inn

*232 W 5th St, 95501* **Tel** *(707) 443-2234, (800) 780-7234* **Fax** *(707) 443-3489* **Rooms** *111*    **Road map** *A2*

The rooms at this chain hotel, located close to the coast and near redwood forests, are clean and comfortable. On-site amenities include indoor and outdoor heated swimming pools, a business center, a spa, and a nice garden atrium. A complimentary limo service to local restaurants is available on select nights. **www.humboldtbayinn.com**

### EUREKA Carter House Inns

*301 L St, 95501* **Tel** *(707) 444-8062, (800) 404-1390* **Fax** *(707) 444-8067* **Rooms** *32*

**Road map** *A2*

Rooms at this gracious hotel are in four different Victorian-era buildings, including cozy cottages and a renovated historic house. All rooms are well appointed and come with breakfast and evening wine service. The restaurant is memorable, the wine shop boasts an excellent collection, and the service is friendly. **www.carterhouse.com**

### FERNDALE The Victorian Inn

*400 Ocean St., 95536-0096* **Tel** *(888) 589-1808* **Rooms** *12*

**Road map** *A2*

Built with the area's redwoods in 1890, the Victorian Inn has been well preserved. Rooms are decorated in Victorian style, with beautiful antique beds, printed wallpaper, and clawfoot tubs. A full breakfast is served in the dining room each morning. The perfect spot from which to explore Ferndale or the redwood forests. **www.victorianvillageinn.com**

### GARBERVILLE Best Western Humboldt House Inn

*701 Redwood Dr, 95542* **Tel** *(707) 923-2771, (800) 780-7234* **Fax** *(707) 923-4259* **Rooms** *76*    **Road map** *A2*

This clean and well-kept motel is near the entrance to Redwoods State Park, and features spacious, nicely appointed rooms. Additionals at the property include meeting facilities, high-speed Internet access, a spa, and a heated swimming pool. Complimentary breakfast is provided. **www.bestwestern.com/humboldthouseinn**

### GARBERVILLE Benbow Hotel & Resort

*445 Lake Benbow Dr, 95542* **Tel** *(707) 923-2124, (800) 355-3301* **Fax** *(707) 923-2897* **Rooms** *55*    **Road map** *A2*

A gorgeously preserved historic, Tudor-style inn featuring beautiful rooms of all sizes. All the rooms are furnished with handsome accessories and relaxing beddings. The property has an excellent restaurant and lounge; live entertainment is featured on occasion. Guests are also provided use of bicycles. **www.benbowinn.com**

### MCCLOUD The McCloud Guest House

*606 W Colombero Dr, 96057* **Tel** *(530) 964-3160, (866) 964-3160* **Fax** *(530) 964-3202* **Rooms** *5*    **Road map** *B1*

McCloud Guest House is a stately former private home, built by a lumber baron, set among towering trees. Each room is cozy and well appointed with fine antiques. Stay includes a hearty breakfast, which can be enjoyed on the large wraparound porch. **www.historicalmccloudguesthouse.com**

### MOUNT LASSEN Roseberry House B&B

*609 North St., Susanville, 96130* **Tel** *(530) 257-5675* **Fax** *(530) 257-8739* **Rooms** *4*

**Road map** *B2*

Roseberry House is a charming, restored Victorian home, complete with white picket fence and hand-painted sign. Built in 1902, its four rooms hold an assortment of treasured antiques. Roseberry has a private entrance for guests to come and go as they please, and breakfast is served in the dining room. **www.roseberryhouse.com**

## MOUNT SHASTA Mount Shasta Ranch Bed & Breakfast ⑤

*1008 W A Barr Rd, 96067* **Tel** *(530) 926-3870* **Fax** *(530) 926-6882* **Rooms** *12* **Road map** *A2*

The rooms at this B&B are spacious and well equipped with minimalist facilities. Most have views of the mountain, and are decorated with antiques and queen size beds. The main house features rooms with huge baths. They also have a games room with a pool table. **www.stayinshasta.com**

## MOUNT SHASTA Best Western Tree House Motor Inn ⑤⑤

*111 Morgan Way, 96067* **Tel** *(530) 926-3101, (800) 780-7234* **Fax** *(530) 926-3542* **Rooms** *99* **Road map** *A2*

Part of the Best Western chain, this comfy hotel is outfitted with redwood furniture, and has nice rooms as well as a welcoming lounge and a lobby with a fireplace. Tree House Inn has a business center, an indoor swimming pool, non-smoking rooms, and a restaurant. Complimentary breakfast. **www.bestwestern.com**

## MOUNT SHASTA Cold Creek Inn & Suites ⑤⑤⑤

*724 N Mount Shasta Blvd, 96067* **Tel** *(800) 292-9421* **Fax** *(530) 926-9852* **Rooms** *18* **Road map** *A2*

Rooms at this friendly hotel are simple, but offer such facilities as pillowtop beds, cable TV, air conditioning, and high-speed data ports. Most rooms have great views of the mountain. Many suites have two and three beds. Non-smoking, and pets are welcome. **www.coldcreekinn.com**

## MOUNT SHASTA Mount Shasta Resort ⑤⑤⑤⑤

*1000 Siskiyou Lake Blvd, 96067* **Tel** *(530) 926-3030, (800) 958-3363* **Fax** *(530) 926-0333* **Rooms** *64* **Road map** *A2*

Set below the towering Mount Shasta, this tranquil recreational resort offers rooms in private chalets, as well as more basic woodland accommodation. Rooms are decently furnished and equipped with all the necessary amenities. They also have a spa and an 18-hole golf course on the premises. **www.mountshastaresort.com**

## WEAVERVILLE Weaverville Victorian Inn ⑤

*2051 Main St, 96093* **Tel** *(530) 623-4432* **Fax** *(530) 623-4264* **Rooms** *65* **Road map** *A2*

This clean, well-run hotel is outfitted in a Victorian motif. The rooms are tidy, comfortable, and nicely appointed. On-site amenities include meeting rooms, an outdoor pool, free Continental breakfast, and parking. Friendly staff can arrange activities such as golfing, fishing, boating, jet skiing, and much more. **www.trinitycounty.com**

## WEAVERVILLE The Whitmore Inn ⑤⑤

*761 Main St., 96093* **Tel** *(530) 623-2509* **Rooms** *5* **Road map** *A2*

This large rambling, turn-of-the-century B&B is in historic downtown Weaverville, within easy driving distance of Trinity and Shasta lakes. It has a pleasant wrap-around veranda, lush gardens, hot tub, tastefully arranged antiques and free Internet access. **www.whitmoreinn.com/**

## WEAVERVILLE Weaverville Hotel & Emporium ⑤⑤⑤⑤

*481 Main St, 96093* **Tel** *(530) 623-2222, (800) 750-8853* **Rooms** *8* **Road map** *A2*

Set in the upper floors of a historic building in the heart of town, this old-fashioned hotel names its cozy rooms after the county's former gold mines. Some rooms have charming four-poster beds and clawfoot tubs. The Victorian-style parlor has an attractive fireplace where you can relax with a book from their library. **www.weavervillehotel.com**

# WINE COUNTRY

## BODEGA BAY Bodega Coast Inn & Suites ⑤⑤

*521 Coast Hwy 1, 94923* **Tel** *(707) 875-2217, (800) 346-6999* **Fax** *(707) 875-2964* **Rooms** *44* **Road map** *A3*

A property on the coast, surrounded by cypress trees. All the rooms are bright, spacious, and well appointed. Suites have color TVs, coffee makers, refrigerators, fireplaces, and whirlpool tubs. Close to a golf course and other recreation areas. Also suited to business travelers. **www.bodegacoastinn.com**

## BODEGA BAY Bodega Bay Lodge 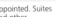 ⑤⑤⑤⑤⑤

*103 Highway 1, 94923* **Tel** *(707) 875-3525* **Fax** *(707) 875-2428* **Rooms** *64* **Road map** *A3*

Above the bay and marshlands, this lodge has spacious rooms and luxury suites with sea views, Jacuzzi tubs, and room service. Lounge by the giant lobby fireplace, walk to the beach, and float in the ocean-view pool. There's a full-service spa, fine dining at the Duck Club, plus free bicycles, sauna, and evening wine reception. **www.bodegabaylodge.com**

## BOYES HOT SPRINGS Fairmont Sonoma Mission Inn & Spa ⑤⑤⑤⑤⑤

*18140 Sonoma Hwy, 95476* **Tel** *(707) 938-9000* **Fax** *(707) 938-4250* **Rooms** *226* **Road map** *A3*

A beautiful hotel set on secluded grounds close to a golf course and many local wineries. The luxurious rooms are equipped with minibars and air conditioning, while the hotel's grounds are home to a top-rated spa and an excellent restaurant. **www.fairmont.com/sonoma**

## CALISTOGA Dr Wilkinson's Hot Springs Resort  ⑤⑤

*1507 Lincoln Ave, 94515* **Tel** *(707) 942-4102* **Fax** *(707) 942-4412* **Rooms** *42* **Road map** *A3*

Since 1952 this modest hotel has placed Calistoga on the map with its hot springs and rejuvenating mud baths. Still family-run, the property features the latest facilities in each room, as well as an enhanced menu of spa services. The front veranda is perfect for people watching. **www.drwilkinson.com**

## CALISTOGA Calistoga Spa Hot Springs    $$$

*1006 Washington St, 94515* **Tel** *(707) 942-6269, (866) 822-5772* **Fax** *(707) 942-4212* **Rooms** *57* **Road map** *A3*

This modest hotel offers good value with its comfortable rooms, all with kitchenettes. There are four naturally heated pools on the property. They also have a meeting room with a wet bar and an outdoor deck offering panoramic views. The staff are friendly, and the property is close to town. **www.calistogaspa.com**

## CALISTOGA Indian Springs Resort and Spa    $$$$$

*1712 Lincoln Ave, 94515* **Tel** *(707) 942-4913* **Fax** *(707) 942-4919* **Rooms** *17* **Road map** *A3*

A classic spa resort that helped start the mud bath trend, this friendly hotel sits on thermal geysers and volcanic ash, and uses both for relaxing and rejuvenating its guests. The rooms and bungalows are well appointed, situated around a central courtyard. The historic mineral water pool is the best in town. **www.indianspringscalistoga.com**

## CALISTOGA Solage Calistoga    $$$$$

*755 Silverado Trail, 94515* **Tel** *(866) 942-7442* **Fax** *(707) 226-0809* **Rooms** *89* **Road map** *A3*

Contemporary-chic eco-resort with a wine- and hot springs-focused spa, with adult and childrens' pools, popular indoor-outdoor lounge, and bocce courts. Studio suites have soaking tubs, patios, and some have fireplaces. Free daily fitness classes, cruiser bikes, and access to Auberge du Soleil and Calistoga Ranch facilities. **www.solagecalistoga.com**

## GEYSERVILLE Geyserville Inn    $$$

*21714 Geyserville Ave, 95441* **Tel** *(707) 857-4343, (877) 857-4343* **Fax** *(707) 857-4411* **Rooms** *38* **Road map** *A3*

A great location as there are more than 70 wineries within a 15-mile (24-km) radius of this friendly, family-run hotel. Rooms are spacious and some have views of wineries. Some feature fireplaces and balconies. Geyserville Inn also has a swimming pool, spa, and a good restaurant. **www.geyservilleinn.com**

## GUALALA Whale Watch Inn    $$$$

*35100 Hwy 1, 95445* **Tel** *(800) 942-5342* **Fax** *(707) 884-4815* **Rooms** *18* **Road map** *A3*

If the time of year is right, you might actually see a whale from your room at this intimate, secluded inn perched above the shore on a cliff. Accommodation ranges from luxurious suites to cozy, inn-style rooms, with no phone or TV. Fireplaces, refrigerators, and private baths are a plus. **www.whalewatchinn.com**

## HEALDSBURG Best Western Dry Creek Inn    $$

*198 Dry Creek Rd, 95448* **Tel** *(707) 433-0300, (800) 222-5784* **Fax** *(707) 433-1129* **Rooms** *163* **Road map** *A3*

A budget-conscious hotel near the town plaza and many wineries, this Spanish-motif inn has spacious rooms with comfortable amenities, including cable TV, refrigerators, and free high-speed Internet access. Complimentary breakfast and wine tasting. There is also a fitness center and a pool. **www.drycreekinn.com**

## HEALDSBURG Camellia Inn    $$$$$

*211 North St, 95448* **Tel** *(707) 433-8182, (800) 727-8182* **Fax** *(707) 433-8130* **Rooms** *9* **Road map** *A3*

Romantic inn near the town center, occupying a Victorian house dating to 1869. The hotel is set among gardens of the namesake flower, and features comfortably appointed guest rooms, with fireplaces and whirlpool tubs. Service is exceptional. Staff can arrange activities such as fishing, boating, waterskiing, and more. **www.camelliainn.com**

## HEALDSBURG Hotel Healdsburg    $$$$$

*25 Matheson St, 95448* **Tel** *(707) 431-2800, (800) 889-7188* **Fax** *(707) 431-0414* **Rooms** *55* **Road map** *A3*

Located in the heart of town, this sleek, stylish hotel features extravagant guest rooms, many with huge soak tubs and private balconies, as well as every conceivable amenity. The atmosphere is completed by an on-site spa and restaurant, both outstanding. They have live jazz on Friday and Saturday evenings. **www.hotelhealdsburg.com**

## MENDOCINO Mendocino Hotel & Garden Suites    $$$

*45080 Main St, 95460* **Tel** *(707) 937-0511, (800) 548-0513* **Fax** *(707) 937-0513* **Rooms** *51* **Road map** *A3*

A Victorian-era hotel overlooking the coast, featuring period furnishing in its well-kept guest rooms. Some rooms have commanding ocean views. The garden suites are a contemporary alternative to the historic original house. It also caters to business travelers. **www.mendocinohotel.com**

## MENDOCINO MacCallum House Inn    $$$$

*45020 Albion St, 95460* **Tel** *(707) 937-0289, (800) 609-0492* **Fax** *(707) 937-2243* **Rooms** *19* **Road map** *A3*

Rooms at this charming coastal inn are set in various historic structures, and range from the antiques-filled main house to private cottages with fireplaces and decks. The landscaped gardens are lovely. Within walking distance to various shops and galleries in town. **www.maccallumhouse.com**

## NAPA Avia Napa Hotel    $$$

*1450 First Street, 94559* **Tel** *(707) 224-3900* **Rooms** *141* **Road map** *B3*

Urban-chic, four-diamond-rated hotel in downtown Napa with spacious, luxurious, contemporary rooms that have huge showers, separate tubs, fireplaces, sitting areas, and roomy workspaces. To top it off there's a trendy wine bar and restaurant, fire-feature terrace lounge, and a very knowledgeable Wine Country concierge. **www.aviahotels.com**

## NAPA Best Western Premier Ivy Hotel Napa    $$$

*4195 Solano Avenue, 94558* **Tel** *(707) 253-9300* **Fax** *(707) 253-0906* **Rooms** *115* **Road map** *B3*

With contemporary decor and up-to-date amenities, like fridges, microwaves, pillow-top beds, and room service, this convenient hotel includes Continental breakfast, parking, and Wi-Fi in the price. There's an on-site café and cocktail lounge, and it's near downtown Napa, the Wine Train, shopping, and restaurants. **www.bestwesterncalifornia.com**

**Key to Price Guide** *see p524* **Key to Symbols** *see back cover flap*

## NAPA Silverado Resort and Spa

$$

*1600 Atlas Peak Rd, 94558* **Tel** *(707) 257-0200* **Rooms** *435*    **Road map** *A3*

A Dolce resort now owned by a golf icon, Sliverado is famous for its golf and offers a glamorous spa with salon and lap pool, a huge tennis complex, and nine pools. Towering trees grace an antebellum-style mansion where a terrace bar overlooks glorious gardens. Offers suites plus 1–3-bedroom condos and cottages. **www.silveradoresort.com**

## NAPA Best Western Elm House Inn

$$$

*800 California Blvd, 94559* **Tel** *(707) 255-1831, (888) 849-1997* **Fax** *(707) 255-8609* **Rooms** *22*    **Road map** *A3*

Surprising charm and value are in equal measure at this small property, which has some fireplace rooms, as well as a spa and lovely gardens. They also have conference facilities, and a wine tasting service. A complimentary breakfast buffet is offered. Elm House Inn is near downtown. **www.bestwestern.com/elmhouseinn**

## NAPA Carneros Inn

$$$$$

*4048 Sonoma Hwy, 94559* **Tel** *(707) 299-4900, (888) 400-9000* **Fax** *(707) 299-4950* **Rooms** *86*    **Road map** *B3*

Operated by the owners of a popular Napa winery, this inn makes an effortless blend of Wine Country charm and urban sophistication. Situated on a sprawling vineyard, the luxurious property features stylish rooms designed to reflect the bucolic surroundings. Also has an excellent restaurant and a serene pool. **www.thecarnerosinn.com**

## NAPA Embassy Suites Napa Valley

$$$$$

*1075 California Blvd, 94559* **Tel** *(707) 253-9540* **Fax** *(707) 253-9202* **Rooms** *205*    **Road map** *B3*

Centrally located with easy access to downtown shops and restaurants and to the area's wineries, this well-run hotel has surprising charm and comfortable amenities. Rooms are suite size and feature wet bars, and refrigerators. The grounds have two swimming pools, a cocktail lounge, and a spa. Free breakfast. **www.embassysuites.com**

## NAPA Poetry Inn

$$$$$

*6380 Silverado Trail, 94558* **Tel** *(707) 944-0646* **Fax** *(707) 944-9188* **Rooms** *5*    **Road map** *A3*

Set on a hillside overlooking the Stags Leap district vineyards, this wonderful new inn offers casual ambience and exceptional luxury in each of its spacious rooms. Every amenity is present, from soft linen and huge tubs to outdoor showers. A gourmet breakfast is offered each morning. The balloon flights are an attraction. **www.poetryinn.com**

## RUTHERFORD Auberge du Soleil

$$$$$

*180 Rutherford Hill Rd, 94573* **Tel** *(707) 963-1211, (800) 348-5406* **Fax** *(707) 963-8764* **Rooms** *50* **Road map** *A3*

Among the top destination spa resorts in the Wine Country, this property has stylish, comfortable rooms with fireplaces, Italian linen, flat-screen TVs, coffee makers, and Internet access. Rooms offer spectacular views of the valley. They also have an exceptional restaurant. **www.aubergedusoleil.com**

## SANTA ROSA Hotel La Rose

$$$

*308 Wilson St, 95401* **Tel** *(707) 579-3200, (800) 527-6738* **Fax** *(707) 579-3247* **Rooms** *49*    **Road map** *A3*

A historic hotel in the heart of the downtown district, with simple rooms and country ambience. Rooms are well appointed and offer some updated features. Well suited to business travelers as they also have conference rooms. Complimentary breakfast is served, and there is a popular restaurant at lobby level. **www.hotellarose.com**

## SANTA ROSA Vintners Inn

$$$$$

*4350 Barnes Rd, 95403* **Tel** *(707) 527-7687* **Fax** *(707) 575-1202* **Rooms** *44*    **Road map** *A3*

With European style and country charm, this inn offers a quintessential Wine Country experience. The hotel is set amid working vineyards, and provides luxuriously appointed rooms and suites arranged around a central fountain. Top-notch bath accessories are a plus. The restaurant is one of the region's best dining spots. **www.vintnersinn.com**

## SONOMA El Pueblo Inn

$$$

*896 W Napa St, 95476* **Tel** *(707) 996-3651, (800) 900-8844* **Fax** *(707) 935-5988* **Rooms** *53*    **Road map** *A3*

Located close to the town's plaza, this charming, family-run inn has lovely grounds and rooms appointed with modest style and casual comfort. Most rooms face the garden and offer privacy. The Sonoma rooms' facilities include DVD players and private patios. Guests can also enjoy the spa whirlpool. **www.elpuebloinn.com**

## SONOMA Lodge at Sonoma

$$$$$

*1325 Broadway, 95476* **Tel** *(707) 935-6600* **Fax** *(707) 935-6829* **Rooms** *182*    **Road map** *A3*

This large, family-friendly hotel is located near the historic plaza, and offers comfortable, luxurious rooms arranged around a swimming pool and deck. The service is top quality and there is a fine spa and restaurant on premises. Guests can also rent bikes or enjoy golf nearby. **www.thelodgeatsonoma.com**

## SONOMA MacArthur Place

$$$$$

*29 E MacArthur St, 95476* **Tel** *(707) 938-2929, (800) 722-1866* **Fax** *(707) 933-9833* **Rooms** *64*    **Road map** *A3*

This historic inn near the town's central plaza has cottages, wonderfully appointed with overstuffed beds, fireplaces, and DVD players. A state-of-the-art fitness center, spa, and pool are add-ons. The grounds are well manicured and private. There is an excellent steak house on-site. **www.macarthurplace.com**

## ST. HELENA The Ambrose Bierce House B&B

$$$$$

*1515 Main St, 94574* **Tel** *(707) 963-3003* **Fax** *(707) 963-9367* **Rooms** *4*    **Road map** *A3*

All rooms at this B&B are individually decorated and come with wireless high speed Internet access. Guests can enjoy a soothing dip in the hot tub in the hotel's private courtyard. A complimentary full gourmet champagne breakfast is served daily. **www.ambrosebiercehouse.com**

### ST. HELENA Harvest Inn
$$$$$

*One Main St, 94574* **Tel** *(707) 963-9463, (800) 950-8466* **Fax** *(707) 963-4402* **Rooms** *74*      **Road map** *A3*

Though it is just off the highway, this cozy inn feels a world away. Rooms are rustic, but perfectly appointed; most have fireplaces and private decks overlooking vineyards. Leisure facilities includes a swimming pool, two massage and spa treatments, or mountain biking. Close to various shops and restaurants in town. **www.harvestinn.com**

### ST. HELENA Meadowood Resort Hotel
$$$$$

*900 Meadowood Lane, 94574* **Tel** *(707) 963-3646, (800) 458-8080* **Fax** *(707) 963-3532* **Rooms** *85*     **Road map** *A3*

Tucked in the hills of the Stags Leap district, this intimate retreat features simply elegant rooms, appointed with casual sophistication. The resort presents a lifestyle of health and recreation; grounds feature tennis courts, pool, and health spa, a croquet lawn, and a golf course. The restaurant serves delicious cuisine. **www.meadowood.com**

### YOUNTVILLE Bardessono
$$$$$

*6526 Yount Street, 94599* **Tel** *(707) 363-7295* **Rooms** *62*       **Road map** *B3*

Uscale lodge famous for sustainable design, with a star-chef restaurant. Luxurious villa-style suites in a Mediterranean setting – olive trees, stone sculptures, water features – each with fireplaces, soaking tubs, and outdoor showers. Sip wine in the garden, by the rooftop pool, or in the bar by the fireplace. Free wine-tasting and bikes. **www.bardessono.com**

### YOUNTVILLE Napa Valley Lodge
$$$$$

*2230 Madison St, 94599* **Tel** *(707) 944-2468, (888) 944-3545* **Fax** *(707) 944-9362* **Rooms** *55*     **Road map** *A3*

Situated at the edge of town, this friendly hotel has simple, but spacious rooms, some with fireplaces and balconies. A complimentary breakfast buffet is offered each morning. Complete business amenities are available as well. The pool, spa, sauna, and fitness center are a plus. **www.napavalleylodge.com**

### YOUNTVILLE Villagio Inn & Spa
$$$$$

*6481 Washington St, 94599* **Tel** *(707) 944-8877, (800) 351-1133* **Fax** *(707) 944-8855* **Rooms** *112* **Road map** *A3*

At once casual and elegant, this centrally located inn features guest rooms with large baths, luxurious robes, balconies, and fireplaces. Other amenities include a business center, a swimming pool with a trellis-covered deck, full spa, and Jacuzzi. Complimentary champagne breakfast. Staff can arrange outdoor activities as well. **www.villagio.com**

## GOLD COUNTRY AND THE CENTRAL VALLEY

### AMADOR CITY Imperial Hotel
$$

*14202 Hwy 49, 95601* **Tel** *(209) 267-9172* **Fax** *(209) 267-9249* **Rooms** *6*      **Road map** *B3*

Set in a restored brick structure dating to 1879, this charming little hotel offers comfortable rooms decorated in whimsical Victorian-era style. Service is friendly, and the location offers convenient access to the region's vineyards. Good restaurant on-site, and the bar has fine Californian and imported wines and beers. **www.imperialamador.com**

### AUBURN Power's Mansion Inn
$$$$

*164 Cleveland Ave., 95603-4801* **Tel** *(530) 885-1166* **Rooms** *15*      **Road map** *B3*

A popular spot for local weddings and a great base for exploring Gold Country. With its parlors and antiques, this hotel feels like a step back in time, and it even has a ghost story dating back to the gold rush days. Each room has its own design, but all include private bathrooms. A full cooked breakfast is included. **www.powersmansioninn.com**

### GRASS VALLEY Holbrooke Hotel and Restaurant
$$

*212 W Main St, 95945* **Tel** *(530) 273-1353, (800) 933-7077* **Fax** *(530) 273-0434* **Rooms** *28*     **Road map** *B3*

Established in 1851, this historic landmark property is still a standard of hospitality in the Gold Country. The hotel retains its Old West charm, but at the same time offers many modern conveniences. Rooms have exposed brick walls, private baths, and clawfoot tubs. They also have a library. **www.holbrooke.com**

### GRASS VALLEY Grass Valley Courtyard Suites
$$$$

*210 North Auburn St., 95945* **Tel** *(530) 272-7696* **Rooms** *35*      **Road map** *B3*

This place has a lot more going for it than meets the eye. Decor is a bit nondescript, but there are extra-large rooms with super-comfortable Tempur-Pedic mattresses, and many suites include full kitchens, cable, and high-speed Internet. Grass Valley Suites are within walking distance of several restaurants and shops. **www.gvcourtyardsuites.com**

### MURPHYS Murphys Historic Hotel
$$

*457 Main St, 95247* **Tel** *(209) 728-3444, (800) 532-7684* **Fax** *(209) 728-1590* **Rooms** *35*     **Road map** *B3*

Like a story from California's Wild West, this historic stone-made hotel has old-time charm and a lively saloon. Most rooms are decorated in period style, but there are some updated rooms available in the "modern" wing. Free Continental breakfast. It is also close to wineries, galleries, and recreational centers. **www.murphyshotel.com**

### MURPHYS Murphys Suites
$$$

*134 Hwy 4, 95247* **Tel** *(209) 728-2121, (877) 728-2121* **Fax** *(209) 728-9442* **Rooms** *70*     **Road map** *B3*

This friendly inn is close to the Ironstone winery, and is among the more popular in the area, beloved for its value and attention to guest comfort. It has spacious rooms and suites, all with fridges and microwaves. Luxurious bed linen and bath accessories are provided, and free muffins and juice delivered to your room. **www.murphyssuites.com**

**Key to Price Guide** *see p524* **Key to Symbols** *see back cover flap*

### NEVADA CITY National Hotel

*211 Broad St, 95959* **Tel** *(530) 265-4551* **Fax** *(530) 265-2445* **Rooms** *38*      **Road map** *B3*

This Victorian-style hotel has been in operation since 1855 and still recalls the thriving Gold Rush era, from the friendly staff to the covered sidewalk. The rooms are quaint and outfitted in period decorations; most have private baths. The swimming pool is perfect for sunny afternoons. **www.thenationalhotel.com**

### NEVADA CITY The Parsonage Bed and Breakfast

*427 Broad St, 95959* **Tel** *(530) 265-9478, (800) 916-3662* **Fax** *(530) 265-8147* **Rooms** *6*      **Road map** *B3*

This Victorian-era B&B is quiet and romantic, and offers an excellent country-style breakfast, which is included in the room rate. The rooms are comfortable, each with a private bath, and most are furnished in period detail. Conveniently located close to Sacramento and Reno. **www.theparsonage.net**

### NEVADA CITY Emma Nevada House

*528 E Broad St, 95959* **Tel** *(530) 265-4415* **Fax** *(530) 265-4416* **Rooms** *6*      **Road map** *B3*

A charming B&B furnished with beautiful antiques, featuring a relaxing sunroom for afternoon reading. The rooms are tidy and comfortably appointed with Jacuzzis or walk-in showers. The inn has been completely restored and given modern amenities. **www.emmanevadahouse.com**

### SACRAMENTO Sterling Hotel

*1300 H St, 95814* **Tel** *(800) 365-7660* **Fax** *(916) 448-8066* **Rooms** *17*      **Road map** *B3*

This elegant inn, set in a beautifully restored Victorian mansion, has period furnishings in its rooms, plus select Asian pieces. Accommodations are large, and feature marble baths, Jacuzzis, and lavish linen. Staff are helpful and chivalrous. Complimentary Continental breakfast is served. Popular wedding venue. **www.sterlinghotelsacramento.com**

### SACRAMENTO Riverboat Delta King Hotel

*1000 Front St, 95814* **Tel** *(916) 444-5464, (800) 825-5464* **Fax** *(916) 444-5314* **Rooms** *44*      **Road map** *B3*

Set in a permanently docked historic paddle wheeler, this charming hotel features comfortable rooms with period furnishings, many with superb river views. The boat also has a theater, and a restaurant that is quite good. It holds regular wine classes, and hosts a business center as well. **www.deltaking.com**

### SACRAMENTO Sheraton Grand Sacramento

*1230 J St., 95814* **Tel** *(916) 447-1700* **Fax** *(916) 447-1701* **Rooms** *503*      **Road map** *B3*

Located in a charming, old, red-brick building in downtown Sacramento, the Sheraton Grand is a big, chain hotel that feels like a small, boutique hotel. Rooms are generously sized with modern decor and flat creen TVs; service is very attentive. Walking distance to several great downtown restaurants and shops. **www.starwoodhotels.com**

### SACRAMENTO Le Rivage

*4350 Riverside Blvd., 95822* **Tel** *(916) 443-8400* **Fax** *(916) 706-3384* **Rooms** *100*      **Road map** *B3*

Le Rivage features lovely river-front rooms, but even those facing the parking lot are pleasant, with large soaking tubs in the bathrooms and large high-definition flatscreen TVs in the bedrooms. The hotel is also home to Scott's Seafood, one of the best restaurants in Sacramento. **www.lerivagehotel.com**

### SOMERSET Fitzpatrick Winery and Lodge

*7740 Fair Play Rd, 95684* **Tel** *(800) 245-9166* **Fax** *(530) 620-6838* **Rooms** *5*      **Road map** *B3*

This quaint B&B is set in the hills above El Dorado wine country. Rooms are rustic and comfortably appointed, and the inn is run with family-like zeal. Features include a lap pool and an outdoor hot tub. A hearty breakfast is included. They also have a wine cellar where wine tasting is held. **www.fitzpatrickwinery.com**

### SONORA Gunn House Hotel

*286 S Washington St, 95370* **Tel** *(209) 532-3421* **Fax** *(209) 533-3835* **Rooms** *20*      **Road map** *B3*

Quaint, with a rich history, this eclectic inn dates to 1850 and has the distinction of being the first two-story structure in town. The meticulously restored property is now a well-run hotel, with period antiques and mementos. Rooms are cozy and quiet. Grounds feature lovely gardens, a nice pool, and a patio. **www.gunnhousehotel.com**

### SONORA Sonora Days Inn

*160 S Washington St, 95370* **Tel** *(209) 532-2400, (866) 732-4010* **Fax** *(209) 532-4542* **Rooms** *64* **Road map** *B3*

Set in a historic Spanish-style structure, this friendly hotel has hosted the likes of Grace Kelly and Drew Barrymore. The facility has well-furnished rooms and an annex with microwaves and refrigerators. They also have conference facilities and a rooftop swimming pool. **www.daysinn.com**

### SONORA Barretta Gardens Inn

*700 Barretta St., 95370* **Tel** *(209) 532-6039* **Fax** *n/a* **Rooms** *8*      **Road map** *B3*

A beautiful California Craftsman home that welcomes with little touches like fresh flowers in the rooms, a nightly drinks reception, and home-cooked breakfast every morning. Each room is named after a different wine and decorated accordingly, and each has its own bathroom, including some with large soaking tubs. **www.barrettagardens.com**

### SUTTER CREEK Hanford House Inn

*61 Hanford St., 95685* **Tel** *(209) 267-0747* **Fax** *n/a* **Rooms** *14*      **Road map** *B3*

An adorable red-brick inn that is all about the details. The walls are adorned with vintage newspaper clippings from the area, and nightly wine and cheese pairings feature local favorites. Warm scones are delivered to guests' rooms every morning, paired with local coffee or tea. **www.hanfordhouse.com**

### SUTTER CREEK Sutter Creek Inn $$$

*75 Main St, 95685* **Tel** *(209) 267-5606* **Fax** *(209) 267-9287* **Rooms** *17*       **Road map** *B3*

Built in 1859, this country-style inn has private cottages with wood-burning fireplaces, and is surrounded by shady gardens laced with walkways and hammocks. Some rooms have beds that swing from the ceiling. Sutter Creek Inn is a good base for exploring the Amador County wineries and other historic sites. **www.suttercreekinn.com**

### SUTTER CREEK Grey Gables Inn 🔲 $$$$

*161 Hanford St, 95685* **Tel** *(209) 267-1039, (800) 473-9422* **Fax** *(209) 267-0998* **Rooms** *8*       **Road map** *B3*

There's a fireplace in every room at this historic inn, which has English-like country charm and friendly staff. Features include individually air-conditioned rooms, free Wi-Fi access, and a full breakfast, as well as tea service in the afternoon. Ideally suited for water sports. Not suitable for children under 12. **www.greygables.com**

# THE HIGH SIERRAS

### BISHOP Best Western Creekside Inn 🔲🈺🏃🎦🍴🈺 $$$

*725 N Main St, 93514* **Tel** *(760) 872-3044, (800) 780-7234* **Fax** *(760) 872-1300* **Rooms** *89*    **Road map** *C4*

A comfortable, chain-run inn set on landscaped grounds alongside a stream. Rooms are spacious and comfortably appointed; all have a patio overlooking the creek. Only a few rooms have air conditioning, private baths, and kitchenettes. Amenities include a pool and Jacuzzi. **www.bestwestern.com**

### BISHOP Joseph House Inn $$$

*376 West Yaney St., 93514* **Tel** *(760) 872-3389* **Rooms** *5*       **Road map** *C3*

An oasis on the road between Death Valley and Yosemite, Joseph House sits on 3 acres (1.2 ha) of landscaped gardens. Rooms are furnished in American country style (wooden/iron beds, thick quilts, fresh flowers), and the owner cooks up a gourmet breakfast for guests and will happily pack a lunch for the day. **www.josephhouseinn.com**

### FISH CAMP Narrow Gauge Inn 🔲🍴🈺🏃🎦🈺 $$

*48571 Hwy 41, 93623* **Tel** *(559) 683-7720, (888) 644-9050* **Fax** *(559) 683-2139* **Rooms** *26*    **Road map** *C4*

This romantic gem is located at the southern end of Yosemite, and features quaint, comfortable rooms, some with private decks. Amenities include a swimming pool and a fabulous restaurant. The staff are attentive, friendly, and can arrange outdoor activities for guests. **www.narrowgaugeinn.com**

### JUNE LAKE Gull Lake Lodge 🈺 $$$

*132 Bruce St., 93529* **Tel** *(760) 648-7516* **Rooms** *25*       **Road map** *C3*

Pet-friendly lodge in a residential neighborhood, within walking distance of June Lake and Gull Lake, and a short drive from Yosemite, Mammoth, and Mono Lake. Rooms are one-bedroom apartments with kitchenette. Larger groups can book the two-bedroom bungalow with its wood-burning stove. Free high-speed Internet. **www.gulllakelodge.com**

### KINGS CANYON NATIONAL PARK Sequoia Lodge 🔲🍴🈺🏃🎦🈺 $$$

*63410 Generals Hwy, 93633* **Tel** *(559) 565-3388, (800) 227-9900* **Fax** *(559) 565-3223* **Rooms** *52* **Road map** *C3*

With ample activity options, this mountain lodge appeals to families and large groups year-round. Rooms are lodge-style or in cabins, and feature large beds, deluxe bunks, and complete bath amenities. Camp-style activities are planned regularly for guests. Meals are included in the price. **www.sequoia-kingscanyon.com**

### KIRKWOOD Kirkwood Mountain Resort 🔲🍴🈺🏃🎦🈺🈺 $$$

*1501 Kirkwood Meadows Dr, 95646* **Tel** *(209) 258-6000* **Fax** *(209) 258-7400* **Rooms** *120*    **Road map** *C3*

Kirkwood is a popular year-round resort featuring well-appointed rooms and suites, many with fireplaces and balconies. There are numerous activities readily available, from fishing and golf to snow skiing. The grounds host live performances and other events. The Bub's Sports Bar is lively and has huge TV screens. **www.kirkwood.com**

### LEE VINING Lake View Lodge 🔲🏃🈺 $$

*51285 Highway 395, 93541* **Tel** *(760) 647-6543, (800) 990-6614* **Fax** *(760) 647-6325* **Rooms** *46* **Road map** *C3*

The clean, simple rooms at this friendly hotel on the western edge of Mono Lake make a nice overnight rest spot between Southern California and Tahoe. Some rooms have kitchens. Lake-view cottages with full amenities are available as well. There are a few especially adapted rooms for disabled guests. **www.bwlakeviewlodge.com**

### LONE PINE Best Western Frontier Motel 🔲🈺🈺 $$

*1008 S Main St, 93545* **Tel** *(760) 876-5571, (800) 780-7234* **Fax** *(760) 876-5357* **Rooms** *73*    **Road map** *C3*

Modest motor inn with rustic accommodation, close to many outdoor recreational activities including hiking, fishing, and golf. Rooms are basic with few frills, and some have mountain views. A large Continental breakfast and high-speed Internet access is included. Business facilities and an outdoor pool are add-ons. **www.bestwestern.com**

### MAMMOTH LAKES Westin Monache 🔲🍴🈺🏃🎦🈺🈺 $$$

*50 Hillside Dr., 93546* **Tel** *(760) 934-0400* **Rooms** *230*       **Road map** *C3*

Right in the middle of the action, steps from the gondola at Mammoth Resort, the hotel features Westin's trademark Heavenly beds in simple, tasteful rooms (white linens, muted colors, nothing too outrageous), along with a decent restaurant and a large swimming area with multiple pools and a hot tub. **www.westinmammoth.com**

## MAMMOTH LAKES Austria Hof Lodge  $$$$$

*924 Canyon Blvd, 93546* **Tel** *(760) 934-2764, (866) 662-6668* **Fax** *(760) 934-1880* **Rooms** *22* **Road map** *C4*

Rooms at this charming mountain lodge feature facilities such as marble bathroom fixtures, DVD players, and free wireless Internet access. Some rooms have fireplaces, Jacuzzis, and kitchenettes. The staff are friendly and accommodating. **www.austriahof.com**

## SOUTH LAKE TAHOE Best Western Timber Cove Lodge Marina Resort $$

*3411 Lake Tahoe Blvd, 96150* **Tel** *(530) 541-6722* **Fax** *(530) 542-1428* **Rooms** *262* **Road map** *C3*

This full-service establishment offers great value for its lakeside location. Rooms are spacious and well appointed, with fireplaces and balconies overlooking the beach. Added attractions include in-room movies and Nintendo games. Close to many winter and summer recreational opportunities. **www.timbercovetahoe.com**

## SQUAW VALLEY Resort at Squaw Creek $$$$$

*400 Squaw Creek Rd, 96146* **Tel** *(530) 583-6300, (800) 327-3353* **Fax** *(530) 581-6632* **Rooms** *404* **Road map** *B3*

This beautiful, luxuriously appointed resort features top-notch rooms with plush beds, nice bath supplies, and full amenities. It also provides spa services and abundant recreation options to choose from, including golf and skiing. It offers free transportation to Squaw Valley. **www.squawcreek.com**

## TAHOE CITY Chaney House $$$$

*4725 W Lake Blvd, 96145* **Tel** *(530) 525-7333* **Fax** *(530) 525-4413* **Rooms** *4* **Road map** *B3*

Chaney House is a charming, traditional stone and timber lodge recalling Lake Tahoe the way it used to be. It has cozy, romantic rooms, and features a large fireplace in the main room and private beach access. A good breakfast is offered each morning. Nearby activities include biking, fishing, hiking, and rafting. **www.chaneyhouse.com**

## TAHOE CITY Sweet Dreams Cabin $$$$

*Bunker Rd., 96145* **Tel** *(800) 581-8828* **Rooms** *3* **Road map** *C3*

This adorable, authentic red log cabin is equipped with a fireplace and full kitchen, three bedrooms, two bathrooms, and a hot tub on the deck, looking out over the pines. The cabin has a great blend of antiques and vintage California accessories, all highlighted by the log walls and ceilings. **www.tluxp.com/bre/properties/Sweet-Dreams**

## TRUCKEE Donner Lake Village Resort 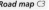 $

*15695 Donner Pass Rd, 96161* **Tel** *(530) 587-6081, (800) 621-6664* **Fax** *(530) 587-8782* **Rooms** *64* **Road map** *B3*

Set on the shore of crystal blue Donner Lake and featuring its own marina, this rustic-style lodge offers condominium-style accommodations. Fully equipped kitchens come with two-bedroom suites and two-bath town homes. Reno's nightlife is only a 45-minute drive from this resort. **www.donnerlakevillage.com**

## TRUCKEE The Richardson House $$$$$

*10154 High St., 96160* **Tel** *(530) 563-6874* **Rooms** *6* **Road map** *B3*

An old flop house and brothel, the Richardson House is a big part of local mining history. In the middle of historic downtown Truckee, it's walking distance to restaurants, shops, and bars, and driving distance to Lake Tahoe and ski resorts. Impeccably restored with a fantastic chef's kitchen and a landscaped, fenced yard. **www.therichardsonhouse.com**

## YOSEMITE NATIONAL PARK Cedar Lodge  $$

*9966 Hwy 140, 95318* **Tel** *(209) 379-2612, (866) 875-8465* **Fax** *(209) 379-2712* **Rooms** *211* **Road map** *C3*

Rooms at this family-friendly hotel range from standard size to a suite that sleeps 14. Facilities include two pools, a spa, and private river access. Grounds feature two restaurants, a cocktail lounge, and a gift shop. Cedar Lodge is located close to the entrance of Yosemite National Park *(see pp488–91)*. **www.nationalparkreservations.com**

## YOSEMITE NATIONAL PARK Wawona Hotel $$$$

*State Hwy 41, 95389* **Tel** *(559) 253-5636* **Fax** *(209) 375-6601* **Rooms** *104* **Road map** *C3*

A landmark of the High Sierras, this charming hotel is straight out of the Old West, and is popular for its historic ambience, comfortable rooms, and its location near meadows and streams. Well suited for adventure activities, and an on-site, nine-hole golf course is available as well. Book well in advance for summer. **www.yosemitepark.com**

## YOSEMITE NATIONAL PARK Yosemite Lodge At The Falls  $$$$

*Yosemite Valley, 95389* **Tel** *(559) 253-5635* **Fax** *(209) 372-1444* **Rooms** *245* **Road map** *C3*

This large and popular lodge is situated on the valley floor close to the village. It offers a wide selection of accommodation, from cabins to modern-style lodge rooms with patios or balconies. Attractions include an amphitheater, food court, shops, and a post office. Internet access is available. **www.yosemitepark.com**

## YOSEMITE NATIONAL PARK The Ahwahnee $$$$$

*Yosemite Valley, 95389* **Tel** *(559) 253-5636* **Fax** *(209) 372-1463* **Rooms** *123* **Road map** *C3*

This famed historic hotel is synonymous with the valley. Opened in 1927, it is elegant and rustic, built of stone and timber, with a Native American ambience. The lodge features a soaring lobby, well-appointed rooms, and an excellent restaurant. The solarium and winter club room are great. **www.yosemitepark.com**

## YOSEMITE NATIONAL PARK Tenaya Lodge  $$$$$

*1122 Hwy 41, 93623* **Tel** *(559) 253-2005, (888) 514-2167* **Rooms** *244* **Road map** *C4*

A Yosemite landmark and a fantastic base for exploring the park. The spa features organic, locally sourced products, and the lodge has cathedral ceilings, exposed beams, and huge windows looking out at the park. Rooms are simple and comfortable with a Native American theme. Indoor and outdoor pools, plus hot tubs. **www.yosemitepark.com**

# NORTH CENTRAL CALIFORNIA

### APTOS Best Western Seacliff Inn
$$

7500 Old Dominion Court, 95003 **Tel** (831) 688-7300 **Fax** (831) 685-3603 **Rooms** 149     **Road map** B4

Located close to Seacliff State Beach, this modest hotel features friendly service and surprisingly comfortable rooms, complete with upscale bath amenities, high-speed Internet access, and video games. The suites are large and have a Jacuzzi. There is also a full-service restaurant available. **www.seacliffinn.com**

### APTOS Rio Sands Motel
$$$

116 Aptos Beach Dr, 95003 **Tel** (831) 688-3207 **Fax** (831) 688-6107 **Rooms** 51     **Road map** B4

A well-operated motel near the beach, with rooms ranging from standard to suites with kitchenettes; many feature balconies overlooking the gardens. Amenities include a swimming pool, spa, and barbecue and picnic areas. A complimentary Continental breakfast is included. Check for special off-season weekly rates. **www.riosands.com**

### APTOS Seascape Beach Resort
$$$$$

1 Seascape Resort Drive, 95003 **Tel** (831) 688-6800 **Rooms** 283     **Road map** B4

For the ultimate Santa Cruz family break, this resort has nautical-themed suites and villas for 2–8 people, with fireplaces and kitchens. There are three oceanview pools, a supervised kids' club, tennis courts, and a golf course. Excellent on-site restaurants are pricey for families, but cafés and a grocery store are nearby. **www.seascaperesort.com**

### BIG SUR Big Sur River Inn
$$$

Hwy 1, Pheneger Creek, 93920 **Tel** (831) 667-2700 **Fax** (831) 667-2743 **Rooms** 20     **Road map** B4

A quaint, historic inn set on secluded grounds among massive redwoods along the river. Rooms are intimate, well appointed, and many have balconies overlooking the water. Big Sur River Inn also has a heated outdoor pool, an on-site general store, and a gift shop. **www.bigsurriverinn.com**

### BIG SUR Deetjen's Big Sur Inn
$$$$

48865 Hwy 1, 93920 **Tel** (831) 667-2377 **Fax** (831) 667-0466 **Rooms** 20     **Road map** B4

Known as much for its restaurant as its cozy, eclectic rooms, this popular inn has a personality of its own. Rooms are private and quiet, and each is furnished with a whimsical artistic touch. Guests can choose rooms with private or shared bathrooms. The staff are friendly and attentive. **www.deetjens.com**

### BIG SUR Post Ranch Inn
$$$$$

PO Box 219, Hwy 1, 93920 **Tel** (831) 667-2200 **Fax** (831) 667-2512 **Rooms** 30     **Road map** B4

Architecturally stunning, this away-from-it-all resort features sumptuously appointed rooms, with dazzling ocean views and romantic seclusion – an unforgettable experience. Morning yoga is offered. They also have a spa, pool, and fitness center. The restaurant is exceptional. **www.postranchinn.com**

### BIG SUR The Ventana Inn and Spa
$$$$$

Hwy 1, 93920 **Tel** (831) 667-2331 **Fax** (831) 667-2419 **Rooms** 63     **Road map** B4

This gorgeous cliffside property is one of the most stunning on the coast. It has rooms with romantic charm, as well as fireplaces, luxurious bath areas, and redwood decks; some have spectacular ocean views. The restaurant and spa are top-notch. They also have a spa boutique selling unique items. Free yoga classes and breakfast. **www.ventanainn.com**

### CARMEL Carmel Wayfarer Inn
$$

24815 Carpenter St, 93921 **Tel** (831) 624-2711, (800) 533-2711 **Fax** (831) 625-1210 **Rooms** 17    **Road map** B4

Located in a wooded area outside downtown Carmel, this cozy and romantic inn is secluded, but within an easy walk to the shops, galleries, and restaurants. Rooms are well appointed, some with kitchenettes, microwaves, and wet bars. Breakfast is included. **www.carmelbytheseawayfarerinn.com**

### CARMEL Los Laureles Lodge
$$$$

313 W Carmel Valley Rd, 93924 **Tel** (831) 659-2233 **Fax** (831) 659-0481 **Rooms** 31     **Road map** B4

Rooms at this eclectic, relaxed inn are built into former horse stables. The hotel features generous amenities in each of its rooms. The grounds boast a patio, a lovely garden, and a good restaurant and bar. Nearby recreational activities include hiking, fishing, horse riding, and tennis. **www.loslaureles.com**

### CARMEL Pine Inn
$$$$

Ocean Ave & Monte Verde, 93921 **Tel** (831) 624-3851 **Fax** (831) 624-3030 **Rooms** 49     **Road map** B4

Iconic and regaled, this charming inn is the oldest in town, and still sets the tone for Carmel hospitality with its gracious rooms and friendly service. The rooms have been updated over the years to offer modern comforts to guests, including free Wi-Fi. The restaurant, Il Fornaio, serves excellent authentic Italian cuisine. **www.pineinn.com**

### CARMEL La Playa Hotel
$$$$

Camino Real at Eighth, 93921 **Tel** (831) 624-6476 **Fax** (831) 624-7966 **Rooms** 75     **Road map** B4

This Mediterranean-style hotel has comfortable rooms offering friendly service along with all the latest facilities. A variety of room types are available, including cottages that feel like a private vacation home. La Playa has a full spa on the premises, and is close to Monterey Bay Aquarium, Pebble Beach, and Big Sur. **www.laplayahotel.com**

**Key to Price Guide** see p524 **Key to Symbols** see back cover flap

### CARMEL Cypress Inn  $$$$$

*Lincoln & 7th, 93921* **Tel** *(831) 624-3871, (800) 443-7443* **Fax** *(831) 624-8216* **Rooms** *44*     **Road map** *B4*

An elegant inn with Spanish-style architecture, located just a few blocks from the beach. The property has well-furnished rooms with basic facilities; some have ocean views and fireplaces. Pets are welcome. Personal service is provided by the attentive staff. Actress Doris Day is the owner of this inn. **www.cypress-inn.com**

### CARMEL Carmel Valley Ranch $$$$$

*1 Old Ranch Rd, 93923* **Tel** *(831) 625-9500, (800) 282-4745* **Fax** *(831) 624-2858* **Rooms** *144*     **Road map** *B4*

This luxurious resort set on a 400-acre (121-ha) estate has a peaceful and relaxing atmosphere that makes for a memorable stay. The hotel offers oversized suites, with fireplaces and plush bath amenities. Additionals include a golf course and a spa among its facilities. Suits business travelers as well. **www.carmelvalleyranch.com**

### CARMEL Highlands Inn Hyatt Carmel $$$$$

*120 Highlands Dr, 93923* **Tel** *(831) 620-1234* **Fax** *(831) 626-1574* **Rooms** *142*     **Road map** *B4*

Long a Carmel favorite, this splendidly rustic inn is set on an ocean bluff among coastal pines offering fabulous views. Rooms have all the modern facilities such as CD players, coffee makers, full bath amenities, refrigerators, and data ports. The restaurant is a destination unto itself. **www.highlandsinn.hyatt.com**

### MONTEREY Lone Oak Lodge $

*2221 North Fremont Street, 93940* **Tel** *(831) 372-4924* **Fax** *(831) 372-4985* **Rooms** *46*     **Road map** *B4*

Popular with scuba divers and the best-kept secret for reasonable family lodgings on Monterey Bay, Loan Oak Lodge is on a street lined with motels, but is close to the beach, aquarium, Cannery Row, a golf course, and downtown. Rooms are basic but suites offer kitchenettes, fireplaces, and Jacuzzis. Free sauna and barbecues. **www.loneoaklodge.com**

### MONTEREY Monterey Bay Lodge $$$

*55 Camino Aguajito, 93940* **Tel** *(831) 372-8057, (800) 558-1900* **Fax** *(831) 655-2933* **Rooms** *45*     **Road map** *B4*

Great value and friendly service are the hallmarks of this tidy hotel situated near the Wharf and other popular attractions. Surrounded by nice gardens, the rooms feature comfortable bedding and the latest conveniences. It also has family suites and deluxe rooms with a fireplace and spa. **www.montereybaylodge.com**

### MONTEREY Casa Munras Garden Hotel $$$$

*700 Munras Ave, 93940* **Tel** *(831) 375-2411, (800) 222-2446* **Fax** *(831) 375-1365* **Rooms** *166*     **Road map** *B4*

Settled on wonderfully manicured gardens, this charming hotel has cozy rooms of all sizes located in structures throughout the property. The property is close to many major local attractions such as Colton Hall Museum, California's First Theater, Fisherman's Wharf, and downtown Monterey *(see pp508-11)*. **www.hotelcasamunras.com**

### MONTEREY InterContinental the Clement Monterey $$$$

*750 Cannery Row, 93940* **Tel** *(831) 375-4500* **Fax** *(831) 375-4501* **Rooms** *208*     **Road map** *B4*

Luxury hotel on Cannery Row with upscale contemporary decor, high-tech amenities, health club, pool, supervised kids' club, spa, business center, and elegant restaurant/bar. Most rooms and suites have fireplaces and oceanview balconies, while bars on the oceanfront patio serve drinks and appetizers. Executive club level perks. **www.ichotelsgroup.com**

### MONTEREY Monterey Bay Inn  $$$$$

*242 Cannery Row, 93940* **Tel** *(831) 373-6242, (800) 424-6242* **Fax** *(831) 373-7603* **Rooms** *49*     **Road map** *B4*

This friendly, centrally located inn features modern, comfortable rooms, with excellent bath and business amenities. Many have spectacular bay views. In-room delivery of a complimentary breakfast is provided. They also have various massage treatments. **www.montereybayinn.com**

### MONTEREY Monterey Plaza Hotel & Spa $$$$$

*400 Cannery Row, 93940* **Tel** *(831) 646-1700, (800) 334-3999* **Fax** *(831) 656-0439* **Rooms** *290*     **Road map** *B4*

One of the best-known hotels in the area, this well-run establishment has European styling and is situated centrally on the bay. Spacious rooms have all the facilities, including fantastic bath accessories and high-speed Internet connections. There is a notable restaurant on the premises. **www.montereyplazahotel.com**

### SANTA CRUZ Beach Street Inn and Suites $$$$$

*125 Beach Street, 95060* **Tel** *(831) 423-3031* **Fax** *(831) 423-2607* **Rooms** *40*     **Road map** *B4*

This old favorite beach-side motel has transformed into a bright, fresh, fun place to stay. The inn has a retro look, ocean views, and a good location adjacent to the boardwalk and the wharf (formerly the Terrace Court). Kitchens and multi-bed units are available. Ocean view pool, free parking, and Wi-Fi. **www.beachstreetinn.com**

### SANTA CRUZ Dream Inn $$$$$

*175 W Cliff Dr, 95060* **Tel** *(800) 716-6199, (866) 774-7735* **Fax** *(831) 427-2025* **Rooms** *163*     **Road map** *B4*

Located two blocks from Boardwalk, this chain hotel offers exceptional value for its beachfront location. The rooms offer all the comfortable amenities such as refrigerators, coffee makers, and air conditioning. Many have balconies and splendid views of the ocean. **www.dreaminnsantacruz.com**

### SANTA CRUZ Sea and Sand Inn $$$$$

*201 West Cliff Drive, 95060* **Tel** *(831) 427 3400* **Rooms** *22*     **Road map** *B4*

These oceanview motel rooms are on the clifftop near the boardwalk and the beach and offer spacious suites and studios with sitting area, fridge, microwave, and fireplace. Some have the added bonus of hot tubs on private patios. A Continental breakfast is included in the price, and free Wi-Fi is available. **www.santacruzmotels.com**

# WHERE TO EAT

Of all the states in the US, California has perhaps the widest variety of places to eat. "California cuisine" – light food prepared in a range of international styles using locally grown ingredients – was pioneered by chefs such as Jeremiah Towers, Wolfgang Puck, and Alice Waters and is now internationally recognized. There is an ample number of Italian and Mexican restaurants, but many other international cuisines are also available. In every city you can eat Japanese sushi, Thai noodles, Chinese dim sum, Middle Eastern falafel, or Indian tandoori. While ethnic cooking reflects the state's many cultures, there is also no shortage of that classic all-American meal: hamburger, French fries, and soda. The restaurants listed on pages 568–605 have been selected for their variety, service, and good value. Some typical meals served in California are shown on pages 564–5.

California diner sign

## CALIFORNIA EATING PATTERNS

Some say Americans make the best breakfast in the world, and this is evident in California. From diners to top restaurants, the breakfast menu is vast. Omelettes with fries and toast, pancakes or waffles topped with fruit and syrup, and eggs, bacon, or sausage served with toast or a muffin are popular options. Less filling choices are coffee with a bagel or pastry, or cereal topped with raisins or bananas. Breakfast is served from 6am to 11am (all day in some diners). Brunch on Sundays, and sometimes Saturdays, adds main courses, salads, and desserts to the breakfast menu from around 11am to 3pm (in moderate to expensive restaurants).

California lunch is light – soup and salad or a sandwich. Dinner is the main meal of the day for Americans. Many restaurants make dinner a special occasion by setting out candles and tablecloths. Dinner is served from 5:30pm to 10:30pm.

## PRICES AND TIPPING

Eating out is very reasonable. A snack in a café should cost no more than $8 per person. A main meal in a diner will set you back up to $15. A three-course meal in an average restaurant, excluding wine, will cost $25–$30, but gourmet meals can begin at $40. Fixed-price menus are rare, but lunch menus are much cheaper and are generally very similar to the dinner menu.

Tipping should be based on service: if satisfactory, leave 15 percent; if superlative, leave 20 percent. Make sure the tip

Planet Hollywood

is calculated on the net cost of the meal and does not include the tax. Restaurant tax in California is up to 8.25 percent.

## FAST FOOD

A ubiquitous feature of the California landscape, fast-food outlets are rarely more than five minutes away. They offer filling, inexpensive food, which stretches the travel budget for families. Chain-owned diners include Denny's, Sizzlers, and Marie Callendar's. While the seating areas are large and the selections on the menu are extensive, the food is prepared in bulk and may therefore be rather ordinary.

## HEALTHY EATING

A number of restaurants in California now follow the American Heart Association's guidelines for reducing cholesterol and dietary fat. A red heart beside a dish denotes an AHA-approved "Healthy Heart" meal, low in calories and cholesterol. If a restaurant does not offer such meals, you can ask your waiter to omit certain ingredients where appropriate.

Vegetarian cuisine is becoming more popular in California restaurants. They all offer salads and many of them will make up meat-free meals for customers if requested.

Campanile Restaurant, Hollywood *(see p571)*

## COFFEE HOUSES, TEA HOUSES, AND CAFÉS

Coffee houses can be found all over California. They specialize in Italian favorites like cappuccino and latte and assortments of sweets to go with them. Some serve as Internet cafés, offering use of their computers or wireless connection. Some of the bigger bookstores now have small cafés for their customers. Southern California's climate lends itself to outdoor living, so many eateries have sidewalk or patio tables.

For afternoon tea, many of the upscale hotels, especially in Los Angeles, offer very elegant tea services.

Gott's Roadside Tray Gourmet, St. Helena *(see p600)*

Ratto's Italian delicatessen in Oakland

## PICNICS AND TAKEOUTS

Delicatessens and super-markets with deli counters stock cold meats, cheeses, pickles, and salads. They will also make up fresh sandwiches to your personal order to take-out and enjoy in one of the parks or open areas that abound in California.

You can also order takeouts from any restaurant, although the prices for this are the same as eating in the restaurant itself.

## MICROBREWERY BARS

In the world of beer, micro-breweries are big news. In every city there is a healthy number of on-site brewmasters with bars serving a selection of national and international beers, but also brewing their own specials, such as Anchor Steam in San Francisco and Karl Straus Amber Lager in San Diego *(see pp566–7)*. If a beer proves successful locally, it can then go on to earn national and sometimes international recognition.

A variety of snack foods is also served at microbrewery bars to soak up the beer.

## SMOKING

California is an antismoking state, and the California State Legislature has banned smoking in all restaurants, and in all public places. Some restaurants that have outdoor tables may turn a blind eye however and allow you to smoke outside. Cigars are rarely allowed. Note that in some places you may not be able to smoke on the beach.

Sidewalk patio of the rustic Los Olivos Wine Merchant Café *(see p576)*

## WHEELCHAIR ACCESS

All new restaurants in Cali-fornia, and old restaurants undergoing renovation, must make their site accessible to wheelchair users. This means that there should be no steps into the restaurant or to the tables, and that there should be wide bathroom doors.

## CHILDREN'S FACILITIES

Most restaurants are children-friendly and offer a children's menu and high chairs or booster seats. However, in the quieter, upscale restaurants, parents are expected to keep children seated at the table, and take noisy or upset children out-side until they calm down.

## DRESS CODES

With California's leisurely lifestyle, many gourmet restaurants do not require men to wear jackets and ties or women to wear dresses, although jeans, shorts, sneakers, and T-shirts are definitely frowned upon.

## BOOKING AHEAD

It is always best to make a reservation in advance to avoid disappointment. City restaurants, in particular, are often very busy, and estab-lished or fashionable spots are sometimes booked up more than a month in advance. If you make a reservation that you later cannot keep, call the restaurant and cancel.

# The Flavors of California

One heady whiff of a California farmer's market and you'll understand how California cuisine – rooted in the simple concept that ingredients should be fresh, healthful, and homegrown – developed in the sun-kissed Golden State. Ethnic cuisine, too, especially sizzling Mexican but also Mediterranean and spicy Chinese and Thai, makes a bold appearance across the state. And, of course, traditionalists can indulge in the all-American burger and fries at a classic diner. Better yet, for a quintessential California car culture moment, pull into a drive-through for a burger-on-the-dash meal.

**Coriander and bay leaves**

A birds-eye view of the state reveals verdant herb gardens unfolding from one end to the other; wild mustard fields giving way to scented swathes of cilantro (coriander), bay, and basil, to be used in everything from sauces to salads.

## FRESH FRUITS AND NUTS

Fruits and nuts flourish in California's year-round sunny climate. The healthy soil, fed by an abundance of fresh water, yields downy-skinned peaches, caramel-sweet dates, and the state's famed avocados. The world's most popular avocado is the rough-skinned Haas variety, a California native, prized for its silky texture and mild, nutty flavor and used extensively in salads and sandwiches and to concoct velvety dips. The thin-skinned, green Fuerte

**Stalls at a Californian market, laden with local produce**

## LOCALLY GROWN VEGETABLES AND HERBS

The seasons reign supreme in California cuisine and chefs develop their menus around what's fresh at the market. The summer warmth brings forth heavy vine tomatoes and a rainbow of peppers, while the autumnal cool reaps lush broccoli, artichokes and acorn squash.

White peaches  Persimmons

Dates  Papaya  Mango

Kumquats  Fresh figs

**Mouthwatering selection of ripe Calfornian fruits**

## CALIFORNIAN DISHES AND SPECIALTIES

Food in California reflects the ethnic diversity of the state's population as well as the natural bounty of produce available year-round. Due to similarities in climate, Californian cooking is also strongly influenced by Mediterranean cuisine. However, traditional Italian or Provençal recipes are often given a twist with the addition of New World ingredients, resulting in innovative pizzas and pasta dishes and exotic, colorful salads. Sauces and salad dressings tend to be light and fresh, designed to enhance and complement the key ingredients of the dish. Locally produced goat cheese is used liberally, its tangy flavor pairing beautifully with vegetables and meat. Desserts make the most of local fruits, and will often be as simple as a mixed-fruit platter with a passion-fruit sauce or home-made ice cream.

**Jalapeño chilis**

**Mesclun salad with dates and goat cheese** *Mixed baby greens mingle with sweet dates and crumbled cheese.*

A bustling Mexican snack bar in San Francisco's lively Haight neighborhood

## MEXICAN CUISINE

There's no need to head south of the border for *comida mexicana*. Nearly every town has its share of casual, colorful *taquerias* where you can dig into Mexican fare at a price that's easy on the wallet. At less than $10 for a blimp-sized burrito or platter overflowing with seasoned rice, beans and chicken, a Mexican meal remains one of the best bargains in the state.

### THE MEXICAN MENU

**Tortilla** A Mexican staple, this is a round, flat unleavened corn- or wheat-flour bread.

**Burrito** Warmed tortilla, filled with *arroz* (rice), *frijoles* (beans), and *pollo* (chicken), *carne* (meat) or veggies.

**Quesadilla** Tortilla stuffed with *queso* (cheese) and other fillings, then grilled or pan-fried to melt the cheese.

**Taco** A crisp tortilla, usually deep-fried, folded, and stuffed with a savory filling.

**Chile Relleno** Stuffed green chili pepper fried in batter.

**Salsas** Spicy fresh sauces, from traditional chunky tomato to trendy slivers of papaya, mango or peach to vegetable salsas with corn and black beans.

**Mole** This rich, dark sauce is an aromatic blend of bitter chocolate, spices, and chilis, often drizzled over chicken.

avocado is another creamy favorite, as are California black walnuts, whose rock-hard shells hide an intensely flavorful meat used by chefs as a nutty seasoning.

## FISH AND SEAFOOD

California's seas and rivers abound with fish and shellfish, from delicate Dungeness crab to meaty swordfish and albacore tuna, and many waterfront restaurants serve up fish so fresh it's practically flopping on your plate. Petrale sole, found everywhere from Fort Bragg to Monterey, is the premium flatfish at the market, with a fine-textured, low-fat flesh that grills to perfection. Named after their rock-hard shell, Ridgeback Santa Barbara shrimp can be tough little guys to peel but

boast the sweetest tasting meat in the Pacific. The best freshwater fish is the state's king salmon, which spawns in the Sacramento and San Joaquin rivers and is prized for its delicate, velvety meat that melts on the tongue.

Succulent crabs plucked straight from the Pacific ocean

**Salmon on watercress with citrus vinaigrette** *Local fish and peppery leaves are offset by a piquant vinaigrette.*

**Grilled chicken breasts with tomato salsa** *Whole black beans and guacamole complement this healthy dish.*

**Poached fresh persimmons** *A luscious concoction of silky persimmons are draped over vanilla ice cream.*

# What to Drink in California

**Beer label**

Californians are devoted to the consumption of beverages, partly because they tend to do so much outdoor exercise in the heat and partly as a social activity. Soft drinks, or sodas, play the largest role in the state's beverage culture, although hard liquor is still popular. Many restaurants tempt weekend customers with champagne brunches. Beer can be enjoyed on the beach or while watching a game of baseball. Wine, particularly local California wine *(see pp438–9)*, is popular with dinner.

**Sign in the Napa Valley wine-producing region in Northern California**

**Tequila bottle**     **Colorful Sunset Strip**     **Strawberry Daiquiri**     **Margarita with slice of lime**

## SOFT DRINKS

Californians are generally very health-conscious, and they consume a lot of fruit juice. Staff at juice stalls in shopping centers or on the street will squeeze juice from

**Iced cola**

almost any kind of fruit, or a mixture of fruit and vegetables, while you wait.

Most fast-food outlets offer a range of soft drinks in three sizes, although the same products can usually be purchased much less expensively from shops or supermarkets.

The most popular nonalcoholic drink in the state remains the all-American cola. However, health awareness has led to a growth in the consumption of diet and caffeine-free versions of colas and other carbonated soft drinks.

Sports-loving Californians often carry bottled water or flexible thermos flasks filled with drinks chilled overnight in the refrigerator.

**Freshly squeezed strawberry juice**

## COCKTAILS

Sipping cocktails beside the ocean at sunset is part of the popular image of the "California dream." The margarita cocktail still ranks as the firm favorite throughout the state. Served in ever-wider glasses, margaritas are a blend of tequila, lime juice, and an orange-flavored liqueur, with the rim of the glass dipped in salt.

The Sunset Strip, named after the once infamous section of Sunset Boulevard *(see pp102–7)*, consists of equal parts of gin, rum, triple sec, vodka, pineapple juice, and lemonade. Another cocktail popular in the state is the piña colada. This is a blend of fresh pineapple juice, cream of coconut, and sometimes papaya juice, lime, and orange juice. A shot of rum is added, and the finished drink is served over ice in tall, elegant glasses.

## TEA AND COFFEE

People in California consume large quantities of "designer" coffee. Café latte, café au lait, cappuccino, frappuccino (iced coffee), and flavored brews, such as almond and mocha, are on hand at coffee houses. Tea is also becoming increasingly popular, and imported teas come in every imaginable flavor.

**Cappuccino**       **Café latte**

**Frappuccino**       **Lemon tea**

## WINE

Grape vines thrive in the mild climate of Northern California, where cooling fogs help the fruit to reach perfection. The main red wine varieties grown in the region are Cabernet Sauvignon, Pinot Noir, Merlot, and Zinfandel *(see pp438–9)*. White wines are also classified by grape variety, with Chardonnay by far the most popular of recent years. Grown throughout the West Coast region, this prestige grape produces wines varying in character from dry, light, lemon, and vanilla-scented to the more headstrong and oaky.

California has acquired an international reputation for excellent champagne-style wines at the right price, reflected in the fact that the finest French producers have huge investments in the state. Moët & Chandon and Mumm, among others, have set up wineries in the Napa Valley and elsewhere.

Wine is much cheaper in supermarkets or liquor stores than in restaurants. State law allows customers to take their own bottles into restaurants; the corkage fee generally starts at $10.

Sparkling Cuvée Napa by Mumm

Rosé or blush wine

Napa Chardonnay

Cabernet Sauvignon

## WATER

A variety of mineral waters is produced in the state, the best of which comes from the spa town of Calistoga in the Napa Valley *(see p461)*. Many mineral waters are flavored with fresh fruit and most are carbonated. Most public places, including office buildings, have water dispensers. California tap water is fresh, clean, and safe to drink.

Calistoga mineral water

## ALCOHOLIC DRINKS

Alcohol cannot be purchased or consumed in California by anyone under the age of 21. It is not uncommon for shops and bars to refuse service or admittance to anyone not carrying documents proving that they are at least 21 years old. Licensing hours, however, are relaxed; those old enough to drink legally can buy or consume alcohol from 6am until 2am, seven days a week.

Busy bar in Santa Barbara

## BEER

Anchor Steam Beer

Red Tail Ale

Liberty Ale

Beers of every variety – foreign, American, even homemade – have become highly desirable. The recent resurgence in small breweries across the United States can be credited to the success of San Francisco's Anchor Brewery, whose Steam Beer, Liberty Ale, and other products show that American beer need not be bland and tasteless. Other excellent local brews to look out for include Mendocino County's rich Boont Amber and Red Tail Ale.

Copying the self-brewing concept that began in Canada, a few Californians are now opening do-it-yourself breweries. Experts are on hand to assist with malting, boiling, carbonating, hopping, fermenting, and bottling. A personal-label brew takes two to six weeks to ferment. Microbrewery beers, brewed on the premises of a bar *(see p563)*, are also extremely popular.

# Choosing a Restaurant

The restaurants in this guide have been selected across a wide range of price categories for their exceptional food, good value, and interesting location. These listings highlight some of the factors that may influence your choice. Entries are listed by region, beginning with Los Angeles.

**PRICE CATEGORIES**
For a three-course meal for one, a glass of house wine, excluding tax and service charges.

$ under $25
$$ $25–$35
$$$ $35–$50
$$$$ $50–$70
$$$$$ over $70

# LOS ANGELES

### AIRPORT/WESTCHESTER Truxton's American Bistro
$$

*8611 Truxton Ave, Westchester, 90045* **Tel** *(310) 417-8789*                    **Road map** *inset A*

Fine meals at very affordable prices spells success for this American restaurant with simple decor – just a step above a coffee shop – and a lively bar. Regulars show up for their *fritto misto* appetizer, Thai Cobb salad, the buttermilk-fried chicken, spaghetti and meatballs, even a marinated tofu steak. Outrageously rich desserts.

### BEL AIR Vibrato Grill Jazz etc.
$$$$$

*2930 Beverly Glen Circle, 90077* **Tel** *310-474-9400*                    **Road map** *inset A*

This restaurant was conceived by jazz trumpeter Herb Alpert, and the jazz artists who play here Tuesday through Sunday add a hip edge to the American cuisine. Sip a martini at the bar and dine on prime beef, lamb chops, seafood, or mac and cheese with a bacon and brioche crust. Closed Mondays.

### BEVERLY HILLS Barney Greengrass
$$

*Barneys New York, 9570 Wilshire Blvd, 90212* **Tel** *(310) 777-5877*                    **Map** *5 F4*

Tucked into the swanky Barneys department store, this is not your average kosher deli, but you can still find your familiar corned beef or pastrami sandwich and a tremendous selection of smoked fish. The terrace provides a great view of downtown Beverly Hills, and lunch is popular with both celebrities and transplanted New Yorkers.

### BEVERLY HILLS Nate 'n Al
$$

*414 N Beverly Dr, 90210* **Tel** *(310) 274-0101*                    **Map** *5 F3*

It may be in one of the fanciest neighborhoods in town, but this unassuming traditional deli could just as easily be found on a Brooklyn side street – and that is the beauty of it. Homesick New Yorkers or anyone looking for simple treats such as pastrami on rye or potato knishes head to Nate 'n Al's, where the Beverly Hills glitz is left at the door.

### BEVERLY HILLS Da Pasquale Trattoria
$$$

*9749 Little Santa Monica Blvd, 90210* **Tel** *(310) 859-3884*                    **Map** *5 E3*

In the midst of ritzy Beverly Hills, Da Pasquale is a friendly, family-operated restaurant that celebrates the cuisine of Naples. Decorated with murals and vintage photos of Old Napoli, this place is famous for its thin-crust pizzas and excellent pastas. While it may attract movie industry folks from nearby offices, this is still a "regular" joint.

### BEVERLY HILLS Enoteca Drago
$$$

*410 N Cañon Dr, 90210* **Tel** *(310) 786-8236*                    **Map** *5 F3*

An *enoteca* is an Italian wine bar serving tapas-like snack foods, and this casual but sophisticated eatery, sheathed in rich wood, offers an abundance of interesting delicacies. Items such as deep-fried olives and grilled octopus are paired with a glass of wine from one of the most interesting lists in town. Full-sized entrées are also available.

### BEVERLY HILLS Kate Mantilini
$$$

*9101 Wilshire Blvd, 90210* **Tel** *(310) 278-3699*                    **Map** *6 F4*

With its casual but clubby ambience, endless menu, and convenient late hours, this cavernous eatery is a great place to visit. The fare is primarily American comfort food, and the kitchen does a fine job with dishes such as chicken potpie, mac and cheese, and meatloaf. It is a good spot to go after a movie or simply grab a martini after shopping.

### BEVERLY HILLS Crustacean
$$$$

*9646 Little Santa Monica Blvd, 90210* **Tel** *(310) 205-8990*                    **Map** *5 E3*

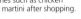

A modern LA interpretation of colonial Saigon, the decor at this trendsetting venue includes a floor-to-ceiling aquarium and a meandering glass-topped "stream" embedded into the marble floor. From the owners' "secret kitchen" come addictive garlic noodles, massive prawns, and crab simmered in Chardonnay, sake, and cognac.

### BEVERLY HILLS The Farm of Beverly Hills
$$$$

*439 N Beverly Dr, 90210* **Tel** *(310) 273-5578*                    **Map** *5 F3*

Bringing a refreshing bit of the Heartland to downtown Beverly Hills, the Farm provides a wide array of classic American foods, such as meatloaf and fried chicken, along with new twists on old favorites. It is an airy, unpretentious setting, with a great sidewalk patio for viewing the street scene. The brownie sundaes are great.

**Key to Symbols** *see back cover flap*

## BEVERLY HILLS Lawry's Prime Rib

$$$$

*100 N La Cienega Blvd, 90211* **Tel** *(310) 652-2827*

**Map** 6 C4

A beloved LA dining tradition since 1938, this is the place to go for classic prime rib with all the trimmings. The dining room is grand, but the service is humble. After a signature Spinning Bowl Salad, guests tuck into perfectly cooked prime rib, expertly carved at the table from a massive stainless steel cart. They now also serve salmon.

## BEVERLY HILLS Matsuhisa

$$$$

*129 N La Cienega Blvd, 90211* **Tel** *(310) 659-9639*

**Map** 6 B4

This flagship restaurant in sushi chef Nobu Matsuhisa's worldwide empire is one of LA's most influential eateries. Attracting lots of celebrities despite its ordinary decor, Matsuhisa specializes in modern sushi, incorporating diverse ethnic influences (the chef lived in Peru and uses many Latin ingredients). Ask for the *omakase* (chef's choice).

## BEVERLY HILLS The Grill on the Alley

$$$$

*9560 Dayton Way, 90210* **Tel** *(310) 276-0615*

**Map** 5 F3

One of Beverly Hills' premier power-lunching scenes, this is where studio heads hold court to discuss their next mega-deal over Cobb salads, perfectly grilled steaks, and pastas. The room reflects the traditional sensibilities of a classic chophouse, with high-backed leather booths and lots of polished wood. The service is among the best in the city.

## BEVERLY HILLS Spago

$$$$$

*176 N Cañon Dr, 90210* **Tel** *(310) 385-0880*

**Map** 5 F3

The flagship restaurant of celebrity chef Wolfgang Puck remains one of the most entertaining places in LA to dine. The stylish, contemporary dining room is always filled with recognizable faces, but the average suburban couple is not snubbed. The menu offers Californian cuisine, plus some traditional Austrian dishes.

## CENTURY CITY Clementine

$

*1751 Ensley Ave, 90024* **Tel** *(310) 552-1080*

**Map** 5 D4

Clementine, one of LA's best kept secrets, is a sensational little Parisian-style café, with colorfully draped tables spilling onto the sidewalk. In the morning, it is perfect for breakfast or simply a cup of cappuccino or hot chocolate. Lunch means delicious soups, salads, and sandwiches on freshly baked breads. It closes early in the evening.

## CENTURY CITY La Cachette

$$$$

*10506 Little Santa Monica Blvd, 90025* **Tel** *(310) 470-4992*

**Map** 4 C5

This lovely, flower-laden cottage – the name means "the hideaway" – is an ideal choice for an updated brand of French cooking that's elegant and delicious, but without the burden of heavy, cream-based sauces. Some vegetarian and vegan dishes, prepared with classic French technique, are also offered. One of the most charming restaurants in the city.

## CULVER CITY Tender Greens

$

*9523 Culver Boulevard, 90232* **Tel** *310-842-8300*

**Road map** inset A

Fresh produce from local farms including line-caught tuna, organic meats, fresh breads, desserts, and local wines and beer are the stars in a simple menu that changes with the seasons. Look for outstanding versions of Cobb salad and tuna niçoise. Closed Mondays.

## CULVER CITY Fraiche Restaurant

$$$

*9411 Culver Blvd, 90032* **Tel** *(310) 839-6800*

**Road map** inset A

This restaurant has received much praise from America's leading food critics. The food is rustic French and Italian, emphasizing market-fresh, seasonal ingredients. Signature dishes include *fruits de mer* and roasted chicken with wild mushrooms and onion *soubise*. It is open unusually late for LA - the bar menu is served until midnight.

## DOWNTOWN Philippe The Original

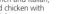

$

*1001 N Alameda St, 90012* **Tel** *(213) 628-3781*

**Map** 11 F3

One of the city's oldest restaurants (founded in 1908) and claiming to be the originator of the French dip sandwich, this downtown landmark serves beef, lamb, pork, and turkey versions of the sandwich. Settle into one of the communal tables and slather on some of the eatery's legendary hot mustard. Coffee is still 10 cents.

## DOWNTOWN Traxx

$$$$

*Union Station, 800 N Alameda St, 90012* **Tel** *(213) 625-1999*

**Map** 11 F3

Tucked into the historic Union Station – one of downtown's landmarks – this Art Deco restaurant is located just off the bustling concourse, but has a hidden outdoor courtyard in the rear. The dishes coming out of the open kitchen possess classic American themes, but are infused with modern touches that always keep the menu interesting.

## DOWNTOWN Cicada

$$$$$

*617 S Olive St, 90014* **Tel** *(213) 488-9488*

**Map** 11 D4

Possibly the grandest dining room in LA, Cicada is housed in the historic Oviatt Hotel, and its dramatic Art Deco design features soaring maple columns, lots of gold leaf, and Lalique glass. The cuisine is a blend between modern Italian and progressive American, with everything from *foie gras* to risotto turning up on the intriguing menu.

## DOWNTOWN Patina

$$$$$

*Walt Disney Concert Hall, 141 S Grand Ave, 90012* **Tel** *(213) 972-3331*

**Map** 11 D3

After many years on Melrose Avenue, this temple of gastronomy moved into the stunning Disney Concert Hall. In a room wrapped in a "curtain" of rich wood, one can expect the highest standards in LA dining: an indulgent caviar cart, major league wine list, and a menu laced with luxurious items. Book well ahead.

### DOWNTOWN Water Grill       $$$$$

*544 S Grand Ave, 90071* **Tel** *(213) 891-0900*     **Map** *11 D4*

Considered by many the city's premier seafood restaurant, this is a hybrid between an old-fashioned oyster bar and sophisticated dining room. The raw bar offers a bounty of wonderful fresh shellfish, and entrées include marvelous dishes such as peeky toe crab salad and slow poached loup de mer that showcase the freshest ingredients.

### GLENDALE La Cabañita    🏃 ♿ V   $

*3447 N Verdugo Rd, 91208* **Tel** *(818) 957-2711*     **Road map** *inset A*

Most Mexican restaurants in LA offer virtually interchangeable menus of tired dishes that are not particularly authentic. La Cabañita is different, serving classics such as *chilies en nogada* (chilies stuffed with meat, fruit, and nuts, finished with a walnut-pomegranate sauce). The small, festive-looking restaurant has a strong local following.

### HOLLYWOOD Canter's Deli and Restaurant    🏃 ♿ 🎵   $

*419 N Fairfax Ave, 90036* **Tel** *(323) 651-2030*     **Map** *7 D2*

Nobody claims Canter's is the best deli in the world, but its attributes are aplenty: it is open 24 hours, which is rare in LA; it offers big portions of classic kosher deli fare; it has a respectable bakery on the premises; and even has an adjacent lounge with live music.

### HOLLYWOOD The Gumbo Pot    🏃 ♿ 🎴 V   $

*Farmers Market, 6333 W 3rd St, 90036* **Tel** *(323) 933-0358*     **Map** *7 D3*

Finding an authentic taste of the Big Easy in LA is not a simple matter, but this little operation, hidden in the historic Farmers Market, is the genuine article. This casual, order-at-the-counter eatery is one of the few places to find authentic beignets and *muffaletta* or po'boy sandwiches, not to mention solid jambalaya and, of course, gumbo.

### HOLLYWOOD Pink's Famous Hot Dogs    🍴 🏃 🎴   $

*709 N La Brea Ave, 90038* **Tel** *(323) 931-4223*     **Map** *7 F1*

Folks line up in the middle of the night at this legendary Hollywood hot dog stand, where Orson Welles once ate 18 frankfurters. The classic chili dog is the favorite, but the menu now includes many specialty hot dogs, such as an Ozzy Osbourne (spicy Polish with the works), and bacon burrito hot dog wrapped in a tortilla.

### HOLLYWOOD Roscoe's House of Chicken & Waffles    🏃 ♿   $

*1514 N Gower St, 90028* **Tel** *(323) 466-7453*     **Map** *3 D5*

Southern-style fried chicken is accompanied by a stack of very tasty waffles, an unlikely combination that proves to be a winner. The menu also features "smothered" or deep-fried chicken livers, chicken sandwiches, collard greens, mac and cheese, and sweet potato pie. Open till 4am.

### HOLLYWOOD Cheebo    🏃 ♿ 🎵 🎴 V   $$

*7533 Sunset Blvd, 90046* **Tel** *(323) 850-7070*     **Map** *1 C5*

A splash of bright paint, reasonable prices, and a terrific rectangular pizza "slab" ordered by the foot makes this a quintessential Hollywood hangout. But Cheebo is no ordinary pizza joint. It also has sandwiches, a signature mesquite-grilled burger with applewood-smoked bacon, and dinner entrées such as rack of lamb and *osso buco*.

### HOLLYWOOD Fred 62    🏃 ♿ 🎴 V   $$

*1850 N Vermont Ave, 90027* **Tel** *(323) 667-0062*     **Road map** *inset A*

An institution on hip Vermont Avenue, Fred 62 has much of what you expect in a traditional American diner, right down to the toasters on the tables. Much of the food is predictable, but some dishes on the pun-filled menu are sophisticated. A diverse crowd, from young rockers to button-down businessmen.

### HOLLYWOOD Geisha House    ♿ 🎴 V   $$$

*6633 Hollywood Blvd, 90028* **Tel** *(323) 460-6300*     **Map** *2 B4*

In a city filled with trendy sushi bars, this is among the hottest, attracting a clientele that includes celebrities. A sake lounge (complete with sake sommeliers), sushi bar, and dining room are filled with patrons enjoying sushi, sashimi, and tempura, or larger plates such as Kobe beef steaks. A hip, dramatic design fits the vibrant scene.

### HOLLYWOOD Tantra    ♿   $$$

*3705 Sunset Blvd, 90026* **Tel** *(323) 663-9090*     **Road map** *inset A*

Tantra is one of the most sensuous Indian restaurants you are likely to encounter. On one side is a sleek, attractive bar, on the other a dining room featuring bold colors, and a dramatic use of contemporary and traditional themes. The modern Indian cuisine, such as green chicken tikka and salmon kebab, is addictive. Open till midnight.

### HOLLYWOOD Angelini Osteria    🏃 ♿ 🎴 V   $$$$

*7313 Beverly Blvd, 90036* **Tel** *(323) 297-0070*     **Map** *7 F2*

Gino Angelini has proven himself to be one of LA's top Italian chefs, turning out a combination of rustic dishes – his grandmother's lasagna with herb sauce is simply marvelous – plus fresher, newer creations. Daily specials run the gamut from veal kidneys to wood-roasted leg of pork. Unfortunately, the dining room is often crowded and noisy.

### HOLLYWOOD Animal    ♿   $$$$

*435 N. Fairfax Avenue, 90048* **Tel** *323-782-9225*     **Map** *7 D3*

Locals rave about the porkbelly sandwich and *foie gras* with biscuits and maple sausage gravy. Sweetbreads and pork star in a lot of dishes, alongside imaginative salads. Staff are professional and friendly and there's a huge selection of wines by the glass. Open until 2am weekends.

**Key to Price Guide** *see p568* **Key to Symbols** *see back cover flap*

## HOLLYWOOD A.O.C.

*8022 W 3rd St, 90048* **Tel** *(323) 653-6359*

**Map** *7 D3*

The acronym for *Appellation d'Origine Contrôlée* (the French regulatory system for wines), A.O.C. offers over 50 wines by the glass and a compendium of tapas-like small bites from around the Mediterranean. It also serves pâtés and sausages from the restaurant's own charcuterie bar, duck confit, fresh fish, salads, and unusual seasonal veg.

## HOLLYWOOD Ca' Brea

*346 S La Brea Ave, 90036* **Tel** *(323) 938-2863*

**Map** *7 F3*

Sharing a street with some of the city's top restaurants and art galleries, Ca' Brea is an appealing Italian restaurant. The multi-tiered, art-filled place is stylish and hip, but not at the expense of comfort. The menu offers some unique items such as a big ball of goat cheese wrapped in pancetta. For dessert, go for the velvety Italian custard.

## HOLLYWOOD Campanile

*624 S La Brea Ave, 90036* **Tel** *(323) 938-1447*

**Map** *7 F4*

Housed in a Mediterranean-style structure built by Charlie Chaplin, Campanile is a revered restaurant in Los Angeles. The open, airy design, with a fountain-laden courtyard, perfectly complements the simple yet stylish Mediterranean cooking. Thursday's grilled cheese sandwich night – with sophisticated renditions – is a favorite event.

## HOLLYWOOD Carlitos Gardel

*7963 Melrose Avenue, 90046* **Tel** *323-655-0891*

**Map** *6 A2*

A beef and wine-lover's paradise, this Argentine steakhouse also has excellent home-made pastas, chicken dishes, and signature garlic fries. Start with mixed tapas, move on to rolled beef filet stuffed with mushrooms and finish with *dulce de leche* pancakes. Excellent service. Live music on weekends.

## HOLLYWOOD Musso and Frank Grill

*6667 Hollywood Blvd, 90028* **Tel** *(323) 467-7788*

**Map** *2 B4*

Hollywood's oldest restaurant never seems to go out of style. It is a classic chophouse – mahogany and red leather – with good martinis and a menu of old-school favorites such as chicken potpie, Welsh rarebit, liver and onions, and steaks. The flannel cakes, served until 3pm, are legendary. It draws a diverse crowd of tourists and locals alike.

## HOLLYWOOD Providence

*5955 Melrose Ave, 90038* **Tel** *(323) 460-4170*

**Map** *8 B1*

Chef/owner Michael Cimarusti offers a sophisticated dining experience at this stylish seafood restaurant, where American classics share a menu with dishes heavy in French and Japanese influences. Purveyors in Maine call the chef every day to report on the catch – that is how dedicated he is to premium ingredients.

## LONG BEACH Parkers' Lighthouse

*435 Shoreline Village Dr, 90802* **Tel** *(562) 432-6500*

**Road map** *inset A*

With a real working lighthouse, this Long Beach landmark has great views of the harbor and the *Queen Mary (see pp134–5).* The menu showcases mesquite-grilled seafood, including salmon, swordfish, mahi mahi, and halibut. Nothing too fancy or cutting-edge, but a bucket of steamed clams on the patio is a great way to spend a summer evening.

## LONG BEACH Sir Winston's

*Queen Mary, 1126 Queen's Hwy, 90801* **Tel** *(562) 435-3511*

**Road map** *inset A*

A grand dining venue on the *Queen Mary,* this is one of Long Beach's most elegant and romantic restaurants. The menu continues the theme, offering caviar service, foie gras and lobster bisque, followed by rack of lamb and, finally, a chocolate soufflé. The Continental fare is traditional.

## MALIBU Duke's Malibu

*21150 Pacific Coast Hwy, 90265* **Tel** *(310) 317-0777*

**Road map** *inset A*

The delicious food and huge picture windows make this a popular ocean-front spot for both locals and visitors. The decor is inspired by the restaurant's namesake, veteran surfer Duke Kahanamoku, with surfing memorabilia lining the walls. Typical dishes include *panko*-crusted calamari and *Huli-Huli* chicken marinated in ginger, garlic, and soy sauce.

## MALIBU Gladstone's Malibu

*17300 Pacific Coast Hwy, 90272* **Tel** *(310) 573-0212*

**Road map** *inset A*

One of the top-grossing restaurants in the nation, this monster-sized beachfront seafood house is famous for its sprawling patio overlooking the Pacific. Big portions of chowder, grilled fish, lobster, *cioppino,* and Cajun-style blackened salmon may not be the world's finest, but most folks are thrilled with its quintessential LA feel.

## MALIBU Geoffrey's

*27400 Pacific Coast Hwy, 90265* **Tel** *(310) 457-1519*

**Road map** *inset A*

There is virtually no interior at this stunning restaurant perched high on a cliff above the Malibu coast. It is casual but high-end, with umbrella-laden tables and fire pits to keep its customers cozy. The California-American menu highlights include Maine lobster, Kobe beef, and Chilean sea bass.

## MALIBU Saddle Peak Lodge

*419 Cold Canyon Rd, 91302* **Tel** *(818) 222-3888*

**Road map** *inset A*

Tucked into the Santa Monica Mountains, this old hunting lodge feels a million miles from chaotic LA. The rustic, multi-tiered restaurant is filled with wall-mounted stag and moose heads, yet an air of elegance permeates the scene with romantic, candlelit tables dressed in white linen. There is no better game – elk, buffalo, or venison – in town.

### MARINA DEL REY C & O Trattoria

$

*31 Washington Boulevard, 90292* **Tel** *310-823-9491* **Road map** *inset A*

An old-fashioned, family-style Italian eatery with a serene garden setting and a friendly, attentive wait staff catering to diners' whims. Come hungry and enjoy portions big enough to share, endless garlic rolls, and traditional Italian fare. Try the popular Chianti carafes. Overlooks the beach.

### MARINA DEL REY The Cheesecake Factory

$$$

*4142 Via Marina, 90292* **Tel** *(310) 306-3344* **Road map** *inset A*

This chain is now found everywhere, but one of its most pleasant branches is right on the marina, where the outdoor terrace overlooks a bay. One can always expect massive portions of well-prepared food from a menu featuring everything from Thai chicken pasta to meatloaf to jambalaya, not to mention a dizzying array of cheesecakes.

### MARINA DEL REY Café Del Rey

$$$$

*4451 Admiralty Way, 90292* **Tel** *(310) 823-6395* **Road map** *inset A*

With its dockside location and expansive windows providing panoramic views of the marina, this is no casual chowder shack, but a sophisticated dining venue. Eclectic but largely Pacific Rim-inspired, the menu ranges from Cuban black bean soup to skate wings. Weekend brunch on the patio is an LA tradition.

### MARINA DEL REY Jer-Ne

$$$$$

*Ritz–Carlton Hotel, 4375 Admiralty Way, 90292* **Tel** *(310) 574-4333* **Road map** *inset A*

Jer-Ne is not what you might expect a Ritz-Carlton dining room to be. Its design is not traditional but cutting-edge, and its menu imports flavors from throughout the Pacific Rim to arrive at imaginative flavor combinations. A bento box of appetizers showcases the chef's innovation, and cherry blossoms or chrysanthemums are used as accents.

### MIDTOWN El Cholo

$$$

*1121 S Western Ave, 90006* **Tel** *(323) 734-2773* **Road map** *inset A*

One of the city's legendary Mexican restaurants, this has been around since 1927, serving what many believe is the best margarita in town. Also famous at this always-mobbed eatery are the fresh-made guacamole, crabmeat enchiladas, and blue corn tamales. The place has the warm, worn look of a true classic. Don't be put off by the neighborhood.

### MIDTOWN Chan Dara

$$$$

*310 N Larchmont Blvd, 90004* **Tel** *(323) 467-1052* **Map** *8 B2*

Known in some circles for its head-turning waitresses, the food here is also well worth commenting on. Housed in a little bungalow just north of Larchmont Village, Chan Dara is a charming, tastefully appointed restaurant where good Thai noodles, soups, satays, and curries can be enjoyed at prices that are every bit as agreeable.

### MIDTOWN Pizzeria Mozza

$$$$

*641 N. Highland Ave, 90036* **Tel** *(323) 297-0101* **Map** *8 A4*

No pizzeria has ever made such a splash as this designer pizzeria owned by three superstar restaurateurs. Creations like fontina, taleggio, and thyme pizza emerge from the stone oven within sight of the diners. Italian wines are modestly priced. Sister restaurant Osteria Mozza is open next door. Reserve early.

### MONROVIA LeRoy's Highland Restaurant

$

*523 W. Huntington Drive, 91016* **Tel** *626-357-5076* **Road map** *inset A*

A good choice for hearty breakfasts and lunches, LeRoy's makes up in portion size and service for what it lacks in atmosphere. This is the place to feed the family on budget, with giant omelets, hot turkey sandwiches, and juicy pork chops served with endless coffee. Expect long lines.

### PASADENA Yujean Kang's

$$

*67 N Raymond Ave, 91103* **Tel** *(626) 585-0855* **Road map** *inset A*

This is not your typical neighborhood Chinese restaurant. The dining room is elegant and tasteful, the service polished, and the menu unique. Innovative chef/owner Kang incorporates non-traditional ingredients, like Parma ham and salmon, into unique dishes prepared with classic Chinese technique. Delicious desserts and good wines.

### PASADENA Saladang Song

$$$

*383 S Fair Oaks Ave, 91105* **Tel** *(626) 793-5200* **Road map** *inset A*

Next door to its sister restaurant, Saladang, and with a traditional Thai menu, this establishment is architecturally acclaimed, as high walls with laser-cut ironwork enclose a sprawling patio. Here you can forgo the standard Thai fare, indulging instead in unique breakfasts, spicy fish cakes, and salmon with curry sauce.

### PASADENA Mi Piace

$$$$

*25 E Colorado Blvd, 91105* **Tel** *(626) 795-3131* **Road map** *inset A*

Always packed with a youthful crowd, this trattoria offers traditional pastas and pizzas, plus a few more innovative dishes. The desserts are famous and an adjoining lounge is a popular hangout. Mi Piace opens for breakfast and closes at 1am.

### PASADENA Shiro

$$$$

*1505 Mission St, South Pasadena, 91030* **Tel** *(626) 799-4774* **Road map** *inset A*

This pioneering Asian-French restaurant never grows old, and it remains very good indeed. The digs are modern and cool, as befits the snappy South Pasadena. The sophisticated California-Asian cuisine includes a signature whole deep-fried catfish with ponzu sauce.

**Key to Price Guide** *see p568* **Key to Symbols** *see back cover flap*

### PASADENA Parkway Grill

510 S Arroyo Pkwy, 91105 **Tel** (626) 795-1001 **Road map** inset A

A favorite since 1985, this place is nicknamed "Spago of Pasadena," thanks to its exhibition kitchen, wood-fired pizzas, and creative California cuisine. Southwestern influences abound, an adjacent organic garden ensures great salads, and wild game is a specialty. The wine list is solid and the garden-like setting is casually elegant.

### PASADENA The Royce

Langham Huntington Hotel & Spa, 1401 S Oak Knoll Ave, 91106 **Tel** (626) 568-3900 **Road map** inset A

For many years a stodgy hotel dining room, the restaurant at this historic hotel has upgraded its cuisine to the ranks of LA's finest. Luxury ingredients from around the world are flown in to benefit lucky diners selecting elegant renditions of California-French cuisine or opting for memorable multicourse tasting menus paired with fine wines.

### PLAYA DEL REY Bistro du Soleil

6805 Vista del Mar Lane, 90293 **Tel** (310) 823-1530 **Road map** inset A

This appealing neighborhood bistro offers a casual dining experience. The menu contains a mixture of classic French cuisine as well as interesting variations on the standards. Accompanying the dishes are a good selection of French and California wines available by the glass.

### REDONDO BEACH Chez Mélange

Palos Verdes Inn, 1611 S Catalina Ave, 90277 **Tel** (310) 540-1222 **Road map** inset A

Pioneering a sophisticated modern cuisine in the South Bay, this restaurant remains one of the area's most popular. The airy dining room, adjoining a modest inn, is relaxed and comfortable. The cuisine is eclectic, with inspirations ranging from Louisiana to Thailand to Italy, and there's even a Sushi bar.

### SAN PEDRO Raffaello's Italian Ristorante

400 S. Pacific Avenue, 90731 **Tel** 310-514-0900 **Road map** inset A

Simple, rustic dishes made with fresh ingredients and family-oriented staff keep regulars happy. Sample the roasted peppers, fried mozzarella, osso bucco, fettucine Alfredo, seafood risotto, and rich tiramisu. A solid wine list, fresh bread, and crisp salads. Good for groups and celebrations.

### SANTA MONICA Border Grill

1445 4th St, 90401 **Tel** (310) 451-1655 **Road map** inset A

A local institution founded by TV chefs Mary Sue Milliken and Susan Feniger, the Border Grill presents an alternative to the Sonora-style Mexican cuisine common in LA. While they may have incorporated some of their own ideas, their inspiration is derived from authentic recipes gathered throughout Mexico. The results are memorable.

### SANTA MONICA Chinois on Main

2709 Main St, 90405 **Tel** (310) 392-9025 **Road map** inset A

Despite the wild, wacky design of this pioneering Wolfgang Puck restaurant, the Asian-French fusion cuisine served here is serious stuff. The menu remains fresh and exciting after many years, and items such as Chinois (Chinese) chicken salad, Mongolian lamb chops, and Shanghai lobster with ginger-curry sauce have become cult classics.

### SANTA MONICA Drago

2628 Wilshire Blvd, 90403 **Tel** (310) 828-1585 **Road map** inset A

Superchef Celestino Drago's flagship restaurant offers a sleek, whitewashed decor, but much of his menu reverts to his rustic Sicilian roots. This is the kind of place you might order spaghetti with bottarga (pressed tuna roe) or pappardelle with pheasant and morel ragu. For dessert, try the panna cotta pudding.

### SANTA MONICA JiRaffe

502 Santa Monica Blvd, 90401 **Tel** (310) 917-6671 **Road map** inset A

More stylish than a bistro but without much pretension, this two-story restaurant's California cooking is among the best in town. Starters include items such as a roasted tomato tart or beet salad, while entrées involve items such as crispy-skinned salmon with parsnip purée and balsamic nage. Produce comes directly from the Farmers Market.

### SANTA MONICA The Lobster

1602 Ocean Ave, 90401 **Tel** (310) 458-9294 **Road map** inset A

At the foot of the Santa Monica pier, this slick fish house is lively and fun, with a wraparound terrace that provides wonderful sunset views. Naturally, lobster shows up in a variety of wonderful forms: lobster cocktail, lobster salad, classic live Maine, or the alternative Pacific spiny lobster. Other seafood and meats are also well prepared.

### SANTA MONICA Ocean Avenue Seafood

1401 Ocean Ave, 90401 **Tel** (310) 394-5669 **Road map** inset A

With a view of the ocean and an elegant atmosphere that suits virtually any occasion, Ocean Avenue's diverse menu offers a solid selection of multicultural seafood specialties from tuna tartare to lobster taquitos to paella. The raw bar always has a wide selection of oysters on hand, which seem to taste best on the patio.

### SANTA MONICA Mélisse

1104 Wilshire Blvd, 90401 **Tel** (310) 395-0881 **Road map** inset A

One of the city's most glamorous and serious restaurants, Mélisse specializes in modern French cuisine fueled by farm-fresh California ingredients. For a true gastronomic experience, consider a multicourse tasting menu paired with wines from a world-class cellar. Diners can also indulge in one of the best cheese boards in Los Angeles.

### SANTA MONICA Valentino

*3115 Pico Blvd, 90405* **Tel** *(310) 829-4313*  **Road map** *inset A*

Suave, sophisticated owner Piero Selvaggio has built his flagship restaurant into one of the finest Italian restaurants in the nation. Regulars do not even look at the menu, but defer to Selvaggio or his staff to create a memorable tasting experience. The wine list, literally the size of a phone book, is backed by a cellar of 200,000 bottles.

### SHERMAN OAKS Café Bizou

*14016 Ventura Blvd, 91423* **Tel** *(818) 788-3536*  **Road map** *inset A*

Housed in an inviting old bungalow, Bizou is very popular due to its solid California-French cooking and extremely reasonable prices. Soup or salad can be added for just a dollar and the corkage fee is only $2, encouraging guests to raid their own cellars. The menu offers everything from salmon to sweetbreads to short ribs. Reserve in advance.

### STUDIO CITY Art's Deli

*12224 Ventura Blvd, 91604* **Tel** *(818) 762-1221*  **Road map** *inset A*

Art's is a bit more expensive than many delis, but its affluent Valley clientele and patrons from nearby studios do not mind. The sandwiches, which are "works of art" according to the proprietor, are really too large for the average person to handle alone. In addition to the pastrami sandwiches, smoked fish and big breakfasts are favored here.

### STUDIO CITY Pinot Bistro

*12969 Ventura Blvd, 91604* **Tel** *(818) 990-0500*  **Road map** *inset A*

The first, and arguably the best, of a local chain of upscale bistros, this is an attractive restaurant offering good-value food. The varied menu includes fancy fare such as foie gras and lobster, but also plenty of bistro favorites such as steak frites and lamb shank. The staff are friendly, and the charming bar area is reminiscent of a true Parisian bistro.

### UNIVERSAL CITY Ca' del Sole

*4100 Cahuenga Blvd, 91602* **Tel** *(818) 985-4669*  **Road map** *inset A*

The dining room here resembles an old home, with a fireplace, hanging copper pots, and cozy booths. The patio, despite being separated from the heavy LA traffic by a single wall, feels like a Tuscan garden. The salads are fresh, pastas, such as ravioli stuffed with lobster or pumpkin, are first-rate, and the main courses are attractively priced.

### VAN NUYS 94th Aero Squadron

*16320 Raymer Street, 91406* **Tel** *818-994-7437*  **Road map** *inset A*

More loved for its atmosphere, with views of the planes taking off on the Van Nuys airport runways, than for its cuisine, this restaurant serves Sunday brunch, with lots of champagne, an omelet bar, fresh fruit, and excellent desserts. A popular choice is the *filet mignon* steak.

### VENICE Jody Maroni's Sausage Kingdom

*2011 Ocean Front Walk, 90291* **Tel** *(310) 822-5639*  **Road map** *inset A*

Although there are now franchises around town, this original venue is a true Venice Beach landmark. Jody's offers stellar sausages, served on freshly baked rolls like hot dogs. Among the dozen-plus varieties are innovations such as tequila-chicken or Bombay curried lamb. The boardwalk setting provides great people-watching opportunities.

### VENICE Rose Café

*220 Rose Ave, 90291* **Tel** *(310) 399-0711*  **Road map** *inset A*

Representative of the old bohemian Venice that is gradually disappearing in favor of rapid gentrification, the Rose Café has a roomy interior and a pleasant, sunny patio. An assortment of pastries, quiches, and salads are what the regulars return for. A cappuccino and a croissant, with a book on the patio, is a good way to spend time here.

### VENICE Joe's Restaurant

*1023 Abbot Kinney Blvd, 90291* **Tel** *(310) 399-5811*  **Road map** *inset A*

Chef/owner Joe Miller has more competition these days, but this Venice pioneer is still one of the neighborhood's favorites. His California cuisine has subtle French and Mediterranean themes, reflected in items such as potato-scaled red snapper with red wine sauce. Desserts are recommended at this sophisticated but laid-back eatery.

### VENICE BEACH Cantalini's Salerno Beach Restaurant

*193 Culver Boulevard, 90293* **Tel** *310-821-0018*  **Road map** *inset A*

Freshly made pastas and New York style pizzas, fresh seafood, and a good children's menu make this a great stop for families who want a casual, affordable place with excellent food. Try the signature gnocchi salerno with prosciutto, peas, and mushrooms. Just a block from the beach.

### WEST HOLLYWOOD Mandarette Café

*8386 Beverly Blvd, 90048* **Tel** *(323) 655-6115*  **Map** *6 C2*

A casual spin-off of a fancy Beverly Hills restaurant, this cozy Chinese café has lots of character and good taste, not to mention a value-oriented menu of intriguing items. Noodle dishes, fresh salads, curried chicken dumplings, and entrées such as Kung Pao chicken or unusual strawberry shrimp make a visit to Mandarette a rewarding experience.

### WEST HOLLYWOOD Bossa Nova Brazilian Cuisine

*685 N. Robertson Boulevard, 90069* **Tel** *310-657-5070*  **Map** *6 A2*

Order the Caipirinha drink of rum, lime, and sugar to go with grilled chicken, black beans, plantain, and salsa or salad with sea bass. Portions are enormous and there's always a line for outside tables along Robertson – prime people-watching territory.

**Key to Price Guide** *see p568* **Key to Symbols** *see back cover flap*

### WEST HOLLYWOOD Jinpachi

$$$

*8711 Santa Monica Blvd, 90069* **Tel** *(310) 358-9134*

**Map** *6 C1*

Served in an elegant dining room are impeccable fresh sushi and sashimi, plus desserts made on site by a skilled pastry chef. Specials include halibut *carpaccio*, Scottish salmon with jalapeño, and blue-fin tuna. Cooked dishes such as rock shrimp tempura are outstanding. On a warm night, dine outside on the lovely, candle-lit balcony.

### WEST HOLLYWOOD La Bohème

$$$

*8400 Santa Monica Blvd, 90069* **Tel** *(323) 848-2360*

**Map** *6 C1*

This Gothic-like space is an extremely romantic setting, with an oversized fireplace, Italian crystal chandeliers, and draping velvet curtains. Outside there is a patio area in a lush green setting. They offer an eclectic cuisine, which is always made with fresh ingredients from the farmers' market.

### WEST HOLLYWOOD The Spanish Kitchen

$$$

*826 N La Cienega Blvd, 90069* **Tel** *(310) 659-4794*

**Map** *6 C1*

This handsome hacienda-style restaurant, inspired by the diverse cooking methods of the southern regions of Mexico (*Chiapas*, *Yucatan*, and *Oaxaca*), offers many intriguing dishes. A lively cocktail bar dispensing flavored margaritas and the *mariscos y mescal* bar, are part of the festive atmosphere. Rather upscale for a Mexican eatery in LA.

### WEST HOLLYWOOD BOA Steakhouse

$$$$

*Grafton Hotel, 8462 Sunset Blvd, 90069* **Tel** *(323) 650-8383*

**Map** *6 C1*

BOA Steakhouse serves delicious aged USDA Prime beef. With its trendy modern design as a backdrop, this restaurant offers great steaks complemented by an assortment of unusual rubs, sauces, and condiments. Excellent seafood is on offer here, too. Specials at bargain prices are available.

### WEST HOLLYWOOD RH Restaurant

$$$$

*Andaz Hotel, 8401 W Sunset Blvd 90069* **Tel** *(323) 785-6090*

**Map** *6 C1*

A quiet, romantic spot in spite of its bustling open kitchen, this restaurant serves traditional Southern French cuisine prepared with local and organic ingredients. Menus change seasonally and use the freshest vegetables and organic beef, pork, chicken, fish, and shellfish. A fine wine selection is available.

### WEST HOLLYWOOD Wa Sushi & Bistro

$$$$

*1106 N La Cienega Blvd, 90069* **Tel** *(310) 854-7285*

**Map** *6 C1*

A trio of chefs from the renowned Matsuhisa *(see p568)* opened this little spot with a hillside view of the city. In addition to superb sushi and sashimi, these chefs use an old range behind the sushi bar to prepare some classic French-inspired sauces to go into their intricately cooked dishes.

### WEST HOLLYWOOD Ago

$$$$$

*8478 Melrose Ave, 90069* **Tel** *(323) 655-6333*

**Map** *6 C1*

Backed by Robert De Niro and film directors Tony and Ridley Scott, this celebrity-driven restaurant is packed all the time. Its fans suggest it serves some of the best Italian cuisine in the city, while its detractors complain about the service (if you are not a celebrity) and the high prices for average quality food. Great for stargazers and wine lovers.

### WEST HOLLYWOOD Jar

$$$$$

*8225 Beverly Blvd, 90048* **Tel** *(323) 655-6566*

**Map** *6 C2*

This restaurant takes the comfort foods of our youth – familiar items such as deviled eggs and pot roast – and presents them with a polished, sophisticated spin. Sauces like lobster Béarnaise enhance the steaks. With its zinc bar, deep wood tones, club chairs, and cork floor, Jar has a stylish retro feel to it.

### WEST HOLLYWOOD Lucques

$$$$$

*8474 Melrose Ave, 90069* **Tel** *(323) 655-6277*

**Map** *6 C2*

Chef/owner Suzanne Goin is one of the city's top chefs, and her menu is both contemporary and traditional. The food is hearty – main courses like braised beef ribs, richly sauced, for instance. The stylish dining room is carved out of the former carriage house of silent star Harold Lloyd.

### WEST HOLLYWOOD The Palm

$$$$$

*9001 Santa Monica Blvd, 90069* **Tel** *(310) 550-8811*

**Map** *6 A2*

A branch of the famous Manhattan eatery, The Palm is a serious steakhouse, and its dark wood and brass help it look the part. Caricatures of celebrities clutter the walls around diners tucking into pricy steaks and even pricier gargantuan lobsters. Cheesecake is flown in from New York. The service here sometimes feels rushed.

### WEST HOLLYWOOD Petrossian

$$$$$

*321 N Robertson Blvd, 90048* **Tel** *(310) 271-6300*

**Map** *6 C1*

Caviar lovers will find a bit of heaven here – poached eggs with caviar and smoked salmon, duck confit salad with caviar, sea bass with caviar, even dessert with caviar. For a splurge, go for the full caviar tasting menu. Service is impeccable as is the interior, with white chairs and lively paintings by local artists.

### WESTWOOD/WEST LA Apple Pan
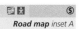

$

*10801 W Pico Blvd, 90064* **Tel** *(310) 475-3585*

**Road map** *inset A*

One of the city's most endearing places, this diner consists solely of a horseshoe-shaped counter, and you usually have to patiently wait for your turn. But the wait is worth it, particularly for the legendary burgers topped with Tillamook cheddar or the barbecue burger. For dessert, go for the apple pie or the delicious banana cream pie.

### WESTWOOD/WEST LA John O'Groats

*10516 Pico Blvd, 90064* **Tel** *(310) 204-0692* — **Road map** *inset A*

This old-fashioned little coffee shop serves some of the best breakfasts in LA, complete with perfect home-made biscuits. Popular items include pumpkin or blueberry pancakes and their own rendition of *huevos rancheros*. Fish and chips are a midday favorite at this friendly place. Expect a wait in the morning. They do not serve dinner.

### WESTWOOD/WEST LA Versailles

*10319 Venice Blvd, 90034* **Tel** *(310) 558-3168* — **Road map** *inset A*

The most popular spot for Cuban cooking in LA, this no-frills eatery has a big menu of Cuban specialties. Among the favorites are the shredded pork, *ropa vieja*, paella, and a garlic chicken dish that has diners literally lining up. Accompanied by black beans, rice, and plantains, these are filling meals often concluded with flan or bread pudding.

### WESTWOOD/WEST LA Bombay Café

*12021 W Pico Blvd, 90064* **Tel** *(310) 473-3388* — **Road map** *inset A*

There are some dishes on the menu of this Indian restaurant that are fiercely authentic, including some hard-to-find snack food. You may order the tandoori thali or South Indian thali for a complete meal. There are also some lighter, more refined creations that appeal to health-conscious Angelenos. They have a wonderful selection of chutneys.

### WESTWOOD/WEST LA La Serenata de Garibaldi

*10924 W Pico Blvd, 90064* **Tel** *(310) 441-9667* — **Road map** *inset A*

A casual spin-off of a venerable East LA restaurant, this place is always packed with loyal customers getting their fix of outstanding Mexican seafood. Dishes include ceviche, mahi mahi tacos, *gorditas* (thick cornmeal griddle cakes) stuffed with shrimp, or salmon in fresh spinach sauce. This kind of refined Mexican cooking is rare in LA.

### WESTWOOD/WEST LA Mori Sushi

*11500 W Pico Blvd, 90064* **Tel** *(310) 479-3939* — **Road map** *inset A*

This unassuming establishment is among the most elite purveyors of sushi in LA. The chef is a master at refined, highly aesthetic creations presented on unique plates fired in his own kiln. Rare species of fish, hand-picked at the fish market, are crafted into delicious, edible works of art. The personalized service is extremely gracious.

### WESTWOOD/WEST LA Tanino

*1043 Westwood Blvd, 90024* **Tel** *(310) 208-0444* — **Map** *4 A4*

Housed in a splendid building designed by legendary architect Paul Williams, Tanino's ornate dining room is filled with rich handcrafted wood, marble, and glass. But the architecture is not the only reason to dine here, as the menu features excellent risotto and pasta dishes, osso buco, and seafood. This is one of Westwood's best dining options.

## SOUTH CENTRAL CALIFORNIA

### BAKERSFIELD Wool Growers

*620 E 19th St, 93305* **Tel** *(661) 327-9584* — **Road map** *C5*

One of the most prominent restaurants in a region with a strong Basque heritage, Wool Growers serves plenty of side dishes – soup, beans, pasta, potatoes, and veggies – with every family-style meal. Choices for the main course include everything from lamb chops to oxtail stew to fried chicken. Portions are substantial and reasonably priced.

### BUELLTON The Hitching Post II

*406 E Hwy 246, 93427* **Tel** *(805) 688-0676* — **Road map** *B5*

Prominently featured in the movie *Sideways*, this place is famous for its oak wood-grilled steaks. At this Wine Country favorite, rustic charm is enhanced with a touch of elegance. Appetizers and sides are included, and the steaks and chops are complemented by a good selection of local wines (including their own).

### CAMBRIA Wild Ginger

*2380 Main St, 93428* **Tel** *(805) 927-1001* — **Road map** *B5*

Locals flock here for what many consider to be the best Asian and Pacific Rim food on the Central coast. The menu features dishes such as Singapore chicken satay, Thai chicken wings, and Vietnamese caramelized prawns. Wash it all down with wine, beer, or sake, and don't miss the desserts.

### CAYUCOS Hoppe's Garden Bistro

*78 N Ocean Ave, 93430* **Tel** *(805) 995-1006* — **Road map** *C5*

Possibly the busiest spot in the sleepy beach town of Cayucos, this acclaimed Central Coast eatery is famous for the chef/owner's signature dish: Cayucos red abalone in hazelnut-mango butter. The extensive menu also offers every-thing from prime rib to seared bison to wild king salmon. There is a reasonable Chef's menu. Closed Mon & Tue.

### LOS OLIVOS Los Olivos Wine Merchant Café

*2879 Grand Ave, 93441* **Tel** *(805) 688-7265* — **Road map** *C5*

Located in the heart of quaint Los Olivos, this is an ideal spot to recharge after a day's wine tasting. A rustic little dining room is paired with a charming wisteria-covered sidewalk patio. For nibbling, there are pizzas, olives, and artisan cheeses, and for serious appetites order pastas, lamb shank, or pot roast. There is also a wine shop and wine bar.

## MONTECITO Lucky's

$$$$$

*1279 Coast Village Rd., 93108* **Tel** *(805) 565-7540*                **Road map** *C5*

Lucky's has the whiff of old money about it that permeates most of Montecito. Local millionaires come here to get a decent steak and a martini, with a healthy side of Rat Pack ambiance. Lucky's serves some of the best food in the area. In addition to steaks with various sides, the desserts are out of this world, and Sunday brunch is outstanding.

## MORRO BAY Windows on the Water

$$$

*699 Embarcadero, 93442* **Tel** *(805) 772-0677*                **Road map** *B5*

The inviting name says it all, as generous windows provide striking views of the water and Morro Rock from every table of this big, airy restaurant. People love the crab cakes with jalapeño aïoli, and cedar-planked salmon, Pacific bouillabaisse, and steaks complete the menu. There is live jazz. Opens at 5pm daily.

## OJAI Suzanne's Cuisine

$$$

*502 West Ojai Ave., 93023* **Tel** *(805) 640-1961*                **Road map** *C5*

Suzanne's was one of the first restaurants to take the local cuisine in Ojai up a notch. Now the chef's commitment to local, organic ingredients, prepared with a French twist, seems almost typically Californian. Suzanne's is considered the best restaurant in town by many, including celebrities who have made Ojai a second home.

## PASO ROBLES Bistro Laurent

$$$$

*1202 Pine St, 93446* **Tel** *(805) 226-8191*                **Road map** *B5*

Bistros and the Wine Country go together marvelously, as is the case with this place. The modern mustard-colored dining room with white linen-topped tables is tucked into an old brick structure and the patio is a good place for sipping local wines. The menu offers French bistro favorites such as roasted chicken, as well as California dishes.

## PISMO BEACH Splash Café

$

*197 Pomeroy Ave, 93449* **Tel** *(805) 773-4653*                **Road map** *B5*

Exactly the sort of funky beachside spot you'd expect here, Splash Café serves outstanding clam chowder (try it in the sourdough bread bowl) and baskets of fish 'n' chips to the town's local surfers, who happily line up for the grub. There's rarely a table inside, but grab a seat on the seawall outside and watch the ocean while sipping chowder.

## SAN LUIS OBISPO Buona Tavola

$$$

*1037 Monterey St, 93401* **Tel** *(805) 545-8000*                **Road map** *B5*

Next to the historic Fremont Theatre, this is a cosmopolitan, art-filled trattoria with a lovely garden patio that is more serene than the bustling interior. The moderately priced menu offers a wide choice of antipasti, pastas such as agnolotti stuffed with scampi in saffron sauce, steaks, and chicken. A good wine list is featured here as well.

## SAN LUIS OBISPO Novo Restaurant and Lounge

$$$

*726 Higuera St., 93401* **Tel** *(805) 543-3986*                **Road map** *B5*

A surprisingly modern, urban space in the middle of quaint downtown San Luis Obispo, Novo specializes in tapas with a twist. Fusing South American and Southeast Asian flavors with Spanish classics, the kitchen turns out small bites like prawns *moqueca* (a Brazilian stew) and *piquillo* (stuffed pepper) and cheese empanadas with chutney.

## SANTA BARBARA La Super-Rica

$

*622 N Milpas St, 93103* **Tel** *(805) 963-4940*                **Road map** *C5*

The devoted locals who patiently stand in line at this little roadside shack can tell you it is one of their city's true culinary treasures. The blackboard menu features simple Mexican street vendor fare. Tacos, made from freshly-grilled tortillas, are filled with marinated pork, beef, chicken, or chorizo. Even super-chef Julia Child loved this place.

## SANTA BARBARA Cold Spring Tavern

$$

*5995 Stagecoach Rd, 93105* **Tel** *(805) 967-0066*                **Road map** *C5*

A must-stop for anyone in the area, this longtime local favorite and former stagecoach stop is popular with motorcyclists cruising the mountains behind Santa Barbara. Though a bit of a drive from town, it's worth it both for the food (outstanding chilies at lunch and inventive meat dishes for dinner) and the old California miner feel to the place.

## SANTA BARBARA Arigato Sushi

$$$

*1225 State St, 93101* **Tel** *(805) 965-6074*                **Road map** *C5*

Consistently voted the best sushi restaurant in town, Arigato is a sure hit for any sushi lover. In addition to super-fresh fish, the restaurant features a few inventive rolls, plus dozens of cooked options, including a delicious teriyaki chicken and several light and tasty tempura dishes.

## SANTA BARBARA Brophy Bros. Restaurant & Clam Bar

$$$

*119 Harbor Way, 93109* **Tel** *(805) 966-4418*                **Road map** *C5*

This dockside eatery with great harbor views is where big groups of locals gather for well-prepared fresh fish. Solo diners cozy up to the clam bar for raw shellfish, bowls of legendary chowder, or *cioppino*. Drawing a diverse crowd, fishermen and office workers alike are found waiting for tables.

## SANTA BARBARA Emilio's Ristorante & Bar

$$$

*324 W Cabrillo Blvd, 93101* **Tel** *(805) 966-4426*                **Road map** *C5*

One of the area's more romantic restaurants, Emilio's is noted for its charming patio, friendly staff, and its very own organic farm. The seasonal menu features many Italian specialties but is eclectic enough to include lobster, corn, and potato chowder. Portions are generous and the candlelit, art-filled dining room is delightful.

### SANTA BARBARA The Palace Grill

*8 E Cota St, 93101* **Tel** *(805) 963-5000*

**Road map** *C5*

If you fancy a traditional New Orleans-style good time, there is no better place to be. Start with a Cajun martini or Dixie beer with your crawfish popcorn or gumbo, move on to *étouffée* or blackened redfish flown in from the Big Easy, and finish with Banana Foster. The Palace Grill also has zydeco music on Saturday nights.

### SANTA BARBARA Trattoria Vittoria

*30 East Victoria St., 93103* **Tel** *(805) 962-5014*

**Road Map** *C5*

This trattoria is run by a traditional Italian family and the food reflects this. The pasta is handmade in house, the soups are made from scratch, and the sauces have the sort of layered, deep flavors that come from cooking over multiple days. In addition to all this, it is one of the most reasonably priced restaurants in the area.

### SANTA BARBARA Bouchon

*9 W Victoria St, 93101* **Tel** *(805) 730-1160*

**Road map** *C5*

A classy, inviting bistro that exudes a warm, comfortable aura, Bouchon offers a terrific array of French classics. Favorites include bourbon and maple-glazed duck, buffalo tartare, and warm chocolate molten lava cake. They offer expert advice on pairing wine with food.

### SANTA BARBARA Downey's

*1305 State St, 93101* **Tel** *(805) 966-5006*

**Road map** *C5*

More restrained than many State Street eateries, Downey's represents a classic California cuisine experience in a simply elegant, unstuffy dining room. Crab, lobster, and mussels from local waters often appear on the daily-changing menu, and meats are finished with uncomplicated but perfect sauces.

### SANTA BARBARA The Hungry Cat

*1134 Chapala St., 93101* **Tel** *(805) 884-4701*

**Road Map** *C5*

It can be strangely difficult to find good seafood in California's beach cities. In Santa Barbara, look no further than the Hungry Cat. Small and always crammed, this place serves the best oysters, fried shrimp, and fish and chips in town. It's also one of Santa Barbara's best people-watching spots.

### SANTA BARBARA Louie's California Bistro

*Upham Hotel, 1404 de la Vina St, 93101* **Tel** *(805) 963-7003*

**Road map** *C5*

A charming, unfussy restaurant tucked into a historic boutique hotel (founded in 1871), this is a place to score some exceptional California cuisine at reasonable prices. At night it turns quietly romantic, and the patio is lovely on a summer evening. Gourmet pizzas and pastas share a menu with regional American classics.

### SANTA BARBARA Olio e Limone

*17 W Victoria St, 93101* **Tel** *(805) 899-2699*

**Road map** *C5*

This intimate, sparingly appointed dining room is one of the city's favorite trattorias. Some authentic Sicilian specialties are offered, while other pastas are more familiar, and the veal and chicken dishes are good bets. The Italian staff are gracious and the wine list is very respectable. They now also serve cocktails and spirits.

### SANTA BARBARA Bella Vista

*Four Seasons Biltmore Hotel, 1260 Channel Dr, 93108* **Tel** *(805) 565-8237*

**Road map** *C5*

This is where locals come for special occasions – with large windows overlooking the ocean, Bella Vista just feels like a treat. In addition to the popular Sunday brunch, sunset dinners are spectacular here. Between the view and the menu – focused heavily on local produce and seafood with an Italian twist – it's hard to do better for a romantic evening.

### SANTA BARBARA Julienne

*138 E. Canon Perdido, 93101* **Tel** *(805) 845-6488*

**Road Map** *C5*

With a focus on sustainably sourced, local ingredients, Julienne's menu changes daily. The commitment to quality is evident in delicious meals anchored by fresh seafood or meat. The restaurant has Santa Barbara's only traditional French *charcuterie*. Although not cheap, Julienne's prix-fixe menus are incredible value, especially when paired with wine.

### SANTA YNEZ Trattoria Grappolo

*3687 Sagunto St, 93460* **Tel** *(805) 688-6899*

**Road map** *C5*

A bustling mural-laden trattoria with good service, a wide selection of pizzas, generously plated pastas, and hearty main courses, too. The wine list, with moderate prices, honors both local wineries and esteemed vintages from the Tuscan countryside. The traditional chocolate tartufo and tiramisu are among the desserts.

### SOLVANG Solvang Restaurant

*1672 Copenhagen Dr., 93463* **Tel** *(800)-654-0541*

**Road Map** *C5*

You must go to at least one corny Scandinavian-themed restaurant while in Solvang, and this one is the best. People travel for miles for the restaurant's popular *aebleskiver*, a sort of Danish pastry topped with raspberry jam and powdered sugar. For those just passing through, the restaurant has a little window on the street where it sells *aebleskiver* to go.

### SOLVANG Root 246

*420 Alisal Rd., 93463* **Tel** *(805) 686-8681*

**Road Map** *C5*

Celebrity chef Bradley Ogden was brought in by the local Chumash tribe to open Root 246 out of what was The Meadows restaurant. Ogden has turned the spot into an oasis of contemporary design and food in the middle of kitschy Solvang. The hand-cut fries, braised meats, and fresh local salads are the perfect end to a day's wine tasting.

**Key to Price Guide** *see p568* **Key to Symbols** *see back cover flap*

### VENTURA Andria's Seafood Restaurant & Market

*1449 Spinnaker Dr, 93001* **Tel** *(805) 654-0546*       **Road map** *C5*

This favorite with locals, right on the harbor, is the ultimate in casual dining. Go to the counter, order up anything from fish and chips to lobster or whatever the fishing boats have delivered that day. Take it outdoors or sit inside. No fuss, no table cloths, no dress-up – just the freshest seafood at affordable prices.

### VENTURA Watermark on Main

*598 East Main St., 93001* **Tel** *(805) 643-6800*       **Road map** *C5*

Owned by a successful music producer, the Watermark was initially better known for its upstairs lounge than its menu. The perfectly cooked steaks and fresh, local seafood served in the stunning downstairs dining room soon changed that. The Watermark is now as popular for a special occasion dinner as it is for a Saturday night out in downtown Ventura.

# ORANGE COUNTY

### ANAHEIM Mimi's Café

*1400 S. Harbor Boulevard, 92802* **Tel** *714-956-2223*       **Road map** *D6*

An institution in the neighborhood, Mimi's serves standard American classics such as eggs Benedict, quiche, flat iron steak, chicken pot pie, broiled salmon, crab cakes, bread pudding, and chocolate brownies. A good family choice close to the Disneyland® resort.

### ANAHEIM Goofy's Kitchen

*Disneyland Hotel, 1150 Magic Way, 92803* **Tel** *(714) 781-3463*       **Road map** *D6*

A popular attraction for kids at the Disneyland® Hotel, Goofy's Kitchen offers a kid-friendly buffet, with items such as Mickey Mouse-shaped waffles, peanut butter and jelly pizza, and chocolate cake. Naturally, Goofy and all his friends are present to keep the kids busy. This place provides a taste of Disneyland® even before entering the park.

### ANAHEIM Napa Rose

*Disney's Grand Californian Hotel, 1600 S. Disneyland Dr, 92803* **Tel** *(714) 781-3463*   **Road map** *D6*

Don't expect to see Mickey or Minnie in this fine-dining restaurant. It's a well-heeled gourmet crowd that flocks here to rediscover the freshness and flavor of the Californian wine country with its farm-fresh cheeses and herbs, and world-renowned vintages. A cut above many Disney® Park eateries and critically acclaimed.

### ANAHEIM Anaheim White House Restaurant

*887 S Anaheim Blvd, 92805* **Tel** *(714) 722-1381*       **Road map** *D6*

The grand façade of this old home, with colonial columns and a sprawling veranda for after-dinner drinks, hints at the elegant, romantic interior. A refined Northern Italian cuisine with indulgent French influences and occasional Asian accents is artfully presented, from soup to soufflés. Intimate rooms are named after presidents.

### ANAHEIM Mr. Stox

*1105 E Katella Ave, 92805* **Tel** *(714) 634-2994*       **Road map** *D6*

One of Orange County's top tables, its polished wood-clad dining rooms have been drawing gourmets since 1968: The menu is filled with familiar dishes such as lobster bisque, grilled salmon, and filet mignon, all prepared with subtle modern twists. The wine list, supported by a 25,000-bottle cellar, is nationally recognized.

### BUENA PARK Mrs. Knott's Chicken Dinner Restaurant

*8039 Beach Blvd, 90620* **Tel** *(714) 220-5080*       **Road map** *D6*

For natives of Southern California, this place is a part of growing up. In fact, Mrs. Knott started serving her chicken in 1934, and millions of people have been lining up ever since. Biscuits, mashed potatoes, gravy, and veggies come with the chicken, which is best followed by Knott's signature boysenberry pie. Non-chicken dishes are served too.

### CATALINA ISLAND The Landing Bar & Grill

*El Encanto Market Place, Avalon, 90704* **Tel** *(310) 510-1474*       **Road map** *C6*

Sitting on the patio with a cold drink overlooking the blue Pacific is what being on Catalina Island is all about. Sandwiches and quesadillas are offered at lunch, while dinner is geared more to pastas, steaks, and grilled fish. A big selection of international beers and microbrews is available, including a local Catalina one, along with stronger drinks.

### CORONA DEL MAR Five Crowns

*3801 E Pacific Coast Hwy, 92965* **Tel** *(949) 760-0331*       **Road map** *D6*

Old fashioned but timeless, this Tudor-style dining house is homey but elegant, with rich wood, crackling fireplaces, and crisp white linen. Beef is the specialty of the house, particularly prime rib, but you will also find rack of lamb, duck, and seafood. Locals enjoy Sunday brunch and the garden is particularly appealing when the weather permits.

### COSTA MESA Memphis Café

*2920 S Bristol St, 92626* **Tel** *(714) 432-7685*       **Road map** *D6*

The spare decor is straight out of the 1960s, and this is a favored spot of the young, hip crowd. The cuisine is surely inspired by the jazz-crazed city for which it is named, but most dishes are updated versions of traditional soul food favorites. Pulled-pork sandwiches, jambalaya, gumbo, and catfish omelets (for breakfast) are menu highlights.

### COSTA MESA Scott's Restaurant & Bar

$$$$

*3300 Bristol St, 92626* **Tel** *(714) 979-2400* — **Road map** *D6*

A San Francisco import, this seafood house offers a warm, inviting dining room with a big central chandelier and prominent fireplace. Mostly old school, the kitchen turns out classics such as oysters Rockefeller, lobster bisque, and *cioppino*, along with USDA Prime steaks with optional blue cheese on top. Finish with bread pudding or cheesecake.

### COSTA MESA Mastro's Steakhouse
$$$$$

*633 Anton Blvd, 92626* **Tel** *(714) 546-7405* — **Road map** *D6*

The sophisticated and contemporary decor exudes the ambiance of fine dining, with subdued lighting, marble floors, and 18,000 bottles of wine. Prime steaks are the house specialty but the menu also includes prime rib and fresh seafood. There is live music every evening.

### HUNTINGTON BEACH The Californian
$$$$

*Hyatt Regency Huntington Beach Resort & Spa* **Tel** *(714) 845-4775* — **Road map** *D6*

Upscale contemporary Californian cuisine accompanied by spectacular sunsets in a richly decorated dining room with attentive service. Ask for the made-to-order dessert first, then relax and enjoy entrées like chili-rubbed rib eye, lobster rigatoni, or sesame-crusted scallops. There is also a large selection of Californian wines.

### IRVINE Javier's Cantina & Grill
$$

*45 Fortune Dr, #400, 92618* **Tel** *(949) 872-2101* — **Road map** *D6*

Regional homestyle Mexican cuisine is served in a sophisticated setting in the Irvine Spectrum Center mall. Favorites here include Dungeness crab enchiladas in tomatillo sauce, tamales, and carnitas. The bar, boasting a huge selection of tequilas and dispensing potent margaritas to a hip, good-looking crowd, is always packed.

### IRVINE Bistango

$$$$

*19100 Von Karman Ave, 92612* **Tel** *(949) 752-5222* — **Road map** *D6*

Irvine's most prominent restaurant, Bistango is tucked into the stylish Atrium Building, where rotating modern art, a lively bar scene, and nightly live jazz are part of the vibe. Befitting the environment, the cuisine is contemporary California, including pizzas, ahi tuna, and surf 'n' turf paella. It has a winning wine list, too.

### LAGUNA BEACH Zinc Café & Market
$$

*350 Ocean Ave, 92651* **Tel** *(949) 494-6302* — **Road map** *D6*

This combination café and market is open for breakfast and lunch. Locals and visiting picnickers stock up on salads, soups, and gourmet items. Specialties include Tuscan white bean soup, vegetarian chili, and personal-size pizzas. An umbrella-laden garden patio makes this an ideal place to recharge before hitting the beach or the boutiques.

### LAGUNA BEACH 230 Forest Avenue Restaurant & Bar
$$$

*230 Forest Avenue, 92651* **Tel** *949-494-2545* — **Road map** *D6*

A bistro and martini bar across from the beach in downtown, this intimate spot specializes in fresh seafood. Try the large chopped seafood salad, or rich Chilean sea bass, and end with the chocolate croissant bread pudding. The wine list and martini selections are wide.

### LAGUNA BEACH The Common Table Kitchen and Drink
$$$

*370 Glenneyre, 92651* **Tel** *(949) 494-8686* — **Road map** *D6*

Rustic decor and industrial accents are the setting for a globally influenced but locally sourced cuisine at this restaurant. Chef Ryan Adams's farm-to-fork philosophy influence both the menu and the laid-back casual ambience. Dinner only.

### LAGUNA BEACH Las Brisas
$$$

*361 Cliff Dr, 92652* **Tel** *(949) 497-5434* — **Road map** *D6*

A popular place to get married, this sprawling coastal restaurant offers spectacular ocean views. The cuisine is upscale Mexican, including specialties such as ceviche, red snapper stuffed with shrimp, and a bouillabaisse-like seafood stew. A wide array of tequilas is offered and the bar is adept at potent margaritas, ensuring a festive vibe.

### LAGUNA BEACH Ti Amo
$$$

*31727 S Coast Hwy, 92651* **Tel** *(949) 499-5350* — **Road map** *D6*

Ti Amo is pure romance, thanks to a roaring fire, flattering candlelight, copious flowers, and classical guitar music. Beyond the Tuscan villa-atmosphere, the menu delivers high-quality Italian-Mediterranean fare such as rigatoni with tomato sauce, and grilled salmon and artichoke hearts.

### LAGUNA BEACH Splashes
$$$$

*Surf & Sand Resort, 1555 S Coast Hwy, 92651* **Tel** *(888) 869-7569* — **Road map** *D6*

Tucked into one of Orange County's top resorts, this restaurant offers dramatic ocean views from virtually every table, but the best seating is on the palm-shaded terrace overlooking the crashing waves. Innovative, seasonal, and always interesting.

### LAGUNA BEACH Studio
$$$$$

*Montage Resort & Spa, 30801 S Coast Hwy, 92651* **Tel** *(949) 715-6420* — **Road map** *D6*

Housed in a freestanding building on the grounds of the exclusive Montage Resort, Studio is coveted for its sensational ocean views and exquisite cuisine. It feels like an elegant beachfront home and the menu, eschewing heavy sauces, reflects a modern French approach with imaginative uses of artisanal California ingredients.

### NEWPORT BEACH Tradition By Pascal

*1000 N Bristol St, 92660* **Tel** *(949) 263-9400*  **Road map** *D6*

Chef/owner Pascal Olhats prepares some of the finest French cuisine in Orange County. Specialties such as sautéed *foie gras*, rabbit with wild mushrooms, and *coq au vin* are served in an elegant, yet welcoming dining room. An adjoining gourmet shop offers a selection of cheeses, pâtés, and other picnic items.

### NEWPORT BEACH The Ritz Restaurant & Garden

*880 Newport Center Dr, 92660* **Tel** *(949) 720-1800*  **Road map** *D6*

For more than two decades, this restaurant has been a favorite for social and business entertaining. The signature "carousel" is a Lazy Susan for the table, loaded with smoked fish, pâtés, steak tartare, and more. Entrées include rack of lamb, steak Diane, and other Continental dishes. There is live entertainment Wed–Sat nights.

### ORANGE The Hobbit

*2932 E Chapman Ave, 92669* **Tel** *(714) 997-1972*  **Road map** *D6*

This is one of Southern California's most unique restaurants. This place specializes in seven-course prix-fixe feasts, which begin with hors d'oeuvres and champagne in the wine cellar before moving upstairs for substantial French-Continental dishes. There's also a tour of the kitchen to meet the chef. Reservations required.

### SAN CLEMENTE Iva Lee's

*555 N El Camino Real, 92672* **Tel** *(949) 361-2855*  **Road map** *D6*

Iva Lee's celebrates the cooking of the South, with beautiful presentations of dishes like fried green tomatoes layered with goat's cheese, and grilled por . chop with a brown sugar-pecan glaze. The setting, enhanced by live blues and jazz acts from Thu–Sat, possesses the warmth of the jambalaya and sweetness of the bananas foster. Dinner only.

### SAN JUAN CAPISTRANO Cedar Creek Inn

*26860 Ortega Hwy, 92675* **Tel** *(949) 240-2229*  **Road map** *D6*

A good looking Spanish mission-inspired design contributes to the inviting, casually elegant location. The extensive menu is straightforward and moderately priced, with everything from pastas to fish and chips and rack of lamb to prime rib. The patio has a view of Mission San Juan Capistrano. Live entertainment Fri & Sat.

### SANTA ANA Antonello Ristorante

*3800 S Plaza Dr, 92704* **Tel** *(714) 751-7153*  **Road map** *D6*

From businessmen power-lunching to couples dining under the stars, this is a highly revered restaurant. A very impressive wine list accompanies a menu that boasts mostly traditional dishes such as spaghetti alla puttanesca, *cioppino*, scampi, and risotto laced with Gorgonzola. The ambience, like the menu, is Old World.

### SUNSET BEACH Harbor House Café

*16341 Pacific Coast Hwy, 90742* **Tel** *(562) 592-5404*  **Road map** *D6*

This roadside café is decorated with surfing and nautical gear, movie posters, and other collectables. The cluttered decor gives the place an inviting, lived-in look. Slide into a cozy booth and enjoy one of nearly 30 omelets, great burgers, malts, and other all-American food from the extensive, modestly priced menu. Open 24 hours.

### TUSTIN Zov's Bistro

*17440 E 17th St, 92780* **Tel** *(714) 838-8855*  **Road map** *D6*

A beloved local favorite bistro, café, and bakery in a contemporary setting. The Mediterranean menu features influences from Greece, Italy, Lebanon, Morocco, and beyond. Prices are reasonable, a versatile wine list is provided, and the on-site bakery turns out an impressive array of cakes, tarts, cookies, and breads.

## SAN DIEGO COUNTY

### CORONADO Mistral

*Loews Coronado Bay Resort, 4000 Coronado Bay Rd, 92118* **Tel** *(619) 424-4000*  **Road map** *D6*

With panoramic views of the Coronado Bay bridge and the glistening city skyline, the former Azzura Point is a dazzling contemporary room that is not overly formal and offers a diverse Californian-Mediterranean menu. Linger over the view with fine wine, cheeses, and winning desserts.

### CORONADO 1500 Ocean

*Hotel Del Coronado, 1500 Orange Ave, 92118* **Tel** *(619) 522-8490*  **Road map** *D6*

After 36 years, the Prince of Wales Grille was replaced by this beautiful restaurant under chef Brian Sinnott. The menu features the freshest Southland coastal cuisine, with selections from Santa Ynez to Cabo San Lucas, and wines to match. Dine on the terrace for sunset views. Dinner only.

### DEL MAR Kitchen 1540

*L'Auberge Del Mar Resort & Spa, 1540 Camino Del Mar, 92014* **Tel** *(858) 793-6460*  **Road map** *D6*

Relaxed, modern, and comfortable, Kitchen 1540 has an open presentation kitchen, wine bar, and outdoor dining terrace cooled by ocean breezes. The varied menu offers American farm-to-plate cuisine with traditional classics and innovative creations.

### DEL MAR Market Restaurant & Bar

*3702 Via de la Valle, 92014* **Tel** *(858) 523-0007*                    **Road map** *C6*

Hearty dishes prepared with finesse and using the freshest local vegetables and greens make this sleek, yet cozy, restaurant with views of the Del Mar Racetrack a popular dining spot. Their steaks draw rave reviews. Dine inside at a table, at the cocktail bar, or at the sushi bar.

### LA JOLLA Harry's Coffee Shop

*7545 Girard Avenue, 92037* **Tel** *(858) 454-7381*                    **Road Map** *D6*

Friendly servers who seem to have been here forever and big portions of breakfast comfort food add up to a typical old-timer coffee shop in an area of trendy shops. You'll find creamed chipped beef, pancakes, bagels, bacon and eggs, and fair prices that keep locals coming back.

### LA JOLLA Living Room Café

*1010 Prospect Avenue, 92037* **Tel** *(858) 459-1187*                    **Road Map** *D6*

An extensive menu at breakfast, lunch, and dinner includes freshly made waffles and bagels, soups, sandwiches such as turkey lasagna, tuna melt with grilled vegetables and olive tapenade, fresh fruit tarts, cheesecakes, and a huge selection of cookies and coffees.

### LA JOLLA Alfonso's of La Jolla

*1251 Prospect Ave, 92037* **Tel** *(858) 454-2232*                    **Road map** *D6*

A La Jolla institution, this family-operated Mexican eatery unites a fresh Pacific catch and the spices of Mexican cooking in a casual, festive setting. Shrimp *ceviche*, lobster fajitas, and lobster burritos join familiar chicken and beef dishes on the menu. Sitting on the front patio, people-watching over a margarita, is a long-standing tradition.

### LA JOLLA Roppongi

*875 Prospect St, 92037* **Tel** *(858) 551-5252*                    **Road map** *D6*

With a huge list of Pacific Rim-style tapas, sushi, and sashimi, as well as innovative specialties inspired by every corner of Asia, Roppongi's menu is one of the most intriguing in San Diego. For lunch, cross-cultural bento boxes are offered. Asian antiques fill a stylish dining room, while a sleek lounge and a charming patio draw a diverse crowd.

### LA JOLLA The Cottage

*7702 Fay Avenue, 92037* **Tel** *858-454-8409*                    **Road Map** *D6*

Breakfast and brunch are local favorites here. Try stuffed French toast with strawberry compote and mascarpone, polenta or crab cakes Benedict, specialty omelets, the breakfast burrito, or fresh scones. Burgers, flat-iron steak, and meatloaf are signature dishes.

### LA JOLLA Whisknladle

*1044 Wall St, 92037* **Tel** *(858) 551-7575*                    **Road map** *D6*

This stylish restaurant offers an eclectic array of seafood specialties, featuring sesame-crusted ahi tuna and a glistening raw bar. Everything is prepared with classic technique, imaginative flair, and a strong sense of seasonality. A wide selection of small tapas-sized plates and seasonal cocktails make it ideal for an upscale happy hour.

### LA JOLLA Tapenade

*7612 Fay Ave, 92037* **Tel** *(858) 551-7500*                    **Road map** *D6*

A bit of Nice in the heart of La Jolla, this casually elegant restaurant derives its cuisine from the south of France. Escargots, duck, and steak *au poivre* are offered. The Maine lobster here comes in many forms, such as salad, soup, and risotto. Desserts are decadent, and a fine plate of cheeses is also available. Children's and vegetarian menu, too.

### LA JOLLA George's California Modern

*1250 Prospect St, 92037* **Tel** *(858) 454-4244*                    **Road map** *D6*

People who knew the aging elegance of George's at the Cove are excited about its new hip decor and the savvy younger crowd it now attracts. Cleverly conceived seafood dishes are the stars of the menu as usual, though there's something for everyone. Communal dining table, lounge, and gorgeous ocean views.

### LA JOLLA The Marine Room

*2000 Spindrift Dr, 92037* **Tel** *(877) 248-6926*                    **Road map** *D6*

Of the many venerable La Jolla oceanfront restaurants, The Marine Room arguably has the most dramatic views, with waves crashing just outside its reinforced windows. A pricy bastion of innovative California cuisine, this place harmonizes Asian twists and French influences on a menu laced with lobster and caviar.

### LA JOLLA The Sky Room

*La Valencia Hotel, 1132 Prospect St, 92037* **Tel** *(858) 454-0771*                    **Road map** *D6*

Perched atop the historic La Valencia Hotel, this exclusive room with only a dozen tables offers unobstructed ocean views. In this strictly romantic, special-occasion territory, big money can buy you luxury items such as prime New York strip steak with *foie gras* mousse in a rich bouillabaisse. Dinner only.

### PACIFIC BEACH Nick's at the Beach

*809 Thomas Ave, 92109* **Tel** *(858) 232-2436*                    **Road map** *D6*

A wide selection of dishes is available at this casual oceanfront restaurant. The diverse menu includes seafood dishes at breakfast, lunch, and dinner, and there's a children's menu. Happy hour, offering good finger foods, draws a lively crowd to the upstairs bar. This is a locals' favorite.

**Key to Price Guide** *see p568* **Key to Symbols** *see back cover flap*

## RANCHO SANTA FE Mille Fleurs

 $$$$$

*6009 Paseo Delicias, 92067* **Tel** *(858) 756-3085* **Road map** D6

Hidden away in an exclusive suburb, Mille Fleurs is one of the most romantic restaurants in the area. The brilliant cooking is a worthy complement to the lovely surroundings and impeccable service. Superb ingredients, flown in from around the world or plucked from nearby farms, enhance the creative modern French cuisine served here.

## SAN DIEGO Burger Lounge

⑤

*4116 Adams Ave, 92116* **Tel** *(619) 584-2929* **Road map** D6

Burger Lounge's great hamburgers, made with organic grass-fed beef, the fresh-cut French fries, the home-made onion rings, and the home-style buns are a local favorite. Fresh tossed salads, turkey burgers, and vegetarian burgers are also on the menu, as are milkshakes, microbrews, and wine.

## SAN DIEGO Big Kitchen Café

⑤

*3003 Grape St, 92102* **Tel** *(619) 234-5789* **Road map** D6

Located behind Balboa Park, this little gem of a diner, with a nice little patio, is extremely popular for its huge breakfasts. The omelets, pancakes, and *huevos rancheros* are quite good. Its owner has a strong personal following, and artistic and cultural groups often meet over coffee at this quirky, but endearing, eatery. Open 8am–2pm.

## SAN DIEGO Karl Strauss Brewing Company

⑤

*1157 Columbia St, 92101* **Tel** *(619) 234-2773* **Road map** D6

Now part of a burgeoning chain, this downtown microbrewery is a great place for a casual but compelling menu of comfort foods featuring blackened salmon, steaks, and meatloaf. The pub fare is an ideal complement to the wide assortment of handcrafted beers on tap. Many seasonal beers are offered.

## SAN DIEGO Regents Pizzeria

⑤

*4150 Regents Park, Row #170, 92037* **Tel** *(858) 550-0406* **Road Map** D6

Serving both New York-style thin pizza and stuffed, double-layer Chicago-style, this is a favorite with nearby office workers and university students. Standouts are the meat-lover's pizza with sausage, meatballs, and pepperoni, and chicken Alfredo with garlic cream sauce.

## SAN DIEGO Alchemy

 $$$

*1503 30th St, 92102* **Tel** *(619) 255-0616* **Road map** D6

This gleaming South Park neighborhood restaurant is all about fusion, combining California cuisine with an eclectic, soothing blend of art, music, and contemporary wood furnishings. The creative menu offers simple, artfully presented fare, with entrées such as crispy-skinned Jidori half-chicken or grass-fed beef burger with Manchego cheese.

## SAN DIEGO Trattoria Fantastica

$$$

*1735 India St, 92101* **Tel** *(619) 234-1735* **Road map** D6

At this homey spot in Little Italy, rustic Sicilian flavors are featured on the extensive, traditional menu. Regulars tuck into wonderful pizzas from a wood-burning oven, hearty pastas, gnocchi, veal, and chicken. The family-operated restaurant offers a casual dining room with muraled walls and a charming courtyard patio that is recommended.

## SAN DIEGO Zenbu

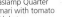 $$$

*7660 Fay Avenue, 92037* **Tel** *(858) 454-4540* **Road Map** D6

Zenbu uses its own seafood company for fresh fish daily, and serves locally raised, grass-fed beef. Expect traditional sushi and tempura, rice bowls, grilled fish, salads, and prime beef, and an extensive sake list. The wasabi-seared tenderloin and scallop combo is delicious.

## SAN DIEGO Candelas

 $$$$

*416 3rd Ave, 92101* **Tel** *(619) 702-4455* **Road map** D6

Mexican cooking is raised to new heights, well beyond the ubiquitous burrito, at this lovely Gaslamp Quarter restaurant. Innovative dishes are served in the stylish, candlelit dining hall. Try the stuffed calamari with tomato and blue cheese sauce, the creamed black bean soup, or the mushroom- and jalapeño-stuffed lobster.

## SAN DIEGO Dobson's

$$$$

*956 Broadway Circle, 92101* **Tel** *(619) 231-6771* **Road map** D6

Serving a California cuisine laced with European and Asian influences, Dobson's always comes through with beautifully presented items, such as the impressive mussel bisque *en croûte*, sautéed salmon, rack of lamb, and pastas. At lunch, politicians crowd the old-fashioned dining room and the antique bar.

## SAN DIEGO El Agave

 $$$$

*2304 San Diego Ave, 92110* **Tel** *(619) 220-0692* **Road map** D6

The tequila is reason enough to visit this Old Town favorite that boasts one of the nation's largest selections. The hacienda-style dining room, sunny patio, and shady deck are attractive features. The kitchen turns out gorgeous presentations of ancient Aztec recipes with sophisticated European influences. Do not pass on the mole.

## SAN DIEGO Indigo Grill

$$$$

*1536 India St, 92101* **Tel** *(619) 234-6802* **Road map** D6

Indigo Grill is a popular spot to explore an innovative "New Western" cuisine. The totem poles and Latin artifacts decorating the contemporary dining room signal a celebration of all indigenous cultures in the Americas. The menu follows through with modern twists on cooking, from Alaska to Mexico. Dinner only.

### SAN DIEGO The Prado

$$$$

*House of Hospitality, 1549 El Prado, Balboa Park, 92101* **Tel** *(619) 557-9441*  **Road map** *D6*

In Balboa Park's ornate House of Hospitality, this restaurant takes full advantage of its majestic architecture in the interior and patio areas. The fusion menu is laced with Italian, Latin, and Asian influences, reflected by dishes like the hamachi fish tacos and the Prado Paella with lobster saffron broth.

### SAN DIEGO Sushi Ota

$$$$

*4529 Mission Bay Dr, 92109* **Tel** *(858) 270-5670*  **Road map** *D6*

The modest, minimal location may not look promising, but Sushi Ota is among the area's best purveyors of sushi. Try ordering something more authentic than the California roll. The skilled chefs love to make traditional, serious sushi crafted from impeccable ingredients. Expect a wait.

### SAN DIEGO Trattoria La Strada

$$$$

*702 5th Ave, 92101* **Tel** *(619) 239-3400*  **Road map** *D6*

A favored option for Tuscan cuisine in the Gaslamp Quarter, both the patio and coveted window tables provide a great view of the lively street scene. To start, several *carpaccios* are among the house specialties, and pastas exceed the usual trattoria fare. Prices are high for this neighborhood, but dishes are deftly prepared and presented.

### SAN DIEGO The Westgate Room

$$$$

*Westgate Hotel, 1055 2nd Ave, 92101* **Tel** *(619) 557-3655*  **Road map** *D6*

Despite its modern façade, the interior of the Westgate has a distinct hint of Versailles, and this striking restaurant is ideal for special occasions. The Continental-California menu with game and seafood is perfectly executed and formally presented in a glamorous, opulent setting.

### SAN DIEGO Bertrand at Mister A's

$$$$$

*2550 5th Ave, 92103* **Tel** *(619) 239-1377*  **Road map** *D6*

On the 12th floor of a downtown office building, this posh restaurant has spectacular views of the skyline and incoming jetliners. The food is delicious, with the likes of tempura lobster tail and jumbo shrimp, and Kobe flatiron steak. In a city filled with ocean vistas, here is a delightful, breathtaking alternative that pampers its guests.

### SAN DIEGO El Bizcocho

$$$$$

*Rancho Bernardo Inn, 17550 Bernardo Oaks Dr, 92128* **Tel** *858 675-8500*  **Road map** *D6*

Hidden in the exclusive Rancho Bernardo Inn, this understated dining room is one of the area's most honored restaurants. The elegant interior features warm earth tones, fireplace, a view of the golf course, and finely appointed tables. Modern French cooking is artistically presented by a polished staff. This place is great for a special occasion.

### SAN DIEGO WineSellar & Brasserie

$$$$$

*9550 Waples St, 92121* **Tel** *(858) 450-9557*  **Road map** *D6*

Off the beaten path but worth the trip, this acclaimed restaurant began as a modest complement to the downstairs wine shop, whose inventory now supports one of the nation's most honored wine lists. The California-French cuisine, creative but built on a strong classic foundation, is served in a lovely room that's charming and unpretentious.

## THE INLAND EMPIRE AND LOW DESERT

### BIG BEAR CITY Old Country Inn

$$

*41126 Big Bear Blvd, 92315* **Tel** *(909) 866-5600*  **Road map** *D6*

Breakfasts are elaborate in the mountains, and this place offers hearty options to start the day. Salads and sandwiches are offered at midday, and for dinner there is everything from prime rib to seafood. A selection of authentic German specialties sets this homey place apart. There are good German beers to go with your schnitzel. Full bar.

### BIG BEAR CITY Peppercorn Grille

$$

*553 Pine Knot Ave, 92315* **Tel** *(909) 866-5405*  **Road map** *D6*

After a day of skiing, fishing, or hiking, this small, cozy, welcoming restaurant in the heart of Big Bear Village is just the place to relax. Choose from pizza, pasta, or high-quality fresh meats and seafood, or vegetarian specials. There is a good wine list, too.

### BORREGO SPRINGS The Arches

$$

*Borrego Springs Resort, 1112 Tilting T Dr, 92004* **Tel** *(760) 767-5700*  **Road map** *D6*

This quiet desert resort enjoys a view of the Santa Rosa mountains. The ornate but informal Arches' dining room features an all-American menu at linen-clad tables. Items such as Southwest chicken, *filet mignon*, salmon, and sea bass reflect the varied but straightforward fare. It is immensely popular for happy hour and Sunday brunch.

### CHINO Centro Basco

$$

*13432 S Central Ave, 91710* **Tel** *(909) 628-9014*  **Road map** *D6*

Formerly part of an old lodging house for Basque sheep herders, this sprawling dining room provides hearty meals. A Basque meal includes a massive tureen of soup, salad, pickled beef tongue, pasta, rotisserie chicken, rack of lamb, trout, or prime rib. Eat at a community table or have your own.

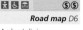

**Key to Price Guide** *see p568* **Key to Symbols** *see back cover flap*

## CORONA BJ's Restaurant Brewhouse
 ⑤

*2520 Tuscany Rd, 92879* **Tel** *(951) 271-3610*    **Road map** D6

Good pub food and a busy bar, if you can get near it, is what awaits you at this friendly place in Corona Crossing's Shopping Center. Order a beer sampler and watch the game or chat up your neighbor. Try the deep dish pizza, balsamic chicken, or an over-the-top ice-cream sundae. There is also a children's menu.

## IDYLLWILD Restaurant Gastrognome
 ⑤⑤⑤

*54381 Ridgeview Dr, 92549* **Tel** *(951) 659-5055*    **Road map** D6

The "Gnome", as the locals call it, boasts a delightfully rustic, timbered dining room with a prominent stone fireplace. A perfect mountain retreat, the hearty fare includes crab cakes, orange-glazed roast duck, salmon with Hollandaise, and lobster tacos. At lunch, you can enjoy a burger on the deck and admire the forest.

## LA QUINTA Louise's Pantry
⑤⑤

*47150 Washington Street, 92253* **Tel** *(760) 360-5991*    **Road map** D6

Originally founded in Palm Springs in 1945, this old-style coffee shop still offers familiar all-American foods. Locals seem happy to stand in line for specialties such as big old-fashioned breakfasts, chicken dumplings, grilled cheese sandwiches, and apple pie that come fresh from the oven. The Reuben sandwich is a particular favorite.

## LA QUINTA La Quinta Cliffhouse
⑤⑤⑤⑤

*78250 Hwy 111, 92253* **Tel** *(760) 360-5991*    **Road map** D6

In a historic ranch house with a rustic beamed ceiling, stone fireplace, and a terrace carved out of rock, La Quinta Cliffhouse is one of the desert's most popular dining venues. The menu features USDA prime beef and the freshest seafood, including lobster, and a legendary burger. With a loyal following, the place can get crowded. Dinner only.

## PALM DESERT Ristorante Tuscany
 ⑤⑤⑤⑤

*JW Marriott Desert Springs Resort & Spa, 74855 Country Club Dr, 92260* **Tel** *(760) 341-2211*    **Road map** D6

Better than most hotel dining rooms, this place is one of the desert's preferred northern Italian restaurants. The main room is a soaring space with floor-to-ceiling murals and elegantly appointed tables. The diverse menu features fresh seasonal ingredients and a superb selection of seafood. Tasting menu also available. Dinner only.

## PALM DESERT Cuistot
⑤⑤⑤⑤⑤

*72595 El Paseo, 95562* **Tel** *(760) 340-1000*    **Road map** D6

The chef/owner worked with the great Paul Bocuse in France and his modern French cuisine has long been one of the desert's premier culinary attractions. Inspired by a French country farmhouse, the restaurant features a beamed ceiling, a stone fireplace, and a patio. From the exhibition kitchen come spectacular looking and tasting creations.

## PALM DESERT Jillian's
⑤⑤⑤⑤⑤

*74155 El Paseo, 92260* **Tel** *(760) 776-8242*    **Road map** D6

Intimate rooms face a charming courtyard at this rustically elegant, romantic venue. The menu provides familiar American roasted meats and grilled fish, dressed up with subtle innovative twists, complemented by an award-winning wine list. Dine with music under the stars. Dinner only.

## PALM SPRINGS Europa
⑤⑤⑤

*Villa Royale Inn, 1620 S. Indian Trail, 92264* **Tel** *(760) 327-2314*    **Road map** D6

Europa is one of Coachella Valley's most romantic restaurants, tucked into a charming little inn. Guests can enjoy modern Continental cuisine either in the intimate dining room by the fireplace, or out on the poolside patio. Menu highlights include rack of lamb, salmon *en papillote*, and duck *confit*. Sunday brunch.

## PALM SPRINGS Le Vallauris
⑤⑤⑤⑤

*385 W Tahquitz Canyon Way, 92262* **Tel** *(760) 325-5059*    **Road map** D6

The grande dame of the Palm Springs dining scene, this restaurant is still going strong. The main dining room is a study in refined elegance, while the garden patio is shaded by ficus trees. French specialties like *escargots* and *foie gras*, share a menu with seared white fish with mustard sauce. Impressive list of Bordeaux. There is a Sunday brunch.

## PALM SPRINGS Melvyn's Restaurant
⑤⑤⑤⑤

*200 W Ramon Rd, 92260* **Tel** *(760) 325-2323*    **Road map** D6

Located on the premises of the legendary Ingleside Inn, Melvyn's has been a special occasion restaurant for over 30 years. Antiques, waiters in linen jackets, and photographs of past eras make dining here a unique experience. The food is well regarded – try the Veal Ingleside – and the wine list is good. Film stars are regularly spotted here.

## PALM SPRINGS Palm Springs Chop House
⑤⑤⑤⑤

*262 S. Palm Canyon Drive, 92262* **Tel** *760-320-4500*    **Road map** D6

In the heart of downtown is this locals' favorite for fresh salads, prime beef, seafood, and an encyclopedic wine list, this is also a great spot for people-watching from the patio tables in the heart of downtown. Rack of lamb, prime double pork chops, bone-in beef rib chops, and brussels sprouts hash are signature dishes.

## RANCHO MIRAGE Las Casuelas Nuevas
 ⑤⑤

*70-050 Hwy 111, 92270* **Tel** *(760) 328-8444*    **Road map** D6

This handsome hacienda-style restaurant specializes in familiar Mexican dishes such as enchiladas, fajitas, tostadas, and carnitas. There is live entertainment nightly and potent margaritas can be chosen from over a dozen varieties. The busy bar also stocks an endless list of premium tequilas. A favored destination for Sunday brunch.

### RANCHO MIRAGE Roy's Hawaiian Fusion Cuisine

$$$

*71959 Hwy 111, 92270* **Tel** *(760) 340-9044*        **Road map** *D6*

Celebrity chef Roy Yamaguchi brings his acclaimed regional Hawaiian cuisine to this sprawling, bustling restaurant. The food is consistently well prepared and beautifully presented. Seared ahi tuna, with a sweet and a hot sauce, is a specialty, and so is the macadamia-crusted mahi mahi in a lobster butter sauce.

### RANCHO MIRAGE Fleming's Steakhouse & Wine Bar
$$$$

*71800 Highway 111, 92270* **Tel** *(760) 776-6685*        **Road map** *D6*

A bustling, noisy place located in The River entertainment area. Fleming's has 100 wines by the glass, serves USDA prime beef and fresh seafood, along with rich sides such as potatoes with jalapeño, cream, and cheddar. A popular place to stop off before or after a movie.

### RANCHO MIRAGE Wally's Desert Turtle
$$$$$

*71775 Hwy 111, 92270* **Tel** *(760) 568-9321*        **Road map** *D6*

One of the grand dining rooms of the desert, Wally's is the kind of place guests come dressed to the nines. Mirrored ceilings, Peruvian artifacts, and elegant murals contribute to the dramatic decor. Prices are high, but top ingredients go into the rack of lamb and filet of beef with a peppercorn or Béarnaise sauce. Closed mid-Jun–early Oct.

### REDLANDS Joe Greensleeves
$$$$

*220 N Orange St, 92373* **Tel** *(909) 792-6969*        **Road map** *D6*

This endearing restaurant inhabits an old building in downtown Redlands. A fireplace, cozy booths, and flattering lighting create a subtly romantic ambience. However, the prime attraction comes out of the glass-enclosed kitchen: wild game, ravioli lobster, pastas, and steaks cooked over a wood grill.

### RIVERSIDE Las Campanas

$$$

*Mission Inn, 3649 Mission Inn Ave, 92501* **Tel** *(888) 326-4448*        **Road map** *D6*

This courtyard charmer is shaded by towering palms in a gracious garden. Fountains and flowering cacti and, at dinner, candles create a romantic setting fit for the gourmet Mexican menu featuring, for example, *filet mignon flautas* or rotisserie chicken topped with apricot chipotle sauce. Try a fresh fruit signature margarita.

### RIVERSIDE Duane's Prime Steak & Seafood
$$$$

*Mission Inn, 3649 Mission Inn Ave, 92501* **Tel** *(888) 326-4448*        **Road map** *D6*

By the time you sit down at your table, you will have already had the pleasure of walking through the magnificent Mission Inn, one of California's most historic hotels. Wood-clad Duane's is dignified and stately, with splendid art and elegant table settings. The USDA Prime steaks are superb and the elaborate Sunday brunch is an experience.

### RIVERSIDE Mario's Place
$$$$

*3646 Mission Inn Ave, 92501* **Tel** *(951) 684-7755*        **Road map** *D6*

Just across from the historic Mission Inn, Mario's is a sleek, cosmopolitan restaurant with sensuous Art Deco touches. The kitchen skillfully plays with both Asian and French technique, as well as serving up traditional Italian specialties from a wood-burning oven. Jazz on weekends. Open dinner Mon–Sat, lunch Fri only.

### TEMECULA Café Champagne
$$$

*Thornton Winery, 32575 Rancho California Rd, 92591* **Tel** *(951) 699-0088*        **Road map** *D6*

Diners have sweeping views of the nearby rolling vineyards from Café Champagne; you will think you are in the Napa Valley. Freshness is a priority here, evidenced by the restaurant's own herb garden. Here fusion cuisine is paired with the winery's own bottles. The delightful patio is an occasional live jazz venue.

## THE MOJAVE DESERT

### BAKER The Mad Greek

$

*72112 Baker Blvd, 92309* **Tel** *(760) 733-4354*        **Road map** *D5*

Whether headed to Las Vegas or Death Valley, weary drivers are advised to skip the big national chains and stop instead at the Mad Greek's. Besides the usual burgers, tasty gyros, hummus, kebabs, and other Mediterranean fare are on the menu. The strawberry shakes are famous, and tourist assistance is offered in several languages.

### BARSTOW Idle Spurs Steak House

$$$

*690 Hwy 58, 92311* **Tel** *(760) 256-8888*        **Road map** *D5*

This traditional, Western-style steakhouse is a good, relaxing place to recharge after a long day of driving. The jalapeño poppers and chicken wings are popular starters, followed by tender aged steaks. The old school bar is a popular watering hole for locals. The attractive patio, dominated by a massive tree, offers a pleasant alfresco option.

### DEATH VALLEY Wrangler Steakhouse

$$$

*Furnace Creek Resort, Hwy 190, 92328* **Tel** *(760) 786-2345*        **Road map** *D4*

Not as formal as the dining room at the adjoining Furnace Creek Resort, this restaurant is housed in a former working ranch, beautifully preserved to reflect the mystique of this desert oasis. The restaurant features a Western steakhouse menu and a good variety of California wines.

### DEATH VALLEY Inn at Furnace Creek Dining Room  $$$$$

*Furnace Creek Resort, Hwy 190, 92328* **Tel** *(760) 786-3385* **Road map** *D4*

Housed in a historic adobe and stone resort, this rather upscale dining room is noted for its Sunday brunch and afternoon tea. The sophisticated dinner menu, with Southwestern and Asian accents, reflects the desert environment in its cactus salad and rattlesnake empanadas. The steaks are also popular. Dinner only, closed mid-May–mid-Oct.

### LAKE HAVASU Barley Brothers Restaurant & Brewery $$

*1425 McCulloch Blvd, 86403* **Tel** *(928) 505-7837* **Road map** *E5*

Offering a view of London Bridge, this versatile place is great for families, yet can also be somewhat romantic, given the view, soft lighting, and conversation-conducive atmosphere. Wood-fired pizzas complement a choice of handcrafted beers, and entrées include seafood, burgers, pastas, ribs, and steaks.

### LAKE HAVASU Shugrue's Restaurant $$$

*1425 McCulloch Blvd, 86403* **Tel** *(928) 453-1400* **Road map** *E5*

With a next-door brewpub catering to a livelier crowd, this quiet family restaurant offers a fine view of London Bridge and its tasteful interior makes for a pleasant respite. Steaks, seafood, burgers, and pastas are the main attractions. Excellent desserts are made on the premises. Bargain-priced early bird dinners are also available.

## SAN FRANCISCO

### CHINATOWN AND NOB HILL Golden Star Vietnamese Restaurant $

*11 Walter U Lum Place, 94108* **Tel** *(415) 398-1215* **Map** *5 C3*

Situated across from the Transamerica Pyramid, the Golden Star is narrow and crowded, and the decor is as plain as a school cafeteria. Nonetheless, this little gem serves up big rice dishes and meat portions for very little money. The lunch specials are of exceptional value.

### CHINATOWN AND NOB HILL House of Nanking $

*919 Kearny, 94133* **Tel** *(415) 421-1429* **Map** *5 C3*

The good, traditional menu at the tiny House of Nanking attracts a loyal clientele. Even though the waiters here are a little unfriendly, food comes in generous portions and the prices are reasonably low. The menu offers favorites like sesame chicken and a good selection of vegetarian dishes. Service is amazingly brisk.

### CHINATOWN AND NOB HILL Yuet Lee $

*1300 Stockton St, 94133* **Tel** *(415) 982-6020* **Map** *5 B3*

Yuet Lee's excellent fresh seafood menu and low prices are the reasons locals flock here. There is a live fish tank and the chef will cook a whole fish or crab to order. Specialties include steamed fish and seafood, salt-and-pepper squid, and an array of vegetables such as long bean and asparagus. It is open until 3am.

### CHINATOWN AND NOB HILL Great Eastern $$$

*649 Jackson St, 94133* **Tel** *(415) 986-2500* **Map** *5 C3*

A longtime favorite in Chinatown, Great Eastern has a menu featuring reliable, if not inspired, Mandarin dishes. The real draw here is the fresh seafood swimming in the tanks – make sure to ask the waiter for the day's specials to sample the best that the restaurant has to offer.

### CHINATOWN AND NOB HILL Nob Hill Café $$$

*1152 Taylor St, 94108* **Tel** *(415) 776-6500* **Map** *5 B4*

Nob Hill Café is a local favorite, frequently crowded to the rafters, as diners enjoy home-style Italian dishes. The bistro-type decor is matched by an easy-going ambience. Visitors often spot "The Twins" – the delightful Brown sisters – here. The similarly dressed duo is as much a San Francisco institution as Nob Hill itself.

### CHINATOWN AND NOB HILL Street $$$

*2141 Polk St, 94109* **Tel** *(415) 775-1055* **Map** *5 A3*

Comfort food at its finest makes this neighborhood restaurant a favorite. Street is noisy and crowded, but the platters are ample. Try one of the best seafood entrées – big, juicy Gulf prawns served in a saffron-laced lobster broth over buttery home-made pasta. Finish with the not-too-sweet pecan bread pudding.

### CHINATOWN AND NOB HILL Venticello Ristorante $$$

*1257 Taylor St, 94108* **Tel** *(415) 922-2545* **Map** *5 B3*

At Venticello, a trattoria serving fine Northern Italian cuisine, romance is not about holding hands by the fireplace – it is on the menu. The laid-back ambience encourages one to linger with a decaffeinated espresso and port after enjoying a perfectly seasoned plate of scampi. There is an impressive wine list.

### CHINATOWN AND NOB HILL The Big Four Restaurant $$$$

*1075 California St, 94108* **Tel** *(415) 771-1140* **Map** *5 B4*

Named after the enormously wealthy railroad barons, Big Four is the chosen place for the Nob Hill elite to hobnob. The dark polished-wood paneling and formal service are an appropriate setting for business people and financiers in particular. The top-quality menu includes rack of lamb and a whiskey-marinated buffalo steak.

## CHINATOWN AND NOB HILL Acquerello $$$$$

*1722 Sacramento St, 94109* **Tel** *(415) 567-5432*

**Map** 5 A4

An exquisite wine list, knowledgable waiters who are happy to recommend food-and-wine pairings, carved glass decanters, and fine linen set the stage for a truly memorable experience in this former chapel. A rich, Venetian-themed menu makes for sumptuous dining. There is a unique collection of Italian cheeses.

## CHINATOWN AND NOB HILL The Dining Room at the Ritz Carlton $$$$$

*603 Stockton St, 94108* **Tel** *(415) 296-7465*

**Map** 5 C4

Ranked number one in many city and travel magazine surveys, the elegant Dining Room is a perfect example of premium service in the grand European tradition. The highly praised menu exhibits an Asian influence, introducing ingredients found in local markets. The cheese board features a wide variety of artisanal cheeses.

## CHINATOWN AND NOB HILL Fleur de Lys $$$$$

*777 Sutter St, 94109* **Tel** *(415) 673-7779*

**Map** 5 B4

The prix-fixes on the French *nouvelle cuisine* menu at Fleur de Lys are the ultimate in gourmet dining, and the waiters flawlessly guide diners from one dish to the next in a lovely tented room. The restaurant also serves a superb vegetarian prix-fixe dinner. Try the oven-roasted yellow and red beet salad and artisanal French cheeses.

## CHINATOWN AND NOB HILL Jai Yun $$$$$

*1080 Clay St, 94111* **Tel** *(415) 981-7438*

**Map** 5 B3

Set in a small space and simply decorated, Jai Yun is full of surprises. The daily prix fixe includes a series of constantly changing, small dishes containing fresh ingredients purchased the same morning from the markets. The excellent seafood menu features abalone, squid, and shrimp dishes.

## CHINATOWN AND NOB HILL Masa's $$$$$

*648 Bush St, 94108* **Tel** *(415) 989-7154*

**Map** 5 B4

In Masa's stylish, urbane setting, diners are treated like royalty as they sample exquisite *nouvelle cuisine*. Benefitting from a celebrated local chef for several years, this well-renowned restaurant continues to beguile diners by changing much of the menu every day, based on fresh market buys.

## CIVIC CENTER Mifune $$

*1737 Post St, 94115* **Tel** *(415) 922-0337*

**Map** 4 E4

Big steaming bowls of Japanese-style noodle soups delivered to your table within minutes of ordering, make this Japantown hub a favorite for fans of fresh food and those with limited time. Mifune also serves bento boxes and other non-soup items. There is also a good selection of vegetarian choices.

## CIVIC CENTER Absinthe Brasserie and Bar $$$

*398 Hayes St, 94102* **Tel** *(415) 551-1590*

**Map** 3 B5

Recreating the 1940s era, this dark romantic setting is among the best European-style brasseries in town. Vintage cabaret music and cocktails are on the menu, along with an array of oysters, the best French onion soup, and hearty bistro food such as *cassoulet*, slow-cooked pork, and cinnamon-braised lamb. The wine list is excellent.

## CIVIC CENTER Hayes Street Grill $$$

*320 Hayes St, 94102* **Tel** *(415) 863-5545*

**Map** 4 F5

A reliable favorite for diners attending the nearby symphony, opera, or ballet, Hayes Street Grill pairs your choice of freshly caught fish and accompanying sauce with crispy french fries, among other dishes. The service is efficient and will get you to your seat in time for the start of the show.

## CIVIC CENTER Indigo $$$

*687 McAllister St, 94102* **Tel** *(415) 673-9353*

**Map** 4 F5

With its cool, blue-themed interior, Indigo lives up to its name. The restaurant is celebrated for its phenomenal wine list and New American menu. The best bargain offered is the Wine Dinner after 8pm, with specially chosen wines and champagnes to accompany and enhance the chef's specialties.

## CIVIC CENTER Jardinière $$$$

*300 Grove St, 94102* **Tel** *(415) 861-5555*

**Map** 4 F5

Thoughtful, efficient service, an elegant atmosphere, and sumptuous California-inspired French food make the popular Jardinière a top choice for special occasions. The jazz duo plays quietly in the background while diners enjoy onion *tarte* and a Dubonnet from the mahogany and marble bar.

## DOWNTOWN Delancey Street Restaurant $

*600 Embarcadero, 94107* **Tel** *(415) 512-5179*

**Map** 6 E5

A wonderful place for dining, Delancey Street Restaurant serves delicious comfort food, including the excellent meatloaf and ribs, and other American dishes. The service is beyond good. The restaurant supports a respected substance-abuse recovery program. Reservations are recommended.

## DOWNTOWN Café Bastille $$

*22 Belden Place, 94104* **Tel** *(415) 986-5673*

**Map** 5 C4

Tucked away in a traffic-free alley, this mini-Paris is often crowded with diners enjoying the fine weather at the out-side tables during the day or jazz in the evenings. Basic bistro soups, salads, beer, and wine are served along with French specialties such as *moules marinières* with *harissa* (red chili) sauce, and tripe sausage with caramelized onions.

**Key to Price Guide** *see p568* **Key to Symbols** *see back cover flap*

### DOWNTOWN Sanraku at Metreon
*101 4th St, 94103* **Tel** *(415) 369-6166*      **Map** 5 C5

Set amidst the noisy whirl of the Metreon, with its multiple theaters, children's attractions, and a video-game floor, Sanraku serves a dependable lunch and dinner. Japanese fare, such as crispy *gyoza* and wet and dry noodles, is served at good prices. They also offer a superb sushi menu.

### DOWNTOWN Yank Sing
*101 Spear St, 94105* **Tel** *(415) 957-9300*      **Map** 6 E4

Much loved for its exquisite dim sum, Yank Sing allows diners to choose from over 100 different items, including the signature Shanghai dumpling with ginger-wrapped minced pork, displayed on the constantly circulating carts. The upscale surroundings make this a cut above most dim sum parlors.

### DOWNTOWN Gott's Roadside
*One Ferry Building, 94111* **Tel** *(866) 328-3663*      **Map** 5 E3

In the foodies' paradise, Ferry Building Marketplace, is this urban version of a 1950s roadside eatery famous for burgers, fish tacos, garlic fries, and hand-scooped milkshakes. Specials include soft shell crab tacos, portobello Reuben sandwiches or other seasonal and whimsical choices, mostly from locally sourced ingredients.

### DOWNTOWN Gordon Biersch Brewery Restaurant
*2 Harrison Street, 94105* **Tel** *(415) 243-8246*      **Map** 5 E4

On the Embarcadero, this is a busy, noisy industrial-style place with huge pub and bar menus offering garlic fries, pizza, steak, seafood, mac and cheese, pastas, and kobe sliders. There is a long list of brewed-on-site brews, and fancy, expensive cocktails. Popular with Giants baseball stadium and gangs of other sports fans. Parking validation.

### DOWNTOWN Out the Door
*845 Market Street, 94013* **Tel** *(415) 321-3740*      **Map** 5 C5

A good stop off after shopping in the massive Westfield San Francisco Centre, enjoy a healthy snack or meal at the food court serving Vietnamese food to eat in or take out. The menu includes imperial rolls, noodle and rice dishes, stir-fries, grills, and steam buns. There is also a selection of desserts.

### DOWNTOWN Sam's Grill and Seafood Restaurant
*374 Bush St, 94104* **Tel** *(415) 421-0594*      **Map** 5 C4

Founded in 1867, Sam's Grill is the oldest seafood restaurant in the city. It has been serving outstanding sand dabs and other fresh fish to generations of visitors. At midday, one can can hear the murmur of businesspeople closing deals in the high-backed booths. It is closed on weekends.

### DOWNTOWN Sears Fine Food
*439 Powell Street, 94102* **Tel** *(415) 986-1160*      **Map** 5 B4

Located on Union Square since 1938, Sears is best for breakfasts. The menu varies from sourdough French toast and tiny Swedish pancakes to strawberry-raised waffles, shrimp and crab omelet, or fresh fruit. There is a large comfort food menu for lunch and dinner, in-house-made pastries, and desserts. If there is a line waiting, sit at the counter.

### DOWNTOWN Silks at the Mandarin Oriental Hotel
*222 Sansome St, 94104* **Tel** *(415) 276-9888*      **Map** 5 C4

Dazzling with silken wall-hangings, floor coverings, and hand-painted silk chandeliers, Silks is a good spot for an intimate conversation and celebrity spotting. The efficient service underscores imaginative New Asian cuisine such as soy-glazed suckling pig, and Szechuan-crusted Pacific yellow-fin tuna.

### DOWNTOWN The Slanted Door
*One Ferry Building, 94111* **Tel** *(415) 861-8032*      **Map** 5 E3

In the Ferry Building Marketplace is this nationally acclaimed, wildly popular, Vietnamese restaurant overlooking the bay. From street food to French-inspired dishes, it serves the best Vietnamese food – caramelized shrimp, cellophane crab noodles, lemongrass tofu, and a myriad of veggie dishes. Book well ahead.

### DOWNTOWN Swan Oyster Depot
*1517 Polk Street, 94109* **Tel** *(415) 673-1101*      **Map** 5 A4

Since 1912, Swan Oyster Depot has served food at the counter with only 18 stools and some of the best clam chowder, and fresh seafood in town. With a lively atmosphere and a super-friendly crew, it is open for breakfast and lunch as well as drinks. Takeout is also available.

### DOWNTOWN Tadich Grill
*240 California St, 94111* **Tel** *(415) 391-1849*      **Map** 6 D4

Founded during the Gold Rush, Tadich Grill is the oldest continuously operating restaurant in the state. It serves excellent *cioppino* and the fresh grilled fish is a tradition among seafood lovers. The wait for a table can be long in the evenings, but lunch is always a good bet. The old-fashioned waiters serve with great style.

### DOWNTOWN Tommy Toy's
*655 Montgomery St, 94111* **Tel** *(415) 397-4888*      **Map** 5 C3

The tasting menu at Tommy Toy's is a great way to enjoy the elegant four-star Chinese cuisine served here. There are also sophisticated dishes, such as prawns in a ginger glaze, made with the freshest ingredients and inspired by *nouvelle cuisine*. The dining room is softened with tapestries, etched-glass, antique mirrors, and lamplight.

## DOWNTOWN Bix      ⑤⑤⑤⑤

*56 Gold St, 94133* **Tel** *(415) 433 6300*      **Map** *5 C3*

The slick Art-Deco interior in this swanky supper club, named after jazz great Bix Beiderbecke, is a sophisticated setting for French-American dishes impeccably served with a tinkling jazz piano. Locally produced ingredients are used in the cooking. Bix has great martinis and a see-and-be-seen afterwork crowd.

## DOWNTOWN Campton Place Restaurant      ⑤⑤⑤⑤

*340 Stockton St, 94108* **Tel** *(415) 781-5555*      **Map** *5 C4*

A serene room classically styled in the subtle colors of an Italian villa, Campton Place exudes elegance. The kitchen creates some of the best Provençal-Mediterranean fusion food in the area, accompanied by a top-notch wine list. This and the smooth service makes for a special night out. A good brunch menu is offered on Sunday.

## DOWNTOWN Farallon      ⑤⑤⑤⑤

*450 Post St, between Mason & Powell Sts* **Tel** *(415) 956-6969*      **Map** *5 B5*

The enchanting undersea decor, from jellyfish-shaped chandeliers to marine-life mosaics, is an appropriate back-drop for the superb seafood served here. The sophisticated menu created by chef Mark Franz includes delights such as champagne-cured sardines and olive oil-poached halibut.

## DOWNTOWN Kokkari Estiatorio      ⑤⑤⑤⑤

*200 Jackson St, 94111* **Tel** *(415) 981-0983*      **Map** *6 D3*

The Kokkari serves stylish Greek food in a large, comfortable dining area with darkwood floors and a big, cozy fireplace. The signature moussaka and perfectly grilled lamb are top picks. The restaurant features an extensive list of Greek wines. The staff can guide your choices.

## DOWNTOWN La Scene Café & Bar      ⑤⑤⑤⑤

*490 Geary St, 94102* **Tel** *(415) 345-2318*      **Map** *5 B5*

Simple French bistro-style food such as *cassoulet* and lamb shank makes this unpretentious restaurant a favorite with theatergoers. The prix-fixe menu is a bargain. The service is prompt, and the waitstaff are guaranteed to get you out of the door on time. Tasty weekend brunches are offered.

## DOWNTOWN Palomino      ⑤⑤⑤⑤

*345 Spear St, 94105* **Tel** *(415) 512-7400*      **Map** *6 E4*

Palomino is a business-lunch favorite. Though part of a chain, it offers an extremely broad menu that features Italian, French, and American favorites. The convenient location features a gorgeous view of the Bay Bridge from the outdoor tables. The atmosphere is pleasantly upbeat in this classy restaurant.

## DOWNTOWN Boulevard      ⑤⑤⑤⑤⑤

*1 Mission St, 94105* **Tel** *(415) 543-6084*      **Map** *6 E4*

The artistic creations of chef Nancy Oakes have earned fame for Boulevard, a Bay Area icon. The menu is a cross between American comfort food and French favorites. The interior is elegant and welcoming. Try to be seated in the back section to take advantage of the wonderful Bay Bridge views.

## DOWNTOWN Coi       ⑤⑤⑤⑤⑤

*373 Broadway, 94133* **Tel** *(415) 393-9000*      **Map** *5 C3*

Coi does "New American cuisine," and does it well. With French Laundry alum Daniel Patterson helming the kitchen, diners can – and do – expect a lot here. Enter through the elegantly trellised entrance and let your tastebuds tantalized by the 11-course culinary adventure with such specialties as the beet rose, beef tenderloin, and crab melt.

## DOWNTOWN Kuleto's      ⑤⑤⑤⑤⑤

*221 Powell St, 94102* **Tel** *(415) 397-7720*      **Map** *5 B5*

The exceptionally pretty Kuleto's is primarily frequented by those looking for a people-watching spot. It has an interior salvaged from an elegant old San Francisco hotel. Standard, if not spectacular, North Italian dishes make up the menu. Enjoy appetizers at the bar for the best view.

## DOWNTOWN Michael Mina      ⑤⑤⑤⑤⑤

*252 California St, 94111* **Tel** *(415) 397-9222*      **Map** *5 C4*

Replacing the venerable Oak Room at Westin St. Francis Hotel, this restaurant serves an American prix-fixe menu built around a single ingredient prepared in three different styles. The eponymous chef, who was formerly at Aqua, also offers American classics along with 2,000 wines. The surroundings are ultra luxurious.

## FISHERMAN'S WHARF AND NORTH BEACH Brandy Ho's Hunan Food      ⑤⑤

*217 Columbus Ave, 94133* **Tel** *(415) 788-7527*      **Map** *5 C3*

Renowned for its hot and sour curries, this hole-in-the-wall restaurant earned a fiery reputation for delicious, authentic Hunan dishes. Be forewarned – "medium spicy" means hot, while "hot" is alarming. Savvy diners know to quell the fire with rice, not water. Order a "mild" plate and enjoy.

## FISHERMAN'S WHARF AND NORTH BEACH Buena Vista Café      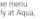 ⑤⑤

*2765 Hyde St, 94109* **Tel** *(415) 474-5044*      **Map** *5 A2*

The original building was a boarding house until 1916, when the Buena Vista Saloon opened. Irish coffee here has been a San Francisco tradition since the drink was created here in 1952. A hearty American breakfast is served all day, and other dishes include steaks, burgers, sandwiches, salads, meatloaf, and crabcakes. There's a view of the bay.

**Key to Price Guide** *see p568* **Key to Symbols** *see back cover flap*

### FISHERMAN'S WHARF AND NORTH BEACH Capp's Corner

*1600 Powell St, 94133* **Tel** *(415) 989-2589*

**$$**

**Map** *5 B3*

A lower-cost option popular with families, Capp's Corner serves up an Americanized version of Italian cooking. Do not expect fine cuisine, but generous portions of all the traditional favorites. Opened in 1960, the restaurant features a photographic gallery of famous former diners.

### FISHERMAN'S WHARF AND NORTH BEACH Alioto's

*8 Fisherman's Wharf, 94133* **Tel** *(415) 673-0183*

**$$$**

**Map** *5 A1*

Lit by spectacular sunsets filtered through the Golden Gate, Alioto's has been serving well-prepared Sicilian-style seafood since 1925. The food is good, especially the bountiful shrimp or crab Louies (juicy seafood on a bed of crisp romaine lettuce). The kitchen uses fresh seasonal ingredients, sourced locally.

### FISHERMAN'S WHARF Boudin at the Wharf

*160 Jefferson Street, 94133* **Tel** *(415) 928-1849*

**$$$**

**Map** *5 A1*

The aroma of sourdough bread will lure you into this touristy, fun place with a casual and noisy café downstairs, and a bistro and bar upstairs. The menu includes chowder in bread bowls, fresh seafood, and sourdough pizza. Stay for the bakery tour to see the famous sourdough bread being made. Several locations in California.

### FISHERMAN'S WHARF AND NORTH BEACH Caffe Sport

*574 Green St, 94133* **Tel** *(415) 981-1251*

**$$$**

**Map** *5 C3*

Big, family-style platters of garlic-infused vegetables, *cioppino* (seafood stew), and other Italian favorites, are served by waiters known for their bossy attitude in this loud, busy eatery. They are happy to tell diners what to order – just ask.

### FISHERMAN'S WHARF AND NORTH BEACH Fog City Diner

*1300 Battery St, 94111* **Tel** *(415) 982-2000*

**$$$**

**Map** *5 C2*

Glorified comfort foods, such as Cheddar biscuits and pulled pork sliders are on the menu, alongside burgers and fries at this chrome-trimmed diner lookalike. Weekend brunch features new twists on old favorites such as smoked chicken hash and eggs.

### FISHERMAN'S WHARF AND NORTH BEACH Il Fornaio

*1265 Battery St, 94111* **Tel** *(415) 986-0100*

**$$$**

**Map** *5 C2*

A chain that built its reputation on outstanding baked goods, Il Fornaio continues to attract diners with fresh breads, delicious pastas, and grilled meats and fish. The superb butternut squash ravioli in butter sauce is served as both an appetizer and entrée. The well-chosen wine list represents small, regional wineries.

### FISHERMAN'S WHARF AND NORTH BEACH The Stinking Rose

*325 Columbus Ave, 94133* **Tel** *(415) 781-7673*

**$$$**

**Map** *5 C3*

True to its name, The Stinking Rose uses garlic in every dish – including dessert. This Californian-Italian-style pasta and pizza restaurant is often crowded with those curious about the unusual name, though service and quality can be uneven at times. Be adventurous and try their garlic ice cream.

### FISHERMAN'S WHARF AND NORTH BEACH Tommaso's Ristorante Italiano

*1042 Kearny St, 94133* **Tel** *(415) 398-9696*

**$$$**

**Map** *5 C3*

In a charming old building in the heart of North Beach, well-established Tommaso's is a quaint, family oriented restaurant, offering Italian food with an emphasis on seafood and pizza. It's a treat for foodie and armchair historian alike, serving its fêted spinach parmesan pizza to returning guests including jazz musicians and celebrities over the years.

### FISHERMAN'S WHARF AND NORTH BEACH Zarzuela

*2000 Hyde St, 94109* **Tel** *(415) 346-0800*

**$$$**

**Map** *5 A3*

A variety of tasty tapas and strong, fruity sangria combined with a caring staff and charming dining room make Zarzuela a favorite for an authentic light meal or more. The best Spanish food in the city according to those who swear by its paella. There may be a wait for a table in the evenings.

### FISHERMAN'S WHARF AND NORTH BEACH Ana Mandara

*891 Beach Street, 94109* **Tel** *(415) 771-6800*

**$$$$**

**Map** *4 F1*

Ana Mandara translates as "beautiful refuge" and this restaurant lives up to its name with its majestic decor and theatrical lighting. The chef/owner Khai Duong is renowned for his creative cuisine, combining modern French and Vietnamese dishes.

### FISHERMAN'S WHARF AND NORTH BEACH Scoma's

*Pier 47, 1 Al Scoma Way, 94133* **Tel** *(415) 771-4383*

**$$$$**

**Map** *5 A1*

To have a street named after you means you've been here awhile, and critically acclaimed Scoma's started out in 1965 as a coffee shop for local fishermen. A standard-bearer for well-cooked, big portions of fresh fish, this restaurant features an impressive menu of over 90 dishes. Pretty views of the bay enhance the dining experience.

### FISHERMAN'S WHARF AND NORTH BEACH Gary Danko

*800 North Point St, 94109* **Tel** *(415) 749-2060*

**$$$$$**

**Map** *5 1A*

In spite of the exorbitant prices, Gary Danko has remained one of the favored restaurants in the city for its New American prix fixes. Three-, four-, or five-course dinners provide hours of carefully choreographed courses, efficient service, and elegant surroundings. The selection of cheeses is a must-sample.

### GOLDEN GATE PARK AND THE PRESIDIO Good Luck Dim Sum 🚹 ⬤ V ⑤

*736 Clement St, 94118* **Tel** *(415) 386-3388*  **Map** *3 5A*

A local favorite, this joint is known to serve the freshest dim sum at rock-bottom prices. Those joining the long queues usually come for take-out. The Formica tables in the back provide a steady surface to eat from if not much else. Good Luck always sells out by early afternoon, so get there in the morning for the best selection.

### GOLDEN GATE PARK AND THE PRESIDIO King of Thai Noodle House 🚹 ⬤ V ⑤

*639 Clement St, 94118* **Tel** *(415) 752-5198*  **Map** *3 A5*

The late-night hours and extremely inexpensive steaming noodle dishes make King of Thai a great hit. Many branches of this citywide chain are open late, and none take credit cards or checks. Spiciness can be adjusted according to each diner's preference. Vegetarian entrées are available.

### GOLDEN GATE PARK AND THE PRESIDIO Khan Toke Thai House 🚹 ⬤ V ⑤⑤

*5937 Geary Blvd, 94121* **Tel** *(415) 668-6654*  **Map** *8 E1*

A temple-like interior and colorfully dressed staff transport diners to Thailand. Featuring both floor- and Western-style seating, this long-established restaurant serves tasty Thai standards for mains, which should be topped off with the delicious banana and coconut ice cream. Reservations are recommended.

### GOLDEN GATE PARK AND THE PRESIDIO Marnee Thai 🚹 ⬤ V ⑤⑤

*2225 Irving St, 94122* **Tel** *(415) 665-9500*  **Map** *8 E3*

Large servings of consistently good Thai food have made this cozy, friendly restaurant a dependable choice. Marnee Thai's green curries are quite good. The tight seating and sometimes long waits for a table do not deter loyal fans. Another location at 1243 Ninth Avenue expands diners' choices.

### GOLDEN GATE PARK AND THE PRESIDIO Pacific Café 🚹 ⬤ ⑤⑤

*7000 Geary Blvd, 94121* **Tel** *(415) 387-7091*  **Map** *7 C1*

Pacific Café was opened in the 1970s and is redolent of the era, down to the stained-glass windows. Good, reliable seafood is freshly prepared and served to one's liking. Those diners who have to wait for a table are often treated to a glass of wine on the house.

### GOLDEN GATE PARK AND THE PRESIDIO Beach Chalet Brewery 🚹 ⬤ 🎵 ⑤⑤⑤

*1000 Great Hwy, 94121* **Tel** *(415) 386-8439*  **Map** *7 A2*

Craft brews, big hamburgers with side dishes of crispy fries, and a spectacular view of the Pacific make Beach Chalet Brewery a promising destination after a day in Golden Gate Park. The WPA murals on the first floor and carved stone stair-rails are a must-see. An excellent brunch is served at weekends and there's live music on Tuesdays.

### GOLDEN GATE PARK AND THE PRESIDIO Ebisu 🚹 ⬤ ⑤⑤⑤

*1283 9th Ave, 94122* **Tel** *(415) 566-1770*  **Map** *8 F3*

Often crowded, this sushi restaurant has visitors lined up to sample what some say is the best and freshest sushi in town, served by laughing, cleaver-flashing chefs at the bar. Try the house specialty, Ebisu maki, featuring salmon and vegetables. Ebisu is seafood-as-entertainment, and queues for table space are not uncommon.

### GOLDEN GATE PARK AND THE PRESIDIO La Vie 🚹 ⬤ V ⑤⑤⑤

*5830 Geary Blvd, 94121* **Tel** *(415) 668-8080*  **Map** *8 E1*

A wonderful neighborhood find in the outer Richmond area – a good stop before or after a visit to Golden Gate Park – La Vie gets consistently good reviews for its Vietnamese menu prepared and served with a French flair. The flaming beef and prawns are a favorite.

### GOLDEN GATE PARK AND THE PRESIDIO Magic Flute Garden Ristorante 🚹 ⬤ 🔳 ⑤⑤⑤

*3673 Sacramento Street, 94118* **Tel** *(415) 922-1225*  **Map** *3 B4*

Magical, enchanting, and quaint, this small restaurant (it seats about 30) is a great place to chill out and enjoy a quiet dinner with someone special. The cuisine is Italian and the service is very attentive and warm. There is also a garden, which is used when the weather is fine.

### GOLDEN GATE PARK AND THE PRESIDIO Park Chalet 🚹 ⬤ 🎵 🔳 ⑤⑤⑤

*1000 Great Hwy, 94121* **Tel** *(415) 386-8439*  **Map** *7 A1*

The view is of a garden rather than the ocean, but the big stone fireplace and retractable glass walls of this Beach Chalet addition make dining here an alfresco experience even on chilly days. Serves great beers from the Beach Chalet brewery, plus *cioppino* and fancified pub specialties.

### GOLDEN GATE PARK AND THE PRESIDIO Ton Kiang 🚹 ⬤ V ⑤⑤⑤

*5821 Geary Blvd, 94121* **Tel** *(415) 752-4440*  **Map** *8 E1*

Ton Kiang is one of the best and most popular dim sum restaurants in town – beware of the queues down the block on weekends. The huge variety of dishes is always fresh, and always rolling your way on cart after cart. Full plate dishes are also served. Do not miss the minced squab with lettuce leaves.

### GOLDEN GATE PARK AND THE PRESIDIO Aziza ⬤ V ⑤⑤⑤⑤

*5800 Geary Blvd, 94121* **Tel** *(415) 752-2222*  **Map** *8 E1*

At Aziza, guests are welcomed by sprinkling rosewater over their hands. Exotic Moroccan specialties are brought to the table, as diners lounge on luxurious cushioned seats. Moroccan classics are prepared with a modern twist. The meal is finished with sweet mint tea. On weekends, belly dancers perform while you dine.

### GOLDEN GATE PARK AND THE PRESIDIO The Cliff House Bistro 🏃 ♿ ⑤⑤⑤⑤
*1090 Point Lobos Ave, 94121* **Tel** *(415) 386-3330*      **Map** *7 A1*

The original Cliff House, built in 1863, was where rich San Franciscans brunched. Twice destroyed by fire, the renovated fresh seafood place has the best views of the barking seals below on Seal Rocks. The formal restaurant is open for lunch and dinner, and the informal bistro for all meals daily.

### HAIGHT ASHBURY AND THE MISSION DISTRICT Axum Café 🏃 ♿ Ⓥ ⑤
*698 Haight St, 94117* **Tel** *(415) 252-7912*      **Map** *10 D1*

Considered to be the best place in the city to sample Ethiopian food, Axum Café is also popular for its rock-bottom prices. Primarily a hole-in-the-wall, it serves spicy and abundant portions of meat and vegetable stews and pancake-like bread, *injera*. Weekends are usually bustling, with a local clientele. Beer on tap is available.

### HAIGHT ASHBURY AND THE MISSION DISTRICT Kate's Kitchen 🍽 🏃 ♿ Ⓥ ⑤
*471 Haight Street, 94117* **Tel** *(415) 626-3984*      **Map** *9 D1*

Checked tablecloths add to the homey feel in this noisy locals' place, which is famous for its breakfasts of French toast, biscuits, and sausage gravy, plus the piles of bacon and gigantic scrambled egg dishes. For lunch, try the meat loaf sandwich or a great home-made pie. Comfort food aplenty in this welcoming establishment.

### HAIGHT ASHBURY AND THE MISSION DISTRICT La Oaxaquena Restaurant 🏃 ♿ Ⓥ ⑤
*2128 Mission Street, 94110* **Tel** *(415) 621-5446*      **Map** *9 F2*

Loosen your belt for this locals' favorite casual place in the Mission District. Awarded "Best New Mexican Hole-in-the-Wall," it serves dynamite burritos and luscious *tamales*, venison, ostrich, and salmon tacos, and Mexican hot chocolate.Some of the best southern Mexican food in San Francisco.

### HAIGHT ASHBURY AND THE MISSION DISTRICT La Taqueria 🏃 ♿ Ⓥ ⑤
*2889 Mission St, 94110* **Tel** *(415) 285-7117*      **Map** *10 F4*

Flavorful marinated beef, pork or chicken layered with firm, tasty beans or rice, fresh lettuce, and tomato make for perfect burritos, at great prices. Another specialty here is the guacamole. The cafeteria-style line moves quickly. Table seating is often filled during lunch, but the turnover is great here.

### HAIGHT ASHBURY AND THE MISSION DISTRICT Pomelo 🏃 ♿ 🚻 Ⓥ ⑤
*1793 Church St, 94131* **Tel** *(415) 285-2257*      **Map** *10 E5*

Noodles and rice plates from around the world – Chinese, Japanese, Indian, African, and European – are on the everchanging menu of Pomelo, a restaurant frequented by locals. Another location, with indoor seating only, is situated at 92 Judah Street.

### HAIGHT ASHBURY AND THE MISSION DISTRICT Rosamunde Sausage Grill 🍽 🏃 ♿ ⑤
*545 Haight St, 94117* **Tel** *(415) 437-6851*      **Map** *10 E1*

The menu at Rosamunde's specializes in one dish, and excels in it. Order a sausage – in the German, Italian, or California style – and layer on the condiments. Eat at the eight-stool counter, take your order to the bar next door, or have Rosamunde's deliver it there for you.

### HAIGHT ASHBURY AND THE MISSION DISTRICT Andalu 🏃 ♿ Ⓥ ⑤⑤
*3198 16th St, 94103* **Tel** *(415) 621-2211*      **Map** *10 E2*

An international version of "small plates" (the Spanish tapas concept) using local, global-inspired ingredients are served at this popular restaurant. Andalu also boasts excellent sangria and an expansive wine list. A festive, informal atmosphere prevails throughout. Public transport is the best way to get here.

### HAIGHT ASHBURY AND THE MISSION DISTRICT Kasa Indian Eatery 🏃 ♿ 🚻 Ⓥ ⑤⑤
*4001 18th Street, 94114, 94119* **Tel** *(415) 621-6940*      **Map** *9 D3*

Inexpensive, outstanding, home-style East-Indian food on a limited menu, offering big portions of chicken tikka, lamb curry, turkey kabobs, and luscious veggie specials. The home-made *roti*, chutneys, *riata*, and lentils are also good. Offers a different vegetarian daily special.

### HAIGHT ASHBURY AND THE MISSION DISTRICT Memphis Minnie's 🏃 ♿ ⑤⑤
*576 Haight St, 94117* **Tel** *(415) 864-7675*      **Map** *10 E1*

A takeout place and a sit-down restaurant, the Memphis Minnie is all about the slow-smoked Southern-style fork-tender sausage, chicken, beef, ribs, and pork, dripping with barbecue sauce. Order a combo, and do not leave out the handcut fries and barbecued brisket chili. In true San-Francisco style, sake is served here.

### HAIGHT ASHBURY AND THE MISSION DISTRICT Cha Cha Cha 🏃 ♿ Ⓥ ⑤⑤⑤
*2327 Mission St, 94110* **Tel** *(415) 648-0504*      **Map** *10 F3*

As much a lively nightlife scene as a restaurant, Cha Cha Cha serves small tapas plates, from mussels to fried cala-mari, and excellent sangria against a background of foot-tapping Latin music. Ever buzzing with an upbeat crowd, this place is not meant for a romantic dinner. Be prepared to wait, as it gets crowded on Friday and Saturday nights.

### HAIGHT ASHBURY AND THE MISSION DISTRICT Delfina 🏃 ♿ 🚻 ⑤⑤⑤
*3621 18th St, 94110* **Tel** *(415) 552-4055*      **Map** *10 E3*

Validated parking in a tough-to-park area makes this restaurant's simple, impeccably seasoned Northern Italian cuisine even better. Ingredients are ultra-fresh, from the morning markets. The wine list is excellent. Delfina is popular, and dining space is at a premium, so get there early.

### HAIGHT ASHBURY AND THE MISSION DISTRICT Thep Phanom Restaurant 🚶 ♿ Ⓥ  $$$

*400 Waller St, 94117* **Tel** *(415) 431-2526* **Map** *10 E1*

Dinner reservations are a must at this popular Thai restaurant, though lunch is more flexible. An accommodating staff serves well-seasoned Thai favorites, such as *yum pla muk* (spicy, crisp, cold calamari salad), in a comfortable, homey setting. The two-course special menu is outstanding.

### HAIGHT ASHBURY AND THE MISSION DISTRICT Tuba Restaurant and Grill ♿ Ⓥ  $$$

*1007 Guerrero St, 94110* **Tel** *(415) 826-8822* **Map** *10 E3*

Though a relative newcomer to San Francisco's lively restaurant scene, Tuba holds its own – and then some. In a neighborhood known for tapas and *tacquerias*, this inviting restaurant serves up authentic Turkish food, from *esme* to *musakka*, in a casual, chic atmosphere. Try the hot appetizer platter for a bit of everything.

### HAIGHT ASHBURY AND THE MISSION DISTRICT Zazie 🚶 ♿ �⬛ Ⓥ  $$$

*941 Cole St, 94117* **Tel** *(415) 564-5332* **Map** *9 B2*

The neighborhood's most popular brunch spot on the weekends, Zazie also serves bistro-style lunches and dinners daily. The bountiful plates are brought by an attentive staff, and the outdoor patio is a lovely place to enjoy a quiet conversation. Zuzie is ideal for a romantic meal.

### HAIGHT ASHBURY AND THE MISSION DISTRICT Zuni Café ♿  $$$$

*1658 Market St, 94102* **Tel** *(415) 552-2522* **Map** *10 F1*

Perfect burgers and juicy roasted chicken, cooked over an open fire, complement a menu offering a variety of Mediterranean dishes. The all-time favorites include roast chicken and Tuscan bread salad. The glass walls overlook Market Street, giving a great view of the city's action until it slows down late at night.

### PACIFIC HEIGHTS Mel's Drive-In 🚶 ♿ 🚛 Ⓥ  $

*2165 Lombard St, 94123* **Tel** *(415) 921-3039* **Map** *3 C3*

This 1950s-style diner is not the real thing, but it comes close enough with period decor, tabletop jukeboxes, and brightly garbed waitresses. Perfect for hamburger-and-fries baskets with thick milkshakes, a late night snack, or an early-morning breakfast of their country eggs and grilled sausage.

### PACIFIC HEIGHTS La Mediterranee 🚶 ♿ 🚛 Ⓥ  $$

*2210 Fillmore St, 94115* **Tel** *(415) 921-2956* **Map** *4 D4*

Taking up only a narrow space, La Mediterranée serves delicious Mediterranean specialties, such as hummus and falafel, with the reasonably priced house wine. For dessert, try the tasty baklava. This old neighborhood haunt still displays the name of the former tenants on the stained glass over the door. Also a branch in Berkeley.

### PACIFIC HEIGHTS Balboa Café ♿ Ⓥ  $$$

*3199 Fillmore St, 94123* **Tel** *(415) 921-3944* **Map** *4 D2*

Dependable lunches and brunches are the mainstay of Balboa Café, the elder statesman of the area known as "the Triangle" for its trendy bars. A must-try are the hamburgers here. After dinner, this restaurant with an elegant decor becomes a meet-and-greet hotspot for 30-somethings.

### PACIFIC HEIGHTS Betelnut 🚶 ♿  $$$

*2030 Union St, 94123* **Tel** *(415) 929-8855* **Map** *4 E2*

Serving contemporary Asian cuisine, Betelnut has been described as everything from "woodsey country Asian" to "sexy back alley." Great variety from salads, dumplings, noodles, and larger plates of seafood, pork, beef and chicken can be found on the menu.

### PACIFIC HEIGHTS Citizen Cake 🚶 ♿ Ⓥ  $$$

*2125 Fillmore Street, 94115* **Tel** *(415) 861-2228* **Map** *3 D4*

A popular, award-winning pastry shop turned casual restaurant, serving an all-home-made menu: bistro fare for dinner (cheese plates, roast beef, seafood); pizza, hearty sandwiches, and soups for lunch. The desserts are amazing, as are the luscious treats to go – cupcakes, gâteaux, tarts, and cakes. Good wine list. Michelin recommended.

### PACIFIC HEIGHTS Fresca Restaurant 🚶 ♿ Ⓥ  $$$

*2114 Fillmore, 94115* **Tel** *(415) 447-2668* **Map** *4 D4*

This Peruvian restaurant has a country-feel interior with an open kitchen. There are plenty of great home-style meat and seafood dishes. Specialties include the ceviche dishes, based on halibut with ginger and *amarillo aji* (yellow Peruvian chili), and seabass with lime and cilantro. The casual ambience adds to its appeal.

### PACIFIC HEIGHTS Greens 🚶 ♿ Ⓥ  $$$

*Building A, Fort Mason Center, 94123* **Tel** *(415) 771-6222* **Map** *4 E1*

Greens is considered by many as the city's most famous vegetarian restaurant. Its elegant, pale walls and views of the Golden Gate Bridge are the perfect setting for the imaginative meat-free delicacies that even a carnivore would love. The bread basket is always heaped with exceptional offerings from the in-house bakery.

### PACIFIC HEIGHTS Liverpool Lil's 🚶 ♿ 🚛  $$$

*2942 Lyon St, 94123* **Tel** *(415) 921-6664* **Map** *3 C3*

Liverpool Lil's fame as a preferred spot for lunch and dinner rests on its strong bar drinks, friendly service, and reliable pub menu featuring big salads, pepper steaks, and an outstanding hamburger. In warm weather, the outside tables look over the west boundary of the Presidio. It opens late and serves till after midnight.

**Key to Price Guide** *see p568* **Key to Symbols** *see back cover flap*

### PACIFIC HEIGHTS Rose's Café

$$$

*2298 Union St, 94123* **Tel** *(415) 775-2200* **Map** *4 D3*

Tables set outside look over the quiet end of Union Street, while the interior features a cheery yellow space with big windows. The restaurant's main draws are the weekday lunches, with good salads and pastas, as well as weekend brunches. Specialties include French toast and breakfast pizzas. Live music on Monday nights.

### PACIFIC HEIGHTS Brazen Head

$$$$

*3166 Buchanan St, 94123* **Tel** *(415) 921-7600* **Map** *4 D2*

This cash-only, dark, pub-like hideaway is the favored destination for those craving a traditional grilled steak, a scotch on the rocks, and quiet conversation late at night after the other local restaurants have closed. The extensive wine list is well chosen. Visitors know the location by the address – there is no sign.

### PACIFIC HEIGHTS Elite Café

$$$$

*2049 Fillmore St, 94115* **Tel** *(415) 346-8400* **Map** *4 D4*

In the middle of the Fillmore shopping area, Elite Café is an institution, with intimate booths and a hopping bar that serves fresh oysters along with stiff drinks. The New Orleans-style gumbos and jambalayas also feature on the weekend brunch menu. Service is warm and attentive.

## THE BAY AREA

### BERKELEY Bette's Ocean View Diner

$

*1807 4th St, 94710* **Tel** *(510) 644-3230* **Road map** *inset B*

A local classic in the city's famous shopping block, this 1940s-style eatery features traditional, hearty American food. Patrons line up for hours at the weekend for their share of classic comfort food, prepared simply, and served with a smile. The pancakes, waffles, and orange-cranberry scones are a must-try. The noise level can be deafening at times.

### BERKELEY Celia's Mexican Restaurant
$

*1841 Euclid Ave, 94709* **Tel** *(510) 549-1460* **Road map** *inset B*

This casual, often noisy restaurant in the heart of Berkeley's popular shopping district serves top-notch, platter-style Mexican fare, traditionally prepared. Nachos, fajitas, burritos, and enchiladas are on offer along with a nice selection of seafood and vegetarian dishes. The margaritas are well worth trying, too.

### BERKELEY Plearn Thai Cuisine
$

*2050 University Ave, 94707* **Tel** *(510) 841-2148* **Road map** *inset B*

Having stood the test of time, and the test of the fickle local public, this no-frills Thai house has become a local favorite; no small feat in a city overrun with Thai restaurants. *Pad thai* (a noodle dish with tofu, shrimp, and peanuts) is one of the house specialties. The service is amicable, and the food is reasonably priced.

### BERKELEY Bangkok Thai Cuisine
$$

*1459 University Ave, 94702* **Tel** *(510) 848-6483* **Road map** *inset B*

A clean, bright atmosphere and good food make this a popular spot for Thai cuisine. The fare is well priced and served quickly, especially at lunchtime, when the restaurant can get crowded. It offers meat, chicken, and seafood dishes along with rice and noodles. Favorites include vegetarian spring rolls, and beef with broccoli.

### BERKELEY Chez Panisse Restaurant
$$$$$

*1517 Shattuck Ave, 94709* **Tel** *(510) 548-5525* **Road map** *inset B*

Proprietor and chef Alice Waters is famed as the innovator of California cuisine, which is on offer in this simple wood-framed restaurant where it all began. Dishes are prepared simply with the freshest ingredients. Book well in advance or opt for a more casual meal at the café upstairs.

### BOLINAS Coast Café
$$

*46 Wharf Rd, 94924* **Tel** *(415) 868-2298* **Road map** *inset B*

This fun, friendly restaurant, set in a historic location, has a surfing decor. Coast Café offers well-prepared classic seafood and California cuisine, including Niman Ranch beef, and even specials for kids. Fresh seasonal produce is used to create innovative dishes. Oysters are barbecued on the deck during summer.

### HALF MOON BAY Cameron's Restaurant and Inn

$$

*1410 South Cabrillo Highway, 94019* **Tel** *(650) 726-5705* **Road map** *inset B*

Just south of town, watch for the red phone booth and the London double-decker buses, one of which is a kids' game room at this funky, fun British outpost. Hearty pub food sees fish and chips, bangers and mash, steak, clam chowder, and more comfort food on the menu, and European brews on tap. Games and volleyball out back. Very lively weekend nights.

### HALF MOON BAY Barbara's Fish Trap
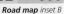
$$$

*281 Capistrano Street, 94018* **Tel** *(650) 728-7049* **Road map** *inset B*

Overlooking Pillar Point Harbor and housed in a little red building on stilts, this fun, noisy, casual place is full of families. Try the daily fresh-fish specials, or chowder, Dungeness crab, burgers, and the delicious thick-cut fries. Take out and eat in the glassed-in patio with outdoor heaters, or choose to dine inside for a harbor view.

### HALF MOON BAY Miramar Beach Restaurant

*131 Mirada Road, 94019* **Tel** *(650) 726-9053*     $$$

**Road map** *inset B*

Once a Prohibition roadhouse from around 1918, this joint jumps with live music on weekends, attracting a lively bar crowd. Fresh seafood and steaks rule, along with paella, pastas, salads, soups, and a host of appetizers. Enjoy the view from the patio and the oceanfront windows, watching the sunset and surfers off Miramar Beach across the road.

### HALF MOON BAY Cetrella

*845 Main St, 94019* **Tel** *(650) 726-4090*     $$$$

**Road map** *inset B*

This top-rated restaurant is at once casual and sophisticated, with Mediterranean touches in the decor and on the menu, which employs the freshest ingredients from the area. Highlights include an impressive assortment of cheeses and an award-winning wine list. Live jazz can be enjoyed from Friday to Saturday. Closed on Mondays.

### LAFAYETTE Postino

*3565 Mount Diablo Blvd, 94549* **Tel** *(925) 299-8700*     $$$$

**Road map** *inset B*

Serving faithful preparations of Italian cuisine, this lively, family-type restaurant attracts visitors from all around the Bay area. Specialties include home-made pastas and cheeses, house-cured meats, and oven-roasted dishes. There is also an array of excellent seafood. The rustic decor adds to the charm.

### LARKSPUR Left Bank

*507 Magnolia Avenue, 94939* **Tel** *(415) 927-3331*     $$$

**Road map** *inset B*

In a circa-1890 building in a charming Marin village, this busy local favorite serves perfectly authentic French brasserie food. Cozy up by the fire to enjoy a tasty steak tartare or steak frites, the luscious Lyonnaise tart, and classic duck à l'orange, buttery mussels, or onion soup, with, of course, profiteroles to finish. Awarded "Best French in Marin."

### LARKSPUR The Tavern at Lark Creek

*234 Magnolia Ave, 94939* **Tel** *(415) 924-7766*     $$$

**Road map** *inset B*

Set in a shaded grove among towering trees, this comfortable, home-like restaurant features award-winning and often inventive American country-style fare, from shrimp and grits to spaghetti with Monterey sardines. There are delicious meat and poultry dishes, as well as a popular Sunday brunch. Dinner only.

### MILL VALLEY Samurai

*425 Miller Ave, 94941* **Tel** *(415) 381-3680*     $

**Road map** *inset B*

Highly renowned, this boisterous Japanese restaurant often has a line lasting as long as an hour or more. However, most diners feel the appetizing fare is well worth the wait. Fried tempura, succulent seafood, and absolutely fresh sushi are some of the house specialties. Closed at lunchtime and on Sundays.

### MILL VALLEY Frantoio Ristorante

*152 Shoreline Hwy, 94941* **Tel** *(415) 289-5777*     $$$

**Road map** *inset B*

Renowned for its home-made olive oil – made by the only on-site olive press in the US – this bright, cheery eatery offers delicious Italian and Mediterranean cuisine, much of it employing its signature ingredient in abundance. Choose from a variety of pizzas, pastas, and seafood, meat, and poultry dishes.

### MILL VALLEY Piazza D'Angelo

*22 Miller Ave, 94941* **Tel** *(415) 388-2000*     $$$

**Road map** *inset B*

A lively atmosphere and well-prepared Italian menu have made this restaurant, set in the downtown plaza, a long-time favorite. The dining room is open and inviting, and the wood-fired pizzas are outstanding, as are the freshly made pastas and seafood dishes. Piazza D'Angelo attracts a mixed crowd, from locals to celebrities.

### MILL VALLEY Buckeye Roadhouse

*15 Shoreline Hwy, 94941* **Tel** *(415) 331-2600*     $$$$

**Road map** *inset B*

Located conspicuously along the freeway, this friendly restaurant is a staple among the area's comfort-food eateries. The atmosphere is neighborly, with a welcoming, roaring fire, and the menu features simple American cooking, including tasty steaks and seafood dishes. The Sunday brunch is worth trying.

### MOSS BEACH Moss Beach Distillery

*140 Beach Way, 94038* **Tel** *(650) 728-5595*     $$$$

**Road map** *inset B*

This is a favorite with locals and visitors alike. The menu serves hearty American and Italian fare and a few good seafood choices. An ever-crowded outdoor deck offers striking views of the ocean, and guests can enjoy a cocktail or sip cocoa while watching the sunset. Moss Beach also features an elaborate brunch on Sunday.

### MOUNTAIN VIEW Tied House Café & Brewery

*954 Villa St, 94041* **Tel** *(650) 965-2739*     $$

**Road map** *B4*

Lively and sometimes raucous, this microbrewery and pub-style restaurant has an amazing selection of home-made beers on tap to complement the better-than-average seafood dishes and other American fare. The menu ranges from Mexican-inspired to New Orleans-style and Italian classics, and is sure to please even fussy diners.

### OAKLAND Rockridge Café

*5492 College Ave, 94618* **Tel** *(510) 653-1567*     $$

**Road map** *inset B*

Styled to resemble a 1940s diner, this casual restaurant is set in the city's busy shopping district. It is extremely popular with students and families, who flock to the eatery on weekend afternoons for a good burger or a rib-sticking breakfast. The atmosphere here is friendly and unpretentious.

**Key to Price Guide** *see p568* **Key to Symbols** *see back cover flap*

### OAKLAND Bay Wolf

$$$

*3853 Piedmont Ave, 94611* **Tel** *(510) 655-6004*

**Road map** inset B

With a reputation for excellence, this long-established, elegant restaurant is set in an old Victorian house, and features dishes inspired by Tuscany and the Basque country. The highly acclaimed menu changes each month to represent a different Mediterranean region. Dinner only.

### OAKLAND Bocanova

$$$

*55 Webster Street, 94607* **Tel** *(510) 444-1233*

**Road map** inset B

At Jack London Square, this hip, rambling place, with lively bar scene and gorgeous contemporary interior, specializes in "Pan-American" food such as gumbo, *mole*, *posole*, and *chimichurri*. Exciting exhibition kitchens cook up sharing portions of roasted and grilled meat dishes, Cuban sandwiches, seafood – try the shrimp *ceviche*. Get here by ferry.

### OAKLAND Oliveto

$$$$

*5655 College Ave, 94618* **Tel** *(510) 547-5356*

**Road map** inset B

A local favorite, this welcoming restaurant has a casual café and a full-service restaurant, where the masterful chef prepares appetizing Italian cuisine using the freshest possible ingredients. The menu changes slightly each day to reflect the fancy of the chef's visit to the market. Oliveto is closed for lunch on Saturdays and Sundays.

### ORINDA Siam Orchid Thai

$$$

*23 Orinda Way, 94563* **Tel** *(925) 253-1975*

**Road map** inset B

Located in a small village 4 miles (6 km) east of Berkeley, this unassuming, yet pleasant restaurant serves up some of the best Thai cuisine in the area, all with friendly service and at bargain prices. The *pad thai* is outstanding as are the daily specials. Expect a brief wait on weekend evenings.

### PALO ALTO Gordon Biersch

$$$

*640 Emerson St, 94301* **Tel** *(650) 323-7723*

**Road map** inset B

Part of a well-known chain of brewery restaurants, this lively, brightly polished eatery features great food that goes well beyond typical pub grub. The menu is rounded off by hearty American and Italian classics. The freshly made pizzas are a good choice to complement the house-made beers.

### PESCADERO Duarte's Tavern

$$

*202 Stage Rd, 94060* **Tel** *(650) 879-0464*

**Road map** inset B

Operated by the same family for more than a century, this unpretentious roadside landmark has a cult-like following for its amiable service and home-made pies. The menu is full of innovative creations, including artichoke omelets, deep-fried sea scallops, and such standards as pork chops and apple sauce.

### POINT REYES STATION Station House Café

$$$

*11180 State Hwy 1, 94956* **Tel** *(415) 663-1515*

**Road map** A3

This unassuming, clapboard-style structure, painted a fire-engine red, houses a friendly restaurant, with surprisingly excellent fare and the freshest seafood. Do not miss the barbecued oysters, which are available in season. The atmosphere here is casual and relaxing. It is closed on Wednesdays.

### SAN JOSE Yankee Pier

$$$

*378 Santana Row, 95128* **Tel** *(408) 244-1244*

**Road map** B4

Set among the fancy shops and restaurants of Santana Row, this family-style, low-key restaurant is a nice respite, and offers delicious seafood. The menu is prepared with a gourmet touch, and includes top-notch clam chowder. The fare is reasonably priced, and the service is fast and friendly.

### SAUSALITO Fish

$$

*350 Harbor Dr, 94965* **Tel** *(415) 331-3474*

**Road map** A3

This small, high-ceiling restaurant at the shoreline has a few tables, and offers its menu by counter service. The specialty here is fresh seafood, simply prepared, and sold at affordable prices. Excellent BBQ oysters, white clam chowder, and grilled calamari. It is extremely busy at lunchtime.

### SAUSALITO Poggio

$$$

*801 Bridgeway, 94965* **Tel** *(415) 332-7771*

**Road map** A3

Situated in the heart of Sausalito village, this comfortable and friendly restaurant serves hearty and appetizing Italian dishes; many are fired in the large wood-burning oven that anchors the space. The chef pays special homage to Italian classics of Tuscany. The service here is impeccable.

### SAUSALITO Murray Circle

$$$$

*601 Murray Circle, 94965* **Tel** *(415) 339-4750*

**Road map** inset B

An urban-chic hideaway within the hip, Cavallo Point Lodge resort, this is located in a lovely historic building and boasts a locally sourced menu by a Michelin-starred chef, with an exceptional 2,000-bottle wine list and cozy bar. The seasonal menu offers seafood, meats, and veggies, from baby beets to veal and grass-fed beef to Dungeness crab.

### STINSON BEACH Sand Dollar Restaurant

$$$

*3458 Shoreline Highway, 94970* **Tel** *(415) 868-0434*

**Road map** inset B

In a charming 1920s building, just a block from the beach, the hearty bistro-style food served in this great restaurant is popular for lunch, dinner, and weekend brunch, offering a varied menu that includes local seafood, steak frites, pasta, and *cioppino*, plus a big wine list. There is a lively bar, and jazz and bluegrass on weekends.

### TIBURON Guaymas
*5 Main St, 94920* **Tel** *(415) 435-6300*

**Road map** *A3*

With sweeping views of the Bay area from its dining room, this stylish restaurant serves high-end Mexican and Latin-American fare, prepared with a gourmet twist and fresh ingredients. The bar mixes excellent margaritas; guests can enjoy them on the pleasant deck. The food is reasonably priced and the service is efficient.

### TIBURON Sam's Anchor Café
*27 Main St, 94920* **Tel** *(415) 435-4527*

**Road map** *A3*

Thanks to its location on the docks of San Francisco Bay, this fun and casual restaurant and cocktail bar attracts visitors from all around the area. The food is serviceable, with tasty fried calamari, some nice seafood dishes, hearty burgers, and Italian-influenced dishes. Sam's draws a lively crowd, especially on summer weekends.

## THE NORTH

### ARCATA Luke's Joint
*887 H St., 95521* **Tel** *(707) 826-0415*

**Road map** *A2*

A little surprise in sleepy Arcata, Luke's Joint is a real find. Brunch features the popular lavender waffles, while lunch is dominated by all manner of pulled pork dishes. Desserts are popular here, too, even the maple bacon cheesecake, which sounds odd but is delicious. The one problem is that the restaurant is tiny and they don't take reservations.

### ARCATA Renata's Crêperie
*1030 G St., 95521*

**Road map** *A2*

There is always a wait for a table at Renata's, but locals keep coming back because the food is that good. With its orange walls and wood floors, Renata's is a nice place to go for a stop-off meal. Try the eclectic crêpe menu from traditional french classics to specialties such as brie, bacon, and scallions.

### EUREKA Brick and Fire Bistro
*1630 F St., 95501* **Tel** *(707) 268-8959*

**Road map** *A2*

Serving home-made, delicious Italian fare in a pleasant, cozy dining room with an exposed brick oven. Brick and Fire feels like just the sort of neighborhood restaurant you'd expect to find in Eureka, but with the quality food you'd expect in a bigger city. Everything is made fresh, from the sauces to the croutons, and it's delicious.

### EUREKA Restaurant 301
*301 L St, 95501* **Tel** *(707) 444-8062*

**Road map** *A2*

The beautiful, historic Hotel Carter is renowned for its restaurant, 301, which offers gourmet preparations of American and Mediterranean dishes, made with fresh seasonal ingredients. The dining room is handsome and romantic, and the wine list is award winning. It is closed for lunch.

### GARBERVILLE Woodrose Café
*911 Redwood Dr, 95442* **Tel** *(707) 923-3191*

**Road map** *A2*

Located in the heart of redwood country, this casual café is a mainstay among locals, especially for breakfast. It offers traditional American cuisine, but also has many vegetarian-friendly options, as well as a range of organic meals. It is closed on Saturdays and Sundays, and for dinner from Monday to Friday.

### MOUNT SHASTA Wayside Grill
*2217 South Mount Shasta Blvd., 96067* **Tel** *(530) 918-9234*

**Road map** *A2*

With its giant A-frame sign, the Wayside feels like a blast from the past. The menu here runs the gamut from pizza and barbecue to Mexican entrées, but all are surprisingly good, as is the service. Packed with après-ski folks during the winter, it gets equally crowded with visitors in summertime, so be prepared for a wait.

### MOUNT SHASTA Lily's
*1013 S Mount Shasta Blvd, 96067* **Tel** *(530) 926-3372*

**Road map** *B1*

This charming restaurant, set in a modest structure surrounded by a white picket fence, offers a little bit of everything on the diverse menu. It features seasonal dishes, a few American classics, and some Mexican and Indian fare. Advance reservations are highly recommended.

### ORICK Snack Shack
*21077 Highway 101, 95555* **Tel** *(707) 488-5305*

**Road map** *A1*

A fresh take on the standard American burger-and-fries joint, this is known for the best fast food in the area. Burgers are cooked perfectly to order with plenty of toppings to choose from, and the menu also offers salads, soups, and sandwiches, as well as thick milkshakes. Service is fast and friendly.

### REDDING Jack's Grill
*1743 California St, 96001* **Tel** *(530) 241-9705*

**Road map** *B2*

A well-run steakhouse serving top-grade meats and poultry to a loyal following since 1940. The fried chicken and huge beef dinners are fantastic. The place is friendly and accommodating, but the lines can be long and reservations are not accepted. It is closed on Sunday, and for lunch from Monday to Saturday.

**Key to Price Guide** *see p568* **Key to Symbols** *see back cover flap*

### REDWAY Mateel Café  $$$

*3342 Redwood Dr, 95560* **Tel** *(707) 923-2030* **Road map** *A2*

Serving health-conscious meals, from fresh fish and hearty salads and pizzas to Mideast-inspired dishes, this casual, out-of-the-way café also doubles as a regional cultural center and a gathering spot for locals sharing news of the day. The freshly baked bread and desserts are delicious. It is closed on Sunday.

### SAMOA Samoa Cookhouse $

*79 Cookhouse Lane, 95564* **Tel** *(800) 487-1659* **Road map** *A2*

Begun as a dining hall for hungry North Coast lumberjacks, this friendly, rustic restaurant still serves huge portions of hearty American fare, including ham and eggs, fried chicken, and such homey touches as fresh-baked bread. The staff are efficient, and there is a logging museum on-site.

### SMITH RIVER Ship Ashore $$$

*12370 Hwy 101 N, 95531* **Tel** *(800) 487-3141* **Road map** *A1*

Part of a resort with the same name, this family-friendly restaurant is set near a permanently docked historic ship. The menu presents straightforward American fare, as well as generous helpings of tasty and fresh seafood dishes. The service is amicable, and the atmosphere congenial.

### SUSANVILLE Black Bear Diner $$

*2795 Main St, 96130* **Tel** *(530) 257-4447* **Road map** *B2*

Although part of a chain of restaurants in the West, this friendly, casual inn has the feel of a one-off diner, with comfortable booths and familiar service. The classic American fare is hearty and well prepared, including excellent burgers and sandwiches, steaks, chops, and huge salads. Breakfasts are very popular here.

### TRINIDAD Larrupin Café 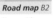 $$$$

*1658 Patrick's Point Dr, 95570* **Tel** *(707) 677-0230* **Road map** *A2*

A favorite among locals, and with views of the Pacific Ocean, this warm little restaurant, just north of Arcata, has a homely ambience and is known for its fresh seafood and gracious hospitality. The barbecued oysters are a popular choice as appetizers. Larrupin's is closed on Wednesdays and for lunch.

### UKIAH Ukiah Brewing Company 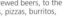 $$

*102 S State St, 95482* **Tel** *(707) 468-5898* **Road map** *A3*

Everything in this bright, lively pub is organically produced, from the wide selection of home-brewed beers, to the complete menu, which features updated American classics. Burgers, hot curries, salads, nachos, pizzas, burritos, sandwiches, filets, and a few vegetarian specials are on offer here.

### WEAVERVILLE La Grange Café  $$

*226 N Main St, 96093* **Tel** *(530) 623-5325* **Road map** *A2*

This cheery café, set in a historic building, serves health-conscious cuisine, from generous portions of organic salads to large sandwiches and a range of vegetarian meals, all offered at affordable prices. La Grange also has an extensive selection of micro-brewed beers on tap. It often attracts a hungry, post river-rafting crowd.

## WINE COUNTRY

### BOONVILLE Boonville Hotel $$$$

*14050 Hwy 128, 95415* **Tel** *(707) 895-2210* **Road map** *A3*

Acclaimed chef Johnny Schmitt is highly regarded for his well-prepared California cuisine, with Mexican and Italian influences. Organic meats and locally grown produce are used at this approachable gourmet dining room. The menu changes often, and there's an excellent wine list. It is closed on Tuesdays, and for lunch from Wednesday to Monday.

### CALISTOGA Buster's BBQ & Bakery  $

*1207 Foothill Boulevard, 94515* **Tel** *(707) 942-5605* **Road map** *A3*

At a roadside BBQ stand at the gateway to Calistoga, pork loin, ribs, and other meats are cooked over an oak fire and served as sandwiches or platters with slaw and baked beans outdoors at picnic tables. Shakes, beer, and espresso drinks wash it down nicely. Servings are large and reasonably priced.

### CALISTOGA Brannan's Grill $$$$

*1374 Lincoln Ave, 94515* **Tel** *(707) 942-2233* **Road map** *A3*

Occupying a historic structure in the heart of town, this handsome restaurant has a thoughtful menu of American grilled cuisine and some Mediterranean-inspired classics. It offers a wide range of gnocchi, steaks, salads, and filet mignons, and boasts an award-winning wine list. The service is friendly and the ambience impressive.

### CALISTOGA All Seasons Café $$$$$

*1400 Lincoln Ave, 94515* **Tel** *(707) 942-9111* **Road map** *A3*

One of the most popular spots in town, this charming restaurant is renowned for its extensive wine list and frequently changing menu of seasonal classics. Do not miss the home-made breads and freshly made pastas. A wine shop and tasting area are also featured on the premises. The service here is impeccable.

### FORESTVILLE Farmhouse Inn & Restaurant

*7871 River Rd, 95436* **Tel** *(707) 887-3300, (800) 464-6642*

**Road map** *A3*

This charming restaurant is situated in a quaint yellow farmhouse and offers a refined, relaxed atmosphere along with top-notch French country-style cuisine. The menu features local and seasonal ingredients and changes often. Meals are accented with a wonderful selection of cheeses and an exceptional wine list.

### HEALDSBURG Charlie Palmer's Dry Creek Kitchen

*317 Healdsburg Ave, 95448* **Tel** *(707) 431-0330*

**Road map** *A3*

This sleek restaurant in the equally stylish Hotel Healdsburg, run by famed chef Charlie Palmer, has a frequently changing menu of seasonal dishes inspired by local ingredients. The ambience is big-city cachet, with small-town charm. There is a great wine list, exclusively from the area. It is closed for lunch from Monday to Thursday.

### NAPA Bistro Don Giovanni

*4110 Howard Lane, 94558* **Tel** *(707) 224-3300*

**Road map** *A3*

This inviting dining room of this extremely popular Napa Valley restaurant has a large wood-burning fireplace and a lovely outdoor terrace. The menu has a delicious offering of rustic Italian fare, with French influence, and an excellent wine list. It presents striking views of magnificent mountains and extensive, well-kept gardens.

### NAPA Cole's Chop House

*1122 Main St, 94559* **Tel** *(707) 224-6328*

**Road map** *A3*

The dining room, with stone walls and wood beams, creates a casual, yet elegant setting for the signature dry-aged steaks and chops on offer here. Start with a martini, then select something from the extensive Cabernet Sauvignon-oriented wine list. The service is exemplary and knowledgeable. Cole's is closed for lunch.

### RUTHERFORD Auberge du Soleil

*180 Rutherford Hill Rd, 94573* **Tel** *(707) 967-3111*

**Road map** *A3*

This handsome, elegant restaurant is a must for any serious food lover with time and disposable income. The cuisine, made with fresh regional products, is inventive and appetizing, and the service is polished and deft. The views from the terrace are second-to-none. A truly memorable dining experience.

### SONOMA Red Grape

*529 1st Street West, 95476* **Tel** *(707) 996-4103*

**Road map** *A3*

Specializing in "New Haven" style, thin-crust pies with traditional and exotic toppings, plus pasta and salads, this light, airy restaurant and leafy patio bustle with families and tourists. Winner choices on the pizza menu vary from pear and gorgonzola to spinach and sausage. Top-notch wine list and beer from the small bar.

### SONOMA Girl and the Fig

*110 West Spain Street, 95476* **Tel** *(707) 938–3634*

**Road map** *A3*

This is one of the region's most highly rated restaurants, serving a seasonal, locally based menu of Country French cuisine with exceptional cheeses, seafood, steaks, and creative veggies. Situated on the plaza, sharing a charming historic building with the Sonoma Hotel, it offers diners an artful setting with a garden patio.

### SONOMA Maya Restaurant

*101 E Napa St, 95476* **Tel** *(707) 935-3500*

**Road map** *A3*

Casual and fun, this bright restaurant is located right on the downtown plaza, and features Latin-American specialties, prepared with a gourmet twist and using the freshest ingredients. The carnitas are the best around. There are good margaritas, as well as a lengthy list of specialty tequilas. It is closed on Mondays.

### SONOMA The Swiss Hotel

*18 W Spain St, 95476* **Tel** *(707) 938-2884*

**Road map** *A3*

One of the best meals in town can be found at this historic restaurant on the plaza, with an appetizing menu of rustic Italian classics and pizzas from a wood-burning oven. The atmosphere is convivial and welcoming, and the clientele consists of tourists and locals alike.

### ST. HELENA Gott's Roadside Tray Gourmet

*933 Main Street, 94574* **Tel** *(707) 963-3486*

**Road map** *A3*

An upscale, 21st-century version of a 1950s roadside stand, with outdoor tables, exotic burgers, calamari, plus beer and an extensive wine list – think classic Americana with a Wine Country twist. The shakes are also good, with espresso bean, mint chip, and white pistachio flavors, and the all-time favorite root beer float.

### ST. HELENA Market Restaurant

*1347 Main St, 94574* **Tel** *(707) 963-3799*

**Road map** *A3*

This comfortable restaurant provides an experience of fine dining without fuss. The service is top-notch and the food excellent. It offers traditional American fare, from steaks and poultry dishes to seafood and pasta, prepared with fresh seasonal ingredients and gourmet touches.

### ST. HELENA Tra Vigne

*1050 Charter Oak, 94574* **Tel** *(707) 963-4444*

**Road map** *A3*

One of the best-loved restaurants in the region, this lively spot is set among trees and foliage and vine-covered stone walls. The menu offers rustic Italian specialties as well as fresh treats from its on-site bakery. Request a table on the secluded courtyard for a complete Wine Country experience.

---

**Key to Price Guide** *see p568* **Key to Symbols** *see back cover flap*

### ST. HELENA Meadowood Restaurant

$$$$$

*900 Meadowood Lane, 94574* **Tel** *(707) 963-3646, (800) 458-8080* **Road map** *A3*

This elegant restaurant at the famed Meadowood Napa Valley resort features fresh inventions of Provençal cuisine, served in a serene environment with white tablecloths and large windows. There is also a less formal grill on the premises. The atmosphere is bright and inviting.

### ST. HELENA Press Restaurant

$$$$$

*587 St. Helena Hwy, 94574* **Tel** *(707) 967-0550* **Road map** *A3*

In the heart of St. Helena, the sophisticated Press Restaurant serves skillfully prepared dry-aged beef, whole roasted chicken, and other specialties from the wood-burning grill and rotisserie. The atmosphere is casual, yet elegant. The service is exceptional. It is open for dinner only.

### YOUNTVILLE Bottega Napa Valley

$$$$

*6525 Washington Street, 94599* **Tel** *(707) 945-1050* **Road map** *B3*

In an old brick winery building with timbered ceilings, Murano glass accents, and a pleasant fireplace terrace, is Food Network star Michael Chiarello's restaurant. Popular with celebrities and winery owners, the menu offers contemporary Italian cuisine with nearly all local ingredients. Well-priced wine list and bar.

### YOUNTVILLE Mustards Grill

$$$$

*7399 St. Helena Hwy, 94558* **Tel** *(707) 944-2424* **Road map** *B3*

A Napa Valley staple, this roadside restaurant has a lovely setting among vineyards. Well-prepared California cuisine is served in a vibrant atmosphere. Try the famed Mongolian pork chop with homemade mustard sauce or the lemon-lime pie with brown sugar meringue. Book dinner early, or drop in for a seat at the bar during lunch.

### YOUNTVILLE Bouchon

$$$$

*6534 Washington St, 94599* **Tel** *(707) 944-8037* **Road map** *B3*

Sample the skill of critically acclaimed chef Thomas Keller at this excellent bistro. Every dish on the menu is exquisite, especially the steak frites. For starters, choose from the extensive raw bar. Mouthwatering fresh breads and pastries are available from the bakery next door.

### YOUNTVILLE The French Laundry

$$$$$

*6640 Washington St, 94599* **Tel** *(707) 944-2380* **Road map** *B3*

This is the famed little house in which chef Thomas Keller built his reputation, and it offers dining at its very best. Book a month in advance, and once you get a reservation, expect to spend a few hours enjoying a monumental dining experience. It is open all days for dinner, with lunch only served on Fridays, Saturdays, and Sundays.

## GOLD COUNTRY AND THE CENTRAL VALLEY

### AMADOR CITY Imperial Hotel and Restaurant

$$$$

*14202 Hwy 49, 955601* **Tel** *(209) 267-9172* **Road map** *B3*

Housed in the Imperial Hotel, this popular restaurant is charming and bright, with a dining room overlooking flower gardens. The seasonal menu features Continental cuisine and many Italian-inspired dishes. Fresh fish and grilled steaks make a regular appearance. It is open for dinner only, and closed on Mondays and Tuesdays.

### CHICO Sierra Nevada Tap Room and Restaurant

$$$

*1075 E 20th St, 95928* **Tel** *(530) 345-2739* **Road map** *B2*

Wildly popular for its microbrewed beer, the restaurant at this working brewery serves up such memorable fare as apple-malt pork loin and delicious pizzas from a wood-burning oven. Frequented by a young crowd, the place is upbeat and lively, especially on weekend nights. It is closed on Mondays.

### GRASS VALLEY Swiss House Restaurant

$$

*535 Mill St, 95945* **Tel** *(530) 273-8272* **Road map** *B3*

This family-friendly restaurant is popular for its Swiss and German specialties, which co-exist on an eclectic menu alongside a few Chinese and Asian dishes. The soups are home-made, as is such traditional fare as sauerbraten, Jaeger schnitzel, and bratwurst. Service is prompt and amicable. It is closed on Mondays, Tuesdays, and for lunch.

### JAMESTOWN National Hotel Restaurant

$$$$

*18183 Main St, 95370* **Tel** *(209) 984-3446* **Road map** *B3*

Set in a historic Gold Rush-era structure, this cheery restaurant offers a long, impressive menu that stresses mainly Mediterranean cuisine. Create a light meal from the extensive appetizer menu. Home-made desserts, particularly the crème brulée, are superb. There is an excellent wine list on offer at the saloon here.

### NEVADA CITY Matteo's Public

$$$

*300 Commercial St, 95959* **Tel** *(530) 265-6248* **Road map** *B3*

With a bustling atmosphere and casual decor, this restaurant is among the most prolific in the area. The food is French country-inspired, skillfully prepared and presented artistically by the inventive kitchen staff. Service is friendly and spirited. There is occasional live music played in the dining room.

## NEVADA CITY New Moon Café
*203 York St., 95959* **Tel** *(530) 265-6399*      **Road map** *B3*    $$$$

The chef and maître'd are co-owners here and their commitment to customers shows in the exceptional service and food. A small but cozy spot, New Moon taps in to local ingredients to produce a fresh, inventive, and always-changing menu. The chef makes a different fresh ravioli every night, served either as an appetizer or an entrée.

## SACRAMENTO Chando's Tacos
*863 Arden Way, 95815* **Tel** *(916) 641-8226*      **Road map** *B3*    $

A bright red-and-orange stand on the side of the road that is consistently named as one of Sacramento's best restaurants, Chando's serves amazing tacos in a town with a lot of good Mexican food. All of the meats and fish are done on the grill, perfectly spiced, and placed in fresh-made tortillas.

## SACRAMENTO Morant's Old-Fashioned Sausage Kitchen
*5001 Franklin Blvd, 95820* **Tel** *(916) 731-4377*      **Road map** *B3*    $

True to its name, Morant's specializes in sausages – mostly German sausages, but they make a number of other types as well. One part old butcher shop, one part deli, Morant's is super casual, but the shop's commitment to quality ingredients attracts local chefs and foodie types, despite the paper menu and strip mall location.

## SACRAMENTO Tower Café
*1518 Broadway, 95818* **Tel** *(916) 441-0222*      **Road map** *B3*    $$$

Immensely popular Tower Café is ideal for sitting in the palm-shrouded courtyard on long evenings and sipping imported beers or teas. The menu is casual and eclectic, influenced by regions from Asia to Africa. Service is informal. The interesting beer and wine list features remote global regions.

## SACRAMENTO Esquire Grill
*1213 K St, 95814* **Tel** *(916) 448-8900*      **Road map** *B3*    $$$$

A New York-style American bistro, Esquire Grill draws a good-looking downtown crowd and the occasional minor celebrity. The menu features well-executed steaks and chops as well as a few seafood highlights. There is a good bar scene on weekends. Closed for lunch on Saturdays and Sundays.

## SACRAMENTO Fat City Bar & Café
*1001 Front St, 95814* **Tel** *(916) 446-6768*      **Road map** *B3*    $$$$

The food is not going to win any Michelin stars, but it is decent and Fat City is worth a visit for the ambience alone. Located in Old Sacramento, it has a real California pioneer vibe to it, complete with old wooden bar and ornate stained-glass windows. The Fat family owns several restaurants in the area, and they know what they're doing.

## SACRAMENTO The Press Bistro
*1809 Capitol Ave., 95811* **Tel** *(916) 444-2566*      **Road map** *B3*    $$$$

Above and beyond its lovely communal table, the Press Bistro has a warm, community vibe to it. Its barrel-poured house wines are made locally, and sharing is encouraged via an assortment of Italian-influenced tapas. Chef David English is well known in the area, making Press one of those spots that other chefs dine at and recommend to friends.

## SACRAMENTO The Firehouse
*1112 Second St., 95814* **Tel** *(916) 442-4772*      **Road map** *B3*    $$$$$

In a historic landmark building in the heart of Old Sacramento, this is known for its top-flight service, extensive wine collection, and creative menus. Start with a martini and the white corn lobster bisque and go on to delicious duck with fresh vegetables, pork tenderloin, or mouthwatering *frutti de mare*. Weekday lunch and dinner nightly.

## SACRAMENTO The Kitchen
*2225 Hurley Way, 95825* **Tel** *(916) 568-7171*      **Road map** *B3*    $$$$$

Sacramento's over-the-top special occasion restaurant, The Kitchen doesn't disappoint. There's one fixed, five-course menu per month, so call ahead before booking, but it's hard to imagine anyone not loving absolutely everything these chefs put out. With white tablecloths and an exposed kitchen, The Kitchen feels as elegant as the food tastes.

## SONORA Talulah's
*13 S. Washington St, 95370* **Tel** *(209) 532-7278*      **Road map** *B3*    $

In its simple, pleasant dining room – all blond wood tables with white tablecloths – Talulah's serves up delicious Italian meals. The ravioli sampler and the gorgonzola-stuffed chicken are both favorites, and everything is served with fresh, perfectly cooked vegetables.

## SONORA The Diamondback Grill
*93 S. Washington St, 95370* **Tel** *(209) 532-6661*      **Road map** *B3*    $$

Though it always has a few specials scrawled on a giant black chalkboard, the Diamondback's real specialty, and the reason people come here, is the burgers, and they are simply delicious. The restaurant's turkey burgers are mouthwateringly juicy.

## SONORA Banny's Café
*83 S Stewart St, Suite 100, 95370* **Tel** *(209) 533-4709*      **Road map** *B3*    $$$

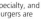

Amicable service and a bustling atmosphere set this otherwise nondescript café apart. The menu features an interesting mix of regional styles, including Californian, European, and Asian, though some are better executed than others. There is also a wine bar, with an extensive list of local vintages.

**Key to Price Guide** *see p568* **Key to Symbols** *see back cover flap*

## THE HIGH SIERRAS

### BIG PINE Rossi's Steak & Spaghetti Restaurant

*100 N Main St, 93513* **Tel** *(760) 938-2254* **Road map** *C4*

This cheerful family-run restaurant, with a long history in the area, sits in an unassuming corner building. The menu is simple, with many steaks, chops, and pasta specialties, but the dishes are perfect every time. The big steaks and huge bowls of spaghetti are well renowned. Service is amicable and intimate.

### BISHOP The Village Café

*965 N See Vee Ln, 93515* **Tel** *(760) 872-3101* **Road map** *C3*

Located in an old house, the Village Café is a popular breakfast spot, known for its large portions and its variety of options. Sandwiches are decent for lunch as well, but breakfast – everything from a variety of eggs Benedict to assorted grilled meats with eggs – served with strong coffee, is what draws locals back time and again.

### FISH CAMP Narrow Gauge Inn

*48571 Highway 41, 93623* **Tel** *(559) 683-7720, (888) 644-9050* **Road map** *C4*

This restaurant in the historic Narrow Gauge Inn is renowned in the region for its high-quality rustic American cuisine. The steaks, fresh fish, and poultry are not to be missed. The lodge-style dining rooms are very romantic, with large stone fireplaces and antique appointments. It is closed on Mondays and Tuesdays, and in winter.

### MAMMOTH LAKES Whiskey Creek Mountain Bistro

*24 Lake Mary Rd, 93546* **Tel** *(760) 934-2555* **Road map** *C4*

Part popular nightclub, part restaurant, this long-standing local favorite has a lively atosphere, with occasional live music or DJ-spun sounds. The restaurant offers a changing menu of seasonal selections, as well as a list of reliable favorites, including grilled steaks, ribs, and prime rib. It is closed for lunch.

### MAMMOTH LAKES The Restaurant at Convict Lake

*HCR - 79, 93546* **Tel** *(760) 934-3803* **Road map** *C3*

This is a beautiful spot 15 minutes' drive from Mammoth, with a fireplace and lots of windows looking out on the lake and the forest outside. Popular as a special-occasion restaurant, it's pricey, but the atmosphere is wonderful and the food surprisingly good. Perfectly cooked local meats and fish are paired with an excellent wine list.

### NORTH LAKE TAHOE Bridgetender Tavern and Grill

*65 West Lake Blvd, 96145* **Tel** *(530) 583-3342* **Road map** *C3*

A long-time popular gathering spot for locals and visitors alike, this casual tavern has a great outdoor seating area overlooking Lake Tahoe and the Truckee River inlet. The kitchen is known for its delicious burgers and fries, but also offers some good grilled seafood choices.

### NORTH LAKE TAHOE Sunnyside Restaurant

*1850 West Lake Blvd, 96145* **Tel** *(530) 583-7200, (800) 822-2754* **Road map** *C3*

This popular restaurant at a lakeside lodge has a spacious dining room with large wooden beams and huge windows, as well as a sizeable deck that gets packed on pleasant afternoons. The menu features good American fare and some lovely seafood dishes. Sunday brunch is a summertime ritual.

### SOUTH LAKE TAHOE Lake Tahoe Pizza Company

*1168 Lake Tahoe Blvd, 96150* **Tel** *(530) 544-1919* **Road map** *C3*

Well-cooked food and excellent prices is the key at this friendly, family-style pizza parlor that uses a special brick oven to make pizzas. The menu mainly features traditional Italian favorites, including barbecued chicken pizza, salads, sandwiches, and pasta. There is also a lean-calorie menu for weight-watchers and a good beer selection.

### SOUTH LAKE TAHOE Fresh Ketch

*2435 Venice Dr, 96150* **Tel** *(530) 541-5683* **Road map** *C3*

Impressive cooking, attentive service, and lovely views make a winning combination at this casual restaurant in the Tahoe Keys area. The menu features mostly seafood, with preparations influenced by the Pacific Rim. There is casual dining downstairs and on the lawn, while fine dining is in an intimate upstairs dining room.

### STATELINE Sage Room Steakhouse

*Hwy 50 at Stateline Ave, NV 89449* **Tel** *(775) 588-2411* **Road map** *C3*

This fine-dining restaurant at Harvey's Casino has been open since 1947 and has amassed a loyal following. The menu includes standards such as great steaks and chops served in a Western-themed setting. There are also select wild game dishes available on occasion. Bananas Foster is a dessert specialty. It is closed for lunch.

### TAHOE CITY Tahoe House

*625 West Lake Blvd, 96145* **Tel** *(530) 583-1377* **Road map** *B3*

There is a great full-service bakery at this interesting restaurant that attracts many people in the morning hours. The Swiss-themed restaurant is also a takeaway deli where picnickers stock up on fresh breads, cheeses, and cakes. There is also an interesting, but approachable, menu of traditional Swiss dishes.

### TAHOE CITY Christy Hill Restaurant

*115 Grove St, 96145* **Tel** *(530) 583-8551*          **Road map** *B3*

A great Tahoe lake-front restaurant, Christy Hill features a large wooden deck with a handful of lovely outdoor tables; be sure to ask for one in the summer, and make a reservation any time of year if you want to ensure a window-side seat. The menu is a bit all over the place, but it's all prepared perfectly and the wine list is superb as well.

### TAHOE CITY Evergreen

*475 N Lake Blvd, 96145* **Tel** *(530) 581-1401*          **Road map** *B3*

Evergreen is one of the few lakeview restaurants at Lake Tahoe where the food is almost as big a draw as the view. Known for their burgers (all natural angus beef), the restaurant also makes terrific salads, soups, and more substantial entrées, including pork chops, steak, and a delicious vegetarian strudel. Reservations are recommended.

### TRUCKEE Moody's Bistro & Lounge

*10007 Bridge St, 96161* **Tel** *(530) 587-8688*          **Road map** *B3*

Toward the end of charming downtown Truckee, Moody's looks like a swanky pioneer-style spot from outside, carried through to the inside with dark wood and a large bar, but the menu is 100% modern. Inventive salads, fresh pastas, and large slabs of grilled meats are specialties here, all done exceedingly well and paired with an excellent wine list.

### TRUCKEE Pianeta

*10096 Donner Pass Rd, 96161* **Tel** *(530) 587-4694*          **Road map** *B3*

Located in downtown Truckee, this neighborly restaurant offers a reliable menu of rustic Italian fare served in a room with a welcoming mountain ambience. The comfortable booths are the prime seating choice. The service is well-honed and amicable. A full bar and wine list are on offer. It is open for dinner daily.

### YOSEMITE NATIONAL PARK Wawona Dining Room

*State Hwy 41, 95389* **Tel** *(559) 252-4848*          **Road map** *C3*

This restaurant in the historic Yosemite Park hotel is popular for its friendly ambience and service. The basic American fare, prepared without much discipline, features flavorful steaks and trouts. The Victorian dining room, with a delightful rustic flair, can get crowded and noisy, which is all part of the charm. Closed November to March.

### YOSEMITE NATIONAL PARK Ahwahnee Dining Room

*Yosemite Valley, 95389* **Tel** *(559) 252-4848*          **Road map** *C3*

The highlight of dining here is the beautiful setting, although the food has improved recently to match the memorable atmosphere. Mostly American standards find a place on the menu here; the best choices are the grilled steaks and chops. Save some room for the delectable desserts.

# NORTH CENTRAL CALIFORNIA

### APTOS Bittersweet Bistro

*787 Rio Del Mar Blvd, 95003* **Tel** *(831) 662-9799*          **Road map** *B4*

One of the best gourmet dining options in the area, this inviting restaurant offers excellent food at great prices. The menu is American bistro with Mediterranean influences, but the quality lies in the fine execution and artful presentation. Premium ingredients are used, with an emphasis on local produce. It has an impressive wine list.

### BIG SUR Nepenthe Restaurant

*Hwy 1 CA, 93920* **Tel** *(831) 667-2345*          **Road map** *B4*

This restaurant, with its stunning coastside setting, has a cult-like following, though the food is not quite as dazzling. The simple preparations of American fare are comforting, as are the freshly made breads and desserts. The ambrosia burger, a ground-steak sandwich with the house-made ambrosia sauce, is a favorite.

### BIG SUR Sierra Mar

*Hwy 1, 93920* **Tel** *(831) 667-2800*          **Road map** *B4*

Part of an inn, this award-winning restaurant has magnificent views from its dining room. The innovative menu of seasonally inspired fare changes daily and is presented prix fixe, however it can be ordered à la carte. Sierra Mar has one of North America's most extensive wine cellars.

### BIG SUR Deetjen's

*48865 Hwy 1, 93920* **Tel** *(831) 667-2378*          **Road map** *B4*

The secluded setting is wonderful at this hotel-restaurant, as is the amicable service. The dining room is divided into four eclectically decorated spaces. The menu features interesting dishes in the California cuisine style. The colorful breakfast menu of sweets and savories is hugely popular. Reservations are recommended. Closed for lunch.

### CARMEL Katy's Place

*Mission Street betw. 5th and 6th, 93921* **Tel** *(831) 624-0199*          **Road map** *B4*

Sweet little place downtown, famous for French toast with strawberries, pecan waffles, nine kinds of eggs Benedict, and a variety of omelets. This is a local favorite, serving breakfast and lunch like Grandma used to make. Burgers, quesadillas, crab cakes, salads, and sandwiches are also good. Eat at the counter to watch the action in the kitchen.

### CARMEL Hog's Breath Inn

$$$

*Corner of San Carlos Ave & 5th St, 93921* **Tel** *(831) 625-1044*

**Road map** B4

With a famous owner – Clint Eastwood – this rustic, cozy bar and restaurant has a great patio upon which to enjoy the hearty California and American cuisine. The ribs are a specialty as is the extensive list of appetizers, which many diners choose to graze their way through on foggy afternoons by the fire.

### CARMEL The Terrace Grill, La Playa Hotel

$$$

*Corner of 8th Ave & Camino Real, 93920* **Tel** *(831) 624-6476*

**Road map** B4

One of the best hotel restaurants in the area, this open-air terrace dining room offers splendid ocean views. The menu here is comprised of fresh California cuisine dishes made with local ingredients artfully presented. There is a great wine selection at the wood-paneled lounge.

### CARMEL Anton & Michel

$$$$$

*Corner of Mission Ave & 7th St, 93921* **Tel** *(831) 624-2406*

**Road map** B4

A Carmel landmark, this downtown restaurant is popular for its contemporary French-inspired cuisine and sophisticated ambience. The fare is reliably prepared using seasonal ingredients. The pan-roasted duck breast is an all-time favorite. The dining room tends to get a bit touristy. Book in advance, and request a patio seat.

### CARMEL Restaurant at Mission Ranch

$$$$

*26270 Dolores Street, 93923* **Tel** *(831) 624–6436*

**Road map** B4

Kick back with cowboys and movie stars in a casual, country setting, either by the fireplace or on the heated patio overlooking Carmel River and Bay, and Point Lobos. The food is a traditional diner house menu done very well, with steak and local fresh seafood. You can stay here, too, in lovely inn rooms and cottages. Piano bar and Sunday jazz brunch.

### CARMEL Pacific's Edge

$$$$$

*120 Highlands Drive, 93923* **Tel** *(831) 622-5445*

**Road map** B4

Just south of town, in the Hyatt Carmel Highlands resort, this elegant, romantic, four-diamond-rated restaurant serves California cuisine with a stunning ocean view. Kansas City beef, Colorado lamb, and extensive seafood choices don the menu. Chef's tasting menu, bar menu, and cigar menu also available, plus an award-winning wine list.

### CARMEL VALLEY Running Iron Restaurant and Saloon

$$

*24 East Carmel Valley Road, 93924* **Tel** *(831) 659-4633*

**Road map** B4

Valley farmers and winemakers have bellied up to this watering hole since the 1940s. The place is a sort of Western museum, with cowboy boots and spurs hanging from the ceiling. Steaks and south-of-the-border specialties are favorites, along with fresh local seafood, fried chicken, burgers, pastas, and yet more comfort food.

### MONTEREY Stokes Restaurant

$$$$

*500 Hartnell St, 93940* **Tel** *(831) 373-1110*

**Road map** B4

Built into a 200-year-old adobe structure, this handsome restaurant is renowned for its expertly cooked Mediterranean cuisine. Ingredients from local producers, from meats and cheeses to wild mushrooms, are prepared with a deft touch. The wine list is excellent. It is closed for lunch on Saturdays and Sundays.

### MONTEREY Tarpy's Roadhouse

$$$$

*2999 Monterey-Salinas Hwy, 93940* **Tel** *(831) 647-1444*

**Road map** B4

Built in an old ranch house, this rustic and appealing restaurant has friendly service and a devoted following. The wide-ranging menu includes wood-fired wild game, great steaks, fresh seafood, salads, and burgers. Select a seat on the patio on warm evenings. There is a full bar and a critically acclaimed wine list. Service is professional.

### PACIFIC GROVE Fandango

$$$$$

*223 17th St, 93950* **Tel** *(831) 372-3456*

**Road map** B4

A long-standing neighborhood spot, this cheery restaurant serves reliable preparations of seafood and steak in different dining rooms. The colorful upstairs room, alcove, cellar, and main dining room all have individual character. The rack of lamb, scampi, and bouillabaisse are highly regarded. A full-service bar is located on site.

### SANTA CRUZ The Crêpe Place

$$$

*1134 Soquel Ave, 95062* **Tel** *(831) 429-6994*

**Road map** B4

This quirky, friendly crêperie is a long-time local favorite, with a wide array of crêpes. Create your own variety, choosing from seafood, meat, or vegetarian options. Additional menu items include soups and salads. The dimly lit indoor dining room is ideal for couples. For families and large groups, there is a bright patio area.

### SANTA CRUZ Crow's Nest

$$$$

*2218 E Cliff Dr, 95062* **Tel** *(831) 476-4560*

**Road map** B4

An icon of the harbor since 1969, this simple, friendly, and entertaining restaurant serves great seafood specialties as well as pasta, steaks, and chops. The upstairs bar, Breakwater, has a more casual atmosphere, serving a selection of sandwiches, burgers, and small seafood plates. There is live music on select nights.

### SEASIDE El Migueleno

$$$

*1066 Broadway Ave, 93955* **Tel** *(831) 899-2199*

**Road map** B4

One of only a handful of Salvadoran restaurants in Northern California, this modest-looking dining room is worth a stop. Thoughtfully blending the culinary traditions of Mexico and El Salvador, the menu features some interesting dishes. The seafood stew is made with fresh locally caught fish. The service is efficient and the prices are attractive.

# SHOPPING IN CALIFORNIA

**Antique Dealers' Association sign**

California is a manufacturing giant and a major player in the global economy. It is the largest producer of children's clothing in the US, and is equally famous for its sportswear and swimwear. Produce from the San Joaquin Valley, including fruit, nuts, and vegetables, feeds the nation. Aside from the shopping districts of LA *(see pp166–7)* and San Francisco *(see* *pp382–3)*, the state's smaller towns and countryside offer a wide range of merchandise and local produce. Roadside food stands, wineries, antique shops, and crafts by local artisans are some of the attractions of California's backroads. Prices tend to be cheaper than in the cities, and in some places, such as flea markets, you will be expected to barter and negotiate.

**Window-shopping along Ocean Avenue, Carmel *(see p510)***

## SHOPPING HOURS

Since the local population tends to view shopping as a recreational activity, most major stores are open for business seven days a week. Typical business hours are 10am–6pm (some 9pm), Monday to Saturday, and 10am–5pm on Sundays. In smaller communities, stores may be closed on Sunday or Monday. Opening hours for these stores are sometimes 11am–7pm.

## HOW TO PAY

Most stores accept credit cards, including MasterCard, American Express, and Visa, and traveler's checks. Paying by traveler's checks requires some form of identification, such as a passport or driver's license. Few stores will accept checks drawn on foreign banks. Cash is the best way to pay for any small purchases *(see pp624–5)*.

## SALES TAX

Sales tax (VAT) in California ranges from 7.25 to 8.5 percent. All items except groceries and prescription drugs are taxed. In general, tax is not included in the advertised price but is added separately at the cash register.

## RIGHTS AND REFUNDS

Merchants are not required by law to give a cash refund or credit for returned goods, although most do so. All stores will refund the cost of a defective item, if it is not marked "flawed" or "sold as is." Inspect the item before you buy it and keep all receipts. If an item is faulty, go back to the store with the receipt and original packaging. Many stores will refund your money up to 30 days after purchase.

## SHIPPING PACKAGES

For a charge, most stores ship goods worldwide, or send your items home by Federal Express or US Express Mail Service *(see pp 626–7)* You will be asked to fill out a form giving a short description of the goods and stating their monetary value. Keep receipts of the transaction in case the items should get lost in transit.

## WHERE TO SHOP

A number of coastal towns noted for their locally owned shops can be found along Hwy 1 or US 101. These include Santa Barbara *(see pp220–21)*, Big Sur *(see pp514–15)*, Carmel *(see p510)*, Santa Cruz *(see pp506–7)*, and Sausalito *(see pp414–15)*.

On Hwy 99 and other roads that cross the San Joaquin Valley, many farms sell locally grown fruit and vegetables. Palm Springs *(see pp274–5)* is known for its fashion and second-hand stores. Antique dealers are plentiful in towns in the Sierra foothills, such as Sutter Creek *(see p476)*.

## FASHION

California is known for its casual clothing – the dress-down Friday business look was invented here. However, the East Coast also looks to California for the very best of cutting-edge fashion.

Seventy percent of all swimwear designed in the US

**San Franciscan original, The Gap**

is designed here, by big names in their field and can be found at chainstores like **Diane's Beachwear**. Sixty-five percent of the country's younger female fashion is also produced here. Children's wear is a specialty of the state. **The Children's Place, Gymboree**, and **Levi Strauss** are good.

Other local heroes include designer **Jessica McClintock Inc**, known for her ballgowns and bridal wear, as well as the teen chainstore **Forever 21**, and **Chico's for Women**. **The Gap**, now an international retail giant, originated in San Francisco in 1969 and was the first store to mass-market denim jeans.

## FLEA MARKETS

Flea markets (also called swap meets) are held on weekends, usually on Sundays. Vendors set up booths within a vast parking lot, football stadium, or even in the grounds of one of the famous missions. Just about everything imaginable is for sale. It is often possible to find a one-of-a-kind treasure at a good price, but don't accept the quoted price – bargaining is *de rigueur*. Be sure to bring cash with you because most vendors will not accept credit cards or traveler's checks.

Notable flea markets include the **Berkeley Flea Market**, the **San Jose Flea Market**, the **Rose Bowl Flea Market** in Pasadena, and **San Juan Bautista Peddlars Fair**. Flea markets may charge a nominal entrance fee of 75 cents or $1.

**Browsers at an open-air flea market in Sausalito**

**Cover of a vintage Hollywood magazine from the 1950s**

## POP CULTURE ANTIQUES

Memorabilia stores are a California specialty. San Fernando's **The Game Doc** sells a variety of old games for all ages. **Hello Central** sells all kinds of antique telephones, from early models to the 1940s black rotary dial telephones. **Sarah Stocking Fine Vintage Posters** specializes in old movie posters. A range of Hollywood memorabilia is easily found in LA *(see pp166–7)* Other stores, such as **Sutter Creek Antiques** in Sutter Creek, also sell such items.

## OUTLET CENTERS

One of the state's most popular retail trends is factory outlet malls. These sell off-season or surplus goods, such as clothing and household items, directly to consumers at prices lower than those in department stores.

Outlet centers usually have at least 20 shops, but the **Vacaville Premium Outlets** has more than 100 stores. Other popular centers include the **American Tin Cannery Factory Outlets** in Pacific Grove, **Napa Premium Outlets, Cabazon Outlets, Citadel Outlets, Prime Outlets Pismo Beach**, and the **Camarillo Premium Outlets**. For special outlet center tours in San Francisco, contact **Shopper Stopper Tours**.

## SIZE CHART

For Australian sizes follow the British and American conversions.

**Children's clothing**

| | | | | | | | | | |
|---|---|---|---|---|---|---|---|---|---|
| American | 2–3 | 4–5 | 6–6x | 7–8 | 10 | | 12 | 14 | 16 (size) |
| British | 2–3 | 4–5 | 6–7 | 8–9 | 10–11 | | 12 | 14 | 14+ (years) |
| Continental | 2–3 | 4–5 | 6–7 | 8–9 | 10–11 | | 12 | 14 | 14+ (years) |

**Children's shoes**

| | | | | | | | | | |
|---|---|---|---|---|---|---|---|---|---|
| American | 7½ | 8½ | 9½ | 10½ | 11½ | 12½ | 13½ | 1½ | 2½ |
| British | 7 | 8 | 9 | 10 | 11 | 12 | 13 | 1 | 2 |
| Continental | 24 | 25½ | 27 | 28 | 29 | 30 | 32 | 33 | 34 |

**Women's dresses, coats and skirts**

| | | | | | | | | |
|---|---|---|---|---|---|---|---|---|
| American | 4 | 6 | 8 | 10 | 12 | 14 | 16 | 18 |
| British | 6 | 8 | 10 | 12 | 14 | 16 | 18 | 20 |
| Continental | 38 | 40 | 42 | 44 | 46 | 48 | 50 | 52 |

**Women's blouses and sweaters**

| | | | | | | | |
|---|---|---|---|---|---|---|---|
| American | 6 | 8 | 10 | 12 | 14 | 16 | 18 |
| British | 30 | 32 | 34 | 36 | 38 | 40 | 42 |
| Continental | 40 | 42 | 44 | 46 | 48 | 50 | 52 |

**Women's shoes**

| | | | | | | | |
|---|---|---|---|---|---|---|---|
| American | 5 | 6 | 7 | 8 | 9 | 10 | 11 |
| British | 3 | 4 | 5 | 6 | 7 | 8 | 9 |
| Continental | 36 | 37 | 38 | 39 | 40 | 41 | 44 |

**Men's suits**

| | | | | | | | | |
|---|---|---|---|---|---|---|---|---|
| American | 34 | 36 | 38 | 40 | 42 | 44 | 46 | 48 |
| British | 34 | 36 | 38 | 40 | 42 | 44 | 46 | 48 |
| Continental | 44 | 46 | 48 | 50 | 52 | 54 | 56 | 58 |

**Men's shirts**

| | | | | | | | | |
|---|---|---|---|---|---|---|---|---|
| American | 14 | 15 | 15½ | 16 | 16½ | 17 | 17½ | 18 |
| British | 14 | 15 | 15½ | 16 | 16½ | 17 | 17½ | 18 |
| Continental | 36 | 38 | 39 | 41 | 42 | 43 | 44 | 45 |

**Men's shoes**

| | | | | | | | | |
|---|---|---|---|---|---|---|---|---|
| American | 7 | 7½ | 8 | 8½ | 9½ | 10½ | 11 | 11½ |
| British | 6 | 7 | 7½ | 8 | 9 | 10 | 11 | 12 |
| Continental | 39 | 40 | 41 | 42 | 43 | 44 | 45 | 46 |

Antique shops in Temecula, near Carlsbad

## BOOKS, MUSIC, AND CRAFTS

Bookstores, whether part of a large chain or independent, are a feature of even the smallest California town.

The best selection of music and books is generally available only in big cities, in chains such as **Barnes & Noble**. If a town has a university, head toward the student district for new and used record stores.

Native American arts and crafts are available; contact the **California Indian Museum and Cultural Arts Center** for more information.

Mexican arts and crafts can be found at San Diego's **Fiesta de Reyes**.

## ANTIQUES

California's small towns are awash with traditional antiques such as fine gold and silver jewelry, Native American Indian artifacts, textiles, antique clothing, Bakelite jewelry, and period furniture dating back to the 18th and 19th centuries.

The West Coast is the port of entry to the US for many Pacific Rim countries and, as a result, many antique porcelain sculptures from Japan and China, and antique Asian furniture are available. Twentieth-century collectables include Arts and Crafts and Art Deco furniture, clothing, posters, prewar tin toys, blown glass, and pottery.

Antique dealers often rent space together in one large mall, barn, or warehouse building that is open to the public. Located north of Balboa Park in San Diego, is **Antique Row**, featuring antiques and collectible stores, vintage-clothing boutiques, and used bookstores.

## FOOD

Many of California's farms, particularly in Sonoma or Fresno counties, sell their produce to visitors on self-guided farm trails. In Sonoma, contact the **Sonoma County Farm Trails** or the **Sonoma Valley Chamber of Commerce**. The Fresno County Blossom Trail is a 62-mile (100-km) trail passing through groves, orchards, and vineyards. It begins at **Simonian Farms**, which sells local fruits, honey, and mustards. Contact the **Fresno County Farm Bureau** for information.

California has a number of unique food shops scattered around the state. In Napa's Anderson Valley, the **Apple Farm** is a year-round fruit

Fresh local produce at a farmers' market

stand selling locally grown apples and pears. Also in Napa, the **Jimtown Store** sells local jams, honey, olives, mustards, vinegars, and salad dressings. On Hwy 152, east of Gilroy, **Casa de Fruta**, which began as a simple cherry stand in the 1940s, has grown into a vast complex with a fruit stand, coffee shop (Casa de Coffee), restaurant (Casa de Burger), and gift shop (Casa de Gift).

**Harris Ranch**, almost midway between LA and San Francisco on I-5, is a vast complex set amid a working cattle ranch. The Spanish-style hacienda has a gift shop featuring Harris Ranch produce and fresh meat, as well as a restaurant, coffee shop, and overnight lodging.

Italian Marketplace at the Viansa Winery

## WINERIES

In addition to the fine wine of Napa and Sonoma counties, wineries are known for the shops located inside their tasting rooms. A range of merchandise related to wine is for sale. For a list of California's wineries, contact the **Wine Institute of San Francisco**.

The Italian Marketplace at the **Viansa Winery** sells Italian cheeses and breads, cookbooks, and kitchenware. The **Sebastiani Vineyards** sell a variety of wine-related souvenirs. The gift shop in the **Sterling Vineyards** offers silk scarves, silver jewelry, and regional history books.

Family-owned **V. Sattui Winery** has a gourmet deli, as well as a shaded picnic area to eat your purchases.

# DIRECTORY

## FASHION

**Chico's**
1314 Montana Ave,
Santa Monica, CA 90403.
*Tel (310) 394-2481.*

**The Children's Place**
Stonestown Galleria,
3251 20 Ave,
San Francisco, CA 94132.
*Tel (415) 682-9404.*

**Diane's Beachwear**
116 Main St, Huntington
Beach, CA 92648.
*Tel (714) 536-7803.*

**Forever 21**
Beverly Center, 8522
Beverly Blvd #849 & #852,
Los Angeles, CA 90048.
*Tel (310) 659-9611.*

**Gap**
1355 3rd St, Promenade,
Santa Monica, CA 90401.
*Tel (310) 393-0719.*

**Gymboree**
421 N Beverly Dr,
Beverly Hills, CA 90210.
*Tel (310) 278-0312.*

**Jessica McClintock Inc**
180 Geary St, 4th floor,
San Francisco, CA 94108.
*Tel (415) 398-9008.*

**Original Levi's Store**
300 Post St,
San Francisco,
CA 94111.
*Tel (415) 501-0100.*

## FLEA MARKETS

**Berkeley Flea Market**
1937 Ashby Ave,
Berkeley, CA 94703.
*Tel (510) 644-0744.*
www.berkeleyfleamarket.com

**Pasadena's Rose Bowl**
1001 Rose Bowl Drive,
Pasadena, CA 91103.
*Tel (323) 560-7469.*
www.rgcshows.com

**San Jose Flea Market**
1590 Berryessa Road,
San Jose, CA 95133.
*Tel (408) 453-1110.*
www.sjfm.com

**San Juan Bautista Peddlers Fair**
115 3rd St, San Juan
Bautista, CA 95045.
*Tel (831) 623-2454.*
www.sjbchamber.com

## POP CULTURE ANTIQUES

**The Game Doc**
535 4th St., San Fernando,
CA 91340.
*Tel (818) 504-0440.*

**Hello Central**
2463 Ladera Court,
San Luis Obispo,
CA 93401.
*Tel (805) 541-9123.*

**Sarah Stocking Fine Vintage Posters**
368 Jackson St,
San Francisco, CA 94111.
*Tel (415) 984-0700.*

**Sutter Creek Antiques**
28 Main Street,
Sutter Creek,
CA 95685.
*Tel (209) 267-5574.*

## OUTLET CENTERS

**American Tin Cannery Factory Outlets**
125 Ocean View Blvd,
Pacific Grove, CA 93950.
*Tel (831) 372-1442.*

**Cabazon Outlets**
48750 Seminole Rd,
Cabazon, CA 92230.
*Tel (951) 922-3000.*
www.cabazonoutlets.com

**Camarillo Premium Outlets**
740 E Ventura Blvd,
Camarillo,
CA 93010.
*Tel (805) 445-8520.*

**Citadel Outlets**
100 Citadel Drive, Los
Angeles,
CA 90040.
*Tel (323) 888-1724.*
www.citadeloutlets.com

**Napa Premium Outlets**
629 Factory Stores Drive,
Napa, CA 94558.
*Tel (707) 226-9876.*

**Prime Outlets Pismo Beach**
333 Five Cities Drive,
Pismo Beach, CA 93449.
*Tel (805) 773-4661.*

**Shopper Stopper Tours**
2489 Schaeffer Rd,
Sebastopol,
CA 95473.
*Tel (707) 829-1597.*

**Vacaville Premium Outlets**
321-2 Nut Tree Rd,
Vacaville, CA 95687.
*Tel (707) 447-5755.*

## BOOKS, MUSIC, AND CRAFTS

**Barnes & Noble**
791 S Main St, Orange,
CA 92868.
*Tel (714) 558-0028.*

**California Indian Museum and Cultural Center**
5250 Aero Dr,
San Rosa, CA 95403.
*Tel (707) 579-3004.*
www.cimcc.indian.org

**Fiesta de Reyes**
Old Town, San Diego,
CA 92110.
*Tel (619) 296-3161.*
www.fiestadereyes.com

## ANTIQUES

**Antique Row**
308 Adams Ave,
San Diego,
CA 92103.
*Tel (619) 282-7329.*

## FOOD

**Apple Farm**
18501 Greenwood Rd,
Philo, CA 95466.
*Tel (707) 895-2333.*

**Casa de Fruta**
10021 Pacheco Pass Hwy,
Hollister, CA 95023.
*Tel (408) 842-7282.*

**Fresno County Farm Bureau**
1274 West Hedges,
Fresno, CA 93728.
*Tel (559) 237-0263.*

**Harris Ranch**
24505 West Dorris Ave,
Coalinga, CA 93210.
*Tel (800) 942-2333.*
www.harrisranch.com

**Jimtown Store**
6706 Hwy 128,
Healdsburg,
CA 95448.
*Tel (707) 433-1212.*

**Simonian Farms**
2629 S Clovis Ave,
Fresno, CA 93725.
*Tel (559) 237-2294.*

**Sonoma County Farm Trails**
PO Box 6032,
Santa Rosa, CA 95606.
*Tel (800) 207-9464.*

**Sonoma Valley Chamber of Commerce**
651-A Broadway,
Sonoma, CA 95476.
*Tel (707) 996-1033.*

## WINERIES

**Sebastiani Vineyards**
389 Fourth St East,
Sonoma, CA 95476.
*Tel (800) 888-5532.*
www.sebastiani.com

**Sterling Vineyards**
1111 Dunaweal Loane,
Calistoga, CA 94515.
*Tel (707) 942-3300.*

**V. Sattui Winery**
1111 White Lane,
St Helena, CA 94574.
*Tel (707) 963-7774.*

**Viansa Winery**
25200 Arnold Drive,
Sonoma, CA 95476.
*Tel (707) 935-4700.*

**Wine Institute of San Francisco**
425 Market St, Suite 1000,
San Francisco, CA 94105.
*Tel (415) 512-0151.*
www.wineinstitute.org

# SPECIAL INTEREST VACATIONS AND ACTIVITIES IN CALIFORNIA

alifornia is practically synonymous with the great outdoors. The state has protected its landscape so that future generations can visit places of beauty. The deserts, redwood forests, alpine meadows, granite mountains, lakes, and sandy beaches all welcome visitors.

Whitewater rafting on the Merced River (see p612)

California has a culture rich with physical activity, and wilderness is never far from any city. Golfers are well provided for around the Monterey Peninsula (see p511) and winter skiers flock to Lake Tahoe (see p487). For details of main events in the sports calendar, see pages 36–7.

Tahquitz Golf Course, Palm Springs

## SPECIAL INTEREST VACATIONS

Details of special interest vacations are available from the **California Office of Tourism**. One of the most popular of these are tours of California's missions along El Camino Real (see pp46–7).

Writers who make California their home often give readings at local writers' workshops. The best of these are the **Santa Barbara Writers' Conference** and the **Squaw Valley Community of Writers.**

Artists can take advantage of the state's various craft centers. Nationally renowned artists hold painting courses at the **Mendocino Arts Center.**

Institutes such as **Gourmet Retreats** at Casa Lana in the Napa Valley and **Tante Marie's Cooking School** in San Francisco provide accommodations, cooking classes, shopping tours, visits to the Wine Country, and fine meals during week-long intensive courses in the summer months.

## CAMPING

California has always valued its wilderness: Yosemite Valley (see pp488–9) and the Mariposa Grove of giant redwoods were protected parkland as early as 1864. Today there are more than 250 places classified as either state parks, wilderness areas, historic sites, or recreation areas.

At every site, there are hiking trails and parking lots. Many also provide bathrooms and camp sites. All state and federal parks allow day-use visitors, charging a small parking fee. For camping, reserve a site with **State Park Reservations** or **Yosemite Reservations**. It is advisable to book in advance.

Camping trips into the state's desert are organized by **Desert Survivors.** They include environmental information.

## HIKING

Day hikes and longer trips in the country are popular with both residents and visitors. There are more than 1 million miles (1.6 million km) of trails in California, the longest being the Pacific Crest Trail. The 2,640-mile (4,245-km) route stretches from Canada to Mexico. One of its highlights is the 200-mile (320-km) John Muir Trail, from Yosemite's high country to Mount Whitney (see pp488–95). The **Sierra Club** organizes guided outings and provides detailed maps.

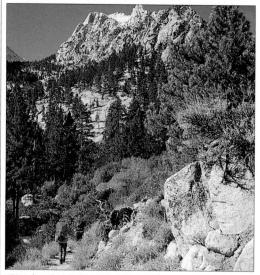

Hiking along the John Muir Trail at Mount Whitney

## HORSEBACK RIDING

Equestrians will find a wide variety of riding trails in California, across all types of landscape – pine-covered mountains, lush meadows, chaparral hills, and dry valleys. Many state and national parks allow horses and pack mules on their trails.

Traditional cowboy life can still be found at privately owned ranches. These are working ranches, and guests can ride with the ranch hands and herd animals, or simply ride for pleasure on their extensive network of trails. **El Alisal Guest Ranch and Resort** holds annual roundups and cattle drives or just let **Hidden Trails** organize a ranch holiday for you.

Horseback riding in Ventura County

## MOUNTAIN BIKING

Many state parks allow cyclists on their hiking trails. One spectacular trail for cyclists begins at High Camp in Squaw Valley, Lake Tahoe (see p487). A 2,000-ft (610-m) ascent via an aerial tram is followed by a downhill ride to Shirley Lake. Contact the **Northern California Nevada Cycling Association** to find out where mountain bikes are welcome in Northern California.

Outfitters such as **Backroads** also lead groups of cyclists on tours of the state's countryside, often with stops for leisurely gourmet lunches. Transport vans accompany the cyclists, carrying heavy equipment and camping gear for week-long trips. Popular destinations

Mountain biking in Marin County

include the Napa Valley (see pp462–3) and the country lanes of Sonoma, Monterey, and Santa Barbara Counties.

## BEACHES

Beaches along California's 900-mile (1,450-km) coastline vary considerably. Some have rough waves and rocky beaches, ideal for rock pool exploration and quiet reflection. Others have the white sand, arching waves, and warm water that attract the surfers of California legend.

Whether you want to surf or simply watch the golden boys of summer, the best beaches include the Leo Carrillo State Beach north of Malibu (see p67), Windansea Beach in La Jolla (see pp248–9), and Corona del Mar in Newport Beach (see pp230–31). The **Club Ed Surf School** offers a 7-day surfing camp for beginners to the sport, which is held between April and October.

Many spots along the coast are good diving areas, including Scripps Shoreline Underwater Preserve in La Jolla (see p249), the coves of Laguna Beach (see p231), and Monterey Bay (see p511). Equipment can be rented from the **Glen's Aquarius 2 Dive Shop**. The **Underwater Schools of America** in Oceanside also offers diving lessons for beginners.

Natural Bridges State Park in Santa Cruz (see pp506–7) and Pfeiffer State Beach in Big Sur (see pp414–15) are good sites for rock pool exploration, where the ocean has eroded the rock in unusual formations. Torrey Pines State Beach (see p248) offers forests and dramatic white-capped swells. Pismo Beach is famous for its sand dunes, surfing, and clam digging (see p208).

Southern California's water is warm enough for swimming from April to November. In the sea north of San Francisco a wet suit should be worn at all times of the year.

Golden beaches of La Jolla cove

## WHITEWATER RAFTING AND KAYAKING

Whitewater rafting is like a thrilling roller-coaster ride combined with stunning scenic views. Specialty outfitters such as **Outdoor Programs Unlimited** and **Whitewater Voyages** provide rafts, paddles, and life jackets. They take groups of six to eight people, accompanied by a guide, down a tributary of one of California's major rivers. Trips may last one day only or include an overnight stay.

The rafting season lasts from April to September. Trips are graded by their level of difficulty: Classes I and II are relatively safe, with a few exciting twists and turns. Beginners wanting a safe but more exciting ride should book a trip on a Class III river. Only experienced rafters should go on a Class IV, or higher, trip.

Most organizations that offer river rafting also provide kayak and canoe trips. For more information on this, contact the **American River Touring Association**.

**Waterskiing in San Diego**

## WATER SPORTS

The lakes and beaches in California offer a variety of activities. Houseboats are available to rent for a slow cruise through the maze of inlets in the Sacramento Delta. Speedboats are available at Lake Tahoe (see p487), Lake Shasta (see p452), and the man-made lakes that are part of the state recreation system.

One of the newest sports is parasailing. With waterskis and a parachute, participants are harnessed to a speedboat and launched into the air for an exhilarating ride. It's a safe sport, but life jackets should be worn. Contact **Parasailing Catalina** for details.

## BIRD-WATCHING

In autumn, ducks, geese, and other shorebirds leave Canada to winter in South America, stopping in California along the way. The Point Reyes National Seashore (see pp412–14) supports at least 45 percent of US bird species. More than 425 species have been sighted here. **Shearwater Journeys** offers bird-watching cruises from Monterey. In southern San Diego, the **Tijuana River National Estuarine Research Reserve** hosts some 400 species, best seen in spring and autumn.

**Bird-watching in La Jolla** (see p261)

## FISHING

California is an angler's paradise. From the end of April through to the middle of November, anglers head to the rivers and streams of the Sierra Nevada Mountains for trout fishing. Bass fishing in California's multitude of lakes and reservoirs is plentiful throughout the year. During the autumn and winter months, schools of salmon and steelhead make their way upriver, with especially good fishing in the Klamath, American, Eel, and Sacramento rivers. Sturgeon and striped bass can also readily be caught in the Sacramento River Delta.

Almost every coastal city in the state offers charter boats for deep-sea ocean fishing. In Northern California, the summer months are particularly good for halibut and ocean salmon, but throughout the Pacific, from autumn to early spring, 40–50-lb (18–23-kg) hauls of cod and rock fish are not unusual. In the warmer waters off Southern California, blue fin, yellow fin, and

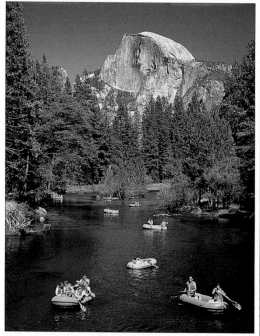
**Rafting at Yosemite National Park** (see pp488–91)

Fishing on Lake Molena in San Diego

skipjack tuna, as well as barracuda are particularly plentiful during the summer. To rent a charter boat for fishing contact **Helgren's Sportfishing Trips**, in southern California or **Anchor Charter Boats** and **Stagnaro's Sport Fishing** in the north.

To find out which fish are in season, contact the **State Department of Fish and Game**. Information on fly fishing, another popular California sport, is available from the **Troutfitter Guide Service** at Mammoth Lakes.

## ROCK CLIMBING AND CAVING

Rock climbing combines the dexterity of gymnastics with the grace of dance, as individuals scale vertical rock walls using only their hands

and high-friction shoes. The sport can be practiced throughout the year in rock-climbing gyms in major cities. Other places to learn how to rock climb or simply to watch others in action are the Joshua Tree National Park *(see pp278 –9)*, Idyllwild, near Palm Springs *(see p276)*, and Squaw Valley in Lake Tahoe *(see p487)*. Contact the **American Mountain Guides Association** or **Mission Cliffs Climbing School** for information.

Spelunkers (cave explorers) should head for the Pinnacles National Monument *(see p517)* or Lassen Volcanic National Park *(see p453)*, where volcanoes have created unusual caves and rock formations.

## HANG GLIDING

If you've ever wanted to ride the thermal air currents at speeds of 25–50 mph (40–80 km/h), this is the sport for you. A hang glider is a kite-shaped, plastic-covered light metal frame. The harnessed rider hangs onto a triangular control bar, jumps from the top of a cliff or hill, and, supported by air currents, glides to the ground. For beginners, flights can be made in tandem with a qualified pilot, equipped with a safety parachute.

The main hang-gliding areas, for both participants and spectators, are

Fort Funston off the Bay Area coastline *(see pp412–13)*, **Torrey Pines Gliderport** in San Diego, or Vista Point in Palm Desert *(see p274)*. If you want to learn the sport, they will recommend instructors. They also sell and rent gliding equipment.

## GARDENS

The warm, sunny climate of California has inspired numerous skilled and amateur gardeners to experiment with horticulture. The result is a rich variety of arboretums, botanical gardens, city parks, and private estates all over the state that are now open to the public.

Huntington Library Art Collections and Botanical Gardens are Henry Huntington's idealistic monument to art and culture. Work began on the gardens in 1904. They cover three-quarters of the 200-acre (80-ha) estate and are among the finest of their kind in California *(see pp158–61)*.

The **Descanso Gardens** in La Cañada offer 4 acres (1.6 ha) of roses, an impressive 30-acre (12-ha) grove of live oaks, and a protected forest of camellia trees. William Bourn's landscaped grounds and elegant estate of Filoli in the Bay Area town of Woodside *(see p427)* and **Villa Montalvo Arboretum** in Saratoga are both carefully tended so that their flowers are in bloom all year long. Weekend jazz concerts are held at Saratoga during the summer months, adding to the cultured environment.

Rock climbing at Joshua Tree National Park

Hot air ballooning over California's landscape

## HOT AIR BALLOONING

Hot air ballooning is a popular excursion in the Napa Valley *(see pp462–3)*, Monterey *(see pp510–11)*, Palm Springs, and Temecula. The rides are taken at sunrise or sunset when there is the least wind and are quiet and gentle, offering incomparable panoramic views of the countryside. Outfitters such as **Panorama Balloon Tours** and **Napa Valley Balloons** provide private and group outings, which are then followed by a picnic.

## WHALE WATCHING

From December through to April, gray whales journey 7,000 miles (11,260 km) along the California coast, having left Alaska's Bering Strait for the warmer climate of Mexico's Baja Peninsula. Ocean cruises offer views of these impressive mammals. Humpback, killer whales, pilot, and blue whales also frequent the coast between San Francisco and Monterey in late summer. Charter operators provide a glimpse of the gray whales, as well as the dolphins and porpoises that accompany them on their trips. For more information, contact **Oceanic Society Expeditions**.

## HOT SPRINGS

A long soak in a hot spring (a bubbling tributary of an underground river, heated by the earth) is said to be very good for one's health. Calistoga in Northern California *(see p461)* has numerous spas, offering everything from heated pools with mineral water to mud baths, steam baths, and massages. Contact the **Calistoga Chamber of Commerce** for a full list of area resorts.

## ISLAND HOPPING

Five volcanic islands off the coast of Southern California make up the Channel Islands National Park *(see p224)*. This stark nature preserve is ideal for hiking, viewing wildlife, and exploring rock pools. It is also an excellent spot to see whales and dolphins, as well as many species of shore birds. Ferries depart from Ventura and Santa Barbara harbors. Reserve your trip with **Island Packers**.

Catalina Island is accessible by ferry from San Pedro, Long Beach, and Dana Point. It is more developed than the Channel Islands National Park, with shops, restaurants, and accommodations. Developed as a summer resort in the 1920s by chewing-gum magnate William Wrigley, Jr, the island offers trails for cycling, hiking, and opportunities for diving and snorkeling *(see pp242–3)*. You can also take a trip into the mountains to see the bison.

Farther north, **Angel Island**, in San Francisco Bay, is a 740-acre (300-ha) marine sanctuary, reached by ferry from Fisherman's Wharf. Extensive hiking trails, picnic areas, and camp sites are available to visitors. Gray whales and a wide range of shore birds can be observed.

Two Harbors on Catalina Island

# DIRECTORY

## SPECIAL INTEREST VACATIONS

**California Office of Tourism**
PO Box 1499, Sacramento, CA 95812.
*Tel (916) 444-4429.*
www.visitcalifornia.com

**Gourmet Retreats**
Casa Lana, 1316 S Oak St, Calistoga, CA 94515.
*Tel (877) 968-2665.*
www.gourmet
retreats.com

**Mendocino Arts Center**
PO Box 765, Mendocino, CA 95460.
*Tel (707) 937-5818.*
www.mendocinoarts.org

**Santa Barbara Writers' Conference**
PO Box 6627, Santa Barbara, CA 93160.
*Tel (805) 964-0367.*
www.sbwriters.com

**Squaw Valley Community of Writers**
PO Box 2352, Olympic Valley, CA 96146. *Tel (530) 470-8440.* www.
squawvalleywriters.org

**Tante Marie's Cooking School**
271 Francisco St, San Francisco, CA 94133.
*Tel (415) 788-6699.*
www.tantemarie.com

## CAMPING

**Desert Survivors**
PO Box 20991, Oakland, CA 94620-0991.
*Tel (510) 357-6585.*
www.desert-survivors.org

**Sequoia National Park Reservations**
*Tel (877) 444-6777.*
www.reserveamerica.com

**State Park Reservations**
*Tel (800) 444-7275.*
www.parks.ca.gov

**Yosemite Reservations**
*Tel (877) 444-6777.*
www.reserveamerica.com

## HIKING

**Sierra Club**
85 Second St, San Francisco, CA 94105.
*Tel (415) 977-5500.*

## HORSEBACK RIDING

**El Alisal Guest Ranch and Resort**
1054 Alisal Rd, Solvang, CA 93463. *Tel (805) 688-6411.* www.alisal.com

**Hidden Trails**
202–380 West 1st Ave Vancouver, BC V5Y3T7.
*Tel (888) 9-TRAILS.*
www.hiddentrails.com

## MOUNTAIN BIKING

**Backroads**
801 Cedar St, Berkeley, CA 94710. *Tel (800) 462-2848.* www.backroads.com

**Northern California Nevada Cycling Association**
www.ncnca.org

## BEACHES

**Club Ed Surf School**
2350 Paul Minnie Ave, Santa Cruz, CA 95062.
*Tel (800) 287-SURF.*
www.club-ed.com

**Glen's Aquarius 2 Dive Shop**
32 Cannery Row, Monterey, CA 93940.
*Tel (866) 375-6605.*

**Underwater Schools of America**
225 Brooks St, Oceanside, CA 92054. *Tel (877) 896-3483.* www.usascuba.com

## WHITEWATER RAFTING AND KAYAKING

**American River Touring Association**
24000 Casa Loma Rd, Groveland, CA 95321.
*Tel (800) 323-2782.*
www.arta.org

**Outdoor Programs**
500 Parnassus Ave, San Francisco, CA 94143.
*Tel (415) 476-2078.*
www.outdoors.ucsf.edu

**Whitewater Voyages**
5225 San Pablo Dam Rd, El Sobrante, CA 94820.
*Tel (800) 400-7238.* www.
whitewatervoyages.com

## WATER SPORTS

**Parasailing Catalina**
PO Box 2275, Avalon, CA 90704. *Tel (310) 510-1777.* www.para
sailingcatalina.com

## BIRD-WATCHING

**Shearwater Journeys**
PO Box 190, Hollister, CA 95024. *Tel (831) 637-8527.* www.shearwater
journeys.org

**Tijuana River National Estuarine Research Reserve**
301 Caspian Way, Imperial Beach, CA 91932.
*Tel (619) 575-2704.*

## FISHING

**Anchor Charter Boats**
PO Box 103, Fort Bragg, CA 95437.
*Tel (707) 964-4550.*

**Stagnaro's Sport Fishing**
PO Box 1340, Santa Cruz, CA 95061.
*Tel (212) 209-3370.*
www.stagnaros.com

**State Department of Fish and Game**
1416 9th St, 12th Floor, Sacramento, CA 95814.
*Tel (916) 445-0411.*
www.dfg.ca.gov

**Troutfitter Guide Service**
PO Box 1734, Mammoth Lakes, CA 93546.
*Tel (800) 637-6912.*
www.thetroutfitter.com

## ROCK CLIMBING AND CAVING

**American Mountain Guides Association**
1209 Pearl St, Boulder, Colorado 80302.
*Tel (303) 271-0984.*
www.amga.com

**Mission Cliffs**
2295 Harrison St, San Francisco, CA 94110. *Tel (415) 550-0515.* www.
touchstoneclimbing.com

## HANG GLIDING

**Torrey Pines Gliderport**
2800 Torrey Pines Scenic Drive, La Jolla, CA 92037.
*Tel (858) 452-9858.*

## GARDENS

**Descanso Gardens**
1418 Descanso Drive, La Canada, CA 91011.
*Tel (818) 949-4200.* www.
descansogardens.org

**Villa Montalvo Arboretum**
15400 Montalvo Rd, Saratoga, CA 95071.
*Tel (408) 961-5800.*
www.villamontalvo.org

## HOT AIR BALLOONING

**Napa Valley Balloons**
6795 Washington St, Yountville, CA 94599. *Tel (800) 253-2224.* www.
napavalleyballons.com

**Panorama Balloon Tours**
PO Box 218, Del Mar, CA 90214. *Tel (800) 455-3592.* www.gohotair.com

## WHALE WATCHING

**Oceanic Society Expeditions**
Fort Mason Center, San Francisco, CA 94123.
*Tel (415) 441-1106.*
www.oceanicsociety.org

## HOT SPRINGS

**Calistoga Chamber of Commerce**
1506 Lincoln Ave, Calistoga, CA 94515.
*Tel (707) 942-6333.*

## ISLAND HOPPING

**Angel Island Ferry**
*Tel (415) 435-2131.* www.
angelislandferry.com

**Island Packers**
*Tel (805) 642-1393.*
www.islandpackers.com

# SURVIVAL GUIDE

# PRACTICAL INFORMATION

California is a vibrant state with something to appeal to every taste: from the clubs, restaurants, and bustling downtowns of San Francisco and Los Angeles to the charming plazas and peaceful vistas of rural towns; from the snow-capped mountains and redwood forests of the north to the surfer haunts of San Diego. And no matter where you go in the "Golden State," you'll be

California tourist office logo

welcomed and looked after. Even so, it is advisable to plan ahead to ensure that you experience the best the state has to offer. Most places will have knowledgable visitors' centers offering travel advice and information on sights and visits and this Survival Guide contains valuable information to help you plan your visit. Personal Security and Health *(pp622–3)* outlines some recommended precautions.

Cross-country skiers overlooking the forest above Lake Tahoe

## WHEN TO GO

The season from mid-April to September sees a rush of visitors to the state's major tourist destinations, but be advised that summer often brings San Francisco's foggiest weeks. The winter months are also popular with visitors, either for the warm climate of the south or for the ski slopes of Lake Tahoe. During the quieter off-season in April or November it is possible to visit many of the attractions at lower admission prices and without the usual crowds.

## VISAS AND PASSPORTS

Canadian or EU passport holders who plan to stay less than 90 days do not require a visa. However, visitors must apply for entry in advance via the Electronic System for Authorization (https://esta.cbp.dhs.gov), which will charge all applicants a $14 processing fee. Visitors from other parts of the world need

a valid passport and a non-immigrant visitor's visa. This can be obtained from a US Embassy or Consulate.

## CUSTOMS INFORMATION

Visitors arriving in the US by air and sea are issued with customs declaration forms before arrival, these need to be filled in and handed to passport control. If you are an adult non-resident, you are permitted to bring in a limited amount of duty-free items. These include 0.2 gal (1 liter) of alcoholic beverages (beer, wine, or spirits), 200 cigarettes, 50 cigars (but not Cuban), or 4.4 lb (2 kg) of smoking tobacco, and $100 worth of gifts for other people. Non-residents will be subjected to a retina scan and be fingerprinted and asked a handful of questions about the purpose of their visit.

## TOURIST INFORMATION

Advance information can be obtained from the **California Division of Tourism** or the

nearest **California Welcome Center**. Maps, guides, event listings, and discount passes for public travel and tourist attractions are available from both state and local Visitors' and Convention Bureaus. Welcome Center offices are open from 9am–5:30pm, Monday to Friday.

The Directory below right provides the addresses and telephone numbers of the primary tourist information offices throughout the state.

## CONSULATES

Most countries have consulates in both San Francisco and Los Angeles. Consulates are generally open from 9am to 5pm, Monday to Friday. Although they are not in existence expressly to deal with visitors' problems, staff can help with lost passports and give advice on legal matters in emergencies.

The address of the nearest consulate office in each city can be found in the local telephone directory or through a local website.

California Welcome Center, Santa Rosa

## ADMISSION CHARGES

Major museums, theme parks, art galleries, and other attractions generally charge an admission fee. Entry fees range from $10 to $20 (up to $80 per person for amusement parks), and there are often discounts for the disabled, students, senior citizens, and children *(see p620)*. Smaller sights are either free or request a small donation. At many larger institutions entrance is free on one day a month (call for details). Visitors can get discounted admission to a number of venues by purchasing "Fun Spots" coupons from the Visit California website (www.visitcalifornia.com). These provide money off entry to many sights. Discounts to San Francisco attractions are available with a CityPass (www.citypass.com; $69 adults, $39 children), which also covers a week's public travel, including cable car rides.

## OPENING HOURS

Most businesses are open from 9am–5pm, Monday to Saturday and do not close for lunch. Many are also open 11am–5pm Sundays. Some

Spanish colonial façade of the San Diego Museum of Art *(see p257)*

groceries, drugstores, and gas stations in the larger towns and cities are open 24 hours a day. In large cities, most shops will often stay open until 7pm or 8pm.

Many museums close on Mondays and/or Tuesdays and on major public holidays, but on some days they stay open until early evening.

Californians tend to eat early in the evenings, and some restaurants often have their last sitting at about 10pm. You may find that restaurants will be closed on Monday or Tuesday evenings, so be sure to check this before heading out for dinner.

Most bars are open until 2am, particularly on Fridays and Saturdays.

## SMOKING

It is illegal to smoke in any public building throughout the entire state of California. Ask about smoking policies when reserving a hotel room if you are concerned about it. Remember that in California smoking is banned in restaurants, bars, and in all public places. However, in Los Angeles and San Francisco, several bars are employee-owned and can decide whether or not to allow smoking, and, in an effort to attract more patrons, many of them do. Visitors can ask around to find these spots, or search a local website for details, such as www.yelp.com.

# DIRECTORY

## TOURIST INFORMATION

### California Division of Tourism
PO Box 1499, Sacramento, CA 95814. **Tel** *(800) 862-2543*. **Fax** *(916) 322-2881*. **www**.visitcalifornia.com

## WELCOME CENTERS

### Central Coast
Pismo Beach, 333 Five Cities Drive, Ste 100. **Tel** *(805) 773-7924*. **www**.visitcwc.com

### Downtown
685 S. Figueroa St. **Tel** *(213) 689-8822*. **www**.discoverlosangeles. com

### High Sierras
Truckee, 10065 Donner Pass Rd. **Tel** *(530) 587-2757*. **www**.visitcwc.com

### Local Bay Area
San Francisco, 39 Pier, #B12, 2nd Level. **Tel** *(415) 981-1280*. **www**.visitcwc.com

### Orange County
Anaheim, 800 W Katella Ave. **Tel** *(714) 765-8888*. **www**.anaheimoc.org

### San Diego
San Diego, 1040¹/² W Broadway. **Tel** *(619) 236-1212*. **www**.sandiego.org

### South Central
Santa Barbara, 1601 Anacapa St. **Tel** *(805) 966-9222*. **www**.santabarbaraca.com

### Southern California
Oxnard, 1000 Town Center Drive, Ste 135. **Tel** *(805) 988-0717*

### Wine Country
Santa Rosa, 9 4th St. **Tel** *(800) 404-7673*.

## CONSULATES

### Australian Consulate
625 Market, Suite 200, San Francisco. **Map** 5 C4. **Tel** *(415) 536-1970*.

### British Consulate General
1 Sansome St, San Francisco. **Map** 5 C4. **Tel** *(415) 617-1300*.

### Canadian Consulate
550 S Hope St, 9th floor, Los Angeles. **Map** 11 D4. **Tel** *(213) 346 -2700*.

### French Consulate
540 Bush St, San Francisco. **Map** 5 C4. **Tel** *(415) 397- 4330*.

### German Consulate
1960 Jackson St, San Francisco. **Map** 4 C3. **Tel** *(415) 775-1061*.

### Japanese Consulate
50 Fremont, 23rd Floor, San Francisco. **Map** 6 D4. **Tel** *(415) 777-3533*.

## TAXES AND TIPPING

The California State Government levies an 8.25 percent general sales and use tax. In major cities, an additional 1–1.5 percent tax is added to all bought items except those for out-of-state delivery, to-go food, and food for preparation. There are no sales tax charges on hotel rooms, but a 12–14 percent transient occupancy tax is generally incurred.

In restaurants, it is normal to tip 15–20 percent of the total bill. Allow for a tip of 15 percent for taxi drivers, bar staff, and hairdressers. Porters at hotels and airports expect $2 per bag. It is also common to leave hotel chambermaids $1–2 for each day of your stay.

## TRAVELERS WITH SPECIAL NEEDS

California law requires that every public building is accessible to people with disabilities, which includes not only ramps and accessible bathrooms, but also clearly marked disabled parking. Direction signs and entrances are also specially adapted for blind and disabled visitors. Disabled people also receive privileges such as reserved seating at event venues and on public transport, free parking, and admission reductions to many national and state parks.

It is advisable to notify sights and hotels in advance

**Parking bays for the disabled are clearly marked**

of your arrival, so that they can prepare for any special needs that you require.

The Society for the Advancement of Travel for the Handicapped (SATH) uses a blue H sign to symbolize special facilities in restaurants, hotels, and at tourist sights. For further information on disability rights in California, contact the **Disability Rights, Education, and Defense Fund**.

## TRAVELING WITH CHILDREN

California has some of the country's best child-friendly attractions, such as Disneyland® and Hollywood Studios® in Los Angeles, the San Diego Zoo, and the Exploratorium and California Academy of Sciences in San Francisco. And then, of course, there are the state's many beaches and parks, all of which are free. Along Highway 1 from Cambria up to Pt. Reyes, there are numerous wildlife viewing points where kids will love to watch elephant seals, elk, or the area's many birds.

There are discounts for children at many theme parks and museums and kid's menus with discounted meal prices at restaurants all over California. Many hotels offer "kids stay free" or "kids eat free" deals and children aged five and under ride public transport for free as well.

## SENIOR TRAVELERS

Seniors aged 65 and older get discounts at many restaurants, movies, and at most attractions. Discount travel and reserved seating for seniors is available on all public transport. The **American Association of Retired People** offers a website, including recommendations for sights and information on available discounts.

## GAY AND LESBIAN TRAVELERS

California has a long history of celebrating gay rights. The largest Gay Pride Parade in the world is held in San

Francisco each year, and there is a general focus on equality throughout much of the state. California's large gay community is mainly focused in the major cities, particularly in the Castro District of San Francisco (see p360), Hillcrest in San Diego, the West Hollywood area of LA (see pp110–19), and Palm Springs. Free newspapers and magazines that contain large listings include the LA Weekly in Los Angeles and the several magazines in San Francisco, such as Out in San Francisco and The Advocate.

**ISIC student card gives discount entry to many attractions**

## TRAVELING ON A BUDGET

There are many ways to take advantage of the best of California on a budget. Students receive discounted entry to several attractions and movie theaters, as well as discounted lift tickets in Tahoe and Mammoth. Most museums have a discount night, often Tuesday or Thursday, when entry is reduced or free.

There are a number of websites offering discounts on hotel rooms, restaurants, and other activities. Try **Jetsetter** and **Bloomspot** for hotel and spa deals, **Groupon** and **Living Social** for restaurant discounts. To save money on lodging, consider renting a house or apartment. **Vacation Rentals by Owner** or **AirBnB** offer rooms from $75 a night for a studio/1 bed up to $300 a night for a house that sleeps 10. **Hostelling International-American Youth Hostels** provides safe and inexpensive accommodation in both rural and urban areas.

The **Student Travel Association** is one of the biggest travel organizations that specializes in holidays for students and young people.

Self-Realization Fellowship in LA, an alternative place of worship

## RELIGIOUS ORGANIZATIONS

California, and particularly Northern California, has the reputation of attracting unconventional forms of worship *(see pp440–41)*. Sects, cults, and alternative religions seem to thrive in the state as much as the more conventional churches and temples. The Catholic Church has the largest following, with nearly a quarter of its number of Hispanic origin. Los Angeles has the second largest Jewish community in the US, and there are many beautiful synagogues. Hindu temples, Islamic mosques, and a range of shrines, such as the Self-Realization Temple in LA, abound throughout the state. Details of places for every type of worship can be found in the telephone book.

## CALIFORNIA TIME

California is in the Pacific Time Zone. Daylight Saving Time begins on the second Sunday in March (at 2am) when clocks are set ahead one hour. It ends on the first Sunday in November (at 2am) when clocks are set back one hour.

## ELECTRICITY

In the United States all electrical current flows at a standard 110–120 volts AC (alternating current). To operate 220-volt appliances requires a voltage converter

and an adapter plug with two flat parallel prongs to fit US outlets. The same applies to battery pack rechargers. Many hotels have hairdryers mounted on the bathroom wall and special plugs for electric shavers that carry 110- or 220-volt current.

## CONVERSION CHART

Remember to bear in mind that 1 US pint (0.5 liter) is a smaller measure than 1 UK pint (0.6 liter).

US Standard to Metric
1 inch = 2.54 centimeters
1 foot = 30 centimeters
1 mile = 1.6 kilometers
1 ounce = 28 grams
1 pound = 454 grams
1 US quart = 0.947 liter
1 US gallon = 3.8 liters

Metric to US Standard
1 centimeter = 0.4 inch
1 meter = 3 feet 3 inches
1 kilometer = 0.6 miles
1 gram = 0.04 ounce
1 kilogram = 2.2 pounds
1 liter = 1.1 US quarts

Green Spa Network logo

## RESPONSIBLE TOURISM

California leads the way on all things "green" in the United States, from the sustainable food movement to the green building boom. Recycling bins are available everywhere, and plastic reduction is also becoming a focus, with cities throughout the state passing bans on plastic bags and bottles. A number of incentive programs have spurred more renewable energy development, so it's not uncommon to see solar or wind farms along rural roads or solar panels atop high-rises. Green business associations, such as the **Green Hotels Association**, the **Green Spa Network**, and the **Green Chamber of Commerce** make it easy for visitors to find and support green businesses.

## DIRECTORY

### TRAVELERS WITH SPECIAL NEEDS

**Disability Rights, Education, and Defense Fund**
2212 6th St, Berkeley, CA 94710.
**Tel** (510) 644-2555.
www.dredf.org

### SENIOR TRAVELERS

**American Association of Retired People**
**Tel** (202) 434-3525.
www.aarp.org

### TRAVELING ON A BUDGET

**AirBnB**
www.airbnb.com

**Bloomspot**
www.bloomspot.com

**Groupon**
www.groupon.com

**Hosteling International-American Youth Hostels**
733 15th St NW, Suite 840, Washington, DC 20005.
**Tel** (800) 909-4776.
www.hiusa.org

**Jetsetter**
www.jetsetter.com

**Living Social**
www.livingsocial.com

**Student Travel Association**
**Tel** (800) 781-4040.
www.statravel.com

**Vacation Rentals By Owner (VRBO)**
www.vrbo.com

### RESPONSIBLE TOURISM

**Green Chamber of Commerce**
821 Irving St, #225278, San Francisco.
**Tel** (415) 839-9280.
www.greenchamberofcommerce.net

**Green Hotels Association**
**Tel** (713) 789-8889.
www.greenhotels.com

**Green Spa Network**
**Tel** (800) 275-3045.
www.greenspanetwork.com

# Personal Security and Health

**WARNING**
YOU ARE ENTERING BEAR COUNTRY
BEARS ARE ACTIVE DAY AND NIGHT
PROPER FOOD STORAGE REQUIRED BY STATE LAW
PROTECT YOUR PROPERTY AND YOURSELF

visitors will be subject to a $500 fine

**Bear warning in Northern California**

Like most major cities, the cities of California have some dangerous neighborhoods. Check with the tourist office or hotel staff about which parts of town are considered unwise to visit, either alone or at night. San Francisco is believed to be one of the safest large cities in the US; unfortunately, problems are more visible in some areas of LA. When traveling in the countryside, always carry a good local map, particularly in the deserts and the mountains. It is important to take the advice of the local authorities seriously and in cases of all outdoor pursuits, normal safety procedures should be observed.

**Motorcycle police patrolling the streets, San Francisco**

## POLICE

Uniformed and plain-clothes police regularly patrol the streets on foot, as well as in cars and motorcycles. The Highway Patrol monitor speeding on the highways and are first-responders in case of accidents. All non-emergency crimes should be reported to the local police station, the number for which can be found easily online or in the Blue Pages of the telephone book (phone books are placed in all hotel rooms).

## WHAT TO BE AWARE OF

The notorious gangs of California, particularly in Los Angeles, are rarely seen outside their own areas and are not interested in approaching visitors. Visitors are more likely to be the target of theft or car crime. Lock any valuables away in the hotel safe – do not carry

them around with you. If you rent a car, do not leave valuables in view when you park, even if it seems like a safe neighborhood. Make sure you know where you're going so you don't enter a bad neighborhood, especially on your own and at night.

Pedestrians should observe road safety laws: jaywalking, or crossing the road anywhere except at an intersection, can result in a fine.

Outside of the cities, in wilderness areas pay attention to posted warnings and heed the advice of local rangers.

## IN AN EMERGENCY

For emergencies that require medical, police, or fire services, call 911 in the first instance. US hospital emergency rooms can often be crowded and it may take time to be seen. City-owned hospitals, are listed in the Blue Pages of the telephone book, private hospitals in the Yellow Pages. When requested, hotels will usually call a doctor or dentist to visit you in your room. The national organization **Travelers' Aid Society** can also provide some assistance in many kinds of emergency.

## LOST AND STOLEN PROPERTY

Although the chances of retrieving property lost in the street are very slim, telephone the **Police Non-Emergency** Line to report lost or stolen items. If you want to make an insurance claim on your return home, you will need to obtain a copy of the police report to send to the insurance company. In most cities, you can now file the report online at www.sco.ca.gov and print a copy for your records. In case of loss, it is always useful to have a photocopy of all documents kept separately as proof of possession.

If your passport is lost or stolen, get in contact with your consulate immediately *(see p619).* For lost or stolen traveler's checks or credit cards, you should contact the nearest issuing company's office *(see p624).*

## HOSPITALS AND PHARMACIES

There are both public and private hospitals in the US, with private hospitals generally offering nicer facilities and shorter wait times. Low-cost clinics are walk-in clinics that charge a small fee and can be a good

**Fire engine, Santa Rosa**

**Police car, Los Angeles**

**Ambulance, San Bernardino County**

option for travelers in need of care for minor illnesses. The main pharmacies in California are **Walgreens** and **CVS**. Some pharmacies offer clinics, and these will be listed in the phone book and can be easily found online. If you take medication, bring a back-up prescription with you. Pharmacies are open from 9am–6pm; many 24-hour pharmacies exist in the cities.

## TRAVEL AND HEALTH INSURANCE

Travel insurance is strongly recommended for the US. You should take out adequate coverage for emergency medical and dental care while also insuring your personal property. If you visit a doctor's office, hospital, or low-cost clinic in the US without insurance, be prepared to pay exorbitant fees. Even with medical coverage, you may still have to pay for some services, then claim reimbursement from your insurance company.

It is also advisable to make sure your travel insurance covers for lost or stolen baggage and travel documents, accidental death or injury, trip cancellation, and legal advice.

A park fire warning sign indicating the level of risk

## SAFETY OUTDOORS

Outside of the cities, pay attention to posted warnings and heed the advice of rangers and locals. The Pacific Ocean is rarely warm, even in summer. The ocean can also be rough, more suited to surfers than swimmers, with a strong undertow.

It is important to have the proper equipment before hiking in the wilderness.

Ranger with a cross-country skiing group at Yosemite National Park

Notify someone of your plans before setting off. Leave the area as you found it, and be wary of the occasionally dangerous wildlife in many of the parks. As forest fires can start fast, check with the park ranger that camp fires are allowed.

There are services for climbers in many parks (*see p613*). Contact local ranger services via the **California State Parks** for advice on instructors, equipment required, and current weather conditions.

Be careful in the desert. At lower levels, it is usually hot and dry; at high elevations, temperatures often drop below freezing at night. Always carry extra gas and water in your car. If your car overheats, do not leave it to go for help.

It is also worth checking the **California Department of Transportation** websites for updates on road conditions and precautions in the sun.

## EARTHQUAKES

The expectation and fear of earthquakes should not get in the way of everyday activities. You may experience a tremor, but the most important thing is not to panic. Precautions are important, such as keeping shoes and a flashlight by the bed when asleep, in case of broken glass or power cuts. Most injuries occur from falling material so, if indoors, stand in a doorway or crouch under a table. If you are in a car, slow down, pull to the side of the road, and stop. When outside, avoid standing under or being near trees, power lines, or bridges. For further information on earthquake precautions, contact **The United States Geological Survey**.

## DIRECTORY

### POLICE

**Police Non-Emergency Lines**
Los Angeles
*Tel* (877) 275-5273.
San Francisco
*Tel* (415) 553-0123.

### IN AN EMERGENCY

**All Emergencies**
*Tel* 911.

**Travelers' Aid Society**
Los Angeles
*Tel* (323) 644-3500.
San Diego
*Tel* (619) 295-8393.
San Francisco
*Tel* (650) 821-2735.

### PHARMACIES

**CVS**
*Tel* (888) 607-4287.
**www**.cvs.com

**Walgreens**
*Tel* (800) 925-4733.
**www**.walgreens.com

### SAFETY OUTDOORS

**California Department of Transportation**
To check highway and road conditions.
**www**.dot.ca.gov

**California State Parks**
*Tel* 800-777-0369.
**www**.parks.ca.gov

### EARTHQUAKE INFORMATION

**The United States Geological Survey**
Earth Science Information Centers, 345 Middlefield Rd, Menlo Park, CA 94025.
*Tel* (650) 329-4390.
**www**.usgs.gov

# Banking and Currency

San Francisco and LA are major West Coast financial centers. California has a wealth of local, regional, and major national banks, plus some retail branches of the leading foreign banks. For the convenience of residents and visitors alike, there are numerous ATMs that operate 24 hours a day. In smaller towns, some banks may not exchange foreign currency or traveler's checks, so it is best to call the bank in advance. Credit cards are very useful, and are typically required as a form of security for checking-in to a hotel or renting a car.

## BANKS AND EXCHANGE BUREAUS

Bank opening times vary throughout the state, but they usually open between 10am–5pm, Monday to Friday. Banking hours within major cities may be longer: some open as early as 7:30am and close at 6pm, and are often open on Saturday mornings too. Credit Unions serve only their own members and deal with local business, so look for banks that offer services to the general public. **Chase**, **Bank of America**, and **Wells Fargo** all have hundreds of branches throughout the whole of California.

Major banks will exchange currency, but larger exchange bureaus are also available at major airports and in the financial districts of California. Exchange bureaux are open 9am–5pm on weekdays, and note that commissions will be charged. The best-known companies are **Travelex Currency Service** and **American Express Travel Service** and all have offices throughout California.

## ATMS

Most ATMs accept debit cards from the main international banks and many credit cards, and can be found in most bank foyers or on the outside wall near the bank's entrance. The ATM machines that are located in bank foyers can be accessed outside normal banking hours via a card-reader at the door, which accepts all major cards. ATM machines usally issue American banknotes in $20 denominations. Ask your card provider which ATM system your card can access in California and how much each transaction will cost. The more popular systems used throughout California are Cirrus and Plus.

Bars and convenience stores often offer ATMs but these machines will usually charge a fee to every cardholder. Withdrawals from ATMs may provide a better foreign currency exchange rate than cash transactions, but you will be charged.

On a cautionary note, be aware of your surroundings when using any ATM. Make sure you shield your PIN, and if available, use a machine located within a bank. Be careful when removing your card at the machine.

If you are traveling from Europe, and use a chip & pin card, you will need to sign for any transactions you make.

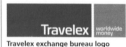
Travelex exchange bureau logo

## CREDIT CARDS AND TRAVELER'S CHECKS

Credit cards are extremely common in the US and can even be used for purchases costing $1, as well as for public transport fares and parking. Most hotels will ask for a credit card number on check-in, and almost all car rental companies require a credit card. Some will accept the use of a debit card. Make sure you know the requirements before going to the rental agency. Hospitals will accept most credit cards in payment. **American Express**, **MasterCard**, and VISA are widely accepted throughout California.

If your credit or debit card is lost or stolen, contact your card company immediately. In order to ensure your card works overseas, it is worth contacting your bank or credit card provider in advance of traveling.

Traveler's checks issued by American Express and Thomas Cook in US dollars are accepted at most hotels, restaurants, and shops without a fee but with a passport as identification. If you lose your checks, contact Thomas Cook Refund Services or the **American Express Helpline**.

Foreign currency traveler's checks may be cashed at a large bank or at major hotels. Rates of exchange are in the newspapers and posted up at banks with exchange services. US dollar traveler's checks can usually be cashed with a recognized form of photographic ID such as a passport or an ISIC card.

ATMs at the Bank of America, San Francisco

## Coins

*American coins come in 1-, 5-, 10-, 25- and 50-cent pieces. The gold-tone $1 coin is also in circulation as are the State quarters, which feature a historical scene on one side. Each coin has a popular name: 25-cent pieces are called quarters, 10-cent pieces are dimes, 5-cent pieces are nickels, and 1-cent pieces are pennies.*

**25-cent coin
(a quarter)**

**10-cent coin
(a dime)**

**5-cent coin
(a nickel)**

**1-cent coin
(a penny)**

## Bank Notes (Bills)

*Units of currency in the United States are dollars and cents. There are 100 cents to a dollar. Notes come in the following denominations: $1, $5, $10, $20, $50 and $100. Security features include subtle color hues and color-shifting ink in the lower right hand corner of the face of each note. Each bank note features a different US president.*

**1-dollar bill ($1)**

**5-dollar bill ($5)**

**10-dollar bill ($50)**

**20-dollar bill ($20)**

**50-dollar bill ($50)**

**100-dollar bill ($100)**

# Communications and Media

As the home of Silicon Valley, California is always ahead when it comes to communication technologies. High-speed Wi-Fi is freely available throughout much of the state, and visitors can pick up pay-as-you-go cell (mobile) phones for use while in California. Public pay phones can still be found in hotels, airports, and some street corners though. Los Angeles is a communications and media hub, and the base of several listings magazines, a variety of national and international newspapers and world news TV channels. No matter where you are in the state, it's generally easy to keep up with what's happening back home.

## INTERNATIONAL AND LOCAL TELEPHONE CALLS

Local calls are free from most hotels, whereas long-distance and international calls are billed at very high rates. Visitors are better off purchasing prepaid phone cards (available at pharmacies and convenience stores, or online) to make calls from pay phones and cell phones, especially if calling international numbers. To use most phone cards you call the toll-free number printed on the card, enter the pin, and then dial the required number. All phone cards have instructions with printed on the card and spoken clearly to the caller when they phone the toll-free number.

To make a call from a public telephone or cell phone, you will need to dial 0 before the number. To call US numbers outside the city you're staying in, you'll need to dial 1 and then the number. To call outside the US, dial 011, the country code and the number.

**at&t**

AT&T cell phone logo

and pay-as-you-go phones and SIM cards for use. Both can be ordered online, however buying in-store ensures that you get a phone or SIM card that is compatible. Calls to phones outside the US are billed at premium rates, while calls to land lines are cheaper.

## PUBLIC TELEPHONES

Modern pay phones have a hand receiver and a 12-button key pad. Pacific Bell (PacBell) operates the majority of public pay phones. Although public phones are becoming increasingly rare, they are still typically available in airports, public transit terminals, and on main streets in large cities. Calls cost a minimum of 50 cents and most phones accept both coins and credit cards. Telephone directories are supplied at most public phones. If you need help or information, call the operator by dialing 0.

## CELL PHONES

Visitors to the US who wish to use their own cell phone will need a tri-band phone and a SIM card that has been activated for "roaming." Ask your cell provider if your phone has been set up to be used abroad.

The primary cell phone providers in the United States are **T-Mobile**, **AT&T**, **Verizon** and **Sprint**. All offer prepaid

## REACHING THE RIGHT NUMBER

- Direct-dial call outside the local area code, but within the US and Canada: dial 1, then the area code and then the local number.
- International direct-dial call: dial 011 followed by country code (UK: 44; Australia: 61; New Zealand: 64), then the city or area code (omit the first 0) and then the local number.
- International call via the operator: dial 01, then the country code, then the city code (without the first 0), and then the local number.
- International directory inquiries: dial 00.
- International operator assistance: dial 01.
- A 1-800, 866, 888, or 877 prefix indicates a free call.
- Local directory inquiries: dial 411.
- For calls within the local area code do not use an area code first. Exceptions: 310, 657, and 714 area codes must be keyed in for all calls, even local.
- For emergency police, fire, or ambulance services, dial 911.

## INTERNET

Visitors can find free wireless Internet access throughout much of California, including on all major public transport systems.

Some hotels provide Internet access for free, while others charge a daily fee. In a few cases, hotels provide hard-wired Ethernet access rather than wireless; such establishments have Ethernet cables available at the front desk. Public Wi-Fi is now so common in California that Internet cafés are becoming rare, but most coffee shops offer Wi-Fi (either free or for an hourly rate), and hotel business centers have Internet-ready computers and printers available to use.

**Cell phones, more popular than public telephones**

A busy café with Wi-Fi facility, San Francisco

**FedEx** offers computers for hire with Internet and printing capabilities, as well as services in store. Libraries also have public computers with free Internet access available.

## POSTAL SERVICES

Apart from post offices, letters can be sent from hotel reception desks or mailed in letter slots in office buildings, in mailboxes on the street, and at rail, air, and bus terminals. Stamps can be purchased at post offices, hotel reception desks, or in some cases from bank ATMs. Different stamps are required for postcards; check postage rules and rates on the **United States Postal Service** website or at the post office. Flat rate envelopes are a great way to reduce postage costs; you can send as much as you can fit into the envelope for a flat $13 rate (available for domestic and international mail).

All domestic mail usually arrives within 1 to 5 days. International airmail to New Zealand, Australia, Canada, Ireland, and the United Kingdom takes 5–10 working days. The federal post office offers Priority Mail, which promises delivery faster than first class mail, and the more expensive Express Mail, which delivers next day within the US, and within 72 hours to many international destinations. Private express and international mail can be arranged through **FedEx**, **DHL**

UNITED STATES POSTAL SERVICE

US Postal Service logo

or **UPS**, the numbers for which are listed in the Yellow Pages.

If you wish to receive mail during your visit it can be sent care of **General Delivery** to a local address. This service is available in the larger city post offices. Undelivered mail sent c/o General Delivery will be held for 30 days before being returned to the sender.

## NEWSPAPERS AND MAGAZINES

The *New York Times*, the *Wall Street Journal*, and *USA Today* are available throughout much of California. There are also several local daily papers, many of which can be bought from street distribution bins or newsstands. Local magazines such as *LA Weekly*, *Angeleno*, and *Los Angeles* magazine in LA and the *SF Weekly*, *Bay Guardian*, and *San Francisco Magazine* in San Francisco provide information on local restaurants and events.

## TELEVISION AND RADIO

The choice of TV stations in California is vast. Much of it is supplied by cable or satellite systems. Most hotel rooms have a TV, with a full range of cable channels, including BBC America and HBO. Bars frequently have screens showing sports. There is a wide selection of national and local channels, most of them showing sitcoms, magazine programs, children's cartoons,

movies, and talk shows. There are also Spanish and Asian foreign-language channels such as KRCA, as well as news and music channels. Most cable or satellite TV set-ups include a menu channel with listings.

There are several radio stations in California; public radio stations run news and talk programs. Wilderness areas typically have a dedicated frequency for news of road closures and weather issues. Hotels may provide a list of radio frequencies, or there are useful websites such as www.radio-locator.com.

## DIRECTORY

### CELL PHONES

**AT&T**
Tel *(800) 225-5288.*
www.att.com

**Sprint**
Tel *(888) 211-4727.*
www.sprint.com

**T-Mobile**
Tel *(800) 866-2453.*
www.tmobile.com

**Verizon**
Tel *(800) 922-0204.*
www.verizon.com

### POSTAL SERVICES

**DHL**
Tel *(800) 225-5345.*
www.dhl.com

**FedEx**
Tel *(800) 463-3339.*
www.fedex.com

**General Delivery**
**Los Angeles**
c/o General Delivery, LA Main Post Office, 900 N Alameda, Los Angeles, CA 90086.
**San Diego**
c/o General Delivery, San Diego Main Post Office, San Diego, CA 92110.
**San Francisco**
c/o General Delivery, Civic Center, 101 Hyde St, San Francisco, CA 94142.

**UPS**
Tel *(800) 742-5877.*
www.ups.com

**United States Postal Service**
Tel *(800) 275-8777.*
www.usps.gov

# TRAVEL INFORMATION

San Francisco and Los Angeles are the two main gateways for visitors traveling to California by air. You can also reach California by car, Amtrak train, long-distance bus, or by ocean liner. Despite continuing problems with traffic congestion and the rapid increase in gas prices, large comfortable cars and a comprehensive network of roads make driving an efficient and pleasurable way to tour the state. Public transportation is also a viable and inexpensive option. In some major cities, historic cable cars and ferries work alongside modern buses and mass transit systems as an efficient way to get around.

**American Airlines aeroplane**

**The modern concourse at San Jose airport, California**

## ARRIVING BY AIR

Air travel is an essential part of exploring America, and California is no exception. All the major airports are efficiently designed, with computerized ticketing systems for faster check-in.

Los Angeles (LAX) and San Francisco (SFO) are the two main airports used by visitors. International flights also land at San Diego (SAN), Oakland (OAK), Ontario (ONT), and San Jose (SJC). With vast numbers of passengers passing through, airports such as LA and San Francisco can be busy and at peak times, lines at customs and immigration are inevitable. It will help to take this into consideration when planning your transport from the airport.

All airports have disabled facilities, although it is advisable to check with the airline if you require help.

## AIR FARES AND TICKETS

Fare prices vary according to the season, with the most expensive fares being during the summer and holiday periods, such as Christmas and Thanksgiving (see p39). It is always cheaper to travel on weekdays rather than on weekends. Tickets can be purchased from a reputable travel agent or they can often be booked for less online with easy to use websites such as **Travelocity** and **Kayak**, which provide airline price comparisons on all flights.

## DOMESTIC AIR TRAVEL

With over 30 airports for domestic flights including Sacramento and Ontario (also international), Santa Barbara, John Wayne/Orange County, and Fresno – air travel within California is easy and fairly cheap with prices starting from around $100 each way. **Southwest**, **Jet Blue**, and **Virgin America** all offer low prices and high quality amenities during the flight. Jet Blue flies out of smaller airports, but offers extra leg room and in-flight satellite TV on personal screens. Southwest will get you anywhere in the US, with a stop over. Virgin America flies to many major airports and boast planes with personal entertainment systems and in-flight Wi-Fi.

| AIRPORT | INFORMATION | DISTANCE FROM CITY |
| --- | --- | --- |
| Los Angeles (LAX) | **Tel** (310) 646-5252 <br> **www**.lawa.org | 15 miles (24 km) from Downtown |
| San Francisco (SFO) | **Tel** (650) 821-8211 <br> **www**.flysfo.com | 14 miles (22 km) from city center |
| Oakland (OAK) | **Tel** (510) 563-3300 <br> **www**.flyoakland.com | 8 miles (12 km) from city center |
| San Diego (SAN) | **Tel** (619) 400-2404 <br> **www**.san.org | 3 miles (5 km) from city center |
| San Jose (SJC) | **Tel** (408) 392-3600 <br> **www**.flysanjose.com | 8 miles (12 km) from city center |
| Sacramento (SMF) | **Tel** (916) 929-5411 <br> **www**.sacairports.org | 12 miles (19 km) from city center |
| Palm Springs (PSP) | **Tel** (760) 318-3800 <br> **www**.palmspringsca.gov | 2 miles (3 km) from city center |

## GETTING INTO THE CITIES FROM THE AIRPORT

Car hire desks (see p632), currency exchange facilities (see pp624–5), and shuttle bus services can be found at all airports. Most car hire companies supply a shuttle bus to the car pick-up points, usually located on the outskirts of the airport.

In San Francisco, the subway Shuttle buses and vans (see p397) can also be called for a door-to-door service to and from the airport and a specific city address. Cheaper than using a taxi, one-way fares vary in price, depending on the distance covered. Bay Area Rapid Transit (or BART) is another option, and has a desk located in the arrivals terminal. It is a 35-minute ride into the city and costs $5 to $7.

Taxi ranks can be found outside most main terminals and will take you into the city. Prices will vary.

## ARRIVING BY LAND AND SEA

The primary interstate freeways into California are the I-80 in the Bay Area and the North, and I-15, I-10, and I-40 in the South. Patrols at state borders will sometimes stop cars to check for illegal substances, but there are no tolls at these crossings and often no one patrolling them.

If driving into California from Las Vegas on the I-15, from Phoenix on the I-10, or from Flagstaff on the I-40, make sure you are well prepared as these roads are quite desolate. Cars can become extremely hot during the summer; drivers are advised to travel in the cooler morning and evening. In winter, cars on I-80 are advised to be equipped with four-wheel drive and snow tires or they will be stopped and made to put on snow chains.

Train travel in the US provides regular and easy connections between all major cities. **Amtrak** runs direct, long-distance routes from LA to Chicago, Seattle, Orlando, San Antonio and Albuquerque. Bus rides from neighboring states cost $80–$100 on average for a round-trip. From Las Vegas it is possible to hop on to a five-hour bus ride with **LuxBus** to LA with minimal stops.

Northern routes and buses originating farther away than Nevada are longer journeys; the ride from Portland to San Francisco is about 20 hours (90 minutes by air). **Greyhound Lines** is the primary bus line with a depot in every major city. **Green Tortoise** offers slower green buses with chances to break the journey at hostels (see p630).

Cruise operators organize trips from ports in the US to ports around the world. The primary ports for the arrival, departure and stopping of cruise ships are Long Beach and San Pedro, in southern California, and San Francisco in northern California.

Greyhound Lines logo

# DIRECTORY

## ARRIVING BY AIR

**American Airlines**
Tel (800) 433-7300.
www.aa.com

**British Airways**
Tel (800) 247-9297.
www.britishairways.com

**Delta**
Tel (800) 221-1212.
www.delta–air.com

**United**
Tel (800) 241-6522.
www.united.com

**US Airways**
Tel (800) 428-4322.
www.usairways.com

**Virgin Atlantic**
Tel (800) 862-8621.
www.virgin-atlantic.com

## AIR FARES AND TICKETS

**Kayak**
www.kayak.com

**Travelocity**
www.travelocity.com

## DOMESTIC AIR TRAVEL

**Jet Blue**
Tel (800) 538-2583.
www.jetblue.com

**Southwest**
Tel (800) 435-9792.
www.southwest.com

**Virgin America**
Tel (877) 359-8474.
www.virginamerica.com

## ARRIVING BY LAND AND SEA

**Amtrak**
Tel (800) 872-7245.
www.amtrak.com

**Green Tortoise**
494 Broadway, San Francisco, CA 94133. **Tel** (800) 867-8647.
www.greentortoise.com

**Greyhound Lines**
Tel (800) 231-2222.
www.greyhound.com

**LuxBus America**
www.luxbusamerica.com

**The Port of Los Angeles**
425 S. Palos Verdes Street P.O. Box 151, San Pedro, CA 90733-0151. **Tel** (310) 732-7678.
www.portoflosangeles.org

An ocean liner arriving at Long Beach

# Getting Around California

Although often more time-consuming, traveling by train, bus, and ferry can be an inexpensive and rewarding way of getting around California. Within the major cities of San Francisco *(see pp396–7)*, Los Angeles *(see pp178–9)*, and San Diego *(see pp266–7)*, there are public transportation networks of buses, trams, Metro trains, ferries, and cable cars although they are very busy during the rush-hour periods. Taxis and shuttle buses are also useful in the cities. The network of Amtrak railroad lines and connecting bus services serves the state's most populous areas and offers some scenic journeys.

**Cycling past Crissy Fields and the Golden Gate Bridge, San Francisco**

## GREEN TRAVEL

Although California may lack the sophisticated rail infrastructure of Europe, California does have some green travel options. In San Francisco, Los Angeles, and San Diego, public transport systems are modern and convenient, easily connecting visitors to the most popular sights and attractions. Many California cities use electric or hybrid buses and there are several "green taxi" fleets with electric and hybrid cars including **Green Taxi Santa Monica**, **San Diego Green Transportation**, and **SF GreenCab**. Most hire car companies also offer a variety of hybrid car options.

While some cities have better public transportation systems than others (San Francisco is leagues ahead of Los Angeles), sustainable transport options are available throughout the state. Cycling is heavily encouraged everywhere with designated lanes along scenic routes and

in towns, and incentives are offered for lower emission vehicles, including carpool lanes for cars with two passengers and lower toll fees.

For those concerned about the carbon emissions from air travel, carbon offsets can be bought through companies such as TerraPass, www. terrapass.com.

## TRAVELING BY RAIL

In California, the rail network, operated by **Amtrak**, is divided into three sections: the Pacific Surfliner Route (Paso Robles to San Diego), the Capitol Corridor (San Jose to Sacramento), and the San Joaquins Route (connecting Emeryville and Bakersfield). The Amtrak Thruway line services all main stations. A bus service also stops along these lines. Local commuter lines include **Caltrain** (linking San Jose and San Francisco); the Coast Starlight Connection (between San Luis Obispo and Santa Barbara); LA Metrolink; and the Coaster (connecting San Diego and Oceanside).

## LONG-DISTANCE BUSES

In California, Greyhound Lines bus services *(see p269)* include scenic coastal connections as well as frequent express routes linking major cities.

Guided tours provide a leisurely way of sightseeing. Several companies offer short package trips in deluxe buses visiting sights such as Hearst Castle *(see pp212–15)*, Yosemite National Park *(see pp488–91)*, and Monterey *(see pp508–11)*. Information about these can be found in the Yellow Pages.

For travelers with more time to spare the Green Tortoise company *(see p629)* offers budget travel between the major cities of the Pacific Coast. Passengers can break their trip to camp, make meals, and explore the area. This company also operates hostels along its routes, which is a great deal for those wanting to book bus and lodging together and is very popular with younger travelers wanting to explore the state.

## TAXIS

Taxis or cabs can usually be found outside all airport terminals, main transportation terminals, and outside most major hotels. Taxis can also be hailed on the street in the downtown areas of all cities. They are expensive and fares are metered according to the distance traveled. Credit cards are often accepted, but it is best to inquire in advance. A tip of 15 percent is expected.

**Pacific-Surfliner Amtrak train, a scenic line at Del Mar, San Diego County**

## BOATS AND FERRIES

Express boat services provide a fast link from Los Angeles to Santa Catalina Island *(see pp242–3)*. In San Francisco you can take a leisurely cruise across the bay *(see pp298–9)* to Sausalito, Alameda, and Larkspur. Most ferries carry foot passengers and bicycles, but not motor vehicles.

Commuter ferries provide a breezy alternative to the smog of rush-hour traffic and congestion. Some routes, such as the San Diego–Coronado ferry, provide a pleasant and reasonably priced way to enjoy traveling to different cities. For ferry timetables, prices, and locations in San Francisco and the Bay Area *(see p399)*; in San Diego *(see p267)*.

## TICKETS AND FARES

The average ticket price on public transport in major cities such as San Francisco and Los Angeles is $2 each way. Although San Diego, San Jose, Los Angeles, and San Francisco transit systems all offer day and weekly passes, only San Francisco's CityPass *(see p397)* is priced to save visitors money. A 7-day unlimited Muni and cable car ticket, plus entry to local attractions costs $69 for adults and $39 for children (aged 5–12).

Ferry fares vary drastically. The ferry from Oakland to San Francisco is only 3 miles (5 km) and is $6.25 each way, while from Long Beach to Santa Catalina island, 22 miles (35 km), it costs $68.25.

# DIRECTORY

### GREEN TRAVEL

**Green Taxi Santa Monica**
*Tel* (310) 430-1882.
**www**.mygreentaxi.com

**San Diego Green Transportation**
*Tel* (888) 473-3605.
**www.**
sandiegogogreentransportation.com

**SF GreenCab**
*Tel* (415) 626-4733.
**www**.626green.com

### TRAVELING BY RAIL

**Amtrak**
*Tel* (800) 872-7245.
**www**.amtrak.com

**Caltrain**
*Tel* (800) 660-4287.
**www**.caltrain.com

## AMTRAK ROUTES

This map shows the main Amtrak routes within California, as well as the Amtrak Thruway feeder services to the main stations. Amtrak also has several interstate services to other major cities in the US.

**Amtrak train**

**KEY**

— Pacific Surfliner Route

— San Joaquins Route

— Capitol Corridor

— Amtrak Thruway

— Connecting Rail service

# Traveling by Car

Driving is an essential part of the California way of life, and for both residents and visitors it is the most convenient way to travel around the state. Roads are well maintained so that they are able to cope with the great volume of rush-hour traffic that pours in and out of the main cities every weekday. The state has an efficient network of major roads linking the cities and towns. In remote areas, such as in the deserts and mountains, it is sometimes necessary to use a four-wheel-drive vehicle.

The Bixby Creek Bridge at Big Sur, part of the scenic Highway 1

## CAR HIRE

It is best to arrange a fly-drive package before arriving in California. Take note of exactly what is included in the deal, and find out whether any extra payments may arise when the car is picked up. These additions – which can include optional fuel purchase, extended insurance cover, collision damage waiver, delivery or drop-off charges, and vehicle rental tax (a daily city vehicle rental tax) – can double the original prepaid fee. It is particularly important to find out exactly what is included in the insurance policy offered by the rental company. Drivers should remember that in California, where litigation is an everyday occurrence, it is sensible to be fully insured.

To rent a car, the driver must be over 25 and have a US or internationally valid driver's license. A major credit card is vital as a guarantee. Some companies may rent to younger drivers or accept a debit card in lieu of a credit card number, but expect higher charges as a result.

Taking a rented car across the border into Mexico is not permitted without prior arrangement.

The gas tank should be full when you return the vehicle, and you must allow sufficient time to process and check your final bill. If you plan on driving around enough to use a full tank of gas, the prepaid fuel option is a good idea to avoid having to stop at the gas station before returning the vehicle, and also paying the local price per gallon rate. Car rental is generally least expensive at airports (*see p629*), but call the free

numbers advertised by rental companies to find out about discounts and deals. Rental cars usually have automatic transmission. If requested, some companies supply cars with manual transmission ("stick-shift"). For alternative hire vehicles, classic cars, Harley-Davidson motorcycles, and RVs (motor homes) can be rented from **USA RV Rentals** and **Dubbelju Motorcycle**.

## ROADS AND TOLLS

The most common routes within the state are Highway 101 from southern California to the north; Highway 1, which provides a scenic, coastal drive from the central coast to Mendocino in the north; and I-80, which runs northeast from San Francisco to Sacramento and Lake Tahoe. Tolls are uncommon on roads, but typical on bridges, mostly around the Bay Area, where it costs between $4 and $6 to cross the region's various bridges.

## RULES OF THE ROAD

AAA sign

Americans drive on the right. Seat belts are compulsory for both driver and passengers. In the US, speed limits are individually set by each state. In California, the maximum speed limit is generally 65 mph (104 kmh) but on selected freeways, 70 mph (110 kmh) limits have now been introduced. In cities, the speed limits are restricted – check road signs as they vary. These limits are rigorously enforced. Drunk driving is a

### TRAFFIC SIGNS

Drivers should take note of the different signs that give warnings and instructions. Speed limits may vary every few miles, depending on the road conditions and the amount of traffic, and should be adhered to. In more remote areas, drivers must look out for wildlife that occasionally strays onto roads. Disregarding traffic signs may result in a Highway Patrol fine.

Traffic flows in a single direction

Wildlife warning      Maximum speed

serious offense and carries heavy penalties. Highways without traffic lights or intersections are called freeways. Bicycles are not allowed on freeways or Interstates. Some freeways have less congested diamond (or carpool) lanes, which only cars with more than one passenger (and in some areas more than two) are permitted to use during rush hour (7–10am and 3–7pm).

Violating carpool lanes carries fines of $250 or more. It is permissible to turn right on red at traffic lights if there is nothing coming the other way, and unless otherwise indicated. The first vehicle to reach a stop sign junction has the right of way.

The **Automobile Association of America** (AAA) supplies maps, has an emergency road service, and offers discounts at hotels and restaurants. It is linked with many automobile clubs abroad, so inquire ahead whether they will honor your membership.

**Signs to prevent cars rolling downhill**

## PARKING

Parking in Californian cities is strictly controlled and can be expensive. Valet parking is obligatory if you pull up outside many hotels and restaurants. Hand the keys to the attendant and pay on departure. Most parking meters accept nickels, dimes, and quarters, but some systems require dollar bills to

be "posted" into the slot for the parking space. Parking lots have their own set prices. Parking is generally free at shopping malls or you can have your ticket validated at any store where you've made a purchase to reduce or eliminate the fee.

Parking restrictions are indicated by curb colors. If the curb is painted red, parking is prohibited; yellow indicates a loading zone; green allows limited parking and white is for drop off and pick up only. Blue curbs are for disabled parking. If parking on a hill in San Francisco, turn your wheels into the road if facing uphill and toward the curb if facing downhill. If your vehicle is towed, contact the local **Department of Parking and Transportation**.

## GASOLINE

Gas, or gasoline, is either unleaded or diesel quality. It is sold in gallons rather than liters. Inexpensive by European standards, the price includes a hefty gasoline tax. Gas stations are not as widespread as many visitors expect, so be sure to fill up the tank before driving into the mountains, desert, or through other remote areas. Few gas stations have pump attendants. Most pumps take credit cards, and it is common to pay for the gas before putting it into the car.

**Driving through the historic district of San Diego's Gaslamp Quarter**

# General Index

# Acknowledgments

Dorling Kindersley would like to thank the following people whose contributions and assistance have made the preparation of this book possible.

**Main Contributor**

**Jamie Jensen** grew up in LA and now lives in Northern California. He contributed to San Francisco in the DK Guides series, and his most recent book is *Road Trip USA: Cross-Country Adventures on America's Two-Lane Highways.*

**Ellen Payne** is Managing Editor of *Los Angeles Magazine* and has worked on numerous travel publications.

**J Kingston Pierce** is a Seattle writer specializing in West Coast history. He is a contributing editor of *San Francisco Focus* and *Seattle* magazines and his book credits include *San Francisco, You're History!*

**Rebecca Poole Forée** is Editor-in-Chief at Foghorn Press, San Francisco. She has written many travel books, including *Northern California Best Places.*

**Nigel Tisdall** is the author of several travel guides. He has contributed to *France, Seville and Andalusia* and *Portugal* in the DK series.

**Stanley Young** lives in LA. He has written several books including *The Missions of California* and *Paradise Found: The Beautiful Retreats and Sanctuaries of California and the Southwest.*

**Contributors and Consultants**

Virginia Butterfield, Dawn Douglas, Rebecca Renner, Tessa Souter, Shirley Streshinsky, Barbara Tannenbaum, Michael Webb, John Wilcock.

**Additional Photography**

Brenna Alexander, Max Alexander, Demetrio Carassco, Steve Gorton, Gary Grimaud, Bonita Halm, Trevor Hill, Kirk Irwin, Neil Lukas, Neil Mersh, Ian O'Leary, David Peevers, Peter Peevers, Erhard Pfeiffer, Chris Stowers, Robert Vente, Paul Whitfield, Francesca Yorke.

**Additional Illustrators**

James A Allington, Arcana Studios, Hugh Dixon, Richard Draper, Dean Entwhistle, Eugene Fleury, Chris Forsey, Andrew Green, Steve Gyapay, Toni Hargreaves, Philip Hockey, John Lawrence, Nick Lipscombe, Mel Pickering, Sallie Alane Reason, Peter Ross, Simon Roulstone, John See, Tristan Spaargaren, Ed Stuart, Paul Williams.

**Cartography**

Lovell Johns Ltd, Oxford, UK; ERA-Maptec Ltd, Dublin, Ireland; Alok Pathak, Kunal Singh. Street Finder Maps based upon digital data, adapted with permission from original survey by ETAK INC 1984–1994.

*Map Co-ordinators* Emily Green, David Pugh

**Design and Editorial**

*Managing Editors* Vivien Crump, Helen Partington

*Deputy Art Director* Gillian Allan

*Deputy Editorial Director* Douglas Amrine

*Senior Editor* Fay Franklin

Emma Anacootee, Lydia Baillie, Shahnaaz Bakshi, Peter Bennett, Marta Bescos Sánchez, Vandana Bhagra, Hilary Bird, Julie Bond, Sophie Boyak, Sherry Collins, Joanna Craig, Cullen Curtiss, Donna Dailey, Stephanie Driver, Caroline Elliker, Michael Ellis, Nicola Erdpresser, Rob Farmer, Emer FitzGerald, Niki Foreman, Anna Freiberger, Rhiannon Furbear, Jo Gardner, Camilla Gersh, William Gordon, Emily Green, Roger Grody, Bonita Halm, Vinod Harish, Paul Hines, Jacqueline Jackson, Stuart James, Claire Jones, Thomas A Knight, Esther Labi, Maite Lantaron, Nicola Malone, Megan McCrea, Kathy McDonald, Alison McGill, Ciaran McIntyre, Annie McQuitty, Sam Merrell, Nancy Mikula, Ella Milroy, Karen Misuraca, Sonal Modha, Mary Ormandy, Catherine Palmi, Carolyn Patten, Mani Ramaswamy, Natalie Rios, Ellen Root, Shailesh Sharma, Marlene Scribner, Jonathan Schultz, Azeem Siddiqui, Meredith Smith, Asavari Singh, AnneLise Sorensen, Alka Thakur, Ingrid Vienings, Marek Walisiewicz, Amy Westervelt, Hugo Wilkinson.

**Special Assistance**

Marianne Babel, Wells Fargo History Museum, San Francisco; Liz Badras, LA Convention and Visitors' Bureau; Craig Bates, Yosemite Museum; Joyce Bimbo, Hearst Castle, San Simeon; Elizabeth A Borsting and Ron Smith, the *Queen Mary*, Long Beach; Jean Bruce-Poole, El Pueblo de Los Angeles National Monument; Carolyn Cassady; Covent Garden Stamp Shop; Marcia Eymann and Joy Tahan, Oakland Museum of California; Donna Galassi; Mary Jean S Gamble, Salinas Public Library; Mary Haas, California Palace of the Legion of Honor; Nancy Masten, Photophile; Miguel Millar, US National Weather Service, Monterey; Warren Morse, LA County Metropolitan Transportation Authority; Anne North, San Diego Visitors' and Convention Bureau; Donald Schmidt, San Diego Zoo; Vito Sgromo, Sacramento State Capitol Museum; Dawn Stranne and Helen Chang, San Francisco Visitors' and Convention Bureau; Cherise Sun and Richard Ogar, Bancroft Library; Gaynell V Wald, Mission San Juan Capistrano; Chris Wirth, Wine Institute, San Francisco; Cynthia J Wornham and Lori Star, the J Paul Getty Trust.

**Photography Permissions**

Dorling Kindersley would like to thank the following for their assistance and kind permission to photograph at their establishments: Balboa Park, San Diego; Columbia State Historic Park; Disney Enterprises, Inc.; J Paul Getty Museum, LA; Hearst Castle, San Simeon; Huntington Library, San Marino; Knotts Berry Farm, Buena Park; Los Angeles Children's Museum; Los Angeles County Museum of Art; Museum of Contemporary Art, LA; Museum of Miniatures, LA; Museum of Television and Radio, LA; Museum of Tolerance, LA; Norton Simon Museum, Pasadena; Petersen Automotive Museum, LA; *Queen Mary*, Long Beach; Sacramento State Capitol; San Diego Aerospace Museum; San Diego Automotive Museum; San Diego Museum of Art; San Diego Wild Animal Park; San Diego Zoological Society; Santa Barbara Mission; Southwest Museum, LA; John Steinbeck Library, Salinas; Tao House, Danville; Timken Museum of Art, San Diego; Universal Studios, LA; University of California, Berkeley; University of California, LA; University of Southern California, LA; Wells Fargo History Room, San Francisco; Winchester Mystery House, San Jose; and all other churches, missions, museums, parks, wineries, hotels, restaurants, and sights too numerous to thank individually. References to various Disney copyrighted characters, trademarks, marks, and registered marks are owned by The Walt Disney Company and Disney Enterprises, Inc.

**Picture Credits**

a = above; b = below/bottom; c = center; f = far; l= left; r = right; t = top.

Works of art have been reproduced with the permission of the following copyright holders:

c.1120–40), tempera colours, gold and silver on vellum bound between paper boards covered with brown calf, 22.8 x 16.4 cm, 85b; GOLDEN GATE HIGHWAY AND TRANSPORT-ATION DISTRICT: 55t, 380tl, 380c, 380b, 380–1t, 381c, 381cb; Charles M Hiller 55t; © J. PAUL GETTYTRUST: (c) 2005 Richard Ross with the courtesy of the J. Paul Getty Trust 86b; GOLDEN GATE NATIONAL RE-CREATION AREA, NATIONAL PARK SERVICE: 339blb, 339bc; RONALD GRANT ARCHIVE: 52tl, 102cr, 105cl, 107cr, 607t; Capitol 198tr; *LA Story*, Warner Bros 25tl; *Rebel Without A Cause*, Warner Bros 68cra; *The Last Ac-tion Hero* Columbia Pictures 68crb; *E.T., The Extra- Terrestrial*, Spielberg/ Universal Studios, 69br; *Gidget*, Columbia Pictures 198c. GREEN SPA NETWORK: 621c; GREYHOUND LINES, INC.: 629; ROBERT HARDING PICTURE LIBRARY: 196t, 203c, 298c, 608t; Bildagentur/Schuster 198b; FPG 24cl, 52cla, 53clb, 55cra; Jon Gardey 497t; Tony Gervis 483; Michael J Howell 23tr; Dave Jacobs 437b, 497c; Robert Landau 73crb; Westlight/Bill Ross 14b, 150tr, Steve Smith 23br 33t; HEARST CASTLE/HEARST SAN SIMEON STATE HISTORICAL MONUMENT: Z Baron 212br; John Blades 212tr, 212clb, 213b, 214c, 215c; V Garagliano 212bc; Ken Raveill 212ca, 213t, 213cra, 214b; Amber Wisdom 213crb; PHOEBE HEARST MUSEUM OF ANTHROPOLOGY: 45crb; HOLLYWOOD ENTERTAINMENT MUSEUM: 108cla; ROBERT HOLMES PHOTOGRAPHY: Markham Johnson 305bl; HOTEL CASA DEL MAR: 174b; HULTON GETTY: 57crb, 105t; HUNTINGDON LIBRARY, ART COLLECTIONS, AND BOTANIC GARDENS: 29b, 158b, 159bl, 159cr, 160b; *Madonna and Child*, Roger van der Weyden 71crb; Gutenberg Bible 159t; *Blue Boy*, Thomas Gains-borough 158cl; *Diana the Huntress*, Houdon 160t; *The Wife of Bath from The Canterbury Tales*, Chaucer (Ellesmere MS), 160c; HUTCHISON LIBRARY: Robert Francis 289t; B Regent 166cl. IMAGE BANK: David Hamilton 23tl; Marvin E Newman 324; Charles C Place 451t; 202clb; Paul Slaughter 512tl; Weinberg-Clark 438tl; IMAGE WORKS: Lisa Law 440–1c; IMPACT: Mike McQueen 203t; KIRK IRWIN: 20b, 197t, 218c, 218b, 291b, 445, 616–17. JOSE CUERVO: 566cla. CATHERINE KARNOW: 200br; KATZ PICTURES: Lamoine 166cr; SABA /Steve Starr 25tl, Lara Jo Regan 69bl; ROBERT F KENNEDY LIBRARY: Special Collections, California Polytechnic State University 215t; KNOTT'S BERRY FARM: 236-237c, 236br, 237br, 274br; KOBAL COLLECTION: *Sabrina*, © 1995 Paramount/Brian Hamill 69tr; HOWARD KOBY: www. photographersdirect.com 107cl; www.KODAKTHEATER. COM: 108cr; *LA Story*, Guild Film Distribution 69cla, *The Big Sleep*, Warner Bros 79b; *The Wild One*, Columbia Pictures 200bl. LA COUNTY MUSEUM OF ART: *La Trahison des Images (Ceci n'est pas une pipe)*, René Magritte, purchased with funds provided by the Mr & Mrs William Preston Harrison Collection, 70t; *In the Woods at Giverny: Blanche Hoschedé at Her Easel with Suzanne Hoschedé Reading*, Claude Monet, Mr & Mrs George Gard De Sylva Collection 114t; *Soap Bubbles* (after 1739) Jean-Baptiste-Simón Chardin Gift of The Ahmanson Foundation 114cla; *The Hope Athena* (2nd century AD) William Randolph Hearst Collection 114c; *Mulholland Drive: The Road to the Studio*, David Hockney, purchased with funds provided by the F Patrick Burnes Bequest 115t; Plate, purchased with funds provided by the Art Museum Council 115cr; Standing Warrior (The King), The Proctor Stafford Collection, purchased with funds provided by Mr and Mrs Allen

C Balch 116tl; *Magdalen with the Smoking Flame*, Georges de La Tour, gift of The Ahmanson Foundation 116tr; *Monument to Honoré de Balzac*, Auguste Rodin, gift of B Gerald Cantor; 116c; *The Cotton Pickers*, Winslow Homer, Acquisition made possible by museum trustees 116b; Pair of Officials, China, 618–907, Gift of Leon Lidow 117t; Dunes, *Oceano*, Edward Weston, © 1981 Center for Creative Photography, Arizona Board of Regents 117b; LA DEPARTMENT OF WATER AND POWER: 52clb, 202b; LADODGERS INC: 152b; Los Angeles Philharmonic: Tom Bonner 125br; LEGOLAND® CALIFORNIA RESORT: 262tr; JACK LONDON COLLECTION: California State Parks 26b. MAGNES MUSEUM PERMANENT COLLECTIONS: 19th-century blue velvet embroidery brocade robe, 419t; MAGNUM PHOTOS: Michael Nichols 57bl; MARINE WORLD AFRICA USA: Charlotte Fiorito 298tr; ANDREW MCKINNEY PHOTOGRAPHY: 47cl, 300tl, 300tr, 301cr, 302tr, 303tr, 303br, 307cr, 307bc, 313crb, 331t, 346c, 369b, 381bl, 414t; MENDOCINO BREWING COMPANY: 567bc; METROPOLITAN TRANSIT DEVELOPMENT BOARD, SAN DIEGO: Stephen Simpson 266cla; METROPOLITAN WATER DISTRICT OF SOUTHERN CALIFORNIA: 202c; MINETA SAN JOSÉ INTERNATIONAL AIRPORT: 628cla; ROBERT MONDAVI WINERY: 464br; JOHN MUIR NATIONAL HISTORIC SITE: National Park Service 415br; MUNI 397t, 397cl, 397b; MUMM NAPA: 567tc; MUSEUM OF TELEVISION AND RADIO: Grant Mudford 90t. THE NAMES PROJECT: AIDS Memorial Quilt © 1988 Matt Herron 57clb; THE NATIONAL MOTOR MUSEUM, BEAULIEU: 201bl; PETER NEWARK'S AMERICAN PICTURES: 47br, 48br, 201tl, 303crb; PETER NEWARK'S WESTERN AMERICANA: 48cla, 48bl, 48–9c, 195 (inset), 253br, 295 (inset), 433 (inset), 519 (inset), 617 (inset); NHPA: Joe Blossom 81tr; Rich Kirchner 39t, 460c; Stephen Krasemann 503cra; P McDonald 242b; David Middleton 436t, 448t; Kevin Schafer 436b; John Shaw 219b, 230b, 279t, 436cl, 491c; Roger Tidman 241b; NEW YORK PUBLIC LIBRARY: I N Phelps Stokes Collection, Miriam and Ira D Wallach Division of Art, Prints and Photo-graphs, The New York Public Library, Astor, Lenox and Tilden Foundations 44clb; THE NORTON SIMON FOUNDATION, PASADENA: *Still Life with Lem-ons, Oranges and a Rose*, Francisco de Zurbaran (1633) 156b; Buddha Enthroned, Kashmir, India (8th century) 157b; *Woman with a Book*, Pablo Picasso (1932), Estate of Robert Ellis Simon, 1969, 156t; *Saints Paul and Frediano*, Filippino Lippi (1483) 157t; *Self-Portrait*, Rembrandt van Rijn (c.1636–38) 156c; *The Little Fourteen-Year-Old Dancer*, Edgar Degas (1878–81) 157bc. COURTESY OF THE OAKLAND MUSEUM OF CALIFORNIA: 425br; Dino Morrow 424bl; Jeff Warrin 425cra; *Yosemite Valley*, Albert Bierstadt (1868) 8–9; *Figure on a Porch*, Richard Diebenkorn (1959) 28cl; *Ocean Park 107* Richard Diebenkorn (1958) 424c; *Afternoon in Piedmont*, Xavier Tizoc Martinez (c.1911) 28br; *California Venus*, Rupert Schmid (c.1895) 29c; The Oakland Museum History Department: 24bl, 43b, 44cla, 44–5cb (2), 45cla, 47cr, 49ca, 49crb, 50tl, 52tr, 53cb, 56cla, 56bl, 379br, 424tl, 424tr, 425t, 441t; The Oakland Museum Kahn Collection 475b; The Oakland Tribune Collection, Gift of Alameda Newspaper Group 54b, 440cl, 440b; LOS OLIVOS: 563bc; OXFORD SCIENTIFIC FILMS: Daniel J Cox 437ca; Michael Fogden 496c; Stan Osolinski 437cr. PALMSPRINGS AERIAL TRAMWAY: 275tl; PALM SPRINGS ART MUSEUM: 275cra; PASADENA CONVENTION AND VISITORS' BUREAU: 154b; EDWARD PFEIFFER: 25tr, 30t, 30b,

31b, 63bl, 72t, 73tl, 88, 89, 90b, 91c, 120, 122cl, 132cla, 132b, 133t, 133c, 133b, 140, 141, 149t; Photolibrary: JTB Photo 123bl; Photo Network: Mary Messenger 608b; Phyllis Picardi 201br; Woodard 36b; Photophile: 34b, 61t, 196c, 244; Jose Carrillo 37b; Scott Crain 18c; Arthur Fox 612t; Mark Gibson 607b; Jim Gray 197b; Michael Hall 68tr, 172t; Matt Lindsay 21b, 37c, 266b, 267b, Sal Maimone 127bl, 167, 196b, 252br, 434b, 522c; LLT Rhodes 46tl; Photo Trek Inc: M J Wickham 434cb; Petersen Automotive Museum: Scott Williamson 118tr; Pictor International—London: 58–9, 62t, 62bl, 62br, 200tr, 236bl; 286–7, 292b, 299tl, 466, 498, 513t; Pictorial Press Ltd: J Cummings 359b; Pictures Colour Library: 22t, 39bl, 74, 123t; Leo de Wys 611c; Popperfoto: 516t. Precita Eyes Mural Arts and Visitors Center: *Balloon Journey* ©2008 Precita Eyes Muralists, by Kristen Foskett 140crb; Hillcrest Elementary School © 2007 Precita Eyes Muralists 140cb; Oakland, *Stop the Violence* © 2007 Precita Eyes Muralists. Directed by Joshua Stevenson. Designed and painted by AYPAL youth (Asian Pacific Islander Youth Promoting Advocacy and Leadership) including Recy, Marcus, and many Others. Acrylic paint on Tyvek 140b; Presidio of San Francisco: NPS staff photos 377tl, 377cra; Presidio Trust: Amy Wolff 377br; Red & White Fleet: 399bl; Retna Pictures LTD: LGI Photo Agency/Marco Shark 27br; Steve Granite 69t; Reuters: Kimberley White 57tr; Rex Features: 360b; Most Wanted 97tl; Riverside Municipal Museum: Chris Moser 44cr. Salinas Public Library: Courtesy of the Steinbeck Archives, 27t, 517b; San Diego Air and Space Museum: 256clb; San Francisco Art Institute: D Wakely 341t; San Francisco Cable Car Museum: 303tl, 303bl; San Francisco Convention and Visitors' Bureau: 39br, Mark Gibson 302c; Courtesy of Brown, Zukov & Associates 382t; San Francisco Museum of Modern Art: *Pohono Bridal Veil 900 Feet, Yo Semite 1861* Purchased through a gift of Gary Sokol and Christine Murray and the Accessions Committee Fund: gift of Barbara and Gerson Bakar, Doris and Donald G. Fisher, Evelyn D. Haas, Mimi and Peter Haas, and Elaine McKeon 319tl; Paul Klee *Blossoms in the Night* 1930 Gift of Charlotte Mack 319cr; *Back View*, 1977, Philip Guston, oil on canvas, gift of the artist, 305cr; *Zip-Light*, 1990, Sigmar Willnauer, leather, polyester, zipper, SFMOMA purchase, 318tl; *Les Valeurs Personnelles*, 1952, by Rene Magritte, purchased through a gift of Phyllis Wattis 318tr; No. 14, 1960 by Mark Rothko 318c; *The Nest*, 1994, by Louis Bourgeois, steel; Points of Departure: Connecting with Contemporary Art, March 23-August 7, 2001 318bl; *Country Dog Gentlemen*, 1972, by Roy De Forest, polymer on canvas, gift of the Hamilton-Wells Collection, 319b; *Orange Sweater*, 1955, by Elmer Bischoff, oil on canvas, gift of Mr and Mrs Mark Schorer, 323cr; San Francisco

Public Library History Room: 54cla, 339bla, 369c; San Mateo County Historical Association: 412t; Santa Barbara Mission Archive Library: 46cl, 47tl; Santa Barbara Museum of Art: *The Ripened Wheat*, Jules Bastien-Lepage (1884), Museum purchase with funds provided by Suzette and Eugene Davidson and the Davidson Endow-ment Fund 220cl; Santa Rosa Convention & Visitors Bureau: 618br, 622cr; Science Photo Library: NASA 284c; George Bernard 428b; Simon Fraser 18t; David Parker 24t; Peter Menzel 24cr, 505b; Sonoma Valley Visitors' Bureau: Bob Nixon 465b; Southwest Museum: ID CT.122, Photo by Don Meyer (491.G.802) 71tr; Spectrum Colour Library: 2–3, 200tl, 265tl, 472tr, 509t, 610b; D&J Heaton 344, 562t; STA Travel Group: 620cra; The Standard, Downtown LA: Martin Kunz 174t; Stanford University Archives: Department of Special Collec-tions, 51b; Stevenson House Collection, Monterey State Historic Park: Sharon Fong 508t, 509cr, 509b Tony Stone Images: 38b, 413crb, 434t, 484; Jerry Alexander 463t; Glen Allison 364; Ken Biggs 36t, 63tl, 178c; James Blank 149; David Carriere 612b; Jim Corwin 310; Chad Ehlers 63tr; Johan Elzenga 280, 283, 290t, 292t; David R Frazier 442; Roy Giles 334cla; Lorentz Gullachsen 19t; Gavin Hellier 494t; John Lamb 332; D C Lowe 487t; David Madison 611t; David Maisel 298b; Ed Pritchard 294–5; A&L Sinibaldi 19br, 435cr; Alan Smith 215b; Larry Ulrich 443; John Warden 450–1; Levi Strauss & Co: 343cr, 343b; Tim Street-Porter: 32b, 33b, 72bl. Tahoe Luxury Properties: 523tl; Tate Gallery London: *It's a Psychological Fact that Pleasure helps your Disposition*, 1948, Eduardo Paolozzi 54–5c; Telegraph Colour Library: 15, 18b; Edward Thomas Photography: 32t. Travelex Currency Services Inc: 624cra; Travelpix: Robert Holmes 630tr; Ulster Museum, Belfast: By kind perm-ission of the Trustees 45cl; © 2000 Universal Studios Inc All Rights Reserved 147b, 148tl, 148cr, 148d, 148br, 149tr, 149bl; By Courtesy of the US Postal Service: 618t; Stamp Designs © 1995, 317c, 627t. Wells Fargo Bank: 49bl, 312b, 314b, 479b; Westfield City Century: 93cr; Westfield Horton Plaza: 250bl; Williams-Sonoma, Inc.: 384cr; World Pictures: 16, 17b, 21t, 34c, 68tl, 136–7, 147c, 166b, 175, 199t, 226, 410, 606c. Yellow Cab Co.: 178tc; Yosemite Museum: National Park Service 44tl, 44cra, Craig & Jennifer Bates 44cl; Michael Dixon 44clb; Yosemite National Park Research Library: 51ca. ©Zefa: 1, 39c, 438cla, 492–3; K. Hackenberg 12b; Bill Zeldis Photography: 42; Zeum: 322clb; Zoological Society of San Diego: 259b.

All other images © Dorling Kindersley. See www.DKimages.com for more information.

Jacket Front - ©Lester Lefkowitz. Back - Alamy Images: Blaine Harrington III tl; AWL Images: Christian Kober clb, bl; Dorling Kindersley: Rough Guides/ Paul Whitfield cla. Spine - ©Lester Lefkowitz: t.

# Road Map of California